Legal Challenges for the Global Manager and Entrepreneur

Second Edition

Frank J. Cavico
Bahaudin G. Mujtaba

Kendall Hunt
publishing company

❧ DEDICATION ☙

This book is dedicated to Nancy and Lisa, who bring about positive changes in our lives and continue to fascinate us with their kindness and understanding. Thanks and we love you!

❧ Contents ❧

🐉 Acknowledgments 🐉

First, we would like to thank the following colleagues for their contributions and guidance in preparing this book:

- Alma M. Sierra
- Andrew E. Trumbach
- Andrés Raúl Pérez Díaz
- Belay Seyoum
- Bina Patel
- Cagri Tanyar
- Carol Pickersgill
- Cuneyt Oskal
- Don Ariail
- Don Valeri
- Elizabeth Danon-Leva
- Erica Franklin
- G. Rauf Roashan
- Hajar Amrani
- J. Preston Jones
- James M. Barry
- John Wayne Falbey
- John W. Palma Jr.
- Josephine Sosa-Fey
- Miguel A. Orta
- Nicolaos Spiliopoulos
- Norman Glick
- Pan G. Yatrakis
- Pedro Pellet
- Ramdas Chandra
- Randolph A. Pohlman
- Regina Harris
- Ronald E. Needleman
- Russell Abratt
- Shakila Faqeeri
- Simone Maxwell
- Stephanie Ferrari
- Stephen C. Muffler
- Steven V. Cates
- Timothy O. McCartney
- Thais Alvarez
- Thomas M. Tworoger
- Trevor Pendleton
- William Freeman
- Daniel Cantillo

Second, we would like to thank all those who have helped us get to this point.

Third, we thank you for reading this material. For suggestions and questions, you can contact us (cavico@nova.edu or mujtaba@nova.edu) at any time.

Frank and Bahaudin

❦ PREFACE ❦

This second edition to this book seeks to make the reader more legally knowledgeable and astute. The book attempts to identify as many legal challenges as possible in establishing, operating, and managing a business in today's very competitive global business environment. The book recommends strategies and tactics to overcome these challenges and to achieve a successful business in a lawful and moral manner. Yet overcoming challenges is not the only goal of this book. The authors naturally want the reader to be able to more clearly foresee legal problems so as to avoid them; but the authors also want the reader to learn how to use the law and the legal system to more effectively establish, manage, and develop the business. Accordingly, an important objective of the second edition of this book is to focus on preventing lawsuits, at times called "preventative law," that is, making the business person aware of the law, its applicability to business, and the legal consequences of business decision-making. The goal is to avoid legal problems before they materialize, as opposed to the "trials and tribulations" (and "trials" perhaps literally) of dealing with them when they occur. One major purpose of this book, therefore, is to help business people recognize legal risks and thus avoid legal liability.

The second edition to the book, moreover, has materially expanded the Constitutional Law chapter by discussing recent very important Supreme Court decisions, particularly First Amendment "commercial speech" cases. The authors also have included in the second edition of book the following sections and expanded sections to chapters:

- Managing attorneys (Legal System of the United States chapter)
- International jurisdiction, international intellectual property agreements, and the Foreign Corrupt Practices Act (International Law chapter)
- Online dispute resolution (Alternate Dispute Resolution chapter)
- Negligent hiring and the duty of landowners pursuant to negligence law (Torts and Business chapter)
- Market share liability and statutes of repose (Products Liability chapter);
- Choice of law and choice of forum provisions in contracts (Contract Law chapter)
- Employment at-will disclaimers in employment contracts and independent contractor (as opposed to employee) status (Agency Law chapter)
- The agent's authority to enter into contracts for business entities, corporate directors rights and responsibilities, right of first refusal, and buy-sell, stock options and warrants, and stock compensation for employees (Business Organizations chapter)

- Choosing the right form of doing business (Business Organizations chapter);
- Landlord-Tenant law (Real Property Law chapter)
- Trademark law, copyright law, non-disclosure agreements and their relationship to trade secret law, covenant-not-to-compete law, non-solicitation and anti-piracy agreements, and employee inventions (Intellectual Property Protection chapter)
- E-contracts and online jurisdiction (Internet Regulation chapter)
- "Going public" (Securities Law and Corporate Governance chapter)
- Employment at-will, "concerted" activity pursuant to the National Labor Relations Act, sexual orientation discrimination, and disparate impact discrimination (Employment, Labor, and Immigration Law chapter).

Particularly noteworthy and important to the second edition is the inclusion of a substantially enlarged chapter on Business Ethics and Corporate Social Responsibility. This expanded chapter deals with philosophy, ethics, morality, business ethics, applied business ethics, corporate social responsibility, corporate governance, and business sustainability. The authors strive to show what ethics is, how ethics can be used to make moral determinations in business, and why business should act not "merely" legally but also in a moral manner. Moreover, the authors discuss what the concept of "social responsibility" means for business today, how the value of social responsibility is distinguished from the law and from ethics, and why a business should be concerned with being a "socially responsible" one. A major objective of the new chapter is not "just" to teach ethics, but also "to do" ethics; that is, the authors' purposes for the new chapter are not merely to deliver moral information in a didactic, sermonizing, or "preachy" way, but also to stimulate and assist the student and reader to do better, clearer, and more well-reasoned ethical thinking about moral questions; and as such to impart the analytical skills needed to apply ethical concepts to business decision-making. Similarly, the authors want the student and reader to be cognizant of the concept of "social responsibility," how that term is applied to business, especially to corporations, what it means to be a socially responsible firm, and why a firm should be a socially responsible one today. The chapter also includes a discussion of codes of ethics, and shows how corporate codes are related to the law, ethics, and social responsibility

Moreover, the authors have developed a text-based website with cases, case studies, case problems, chapter summaries, a Glossary of Terms section, and Powerpoints, as well as other supplemental materials to help the reader comprehend the legal, ethical, and social responsibility concepts and principles, and particularly how they are applied in a modern business environment.

The authors are most grateful for all the support and encouragement to publish the second edition, and particularly for the many most helpful suggestions for improving the book from colleagues, associates, students, friends, and readers. Furthermore, by using this book, you are contributing to the Business Ethics and Global Social Responsibility Scholarship, which has been established at the Huizenga School of Business and Entrepreneurship at Nova Southeastern University to support scholarly research and coursework by students, which will advance the fields of business ethics and global social responsibility. This scholarship was conceived and created by the authors of this book, and Huizenga School professors, Dr. Frank J. Cavico, J.D., LL.M, Professor of Business Law and Ethics, and Dr. Bahaudin G. Mujtaba, Professor of Management. Professors Cavico and Mujtaba are co-funding this academic scholarship initiative with the support of the H. Wayne Huizenga School of Business and Entrepreneurship and Nova Southeastern University. Professors Cavico and Mujtaba continue to provide funds to this scholarship from the royalties from the sale of this book along with their other books. Thank you for exploring and leading discussions, and advancing knowledge on legality, morality and ethics, as well as social responsibility, in the world of business management, entrepreneurship, and leadership!

The two quotes from William Shakespeare's The Merchant of Venice that commence this book underscore the importance of global trade, commerce, and business to the success and fame of Venice, as well as the critical need to conduct business in a principled-based, legal, ethical, and socially responsible environment. Remember that it was the Venetians who first used the term "communally controlled capitalism," that is, capitalism, and very successful capitalism, yet tempered by law, ethics, and social responsibility; and it was also the Venetians who "coined" the concept of commercial paper. Also, recall the motto of the Venetian Republic—"For the honor and profit of Venice." So, like the Venetians of "olden days," the authors want the readers to do well in business, but to do well honorably, and thereby to act in a legal, ethical, moral, and socially responsible manner.

Overall, we sincerely hope that, as with the first edition of this book, you also enjoy this second edition; and that you find it similarly useful and beneficial–academically and practically—as well as intellectually stimulating, thought-provoking, and challenging; and the authors sincerely hope too that all the stated aforementioned objectives are attained in an efficacious and enjoyable manner; and as a result the knowledge of the reader is increased, the mental acuity of the reader is enhanced, and the mental discipline of the reader is strengthened.

Frank and Bahaudin

Now, what news on the Rialto?

William Shakespeare, Merchant of Venice, Act III, Sc. 1

There is no power in Venice can alter a decree established. 'Twill be recorded for a precedent, and many an error by the same example will rush into the state. It cannot be.

William Shakespeare, Merchant of Venice, Act IV, Sc. 1

PART I

FOUNDATION OF THE LEGAL AND REGULATORY ENVIRONMENT OF GLOBAL BUSINESS

ONE

It is becoming more important than ever before in today's global business environment and litigious society to proactively understand and effectively deal with legal issues and challenges. As such, managers and professionals working in a global environment must be aware of the local rules, policies, and practices of the various nations in which they conduct business. Becoming aware of the rules, obeying the rules, and being fair to all parties are legal and moral imperatives for national and global managers. Ethical norms and laws exist in all countries and locations in one form or another. Each country has its own laws and regulations for conducting business—often referred to as antitrust or competition laws, which prohibit unlawful restraint of trade. These national, international, and global laws are designed to protect consumers and competitors against unfair business practices and to promote and protect healthy competition among all parties.

Most of the larger companies tend to be fully committed to observing the applicable antitrust or competition laws of all nations where they operate. Antitrust and other laws that apply to global organizations tend to vary from country to country. However, generally speaking, these laws tend to prohibit unilateral and collective agreements and actions that restrain trade. Such laws are meant to be inclusive of all such restrictive practices that may reduce competition to an unreasonable level without providing beneficial effects to consumers. Activities that are generally found to violate antitrust or competition laws include agreements among two or more competitors to fix or control prices, to boycott certain suppliers or customers, to divide or allocate markets or customers, or to limit the production or sale of products or product lines for anticompetitive purposes.

The ethical issues that a global manager has to deal with can be very complex. For example, what suggestion can one make to a global manager when "bribing" people seems to be the norm in a foreign country where he/she is working? If everyone else is "greasing the wheel" or "bribing" officials to get the routine paperwork completed, shouldn't this particular manager also pay a bribe to get the work done? Ethics and ethical behavior alignment are complex issues. Ethics is not always a "black-and-white" issue and there are many "gray" areas. However, the answers become a bit clearer when the global manager understands the laws and ethical norms of the local culture or country as well as the policies of his/her own company. Starting from this understanding, he/she can work on transcending the legal requirements in order to provide effective leadership in getting the job completed in a manner satisfactory to all parties involved.

Global managers and entrepreneurs must always be aware of laws that not only impact their day-to-day business activities, but also their daily living activities such as driving, shopping, and other community behaviors. For example, Florida and at least ten other states in the U.S. have made it illegal for parents to leave their young children in the car when dropping off mail in the post office or entering a retail outlet in order to get stamps. The temperature can get extremely high during hot summer days and this heat can be extremely dangerous for a child left in a car even for a few minutes. Despite such laws, many children die each year when left alone in a hot car because parents mistakenly think that a few minutes may not make much of a difference. The fact is that a few minutes can make a huge difference, which is why the government has made it illegal to leave children by themselves this way. Sometimes parents forget that they even have a child in the back seat of their car, but such neglect can easily land them in prison if their actions are discovered by authorities. Experts suggest that, as a habit, parents might leave their purses or wallets in the back seat of the car where the child is sitting to remember to take it—and, by extension, the child—with them when leaving a car.

Of course, such a rule is designed as a safeguard to save lives and applies equally to local and global managers who are living in a particular community. So, global managers and entrepreneurs doing business in the United States must be aware of such laws in order for them to, in an extreme case, stay out of prison or have their children taken away from them.

The Structure and Content of the Book

This book is about values, specifically, the value of legality in a global business and entrepreneurial context. A "value" is something that is regarded, esteemed, desired, and possesses worth. Values can be intrinsic (terminal), that is, good in and of themselves, or extrinsic (instrumental), i.e., good only because they lead to or produce other values. For example, happiness is considered to be an intrinsic value, whereas money is considered to be "merely" extrinsic since money can produce other values (and thus money *can* buy happiness!).

This book takes an instrumental approach to the value of legality, thus underscoring why, in very practical business and entrepreneurial terms, it is essential for the global manager to be keenly aware of the law in a global context including a law's reach, scope, and complexity. This book, although predominantly a law book, also succinctly deals with key values, such as the values of morality and ethics as well as corporate social responsibility in the global business milieu. This book is divided into four major parts comprising twenty-four chapters (including this Introduction). The five parts are as follows: *Part I: Foundations of the Legal and Regulatory Environment of Global Business; Part II: The Legal Environment of Global Business; Part III: The Regulatory Environment of Global Business; Part IV: Cases for Analysis; and Discussion and Part V: Glossary of Terms.* The individual chapters are predominantly divided into five main parts, to wit: 1) a brief introduction to the chapter; 2) a detailed explication of certain important U.S. laws affecting business; 3) a section entitled "Global Legal Perspectives" wherein the authors discuss the extraterritorial effect of U.S. law and then succinctly present the laws of selected international jurisdictions; 4) a section called "Management Strategies," wherein the authors provide suggestions and recommendations for global managers and entrepreneurs on how to handle and to avoid legal problems; and 5) a brief summary to the chapter.

Part I: Foundations consists of eight chapters (including the introduction). Chapters 2–8 examine "keystone" legal concepts and principles that underpin national and international legal systems and thus serve as the basic framework for global business and entrepreneurship. Chapter 2: Introduction to Law and Legal Reasoning—provides an introduction to the law, sources of the law, classifications of the law, and legal reasoning. The chapter also differentiates case-made law—that is, the common law—from statutory law. Chapter 3: The Legal System of the United States—affords the reader an overview of the legal system of the United States and also provides a comparative discussion of certain aspects of the U.S. system compared to the legal systems of other countries. Chapter 4: International Law—is a very substantive chapter that first examines the government and legal systems and their relationship to the businesses of several countries. The chapter then includes a discussion of the basics of Islam and Islamic law with application of Islamic legal principles to economic systems and business. Finally, the chapter imparts fundamental material regarding international law, treaties and organizations, international business transactions, and the problem of corruption in the international business arena. Chapter 5: Alternative Dispute Resolution—defines and differentiates arbitration and mediation, discusses the advantages and disadvantages of arbitration as well as the enforceability of arbitration awards, particularly in the international business arena. Chapter 6: Business Ethics and Corporate Social Responsibility—supplies the reader with a philosophical as well as practical framework to business ethics in a global business context and then defines, explains, and illustrates the key term, "corporate social responsibility," in a global context. Chapter 7: Constitutional Law and Business—bestows on the reader an explication of essential U.S. constitutional law doctrines and principles, then, in the Global Legal Perspectives section, compares U.S. law with certain aspects of constitutional law in other countries. Chapter 8: Administrative Law and Business—sets forth basic doctrines and principles of U.S. administrative law and then compares U.S. law with certain aspects of other countries' administrative law and procedure.

Part II: Legal Environment is composed of eight chapters, chapters 9–16, which discuss very basic legal doctrines, principally made by judges, which have been in effect for many years and impact business. Chapter 9: Torts and Business—defines, compares, and contrasts the three main types of torts in the United States: intentional torts, the tort of negligence, and the doctrine of strict liability. In the Global Legal Perspectives section, one important intentional tort in the U.S. is compared with its foreign equivalent. Chapter 10: Products Liability—predominantly focuses on warranty law and the doctrine of strict liability as applied to products, then, in the Global Legal Perspectives section, compares certain aspects of U.S. products liability law with European Community law and the laws of other nations. Chapter 11: Crimes and Business—defines and succinctly explains several types of crimes in the U.S. that impact business. The chapter also addresses corporate criminality and the Federal Sentencing Guidelines in the United States. In the Global Legal Perspectives section, the U.S. Foreign Corrupt Practices Act and the U.S. Economic Espionage Act—as well as their application to international business—are examined. Chapter 12: Contract Law—sets forth the definition, types, and requirements of a valid contract in the U.S. as well as describes various legal doctrines that will invalidate a contract. In the Global Legal Perspectives section, certain aspects of U.S. contract law are compared and contrasted with contract law rules in other countries. Chapter 13: Sales Law—first distinguishes sales law from contract law, and then explains important sales-law doctrines. In the Global Legal Perspectives section, a discussion of international sales law is offered. Chapter 14: Agency Law—defines and explains three key legal relationships: principal-agent, employer-employee, and employer-independent contractor. The chapter also describes the practical functions and legal rights and liabilities of these parties in a business context. In the Global Legal Perspectives section, an important legal principle dealing with agency liability is examined in an international context. Chapter 15: Business Organizations—is another very substantive chapter that offers the reader a detailed explication of the variety of ways available today to conduct business globally. In the Global Legal Perspectives section, business- organization laws of various nations are compared to U.S. law. Chapter 16: Real Property Law—first defines and describes the nature of property, next distinguishes real from personal property, then outlines the basics of transferring real property within the United States, and finally examines landlord-tenant law. In the Global Legal Perspectives section, a discussion of acquiring real property in other nations is offered.

Part III: Regulatory Environment sets forth the final substantive seven chapters, 17–23, which deal with newer bodies of law, principally legislatively created or promulgated through government agencies that regulate business. Chapter 17: Intellectual Property Protection—supplies the reader with a variety of methods by which intellectual property can be protected legally. In the Global Legal Perspectives section, a discussion of the various international treaties dealing with intellectual property is provided. Chapter 18: Internet Regulation—discusses several statutes impacting contracting on the Internet and also discusses privacy and domain name statutes. In the Global Legal Perspectives section, e-commerce and e-contracts are addressed in an international context. Chapter 19: Securities Regulation and Corporate Governance—provides an indepth analysis of several critical statutes in the U.S. that regulate the purchase and sale of securities that materially affect corporate governance. In the Global Legal Perspectives section, certain aspects of U.S. law are compared and contrasted with the laws of other nations. Chapter 20: Antitrust Law—is another very substantive chapter that makes available to the reader a detailed explication of U.S. antitrust law, including the extraterritorial effect of U.S. antitrust law. In the Global Legal Perspectives section, certain aspects of U.S. antitrust law are compared and contrasted with antitrust law in the European Community as well as other countries. Chapter 21: Employer, Labor, and Immigration Law is also quite substantive. The chapter first defines the key legal doctrine of employment "at will" in the United States as well as the exceptions thereto, then carefully delineates several U.S. civil rights, labor, and immigration laws impacting business. In the Global Legal Perspectives section, several key aspects of U.S. law are compared and contrasted with the laws of other nations. Chapter 22: Consumer Protection—sets forth various legal doctrines that protect the consumer, and also discusses in the Global Legal Perspectives section a particular advertising issue with international ramifications. Chapter 23: Environmental Protection—makes available to the reader a succinct examination of several important environmental statutes in the United States, then, in the Global Legal Perspectives section, discusses a major international environmental treaty as well as environmental regulations in several countries.

Chapter 24 comprises the *Conclusion*. In addition to providing a brief summary and restatement of the authors' learning objectives, the Conclusion ends with the fervent hope of the authors that their book serves an even greater purpose in bringing peoples and nations together in a mutually advantageous manner.

Part IV: Cases sets out sample concise case studies, based on very current historical events involving law and business which the authors offer as tools for critical analysis and thought-provoking discussion. To effectuate discussion, the authors have provided after each case a series of discussion questions. A further and full complement of case studies can be found on the supplemental website to this book.

Finally, *Part V: Glossary of Terms provides definitions of key terms used in the book.*
The book ends with the authors' biographies and the biographies of the many academic contributors to this work. The authors could not have achieved such an ambitious project—attaining the substantial, detailed, and far-reaching legal and management explication as presented herein—without the material assistance of a host of contributors, many of whom are faculty colleagues or former students of the authors. For this help, guidance, and encouragement, the authors are very grateful indeed.

Global Legal Perspectives and Management Strategies

Throughout this book, the last part of each chapter, as noted, will include sections entitled Global Legal Perspective and Management Strategies. These sections offer practical views from the authors, contributors, or researchers in the field about the subjects and topics covered in the preceding chapter. These sections are offered for reflective discussions, practical implications, and further research on the relevant topics.

The Global Perspectives are typically contributions which are summarized from the writings of previous researchers, and some are based on the writing or personal experiences of the authors. Interested readers can check out the full reference by the original author's name—included in the bibliography section— read the complete material from the original source, and reflect upon the study's findings and implications for global professionals in the fields of law and business.

Summary

This chapter provided a brief introduction to the need for professionals to study and understand some of the challenges that global managers face today. After understanding these challenges, managers, entrepreneurs, and leaders can properly and proactively prepare their employees to effectively handle such challenges. Each chapter of the book will end with a brief summary of what was discussed in the chapter. The summary will make mention of some of the major topics and/or emphasize one or two main elements of the chapter.

TWO

INTRODUCTION TO LAW
AND LEGAL REASONING

The "law" has many definitions. Fundamentally, the law is the entire body of principles that governs conduct and which can be enforced by the courts or other government tribunals. If there were no societally-made law, many people would still act in a "proper" manner based on societal norms, moral beliefs, conscience, or religion. However, not all people would act in such a "good" manner. Therefore, a basic purpose of the law is to provide a degree of order and control to human activities. The law thus serves as an instrumentality of control by means of substantive legal rules, legal procedures, and mechanisms of legal promulgation, adjudication, implementation, and enforcement.

Sources of the Law

When most people think of the term, the "law," they usually are thinking of a statute enacted by a legislative body, such as the United States Congress or a state legislature. In addition to these concepts, statutory law encompasses the legislative ordinances enacted by constituent government elements of states within the United States—that is, ordinances and codes promulgated by counties and municipalities.

Law also encompasses constitutional law. In the United States, this would be the Constitution itself (federal or national level) as well as state constitutions. Constitutional law in the U.S., as in most legal systems, is supreme.

Law further includes regulatory law—that is, the laws, in the forms of rules and regulations promulgated by administrative agencies, which have been delegated sovereign law-making powers by the legislative bodies. In the United States, a good part of the law that regulates business stems from government administrative agencies on not only the federal level, but also at the state and local level. Law consists, moreover, of case law—called the "common law" in the Anglo-American judicial tradition—which is the law expressed by judges in court decisions.

Treaties are another source of law. As a matter of fact, in the United States, the federal constitution explicitly gives the President the power with the advice and consent of the Senate to enter into treaties with foreign governments. Executive orders, finally, are yet one more source of the law. These are orders from the executive branch of government such as, in the U.S., by the President or the governor of a state. The authority to issue executive orders is either expressly granted to chief executive officers or implied from the federal or state constitutions.

Classification of the Law

There are many different classifications of the law. Generally, law can be divided into "public" law and "private" law. Public law impacts the "people" as a whole who are directly involved with the law. The aim of public law is to serve the societal interest as well as to seek to achieve justice, and "the people's" interests are represented by government agencies and officers. Prime examples are constitutional law, administrative law, and criminal law. Whereas "private" law deals with the legal problems, relations, and interests among private individuals, society and "the people" as a whole are not involved.

Prominent illustrations of private law are the laws of contracts, torts, and property. Related to public and private law, though narrower in focus, are the criminal law and the civil law. Criminal law deals with legal wrongs committed ultimately against society, since society cannot function unless people and their property are protected. Criminal infractions are punished by society, particularly by the sanction of imprisonment—by which the wrongdoer makes amends to society. However, the civil law deals with legal wrongs committed by one private party against another private party, such as a lawsuit for breach of contract or the tort of negligence. The payment of money is the usual means of redress in such situations.

The term "civil law," however, has another meaning. In many legal systems, the sole or primary source of the law is found in detailed statutes, called codes. Court decisions have a secondary importance and, as a matter of fact, in some legal systems they do not even carry the force of law. The civil law in this sense is premised on the Napoleonic Code, but harkens back even further to Roman law. Today, most European countries and all Latin American countries have "civil law" systems. So, to some extent, does the state of Louisiana in the United States, due to its origins from and former rule by the Spanish and the French.

Civil law, moreover, must be differentiated from the "common law," which is a system of law that relies substantially on judicial-made case law. In a common law system, there of course will be statutory law too and, accordingly, the function of the courts will be to not only make law but also to interpret statutory law and review statutory law. One final important classification of the law is the distinction between substantive law and procedural law. The former defines the legal relation of people with other people or the relation of people with the state while setting forth their respective rights and duties. Procedural law is the legal method, means, or process by which the substantive law is administered and the parties' and society's rights and duties are enforced.

Great Britain and the United States are two examples of common law systems.

The Common Law v. Statutory Law

In the Anglo-American legal tradition, it is necessary to explicate the meaning of the core legal concept, the "common law," as well as to explore the relationship between the common law and statutory law. In early English times, the kings and their royal representatives, officiating as courts, made up the law on a case-by-case basis not from a subjective starting point, but rather rooted in the customs and prevailing mores of the community. Over time, as more and more cases were decided, discrete bodies of law were developed. Moreover, after time, courts looked to earlier cases to see what legal principles were enunciated and then, most significantly, ultimately followed these prior legal principles in deciding contemporary cases. Following these foundational legal principles became the heart of the common law of England. The system of English common law was later adopted by courts in the United States.

In common law systems, two concepts are critical: "precedent" and the doctrine of "*stare decisis.*" A precedent is an earlier case with the same or similar facts which has enunciated certain legal rules. *Stare decisis* means that a court will follow established precedents in resolving the case "at bar." Thus, if a similar case comes forth, a court will stick to the same rule in settling the present case. The strength of *stare decisis* is that the system brings order, uniformity, certainty, and predictability to the law. When a rule is applied to more and more cases with the same or similar issues, the likelihood is greater that the rule will be followed in the future and thus an attorney will be better able be to advise his or her client on how a court will decide regarding his client's potential case.

Nevertheless, there are some problems with precedents and the system of *stare decisis.* First, the more dissimilar the issues and factual patterns between the precedent case and the current legal controversy, the more the uncertainty as to legal result. Consequently, the present court now has some flexibility in resolving such a dispute. Secondly, if there are no cases or very few cases with the same or similar issues and facts, then a court similarly will possess more latitude in determining what rule of law to apply. Thirdly, if there are no cases in point anywhere, then a court is free to decide the dispute, yet again based on prevailing customs or, if none exist, upon principles of what is just. The next "precedent" problem arises when there is a "bad" or "unfair" rule that is "stuck" in the system and is applied again and again. Fortunately, this has not been a regular occurrence, and there have not been that many "bad" laws. A court is not bound slavishly to precedent but rather ultimately to justice. Finally, the original reasoning behind a precedent may no longer exist, but the courts may still keep applying the rule. An example of the latter situation was that, in the old common law, hospitals were regarded as charities and thus were "cloaked" with charitable immunity, meaning that a hospital was not legally responsible for the wrongs committed by its employees. Now, obviously, hospitals are responsible due to heightened public policy concerns as well as the fact that hospitals have become "big business" protected by insurance. Yet again, this has not been a widespread problem as courts are very cognizant of constantly changing conditions.

Despite the primacy of case law in common law systems, statutes are important, particularly in the United States. Today, many branches of the law are based on legislatively and formally crafted enactments. For example, corporation law in the U.S. is based predominantly on state corporate codes. However, there are many branches of law that include contracts, agency, and torts, which are all governed by the common law. In examining statutory law, three main areas need to be addressed: 1) the process by which statutory law is created; 2) the differences between statutory law and the common law; and 3) statutory interpretation.

The term "statutory process" connotes the power that legislative bodies have in enacting statutes. There are, however, limitations to this power, specifically: 1) subject matter limitations imposed by the constitutions; 2) procedural requirements; and 3) a requirement that statutes be reasonably definite and not vague. Regarding the first limitation, in the United States the federal constitution sets forth the legal parameters for legislation crafted by the federal (that is, national) legislature and the state legislatures. The U.S. Constitution grants specific powers to the federal government, called enumerated powers, that include the power to declare war, to maintain a postal system, and to make uniform bankruptcy laws. All other powers are reserved to the states. The federal legislature thus must point to an express power or a power implied from a select power, such as the power to create a draft and impose a selective service requirement, in order to legislate.

The states—the original sovereign entities in the United States—have full power to legislate based on their "police power," which is not only a law enforcement tool, but also the authority to pass any legislation which the state legislature deems necessary to promote or protect the health, safety, and welfare of the citizens and people residing in that state. The second limitation in the U.S. comes from the federal constitution as well as the state constitutions, which set forth procedural requirements for promulgating statutes. For example, in the U.S. Constitution, all revenue bills must originate in the House of Representatives. And at the state level, the subject of every bill must be in the title and there can be only one subject per law. Finally, laws must be reasonably certain and definite. Consequently, if a statute is worded so that persons of ordinary intelligence cannot comprehend its meaning, the statute is invalid and illegal.

There are two major differences between the common law and the statutory law: 1) the process of creation, and 2) the form after each becomes operative. The process for legislative enactments is that a statute becomes a law only after passing through formal steps. For example, in the U.S., at the federal level, a bill passes through both houses of Congress and is then approved by the President. Common law rules, by comparison, emanate from the judicial branch of government and are legal rules created by judges in order to settle cases and controversies. A statute is found in an official text, is typically quite specific, and becomes part of a code. Common law decisions are published in casebooks, called "reporters" in the U.S., and are far more general in content.

There are, moreover, other differences between statutes and the common law. Social and political forces have more impact on the formation of statutory law but judges are typically more insulated from such pressures. Legislatures have an option to make laws and legislators individually can refrain from acting. Judges must settle controversies that are presented in their courts, but courts can make law only in deciding cases that come before them. The legislative power, especially at the state level in the United States, is very broad. A legislature can even enact statutes where case law is non-existent. In addition, and most significantly, legislative bodies can pass laws that can expressly overrule the common law. The legislative body, elected by the people, is "closest" to the people so, accordingly, legislative laws will supersede the common law.

The courts, however, do have a role in the statutory process. The legislative bodies, as noted, do have broad power to enact statutes, but the courts also have a corresponding power. That is, the scope and meaning of a statute will not be known until a statute is construed by the courts in settling actual concrete disputes under the statute itself. This search for legislative intent, called statutory interpretation, is a major source of law and one that is performed by the courts. In interpreting a statute, courts will adhere to the "plain meaning" rule, which holds that if the language of the statute is so clear, then only one result can be logically indicated and the court will not consider any other factors, thereby giving deference to the will of the legislative body.

Nonetheless, the "plain meaning" rule may not be appropriate to evaluate many statutes as the statutes themselves may be drafted with imprecise language. (There are very few words that are subject to just one evident meaning.) Moreover, the legislative body may have acted intentionally by being a bit imprecise so as to have some flexibility in the statute's application. Courts will look at the statute as a whole so as to divine its intention as well as to examine the problem that prompted the statute's enactment and refer to the legislative history of the statute in order to look for clues as to legislative intent. Thus, courts have more interpretative power.

Legal Reasoning

Legal reasoning is the process of critical legal analysis that judges use in order to resolve a case. Attorneys and law students also use this process to analyze or "brief" a case.

The first step in legal reasoning is to summarize the facts of the case, paying very close attention to the key or "operative" facts in the case—that is, the facts that will be crucial in the ultimate resolution of the case. The second step is to ascertain the issues in the case. The issues are the legal questions that the court will be asked to resolve. Characteristically, courts start out by addressing general legal issues and then move on to narrower component issues. The third step is to state the rules of law that will be used to decide the case. The fourth step is to apply these rules of law to the unique facts of the case and thereby to render a decision as to who prevails and who does not prevail in the case. Frequently, this decision is designated as a "holding." The final step is to provide the reasoning for the decision. The reasoning typically is based on the law and the application of the law to the concrete facts of a particular case, but the reasoning can extend to the rationale behind the rules of law themselves. Usually at the appellate, or review, level in the United States legal system, these decisions are framed as judicial "opinions." Ascertaining the issues is the crucial step, since how can one know what to answer if one does not know the questions?

It is important to note that these rules have precedent quality, i.e. that they can be used to resolve the case at bar and other cases with the same or similar facts.

Global Legal Perspectives

Regulations, laws, and policies differ across countries, businesses, and local communities.[1] It is for this purpose that global managers and entrepreneurs are often asked to understand and comply with the differing laws and regulations, especially in countries where they conduct business. It is vital, initially, that managers perform business in conformity with legal, ethical, civic, and moral standards in any country, city, or region in which business is performed. They must also earn the respect of the "locals" (such as their immediate communities) through participation in local civic events so as to not only learn the culture, but also, most importantly, to provide a positive image of their company and the country they are representing.

It is for this reason that managers and entrepreneurs must understand how to abide by international laws in order to achieve their goals. Most international businesses are aware of global regulations of employment practices, legal rules for business transactions, environmental protection standards, and so forth so as to teach their employees to respect other business standards as well as help them gain the "know-how" of conducting business in other countries. It is very important for

---

[1] Coauthored with Bina Patel, Nova Southeastern University.

global managers and entrepreneurs to understand local policies as it is a strategic way to help achieve goals. Global managers and entrepreneurs must also understand foreign business policies as well as their home country's business foreign policies. For instance, all firms residing in the United States and those that are based out of the country but conduct business in the other countries that include the U.S. are to comply with the U.S. Foreign Corrupt Practices Act, which states what business information and business performances are considered to be illegal and legal. For example, it typically is considered illegal for firms to gain favorable treatment of local businesses by offering gifts, money, and other bribes to local foreign officials or businesspeople. It is important to note that countries that are members of large organizations, such as the United Nations (UN) or World Trade Organization (WTO), are oftentimes forced to comply with international laws, norms, and regulations in all sectors, including business practices. For example, countries that are members of the UN or WTO must abide by rules that state that firms cannot infringe or violate antitrust or copyright laws.

Global managers and entrepreneurs are often faced with challenges of performing business practices in accordance with all types of laws at the local, state, national, and international levels in countries in which business is conducted, including their home countries. As the rules, regulations, laws, and policies vary across countries, business practices, and local communities, global managers and entrepreneurs must be keenly aware of these differences in order to achieve their goals in a legal and efficacious manner. Therefore, global managers have the responsibility to not only adopt local, national, and international laws, but also to ensure compliance by their employees.

Civil Codes and Latin America[2]

Legal systems and legal practice in Latin America are premised on civil law codes, in particular the so-called Napoleonic Code, which was the French Civil Code of 1804. As early as the 1820s, the civil codes of Haiti and Mexico were taken almost directly from the French Civil Code, and in the mid-1800s, the Brazilian and Argentinian civil codes were also crafted based on the French Code. However, the globalization of law, legal practice, and business; the prevalence of international as well as regional treaties such as the North American Free Trade Agreement, the Andean Community, and the Free Trade Area of the Americas; and the extent of international investment in Latin America have all led to a "sidestepping" of "domestic" civil law and national legal systems in contemporary Latin American countries.

---

[2] See M.C. Mirrow (2005).

Accordingly international rules and norms are becoming more relevant to Latin American business transactions while local laws and customs have become less so. Accelerating this trend is the significant fact that most people now provide, in their international contracts and agreements, choices of forum as well as choices of law provisions. Similarly, many international agreements have alternative dispute resolution provisions, whereby private law and procedure mechanisms, such as arbitration and mediation, are to be utilized to resolve disputes. The contractually agreed-upon rules that are used to resolve these disputes are often rules from other legal systems, principally Anglo-American common law systems. The result is that local Latin American civil codes and laws are becoming increasingly less applicable in today's global business and legal community.

These very important choices of law, choices of forum contract provisions, as well as alternative dispute mechanisms will be covered in the following chapter and other subsequent chapters of this book.

Management Strategies

Global managers are taught to comply with rules and regulations at the business level of their firms.[3] However, they are not always taught how to react or act in accordance with international laws at the local levels. Therefore, it is vital for firms to provide thorough and comprehensive training classes for all global employees, especially managers. For example, firms often have available copies of policies of international companies with which they conduct business on a regular basis. These policies usually summarize the country's laws, business practices, and other practices that are accepted or unaccepted legally and morally, thereby providing a framework of what is to be expected from international managers working abroad.

This knowledge is especially important for global managers performing business in developing countries, where unethical behaviors such as bribes, paying money to gain favors, etc. may be practiced. In most African countries, such as Kenya, Congo, or Egypt, where corruption appears to be very high and readily accepted, global managers and entrepreneurs must be careful not to get caught up in this environment as it can not only hinder the ultimate achievement of their business goals but also could potentially land such managers in prison should they be criminally sanctioned.

In addition, home countries oftentimes do not allow their citizens to conduct business overseas in an illegal manner. For example, countries such as the United States have established the U.S. Foreign Corruption Act to explicitly

---

[3] Coauthored with Bina Patel, Nova Southeastern University.

state that managers may not engage in any illegal business practices and that the U.S. will take legal action in order to ensure that just practices remain the norm.

Furthermore, global firms have the obligation and responsibility to train their managers working abroad to take into account a country's culture, local customs, communities, acceptable business practices, and so on in order to achieve their business goals. It is also important for firms to provide such training courses in risk management, business confidence, and so on as this education will help managers deal with "real life" scenarios that may occur in host countries. For example, according to a survey conducted by the World Economic Forum, global executives were very hesitant to perform business in Middle Eastern countries due to the high market, financial, and operational risks associated with the region. In these situations, where global managers must engage in business practices, firms must provide the proper training, with real scenarios, to help build confidence and find solutions in order to achieve success. It therefore is the responsibility of a firm to provide global managers with the proper resources needed in order to help them conduct successful business practices abroad.

Summary

Each country has its own diversity and uniqueness in regards to its culture, ethical expectations, and laws. Global managers and entrepreneurs should become aware of these laws and customs, respect them, and make sure their employees obey them. As the law continues to serve its purposes through means of legal regulations, procedures, and mechanisms of legal promulgation, adjudication, implementation, and enforcement, global managers and entrepreneurs should be fully prepared to embrace these legalities with dignity. It is especially vital for international managers and entrepreneurs to understand how legal issues and laws affect business practices and performances in various countries as this knowledge can only help in the achievement of their goals. With issues such as the sources of law, classifications of the law, legal reasoning, and global legal perspectives, management is faced with the challenges of establishing successful strategies to help their employees, as well as themselves, to embrace local cultures, laws, policies, and, most importantly, business practices while at the same time respecting their home country's laws and their company's regulations.

THREE

THE LEGAL SYSTEM OF
THE UNITED STATES

The defining of the scope of the United States court system goes back further than early colonial times and continues into the present day. The Founding Fathers of the United States established a federal legal system that allowed for individual states to comprise their own laws in accordance with their beliefs and ideas. But as slavery was a major divisive factor during the 1700s and 1800s, the legal system eventually diverged between the ideals of the Northern and Southern states, culminating in the U.S. Civil War. However, due to President Lincoln's leadership, the union was restored, slavery was abolished, and the legal system was on its way to being seemingly more liberal, justified, and democratic.

Today, the legal system continues to operate in accordance with the United States' Constitution, which was effectively written to allow for flexibility. The powers of government are separated into three areas: judicial, executive, and legislative branches. The powers are then narrowed down to state and local offices, in which officials and representatives are elected by the citizens of the United States.

The differences and similarities between the state and federal court systems in the United States will be examined shortly, along with the conflicts that arise between laws, equity, and court procedures at the federal, state, and local levels. In addition, global legal perspectives and management strategies shall be evaluated to help determine the relationship that exists between the United States' legal system and global management and entrepreneurship. The federal constitution and its application to business will be discussed in U.S. Constitutional Law and Business chapter.

The United States Court System

The courts in the United States are endowed by the federal and state constitutions with judicial power. The judicial capacity encompasses three powers: 1) adjudication—the application of legal principles and rules to factual disputes in order to settle cases and controversies; 2) judicial review—the power for statutes and other actions to be evaluated by the two other branches of government to ensure that they are constitutional; and 3) statutory interpretation—the power to construe and clarify legislation for exact meaning.

As noted, the United States is a federal system of government with two distinct levels of government—the national/federal government and the state governments—and thus there are two separate court systems. Because the fifty state court systems each have their differences, any detailed explication is beyond the scope of this book. Rather, this book will examine the common elements in the state court systems and compare this general state model to the federal court system.

State v. Federal Court Systems in the United States

At the apex of the state court system is the highest court in the state, typically called the state supreme court. A state supreme court possesses appellate jurisdiction, which is the power to hear and decide judgments of the lower courts of the state. A state supreme court decision is final in all cases not involving federal Constitutional law or statutory law or treaties. Below the state supreme court, the intermediate courts form the next level in the state court system. These courts also possess appellate jurisdiction and hear cases from the "inferior" courts within the state system. These intermediate courts typically are called district courts of appeal, but in larger and more populated states, there will be several courts of appeal established in geographic regions throughout the state. Below the courts of appeal is the level of the original jurisdictional courts. These courts possess both civil and criminal jurisdiction and thus they are usually the first courts to hear and resolve disputes between private parties as well as criminal offenses against the state. Typically, these original jurisdictional courts are referred to as circuit courts. Inferior courts also include the county courts, which hear minor civil and criminal matters, but which also possess the original jurisdiction to decide real estate cases within their jurisdiction. Finally, state inferior courts also include small claims courts, at times called summary procedure tribunals, as well as traffic courts.

At the apex of the federal court system is the U.S. Supreme Court, which is the only federal court expressly created by the Constitution. It is the highest court in the United States. The U.S. Supreme Court possesses both original and primary jurisdiction. The former extends to cases concerning ambassadors and public ministers as well as cases in which two states are parties. This is in contrast to the court's appellate jurisdiction, which extends to all cases brought into the federal court system as well as the appellate jurisdiction of certain cases decided by the state supreme courts. The intermediate level in the federal system is composed of the U.S. Courts of Appeal. The United States is divided into eleven judicial circuits and each circuit has a designated court of appeals. These courts have appellate jurisdiction only, and thus review the final decisions of the courts of original jurisdiction in the federal system. The District Courts are the courts of original jurisdiction in almost all cases maintained in the federal court system. They are the trial courts for federal, civil, and criminal matters. Finally, there are specialized federal courts created by Congress to determine specialized matters, such as the Patent Court and the Tax Court.

Courts and Jurisdiction

Legal rights are meaningless unless they are enforceable. Accordingly, one major function of government is to provide a system wherein the rights of parties under the law can be determined and enforced. The instrumentality of government so empowered is known in the Anglo-American system as a "court." A court is a tribunal established by the government to hear and decide cases and controversies properly brought before it, grant redress to aggrieved parties, deter wrongdoing, and enforce punishment against wrongdoers. This legal process ordinarily is called a "lawsuit" for civil cases and a "prosecution" for criminal cases. However, it should be noted here that other instrumentalities of government—for example, administrative agencies—have been created to enforce certain distinct areas of law and thereby determine rights and obligations. The topic of administrative law, particularly the judicial power of agencies, will be discussed in the Administrative Law and Business chapter.

Jurisdiction is the power each court has to try cases and to decide certain types of controversies. As mentioned, original jurisdiction is the power a court has to hear a case when it is first brought into the legal system whereas appellate jurisdiction is the authority a court has to review a judgment of a lower court or an administrative agency. The term "jurisdiction," however, should not be confused with the term "venue." Jurisdiction deals with the original authority of a court to hear a case; but once a court has jurisdiction, venue rules will govern where geographically the case will be heard. The venue of a lawsuit usually is the location of the court nearest to where the defendant to the lawsuit resides or where the incident or transaction at issue occurred. Venue assumes that a court has jurisdiction, and "merely" determines where within the court's jurisdiction the case will be heard.

There are two indispensable prerequisites for a court to obtain original jurisdiction. First, the court must have jurisdiction over the subject matter of the lawsuit, i.e. a case must fall within a court's general, special, limited, or monetary jurisdiction. And second, the court must have jurisdiction over the person against whom the lawsuit is being brought. As a general rule, if a court lacks either requirement and enters a judgment, the judgment is void and thus has no legal effect. Regarding subject matter jurisdiction in a federal system such as the U.S., the general rule is that cases begin in the state courts, however, two very important exceptions hold that if a case is a "federal question" case or if there is "diversity of citizenship" between the litigants, the federal courts properly will assume jurisdiction. A federal question case is any case where the person bringing the lawsuit is basing his or her case on the federal constitution, a federal statute or administrative regulation, or a U.S. treaty. A diversity of citizenship case is when the person bringing the suit, usually called the plaintiff in such a context, and the defendant, the person being sued, are citizens of different states. Significantly, there is no federal question requirement for a "diversity" lawsuit but there is a requirement that the amount in controversy in the lawsuit be over $75,000.

In examining the original jurisdiction of a court, an action *in personam* must be differentiated from an action *in rem*. An action *in personam* is an action wherein the plaintiff is seeking to hold the defendant liable for a personal obligation. To illustrate, this means that the plaintiff is suing the defendant to recover money damages for an alleged breach of contract by the defendant, the plaintiff is suing the defendant to recover a debt allegedly owed by the defendant to the plaintiff, or the plaintiff is suing to recover damages for personal injuries that the defendant purportedly negligently inflicted upon the plaintiff.

When the plaintiff brings an action *in personam*, the court must have jurisdiction over the person of the defendant. A court can acquire *in personam* jurisdiction in a variety of ways. The first method occurs when the defendant resides within the territorial jurisdiction of the court and the defendant is either "served" with a summons and copy of the plaintiff's complaint or the sheriff or other designated court officer leaves the summons and complaint with an adult at the place of the defendant's residence or work. The second method of securing personal jurisdiction occurs when the defendant resides elsewhere but is personally served by the sheriff with a summons and complaint when the defendant resides within the court's territorial jurisdiction.

An action *in rem* is one in which the plaintiff is seeking to enforce a right against certain property owned by the defendant. Such a suit must be brought before the court where the property—the "res"—is located. Ordinarily, there is no need for personal service but there is, however, a service via "publication," wherein a notice of the lawsuit is published in a newspaper which circulates in the geographic area of the lawsuit itself. One such example would be a mortgage foreclosure action against a real estate property, but the suit itself must have been brought in the county court where the property is located. Another example would be a divorce lawsuit. Because a marriage is considered by the law to be a "res," publication usually will be sufficient enough service for a court to obtain jurisdiction over even an out-of-state spouse.

Finally, there are two types of state statutes—Long Arm statutes and Motorist Implied Consent statutes—that directly impact the courts' jurisdiction. A state Long Arm statute permits a cause of action to be instituted against an out-of-state resident defendant in the plaintiff's home state if the defendant himself does business within the state, thereby impliedly giving his or her consent to be sued on a claim arising from that business. The plaintiff typically serves the Secretary of State for that state and thereby acquires jurisdiction over the out-of-state defendant. However, the U.S. Supreme Court has ruled that in order for an out-of-state defendant to be subject to the jurisdiction of a state court, the state must have "minimum contacts" with the defendant. Of course, doing business and having business operations in the state will satisfy that standard, but a contemporary problem exists due to the advent of the Internet: There is not yet a definitive legal answer as to what type and level of Internet activities will satisfy the "minimum contacts" standard. This issue will be discussed in the chapter dealing with Internet Regulation.

Finally, a Motorist Implied Consent statute is a state statute that maintains that when a non-resident operates a motor vehicle within the borders of the state, he or she impliedly consents to appoint the state's Secretary of State as an agent for accepting service if the non-resident is involved in a motor vehicle accident within the state.

Conflict of Laws

A problem arises in a legal system composed of sovereign legal entities—such as the "states" in the U.S.—when a legal situation occurs due to acts or transactions that affect more than one state and/or parties from different states.

Which states' laws will be applicable in such a multiple state case? As an example, let's say that a plaintiff, a citizen of Florida, makes a contract in Georgia with the defendant, a citizen of New York, with agreement for the rendering of a performance in New Jersey. The defendant refuses to carry out the contract and is then sued in federal court in New York (to satisfy personal and diversity jurisdiction, assuming the requisite amount in controversy). What state laws should the federal court apply? In answering this question, the courts will apply Conflict of Laws rules, of which there are three main categories: 1) If the case is a contract case, as above, and if the issue is the validity of the contract, then the law of the state in which the contract was made will govern the case; but if the issue is the performance of the contract, then the law of the state where performance took place or is to take place will govern; 2) If the case is a tort case, the law applicable is the law of the state where the injury occurred; and 3) In all other cases, the law of the state with the "most significant relationship" to the lawsuit will apply to the case.

One way in which the parties to a contract can eliminate "conflicts" and uncertainties as well as jurisdictional disputes is to have in their contracts "forum selection" clauses to designate the court to hear a potential controversy as well as "choice of law" clauses, which will designate the law of a particular jurisdiction as the controlling law of any possible breach of contract lawsuit.

Law v. Equity

In Anglo-American legal history, after the Norman Conquest of England in 1066, the early English kings established a nationwide system of courts with the kings designating individuals as their personal representatives to settle disputes. The system was originally based on the prevailing customs in the community. Controversies were decided on a case-by-case basis and over time, a body of decisions on a variety of subjects was created. These decisions, as noted, became precedents and formed the foundation of the common law.

However, even early on in English jurisprudence, problems with the common law precedent system developed. There was a tendency for too many cases to be decided in the same way with the result that the common law system became rigid. Moreover, since the primary relief which common law could grant was the payment of money damages, there were certain wrongs for which no adequate remedy existed at common law for a court to enforce. Consequently, the parties began to petition the early English kings for particular types of relief that were not available from the ordinary courts of law, which were themselves bound by the common law. The king, of course, was not bound by recognized legal principles but had the power as well as the duty to decide cases based on conscience, fairness, and justice. Gradually, there were so many of these special appeals to the king that the king turned over such cases to his chancellor, ordering him to decide these cases in the king's name in an equitable manner. When deciding these disputes became too demanding even for the chancellor, he then appointed legal representatives to act in his and the king's name in order to decide these cases in an equitable manner. Thus, eventually there evolved in England an additional and different system of law, called Courts of the Chancery and, later, Courts of Equity, which were empowered to provide relief when there was no adequate remedy at law available.

Several equitable remedies were created to mete out justice, but the two most important remedies were the decree of injunction and the decree of specific performance which are still very important legal remedies even today. The injunction originated when a plaintiff asked a common law court of law to stop the defendant from doing a particular act, such as trespassing on the plaintiff's land or committing a nuisance that hindered the plaintiff's enjoyment of his or her property. The court of law had to deny that request as the only type of relief such a court could grant was money damages for past injury; the court did not have the power to prevent future trespass or nuisance. As a result, the plaintiff asked the king for relief, and if the king or chancellor or his representative deemed the request to be justified, an order in the king's name commanding the defendant to stop committing the wrongful act was issued. This order, called an injunction, was enforced by the king's inherent power to do justice and maintain law and order and was specifically enforced by the king's "contempt" power, which included imposing fines and imprisonment for refusing an order of the king.

Specific performance started as a request by a plaintiff for an order commanding a defendant to live up to the terms of a contract made with the plaintiff. However, a court of law once again could only order the defendant to pay money damages for the loss caused by the defendant's breach of contract. So a Court of Equity was asked to issue such a decree and would do so if money damages were inadequate to fully compensate the plaintiff (such as in an instance when the subject matter of the valid and breached contract was a rare heirloom). Today, in Anglo-American jurisprudence, there has been a fusion of courts of law and courts of equity. As a result, today the same court administers both legal and equitable remedies, though in the case of equitable remedies it must be noted that there is no right to a jury trial.

The injunction and the decree of specific performance, as well as other equitable remedies, will be covered throughout this book in a modern-day business context.

Court Personnel, Organization, and Procedure

The most important personnel of the courts are the judge, clerk, and jury. The judge is the primary court officer, who is either appointed or elected and whose function is to preside over and manage trials, maintain the order and dignity of the proceedings, decide questions of law, and to instruct the jury on the applicable law of the case at hand. Each court has the power to make rules to transact legal business before the court as well as to preserve order. As mentioned earlier, a violation of an order from a judge, violation of the court's rules, or an affront to the dignity of the court will result in a party being held in "contempt of court," which can be rendered via fine or imprisonment. The clerk of the court is the court officer whose function it is to keep accurate records of cases and to enter cases on the court calendar. The jury is the body of citizens sworn by the courts to decide questions of fact, to apply the law to the facts, and thereby to render a verdict, which the court will convert to a legally enforceable judgment.

Court procedure is a very consequential area of the law. After all, what good are substantive rights if one does not know how to enforce them procedurally? Yet procedure is a very detailed and complex legal matter. There are many precise and specific procedural rules as to how, when, and where a lawsuit may be brought to the courts and how it is to be maintained in the courts. As noted earlier, in a federal system such as that present in the U.S., there are procedural rules for the federal courts as well as for the state courts. Moreover, at the state level, there is no uniform judicial procedure as the laws of each state differ. Thus, an explication of procedural law is way beyond the purposes of this book. Nevertheless, the authors would like to make some basic and general observations regarding court procedure, using the civil "side" of the courts as the illustration.

A civil lawsuit must be commenced by a party who institutes a cause of action. (A court can only settle disputes between individuals when one of the parties formally requests the court to do so.) A civil suit begins when one party files a written request, called a complaint or a petition. As noted, the plaintiff is the person who initiates the action and the defendant is the person being sued. A person who is contemplating filing a lawsuit must be very careful about the applicable statute of limitations, which establishes the time period within which a lawsuit must be brought forth. Statutes of limitation begin to "run" when the occurrence or transaction first transpires. For example, generally speaking, in a negligence lawsuit, the injured party has two years to bring the lawsuit; in a breach of contract case, the aggrieved party has four years; and in a fraud lawsuit, the victim has six years. If the time period to bring the suit has expired, the statute of limitations is said to "toll" and the plaintiff's lawsuit will then be dismissed.

The ordinary order of civil court events is as follows: 1) The plaintiff files a complaint with the clerk of the court, which sets forth the nature of the claim and the remedy sought; 2) The next step is service of process, whereby the clerk issues a summons with a copy of the complaint attached, which must be served on the defendant. This "service" gives the defendant notice that a cause of action is being brought, and subjects the defendant to the power of the court;) In response, the defendant can file a motion to dismiss the lawsuit for, for example, failing to state a legally recognizable cause of action, or because of a lack of subject matter or personal jurisdiction; 4) If the defendant's motion to dismiss is overruled, or if the defendant did not file one, then the defendant must respond to the complaint. The defendant's response is called the "answer," wherein the defendant either admits to or denies the plaintiff's allegations. If the defendant fails to answer within the prescribed time limits, the defendant is said to "default," resulting in a default judgment being rendered against the defendant and, as a result, the plaintiff winning the case by default. The complaint and the answer are usually called the "pleadings," which are distinguished from "motions," which are "merely" requests to the court for an order.

If the pleadings indicate that the only questions involved in the lawsuit are questions of law, the judge can then decide the case based on the pleadings alone. One party can actually request that the judge decide the case as a matter of law if there are no genuine factual issues to be resolved. This type of request is called a motion for summary judgment. If all parties agree, the case may be tried by the judge alone, without a jury, thereby leaving the judge to decide both questions of law and questions of fact. However, if there are factual issues to be decided, then the case must be turned over to a jury to determine the facts.

In the case of decision by jury case, an example of the uncertainty of "pure" law arises in a question such as: When does an offer to enter into a contract—with no time period specified—expire? In such a case, the judge will instruct the jury that the law holds that such an offer expires at the expiration of a "reasonable" period of time. The thorny question, however, is what exactly constitutes "reasonable"? This question of "reasonableness"—both in contract law and in the greater context of all Anglo-American jurisprudence—is left to the jury to resolve.

Continuing on, if the lawsuit is not resolved on summary judgment motions alone, the next stage is called the "discovery" process. Discovery encompasses the parties asking for and receiving pertinent factual information regarding the case. Such methods of discovery include interrogatories, which term means asking official questions of the opposition. Other methods include asking for admissions, deposing the parties and witnesses under oath, and requesting physical exams, photos, and documents. The purposes of discovery are both to be sure that each side is made fully aware of the facts at hand as well as to encourage settlement.

After discovery, a jury must be selected. The jury selection process is known as "voir dire," which entails the parties and the judge all asking prospective jurors a series of questions designed to ascertain jurors' qualifications, abilities, and biases. The parties to the case at hand typically can challenge jurors for cause, but challenges must be supported with a reason for a juror's dismissal. There is no limit to the number of challenges that can be made. However, a party can also assert "peremptory" challenges to automatically dismiss a juror—even in most cases—without a reason. The number of peremptory challenges is limited, usually to three.

Once selected, the basis for the jury's factual determination is the evidence. Evidence is presented by both parties in conformity with substantive and procedural evidentiary rules. The "trier of fact," usually the jury, can only decide questions of fact on the basis of the evidence presented.

Evidence consists of testimony, that is, answers by persons made to questions asked in court—and "real" evidence, that is, papers, books, records, and other things tangible. As a general rule, evidence, in order to be admissible, must be relevant, material, and unbiased. For example, presenting evidence that one of the parties involved in a breach of contract dispute was previously divorced would be inadmissible on the grounds of irrelevancy.

A "witness" is a person who testifies in court and who has direct connection with the facts of the case. What this means is that a witness saw events occur or heard one of the parties say something. If a witness did not in fact see or hear such things directly, the evidence will be deemed to be "hearsay" and is therefore excludable. A person can be subpoenaed and thus compelled to appear in court as a witness.

The party initiating the lawsuit has certain legal "burdens": the burden of persuasion and the burden of proof. The burden of persuasion refers to the obligation to introduce sufficient evidence to keep the lawsuit moving forward. The burden of proof refers to the obligation of a party to convince a jury of a specific issue at hand. For example, in a criminal case, the state has the burden of proof to prove its case "beyond a reasonable doubt"—that is, to a moral certainty. Whereas in a civil case, the usual standard is a "preponderance of the evidence," meaning that there has been presented a greater evidentiary weight for rather than against a particular argument. In certain civil cases such as fraud, for example, there is an intermediate standard established for the burden of proof: "clear and convincing" evidence.

It is also instructive to briefly outline the ordinary trial procedure, again from a civil case perspective. Initially, the attorney for the plaintiff commences legal proceeding by making an opening statement to the jury in which he or she discusses the nature of the plaintiff's cause of action and what the plaintiff expects to prove. The defendant's attorney then makes a rebuttal statement and also states what the defendant expects to prove. The next step is the direct examination, wherein the plaintiff's attorney presents his or her witnesses and asks questions. Next is the cross-examination stage, where the defendant's attorney asks the plaintiff's witnesses other questions in an effort to disprove previously given answers. The defendant is then allowed the same cross-examination process of his own witnesses by the plaintiff. After all witnesses have been examined and cross- examined, the following step is called the summation, wherein the attorneys for each side summarize the evidence, argue legal and factual points, and then suggest to the jury the particular verdict that the attorneys feel is proper and just. At this stage, the parties can make a motion to the judge for a "directed verdict." Such a motion may argue that one of the parties failed to introduce evidence or that the evidence introduced is so weak that the case should not go to the jury, but rather the judge should immediately direct a verdict favoring a particular party.

Assuming that there is no motion for a directed verdict presented or that such a motion is denied, the judge at that time will "charge" the jury. This means that the judge will instruct the jury as to the rules of law governing the particular case. These points of law are called the jury's "instructions." After receiving its "instructions," the jury will deliberate on the weight and sufficiency of the evidence, decide the facts of the case, apply the law to the facts, and thereby render a decision, called a "verdict." The judge then will enter a judgment in accordance with the jury's verdict.

A party who is dissatisfied with the verdict and judgment can appeal the case to the proper appellate court. However, an appellate court will not retry the case and will not hear witnesses. Rather, the appellate court will perform two functions: It will examine the entire record to see if the lower court judge made an error of law; and second, the appellate court will determine whether the jury's verdict was supported by substantial evidence. If there is an error in the law or if there is insufficient evidence to support the verdict, the appellate court will set the verdict aside and the case will have to be retried.

Assuming no appeal is sought or an appeal is unsuccessful, the losing party must comply with the judgment of the court. If there is non-compliance, the prevailing party can take steps to seek to have the court's judgment carried out. This is typically called "execution" and it can have numerous manifestations (such as, for example, asking the court to compel the sale of the defendant's property). Once the legal matter is decided, it is regarded as "res judicata," meaning the case is final and cannot be re-litigated.

Finally, the "full faith and credit" clause of the U.S. Constitution requires that a court judgment rendered in one state be given complete legal effect in "sister" states.

Global Legal Perspectives

Legal systems vary around the world, and managers from multinational companies[4] must comply with laws not only from their home countries, but also with those laws of regions around the world where they conduct business. Therefore, global managers need to constantly keep abreast of current legal statuses of doing business in and relationships between different countries.

For example, the United States has several treaties with countries including Canada, Mexico, countries within the European Union (EU), and so forth, thus allowing for free trade, liberal laws, etc. The United States court system also treats foreign firms conducting business within its borders as domestic businesses, thus providing for an equal and fair opportunity for all.

However, due to political instability, economic crises, and so on, the same is not always true for U.S. firms conducting business in other countries. Therefore, managers of firms belonging to "the state" of various countries are often forced to solve matters that are not governed exclusively by their home country's laws. The international legal system is then applied in conjunction with national states that accuse one another of violating international laws. To address such problems, the International Court of Justice (ICJ) was established by the United Nations (UN) in the Netherlands during the 1940s. The ICJ has dual roles—providing opinions and suggestions regarding legal questions to foreign agencies

---

[4] Coauthored with Bina Patel, Nova Southeastern University.

and settling court matters that affect different national states. Oftentimes, when state-owned firms have disputes with other firms from foreign countries in areas such as breach of contract law, the ICJ will take over the matter. It is important to note that only national states or member nations of the UN may apply and appear before the ICJ, not private parties.

The World Trade Organization (WTO) also has its own dispute resolution procedure, whereby member nations are entitled to appear before the court in order to solve disputes relating to rules of trade, agreed-upon procedures and other matters. The WTO advises nations to first settle their matters outside of courts due to the simple fact that not all court cases will be heard.

The international legal system is also based upon the morals and ethics shared by various member nations, including adherence to fundamental human rights. In essence, there is no single, defined, superseding international law; however, the rules that do exist are established so as to achieve fairness and equality. Even though the court systems of both the ICJ and WTO vary in comparison to the U.S. legal system, rules and laws are still created in order to provide for a more stable, global, business environment for all.

The European Court of Justice

The European Union (EU) has evolved from a free-trade treaty arrangement organization to an economic union and now to a political power. Fundamental to the formation of the EU as an integrated political union has been the development of a common legal system. Particularly, the role played by the European Court of Justice (ECJ), which was created by the treaty of Rome in 1957, has been indispensable to the formation of this union.

The ECJ was created to resolve disputes concerning European Community (EC) treaties as well as to assist national courts in the consistent interpretation and application of EU treaties and laws. The ECJ is also charged with the legal responsibility to make sure that member states comply with EU laws. According to one commentator,[5] the ECJ has been the "main facilitator" in the legal integration of the European community. The only way, according to this commentator, for the EU to supersede 150 years of different constitutions and civil codes was to grant the ECJ the power to overrule and establish a system of precedents that the national courts would be obligated to follow. Article 234 specifically enables the ECJ, on application by national courts, to provide rulings on the interpretation and validity of EC law. That is, once the ECJ "speaks" on an issue of EC law, a national court is bound by the ECJ's interpretation and therefore "must apply" the Court's ruling to the facts of the particular case at hand.

---

[5] See Gierczyk, Yvonne (2005).

The Court's decision, as noted, bears precedent-effect and thus will apply to future cases that entail the same or similar facts. So, although the Court is grounded in civil law traditions, Article 234 of the Treaty of Rome nonetheless confers to court decisions the power of precedents. Article 234, therefore, is considered by many to be the most important part of the Treaty of Rome.

So, by borrowing the system of precedents and *stare decisis* from the tradition of common law, the ECJ, by adjudicating cases, has created of system of legal and political integration.

Enforcing Legal Judgments in Brazil[6]

Enforcing legal judgments of one legal system in another country's legal system has always been a challenge in the global legal arena. In Brazil, money judgments on business matters, issued by courts in the United States and elsewhere, are enforceable by the Brazilian legal system. The Brazilian system of recognition of foreign judgments does not analyze whether the decision was fair or in accordance with Brazilian law or in accordance with the law of the foreign country where the decision was rendered. Consequently, a Brazilian court will not confirm or deny the merits of the foreign judgment. Rather, it will only cooperate with a foreign court by ascertaining that the judgment was rendered in a sovereign manner by a foreign country's laws and then acknowledging the judgment as such.

There are four mandatory requirements in Brazil for that country's recognition of foreign judgments: 1) the foreign judgment must be based on a decision by a foreign judge of competent jurisdiction; 2) the parties must have been served with notice of process, or if the judgment was a default one, it must have been legally entered based on a non-answer to a complaint; 3) the judgment must be final with the legal force of *res judicata;* and 4) the foreign judgment must be notarized by the Brazilian consul and be accompanied by a Portuguese translation rendered by a sworn translator in Brazil. However, there are three grounds for non-recognition of foreign judgments—that is, when the foreign judgment contravenes the national sovereignty public policy or good mores of the nation of Brazil. These key non-recognition standards, however, are not precisely defined in the governing law, and thus the scope of their application is subject to some debate in Brazil.

What is most interesting to note is that although the "national sovereignty" and "public policy" legal standards do have some explication in the law, in Brazil, the U.S., and internationally, a "good mores" criterion is more of an ethical term that harkens back to the theory of ethical relativism. Consequently,

---

[6] See Oliveira, Maria Angela Jardim de Santa Cruz (Winter 2006).

ascertaining the moral norms of Brazilian society may emerge as more than a "mere" philosophical or ethical exercise for the international business person since a legal judgment must comport to those "good" norms in order to be legally enforceable.

Japan and Litigation

Whether disputes are decided by means of formal legal mechanisms, such as trails, or informally through alternative dispute resolution procedures has always been an interesting and important area of global legal and business practice. Japan always has been regarded as a non-litigious society where disputes are amicably resolved through mediation and conciliation, and where suing a person or even a business was considered to be a shameful act.

However, a recent article reported that cultural norms may be changing (Inagaki, 2006), "thanks" perhaps to the influence of the United States and its adversarial legal system. Thus, a shift in social attitudes toward litigation and lawyers is now occurring in Japan. Yet concomitantly, one problem has emerged: a shortage of lawyers in Japan! Japan has approximately 22,000 lawyers—one for every 5,790 people—compared with one for every 278 in the United States. Moreover, under the current Japanese attorney Bar Examination, which is scheduled to be abolished in 2011, fewer than 1,500 candidates were permitted to pass the exam and become attorneys. To compare, in the U.S., which has about twice the population of Japan, that number is close to 75,000.

In response to Japan's shortage of lawyers, the government plans to more than double the number of legal professionals—lawyers, prosecutors, public defenders, and judges—to 50,000 by 2018. More lawyers and, specifically, more *practically* trained lawyers, are needed. Accordingly, the first U.S.-style law school opened in Japan in 2004, and now Japan has 72 law schools. But it is not just the desire to settle disputes in a more formal, adversarial fashion that is prompting these significant changes. Businesses have begun demanding more specialized legal counsel, especially in the areas of tax law and intellectual property law. Furthermore, bankruptcies are increasing in Japan and, consequently, so are bankruptcy legal filings. Even inheritance and divorce disputes are now being brought to court.

In addition to an increase in legal professionals, juries for serious criminal cases will be introduced in 2009 in order to ease the responsibility of the judiciary. This use of lay juries will be a very significant change for Japan and will give the ordinary Japanese citizen his or her first opportunity to participate as a member of the justice system.

Thus, Japan appears to be moving closer to the more formal, adversarial, attorney-oriented legal system used in the United States.

Management Strategies

It is important to remember that legal systems vary across the world. Therefore, management must be trained in advance in order to overcome legal challenges that may hinder company goals and procedures. Due to the many challenges that have been introduced in this chapter, multinational firms must provide their managers, who may work abroad, with courses that specifically deal with strategic decision making, exercising "teamwork," dealing with "locals," adapting to the surrounding environment, and abiding by local laws and customs. This knowledge will not only make managers better aware of the atmosphere of the countries where they conduct business, but it will also compel them to act accordingly should difficult situations arise.

As global firms engage in foreign business, they are often faced with not only different languages, cultures, and business practices, but also variations in the legal systems and interpretations of the rules. Domestic and international managers, as well as entrepreneurs, will encounter both national and foreign laws when conducting business internationally and these laws affect several areas of a firm's structure, such as accounting procedures. In essence, it would be wise for all managers to conduct research of political issues and local laws before engaging in global business agreements. This knowledge will allow for corporations to conduct more streamlined operations that are in line with the legal requirements of host countries in all regions of the world, including those that are politically unstable. However, managers must exercise care in dealing with politically unstable countries as political insecurity continues to be one of the major causes of reduced profits for businesses due to factors such as the seizure of land and property (among other concerns), especially in countries that may become highly nationalistic.

There are resources available to global managers, such as local American Chambers of Commerce in most countries where U.S. companies are active.[7] Their members are knowledgeable about local business practices and can also advise local attorneys who have worked with U.S. companies. Another source of possible help for global managers, especially if there is an issue with a host government agency, is the Commercial Section of the local American Embassies and Consulate Generals, which are staffed by the Foreign Commercial Service of Commerce Department. These Foreign Service Nationals (FSNs), especially those with long service records, know the local business community and bureaucrats. They may be able to provide insights as to the reputation of individuals the company has dealt with before. They

---

[7] Sources suggested by Dr. Norman Glick, a global educator.

may be able to provide access to government officials who might otherwise be difficult. Initial contact with this resource can be made through a local Commerce District Office, located in 60 cities across the United States. For example, managers and entrepreneurs who live near or travel to South Florida can make use of the office in Miami.

Legal Counsel—Finding and Managing Attorneys[8]

As this book will plainly show in the chapters to come, a company *will* need legal advice and legal counsel. Today, there is simply too much law—substantively, procedurally, as well as domestically and globally—for a company to safely navigate without legal counsel.

Finding the right attorney can be a major challenge for the global manager and entrepreneur. Usually, fellow business managers and business people will make recommendations. National, state, and local bar associations have listings of attorneys according to specialty. In the United States, many states have certification programs whereby an attorney may become certified in the United States in a specialized field and then may be allowed to advertise himself or herself as a legal specialist. Many practicing attorneys also teach on a part-time basis at local business schools as adjunct professors, frequently instructing in business law and government regulation of business subjects or on specialized legal subject matters, such as taxes. Thus, a manager's training—perhaps as an MBA student—typically should bring the student manager into direct contact with practicing attorneys.

When requiring counsel, a company must consider whether it intends to use its own in-house lawyers for routine matters and then retain outside law firms for specialized or trial matters or to use its own employees for these situations as well. The more legal work that can be done in-house, the more money a firm will ultimately save on legal work. Salaried staff lawyers of the firm can perform legal research, provide legal advice, and engage the routine legal tasks, such as compliance reports required by government regulatory agencies.

All legal work that needs to be done at a company, either by its own attorneys or outside counsel, should be condensed and categorized into a readily accessible in-house research "bank" so, for example, the firm will not have to pay to have the same research done by outside counsel and thus have the same legal memos prepared. The expense of legal research, even if done by legal assistants, adds up, and very quickly can turn into one of the most expensive components of legal services. The firm's in-house lawyers will also need to monitor and manage the outside attorneys and in essence "keep them in line." In particular, litigation

---

[8] See Bagley and Dauchy (2008) and Davidson and Forsythe (2011).

strategies, tactics, and efforts should be very closely guarded and supervised. This legal management role is typically performed in a large company by its general counsel.

But not all companies have a general counsel or, for that matter, a legal department at all. So, if an outside law firm is to be used, a decision has to be made as to whether the outside law firm is to be employed on a retainer basis—meaning that the outside firm will have a continuous relationship with the company for advisement and certain prescribed legal matters—or whether the law firm should be employed on more of a short-term *ad hoc* basis.

Another suggestion would be for a company to seek bids for well-defined types of legal work. If the work is litigation, an option would be to break the litigation down into its major components and then to ascertain the work to be done and the cost for each part of the process: The idea is to negotiate the best possible legal deal. Another suggestion is to seek either a standard fee for billable hours or a discount for a certain number of billable hours, or to try to secure a discount for retaining a law firm for a longer period of time, say a year or two. A company should not be shy in firmly telling a law firm the limit it is willing to spend on legal fees and services, from "billable hours" to photocopying expenses. A company should insist on a detailed accounting of every dollar to be spent for legal fees and legal services.

Also, there is nothing wrong with "comparison shopping," which is just as smart in the legal sector as it is in the retail sector. The company should meet regularly with its attorneys, question their work, and gauge what attorneys from the outside law firm are on the "team." If there is a new member of the law firm on the client-company's "team," it is not unreasonable to demand that the "education" of this new attorney regarding the client's case be borne by the law firm and not by the client's time or "dime." A company also should be wary of a law firm asking for too many extensions for a case, especially if new attorneys are to be "brought up to speed" on the company's case.

Costs should be monitored on a daily basis. Indeed, a company may have the requisite leverage to pressure its outside law firms to cut costs, particularly for "everyday" legal work. Today, computer technology and software exist to enable a company to see exactly how much each research project, deposition, or hearing in a case will, or has, cost. Such technology and software exist so that the company itself may reduce paperwork, lessen research needs, facilitate research, and more closely scrutinize billing practices of outside attorneys. For example, computerized fee-tracking systems exist for a company to compare the costs of using the country's major law firms for various types of legal work.

A company should also consider pressuring a law firm to use different types of billing, such as hourly rates, flat fees, and contingency fees, for different kinds of legal work. A company should insist that certain legal assistant personnel perform basic legal tasks, such as research, and that these tasks not be done by more established attorneys who, naturally, would charge more for such services. Of course, the more experienced attorneys would appear in court on behalf of the firm and then bill accordingly. Also, efficiency and results should be rewarded.

Negotiation leading to the settlement of a case is always an option, and one that must be discussed by the firm at every stage with its legal counsel. Lawyers, especially trial lawyers, may have a very aggressive and combative attitude, which may turn out to be very expensive in a protracted, litigious legal matter. An early settlement of a case could save the firm a great deal of money in legal costs.

A company should never merely "rubber-stamp" its law firm's legal bills. The basic idea here is for a company to be an "educated consumer" when it comes to legal services. In essence, the client, the company, must get more actively involved in its own cases.

Expert legal counsel is strongly advised for the entrepreneur as the law is very extensive and very complex, and mistakes and omissions can be quite costly. Moreover, a lawyer will be able to discern issues and foresee potential problems that a lay business person might not have even thought of. As such, bringing a lawyer into the process in the beginning will save the entrepreneur time, effort, and money in the long-term. Should the entrepreneur opt for a large or a small law firm? One advantage of a large firm is that it typically would have legal experts in several specialty areas, such as securities law and intellectual property, which may be important to the entrepreneur. Yet large law firms typically charge more per hour but may be able to accommodate an extended payment schedule. Also, large firms may be more bureaucratic in nature and involve many lawyers and legal assistants and administrative assistants so that dealing with all these personnel, especially less experienced ones, may translate into more time, effort, and money spent by the entrepreneur. Small firms characteristically contain generalist attorneys. An attorney in a small firm usually will charge less and there will be more personal contact. If the entrepreneur initially is seeking advice on what type of business entity to form and to achieve the formation, then a business law attorney at a small firm should suffice. Of course, if the entrepreneur asks his or her generalist attorney to act in specialized legal areas, the entrepreneur should be aware that he or she may wind up "paying" for that education.

How does the entrepreneur find an attorney? There are many lawyer referral services and law directories, such as state and local bar associations, but usually these are impersonal and uncorroborated sources, and thus generally not sufficient. A better way is to seek a referral from family, friends, work colleagues, and other business people and entrepreneurs in the locality. Accountants, financial advisors, and real estate agents and brokers are also good sources for referrals as they regularly work with attorneys. Local universities are another good source of referrals. For example, the professors who teach legal subjects are attorneys, and though most do not practice, they certainly can make recommendations. Also, many universities use adjunct professors, and many of these professors who teach law subjects as adjunct professors are practicing attorneys in the community. Local attorneys often serve as guest speakers at universities and for the local chamber of commerce and local community groups. Whether the attorney works in large or small firm, the entrepreneur must determine the firm's billing procedure. Will the work be billed on an hourly basis or by the project? Charging by the hour is fine if the attorney can efficiently and effectively complete the legal task; yet billing per hour could end up quite costly if there is an educational component for the attorney. Hourly prices can range from $125 to several hundred dollars for each billable hour. If the work is done by the project, the amount asked, for example, to form a limited liability company, would be a "flat fee" and one that can be compared to other attorneys and law firms. It is incumbent on the entrepreneur to ascertain exactly what legal services are included in the flat fee as well as for the billable hour. For example, the entrepreneur must determine how and to what extent travel time, time spent answering emails and phone calls, research and writing of legal memos and documents, and consulting with legal assistants and other attorneys are handled in the fee structure. The entrepreneur should not be shy! That is, ask for price estimates, maximum price limits, and sample bills; ask how long the task is expected to take; ask that administrative and clerical type actions performed by the attorney be billed at a lower rate; ask that telephone calls under a certain number and time not be billed; and review carefully any invoices and challenge any expenditures that the entrepreneur feels are unauthorized, improper, or unreasonable. Of course, as a matter of common sense as well as "good business," the more educated, prepared, organized, and proactive the entrepreneur is when dealing with attorneys, the more efficiently, economically, and effectively will the entrepreneur be able to use the attorneys services. Have the necessary documents readily at hand; explain what is intended and what the situation is clearly and succinctly. "Time is money," thus the advice to the entrepreneur is: "Do not waste the attorney's time, and your money"!

The entrepreneur must be aware of the attorney-client privilege which protects as confidential communications between a lawyer and his or her client who is seeking legal advice. If the client is a corporation, the privilege still exists and protects communications between the company's lawyer and company personnel so long as the nature of the communication relates to the employer's duties and the relationship with the lawyer is directed by the employee's manager or a corporate officer. Note, though, that the privilege belongs to the corporation and not the employee, and thus the employee cannot claim it if his or her corporation brings a lawsuit against the employee.

A major purpose of hiring an attorney is to secure help in avoiding legal problems. Of course, the more the business person knows about the law and the legal risks therein, and the more information the business person has the more accurate and thorough records he or she keeps, the better prepared the business person is to consult with an attorney in a timely manner in order to prevent serious legal problems. The objective is to prevent "small" legal issues from developing into "large" legal problems, which the attorney still may be able to solve, but at a much greater cost in time, effort, and money.

A determination must be made by the entrepreneur as to how to hire an attorney. That is, should be hired on a case-by-case basis or on a continuing basis by means of a retainer. Hiring an attorney on a retainer basis might make sense for an established business with regular legal work, such as drafting or reviewing leases and contracts. In such a case, the attorney is retained with an "upfront fee" for a certain period of time, and the attorney agrees to provide advice and consultation when needed; but if the attorney must perform legal work, then he or she is paid an hourly fee in addition to the retainer fee. Yet for the business person commencing a business as an entrepreneur the hiring of an attorney on a retainer basis early on in the commencement of the business would typically entail a large expenditure of money, which a new business typically would not have. If the attorney is hired on a case-by-case basis, a determination must be made as to how the attorney is to be paid – with a "flat" fee, on an hourly basis, or on a contingency basis. The flat fee, where the attorney is paid a specific dollar amount for a specific legal task, usually is best for relatively simple and straightforward legal matters, such as incorporating a business or forming a limited liability company. Yet if the legal matter is more complicated, an hourly fee might be preferable, though the business person is well-advised to seek an estimate of what the total legal cost might be. The business person also should ask if the hourly fee will be more for trial work or less for work done by "junior" attorneys and legal assistants. Also, the business person must ascertain how much the attorney will bill for taking a phone call or responding to an email, for example, that does not last a full hour. Most firms typically charge ¼ to ½ hour for these tasks even if they take less than the quarter or one-half hour billing increments. Finally, in lieu of a flat fee or an hourly payment, the parties can agree to a contingency fee arrangement, whereby the attorney agrees to represent the client, usually in a tort case, and accept as payment a percentage of the settlement or judgment obtained for the client. If the client does not prevail, the attorney gets nothing. These percentages typically range from 25% to 40%, depending on what stage the lawsuit is resolved, that is, in initial negotiations, when a demand is made, when a complaint is filed, after a jury trial, or after an appeal. The business person contemplating hiring the attorney on a contingency basis must ascertain who will pay for the costs of the litigation beyond the legal representation. That is, who will pay for the filing fees, copying of records, courier services, etc? Usually, the attorney will pay all the costs associated with the litigation, but then, assuming the business person prevails, the attorney will then bill the client for the cost of expenses and take the amount from the client's percentage of recovery.

An entrepreneur or any business person has a variety of methods to find an attorney. In the United States, attorneys are admitted to the Bar Associations of the individual states and are licensed by the individual states and are authorized to practice law only in those states. They cannot practice in other states, unless of course they are admitted to other states Bar Associations; and they cannot practice in foreign jurisdictions. State Bar Associations and local Bar Associations have lists of attorneys who practice in the state as well as locally; and these lists typically will indicate legal specialties practiced by certain attorneys. In order to use a "specialist" designation the state Bar Association typically will require that the attorney take a certain number of specialty courses, practice for a certain amount of time in the specialized field, and/or take a special exam. Lawyer Referral services exist to provide recommendations (for a fee) of attorneys who can handle a legal problem confronting the business person. Recommendations are, of course, a very good means of finding an attorney. Recommendations can come from other attorneys (for example, the business person may have a general practice attorney who can recommend a specialist), from other business people, from family and friends, and may law professors and business law professors who teach at local law schools, universities, and colleges. Attorney advertisements are now ubiquitous, though many attorneys still do not advertise; but the prudent business person is well-advised to check out the advertising attorney credentials and claims with the state Bar Association to determine their veracity. The Martindale-Hubbell Law Directory also lists attorneys and provides information as to their areas of practice and backgrounds. Specialized attorneys, of course, charge more, but then the business person is paying for the attorney's specialized knowledge.

Attorneys, regardless of how paid, are expensive! Accordingly, it is incumbent on the business person to utilize his or her time with the lawyer in the most efficient and effective manner. So the business person must be prepared to discuss with the attorney the facts of the case in a succinct manner and to provide key information, such as people, places, dates, in a clear and organized manner. Copies of any pertinent documents should be provided, as well as proposed terms for a contract or those terms in the articles of incorporation, for example. The attorney, of course, will draft the final legal document. The idea, obviously, is to be prepared so as not to waste the attorney's time and the business person's time and money.

The entrepreneur and business person must be aware of the traditional Attorney-Client Privilege and the protection it affords to communications between the client and the attorney. This privilege protects confidential communications between an attorney and the client for the purposes of obtaining or providing legal representation, advice, and assistance. This privilege prohibits the attorney from revealing any communications between the attorney and the client without the client's permission (unless the client informs the attorney that the client intends to commit a crime in the future). This privilege belongs to the client, and not the attorney, and thus can only be waived by the client.

Summary

The United States legal system was created in order to provide for a fair and equal opportunity for all its citizens as well as to create opportunities for domestic and international businesses. The court system varies at the local, state, and federal levels and elections are held at all levels so that the people can elect representative officials. This chapter provided fundamental information regarding the legl system of the United States as well as extensive guidance to the business person and entrepreneur on how to find and manage attorneys.

Variations among and between the state and federal court systems of the United States, conflicts of laws, equity, and court procedures at all levels have been identified to more clearly illustrate and explain the U.S. legal system. Furthermore, global legal perspectives and managerial strategies were discussed to help clarify the relationship that exists between the United States legal system and other legal systems across the world, as well as to show how this symbiotic relationship influences decisions made by global managers and entrepreneurs. Due to the instability in global political, social, and economic environments, international managers are at times forced to overcome challenges that conflict with the goals of their own companies. Various legal systems have been established in order to help managers resolve such problems.

In addition, the levels of various legal systems from around the world also differ, based on their individual rules. Therefore, foreign managers and entrepreneurs from other countries must learn to abide by the laws not only of their own country, but also the local, state, and federal laws governing business in their host country.

FOUR

FOUR

INTERNATIONAL LAW

Globalization and the internationalization of business and work practices—in the hopes of gaining new market share so as to increase the "bottom line"—also bring about new complexities and legal challenges for a business and its management. The global manager, as well as the entrepreneur, must be respectful of different cultures as well as the local laws and policies of other people. Achieving such respect can be "operationalized" by way of learning about international laws and treaties as well as understanding the "do's and don'ts" of conducting business in today's complex global environment. As such, this chapter covers international law, comparative law, definitions and sources of international law, international trade, challenges associated with conducting business internationally, import and export considerations, and the effective management of various international transactions.

International Law[9]

International law is divided into public international law and private international law. Public international law consists of rules and principles which govern the relations and dealings of nations between one other. Public international law concerns itself only with questions of the rights in question in dealings between several nations or the rights of nations as they relate to the rights of the citizens or subjects of other nations.

In contrast, private international law deals with controversies between private persons—either natural or juridical—and more than one nation; such controversies often entail significant relationships. Private law includes the basic, classic concepts of law in national legal systems: status, property, obligation, and tort. It also includes substantive law, procedure, process, and remedies. In recent years, the line between public and private international law has become increasingly uncertain as issues of private international law may also affect issues of public international law. Furthermore, many matters of private international law bear substantial significance for the international community of nations.

International law is derived from several sources. The most important is treaties between nations. Treaties are contracts or agreements between nations,

---

[9] Contributed by Miguel A. Orta, Nova Southeastern University.

often referred to as covenants, compacts, protocols, or conventions. Such agreements are rooted in the concept of acceptance that the nation states that constitute the system will abide by them.

Customary law and conventional law are also primary sources of international law. Customary international law results when states follow certain practices generally and consistently out of a sense of legal obligation. In 1980, for example, the customary law was codified in the Vienna Convention on The Law of Treaties.

Conventional international law derives from international agreements and may take any form that the contracting parties agree upon. Agreements may be made in respect to any matter except to the extent that the agreement conflicts with the rules of international law, thus incorporating basic standards of international conduct.

International agreements create law for the parties of the agreement. They may also lead to the creation of customary international law when they are intended for adherence generally, and are in fact widely accepted. Customary law and law made by international agreement have equal authority as international law. Parties may assign higher priority to one of the sources by agreement. General principles common to systems of national law are secondary sources of international law. There are situations where neither conventional nor customary international law can be applicable. In this case, a general principle may be invoked as a rule of international law, because it is a general principle common to the major legal systems of the world and not inappropriate for international claims. The law of nations is a part of the law of the United States unless there is some statute or treaty to the contrary. International law is a part of the law of the United States only for the application of its principles on questions of international rights and duties. It does not restrict the United States or any other nation from making laws governing its own territory. A state of the United States is not a "state" under international law, since the Constitution does not vest it with a capacity to conduct foreign relations.

Although, international law exists, it should be pointed out that each sovereign nation is responsible for creating and enforcing laws within its own jurisdiction. Many countries often attempt to enforce their laws outside their borders, and this is referred to as "extraterritorial" application of laws.

International Taxation[10]

International tax laws, administered by the U.S. and foreign governments, can dramatically affect business decision-making, job creation and retention, plant

---

[10] Contributed by Miguel A. Orta, Nova Southeastern University.

location, and competitiveness. The basic tenets of tax policy are that income should be taxed once and only once—as close to the source as possible—and that a tax system should be neutral to business decision-making.

Taxation has many purposes other than to raise revenue for the government. Non-revenue tax purposes include redistributing income from one group to another, discouraging the consumption of products, such as alcohol and tobacco, encouraging the consumption of domestic goods rather than imported goods, discouraging investment abroad, and granting reciprocity to resident foreigners. Special interest groups in every country push for tax policies that favor their interests. These interests differ from country to country and often conflict, accounting at least in part for the complexities of international tax practices.

Taxation levels vary greatly among the nations of the world. Western European countries have relatively high tax rates, while "tax havens" have zero tax. Generally, the U.S. taxes companies on their income at the rate of 35 percent whether it is earned domestically or abroad by a subsidiary. Because foreign subsidiaries of U.S. firms pay income taxes to their host countries, the U.S. addresses the problem of double taxation by allowing firms to take a credit against their U.S. tax for income taxes they have paid to another country.

But because tax rates vary greatly between countries, the U.S. foreign tax credit system is far more complicated than it first appears. For example, suppose that International Widget Makers earns $100 million in U.S. profits and $100 million in profits from its Brazilian subsidiary. Under a purely worldwide tax system, International Widget Makers would owe $35 million—at the 35 percent rate—on its U.S. earnings and another $35 million on its Brazilian earnings. In order to avoid the double taxation of its Brazilian earnings, the U.S. system gives International Widget Makers a $28 million foreign tax credit for income taxes paid to Brazil at its 28 percent corporate rate. However, under the U.S. system, International Widget Makers still owes $7 million in U.S. taxes on those residual Brazilian earnings. This amount represents the difference between what the company paid to the host country versus the amount which that income would have been taxed had it been entirely generated in the U.S.

There is, however, a limit to the foreign tax credits U.S. firms may claim, and this limit is equal to the U.S. tax rate. Let's suppose that International Widget Makers also does business in Belgium, which has a top corporate tax rate of 40.2 percent, 5.2 percentage points higher than the U.S. rate. In this case, International Widget Makers would pay $40.2 million in Belgian taxes on that $100 million in income. However, International Widget Makers could only take a foreign tax credit equal to the U.S. rate, or $35 million. Because International Widget Makers cannot take a full credit for the taxes it paid in Belgium, it is therefore said to be in an "excess credit" position. Complicating this simple example is the fact that the U.S. system does not tax profits earned abroad until companies actually return those profits to the U.S. This part of the U.S. international tax system is called "deferral" because companies are able to defer paying taxes on such foreign-source income as long as they reinvest said income into an active foreign subsidiary. Further complicating things still is that the U.S., like many countries, has a system in place of "anti-deferral" rules: regulations that tax certain kinds of foreign-source income in the year it was earned, even though the U.S. parent company had not repatriated those profits.

There are many techniques multinational firms can employ to minimize their worldwide tax burdens. One method identified by some studies is the aggressive use of "transfer pricing," the price a parent company charges its overseas affiliate for a product, component, or trademark. Although complicated in practice, the simple goal of this technique is to "book" the higher expenses in a high-tax country—thereby minimizing the after-tax profits—and then "book" the profits in the lower-tax country, where they can then be deferred.

Another method firms use to minimize their global taxes is to shift the balance of tax-deductible debt and royalty payments between high-tax and low-tax countries. For example, the tax codes of many countries, including the U.S., grant a tax advantage to debt-financed expansion by allowing firms to deduct the interest costs of their loans from their taxes. However, there is no similar preference for equity-financed investments. Similarly, royalty payments are tax deductible, but dividend payments are not. Because of such incentives, many parent firms will lend capital to their foreign subsidiaries, especially to those in high-tax nations, as this practice allows the subsidiary to deduct interest payments paid to the parent company, thereby lowering its own taxable income. For the parent company, the interest payments are then taxed as income, but presumably at a lower tax rate than would be levied against the profits earned by the subsidiary in the higher-taxing country.

Worldwide, there exists a wide variety of different types and rates of taxes. The capital gains tax, for example, levies a tax liability on income derived from the sale of a capital investment. A capital investment can be almost anything: a home, a farm, a ranch, a family business, or a work of art. In most years, slightly less than half of taxable capital gains are realized on the sale of corporate stock with the capital gain representing the difference between the money received from selling the asset and the price paid for it. In the United States, capital gains tax collections account for just 6 percent of personal and corporate income tax receipts and just 3 percent of total federal tax revenues.

An income tax is a tax levied on the financial income of persons, corporations or other legal entities. Various income tax systems exist, ranging from a flat tax to a progressive, or graduated, tax system. In a flat tax system, all income is taxed at the same rate. In a progressive or graduated tax system, the tax is imposed such that the tax rate increases as the amount to which the rate is applied increases. The term *progressive* in this context refers to the way the rate progresses from low to high.

Income taxes are common in industrialized countries. The United States, for one, relies on income tax for most of its revenue. The following countries often referred to as "tax havens," however do not have an income tax: Andorra, Bahamas, Bermuda, Bahrain, Brunei, Cayman Islands, Kuwait, Monaco, Oman, Qatar, Saudi Arabia, United Arab Emirates, and Vanuatu.

In addition to the income tax, many countries raise revenue through the value-added tax (VAT). The VAT is similar to a sales tax in that it is a tax based on the value of goods and services. The VAT is a levy imposed on businesses at all levels of the manufacture and production of a good or service and is calculated based on the increase in price, or value, provided by each level of production. Because the consumer ultimately pays a higher price for the taxed commodity, a VAT is essentially a hidden sales tax. Originally introduced in France in 1954, VAT is now a major part of the tax structure of most Western European nations.

Consider the following example of a birthday cake to understand how the tax works. A farmer grows and nurtures the wheat that eventually will go into the cake. He then sells the wheat to a miller for 50 cents. Assuming a 10% VAT rate, the farmer will set aside 5 cents of the 50-cent sale price to pay the government. The miller converts the wheat to flour, thereby adding another 50 cents of value. The miller then sells it to the baker for $1.00. Because the miller added 50 more cents of value, he too will pay a VAT of 5 cents. The baker now bakes the cake and in the process adds $2.00 of value. After selling the cake to the retail store, the baker is now liable for 20 cents worth of VAT. The retailer then advertises the cake in displays and eventually sells the cake for $5.00, having added $3.00 in additional value (his VAT liability being 30 cents). All told, the wheat grown by the farmer has generated 60 cents of tax revenue.

VAT rebate enables exporting countries to offer lower-priced and more competitive goods. The World Trade Organization (WTO) permits a rebate of VAT when the product in question is exported but does not allow a rebate of income tax. Opponents of this type of tax argue that it represents a type of consumption tax that bears most heavily on the poor. In the U.S., many favor the imposition of a VAT and the lowering of income taxes. Other proponents argue that the VAT is relatively simple and can be fluctuated to conjure the income desired by a government.

Since there exist innumerable differences between the tax laws of different nations, many countries have executed tax treaties with one another. The presence or absence of a tax treaty is often a factor in the location of an international business investment as tax treaties make business operations more predictable. Most countries regard treaties as providing a standard framework for all countries in allocating taxing jurisdiction and treaties determine which country will tax which income. Tax treaties define such things as income, source, residency, and what income will be taxed within each country. These treaties often address how much the income, earned by a national of one country living or working in another country, may be taxed.

Most treaties contain provisions for the exchange of individuals' financial information between the tax authorities of the two countries in question. The United States presently has tax treaties with over 50 different countries. Under these treaties, residents (not necessarily citizens) of foreign countries are taxed at a reduced rate, or are exempt from U.S. income taxes on certain items of income they receive from sources within the United States. These reduced rates and exemptions vary according to country and specific items of income. If the treaty does not specifically cover a particular kind of income, or if there is no treaty between a certain country and the United States, then the individual or corporation must pay tax on the income without any benefit.

Tax treaties reduce the amount of U.S. taxes that residents of foreign countries must pay. With certain exceptions, treaties do not, however, reduce U.S. taxes imposed on its own citizens or residents. Ergo, U.S. citizens and residents are subject to U.S. income taxes on their worldwide income. Treaty provisions generally are reciprocal (that is, they apply to both treaty countries). Foreign taxing authorities sometimes require certification from the U.S. government that an applicant has filed—as part of the proof of entitlement to the treaty benefits—an income tax return as a U.S. citizen or resident.

International Law, Business, and Government

International law consists of rules and principles which govern the relations and dealings of nations with each other. International Law, which is in most other countries referred to as Public International Law, concerns itself only with questions of rights between several nations or nations and the citizens or subjects of other nations. In contrast, Private International Law deals with controversies between private persons, natural or juridical, arising out of situations having significant relationship to more than one nation. In recent years, the line between public and private international law has become increasingly uncertain. Issues of private international law may also implicate issues of public international law; and many matters of private international law have substantial significance for the international community of nations. International Law includes the basic, classic concepts of law in national legal systems—status, property, obligation, and torts. It also includes substantive law, procedure, process, and remedies. International Law is rooted in acceptance by the nation states which constitute the system. Customary law and conventional law are primary sources of international law. Customary international law results when states follow certain practices generally and consistently out of a sense of legal obligation. That is, the practice, action, or decision is followed in a regular manner and a country recognizes this practice as binding. Recently the customary law was codified in "conventional" international law, which is law derived from international treaties, agreements, or conventions, and which may take any form that the contracting parties agree upon. A treaty, also called a "convention," is an agreement or contract between two or more countries that must be legally authorized and ratified by the legal system in each country. For example, in the U.S., Article II of the Constitution empowers the President to enter into treaties on behalf of the United States, but with the "advice and consent" of the Senate (manifested by a 2/3rd's vote concurring vote of the Senators present). An example of a treaty is the Organization of Economic Cooperation and Development Anti-Bribery Convention (which treaty is patterned after the Foreign Corrupt Practices Act outlined in this chapter). Another example would be NAFTA—the North American Free Trade Agreement—between the U.S., Mexico, and Canada which regulates trade among those countries. Treaties and agreements may be made in respect to any matter except to the extent that the agreement conflicts with the rules of international law incorporating basic standards of international conduct or the obligations of a member state. International agreements create law for the parties of the agreement. They may also lead to the creation of customary international law when they are intended for adherence generally and are in fact widely accepted. Customary law and law made by international agreement have equal authority as international law. Parties may assign higher priority to one of the sources by agreement. However, some rules of international law are recognized by international community as peremptory, permitting no derogation. Such rules can be changed or modified only by a subsequent peremptory norm of international law.

Comity, Act of State, and Sovereign Immunity

The doctrines of comity, Act of State, and sovereign immunity are also very important international law principles. Comity means that countries should comply with international treaties, conventions, customary law, and other sources of international law due to the mutual respect that countries should have for one another as well as the need for effective and harmonious relationships. Of course, comity assumes that a particular country has signed a treaty or convention or has participated in international customs. Comity also entails one country deferring and giving effect to the laws and judicial decisions of another country (assuming they are consistent with the laws and public policy of the country asked to defer). Accordingly, U.S. courts ordinarily will not review laws, acts, or judicial decisions of foreign countries or interfere with foreign government legal and judicial proceedings which are taking place in foreign countries. However, it is important to note that comity is not law per se; that is, countries should abide by international agreements and they should honor foreign legal determinations, but they are not legally required to do so. Related to comity is the Act of State doctrine. This doctrine holds that the judicial system in one country does not have the power or authority to challenge and overrule the acts of another country within that country. To illustrate, if a U.S. citizen has property in a foreign country and that property is seized and expropriated by the foreign government (presumably pursuant to proper legal procedure, for a legitimate public purpose, and with payment of just compensation), nevertheless, based on the Act of State doctrine, that expropriation cannot be challenged in a U.S. court, for example on grounds that the compensation was not sufficient and that the property was really confiscated by the foreign government.

The doctrine of sovereign immunity is another fundamental principle of international law, which is based on the premise that the jurisdiction of a county within its own territory is exclusive and absolute. Consequently, as a general rule, sovereign immunity exempts foreign countries from the jurisdiction of U.S. courts. However, there is a statute in the United States, called the Foreign Sovereign Immunities Act (FSIA), which provides the exceptional circumstances when a foreign country can be sued in a U.S. court, to wit: 1) the foreign country has waived its immunity and has consented to be sued; 2) the lawsuit is based on commercial activity by the foreign country in the U.S. or commercial activity outside the U.S. which has a direct effect in the U.S.; 3) the lawsuit is based on personal injuries caused by the commission of a tort in the U.S. or any torture, extrajudicial killings, aircraft sabotage, hostage-taking, or providing material support and resources for the aforementioned acts. Furthermore, based on U.S. judicial interpretation, the FSIA only provides immunity to foreign governments and not to foreign officials even if they are acting in an official capacity.

International Jurisdiction

As with residents of different states in a federal system, such as the United States, jurisdictional issues also arise with citizens of foreign countries in the international arena, especially regarding the adjudication of disputes and the enforcement of judicial decisions against foreigners. Generally, a country can exercise its jurisdiction to adjudicate and enforce against foreigners when: 1) a person is physically present in a country's territory, except if he or she is merely in transit; 2) a person is domiciled in or a resident of that country; 3) a person regularly carries on business in that country; 4) a person has carried on an activity in the country and that activity is the subject matter of the dispute; or 5) a person has done something outside of a country but that action has a direct and substantial effect within another country. The international jurisdiction issue becomes even more problematical when the Internet is involved (as will be discussed in the U.S. national context in the Internet Law chapter). As difficult as it is to determine the jurisdictional issue involving an out-of-state website owner and business in the U.S., resolving the jurisdiction question will be even more daunting when the website or business owner is located in a foreign country. What is considered a "direct and substantial effect" in the "virtual" world of cyberspace? For example, if a foreign business uses the Internet to target consumers in the U.S., is that action sufficient for the U.S. courts to exercise jurisdiction? Will the courts and legislative bodies in other countries move to the U.S. "minimal contacts" Due Process standard? These difficult global jurisdictional issues will eventually have to be dealt with by the courts.

Another significant jurisdictional legal issue, as well as an ethical one, concerns human right abuses overseas and the use of the courts in the U.S. to seek redress therefor. In 2013, in an important international jurisdiction case involving the Shell oil company, *Kiobel v. Royal Dutch Petroleum Co.*, the Supreme Court ruled that U.S. courts do not have jurisdiction to hear cases of victims of human rights violations and other international law violations that occur in foreign countries and not in the United States. The lawsuit was premised on an 18th century law – the Alien Tort Statute, a very old and vague statute that grants the federal courts the power to resolve claims arising under the "law of nations." The lawsuit was brought by Nigerian refugees who contended that Shell had aided and abetted the Nigerian government in inflicting human rights abuses while suppressing protests against Shell's operations in Nigeria. Shell had denied the allegations; regardless, the Court ruled that the U.S. courts even lacked jurisdiction to decide the case because the allegations were too remote from the United States. The only U.S. connections were that the Nigerians bringing the suit had received political asylum in the U.S. and that Shell, an Anglo-Dutch company, does business in the United States. As construed by the Court, the statute provides redress against violations of international law that occur only within the United States. To hold otherwise, explained Chief Justice John Roberts, would make the courts in the U.S. the forum for deciding disputes from around the world and the U.S. the enforcer of international norms.

International Intellectual Property Agreements

Globally, there are several international agreements in place which protect intellectual property. The main agreements are: the Paris Convention of 1883; the Berne Convention of 1886; the TRIPS Agreement of 1994; the GATT Agreement of 1994; the WIPO Treaty of 1996; and the Madrid Protocol of 2003. The Paris Convention, known fully as the Convention of the Union of Paris, which approximately 175 countries adhere to, allows a party in one signatory country to sue for patent and trademark protection in the other member countries. The Berne Convention is the international copyright treaty, which affords legal protection to copyrighted works in all the member countries. Copyright notice on the work itself is not required for works produced after March 1, 1989 (though such notice is strongly recommended as it will rebut an assertion of "innocent" infringement). TRIPS stand for Trade-Related Intellectual Property Rights. It is an agreement that over 100 countries have signed, which grants legal protection to patents, copyrights, and trademarks. The most important part to TRIPS is the provision that each signatory nation provide in its own domestic laws legal protections for intellectual property rights as well as legal mechanisms and sanctions to enforce these rights. In essence, TRIPS forbids a signatory nation from discriminating in legal processes against foreign owners of intellectual property in favor of their own national citizens. The TRIPS treaty also extends legal protection to computer programs. GATT is the General Agreement on Tariffs and Trade, which established the World Trade Organization (WTO), which is an international trade organization of which the U.S. is a member. GATT's intellectual property provisions, which were ratified by the U.S. Congress, changed U.S. patent law to make patents valid for 20 years, and also changed U.S. law to make the time period run from the date the patent application was filed. WIPO stands for the World Intellectual Property Organization Treaty. The WIPO Treaty upgraded intellectual property protection, particularly on the Internet. It also should be noted that the U.S Digital Millennium Copyright Act implemented the provisions of the WIPO Treaty and established civil and criminal penalties for those violators who circumvent encryption software and anti-piracy protections for protected digital works. Finally, the Madrid Protocol is an international treaty dealing with trademark protection, which has been signed by approximately 80 countries, that seeks to facilitate international trademark protection, in particular by having a simplified and less costly process for multi-country trademark registration. These international agreements will be discussed more fully in the Intellectual Property Protection chapter.

Global Organizations and Legal and Regulatory Responsibilities[11]

Global managers and entrepreneurs have a difficult job. Laws are an important part of doing business and it is important for domestic and global managers and entrepreneurs alike to view law as a process of protecting and facilitating voluntary arrangements in a business environment. This is especially true in today's society, where almost everything seems to take the form of business or economic arrangements. But even more challenging tasks lay ahead: As globalization matures, more opportunities for mutually beneficial trade, investment, and business opportunities will emerge.

The transformation experienced in today's vehemently capitalist macro-environment, coupled with overwhelming thoughts of profit maximization, are some of the most fervent driving forces of current political-legal integration. This trend is not new, but has developed along with international trade and organizations, such as those regulating exports and imports vital to global management and entrepreneurship. These organizations include the International Trade Administration (ITA), the International Trade Commission (ITC), North American Free Trade Agreement (NAFTA), World Trade Organization (WTO), Free Trade Agreement of The Americas (FTAA), and others that have set formidable precedence for the widening of juridical boundaries and applications of laws in even neutral territories where peoples and nations intermingle in social and economic-business exchanges. Constitutional laws in every nation impact business managers. Regulations concerning antitrust, administrative, and regulatory issues, as well as environmental law, product liability law, and securities law all serve to affect managers. The most important laws that affect managers and their businesses are commercial laws, which deal with the principles of the law of contracts, agency, property, sales, and security transactions.

Global managers and entrepreneurs of the 21st century are a new breed of techno-savvy, competitive, and performance-driven individuals who are experimenting and practicing in an arena where change and uncertainty are the major forces undercutting strategic effectiveness. The changing legal environment in which they function also produces uncertainty, with each individual party seeking absolute advantage or mutual advantages. Managers must abide by laws and legal procedures upon which principles, policies, and procedures governing trade are based.

The legal challenges faced by global managers and entrepreneurs cover a broad range of issues, not limited to the following:
- Technological-Legal—Technology "piracy" and other laws, such as monitoring, etc.

---

[11] Contributed by Anthony McFarlane, Nova Southeastern University.

- Economic-Legal—Economic and trade laws: agency regulations such as ITC and ITA, etc.
- Social-Legal—Conduct of behavior premised on ethics, morality, and legal precepts
- Legal-Legal—National and international laws: Islamic, Code Law, Civil, etc.
- Agency-laws and procedural policies governing standards, quality, and exchange relationships
- Labor Laws—Diversity, employment, harassment, and discrimination laws
- The "Unwritten Laws"—"cronyism" and "cronies"

Global managers and entrepreneurs must recognize that although they are functioning in "borderless" business environments—i.e., "market spaces" instead of marketplaces—there are laws, rules, procedures, and regulations governing trade, relationships, methods of doing business, limitations on business, and definitions of ethics (right and wrong, fair and unfair practices) affecting individuals' and entities' rights and well-beings.

The global economy of the 21st century is one in which competition plays a vital role at three important levels: country-specific, firm-specific, and international-specific. As such, competition must be managed, in as much as it can legally and practically be, in order to maintain vital flows at all levels. This is especially the case at the country-specific and firm-specific levels, where it is most true for economies built on and striving for healthy and sustained balanced competition.

The United States economy, for example, is well-regarded for its dependency on progressive competition, which is essential to the continued prosperity of the national economy and wealth and progress of capitalism. Throughout previous decades, the United States government has been adamant in protecting its internal strengths and monitoring competition at all levels. Its many antitrust laws, fair trading practices, and multiple agencies involved in import and export transactions and regulatory practices testify to this notion.

Two powerful organizations that have been formed to regulate import competition are the International Trade Administration (ITA) and the International Trade Commission (ITC). While both organizations use different approaches and function on separate tasks and initiatives, their purpose is essentially the same: regulating import competition in firms, industries, and the economy.

The International Trade Administration (ITA)

The mission of the ITA, which is part of the United States Department of Commerce, is to create prosperity by strengthening the competitiveness of U.S. industry, promote trade and investment, and ensure fair trade and compliance with trade laws and agreements. The ITA is an essential part of the Department of Commerce and consists of several liaisons whose job it is to ensure the agency remains effective in the regulation of import competition.

The ITA regulates import competition through four units or departments. The ITA regulates import competition via three main methodologies:

1. *Through the Promotion of Trade and Investment:* The major goal of the International Trade Administration (ITA) is to help create economic opportunity for American workers and businesses by promoting trade and investment, which lead to prosperity and higher living standards. According to the ITA (2006), in order to increase trade and investment, the ITA helps U.S. companies navigate foreign markets while also educating companies about how to tailor their activities to the specific market with respect to their product slate, financing, marketing, assembly, and logistics. The ITA plays a role in assisting businesses, especially smaller businesses, to become more oriented towards exports. According to the ITA, "While the United States exports more than any other country, making that first export can still be a daunting challenge for a small or medium-sized business. ITA helps equip those businesses with the knowledge and tools that they need to meet that exporting challenge, and by extension, promote the trade and investment that helps us all."

2. *By Strengthening Industry Competitiveness:* In its bid to strengthen competitiveness within and across various industries, the ITA consults with U.S. industry so as to assess the impact of proposed domestic and international regulatory policies that affect American industry's competitiveness as well as the expansion of U.S. exports. As such, ITA ensures that U.S. industry's commercial interests are represented in trade negotiations, bilateral and multilateral discussions, and that the U.S. rulemaking process is maintained. ITA advances policies and strategies that stimulate innovation and investment, enhance economic growth, and support U.S. manufacturing and service industries as competition increases and globalization produces new challenges.

3. *By Ensuring Fair Trade:* ITA monitors industry access to overseas markets and works to remove costly barriers to product and service exports. In addition, in order to ensure fair trade, the ITA enforces trade laws and agreements to prevent unfairly-traded imports and safeguard both jobs and the competitive strength of American industry.

The ITA also functions in regulating import competition through its four subdivisions:

1. *The U.S. Commercial Service:* The U.S. Commercial Service is the trade promotion arm of the International Trade Administration and helps U.S. small and medium-sized businesses increase international sales

by providing world-class market research, trade events that promote a company's product or service to qualified buyers, introductions to qualified buyers and distributors, and counseling and advocacy through every step of the export process.

2. *Manufacturing and Services:* The Manufacturing and Services (MAS) unit of the ITA is dedicated to enhancing the global competitiveness of U.S. industry, expanding its market access, and increasing its exports. As such, the MAS strives to attain the following: Support American industry's global competitiveness through critical analysis of domestic regulations, legislation, trade policy development and negotiations; ensure U.S. industry input into the interagency trade policy, regulatory, and promotion processes; analyze trade data and economic policy to support trade negotiations and bilateral and multilateral discussions; and work with industry and government agencies to reduce costs of regulation and other government policies (ITA, 2006).

3. *Market Access and Compliance:* According to the ITA (2006), the Market Access and Compliance (MAC) identifies and overcomes trade barriers, resolves trade policy issues, and ensures that trading partners fully meet their obligations under trade agreements. MAC ensures access to world markets for American companies and workers so they can compete on a "level playing field." As far as import regulation, MAC focuses on resolving trade complaints and market access issues, which include intellectual property and piracy, quotas, standards, customs, transparency and contract sanctity, national treatment, good governance, and the sanitary and phytosanitary standards.

4. *Import Administration:* The Import Administration is the ITA's lead unit on enforcing trade laws and agreements so as to prevent unfairly traded imports and safeguard jobs and the competitive strength of American industry. Its job ranges from working to resolve disputes to implementing measures when violations and unfair trade practices are discovered.

The Import Administration is the major unit of the ITA when it comes to the regulation of import competition. According to the ITA, the Import Administration fields the majority of responsibilities. The Import Administration focuses more globally, drawing up applications for settling or identifying disputes in trades. The primary role of the Import Administration is to enforce effectively the U.S. unfair trade laws (i.e., the "anti-dumping" and "countervailing duty" laws) and to develop and implement other policies and programs aimed at countering foreign unfair trade practices. The Import Administration also administers the Foreign Trade Zones program, the Statutory Import Program, and certain sector-specific agreements and programs, such as the Textiles and Apparel Program and the Steel Import Monitoring and Analysis licensing system.

The Import Administration's job is overwhelming and more substantive than that of the agency's other three units. Apart from the above tasks in regulating import competition, the Import Administration of the ITA functions through its own four major import monitoring, licensing and compliance programs. These units are:

1. *Steel Import Monitoring and Analysis*—provides steel producers, steel consumers, importers, and the general public with accurate and timely information on anticipated imports of certain steel products;

2. *Subsidies Enforcement*—monitors foreign subsidies and identifies subsidies that can be remedied under the WTO Subsidies Agreement. The Subsidy Library is an easily accessible one-stop shop providing user-friendly information on foreign government subsidy practices;

3. *Textiles and Apparel*—oversees programs and strategies to improve the domestic and international competitiveness of the U.S. fiber, textile, and apparel industries; determines when market-disrupting factors exist in the domestic fiber, textile, and apparel marketplace; and administers U.S. textile quota agreements, formulates trade policy, performs research and analysis, compiles industry data, and promotes U.S. trade events; and

4. *Trade Remedy Compliance*—provides assistance to U.S. businesses that believe their trade problems may stem from unfair practices or the improper application of foreign unfair trade laws. For key countries, it tracks foreign government policies and market developments that might contribute to unfairly traded imports and keeps watch on foreign antidumping and countervailing activity to identify potential difficulties for U.S. exporters and/or conflicts with WTO obligations.

The aforementioned responsibilities are the different functions of the ITA in regulating import competition. Apparently, the ITA uses both internal and external measures in order to ensure that import competition is kept in balance with national competition and firm-specific competitive requirements to secure domestic economic growth and prosperity.

Another agency which functions in regulating import competition is the International Trade Commission (ITC).

The International Trade Commission (ITC)

The ITC, or United States International Trade Commission (USITC), as it is often called, is "an independent, quasi-judicial Federal agency with broad investigative responsibilities on matters of trade. The agency investigates the effects of dumped and subsidized imports on domestic industries and conducts global safeguard investigations. The Commission also adjudicates cases involving alleged infringement by imports of intellectual property rights. Through such proceedings, the agency facilitates a rules-based international trading system. The Commission also serves as a Federal resource where trade data and other trade policy-related information are gathered and analyzed. The information and analysis are provided to the President, the Office of the United States Trade Representative (USTR), and Congress to facilitate the development of sound and informed U.S. trade policy (USITC, 2006)."

The mission of the ITC is to 1) administer U.S. trade remedy laws within its mandate in a fair and objective manner; 2) provide the President, USTR, and Congress with independent analysis, information, and support on matters of tariffs, international trade, and U.S. competitiveness; and 3) maintain the Harmonized Tariff Schedule of the United States (HTS). In accomplishing its mission, the ITC has five major operations that serve its external customers: Import Injury Investigations, Intellectual Property-Based Import Investigations, Industry and Economic Analysis, Trade Information Services, and Trade Policy Support.

The ITC functions in regulating import competition adjudication of import injury cases through three main avenues: trade remedy investigations, industry and economic analysis, and its traffic information center.

1. *Trade Remedy Investigations:* The ITC determines whether imports injure or threaten to injure U.S. industries under a number of trade laws. Trade Remedy investigations include:

   (a) Antidumping and Countervailing Investigations, wherein U.S. industries may petition the government for relief from imports that are sold in the United States at less than fair value ("dumped") or that benefit from countervailed subsidies provided via foreign government programs ("subsidized"). Dumping and certain subsidizing are considered unfair trade practices, as per the 2006 material from ITC. The ITC and the U.S. Department of Commerce both have roles in these investigations, but each addresses a different question. Commerce determines whether the alleged dumping or subsidizing is happening and, if so, the margin of dumping or amount of subsidy. The ITC determines whether the U.S. industry is materially injured or threatened with material injury by reason of the imports under investigation. If both Commerce and the ITC reach affirmative final determinations on their individual questions, then Commerce will issue an antidumping duty order to offset the dumping or a countervailing duty order to offset the subsidy.

   (b) Five-Year (Sunset) Reviews: According to the ITC (2006), the Department of Commerce must revoke an antidumping or countervailing duty order, or terminate a suspension agreement, after five years unless Commerce and the ITC determine that doing so would be likely to lead to continuation or recurrence of dumping or subsidies (Commerce) and of material injury (ITC) within a reasonably foreseeable timeframe. Each agency conducts reviews on its separate question. If either agency makes a negative determination, the antidumping or countervailing duty order will be revoked. If both agencies make affirmative determinations, the antidumping or countervailing duty order will remain in place (ITC, 2006).

(c) Intellectual property rights infringement and other unfair acts (section 337 investigations): The ITC investigates certain alleged unfair practices in import trade. Most complaints under this provision involve allegations of patent infringement or trademark infringement. Parties in these investigations include the complainants, the respondents, and an ITC attorney who represents the public interest. Each investigation is assigned to one of the ITC's four Administrative Law Judges (ALJ), who oversees an extensive discovery process and holds an evidentiary hearing. The ALJ makes an initial determination of whether there is a violation of the law (Section 337 of the Tariff Act of 1930); the ALJ's determination is then subject to review and possible modification by the Commission. Remedies available under this law are exclusion orders, which direct U.S. Customs and Border Protection to exclude infringing products from entry into the United States and/or orders that direct entities to cease and desist from certain actions.

(d) Global and special safeguard investigations: Domestic industries seriously injured or threatened with serious injury by a surge of imports may petition the ITC for import relief. Global safeguard investigations do not require the finding of an unfair trade practice. Relief provided under this law is temporary in order to provide an industry with time to adjust to import competition. The ITC conducts an investigation, and if the Commission makes an affirmative determination, it recommends to the President relief that would remedy the injury and facilitate industry adjustment to import competition. The President makes the final decision whether or not to provide relief as well as the type and duration of relief.

(e) China safeguard investigations: Domestic producers can obtain relief under this provision if the ITC finds that increased imports of Chinese products are causing or threatening to cause market disruption. Similar to global safeguard investigations, if the Commission makes an affirmative determination, it also proposes a remedy to the President. The President makes the final decision whether to provide relief to the U.S. industry and the type and duration of relief.

(f) Trade remedy assistance for small businesses: The ITC's Trade Remedy Assistance Office provides information to small businesses and other small entities concerning the remedies and benefits available under U.S. trade laws and provides technical and legal assistance to eligible small entities seeking remedies.

2. *Industry and Economic Analysis:* The Commission's industry and economic analysis program consists of analysis conducted at the request of the President, Congress, and the Commission, as well as analysis conducted by staff on issues related to the mission of the Commission. Commission analysis draws heavily upon its industry, sector, and economic expertise and databases. The Commission's analysis is used to contribute to the development of sound and informed U.S. international trade policy and to the public debate on issues relating to U.S. international trade and competitiveness. Commission analysis integrates industry, trade, and tariff databases with sectoral and economic expertise and economic models in order to prepare a wide range of official Commission reports and staff-developed articles (ITC, 2006).

The ITC's Industry and Economic Analysis consists of the following: Research and Analysis, Product and Services Analysis, Regional Analysis, External Trade Resources, the Research Program, and U.S. Imports/Export Data (Dataweb).

3. *The Traffic Information Center:* The regulation of import competition by the ITC also takes place via its traffic center functions and initiatives. The Harmonized Tariff Schedule of the United States (HTS) was enacted by Congress and made effective on January 1, 1989, replacing the former Tariff Schedules of the United States. The HTS comprises a hierarchical structure for describing all goods in trade for duty, quota, and statistical purposes. This structure is based upon the international Harmonized Commodity Description and Coding System (HS), administered by the World Customs Organization in Brussels. (The 4- and 6-digit HS product categories are subdivided into unique 8-digit U.S. rate lines and 10-digit, non-legal statistical reporting categories.) Classification of goods in this system must be done in accordance with the General and Additional U.S. Rules of Interpretation, starting at the 4-digit heading level—in order to find the most specific provision—and then moving to the subordinate categories. The "general" rates of duty sub-column contains normal U.S. trade relations duty rates. Products of some NTR countries may be eligible for preferential tariff programs, as reflected in the "special" sub-column. Column 2 (the so-called "statutory rates") applies to countries listed in

general note 3(b). These general notes set forth the rules for applying the HTS. Embargoes, anti-dumping duties, countervailing duties, and other very specific matters administered by the Executive Branch are not contained in the HTS (ITC, 2006).

Both the ITA and ITC have different functions in the regulation of import competition. However, regulating import competition is the major goal of each agency and as such, their work must overlap and they must work closely under the United States Department of Commerce to effectively achieve their goals. They function under the same department and apply the same rigorous economic and legal standards in assessing import injuries, ensuring fair trade practices, investigating and handling cases which violate established rules, standards, and provisions on competition and trade. Furthermore, both their missions involve the promotion of fair trade practices which are healthy to continued competitiveness in industry. They both also promote prosperity of sectors and firms as well as of the entire economy and region. The agencies differ only in their approaches and methods.

Global managers and entrepreneurs invariably become subject to the laws, regulations, and policies put in place by these bodies. Most trade today involves export or import, whether of technology, labor, or other factors of production, and this fact brings in the added challenge of contending with international global laws and regulations.

The European Union and Other International Organizations

The EU, also known as the European Community (EC), and originally known as the European Common Market, is one of the most significant international intergovernmental organizations in the world.

The EU was established in 1957, with the Common Market formed prior in 1951. The EU is composed of 17 European countries (as of the writing of this book), mainly from Western Europe but now also from Eastern Europe, and possibly Turkey in the near future as well. (A unanimous vote is needed to admit a new member to the EU.) Today, the EU is a true economic, monetary, and political union. Accordingly, the people, services, goods, and capital of EU members can move just about as freely within the EU as they can within a member nation. Although a truly detailed explication of the EU is beyond the scope of this book, several important legal components of the EU must be mentioned.

The Council of Ministers, also known as the Council of the European Union, is the main legislative body for the EU. The Council enacts legislation that applies directly to the member states. It must be emphasized that once such legislation is passed, there is no need for the member states to also enact the same legislation. Members are appointed to the Council by the governments of the member states. Some matters before the Council require a unanimous vote, while others require only a majority vote.

The European Parliament is a government body directly elected by the citizens of the member states. The Parliament's main functions are to consult with the Council and to give opinions and make recommendations as to legislation.

In essence, the European Commission is the executive branch of government of the EU. The Commission is composed of representatives of the member states, but it is meant to represent the EU community and not merely to serve the individual interests of the member states. It develops policy, gives opinions, and makes recommendations. It also has some legislative and judicial functions. However, the main authority the Commission has is the executive power to take enforcement actions to ensure that the member states comply with various EU treaties.

The European Court of Justice is the judicial branch of the EU. Each member of the EU appoints one judge to the Court for a six-year term. The Court interprets EU treaties and laws and resolves disputes concerning member states' compliance with EU laws. The Court is the final arbiter of EU law, however, the Court does not have any power to enforce its judgments in member states and must therefore rely on the member states to enforce its judgments. The Court's opinions are given great deference by its members.

The European Court of First Instance is in essence a court of original jurisdiction in the EU. It was established in 1989 in an effort to reduce the caseload of the European Court of Justice. The Court of First Instance has jurisdiction to handle lawsuits initiated by individuals and businesses, i.e., intellectual property and antitrust matters. Appeals from the Court of First Instance are made to the Court of Justice, but appeals can only be made regarding questions of law and not issues of fact.

In addition to the EU, there are many other organizations that global managers and entrepreneurs must be aware of. Therefore, a few will be briefly mentioned here.

NAFTA is a free-trade agreement between the United States, Canada, and Mexico that has removed most barriers to trade and investment. There are several economic agreements which have occurred as a result of NAFTA which include: 1) the elimination of tariffs as well as import and export quotas; 2) the opening of government procurement markets to companies in participating nations; 3) an increase in the opportunity to make investments in one another's countries; 4) an increase in the ease of travel between countries; and 5) the removal of restrictions on agricultural products, auto parts, and energy products. These factors pose legal and restrictive conundrums as well as new challenges for managers in the global business environment.

The World Trade Organization (WTO) is a global organization of countries that oversees rules and regulations for international trade and investment. This includes agriculture, intellectual property, services, competition, and subsidies.

Also noteworthy is the Free Trade Agreement of the Americas (FTAA), which impacts businesses and business activities. FTAA, however, is a proposed free-trade agreement among 34 democratically governed countries of the Western Hemisphere. The negotiations underpinning the development and progress of FTAA have been lagging, due largely to differences existing between developing nations such as Brazil, and developed nations like the United States.

The Islamic World

Many nations around the globe live according to religious rules and this is perhaps nowhere truer than in Islamic nations, which are often governed by non-secular business and economic policies. Because many nations around the globe are Islamic States and their citizens have been brought up with Islamic beliefs and values, it is best to review some foundational elements related to the religion.

Islam implies submission to the one, and only one, God who is the creator of everything in the universe. Anyone who accepts this submission to God and accepts Mohammad as the Messenger of God is considered to be a Muslim.[12] A Muslim uses the *Quran* to study the ways of God and the teachings of his Messenger, Prophet Mohammad (PBUH), who died in 632 AD Prophet Mohammad is the last of all the Messengers in Islam. Prophet Mohammad lived from 570-632 AD and the collection of his sayings and guidance are called *Hadith*. The *Quran*, words of God, was revealed to Prophet Mohammad because he is the last Messenger of God. Quran, the book of God, is every believer's guide to the truth and justice.

Islam is an egalitarian religion where everyone is created by God, and can be taken away by God. Therefore, each person is born equally, meaning no one is born better or worse, and each person may leave this world differently, depending on his/her beliefs and deeds. Muslims are monotheistic, and believe that God is the creator of the universe, omnipotent, fair, and merciful.

The word "Islam" in Arabic means peace. Muslims often greet each other by saying "*Assalam-u-alaikum,*" which simply means "peace be upon you." In Islam, the proper reply for "*Assalam-u-alaikum,*" would be "*Wa`-alai-kum-Assalam*" which means "and peace be unto you." In this respect, Islam is very similar to

---

[12] Originally published in the book, Afghanistan: Realities of War and Rebuilding, 2nd edition, by Bahaudin G. Mujtaba, 2007.

other practices or ways of life. For example, in the tribes of northern Natal in South Africa, people greet each other by saying "*Sawa bona*," which means "I see you," and the other person would reply by saying "*Sikhona*" meaning "I am here." The concept is that by acknowledging that you are seeing the person, you bring them into existence.

Islam's themes include the universal unity of every human being on earth. Therefore, Islam does not discriminate based on race, culture, ethnicity, country of origin, or any other societal factors which one cannot change. Islam is a way of life as it has imposed a complete ethical code that expects honest, fair, generous, and respectful conduct and behavior from its members in all situations. This code also prohibits waste, adultery, gambling, usury, alcoholic beverages, and eating certain meats (such as pork). Each and every Muslim is responsible for his or her own actions to God. Each Muslim declares his/her faith toward the one God, should pray daily, practice almsgiving, fast during the month of Ramadhan, and make a pilgrimage once in a lifetime if financially and physically capable.

There are two major factions of Islam, Sunni and Shia. Both factions believe in God and have the same major values. In Afghanistan, Sunni and Shia practiced their religion often in the same mosques, homes, cities, and provinces. The personal differences between the two factions were fully respected as they were based on each person's personal beliefs, which did not hinder the beliefs of others.

Most people in the United States tend to think that there is no difference between those who are members of the Nation of Islam and those who are orthodox Muslims. They are not the same and it must be clarified that the two groups of people tend to have many different beliefs.

The Nation of Islam was perhaps created as a nationalistic movement in the United States in order to secure equal rights for blacks who had previously faced so much discrimination. The Nation of Islam numbers around 100,000 people living in the United States, while orthodox Muslims make up about one-third of the world's total population (there are around three to ten million Muslims in the United States). Islam is considered a very religious way of life and its tenants were revealed in the seventh century. By contrast, the Nation of Islam was founded by W.D. Farad within the last century. (Farad was considered by many to be God incarnate.) In the Nation of Islam, Elijah Muhammad, who died in the 1960s, is considered a Prophet. The Nation of Islam has adopted many Islamic traditions such as Islamic holidays, dress code, and certain Islamic terms, but they have not yet joined with mainstream Islam. Global managers working in Islamic states and cultures must be careful as to not confuse the Nation of Islam beliefs with traditional Islam, which is practiced in the world.

The Islamic nations not only take care of their own citizens, they are also tasked to play a socially responsible role in the affairs of their neighbors and countries throughout the world. Islamic nations are expected to promote peace and continuously improve and enhance the lives of people throughout the world. This expectation obligates an Islamic state to be friendly and play a pivotal role in the areas of peace, interdependent living, education, economics, international business, and fairness.

Marriage and Women in Islam

One should remember that cultural practices, which are not necessarily driven by religion, can vary drastically from one culture to the next. For instance, Muslim men and women can marry a person of their own choosing, provided the pairing occurs within Islamic guidelines. Muslim men can marry women of other religions, as long as the woman believes in God (such as Christians and Jews, who ascribe to the same monotheistic ideology as Muslims). However, Muslim women are not allowed to marry men from other religions. The reason for this is because Muslims respect Christianity and Judaism as well as their prophets and books (such as the Torah and the Bible), men are able to allow their wives to practice their religion freely, even if they come from a different religion. However, the same is not always true of husbands from other religions, who may not respect their wives practicing Islam. Furthermore, because the father is usually the one who determines the religion of his children, Islam requires that the husband be a Muslim so that his children can freely practice Islamic traditions.

In accordance with Islam, women may work, attend school, and go off to defensive war, all similar to what their male counterparts do. According to Islamic teachings, women, while in the presence of others, should be modest. In Afghanistan, for example, most women choose to wear *chadari*, a traditional dressing borrowed from the ancient Persian culture. *Chadari* provided women privacy and at times protection from thugs, criminals, and rapists. However, during peaceful times, the practice was not commonplace for many Afghan women.

In modern times, many women in Islamic nations go to school and work wearing pants, skirts, and professional work attire, just as they would in modern countries. During a divorce with no circumstantial evidence, generally women are granted custody of their boys until age seven and their girls until the age of nine. The husband is then permitted to seek custody.

Understanding Jihad

In most Western societies, people are being challenged by many of the difficult questions regarding jihad and the moral issues of Islam. The lack of education and understanding about such topics has brought misinterpretation of these terms and also many negative views of Islamic peoples. The media has concentrated on covering the wars and extreme forms of government in many Islamic countries across the developing world, countries where subjective and cultural views are being interpreted in strict accordance with Islamic rules. Many media reports showcase violent conflict and other unfortunate circumstances, which are interpreted by media figures as being instigated by Muslim extremists alone. Other variables, such as freedom, rights, liberty, and other societal or environmental conditions of those countries are completely ignored. Therefore, the global manager must be cautious not to heed erroneous information about the Muslim world, and keep the truths in mind when engaging in dealings with local and/or global Islamic employees during the manager's expatriate assignment.

The term "jihad," in the Arab language, means a great struggling or striving to accomplish something. As children, individuals struggle to crawl, walk, and graduate from high school. Musicians, movie stars, and politicians strive to increase their popularity with members of society. In this context, the term "jihad" can apply to Muslims as well as non-Muslims, meaning that people are engaged in great efforts toward accomplishing something. However, in most contexts, the term "jihad" is generally interpreted to mean "holy war," which is in fact not the correct meaning. This translation of "holy war" has been popularized as a result of century-old media propaganda.

According to Islamic literature, starting a war is discouraged and considered to be unholy, unless it is inevitable. The Quran and the Hadith (encompassing the teachings of Prophet Mohammad) use the word "jihad" in many different contexts. The following are some of the term's applications and explanations:

1. *Recognizing God and loving God unconditionally.* All human beings are generally conditioned to recognize and build an attachment to the physical and what is in the proximity of one's vision and senses. God (Allah) is the creator of the universe and at times, many people have a propensity to ignore and not recognize Him.

2. *Resisting societal pressures.* Many individuals who commit themselves to serve the one and only God and to put Him above all else often feel the outside pressures of others. It may be difficult to resist such pressures and continue striving to stay committed to God over all other pursuits.

3. *Always remaining on the "straight path."* Sometimes Muslims will be harassed and bothered by others. It is the responsibility of each Muslim to strive and struggle for a life that is *Ihsan*, of the highest level of good character. It is the responsibility of Muslims to migrate into other lands if they are being pressured by non-Muslims. They should move to an area that is peaceful and tolerant, where they can continue to strive for the cause of God.

4. *Striving for righteous deeds.* Often people are forced to choose between competing interests, so choosing the right path in effect becomes a jihad, as a person tries to make his/her decision. Prophet Mohammad encouraged

Muslims to strive (participate in jihad) by serving their parents, making a pilgrimage to Makkah (Mecca), to stand for truth, and continually serve God and abandon evil deeds.

5. *Having courage and steadfastness to convey the message of God.* It takes courage and consideration to stay a true Muslim and to educate and invite others to the way of God.

6. *Defending Islam and the community.* Defensive fighting is permitted by the Quran, but it should only be done to defend and protect one's family, property, and community.

7. *Help allies.* God has further encouraged everyone to help allied people who may not be Muslims, as did Prophet Mohammad when Banu Khuza'ah became his ally. God has also encouraged Muslims to fight for what is right and defend those who cannot defend themselves. Muslims are to remove treacherous "warlords" from power whenever possible.

God has further encouraged all believers to strive for continuously educating, informing, and conveying the message of fairness and equality to others in an open and free environment. It is also the responsibility of all individuals to free people from tyranny and exploitation by oppressive systems, as did Prophet Mohammad.

One must keep in mind that Islam did not spread by the use of force, swords, or guns. Rather, Islam has spread through the use of reason, knowledge, self-discovery of God, and continually educating and informing others about the ways of righteous behavior.

Morality in Islam

There are many important and difficult moral issues which many organizations and societies are facing today. Because specific legal rules and regulations often cannot solve certain problems or lend a moral perspective, people often rely on religious belief systems for guidance. Such fundamental beliefs are often the foundation for living a moral life. Learning more about these scriptural beliefs can help people grow mentally, psychologically, and spiritually, allowing them to function in the social mainstream. It is important for global managers to become aware of the important moral issues inherent to various other countries and cultures in which they do business.

In Islamic cultures, for instance, the only valid sexual relationship is that of a legitimately married couple. Muslims have been encouraged by the Prophet Mohammed to get married when they are sexually mature. Islam does not limit the age at which one can marry; the specific time of marriage depends largely on one's own physical (sexual) and mental maturity. However, Muslims believe that humanity has been created in pairs (man and woman), and any deviation would destroy this natural order. Therefore, staying single is not encouraged. Birth control, as suggested by Muslim legal scholars, is allowed and people may use their own choice of birth control. However, this may not be a common or even accepted practice in certain Islamic nations and cultures. Abortion in Islam is acceptable during the first four months of pregnancy, as backdated to the last menstrual period. After the first four months, abortion of any type is prohibited because in Islamic philosophy, after four months, most of the human organs and the brain, with its cortex, are formulated. The embryo thus now functions as a person.

Instead of wishing for panacea or taking "the easy way out," Islamic work ethics have always encouraged hard work, personal commitment, and efforts to accomplish tasks and receive things. All alcoholic beverages, gambling, and drugs are prohibited under Islam because these things prevent the mind from functioning normally. Because all gambling activities and "games of chance" are not productive, they are prohibited in Islam, and this prohibition extends to betting on games and the lottery.

Human Rights and Islam

Islam does not discriminate based on physical differences, such as nationality, race, color, or gender. In Islam, all human beings are substantially the same, and no person should be discriminated against based on his/her physical appearance, ethnicity, or place of birth. Because all human beings are the same, they are related to one another and form a community: as friends, family members, brothers and sisters. A country may have geographical boundaries and may be located in any part of the world, but Islamic rules and guidelines regarding human rights and privileges are not restricted to such limitations. Islam has codified certain universal rights that are basic and applicatory to all persons without regard to circumstances or "man-made" territorial borders. These rights apply whether a person is Muslim or not, and should be obeyed for the sake of society in general. Human life is sacred in all of its forms; human blood should not be "spilled" without justification. Islam equates the killing of one person without just cause to the killing of the entire human race.

Islam does not allow anyone to mistreat in any sense whatsoever, women, children, older people, or people who are sick or wounded badly. As a matter of fact, Islam encourages respect for women, feeding the hungry, treating the injured, and educating children without consideration of their religious beliefs or cultural backgrounds. The fundamental human rights of Islam are believed to have been granted to all people from God, and not from an ad hoc task force or a legislative assembly appointed by human beings. However, in Islam, human rights are fundamental to all human beings, and they are granted to everyone from God. Islam also stresses that all leaders of the government should be elected by the people of the society, without coercion. But whereas things that have been, or will be, created by people can be taken away just as easily because they can prove to be harmful in different situations or as time changes, human rights in Islam will always remain unchanged and will be applicable universally, regardless of race, gender, nationality, and so on.

The following human rights for an Islamic State have been stated and clarified by the Islamic scholars, World Assembly of Muslim Youth (WAMY) and the Institute of Islamic Information and Education (IIIE):

1. The Security of Life and Property
2. The Protection of Honor
3. Sanctity and Security of Private Life
4. The Security of Personal Freedom
5. The Right to Protest Against Tyranny
6. Freedom of Expression
7. Freedom of Association
8. Freedom of Conscience and Conviction
9. Protection of Religious Sentiments
10. Protection from Arbitrary Imprisonment
11. The Right to Basic Necessities of Life
12. Equality Before the Law
13. Rulers are not Above the Law
14. The Right to Participate in the Affairs of State

Islam tries to achieve these human rights, and many others mentioned in the Quran, by providing certain legal safeguards, but mainly by asking all human beings to transcend the lower level of animal life and be able to go "above and beyond" the mere ties fostered by the kinship of blood, racial biases, linguistic arrogance, and economic privileges. Islam invites people to learn to reason with each other, and speak by speaking a language that is understandable to both parties.

Wealth Distribution or Zakat (Zakah) in Islam

Zakat (or *Zakah*) is one form of wealth distribution in Islamic countries, wherein the distribution goes from the rich to the poor among Muslims. Zakah is the third pillar of Islam and an obligation of each Muslim. It prevents the hoarding of wealth, thereby encouraging the fair distribution of income among everyone in the society. It is one way of closing the gap between the wealthy and the poor sectors of the population. Furthermore, Zakah promotes solidarity, equality, fairness, and the Golden Rule. Traditionally, the Golden Rule means that a person should treat others as he or she wishes to be treated. It is a revolutionary system that enables people to purify their wealth, care for one's fellow citizens, empower the less fortunate in the society, invest in the future of upcoming generations, and fulfill a compulsory act of spiritual obligation.

The literal meaning of the word "Zakah" in the Arabic language is "purification" and "growth." Zakah is an amount collected from the surplus wealth of both male and females who hold assets valued at more than the Nisab of Zakah, i.e., the equivalent value of 85 grams of gold. Zakah payments are required by people who have full and legal ownership of an asset for a full calendar year, provided the asset is valued in an amount that exceeds the minimum value of Nisab (based on the market price of 85 grams of gold or about 2.5% of one's accumulated wealth beyond one's immediate needs). Zakat is payable on assets that have been acquired for the sole purposes of earning more income and generating wealth. Of course, Muslims often give beyond the 2.5% requirement as part of their Zakat.

According to Islamic laws, Zakah can only be distributed to one or more of the following eligible beneficiaries: the poor, the needy, the administrators in charge of managing Zakah, slaves or captives (Zakah can be used to free slaves), those who are in debt for acquiring the basic necessities of life, righteous causes that enhance or create an ethical society (scholarship for students, fighting against injustice and oppression, and developing a community's infrastructure), and those who are stranded during a journey (due to loss of money, car breakdowns, illness, etc). Zakah is payable to the leaders of a community or mosque as they are the administrators for the creation of a stable community or society.

An Islamic state is responsible for making available the basic necessities of life, such as food, security, clothing, and education to all of its citizens. Zakat essentially is a welfare system that is more than 1,400 years old, aimed at preventing the unusual disparities in wealth between the "have" and "have not" sectors of the population. But because there is no central authority that administers the distribution of these funds, usually charitable organizations and mosques take the responsibility for spending on the poor or employing appropriate means to enhance the lives of the people.

Economic Systems in Islam

Islam sees life from a systemic or holistic perspective, as one aspect of life tends to impact all others. For example, one person suffering is going to cause the suffering of others; one community suffering from a major disaster is likely to have a negative impact on other communities, etc. The economic system of Islam is one aspect of its ideology that provides guidance and balance for a prosperous life within the community.

According to Islamic views, every rule and tangible commodity on Earth is for the benefit of mankind and society's welfare. Ghulam Sarwar[13] states that economic principles of Islam aim to establish a just and fair society that promotes socially responsible behavior among individuals and corporations. According to Sarwar and other scholars, the Islamic economic system is based on many fundamental principles, including the following:

1. Honestly earning and spending (expenditures). One should not earn income or spend income on illegal or unlawful activities or products. Waste is discouraged in Islam and continuous improvement must be a day-to-day mindset. Every day, one must strive to become better and do his/her job better than the day before.

2. Do what is legal and lawful. One should not lie, falsify evidence, cheat, commit fraud, steal, or acquire property by the use of force from those who cannot protect themselves.

3. Sell fairly and openly. A person or a corporation should not be hoarding food or other basic necessities of life in order to create an artificial shortage in the hopes of creating higher prices and more profits.

4. Earn legally. Citizens must not work in jobs, professions, or practices that are harmful to society.

5. Avoid usury or interest. The economic system in Islamic countries prohibits the paying of interest, which essentially assists the rich to get richer and leads the poor to being poorer. Islam allows for a zero rate of interest and prohibits any and all transactions that are made using interest payments. Islamic scholars state that the practice of paying interest is neither a trade nor a profit. Rather, it is a means of exploiting people and gathering wealth. Muslims believe that an interest-free world would be beneficial to everyone around the globe in all societies. Capitalistic societies practice the payment of interest, wherein wealth is transferred from the poor to the rich; this is the opposite of Zakah. As discussed earlier, Zakah directs wealth from the rich to those who really need it.

In addition to the above guidelines, suggestions, and principles, Islam has many more rules for the creation of a complete economic system. Islamic states attempt to put into good use all of their human and natural resources. Global managers and entrepreneurs must be aware of these principles when operating in Islamic nations.

Furthermore, Islamic states also attempt to eliminate corruption, bribery, and other harmful activities that temporarily lead some individuals to lucrative deals. Muslim scholars and communities often understand that some individual

---

[13] See Sawar's book entitled Islam: Beliefs and Teachings (July 1995).

freedom may have to be sacrificed for the social good of the nation and society. Hammudah Abdalati, in the book entitled *Islam in Focus*, states that in order to effectively combat cheating and exploitation of people, Islam requires honesty in all business dealings, requires the warning of cheaters, encourages decent work, and forbids usury or the taking of interest in return for lending money to a person who needs more than the owner. Of course, earning an honest living through hard work is not only a duty for all Muslims, but also a prime virtue for all of society as well.

Overall, an Islamic economic system encourages simplicity, charity, interdependence, modesty in all activities of life, and complete cooperation with one's colleagues, superiors, and neighbors. While this section has analyzed some of the basic rules and policies of Islam, global managers and entrepreneurs working in Islamic states are encouraged to comprehensively investigate such topics in the standard books about Muslims and their economic systems.

Islamic Law: The Shar'ah

In Islamic states and cultures, there are two main sources of authority, the sayings of God (from the Quran) and the sayings of Prophet Mohammad (known as Hadith). Of course, Islamic laws[14] are also formed and further interpreted by the actions and practices of respected leaders and scholars known as imams. Muslim students, managers, and scholars utilize these sources of authority to understand the principles of *Shari'ah*, or Islamic Law.

By applying these principles, the scholars work to form and develop legal opinions on various situations. The authentic sources serve as measurement "yardsticks" or criteria for differentiating between actions that are based on religious principles and those that are the result of local customs and cultures. For example, while Islamic laws encourage women to cover their bodies except for the face, hands, and feet, some cultural practices require the wearing of a veil, as commonly done in various parts of Afghanistan. But the wearing of a veil is not a requirement of the Shari'ah or Islamic Law.

The term Shari'ah means "the path" or "the way to a watering place" in the Arabic language. The term is used to mean divinely revealed "Islamic Law," which plays a very important role in the lives of people living in Islamic states and cultures.

Muslim scholars recognize at least four main sources for developing and applying Shari'ah to various situations that human beings face in today's workplace: 1) the Quran, 2) the Sunnah, 3) the Jima (consensus among Muslim

---

[14] This material is gleaned from material offered by Islamic Network Group (2002).

scholars and jurists), and 4) the Qiyas (making deductions by analogy or precedent). Of course, global managers and entrepreneurs who are interested in further research on these sources can gather more information from Islamic law
books, which are publicly available in most libraries around the world.

Some Muslim states have implemented Shari'ah as the basis for the judicial
system and for regulating human behavior, whereas others have implemented a
hybrid of Shari'ah and civil law. In non-Islamic states, Muslims can express a
desire for the implementation of Shari'ah for themselves. As a matter-of-fact,
in England, Muslims have established a religious parliament at the government
level to enable the implementation of Islamic laws that deal with issues of marriage, divorce, inheritance, and other such matters.

Fiqh is another Arabic term used to refer to the body of scholarship and
jurisprudence developed over the centuries to interpret and implement the
Shari'ah. Islamic scholars around the world today use the principles of fiqh to
deduce new strategies and approaches to life in the modern society.

International Business and Corruption[15]

Conventional wisdom says that almost all people around the world expect,
respect, and strive for democracy. People tend to think they know what it is, until
asked the very question: So what is it? Examples vary. A thoroughly democratic
acclamation in China is the Maoist party promise of riches first and democracy later. In France, lawmakers are changing the constitution to provide more
democracy in accordance with the laws of the EU. Iraq is drafting a democratic
constitution to replace the strict laws once put in place as a result of one-party
tyranny.

Thus, democracy has become the "solution" to freedom, but has it also
become the cause of corruption? Corruption is a hidden epidemic around the
world and the lack of treatment has allowed it to become a virus that manifests
within its environment and spreads into the minds and eyes of people, cultures,
and nations from generation to generation. Corruption has been in existence
since the birth of civilization, but it has progressively worsened. Different forms
of corruption, their existence and effects on the political and economic realms,
as well as the concerns of corruption for international managers and methods of
preventing it will be further explored.

The definition of corruption varies among different countries, cities, peoples,
and business organizations. The negative implications associated with corruption
in one country may mean quite the opposite in another. However, all definitions

---

[15] Contributed by Bina Patel, Nova Southeastern University. Originally published in Cross-
Cultural Management and Negotiation Practices, by Mujtaba, 2007.

seem to agree that corruption is an act that is conducted with the intent of gaining an unfair advantage. The emergence of trade has brought not only globalization, but also corruption. The essence of corruption has now spread within the corporate world, where it has become one of the most uncontrollable of phenomenon. It is an epidemic, but one where "treatments" prescribed may work.

According to experts, the epidemic of corruption that exists today comes in various forms, including:

1. *Bribery:* the most common form of corruption around the world is bribery. It is the act of offering something, usually money, in order to gain an advantage.
2. *Grand corruption:* a form of corruption that exists between the heads of state, ministers, and other senior officials. It serves the interests of a small group of politicians and businesspeople.
3. *Political corruption:* a form of corruption that involves lawmakers (i.e., monarchs, dictators, legislators, etc) who seek bribes or other financial rewards for their own political or personal benefit. In return, most of these officials provide political favors to their supporters, usually at the expense of the public.
4. *Petty corruption:* exists when small amounts of money are used in transactions involving customs clearance or the issuance of building permits.
5. *Administrative corruption:* includes the usage of favoritism or bribery between certain individuals and private businesses (i.e., to lower taxes, escape regulations, etc).
6. *Systematic corruption:* a form of corruption that pervades throughout all levels of society.
7. *Corporate corruption:* a form of corruption that arises among individuals in private business corporations in dealings with their suppliers and/or clients. Most corporate corruption occurs at the higher levels of a business, wherein it is practice in the pursuit of private gains, usually at the expense of shareholders, who are most oftentimes unaware of these acts.

Corruption is seen both within the public and private sectors of international business. It can result from several different situations including ambiguous laws and regulations, weak enforcement of anti-corruption laws, and the opportunity to abuse power. Corruption is also very common among the political elite throughout the world.

The primary statute in the United States to combat corruption, especially bribery, in international business, is the Foreign Corrupt Practices Act which will be covered in detail in the Criminal Law and Business chapter.

Corruption in the Political Realm

Public authorities around the world are faced with corruption on a daily basis. The majority of the world expects corruption to be of existence in the developing countries, such as in India or Africa or Asia, and it is true that corruption exists in the political arena throughout the Eastern hemisphere. While it is true that all forms of corruption are found in most poor countries, it has also become pervasive within the Western realm. But it is important to note that it is mostly the rich and the elite who utilize corruption on a daily basis, much more so than the poor.

Bribery, of course, can be seen in many countries. The ex-Prime Minister of India, Rajiv Gandhi, for example, claims that at least 15% of aid money India received during the time he served went straight to bribery and other forms of corruption.

Political donation is another form of bribery, and politicians in most countries are notoriously known to accept private support in return for favors. This is most often visible in countries such as Nicaragua, Brazil, Venezuela, and African countries like Nigeria. The Nicaraguan government, for example, concluded that a Canadian mining firm, Greenstone Resources, donated over $20,000 to President Arnoldo Alemán in 1999. Greenstone Resources is known to control over 70% of mined areas in Nicaragua, and in return for the generous donation, the mining company was allowed to get away with violating environmental laws and regulations. This form of corruption is quite common in poor nations, where corporations from industrialized countries use direct foreign investment or some form of bribery in order to circumvent "nagging" laws, which are there to protect a nation's own citizens.

The Japanese government is heavily involved in the private business sector. Consequently, on a typical day in Japan, bribes are offered to secure various business favors from public officials in connection with the granting of licenses or the awarding of contracts for public works. The Japanese parliament party has a very strong connection with specific business industries. These interests often offer favors such as "luxurious business entertainment," to members of the party in order to influence political decisions in their favor as well as receive governmental approval for different products. In fact, such forms of bribery are so common, yet so secretive, that they are almost expected when international managers conduct business with the Japanese.

The Japanese government is not the only national government that is involved in high forms of corruption. Several member countries of the Organization for Economic Co-operation and Development (OECD), including the United States, are involved in corruption within the political realm. In the United States, the Republican and Democratic parties are constantly accusing each other of receiving large donations or favors from powerful corporations or wealthy investors. For instance, in November of 2005, Republican representative Randy Cunningham was forced to resign after he pled guilty to taking more than $2 million in bribes in a criminal conspiracy which involved at least three other defense contractors. Cunningham committed tax evasion, mail and wire fraud, as well as bribery in order to gain enough money to buy his mansion, luxurious cars, and much more.

Instances such as this are common in the United States, just as they are in any other country. The world is filled with corruption at all levels, including the industrialized nations. Corruption not only affects the political realm, but also the world's economic domain.

Corruption in the Economic Domain

Different forms of corruption within any nation can hinder economic growth, which is vital and necessary, especially for Third World and developing nations.

Initially, the notion of corruption begins in the culture itself, where it grows in its environment and spills over into the nearby societies. In the preliminary years, when trade first begins between people of different backgrounds, a breeding ground for corruption is created, and from this, bribery also evolves. Bribery is the main type of corruption that exists in most developing nations and "transition" economies.

As globalization has evolved, the benefits derived from it have also increased. However, the spread of globalization also resulted in a high growth of corruption at all levels. In fact, because of the spread of globalization, industrialized nations began to invest in developing countries through foreign direct investment (FDI), wherein factories were established in the poorer countries. High levels of investments continue today through FDIs in several countries, as it is seen as a major source of capital for most developing nations and their people.

However, the disadvantages of FDI include most forms of corruption being practiced. In fact, it seems that local corruption can dissuade foreign direct investment in several developing nations, thereby deterring multinational firms from investing in other countries. Most international investors who invest heavily in FDI plants and factories in developing countries rarely recognize that their managers are the ones who engage in corruption with the local officials in order to obtain permits, taxes, health inspections, etc. In fact, once the investments have been made, local officials are more than likely to threaten or even complicate matters by creating certain obstacles unless they are bribed. To a certain extent, managers are "pushed" into engaging in the act of bribery due to these barriers from corrupt local officials.

In addition, during times of crisis, which are very common in developing and Third World countries, local corruption actually may discourage FDI when international banks helping international creditors "bail out" of a country faster than international investors, a procedure that will prevent bank loans from defaulting. For example, in countries where there is a high level of political risk, where a military takeover is likely to occur, or in Asia, where the currency crisis occurred, international "bailouts" of creditors took precedence in order to avoid massive defaults. The World Bank, IMF, and the Group of Seven (G-7) countries (Canada, France, Germany, Italy, Japan, the United Kingdom, and the United States) all provide assistance packages during times of crisis for international creditors, but the same is not done for international investors and this deters investors from getting involved in direct investments overseas, especially in countries with a high corruption rate.

Although corrupt local officials are to be blamed most of the time for engaging in any form of corruption, international investors and managers of direct foreign investment are highly prone to initiate bribery or engage in different forms of corruption when conducting business in exploited nations. The deleterious role played by local officials, international banks, and managers, especially during times of crisis, is another way of preventing other sources of capital from being introduced within these countries, thus hindering economic growth.

To plainly illustrate that corruption within the economic domain is a real global business challenge and not merely an "academic" problem, the authors of this book would like to relate the experiences of their MBA students and their many experiences with questionable payments being requested by foreign officials in the course of the students' international business dealings. One student related that in order to process applications for security permits in a South American country, a $100 bill would have to be attached to each application as an additional "processing fee." Another student said that it would cost $200 to have a particular small product or product part released from customs in an Asian country. Yet another student mentioned that in order to have the utility services for a business promptly turned on in a Caribbean nation, an additional payment of $3,500 would be necessary. If the student did not pay, the student would be placed on "the list." The list refers to the very long waiting list to have one's utility services commenced. In a most unusual case, another student related that in another South American country, the local military commander at a security checkpoint required a fee for the prompt processing of a vehicle convoy through the checkpoint. What was interesting was that the official wanted not money, but fancy bathroom tile as his wife had remodeling plans. According to one student, who related his experiences in doing business in an African county, the global manager and entrepreneur should be prepared to deal with a cultural norm expressed by the saying, "Why hire a lawyer when you can buy a judge?"

Whether and under what circumstances it is legal for companies to pay "bribes" will be covered in the Criminal Law chapter's discussion of the U.S. Foreign Corrupt Practices Act and international anti-bribery conventions (treaties).

Global Legal Perspectives

For many organizations, the goal of delivering value to customers by achieving a higher level of client satisfaction has become a fundamental building block of their long-term national and international strategies. Consistently increasing customer satisfaction will regularly expand the opportunity for increased revenues and profitability. For the global manager and entrepreneur, there are many compelling reasons to achieve the objective of client satisfaction in both a legal and ethical manner but also without violating local cultural norms and traditions.

Customers for a global corporation can include the end-users, suppliers, local citizens, local government, third parties, and the "informal channels" for doing business. Whatever the industry and whoever the customer, being able to measure their level of satisfaction and acting appropriately on the results of these data is essential for long-term financial success. Firms that do not consider customer satisfaction as a top priority leave their customers open to the competition that *does* understand the merit of customer satisfaction. Thus, organizations that make the mistake of not prioritizing customer satisfaction will surely lose market share to those who do.

Regarding the topic of the global environment, some professional managers in the 21st century will get the opportunity to work with diverse individuals in decidedly different cultures. This poses rigorous and numerous challenges, not the least of which is the existence of very diverse laws and policies that can lead to culture shock. Culture shock occurs when managers realize that their "old ways" of doing things, which have always made them successful, may not work in the new environment. Hopefully, in a winning scenario, they adapt over time and become successful. This type of success depends on many things, including the manager's personality, his or her flexibility and attitude toward new things and change, his or her ability to rely on local mentors to provide accurate and timely assistance, family support, and willingness to experience a new culture.

In particular, global managers need to pay special attention to the work of Gert Hofstede, who studied the cultural values of many countries through his work with the IBM organization in the early 1980s. Hofstede, in his original profile, found that countries could be profiled on at least four variables: individualism, power distance, masculinity/femininity, and uncertainty avoidance.

(The masculinity/femininity dimension has since been renamed the "achievement versus nurturing" orientation to be more politically correct.) Hofstede added a fifth dimension, long-term versus short-term orientation. All managers and entrepreneurs should understand that national cultural values are often embedded into one's subconscious mind during childhood. Consequently, some individuals are unaware of their own cultural conditioning. On the other hand, organizational values are often taught and internalized later in life, either through general education or workplace training. Because these values are often assimilated into one's conscious level at a later stage of development, they can be changed more quickly via socialization into the new culture.

Understanding the cultural values and the legal system of another economy can be an essential component of success for expatriates, managers, and organizations who want to expand their markets abroad through such means as import/export or various other forms of foreign direct investment.

Management Strategies

Political Risk and its Effects on Multinational Corporations and Managers[16]

Political risk is the chance that change in the political environment may adversely affect the value of a firm's investment. Because the world is getting smaller and foreign direct investment is increasing, the issue of political risk is of paramount importance in contemporary business.

Griffin and Pustay (2003) break political risk into three components: 1) ownership risk, by which property is threatened by confiscation or direct expropriation or where any property of a foreign firm, including profits, is seized by a host government; 2) operating risk, in which activities and operations of the firm are affected by law changes, environmental standards, tax codes, terrorism, etc; and 3) transfer risk, which is the risk that the host government will interfere with a firm's ability to transfer funds out of the country. Firms that are afraid of having their profits, land, and buildings taken away by the host government may be reluctant to locate there, particularly if a nation has a reputation for continual property violations. Transfer risk and ownership risk soon give way to repatriation risk, which means that a government can essentially restrict the free outflow of profits earned by a foreign firm or directly take the earnings of these firms.

Repatriation risk involves the inability of a firm to freely transfer funds out of the host country, and can occur through several channels. The foreign country may outright ban foreign firms from repatriating profits back home. There may be extensive tax laws in place to reduce the overall value of repatriated profits. Currency and exchange controls may also exist that make it difficult for a firm to

---

[16] Contributed by Erica Franklin, Nova Southeastern University.

convert the profits from the host country currency to the home country currency in order to make repatriation easier. One of the other ways that a host government can restrict the repatriation of profits is to confiscate the profits and keep them for government use, either with or without any compensation measures. Profits may include items such as cash, dividends, royalties, financing, and negotiable instruments used in commercial transactions.

Profit expropriation may also occur, when a host government unfairly taxes earnings through operating risk, thereby restricting and reducing the amount of earned profits a foreign multi-national company (MNC) can bring home. In addition, profit expropriation may occur through the taking of shareholder dividends. For example, there is an increasing prevalence of expropriation of a firm's outside shareholders by the firm's controlling shareholders, especially in the Asia region. Financial losses also may occur when large amounts of high returns are siphoned off by controlling investors of low-profit-yielding firms.

All of these actions can hinder businesses from expanding throughout the world, thus forcing concentration into areas of the globe where the risk is minimal. Repatriation risk may also be problematic for the firm that chooses to generate most of its profits from foreign nations. For example, because repatriation risk is inherent both domestically and abroad, U.S. firms face a two-sided problem when it comes to profit remittance from the host nation when most of their profits are generated from a foreign nation.

Because these various risks cause firms to lose future profits and lower after-tax profits on current earnings, they are problematic to companies that generate most of their profits from foreign nations.

All countries have laws on extracting profits—the foreign country may want to restrict outflow of foreign investment, and the U.S. may want to take a portion of the repatriated investment in terms of taxes. China, for example, has an economy with the greatest potential for foreign investment, but operating in China poses its own challenges for managers who wish to locate there. Recently, China has removed restrictions that prohibited the non-repatriation of profits, income, interest, and dividends. China's currency, the renminbi, has also been made fully convertible, thus allowing foreign companies to repatriate their earnings out of the country. Although China does not require foreign firms to reinvest profits into the country, it strongly encourages this type of investment. Firms that reinvest will receive an "escalating" tax refund if they reinvest profits for at least five years in high technology or export-oriented industries.

On the other hand, there are legal processes that may delay profit repatriation. In order to remit profits out of China, firms must go through a cumbersome paper process, entailing various authorizations and approvals through different agencies required by Chinese law. Capital requirements must be met and approval from the board of directors and local tax bureau must be obtained before profits can be repatriated. This process creates delays for firms wishing to repatriate profits. Furthermore, after paying taxes, China earmarks the funds a percentage of profits for government-mandated company funds, an enterprise expansion fund, and a staff bonus and welfare fund.

China has various regulations in place that govern exchange controls; this may also affect profit repatriation. China's Forex regulations specifically stipulate that in order for a firm to convert the renminbi, the bank must present certain sets of documents in order to facilitate the conversion of profits in preparation for repatriation. These documents include a tax certificate, an approval from the board of directors, registered capital verification, and official Forex registration. In the past, enterprises were only allowed to keep a small percentage of their hard currency, forced to give up the majority of it to authorized banks if it was in excess of legal limits. However, the exact limit is undisclosed, and apparently varies according to what the State Administration of Exchange Control determines the limit should be.

Effects of Repatriation Law on Managers and Entrepreneurs[17]

By analyzing laws currently in place regarding the extraction of profits in the United States, in China, and in international law, it can be seen that there are a variety of problems that occur when a U.S. firm generates most of its profits from a foreign subsidiary. The main problem with U.S. firms generating most of their profits from a foreign country is twofold. First, the host nation may expropriate and disallow the repatriation of profits to the U.S. Second, the U.S. has laws that heavily tax foreign-earned income. Both factors significantly decrease overall profits.

Chinese regulations that previously prohibited profit repatriation were harmful to U.S. firms as such laws reduced the amount of profits repatriated back to the U.S. Currency issues, such as devaluation and inconvertibility (especially in China), caused firms to lose most of their profits before they were ever able to take them home. Without convertibility for the renminbi, the profits earned by U.S. firms were stuck in China, where they were unable to be converted to dollars and thus transferred back into the United States.

The Chinese government hopes to use such proceeds to create new jobs for workers, pay down government debt, and run government-sponsored services. Although it gives a tax refund for reinvestment and is not bad for China, this money is not allowed to be invested in the United States even though these funds could, at least in theory, have the same possible effects on America's economy and society.

---

[17] Contributed by Erica Franklin, Nova Southeastern University.

Unspecified compensation measures and ambiguous legality of what exactly constitutes legal expropriation under Chinese law also leave investors without knowledge of whether actions that prevent the extraction of profits are legal or not. The lengthy process prescribed by Chinese banks to remit profits also prohibits firms from extracting their profits in a timely manner for use in other investments, either at home or around the world.

Yet another pitfall of repatriating profits from abroad is the burdensome tax laws the United States implements, which also reduce the value of profits repatriated from abroad. This is also detrimental to the firm that pulls most of its profits from the host country. Many firms allege that double taxation by the U.S. government on repatriated earnings effectively causes them to lose money and reduces the value of the profits they are able to bring home. This is after obtaining what funds they could achieve from a foreign government, funds that were already once devalued by foreign regulations.

Certain other nations do not impose the same restrictions on their firms that operate overseas because these firms usually do not owe tax to the home country on foreign-earned income. According to Hesler and Hiremath (2005), these tax laws often cause U.S. firms to avoid repatriating profits back home, so they reinvest them in other foreign ventures.

As a result of the fear of double taxation and other U.S. measures that may result in profit reduction, U.S. firms often engage in activities to counter the effects of these laws, such as switching ownership of their companies. Some U.S. firms take the initiative to lose their "American" identity and become foreign firms in an attempt to reduce their tax obligation. Firms do this by reincorporating in a foreign country in order to transfer shares from the foreign subsidiary to the U.S. company. The subsidiary effectively becomes the parent and the parent the subsidiary, thereby avoiding tax laws. With the exchange completed, shareholders now own stock in the foreign company, which itself owns the U.S. firm. This process is known as "inversion," and is done to avoid paying double taxes to the U.S. as well as to reduce firms' tax liability on foreign-earned profits. More firms have reportedly made plans to do this in the future.

Although the Subpart F tax law gives U.S. firms tax credits for foreign-paid income tax, some firms do not believe this is enough to discourage them from further expatriating foreign-earned profits, which increases the value of their profits. If these same firms' profits were mostly domestic in nature, U.S. laws perhaps would not have that much of a negative effect on said profits.

In the international arena, loopholes in international law also may pose as a negative of operating globally. As there are no treaties that truly examine the legality of, or make rulings on, regulations that cause repatriation risk, firms do not have any recourse through the international legal system when a nation undertakes such actions. The selected tribunals of each treaty interpret the appropriate laws differently each time government interference prohibits the extraction of profits from the host nation. This situation leaves a shadow of uncertainty in the minds of investors and firms who operate abroad and need to effectively plan for these types of risks. The lack of previous legislation on profit repatriation in international law also negatively affects enterprises as there is no way that countries can be forced to undertake drastic policy changes in taxation, currency controls, or other regulations that affect profits or other investments. This hurts the international company because it is not able to avoid these risks within the host country. Not only do present laws negatively affect international businesses that wish to operate profitably and mainly abroad, there are also deleterious effects on the welfare of society and on the stakeholders as a result of the denial of profit extractions and the expropriation of profits.

International Law and the Global Manager

International laws, both secular and non-secular, apply to all working professionals in today's competitive global environment. In this environment, the manager will need to function in or travel to several different countries as part of his or her professional responsibility. This means that the global manager and entrepreneur must be aware of the world's diverse legal and ethical perspectives, as well as its diverse religions and moral problems. This will apply to matters of corruption, terrorism, and translation.

The "grand epidemic" of corruption, for example, has manifested within various environments throughout the political and economic realms. International managers from Western-based societies are not equipped to understand all of the ins and outs of the culture of corruption nor are they prepared to engage in it. Furthermore, societies within the developed and developing countries are similarly ill prepared for the culture of corruption, and indeed it has been the people of the developing countries and their poorest citizens who have been affected the most by this vicious cycle. Several policies have been conceived by different presidents, officials, and international organizations to combat this problem, but the enforcement of such prescriptions has been weak to nonexistent at best. Fingers are constantly pointed by nations and their people, but it must be understood that all countries share blame for corruption in one form or another. Until sound policies and regulations are enforced, this epidemic will continue with fateful consequences: Not only will nations be affected, but the poor especially will be hurt by such dishonest business methods.

Terrorism, as well as the perception of terrorism, is another risk that global managers and entrepreneurs have to deal with. Prior to the September 11th attacks on the New York Twin Towers, terrorism was not regarded as a very important issue for most people in the United States or other countries around the world. However, terrorism has always been present in many countries such as Spain, Ireland, Israel, and Palestine, where it represents a constant danger to many people. Global terrorism can have a tremendous impact on business as well as almost all other elements of daily living. One of the greatest effects terrorism has had on business is the financial burden it creates. In order to take the proactive stance, it is necessary to implement strategic plans to protect businesses from terrorism and all harmful consequences connected with the perpetration of terrorism. However, such problems can be expensive and taking measures to protect employees, personnel, and even customers has become a great financial burden for many industries, especially the airline industry. But taking such protective measures is not only a necessity, but also an investment to prevent disastrous consequences.

An additional ancillary problem associated with terrorism is that many U.S. universities have become concerned about recruiting foreign students from Islamic cultures, even though these individuals tend to be hard-working graduate assistants. Part of the problem with the additional security is that many gifted foreign students are choosing to attend school in Europe and other developed nations instead of in the U.S. The U.S. government will have to consider what to do in order to continue to have a diverse pool of talented students in its schools. Such diversity is especially valuable to international human resource departments, as companies often seek recent graduates who bring country-specific experience with them.

Translator services are normally used when a conference meeting involves a person who has no English-speaking background. However, this does not mean that if the person speaks English, then he or she will not have a translator. Rather, if someone in the meeting is able to understand and speak English fairly well but still needs the "extra something" to explain what exactly is meant at the time of the conference, then the services of a professional translator should be used.

Therefore, in order to avoid making mistakes with regard to international labor laws and local moral norms, it is best that global managers and entrepreneurs reflect upon questions such as when and how should language translators be used in business meetings and who should provide the translators? Perhaps managers should always have a translator on hand for any meeting, especially if the conference deals with transnational companies and diverse labor laws. Also, the translator should be provided by the company hosting the visitor.

However, with technological advances, the actual translator does not even have to be at the meeting or conference itself. In more advanced scenarios, the translator could even be in a room alone, from where he or she translates the information and sends it back to the listener through audio phones. The translation service can even be done via internet camera or telephone. The disadvantage here is that nonverbal communications may not be apparent to the translator when he or she is not present in the room physically. On the other hand, when there are only one or two people who require a translation, then the translator should sit near them and translate right then and there in a low tone of voice.

So, based on the experiences of the authors, translators always should be used in international scenarios and especially in negotiations.

Summary

Global managers and entrepreneurs are expected to be respectful of different cultures as well as their own local mores and customs. Managers must become familiar with the local laws and policies of each nation or government in which they conduct business. This chapter covered comparative government, laws, international laws, international trade rules, culture, challenges associated with doing business internationally, import and export considerations, and the effective management of various international transactions according to local customs and expectations. The chapter further offered suggestions on how to navigate complex laws when dealing with them for the first time, especially in a foreign language.

FIVE

The enforcement of international awards in the national courts is an important global legal and business issue. Addressing this issue is an important treaty called the United Nations Convention on the Recognition and Enforcement of Foreign Arbitral Awards (also called the "New York Convention"). This treaty obligates member nations to enforce arbitration awards issued outside of their own national territories, presuming that certain requirements—mainly procedural—are met. The treaty now has over 130 members, making it one of the most widely ratified treaties in the world.

Such treaties represent a way of resolving business disputes in lieu of more traditional methods such as litigation. Litigation is often viewed as being too expensive, too time-consuming and, especially in the United States—with its prevalent use of a lay jury to decide the facts of a case—too unpredictable. Therefore, a major global trend has sought the use of alternative dispute resolution (ADR) mechanisms as a substitute for more traditional court procedures. This chapter will examine the main types of alternative dispute resolution, pointing out the advantages and disadvantages of ADR, and paying particular attention to the use of ADR in employer-employee scenarios and within greater global settings.

Definitions and Types of Alternative Dispute Resolution

The two foremost types of ADR are mediation and arbitration. Mediation is a process by which a neutral third party acts as a conciliator and assists the parties to the controversy in reaching a compromise solution. Arbitration is a process whereby the parties to a controversy submit the dispute to a neutral third party—who is not a traditional court judge—for a final and binding decision.

Mediation

Mediation seeks to bring about a compromise solution to the dispute that is satisfactory to all involved parties. It is absolutely fundamental to note upfront that a mediator does not impose a binding solution on the parties; he or she is not a decision maker even though the mediator does in fact enter the decision-making process. In essence, the mediator, a neutral, disinterested, and objective third party, acts as a conciliator and facilitator. The mediator schedules and oversees negotiation sessions, opens up lines of communications, points out the strengths and weaknesses of each party's position, transmits proposals, and proposes compromise solutions. But only the disputing parties themselves can actually adopt any particular resolution.

Key Mediation Issues [18]

Mediation has certain advantages over both litigation and arbitration. It is speedier, less expensive, and certainly more harmonious than litigation, for sure, but also arbitration (where there will be a "winner" and a "loser"). In mediation, as opposed to litigation and arbitration, neither party will have a result forced on him or her. Furthermore, mediation can result in a "win-win" resolution that maintains amicable relations between the parties and that also certainly encourages future business dealings between the parties.

Three important legal issues involving mediation are: 1) the confidentiality of the mediation process, 2) legally requiring mediation, and 3) the conduct of the mediator. First, regarding confidentiality, characteristically most mediations are conducted in a confidential manner and thus the parties thereto have an expectation that the communications made during the mediation will not be disclosed to others or used in court proceedings. Although in the United States there is no common law basis for the confidentiality of the mediator-client relationship, some states now have statutes providing for such confidentiality, in particular protecting settlement negotiations by deeming them inadmissible evidence. The Federal Rules of Evidence in the U.S. also make statements made in the course of settlement negotiations inadmissible in legal proceedings. It is important to note that the federal law just protects settlement negotiation statements and not other communications, such as assertion of legal claims and defenses, such as fraud, and statements of fact, and also just deals with evidence inadmissibility and not ultimate disclosures. What complicates matters, of course, is that the mediator has in fact two clients who typically will possess conflicting interests and objectives. Consequently, one's client's desire to maintain confidentiality may be opposed by another. Furthermore, even if both clients want to waive confidentiality, the mediator may not be willing to do so since the mediator may fear that the whole mediation process could be harmed and that the mediator could be brought into a court case and compelled to testify. Statutes typically do allow confidentiality to be waived but only if the participants and mediator consent. Also, statutes will provide exceptions to confidentiality if there are allegations of malfeasance or malpractice on the part of the mediator, if there is an allegation that fraud or duress occurred during the mediation, if there is evidence of a crime, or if there is an allegation that a party refused to mediate in good faith.

---

[18] See Coltri, Laurie, S. (2010).

The second mediation legal issue arises when there is an attempt to legally mandate that a party mediate. Mediation is supposed to be a voluntary alternative dispute mechanism, so the question of coercing a party to mediate is certainly a problematic one. In order to resolve this problem, it is essential to distinguish purely private and voluntary mediation, where the parties are merely trying to get professional help to solve a dispute that they cannot solve on their own, from court required mediation. In the first situation, there can be no coercion as the process is voluntary and private. However, the parties may have contracted to submit a dispute to mediation, and, if so, the failure to do so could result in a lawsuit for breach of contract for the failure to mediate or the failure to mediate in good faith, for example, by not listening, not making proposals, not making counter-proposals, and not negotiating. Of course, a contract to mediate will be enforced to the same degree as any other contract, which means that the standard contract defenses, such as fraud, can be used to contest the mediation contract. In a court situation, a judge may offer and suggest that the parties attempt mediation as an alternative to litigation. However, a court may have the authority to require some degree of mediation, and then the mediation will have a coercive element because the court may be able to impose sanctions, such as contempt of court, the payment of attorneys' fees, and preventing a party from proceeding in court until the mediation has been conducted. Moreover, in some situations, not only is mediation ordered by the court but the judge is bound to take cognizance of the mediator's evaluation of the case and, in some cases, to take cognizance of the mediator's recommendation.

The third mediation issue deals with the conduct of the mediator. Mediators are bound to be neutral, impartial, and fair. The mediator thus cannot be perceived, as favoring one party or one result over another. Obviously, if a mediator cannot be trusted by the parties to be fair and objective then the entire mediation process will collapse. Clearly, then, if the mediator has any financial interest in a particular outcome, or bias for or against a party, or had a prior relationship with a party, such as a legal one, then the mediator will be seen as not fair and impartial. Furthermore, if the mediator is unfair, biased, or incompetent, these circumstances can be used as defenses in a lawsuit to enforce a contract for mediation. Related to the conduct issue is the issue of the qualifications of the mediator. However, for private mediators, there are few uniform and consistent standards for mediators in jurisdictions in the U.S. and for different types of disputes. However, in the business and commercial arenas, these mediators are usually legal business law experts who have a great deal of knowledge and experience in certain fields. If a mediator is connected to, and referred by, a court, the mediator typically will have to meet that jurisdiction's requirements for a mediator, for example, that the mediator have a college degree, possess mediation training or experience, and be monitored. For private as well as court connected mediators, there are professional organizations, such as the Association for Conflict Resolution and the American Arbitration Association which provide mediation courses and training and grant certificates as to the mediator's professional qualifications.

Arbitration

Arbitration is a process whereby a neutral third party is granted, by the parties in dispute, the power to determine a binding solution to a particular dispute. Such a decision characteristically involves the determination of the rights and liabilities of the parties involved as well as the rendering of a "win-lose" resolution. Typically, the parties will contractually agree that the arbitrator's decision be legally binding. The arbitrator is often referred to as a "private judge" and, in fact, arbitrators very well may be retired judges.

In the United States, most union contracts include arbitration agreements, but such agreements are negotiated by the union with its employers rather than being imposed as a condition of employment. The use of arbitration has also spread from business and employment to other sectors in the United States. Examples include agreements between businesses and consumers, such as contracts covering credit cards, communications, cable television, cell phone services, retail sales, health clubs, travel agencies, summer camps, and various other financial services. Furthermore, the use of arbitration in the U.S. has risen dramatically since a very important Supreme Court decision upheld the use of arbitration in an employment discrimination context.

The U.S. Federal Arbitration Act and the Uniform Arbitration Act

The right to arbitrate arises from an initial contract between the parties in question. The contract can be a preexisting one, in which the parties have agreed to submit all or certain issues for arbitration, or the parties can enter into a present contract to arbitrate an existing dispute. Because arbitration is contract based, the parties are legally obligated to arbitrate only those issues which they agreed to arbitrate in their contract. If a party refuses to arbitrate, the aggrieved party can petition a traditional court for an order directing the arbitration to be rendered. If a party refuses to carry out the terms of the arbitrator's decision, the aggrieved party can seek a court order directing that the arbitrator's decision be carried out.

The key applicable statute in the United States is the Federal Arbitration Act of 1925 which allows for arbitration and makes arbitrators' decisions enforceable in the federal courts. Most states also have statutes under which arbitration agreements are enforced. Statutes at the state level are often premised on the

Uniform Arbitration Act, which seeks to promote the enforceability of arbitration awards as well as the application of arbitration on a consistent basis at the state level.

Advantages and Disadvantages of Arbitration

The advantages of arbitration are many. Arbitration certainly is less expensive and less time-consuming than the traditional judicial manner of resolving disputes. Arbitration also allows for judges to be experts on the subject matter for very complex cases whereas most traditional court judges are "generalists." Arbitration is also less formal than traditional court adjudication: It does not strictly follow the rules of evidence, such as the "hearsay rule." Furthermore, there is no traditional jury in an arbitration proceeding. Juries are very risky, especially for large corporations, and especially when it comes to damages. Class action suits pose an even greater risk to a company. Arbitration is (presumably) voluntary, meaning that it is based on contractual agreement and, therefore, consent. Finally, arbitration is usually a private affair. Businesses and employers usually prefer this method as there is no public record and they are spared any potential bad publicity.

On the other hand, arbitration at times is criticized as being "second-hand," "second-rate," or even "second-class" justice. Such grievances come because arbitration deprives an aggrieved party of his or her "day in court." Moreover, an arbitrator does not have to follow existing federal and state laws—including legal procedures and evidentiary rules—as strictly as would a traditional judge. Furthermore, fact-finding can be more restricted by an arbitrator versus a traditional judge. Damages are often "capped," appeals are very limited (as will be seen), and arbitration itself can be costly, especially for an aggrieved employee or consumer.

Because the clauses are commonly placed as one of many provisions in a larger contract, many employees and consumers may not even realize that they have already agreed to arbitration. Another problem is that the law does not stipulate what rights, obligations, and remedies the arbitration process must include. Arbitration may not be mandatory for a business or employer, but may be mandatory for an employee or consumer, and the business or employer thus may also be able to pursue a traditional court remedy. Furthermore, because arbitration usually is a confidential process, it may keep private matters of societal concern that really should be made public, such as issues regarding product safety and anti-competitive practices.

The Arbitration Process

When a dispute arises, the parties can agree to submit the dispute to arbitration. However, typically, disputes are arbitrated because of an arbitration clause in a contract entered into before the dispute arose. (Usually, such a clause will state that any dispute arising under the terms of the contract will be resolved by means of arbitration.) Virtually any business, commercial, or contract matter can be submitted to arbitration. The submitted issues can be factual, legal, or both and can also entail questions regarding the arbitration agreement and the interpretation thereof.

Arbitration commences with a formal arbitration "submission," which means that the parties officially refer certain issues to the arbitrator for resolution. The next steps in the procedure consist of: the parties being given notice of the time and place of the arbitration hearing; the arbitrator establishing the rules, which again are less formal than a traditional court; a hearing being held, where opening statements are made, testimony is taken (without any formal pleadings or motions and without the strict rules of evidence discovery being followed), evidence is presented, witnesses are examined, and closing arguments are made; and the arbitrator deliberates and renders his or her decision. Often, the decision is made orally and without explanation. The decision of the arbitrator is called the "award," and it is binding for all parties to the dispute on all issues submitted.

Appealing and Overturning an Arbitration Award

In the appeal process, a party may ask the court to render an order compelling the other party to comply with the arbitration award. Also, if one party to an arbitration procedure is dissatisfied with the arbitrator's decision, he or she has the right to appeal it to a traditional court. However, in the United States, the scope of judicial review of an arbitration award is very, very limited, with the scope of judicial review far more restricted than an appellate court's review of a trial court decision.

In an appeal of an arbitration award, a judge will examine the award to see if it covered matters that were beyond the issues submitted. If the arbitrator exceeded his or her conferred powers in deciding the dispute, his or her decision can be overturned by a court. A judge also will always seek to ascertain if there was any fraud, corruption, bribery, conflict of interest, bias, or other misconduct in the rendering of the award. Consequently, an award may be set aside by a court if there is sufficient evidence of an arbitrator's bad faith or misconduct. The refusal or failure of the arbitrator to hear relevant evidence will also be grounds for the reversal of an award, although these types of arbitrator misconduct are rare.

Judges, of course, may be a bit biased towards letting arbitrations stand given the fact that arbitration keeps disputes off of already crowded court dockets. However, a court may need to get involved initially if there is a dispute as to whether a particular matter is even one that can be resolved by arbitration. Such a problem is commonly called an "arbitrability" issue, but it could also very well be a more traditional legal issue as well.

It is important to remember, however, that a traditional court in the U.S. will not review the merits of the decision, whether there was sufficient evidence to support the decision, or even if the award was contrary to the evidence presented.

Arbitration of Employment Discrimination Claims in the United States

Employers naturally want to avoid time-consuming and costly litigation, especially considering the potential for damages and attorneys' fees. They especially want to avoid litigation that involves discrimination claims by employees.

As a result, employers increasingly have been making arbitration a contractual condition of an employee's employment with the employer. Of course, when the employee chooses to work for the employer, he or she "voluntarily" signs the employment contract with the arbitration clause. In such a situation, arbitration is now mandatory for the employee, who has effectively waived, by contract, his or her right to have a traditional court hear his or her employment discrimination claim. However, the employer is still allowed to take the employee to court.

Moreover, an arbitration clause usually "caps" damages as well as disallows "pain and suffering" and punitive damages. Therefore, the monetary damages that an aggrieved and vindicated employee receives from an arbitration award are far less than what the law allows in the U.S. for civil rights discrimination claims. And there is, of course, no jury in an arbitration proceeding.

Recent court decisions in the United States clearly reveal that arbitration can be a viable and legally permissible substitute for traditional court litigation of employment discrimination claims. The leading case was the U.S. Supreme Court's 1991 decision in *Gilmer v. Interstate/Johnson Lane Corp*. The case involved an employee who was a stockbroker and financial manager for a particular corporation. After being terminated by the employer, the employee sued for age discrimination. There was, however, an arbitration clause in the employee's contract, which was required by the New York Stock Exchange for registration as a securities representative. Nonetheless, the employee contended that the termination violated the Age Discrimination in Employment Act. But the Supreme Court stated that nothing in the federal Act itself indicated an intent to preclude enforcement of arbitration agreements. Thus, the Court upheld the arbitrability of the claim.

In 2001, another important Supreme Court case, *Circuit City v. Adams*, the Court again upheld the arbitrability of an employment discrimination claim, this time filed in state court by the employee. In this case, the employee, an electronic salesperson who was homosexual, sued for discrimination and sexual harassment. However, the employee had signed an employment application with a binding arbitration clause, which required all employment disputes to be resolved by arbitration. The employer went to federal court, arguing that under the Federal Arbitration Act, the dispute should have been handled by the arbitration process and not in the state court lawsuit. The Supreme Court agreed with the employer.

The technical legal issue in the *Circuit City* case dealt with an exception to the Federal Arbitration Act for workers engaged in interstate commerce. The lower federal courts had ruled that the employee was involved in "commerce," but the Supreme Court agreed with the employer that the "interstate commerce" exception in the Act was limited to those workers who actually were involved in the movement of goods from one state to another.

However, in 2002, the U.S. Supreme Court made it a bit more difficult for employers to keep employment discrimination cases completely out of court. The Court, in *EEOC v. Waffle House, Inc.*, ruled that even when an employee has agreed to binding arbitration, the federal agency that implements the U.S. Civil Rights Act, the Equal Employment Opportunity Commission (EEOC), can still sue the employer and pursue legal remedies for the employee, such as reinstatement and back pay. The Court explained that a binding arbitration agreement will not prevent this federal agency from exercising its powers, fulfilling its functions, or granting remedies as provided by the U.S. Congress. Yet the ruling has not had a very substantial effect on employers as the EEOC only chooses to file a lawsuit on behalf of an employee in a very small number of the many complaints from employees that the agency regularly receives.

Key Arbitration Issues[19]

A key arbitration legal issue that must be resolved prior to the arbitration is whether a dispute should in fact be arbitrated. Typically this problem arises when a contract has an arbitration clause and one of the contract parties refuses to arbitrate. Then, the legal issue becomes a breach of contract and contract enforceability issue for the courts. As noted, the Federal Arbitration Act (FAA) in the United States decrees that arbitration agreements are enforceable just like any other contract. The courts, moreover, have ruled consistently that a dispute is considered to be appropriate for arbitration unless a statute clearly disallows arbitration. The FAA also provides procedural mechanisms for enforcing arbitration agreements in federal court. Assuming the contract containing the arbitration agreement is not vitiated by fraud or some other legal doctrine, the courts have uniformly held that these arbitration agreements in contracts are

---

[19] See Coltri, Laurie, S. (2010).

legal and enforceable, even when they are imposed on consumers and employees on a "take-it-or-leave-it" basis by large and powerful businesses and employers, and even if the arbitration agreement may adversely affect statutory rights under consumer protection and Civil Rights statutes. In order for an arbitration agreement to not be enforced against a consumer or employee, it would have to be manifestly and grossly unfair and one-sided, for example, if the arbitration agreement allows and employer, but not the employee, to institute legal proceedings in a traditional court. The arbitration award, moreover, can be enforced by traditional judicial remedies for enforcing monetary judgments, such as attachment, seizure, and sale of property and garnishment of funds and wages. Furthermore, since the FAA is a federal statute, the courts have ruled that the FAA and court decisions interpreting and implementing the FAA preempt and conflicting state laws. Accordingly, there evidently is a federal legal policy favoring arbitration of disputes.

Regarding the confidentiality of arbitration, it is interesting and important to note that under the common law and under most states' law and federal law, arbitration is not deemed confidential, though it is private, as opposed to a traditional court trial which the public usually can freely enter. Consequently, as a general rule, arbitration proceedings are discoverable in a court case and can also be admitted into evidence. One must investigate a particular jurisdiction to see if the state has any confidentiality laws protecting arbitration proceedings. Of course, the parties to the arbitration proceeding can, and actually may have very good reasons, to provide that the arbitration proceedings be kept confidential.

Another important legal area regarding arbitration occurs after the arbitration is completed and one of the parties wants to challenge the arbitration decision in a traditional court. As a very firm general rule, rising to the level of a legal presumption, the rule of law holds that arbitration decisions are not appealable to the courts. The rationale is that the parties have freely (presumably) chosen arbitration to resolve their dispute, which includes a non-appealable decision element. However, the FAA does provide some limited circumstances, where an arbitration decision can be appealed and overturned by the courts, for example, where there is evidence of fraud or corruption, misconduct or bias by the arbitrator, or where the arbitrator has exceeded his or her authority granted by the arbitration agreement, for example, by deciding an issue that was clearly not one subject to arbitration. However, unlike a traditional court decision, an arbitrator's decision cannot be overturned by a court if the arbitrator has made a mistake as to the law, for example, in the existence, interpretation, or application of the law. Perhaps if there is evidence that the arbitrator manifestly disregarded the applicable law, a party may be successful in getting a court to vacate the award. Yet arbitration awards can be corrected or modified by the courts if there are clerical or mathematical mistakes. Finally, a traditional court always has the authority, as it does with any type of contract case, to strike down the arbitration award for contravening the public policy of the jurisdiction.

Choice of Law in Arbitration Disputes

Another important legal area in arbitration involves the choice of law for the arbitration proceeding. That is, what jurisdiction's law should apply to the dispute if the parties are from different legal jurisdictions or if the dispute or transaction is multi-jurisdictional or international? The answer to this question is simple. That is, the parties in their arbitration agreement can specify which jurisdiction's laws will apply to the dispute. If the parties fail to do so, they are "asking for trouble" since it is possible that many different sources of law could apply to the transaction, for example, the place where the arbitration agreement was formed, the place where the dispute arose, the place with the most significant relationship to the dispute, or perhaps a statute or treaty which specifies the choice of law. Generally, in the United States, if the dispute arises in the U.S., the choice of law is made by referring to the FAA. The situation is more complicated in international transactions, where there are wide and at times divergent legal systems and bodies of laws. There in order to avoid confusion and unintended consequences, the parties should choose the forum for arbitration, that is, the country where any arbitration will be held, as well as the choice of law for the arbitration. In the international context, of course, reference must be made to international treaties governing arbitration.

Arbitration Clause in Contract

Considering all the advantages to arbitration as an alternative dispute resolution mechanism, employers should seriously consider the placement of an arbitration clause in the employers' contracts with employees, suppliers and distributors, and consumers. The courts consistently uphold arbitration clauses in contracts so long as the arbitration is fair and unbiased and provides all parties with due process. The contract can specify that any dispute will be settled by arbitration or that the parties must first seek a resolution of the dispute by means of mediation before any other method for resolving the dispute can be used. Such a clause will afford the business person the opportunity to settle the dispute in mutually acceptable manner by mediation or if a decision is called for by means of arbitration as opposed to a traditional court trial.

Mediation and Arbitration Services and Online Dispute Resolution

Mediators are people known for their subject matter expertise, "diplomatic" skills, and fairness. They are selected by the parties to a controversy from a mediation service, such as the National Mediation and Conciliation Service in the U.S., which mediates labor disputes. The American Arbitration Service, founded in 1926, is the largest provider of alternative dispute resolution services in the United States. Another large organization is the CPR Institute for Dispute Resolution. Such organizations naturally charge fees for their services.

Arbitration and mediation now can be conducted online where the parties can communicate "virtually" with each other and the arbitrator or mediator. There exist today several entities, such as Cybersettle, ClickNSettle, and Settlement Online, which provide online dispute resolution services. However, before engaging in alternative dispute resolution, or for that matter even negotiation, whether on ground or online, the business person should require an agreement that any statements or offers of settlement made during the course of these processes will not be admissible in a court of law if these alternative processes fail to solve the dispute and the parties end up in litigation.

Online dispute resolution is currently being used to resolve Internet domain name disputes, as will be seen in the Internet Regulation chapter, but online dispute resolution may appear as a viable ADR for smaller companies, who may prefer it to the more costly and more involved "ground" arbitration services. For example, the Virtual Magistrate Project, an affiliation of the American Arbitration Service, provides online arbitration services for the users of online systems as well as provides the resolution of online disputes, including contract, tort, and intellectual property "virtual" controversies.

Global Legal Perspectives

International arbitration agreements can allow companies to decide in advance where disputes will be heard, by whom, and in what language. International arbitration has increased dramatically, mostly because it can provide business partners, suppliers, and customers from different countries and varying legal jurisdictions an unbiased forum in which to resolve disputes. Arbitration is a particularly efficacious way of resolving disputes in those countries and cultures, such as Thailand, where confrontation and litigation are frowned upon, seen as evidence of failure, as well as cause for shame and, consequently, to be strenuously avoided as means of resolving disputes.

Private parties desiring to solve legal disputes often determine the venue of jurisdiction during the time a contract is being written so that the laws of a certain country will be applied during such legal issues. Normally, a central location is determined and agreed upon by both parties ahead of time should legal issues arise. However, as all cultures vary in their proceedings toward issues of legality, there are other ways of resolving disputes, including those of the World Trade Organization (WTO). (Note: This mechanism is only applicable to member states.) The WTO provides legal advice and court appearances to member nation states in conflict with one another over various matters such as business. State-owned firms often appear as players in such disputes, especially if international norms and rules have been violated. Most cases are resolved by separate arbitration committees, which are established specifically for dispute resolution within these organizations.

Further information is provided on the WTO's website, as well as the websites of other relevant organizations to find out more about such disputes.

Arbitration in Indonesia and Brazil

The specific discussion of international arbitration and the New York Convention herein will be focus on two countries, Indonesia[20] and Brazil.[21] While Indonesia is a signatory of the WTO treaty, according to one commentator, it is well-known that local Indonesian courts frequently have intruded into the arbitration process to the extent of adjudicating cases being subject to arbitration agreements, enjoining ongoing arbitration proceedings, and even reopening the merits question of a particular award. The result has been that Indonesian courts have engendered little confidence among foreign businesspeople and investors regarding alternative dispute resolution procedures and, in particular, the enforceability of the arbitration award. This negative perception has hurt Indonesia economically, according to the commentator.

The animus toward alternative dispute resolution by the Indonesian courts, moreover, is a bit strange considering that traditionally, Indonesian society has been somewhat non-litigious. Indeed, conciliation, mediation, and consensus building are more preferable in Indonesian society than arbitration, which is a more adversarial "win-lose" mechanism. Accordingly, Indonesians have been thought of as valuing the preservation of business and commercial relationships and thus preferring to settle disputes amicably through negotiation rather than arbitration.

Therefore, in order to modernize Indonesian arbitration law, make it more consistent with international standards and practices, and ultimately to make the country more attractive to foreign business and capital, in 1999, the country passed a new arbitration law, the Law Concerning Arbitration and Alternative Dispute Resolution. The law first provides for the enforcement of domestic arbitration awards and second, and perhaps most importantly, the law provides for the enforcement of international arbitration awards. This law provides that such a foreign arbitration award will be recognized and enforceable if five conditions are met: 1) The award was rendered in a country that is bound with

---

[20] See Rubins, Noah (2005).
[21] See Pucci, Adriana Noemi (2005).

Indonesia to recognize and enforce arbitration awards; 2) The dispute is commercial in nature; 3) The award does not violate public order; 4) The Chairman of the district court issues an order of execution; and 5) If Indonesia itself is a party in the dispute, the execution order must be issued by the Supreme Court of the Republic of Indonesia. The legal authority to enforce such foreign awards is designated as the District Court of Central Jakarta. This 1999 law thus should make Indonesia more palatable to foreign business and investment.

The arbitration situation in Brazil has been different than the Indonesian experience. Arbitration and alternative dispute resolution long ago attained a high level of acceptance in Brazil and is currently being extensively utilized in that country. Brazil has a modern arbitration law, the 1996 Arbitration Act. In 2002, Brazil ratified the New York Convention on arbitration awards and it has also enacted the International Commercial Arbitration Agreement of Mercosur, which provides for arbitration to resolve commercial disputes. Moreover, in 2001 Brazil's Supreme Court (the Supremo Tribunal Federal) upheld the constitutionality of the country's modern arbitration act.

Brazil's arbitration act provides that if there is an arbitration clause in a contract, in the event one party refuses to arbitrate, the other party can request the intervention of a judge, who has the authority to rule that the court has no jurisdiction of an arbitral dispute and to appoint a sole arbitrator to resolve the dispute. The Arbitration Act also provides that an arbitration award has the same effect as a court decision, which means that an award, including execution on property, can be enforced by a court in order to satisfy the award. The parties to arbitration agreement also have the freedom, under Brazilian law, to choose not only the arbitrators, but also to choose any substantive and procedural laws they deem applicable to their arbitration agreement. However, one superseding factor is that the laws chosen to be applied cannot be contrary to the morality and general public policy of the nation of Brazil.

Presuming that the procedural aspects of the arbitration were complied with, the Brazilian courts have no authority to challenge an arbitration award on its merits. Even a mistake on the part of an arbitrator will not be sufficient grounds for a court to overturn an award in Brazil. Accordingly, when it comes to courts nullifying arbitration awards, the situation in Brazil is very similar to that in the United States. Therefore, arbitration awards are given a great deal of deference in Brazil.

The justification for these legal actions is the recognition by the Brazilian legal and business communities that having an enforceable arbitration system is indispensable to attracting foreign business and investment. The fact that the Brazilian courts are upholding the enforcement of arbitration provisions in contracts as well as upholding the ultimate awards themselves should give international businesspeople and their attorneys the confidence to do business and invest in Brazil as well as to include arbitration clauses in their Brazilian commercial agreements.

Management Strategies

In an effort to further avoid traditional court litigation, companies also can simply make an arbitration provision a part of a contract, a condition of employment, or a condition of doing business with the firm. This puts parties to a commercial or consumer contract in the position of waiving court rights in exchange for binding arbitration. Furthermore, employees and consumers thus may be left with a "take-it-or-leave-it" employment contract-arbitration choice.

At the same time, companies should strive to select arbitrators who are industry and subject matter experts, as well as perceived to be fair and balanced. The arbitration process that a company and its employees and customers agree to must not only be fair, but also must be knowingly and voluntarily agreed upon. Otherwise, a company takes the risk of the judiciary, regulatory agencies, and even the arbitration associations criticizing the process or perhaps even delimiting or overturning arbitration.

For example, if the company solely picks the arbitrator, pays the arbitrator, and limits the employee's rights during the process by not providing documents and witnesses until the hearing, prevents the employee from asking questions, limits the remedies thereafter, and then constrains the arbitrator's freedom to render a decision, a judge, either domestically or internationally, may set aside the very one-sided arbitration agreement as an "unconscionable" or immoral contract. The arbitrator might even turn down such an assignment as being intrinsically unfair.

Summary

Traditional litigation has been highly discouraged in many courts across the world, usually forcing managers, firms, and states to seek other alternative means to resolving disputes. Because court systems across the international arena vary in their accordance to individual laws, ADR has become a very popular method of solving legal issues.

Today, arbitration is one of the most popular methods used to resolve disputes: among private parties, between states, and between state-owned firms. Litigation, mediation, and arbitration vary in their ways of resolving disputes. Such methods of dispute resolution are oftentimes utilized by courts and businesses in varying forms in different countries. Today, traditional court appearances are frequently discouraged and this reluctance to go to court also extends to organizations like the WTO. Therefore, firms are only allowed to present their cases in court if there are no alternate solutions available.

The advantages and disadvantages of ADR methods such as mediation and arbitration were discussed to better provide readers with different perspectives on settling conflicts. Strategies for managers were also examined to help multi-national managers avoid traditional litigation court procedures.

SIX

Moral philosophy is the study of morality and the application of philosophy and ethics to moral thinking, moral conduct, and moral problems. Moral philosophy encompasses various ethical theories that prescribe what is good for people and what is bad for people, what constitutes right and wrong, and what one ought to do and ought not to do. Moral philosophy offers ethical theories that provide a theoretical framework for making, asserting, and defending a moral decision. However, there is not one determinate set of ethical theories. Moral philosophy embraces a wide range of ethical perspectives, and this field concerns itself with analyzing the differences among these ethical views. Nonetheless, each ethical theory underscores some ultimate principle or set of principles which one is obligated to follow in order to ensure the establishment of moral behavior and the "good life."

Business ethics and corporate social responsibility are important aspects of moral maturity in today's global business environment. This chapter in Part I discusses various ethical theories and their application in a modern business environment. Then in Part II the chapter examines the concept of social responsibility and how that concept is applied to business in the form of "corporate social responsibility." The chapter also offers frameworks for effective moral and socially responsible decision-making in the global workplace.

Morality and Ethics[22]

The ultimate aim of moral philosophy is to answer one superseding question: How *should* one live?

The philosophical study of morality is distinguished by the general, systematic, and logical nature of the endeavor itself. The study of morality is the effort to systematize ethically moral judgments as well as to establish and defend ethically moral beliefs and standards. Moral philosophy develops ethical frameworks for evaluating the merits of asserted moral positions and attempts to establish logical thought processes that will determine if an action is right or wrong. The philosophy also seeks to find criteria by which to distinguish good from bad conduct. Moral philosophy endeavors to prove its claims through ethical arguments, which can demonstrate that the ideal thought, conduct, life, and morality are, in fact, ideal.

---

[22] For a comprehensive coverage of this material, see Cavico and Mujtaba's book, entitled *Business Ethics: Transcending Requirements through Moral Leadership.*

Ethics is the theoretical study of morality. It is the sustained and reasoned attempt to determine what is morally right or wrong. Ethics is used to test the moral correctness of beliefs, practices, and rules and necessarily involves an effort both to define what is meant by morality as well as to justify the way of acting and living that is being advocated.

Ethical theories are moral philosophical undertakings that contain bodies of formal, systematic, and ethical principles that are committed to the view that an asserted ethical theory can determine how one should think and act morally. Ethics proceeds from a conviction that moral disagreements and conflicts are resolvable rationally. Ergo, there is one "best" answer to any moral dispute, and this answer can be reached through reasoning.

The purpose of ethics is to develop, articulate, and justify principles and techniques that can be used in specific situations where a moral determination must be made about a particular action or practice. There are, of course, problems in this attempt to formulate principles to resolve concrete moral problems. For instance, to what extent is ethics a source of objective, determinate, and reasoned principles rather than merely personal, political, cultural, legal, or religious "answers" to moral questions?

Moral judgments are deducible based on a hierarchy of ethical principles and it is the moral philosopher's task to articulate such ethical principles and to insist upon their proper application. Presuming that ethical principles are objective and reasoned, how are they to be justified? Is there some independent, overarching principle or mechanism that can arbitrate among various moral philosophies across different cultures and validate the correctness of ethical principles? Even if people around the world agree on general ethical principles, the application of such principles to specific moral problems also causes controversy.

There is a relationship between ethics and morals in the conduct of human affairs. When something is judged to be good or bad, right or wrong, or just or unjust, the underlying standards on which the judgment is based are thus considered moral standards. Moral standards include not only specific moral rules, but also the more general ethical principles upon which the moral rules are based. When a decision involves a moral component, the decision necessarily encompasses moral rules and ethical principles. Morals themselves are beliefs or views as to what is right or wrong or good or bad. Moral norms are standards of behavior by which people are judged and that require, prohibit, or allow specific types of behavior. Moral rules are action-guiding or prescriptive statements about how people ought to behave or ought not to behave.

Ethics deals with matters that are of serious consequence to human beings. Ethics affects human welfare and fulfillment in significant ways as people will be positively or negatively affected by various moral decisions. Ethics, therefore, is concerned with conduct that can benefit or harm human beings.

Values are rankings or priorities that a person establishes for his or her own norms and beliefs. Values express what is the chief end of life, the highest good, and what things in life are worthwhile or desirable. Deeply held values can drive behavior. One very difficult problem with values is placing values in proper relation to one another. Values often are controversial because the norms and beliefs that one person holds in high esteem may conflict with different norms and beliefs that another person holds in equally high esteem.

Moral values are the rankings or priorities that a person establishes for one's own moral norms and moral beliefs. A distinction here must be made between two types of values: instrumental and intrinsic values. Instrumental (or extrinsic values) are good because not adhering to them brings about consequences. Instrumental values are desired as a means to an end, i.e., their worth is not measured in their own right, but rather in relation to what they can bring about in connection with other values (e.g., in the field of economics). Intrinsic values, by contrast, are good in and of themselves. They are an end unto themselves and are desired for their own sake, claiming appraisal in their own right. Intrinsic values are—or claim to be—of absolute worth, e.g., pleasure (to a hedonist), power (to a Machiavellian), knowledge, or self-realization. In philosophic context, moral values are generally considered to be intrinsic.

There are theories of ethics that depend upon some theory of intrinsic value. That is, in order to determine if something is good or right, one first must determine which things are worth seeking, without regard to consequences. But the question of whose intrinsic good is in question and whose should be promoted must be addressed. For example, to an egoist, one should promote one's own greatest good; to a utilitarian, one should promote the greatest good for everyone.

Part I—Business Ethics

Determining whether an action, rule, or law is moral or immoral, right or wrong, or just or unjust perforce brings one into the realm of *ethics*, which is a branch of *philosophy*, and then logically one proceeds to ethical theories, ethical principles, applied ethics, and ethical reasoning to moral conclusions. In the ethics part to this chapter, the authors will explain and then apply four major ethical theories—Ethical Egoism, Ethical Relativism, Utilitarianism, and Kantian ethics—to the subject of bribery to determine if paying a bribe to a foreign government official is moral. These ethical theories were chosen because they represent the essence of ethics as a branch of philosophy in Western Civilization, which obviously is not the only civilization, but it is one that the authors are the most familiar with, including, of course, the ethics component to Western knowledge and thought, as opposed to, for example, Confucian ethical principles and the application thereof, which, although most interesting and intriguing to learn and to apply, practically would be beyond the scope of the authors' objectives for this chapter. These four Western theories also were selected because they are reason-based ethical theories; as such, the authors assume that the readers of this book possess intellect, reason, and logic, and thus will be quite "comfortable" in following the authors' ethical "train of thought," though, of course, perhaps not agreeing with their ultimate moral conclusions. Furthermore, religion-based ethical theories were not chosen because not all the readers of this book will be of the same religion and, for that matter, some may have no religion at all; and, moreover, bringing in a religious-based ethical component to this chapter would be to expand the book beyond the authors' aims. The focus is on Western ethics; and the first ethical theory to be examined will be Ethical Egoism. However, it is first necessary for the authors to explain some key ethical terms and concepts.

Values

The authors believe it is very harmful for people to use continually a wide variety of very general terms without clear meanings. The lack of any fixed meaning, the inability of people to provide proper explanations, the individualistic, expedient decision-making, as well as an emphasis on rhetoric and persuasion, engender relativism, skepticism, and a great deal of confusion, People then will be talking at cross purposes and their discussions will make no progress. Only confusion, skepticism, chaos, and perhaps even conflict, will ensue. Therefore, it is very important for a business leader, academic, and manager to look for, ascertain, and pay special attention to definitions and terms. When one initially encounters the fields of ethics, corporate governance, social responsibility, and stakeholder analysis in a business context, one is confronted with some confusion due to a lack of an agreed-upon terminology and set of definitions. What is social responsibility? How does it differ from the law, ethics, and morality? What exactly do the terms "corporate social responsibility," "stakeholder values," "sustainability," "people, planet, and profits," "going green," and "socially responsible investing" mean? What is a corporate "constituency" statute and how does it compare and contrast to a "social benefit" corporation? So, as will be seen in Part II of this chapter, if one is going to understand what social responsibility is and how it works in a modern global business environment, there must be some agreement on, and some insight into, the meaning and nature of the value of social responsibility especially when juxtaposed with the values of legality, based on the law, and the value of morality, based on ethics. There is, therefore, a need for words, terms, and definitions with precise meaning.

In order to arrive at a precise as possible meaning of the terms ethics and "social responsibility," it is first necessary to define some fundamental terms and concepts. A value is something that possesses worth. *Values* can be *intrinsic* (also called terminal), meaning that they possess value and worth in and of themselves, for example, happiness and aesthetics. Whereas values that are "merely" *extrinsic* (also called instrumental) possess worth and are valuable because they are the means to produce something else of value, for example, money (which can buy happiness!). The value of legality is, of course, based on the law. The value of morality stems from ethics; yet the terms ethics and morals or morality are not synonymous. *Morality* is the conclusion of what is right or wrong or good or bad; whereas ethics is the philosophical framework, consisting of ethical theories and principles that one uses to reason to moral conclusions. Whether morality is an intrinsic value or merely and instrumental one is an issue which the authors will leave to the philosophers. Social responsibility too is a value, related to, but distinct from law and ethics. Social responsibility, particularly in a business sense, as will be addressed in Part II to this chapter, is concerned with a business going "above and beyond" the law as well as acting beyond morality by taking an active part in community and civic affairs and charitable endeavors.

Ethical Egoism

The ethical theory of *Ethical Egoism* harkens back to ancient Greece and the philosophical school of the Sophists and their teachings of relativism and promotion of self-interest. This ethical theory maintains that a person ought to promote his or her self-interest and the greatest balance of good for himself or herself. Since this theory is an ethical theory, one thus has a moral obligation to promote one's self-interest; and so "selfishly" acting is also morally acting; and concomitantly an action against one's self-interest is an immoral action; and an action that advances one's self-interest is a moral action. An ethically egoistic person, therefore, will shrewdly discern the "pros" and "cons" of an action, and then perform the action that performs the most personal good, which also is the moral course of action. However, the Ethical Egoists counsel that one should be an "enlightened" ethical egoist; that is, one should think of what will inure to one's benefit in the long-run, and accordingly be ready to sacrifice some short-term pain or expense to attain a greater long-term good—for oneself, of course. Also, the prudent ethical egoist would say that as a general rule it is better, even if one has a lot of power as well as a big ego, to treat people well, to make them part of "your team," and to "co-op" them. Why should one treat people well? One reason is certainly not because one is beneficent, but rather because one is "selfish." That is, one is treating people well because typically it will advance one's own self-interest in the long-term to do so. One problem with ethical egoism is that one's own "good" must be defined. What exactly is one maximizing? Is it one's knowledge, power, money, pleasure, comfort, prestige, success, or happiness? Ethical egoists agree that people ought to pursue and advance their own good; but they disagree as to the type of good people should be seeking. Yet in business the "good" typically means making money! Another problem with Ethical Egoism is that the doctrine counsels that everyone should pursue his or her own self-interest. Yet what if there is just one job position or one promotion opportunity and two people want to advance themselves by attaining the job or promotion? Now, one would hope that as rational egoists there would be clearly defined, legitimate, job-related criteria for the job or promotion. Yet that is no always the case. Consequently, there is the distinct possibility that the two egos seeking self-advancement will clash; and conflict may result; but there is no mechanism in Ethical Egoism that acts as an arbitrating principle to decide whose ego gets advance. So, who will "win" the job or the promotion? "Might makes right," the Sophists long ago said!

Ethical Relativism

Ethical Relativism as an ethical theory also harkens back to ancient Greece and the philosophical school of the Sophists as well as the philosophical school of the Skeptics. Ethical relativists deny that there are any objective, universal moral rules which one can construct an absolute moral system. Ethical relativists deny that there are moral rules applicable to all peoples, in all societies, and at all times. There thus are no universal moral standards by which to judge an action's morality; rather, morality is merely relative to, and holds for, only a particular society at a particular time. "When in Rome, do as the Romans," said the Ethical Relativists. Morality, therefore, is a societal-based notion; it is nothing more than the morality of a certain group, people, or society at a certain time. What a society believes is right is in fact right for that society; the moral beliefs of a society determine what is "right" or "wrong" in that society. However, different societies may have different conceptions of what is right or wrong. What one believes is right, the other may believe as wrong. Consequently, the same act can be morally right for one society but morally wrong for another. So, one society can believe that the use of partial nudity in advertising is moral; whereas another society may condemn such a practice as immoral. Since pursuant to Ethical Relativism there are no moral standards which are universally true for all peoples, in all societies, and at all times, and since there is no way to demonstrate that one set of beliefs is true and the other false, the only way to determine an action's morality is to determine what the people in a particular society believe is right or wrong at a given time. So, "simply" discern the societal moral precepts, and then conform and adapt; and one will be acting morally, at least pursuant to this ethical theory.

Of course, ascertaining exactly what a "society" is a daunting challenge. Even within a homogeneous society, there are diverse cultures, subcultures, social classes, kinship, and work groups; and in a heterogeneous society there will be many smaller sub-societies that co-exist. All these components of society may reflect different standards, mores, customs, and beliefs, including moral standards and beliefs. Yet pursuant to the doctrine of Ethical Relativism, one must attempt to find the pertinent "society" and then try to ascertain that society's moral beliefs; but when one does ascertain the societal beliefs, standards, and practices regarding morality, one simply has to conform and adopt, and one will be acting morally, at least according to the ethical theory of Ethical Relativism.

Utilitarianism

Utilitarianism is a major ethical theory in Western civilization; it was created principally by the English philosophers and social reformers Jeremy Bentham and John Stewart Mill. Their goal was to develop an ethical theory that not only was "scientific" but also would maximize human happiness and pleasure (in the sense of satisfaction). Utilitarianism is regarded as a consequentialist ethical theory, also called a teleological ethical theory; that is, one determines morality by examining the consequences of an action; the form of the action is irrelevant; rather, the consequences produced by the action are paramount in determining its morality. If an action produces more good than bad consequences, it is a moral action; and if an action produces more bad than good consequences it is an immoral action. Of course, ethical egoism is also a consequentialist ethical theory. The critical difference is that the Utilitarians demand that one consider the consequences of an action not just on oneself, but also on other people and groups who are affected directly and indirectly by the action. The scope of analysis, plainly, is much broader, and less "selfish," pursuant to a Utilitarian ethical analysis. In business ethics texts and classes, the term "stakeholders" is frequently used to indicate the various groups that would be affected by a business decision. Furthermore, the Utilitarians specifically and explicitly stated that society as a whole must be considered in this evaluation of the good and/or bad consequences produced by an action. The idea is to get away from a "me, me, me" mind-set and consider other people and groups affected by an action.

Utilitarianism is a very egalitarian ethical theory since everyone's pleasure and/or pain gets registered and counted in this "scientific" effort to determine morality. Yet, there are several problems with the doctrine. First, one has to try to predict the consequences of putting an action into effect, which can be very difficult if one is looking for longer-term effects. However, the Utilitarians would say to use one's "common storehouse of knowledge," one's intelligence, and "let history be your guide" in making these predictions. Do not guess or speculate, but go with the probable or reasonably foreseeable consequences of an action. Also, if one is affected by an action, one naturally gets counted too, but if that same one person is doing the Utilitarian analysis, there is always the all-too-human tendency to "cook the books" to benefit oneself. The Utilitarians would say that one should try to be impartial and objective in any analysis. Next, one now has to measure and weigh the good versus the bad consequences to ascertain what prevails and thus what the ultimate moral conclusion will be. The Utilitarians said that not only was this ethical theory "scientific," but it was also mathematical ("good old-fashioned English bookkeeping," they called it). But how does one do the math? How does one measure and weigh the good and the bad consequences? And for that matter how does one measure different types of goods? The Utilitarians, alas, provided very little guidance. Finally, a major criticism of the Utilitarian ethical theory is that it may lead to an unjust result. That is, the "ends may justify the means." Since the form of the action is irrelevant in this type of ethical analysis, if the action produces a greater overall good, then the action is moral, regardless of the fact that some bad may be produced in this effort to achieve the overall good. The good, though, outweighs the bad; accordingly, the action is moral; and the sufferers of the bad, who perhaps were exploited or whose rights were trampled, got counted at least. Such is the nature of Utilitarianism.

After determining the action to be evaluated, the next step in the Utilitarian analysis is to determine the people and groups, that is, the stakeholders, affected by the action, then make a determination as to how they are affected (that is, are the reasonably foreseeable consequences good or bad ones), and next make an overall determination if putting the action into effect results in more good or bad. If the former, the action is moral; if the latter, the action is immoral pursuant to Utilitarianism. Although the Utilitarians claim that their ethical theory is objective and scientific, it is difficult to predict, measure, and weigh consequences. Nonetheless, in the next section the authors present a Utilitarian model, specifically a stakeholder, pleasure v. pain, consequentialist version of the Utilitarian ethical theory, originally developed by Professor Richard T. DeGeorge in his book, *Business Ethics* (2006).

In order to determine the morality of an action, practice, rule, or law pursuant to the stakeholder, pleasure v. pain, consequentialist model of the ethical theory of Utilitarianism:

1. Accurately and narrowly state the action to be evaluated (e.g., Is it moral for a particular company or organization to...?);

2. Identify all people and groups who are directly and indirectly affected by the action (including the company's or organization's constituent groups or "stakeholders" as well as society as a whole);

3. Specify for each stakeholder group directly and indirectly affected all the reasonably foreseeable good - pleasurable and bad - painful consequences of the action, as far as into the future as appears appropriate, and consider the various predictable outcomes, good and bad, and the likelihood of their occurring;

4. For each stakeholder group, including society as a whole, measure and weigh the total good consequences against the bad consequences, and determine which predominates for each stakeholder group;

5. Overall, measure and weigh all the good and bad consequences assigned to the stakeholder groups;

6. If the action overall produces more good than bad it is a morally right action; and if the action overall produces more bad than good it is morally wrong based on this model of the Utilitarian ethical theory.

By following the aforementioned Utilitarian model, and being as objective and precise as possible, one can make a determination of what it means to be moral pursuant to the Utilitarian ethical theory. However, as noted, the lynchpin to the Utilitarianism is the focus on consequences. Yet some moral philosophers believe that focusing on consequences is the wrong approach to take in determining the morality of an action.

Kant's Categorical Imperative

The German professor and philosopher, Immanuel Kant, condemned Utilitarianism as an immoral ethical theory. How is it logically possible, said Kant, to have an ethical theory that can morally legitimize pain, suffering, exploitation, and injustice? Disregard consequences, declared Kant, and instead focus on the form of an action in determining its morality. Now, of course, since Kantian ethics is also one of the major ethical theories in Western civilization, a huge problem arises since these two major ethical theories are diametrically opposed. Is one a Kantian or is one a Utilitarian? (Or is it all relative as the Sophists and Machiavelli stated?) For Kant, the key to morality is applying a formal test to the action itself. This formal test he called the *Categorical Imperative*. "Categorical" meaning that this ethical principle is the supreme and absolute and true test to morality; and "imperative" meaning that at times one must command oneself to be moral and do the right thing, even and especially when one's self-interest may be contravened by acting "rightly." The Categorical Imperative has three ways to determine morality. One method is called the *Universal Law* test. Kant is not referring to legal law here; rather, Kant asks one to imagine what would happen if a practice theoretically could be made into a universal law. Would one want to live in such a society where the universal moral norm is that it is permissible to steal, to lie, and to cheat? Of course, one would not want to live in such a society; but then one can logically conclude pursuant to the Universal Law test that stealing, lying, and cheating are immoral actions. Now, Kant does admit that people do steal, lie, and cheat, but he calls these people immoral "parasites" for living off an otherwise moral system where the vast majority of people do not steal, lie, or cheat.

Another method of determining morality is called the *Kingdom of Ends* test. Pursuant to this Kantian precept, if an action, even if it produces a greater good, such as an exploitive but profitable overseas "sweatshop," is nonetheless disrespectful and demeaning and treats people as mere means, things, or as instruments, perhaps as badly as broken pieces of office furniture, then the action is not moral. The goal, said Kant, is for everyone to live in this "Kingdom of the Ends" where everyone is treated as a worthwhile human being with dignity and respect. Related to the Kingdom of Ends precept and also part of the Categorical Imperative is the *Agent-Receiver* test, which asks a person to consider the rightfulness of an action by considering whether the action would be acceptable to the person if he or she did not know whether the person would be the agent, that is, the giver, of the action, or the receiver. If one did not know one's role, and one would not be willing to have the action done to him or her, then the action is immoral. Do your duty, be ethically strong, have a good moral character, declared Kant, and obey the moral "law," based on his Categorical Imperative, and thus do the "right" thing regardless of consequences.

The authors have attempted to explain and illustrate the field of ethics as a branch of philosophy by discussing four major ethical theories. Yet, as the discerning reader can see, these ethical theories can conflict; and there is no "Supreme Court of Ethics" to tell one which ethical theory is the correct, true, and right one! The ethical situation gets even more complicated when these ethical theories are applied to factual situations to determine whether a person or a business is acting morally. In the next section to Part I of this chapter, the authors will show how "applied ethics" works, that is, how these ethical theories can be applied to practices to make moral determinations. The authors will use as their factual situation the paying of a bribe by a U.S. business person to a foreign government official in order to secure a government contract with the business person's corporation.

Applied Ethics—Payments to Foreign Government Officials

Doing business globally raises the difficult issue of payments to foreign officials. A multinational company or international business person may feel pressured into paying money or transferring something of value to a foreign official in order to protect a business investment, secure a business opportunity, to facilitate the performance of some service in the host country. The *Foreign Corrupt Practices Act*, as will be seen in the International Business Law chapter, makes *bribery* a civil and criminal wrong; yet the statute has exceptions which have the potential to legalize "bribery." Yet, assuming a U.S. multinational's or business person's ethical analysis extends, as it should, beyond the law, the issue emerges as to whether it is moral to bribe legally (or for that matter illegally!).

In order to explicate the ethical aspects of bribery in an international setting, assume a situation, as originally proposed by Professor Richard T. DeGeorge in his book, *Business Ethics* (2006), where a sales and marketing representative of a U.S. multinational in precarious financial condition is in the final stages of negotiating a contract for the sale of a substantial quantity of goods to the government of a rapidly developing foreign country. The contract is very important to the company because it provides a significant infusion of money as well as an entry to a foreign market. The contract, moreover, personally is very important to the company's marketing/sales representative and would secure the representative a promotion and substantial raise. All appears to be proceeding very well; and actually the company's offer is viewed very favorably by the foreign government, and the foreign country would in fact secure a very good deal by accepting the U.S. multinational's offer to contract. The U.S. multinational's representative seems assured of success until the representative is confronted by a key foreign government official, who also looks upon the company's offer favorably but demands a large "consulting fee" to process properly the paperwork and thus secure the contract. If the fee is not paid, the official will reopen the bidding and the contract may go to a competitor. The representative is acutely aware of the critical nature of the deal, knows that the sum is immaterial when compared to the contract price and the profits to be realized, and has heard that such payments are a common and lawful practice in the foreign country, but feels that making such payments are not quite right and may be illegal under U.S. law. What is the right and moral decision for the representative to make? Such an inquiry leads one directly into the field of applied ethics.

If one is a Legal Positivist, that is, a person who equates acting legally with acting morally too, one simply would advise the representative to determine the legality of the payment. If it is legal under the foreign country's law, and it is legal under the Foreign Corrupt Practices Act exception for expediting and facilitating payments for ministerial actions (such as, perhaps, the mere processing of the lowest bid), then this legal action is also a moral action pursuant to legal positivism.

If one is an Ethical Emotist, that is, a person who makes moral decisions based on conscience, one would advise the representative to get in "touch" with his or her feelings. If he or she feels "bad" about the payment, then it's immoral; if "good," then it is moral. Of course, he or she can always have a change of heart by merely having a different emotion about the payment at a later, perhaps more critical, date.

If one adheres to the doctrine of Ethical Egoism, the analysis is twofold: is it in the representative's best long-term interest, as agent of the multinational, to pay the bribe; and is it in the interest of the multinational, as the corporate entity, for its representative to pay the bribe? The representative must calculate whether the risks to his or her career, reputation, conscience, and even freedom will supersede the potential personal benefits from paying the bribe, securing the contract, and thus the promotion and raise. The multinational must determine whether the assertion and defense of its legitimate and critical business interests in the foreign country are worth the legal risks as well as risks to the company's reputation. An intelligent ethical egoist also could argue that even if the "bribe" is deemed immoral, the fact that its nonpayment is such a dangerous threat to the company's very existence, the issue of duress as a moral defense arises to counter any charge of immorality.

An Ethical Relativist simply would tell the company and its representative to ascertain whether such payments are an accepted standard and locally unobjectionable practice in the foreign country; if so, paying the "bribe" may be quite moral.

A Utilitarian, of course, would be concerned with the consequences of paying or not paying the bribe. If the bribe is not paid, the company, its shareholders, employees, and suppliers all will suffer a severe financial loss. If, however, the bribe is paid, all these preceding groups benefit, as well as the sales representative, who gets a promotion and raise; the foreign official, who gets the money; the foreign government, which gets a "good" price for a "good" product; and the foreign consumers, who get a quality product. If the bribe is paid, the competition does not get the contract; yet none of the company's competitors had the low bid anyway, so what is the real harm? Paying a bribe, however, usually is construed as adversely affecting the society of the "host" country. Bribery's net effect is to reduce market competition by engendering unequal competition and by erecting additional barriers to market entry. The "best" bribers thus begin to achieve monopoly status, with the distinct possibility of exhibiting the inefficiencies characteristic of monopolies, such as higher prices and lower quality. However, if this instance of bribery under consideration is viewed as an exception, and if one is a utilitarian, the harm to society is reduced accordingly and this "pain" is subject to being outweighed by the greater good produced for all the other affected groups and people.

Disregard these consequences, good ones or otherwise, of paying the bribe, a Kantian would argue. Rather, apply the Categorical Imperative to determine if bribery is moral. Applying the first test, a Kantian would argue that bribery cannot be realized as a consistently universal practice. Assuming everyone bribed in a similar fashion, the action "bribe" would no longer be able to sustain itself. Since everyone is bribing, "bribing" loses its efficacy; it contradicts itself, becomes nonsensical, and self-destructs. Bribery, therefore, is immoral. Bribery with qualification, however, is a different matter. Bribery, in the case herein, saves one's company from financial ruin, secures a contract that is a "good deal" for the host government and country when the bribing company is in fact the lowest bidder, and induces the foreign government official to perform his or her public duty of merely awarding the contract. With such qualifications, "bribery" can be made consistently universal. Not everyone is bribing, and the bribe, because it is qualified, will secure results in the limited circumstances presented.

Although bribery qualified arguably can pass Kant's first test, the issue arises as to whether a qualified bribery action will pass the second and third parts of the Categorical Imperative. Does bribery treat all the parties involved with dignity and respect, particularly the official and the company's representative "pressured" to pay the bribe? Would paying the bribe be acceptable to a rational person if one did not know one's status as the "giver" (or agent) of the action or the receiver? Would a rational person want to be placed in the role of the competition in a bribery scenario? Such questions clearly illustrate the strictness of Kantian ethics and the difficulty of even a qualified "wrongful" action passing the Categorical Imperative.

So, is bribery in the preceding context moral or immoral? Well, the answer is it depends! That is, determining whether a bribe or for that matter any action is moral or immoral often depends on the ethical theory that one is using to make the determination. Differing ethical theories can lead, even logically so, to differing moral conclusions. Yet, the truly egoistic goal of the ambitious yet moral person would be to take a long-term approach and naturally seek to benefit oneself and one's company or organization, but to do so without offending the moral norms of a society where one does business (that is, be "culturally competent"), always seeking to achieve the greater good for all the stakeholders, including society as a whole, but also always mindful not to demean or disrespect anyone in an effort to attain this personal and societal good. The idea is to do well, but also to do good—and "good" meaning in the full ethical sense. In order to keep a company or organization and its employees and associates on this "good" ethical path many companies today have adopted Codes of Ethics.

Corporate Codes of Ethics

Ethics codes have always been adopted by the profession, such as law and medicine. In recent years, however, they also have been adopted by many corporations and businesses. A strong legal impetus for codes of ethics emerged from the Sarbanes-Oxley Act of 2002 (SOX) (discussed in the Liability of Accountants chapter in this book), which was promulgated as a result of the Enron and other corporate accounting and financial scandals, and which was intended to help restore confidence in the corporate financial system. SOX has many provisions; and regarding ethics codes the statute states that companies must have such a code for senior financial executives and officers or to state (to the Securities and Exchange Commission and to the public) why they have not done so. SOX defines an ethics code as one having written standards that are reasonably designed to deter wrongdoing and promote honest and ethical conduct, as well as full disclosure, compliance with the law, prompt reporting of violations, and methods to conform to the standards of the code.

Codes of ethics usually are developed for a company as a whole and form the foundation of the company's ethics program. Codes of ethics serve as the major vehicle for stating the ethical principles, core values, and moral rules the company believes in and follows. A code of ethics helps to make managers and employees aware that moral considerations, as well as economic and legal factors, must be considered when business decisions are made. The code also demonstrates to other stakeholders that the corporation is aware of, and fully committed to, acting morally as well as in a socially responsible manner.

Whistleblowing

"*Whistleblowing*" may be defined as an attempt by a member of an organization to disclose what he or she believes to be wrongdoing in or by the organization. This section focuses on whistleblowing by employees of a corporation. "Wrongdoing" entails not only conduct or conditions that the employee believes are illegal, but also behavior that the employee considers to be immoral. Whistleblowing can be internal, that is, to those higher up in the corporate hierarchy; or it can be external, that is, to the government, such as a regulatory agency, to a public interest group, or to the media. A "*whistle-blower*," of course, is the person, the employee, who attempts to make known the wrongdoing. He or she usually "blows the whistle" for right, as well as rightful, reasons; yet one should not always assume that the whistleblowing employee's motives are meritorious or that he or she is even correct as to the underlying premise of wrongdoing.

Whistleblowing and the Law

While there may exist federal and state statutes that protect public sector employees who blow the whistle from retaliation by their government employers, as well as statutes in the areas of civil rights, labor law, and health and safety law, that prohibit employers from taking retaliatory actions against employees who report statutory violations, there is no general federal statute, and little state law, extending similar protection to private sector employees, the vast majority of whom are employees and "at will." The state *Whistleblower Protection Acts* that do exist usually only protect disclosures of actual legal violations by a company and by its employees. Therefore, reports of suspicious unfounded illegality are usually not protected, nor are disclosures of immoral and unethical conduct which are also not illegal. Thus the whistleblower must be certain of the legal wrongdoing, as in most states erroneous but good faith whistleblowing is not protected. Moreover, the state statutes are uniform in that to be protected the whistleblowing must be made to a government agency or public official and not to the media or a public interest organization. Some, such as Florida's, even require that the whistleblowing employee report the legal wrongdoing to his or her supervisor, then up the corporate "chain-of-command," and also give the employer a reasonable opportunity to correct the problem. Furthermore, in most states, the successful and legally protected whistleblower "only" gets his or her job back (with lost wages, benefits, seniority, etc. but no money damages (though in New Jersey the wrongfully discharges whistleblower can also sue for emotional distress damages). Even if a state does not have a whistleblower protection statute, the wrongfully discharged employee can attempt to bring a suit under the *Public Policy doctrine* if the employee can convince a court that his or her discharge was in violation of the "fundamental public policy" of the state, for example, when the employee disclosed pollution or workplace hazards on the part of the employer. There is also a federal whistleblowing statute in the Sarbanes-Oxley Act (SOX) of 2002 (discussed in the Liability of Accountants chapter), but that law only protects whistleblowing employees of public companies regulated by the Securities and Exchange Commission. Moreover, SOX only protects employees who disclose information pertaining to securities fraud or some other type of fraud or embezzlement against the shareholders. Thus, SOX provides only some protection to whistleblowers. Whistleblowing, finally, should not be confused with disclosing wrongdoing pursuant to *False Claims Acts*, which are federal and state statutes that provide that a whistleblowing employee who discloses wrongdoing by his or her employer in the form of embezzlement or fraud against the government, such as Medicare or Medicaid fraud, is entitled to a percentage (ranging from 10-30%) of the award or settlement against the employer that the government receives. It also should be noted that the 2010 Dodd-Frank Wall Street Reform and Consumer Protection Act has a provision that extends whistleblower protection and rewards to those employees, as well as any others, disclosing financial fraud in private sector contracting and bribery in overseas contracting with foreign governments. Thus, whistleblowing may, or may not be, legally protected, let alone rewarded; and consequently the issue arises, therefore, as to whether ethics extends any moral protection to private sector whistleblowing employees, especially in the corporate context and particularly regarding at-will employees.

Whistleblower Checklist

Assuming that an employee is a "good Kantian" and thus intends to comply with the moral "law" and plans to "blow on the whistle" on his or her employer's wrongdoing, the employee should nonetheless think carefully and plan accordingly. First, the employee should seek legal counsel to ascertain whether he or she is protected by a federal or state whistleblower protection statute. There are whistleblower protection provisions in the Sarbanes-Oxley Act, but they just extend to publicly traded companies and allegations of securities fraud. Moreover, a few states do have general whistleblower protection acts which protect, to a limited degree, private sector workers; and perhaps the morally motivated whistleblowing intending employee will also be legally protected. If there is such a statute, it would be incumbent on the employee to check it very carefully as to the particular state's requirements for legally protected whistleblowing. As previously noted, all state statutes will require that the predicate for protected whistleblowing be a legal violation; and furthermore will require an actual, as opposed to a suspicion of a, legal violation by the employer. Moreover, some statutes require that prior notice of the legal violation be given to the employer, and in some cases in writing, and also in certain cases that the employer be given a reasonable opportunity to correct the violation. Finally, as previously underscored, all whistleblower statutes—federal and state—will require that the whistleblowing to be protected must be reported to an appropriate government agency or public sector official. Second, the capability of the employee to secure sufficient evidence or documentation of a legal violation is critical to ensuring that the employee fulfills his or her legal and ethical duties, as well as to ensure that the whistleblowing actually is efficacious and results in needed changes. Third, the prudent employee should carefully examine his or her motives for the intended disclosure. Granted, legally as well as morally, the employee may be protected in a "mixed motive" situation, but acting out of an improper motive, such as spite, hatred, or revenge, may cause the employee to embellish the case, to jump to conclusions, and to unnecessarily contravene duties of loyalty and confidentiality. Finally, the employee must be fully prepared for the consequences of his or her whistleblowing, especially if the disclosure occurs in a jurisdiction where the employee is a mere employee at-will and not protected regarding job tenure by a contract or a whistleblower protection statute. Can the employee find suitable employment, especially if the employee may be "blacklisted" in the industry or profession as a "snitch," "stoolie," or "informant"? Kant would say that if whistleblowing is morally required, one should "blow the whistle," period, regardless of consequences; yet the prudent person who intends to do his or her moral duty should nevertheless seek legal counsel and "count the cost." In order to determine if one is morally required to act to "blow the whistle" or to take any affirmative action reference must be made to the Ethical Principle of Last Resort.

The Ethical Principle of Last Resort

As can be seen in the Torts and Business chapter that as a general rule (though with exceptions, as noted) based on the common law doctrine of nonfeasance one does not have a *legal* duty to help, aid, or rescue anyone. Consequently, one, again as a general rule, cannot be held legally liable for negligence for not rescuing someone even if one is able or for not warning someone of a peril. That is the law—nonfeasance, not acting, is not actionable legally. Yet when does one have a positive moral obligation to act? Acting morally may involve more than merely avoiding negative harm; acting morally also may require one to perform an affirmative positive action, even though legally one may not be required to take the action. The ethical principle of *"last resort"* indicates when one has a moral duty to act, to aid another, or to rescue. One morally must act when there is a need, proximity, capability, one is the last resort or chance to avoid the peril, and when acting would not cause harm, or threaten to cause harm, equal to or greater than the original peril. The principle is based partially on Kant's admonition that "ought implies can," that is, that one is obligated to do only what one can do. Thus, if one is unable to act and help, due to lack of opportunity, means, or resources, one is not obligated morally to act.

The "last resort" principle usually involves an obligation of immediacy and high priority posed by an emergency; it thus generates a moral obligation to act that one cannot ignore without moral condemnation. The classic example is a drowning case when the five "last resort" factors are present. The problem in successfully applying the "last resort" principle to business, however, emerges the fourth and fifth factors. Who is the last resort for people unemployed and in need, business or government? Would business "rescuing" in fact harm the corporation, or its shareholders, or other stakeholders? A "friendly takeover," a corporation helping an employee pay his or her children's college tuition, may be praiseworthy actions, but are they morally required under the "last resort" principle? Is a corporation immoral for choosing not to act in the preceding circumstances? One example is the case of the Malden Mills Company, whose very compassionate owner rebuilt the facility after a fire without terminating any employees; but due in part to the added financial strain of keeping those employees, he forced his company to file for Chapter 11 bankruptcy protection in order to reorganize its finances, thereby resulting in a considerably, and permanently, diminished workforce. Another example concerns the large, multinational pharmaceutical companies who are providing for free or at greatly reduced cost their patented anti-AIDS drugs to African nations. Yet are they so doing because it is their moral responsibility as the "rescuer" of "last resort" or due to other social pressures? Similarly, corporations may not be the "last resort" to take care of their employees' disabled children, yet companies such as Toyota and Raytheon do provide assistance, for example, by hosting dinners with speakers and holding "networking" events, as well as expanding insurance coverage for "special needs" children. If not moral duty, what motivates these meritorious actions? A most interesting and thought-provoking example concerns Wal-Mart's very meritorious response to the Hurricane Katrina disaster in New Orleans and the Gulf Coast. Was Wal-Mart's "trucking in" tons of relief supplies (literally!) "merely" a socially responsible action, or was Wal-Mart the "last resort" to bring rapid relief to this devastated region of the country; and if the latter, what does that say about the government—all levels of government—federal, state, and local?

A critical point is that even though a company or person may not have a legal obligation to help, aid, or rescue, and, moreover, even if a company or person does not have any moral obligation to act based on the "last resort" principle, nonetheless many people and businesses do "help out" in the community by taking part in charitable and civic affairs. These philanthropic and civic-minded individuals and business today are deemed to "socially responsible" ones. The value of social responsibility will be covered in Part II of this chapter.

Conclusion to Part I

So, what does it mean to be moral? Being moral means being ethical, that is, reasoning from ethical theories and principles to moral conclusions as to right and wrong. This chapter has introduced the reader to the field of ethics, which is a branch of philosophy, and has sought to demonstrate how ethical theories can be applied to modern day business problems to reason to moral conclusions. The four ethical theories examined in this chapter—Ethical Egoism, Ethical Relativism, Utilitarianism, and Kant's Categorical Imperative—are major ethical theories in Western Civilization intellectual thought and tradition. These theories are not, of course, the only ethical theories in Western Civilization; and obviously there are many other ethical theories stemming from other civilizations as well as religions. As noted, the authors selected these four since they are very important ones as well as the fact that the basic tenets of each should be familiar to the reader. Ethics is thus a very large intellectual endeavor. And, as emphasized, to really complicate matters, there is no "Supreme Court of Ethics" to tell the readers, and for that matter the authors, which ethical theory is the "true" and "right" one. There is, however, an element of truth and rightfulness in all four theories. Accordingly, the authors would advise the reader to do the following: first, pursuant to Ethical Egoism improve oneself, empower oneself, and achieve success for oneself and one's company or organization; second, pursuant to Ethical Relativism, when achieving this success be "culturally competent" and thus strive not to contravene a society's moral norms; third, pursuant to Utilitarianism, in addition to achieving one's own and one's company's success similarly strive to find "win-win" scenarios where the good of all the stakeholders including society as a whole is maximized too; and finally, pursuant to Kantian ethics, in attaining this individual and societal good make sure that no person or stakeholder group is disrespected or demeaned. These principles should be manifested in any true Code of Ethics. Then, one will be successful, and rightfully so, in the sense that individual and organizational success will be secured in a truly moral manner. Of course, now that one and one's company has achieved so much success, stature, and money, there very likely will emerge an expectation from the community and society that the company and organization will be not "just" a legal and moral one, but also a "socially responsible" entity. The next part to this chapter, therefore, deals with the very current and relevant topic of social responsibility, or when the term is applied to business—"corporate social responsibility."

Part II—Corporate Social Responsibility

Introduction

Stakeholder analysis has emerged as a critical concern for the modern business leader. Typically, *stakeholder* considerations, above and beyond the interests of the shareholders of the corporation, have been interpreted and examined under the concept of "*corporate social responsibility*." Corporate social responsibility (CSR) now also has become a central issue for business leaders. Moreover, today stakeholder analysis as well as CSR is converging with the notion of "corporate governance," which traditionally has had mainly legal connotations. In this Part II to the chapter, the authors examine stakeholders and CSR in the context of corporate governance. The authors take a broad approach to corporate governance and stakeholders, encompassing legal, moral, social responsibility, and economic values. Stakeholder analysis and CSR are addressed in a global context. The authors discuss the traditional nature of the corporation, with its emphasis on maximizing shareholder value; and then examine corporate constituency statutes which allow corporate boards to consider the values of other stakeholders. Next, the authors examine new socially responsible ways of doing business, social benefit corporations, or B-Corps, and low-profit limited liability companies, which give primacy to stakeholder values beyond the interests of the shareholders in corporate decision-making. The authors principally analyze U.S. law but global legal perspectives are presented too. The critical relationship of corporate social responsibility and stakeholders to corporate governance is emphasized and explicated; and finally implications and recommendations for business leaders are provided to incorporate not only legal and ethical values but also corporate social responsibility and stakeholder values into corporate governance. The imperative of governing the corporation in a profitable, legal, moral, and socially responsible manner is underscored; so that the corporation achieves sustainable economic growth and development and also produces positive value for all the stakeholders of the corporation and betterment for society as a whole.

Corporate Social Responsibility

What exactly is a corporation's "social responsibility"? Does a corporation have a social obligation to take care of the poor, educate the public, give to charity, and fund cultural programs? Social projects and social welfare in the United States traditionally have been viewed as the appropriate domain of government, not of business. Business, of course, is taxed and such taxes may be used for social purposes. The traditional purpose of business as viewed in the U.S., moreover, is the profitable production and distribution of goods and services, not social welfare. Yet by raising the issue of social responsibility, business is forced to concern itself with the "social" dimension of its activities. This issue is now a critical one for business today.

Accordingly, what is the "social responsibility" of business today? The term at a basic philanthropic level may be defined as a business taking an active part in the social causes, charities, and civic life of one's community and society. Newman's Own is a private sector company praised for its philanthropic mission since it donates all of its profits and royalties after taxes for charitable and educational purposes. However, corporate social responsibility (CSR) certainly can be more than "mere" philanthropy. The social responsibility of business can also be thought of in a broader constituency or stakeholder sense, that is, by the corporation considering the values and needs of employees, suppliers, consumers, local communities, and society as a whole. One can also take a "strategic" as well as stakeholder approach to corporate social responsibility by integrating stakeholder, social, environmental, as well as economic concerns into the organization's values, culture, governance, strategy, and decision-making.

The World Business Council for Sustainable Development views social responsibility in a corporate context as a company's continuing commitment to act legally and morally and also to contribute to the economic development of society while improving the quality of life of their employees and their families as well as the local community and society as a whole. This definition evokes another, and even more expansive, concept of the "social responsibility" of business—"sustainability." The sustainability approach to corporate social responsibility is premised on the idea that a company must remain economically viable in the long-term, and that in order to be viable the company must take into consideration other stakeholders beyond the shareholders. The objective is to simultaneously produce economic value for the company, but also value for society as a whole by helping to solve societal needs, particularly by improving the lives of the people (and potential consumers) who live in the communities where the company does business. "Sustainability" is often used when discussing such concepts as corporate citizenship, social responsibility, stakeholder analysis, and social enterprise.

A corporation, of course, is a profit-making entity that exists in a competitive environment, and thus may be limited in its ability to solve a multitude of social problems particularly at the expense of the owners of the corporation—the shareholders. Where are the philanthropic guidelines for corporate contributions and improvements? How should a corporation's resources be allocated, and exactly to whom, to what extent, and in what priorities? What is the proper balance between shareholder and stakeholder interests? The corporate governance policies of the organization must seek to answer these important, yet, difficult questions. If a corporation unilaterally or too generously engages in social betterment, it may place itself at a disadvantage compared to other less socially responsible business entities. Being socially responsible costs money, and such efforts cut into profits. In a highly competitive market system, corporations that are too socially responsible may lessen their attractiveness to investors or simply may price themselves out of the market. One example is the clearly socially responsible firm—Ben & Jerry's, which has long been known and lauded for its civic, community, and environmental efforts. Yet the company may have been too socially responsible and consequently neglectful of basic business concerns. Ultimately, the original former "hippies" Ben Cohen and Jerry Greenfield of Ben & Jerry's sold their interests in their company in 2000 to global consumer products giant, Unilever, which carried on the social responsibility activities of the brand to a degree, but in a more prudent and strategic manner. Nevertheless, despite the saga of Ben & Jerry's, social responsibility, at least to some reasonable degree, may be in the long-term self-interest of business, so long as these activities align with the corporation's long-term objectives. Furthermore, there is some evidence that these socially responsible strategies have been successful.

A corporation cannot long remain a viable economic entity in a society that is uneven, unstable, and deteriorating. It makes good business sense for a corporation to devote some of its resources to social betterment projects. To operate efficiently, for example, business needs educated and skilled employees. Education and training, therefore, should be of paramount interest to business leaders. A corporation, for example, can act socially responsible by providing computers to community schools and by releasing employees on company time to furnish the training. Business also gains an improved public image by being socially responsible. An enhanced social image should attract more customers and investors and thus provide positive benefit for the firm.

Other examples of companies engaging in socially responsible marketing as one way to persuade consumers to spend in a difficult economy, to wit: Sketchers USA launched a brand called BOBS, meaning Benefiting Others By Shoes, which results in the company donating two pairs of shoes for every one sold; Urban Outfitters features clothes by Threads for Thought, which gives part of its sales proceeds to humanitarian groups; Nordstrom sells hats made by Krochet Kids International, which enlists impoverished people in Uganda and Peru, for example, to make hats which are sold in the U.S. for $24; and Feed Projects, which makes T-shirts, handbags, and accessories, donates a percentage of its profits to United Nations anti-hunger programs. When implemented correctly, these socially responsible retailing efforts are "good works" and also good strategies, which may be young consumers who may not have the means to make large charitable contributions but who admire brands that are "trendy" but which also reflect a save-the-planet theme. To further illustrate, the Walt Disney Company, in an effort to portray a socially responsible message, as well as to attract customers to its theme parks, commenced a program, called "Give a Day, Get a Disney Day," whereby the company will give away a million one-day, one-park tickets to people who volunteer at select charities.

A corporation that acts more socially responsible not only secures public favor, but also avoids public disfavor. To illustrate, for many years the large multinational pharmaceutical companies were criticized for not providing AIDS drugs for free or at greatly reduced prices to African governments. In response to public criticism, the pharmaceutical responded in a socially responsible (and also egoistic manner) by giving the drugs away or selling them at cost. Moreover, certain pharmaceutical companies, such as Roche and GlaxoSmithKline, on their social responsibility and sustainability websites, have statements indicating preferential pricing and accessibility as well as limited patent policies for AIDs drugs going to African and other less developed countries. Accordingly, social responsibility and also good public relations are achieved. Wal-Mart, the giant retailer, in response to criticisms from environmentalists and labor activists, now has a director of global ethics, who will be responsible for developing and enforcing company standards of conduct, as well as a "senior director for stakeholder engagement," whose role will be to develop a new model of business engagement that produces value for society. Similarly, clothing and apparel manufacturers, such as Nike and the Gap, in response to criticism by labor and consumer groups about exploitive working conditions in overseas "sweatshops," have ended poor working conditions, and now also report on their social responsibility efforts and achievements overseas. Business is part of society and subject to society's mandates; and if society wants more "responsibility" from business, business cannot ignore this "request" without the risk of incurring society's anger, perhaps in the form of higher taxes or more onerous government regulation. Socially responsible activities may also improve a company's reputation when viewed by external stakeholders, such as bankers, creditors, investors, and government regulators, which not only may avoid economic harm, but also may bring about economic benefits. As such an egoist and rational actor will surely see the instrumental value of a prudent degree of social responsibility in today's global business marketplace.

The topics of social responsibility and stakeholder analysis emerged as a critical one for global business leaders too. A global example would be the Coca-Cola's company's efforts to provide clean water to parts of the developing world, which Coke also hopes to promote goodwill, boost local economies, and broaden its customer base. Royal Caribbean Cruise Company is teaming up with a Haitian non-profit organization to build a primary school, which is located on land the company leases from the government as a stop for its ships in the port town of Labadee. Wal-Mart is now selling online handicrafts made by women artisans in developing countries, such as dresses made in Kenya and jewelry from Guatemala and Thailand. Over 500 items from 20,000 female artisans will be offered for sale, which certainly will help the female artisans but also improve the company's global image. "Sustainability" is also used to support corporate social responsibility efforts globally: For transnational corporations doing business in developed countries, sustainability may require investment in community-level infrastructure development projects, technological innovation, education, and health care. Two excellent examples of global "sustainable" CSR are the Norwegian company, Yara International, the world's largest chemical fertilizer company, has sponsored public/private partnerships to develop storage, transportation, and port facilities in parts of Africa with significant untapped agricultural potential, thereby developing local agriculture, providing jobs and improved incomes for farmers, and at the same time benefiting the company through an increased demand for its fertilizer products. Second, the Nestle Company is working to improve milk production in certain regions of India, by investing in well drilling, refrigeration, veterinary medicine, and training, thereby significantly increasing output and enhancing product quality, certainly beneficial to the company, and at the same time allowing the company to pay higher prices for farmers and their employees, resulting in a higher standard of living for the local community.

The United Nations now has a business initiative on corporate social responsibility, called the United Nations Global Compact, whereby companies can join and thus voluntarily agree to make improvements in human rights, labor, the environment, and combating corruption. The World Bank, moreover, now has an Internet course on social responsibility, called "CSR and Sustainable Competitiveness," offered by its educational and training division. The corporate social responsibility course is designed for "high-level" private sector managers, government officials and regulators, practitioners, academics, and journalists. One major purpose to the course is to provide a conceptual framework for improving the business environment to support corporate governance policies and social responsibility efforts by corporations and business. The course is also designed to assist companies to formulate a social responsibility strategy based on moral and economic values as well as one with a long-term perspective.

Stakeholder Values

Stakeholder theory considers the enterprise as a community with a number of stakeholders—in other words, social groups that are directly and indirectly connected to the enterprise and that are dependent on its success and prosperity. These groups include employees, customers, suppliers, distributors, local communities, and especially the society or societies in which the business has operations.. In order to illustrate the stakeholders and their values involved in business decision-making, as well as to show the relationship among stakeholder values, social responsibility, and sustainability, the authors have prepared Table 6.1, which was based in part on the work of Professor N. Harish (Harish, 2012):

Table 6.1 – Stakeholder Values, Social Responsibility, and Sustainability

Stakeholders	Primary Values	Secondary Values
Owners / Shareholders	Financial Returns and Income	Growth and Added Value
Employees	Jobs and Pay	Job Stability and Satisfaction
Customers and Consumers	Supply of Goods and Services	Quality, Price, and Customer Service
Suppliers / Distributors	Contract Relationships and Payment	Long-term Relationships
Creditors	Payment and Rate of Return	Credit-worthiness and Security
Community	Employment and Tax-base	Philanthropy and Social Responsibility
Government	Legal Compliance and Tax-base	Competitiveness and Entrepreneurship
Competition	Market Share	Legal and Ethical Competition
Society	Growth, Prosperity, Sustainability	Social Responsibility and Environmental Stewardship and Improvement

Table 6.1 shows the typical stakeholders in the business realm, that is, those constituent groups which are directly or indirectly affected by corporate actions. The Table then shows what these stakeholders value, that is, what they deem to possess worth—primarily and secondarily. These stakeholder groups typically are the following: shareholders and owners, employees, customers and consumers, suppliers and distributors, creditors, community, government, competition, and society. Shareholders as the owners are always listed first. Obviously, a corporation cannot survive unless it serves and benefits its shareholders in a financial sense. However, today, shareholders may view their

investment as one that benefits society too and perhaps in a direct manner by means of the social benefit corporation. Regardless, all shareholders are entitled to the honest and efficient management of their investment as well as a fair return on their investment. Employees are of course interested in obtaining and maintaining employment. They value a just wage, fair employment practices and working conditions, and job security. They also may value working for a company that is regarded as a "socially responsible" one. Customers and consumers want access to good and services that are of good quality, at a fair price, and that come with good customer service. Suppliers and distributors want financially rewarding, long-term contractual relationships with the company. Local communities want to see the corporation located in their cities and towns so as to provide employment for the citizens and residents and to support the local tax-base. The local community also values, and very well may expect, that the corporations in its presence participate in civic, charitable, philanthropic, and socially responsible activities. Creditors naturally value being repaid and also expect a fair rate of return as well as adequate assurances of security for the obligation. Government values legal compliance with business laws and business regulations. Government also values business as an important component of its tax-base. Government also values and thus desires to promote entrepreneurship and competition. As to the competition, the competition values its own market share, yet expects in a capitalistic model "tough" and "hard-hitting" competition, but the competition also values completion that is legal and ethical. Society values its survival, of course, and also growth, prosperity for its members, and the sustainability of business and society. Members of society also value today, and thus expect, that the corporation will be a socially responsible one, particularly regarding its stewardship of the environment and efforts to improve the environment.

The goal of the business leader today is to balance and harmonize these values and thus attempt to devise corporate governance policies that maximize these values in a legal, moral, socially responsible, and practically efficacious manner, thereby resulting in "win-win" scenarios for the business and all its stakeholders and attaining a level of continual sustainable business success.

Corporate Constituency Statutes

Socially responsible entrepreneurs and corporate directors and officers who wanted to engage in activities to benefit corporate stakeholders other than shareholders have in the past confronted a serious legal problem. Traditionally, pursuant to state corporation law the directors and officers of a corporation owed legal and fiduciary duties solely to the corporate entity. This overarching duty of the traditional *corpus* of corporate law is to maximize shareholder wealth. In fulfilling this duty, the directors and officers, based on the conventional Business Judgment Rule of corporate law, were required to act based on informed consent, with reasonable care, and in good faith. These legal duties were owed strictly and exclusively to the corporation and to the shareholders and not to any other people or groups, though the shareholders might have to enforce these duties on behalf of the corporation, if a breach of these duties by the directors and officers occurred, by means of a shareholder derivative lawsuit.

Today, however, many states have enacted statutes, called *"constituency statutes,"* or have amended their corporation statutes, to allow the directors and officers to consider other constituent groups, often called "stakeholders," who are directly or indirectly affected by the corporation's activities. To illustrate express constituency statutes in the United States, the Minnesota corporation statute states that "in discharging the duties of the position of director, a director may, in considering the best interests of the corporation, consider the interests of the corporation's employees, customers, suppliers, and creditors, the economy of the state and nations, community and societal considerations, and the long-term as well as short-term interests of the corporation and its shareholders" (*Minnesota Statutes* Section 302A.251(5)). Similarly, in Florida, directors are now permitted to consider in making decisions a variety of factors not directly related to maximizing value for the shareholders. These broader stakeholder factors encompass the long-term interests and prospects of the corporation and its shareholders, as well as the social, economic, legal, or other effects of any corporate action on the employees, suppliers, customers, the communities where the corporation and its subsidiaries operate, and the economy of the state or nation (*Florida Statutes* Section 607.0830(3)). There is some variety among the provisions in the state statutes in the United States; but most statutes limit the consideration of stakeholder interests to those of customers, employees, creditors and the local communities. These permissible constituency groups typically include employees, creditors, suppliers, consumers, and the community at-large. Consequently, constituency statutes typically are limited, since the definition of "constituents" is a "narrow" one which, although including customers, employees, suppliers, and the local communities where the company does business, does not encompass the international community, environmental concerns, or broader human rights issues. Nevertheless, these statutes, whether separate enactments or amendments to state corporation statutes, usually are called "constituency" statutes.

It is critical to note, however, that constituency statutes generally are permissive, and not mandatory; that is, the directors and officers may take into consideration the interests of non-shareholder stakeholders, but the directors and officers are not required to do so. Significantly, however, these statutes only permit a balancing of interests rather than requiring a balance. Corporate boards of directors would thus be free to pursue socially responsible policies, but cannot be sanctioned for choosing not to do so. That is, directors can weigh competing interests at their discretion, and they also can freely disregard particular interests without fear of legal consequences at the hands of shareholders or any other group. These constituency statutes, therefore, do not impose any legal duty on the directors to any stakeholders or constituencies; and also these statutes do not furnish a corporate constituency or stakeholder group with a legal cause of action against the corporation's directors. Rather, these statutes allow boards of directors to consider stakeholder interests in the decision-making process, thereby enabling corporations to justify and to possibly defend a decision that they believe to be in the best interest of the corporation without contravening the duties owed to shareholders. Therefore, regarding non-shareholder interests, these constituency statutes are not mandatory but rather merely "permissive."

Social Benefit Corporations

In marked contrast to the corporate constituency statutes, as well as the traditional corporation itself, is a new legal business concept—the "*social benefit corporation.*" These new entities also are called "benefit corporations," or simply "B-corporations" (as opposed to the traditional business or "C-corporation" of state corporate law). At times, the general term "social enterprise" is used to describe a social benefit corporation. Very recently in the United States, this new form of business enterprise has been created to provide a corporate legal structure for "social entrepreneurs," that is, those business people who aim to deliver not only financial benefits to the shareholders but also social benefits for other stakeholders, including local communities and society at large by means of a "double bottom-line" of profits and social benefits or a "triple bottom-line" of social, environmental, and economic concerns. Social entrepreneurs firmly believe that social good can be produced along with profits, and thus they desire hybrid forms of business organizations to effectuate the achievement of both goals.

The critical difference between a social benefit corporation and a constituency statute in the U.S. is that in a corporation constituency statute the directors of a corporation *may* consider other stakeholder groups than the shareholders, but with a social benefit corporation, the directors *must* consider other stakeholders. In a social benefit corporation, typically in the company's articles of incorporation (which becomes its charter when approved by the state), the corporation will specify its intended social purposes or benefits as well as the stakeholders or constituent groups that it is legally obligated to consider in achieving these objectives. That is, it is pursuant to this new form of doing business the legal duty of corporate directors to consider the consequences of corporate actions, such as moving facilities from one state to another or overseas, lay-offs and downsizing, and takeovers and mergers, on groups other than the shareholders. Moreover, the directors are allowed to consider social responsibility and environmental objectives equal to or even greater than achieving profits. Traditionally, pursuant to state corporation laws, directors were held to a legal duty—a fiduciary duty—to act in the best interests of the corporation and its owners—the shareholders; and consequently directors could not consider stakeholders other than the shareholders. Furthermore, even under constituency states, where directors could consider other non-shareholder stakeholders, the directors had to do so with the aim of maximizing the long-term good, not of the public, but ultimately of the shareholders. For the law in the form of a social benefit corporation to now say that directors have a legal duty, that is, *must*, as opposed to *may*, consider the interests of other stakeholders affected by corporate activities is a very momentous change in the law indeed. It must be emphasized that consideration of the other constituencies beyond the shareholders is mandatory.

Several states in the United States, including Vermont, Hawaii, California, New York, New Jersey, Virginia, North Carolina, Pennsylvania, and Maryland, which in 2010 was the first state, have now promulgated legislation to allow "social benefit" corporations. Legislation has been introduced in Colorado, Michigan, Pennsylvania, North Carolina, and Oregon. The states generally have based their social benefit corporation statutes on a "model" act, called the "Model B-Corp Act." Pursuant to the Model Act as well as the state corporation benefit statutes, typically, the social benefit corporation must be cleared designated as a benefit corporation, and must specify in its social responsibility and environmental objectives in its charter and articles of incorporation, and also in some cases in its bylaws. In Maryland and other states the stock certificates also must be labeled to include the term "benefit corporation." The benefit corporation can pursue a "general public benefit" and/or "specific public benefits," such as providing low income or underserved people or communities with beneficial products or services, promoting economic opportunity for people and communities, preserving, protecting, and improving the environment, improving human health, promoting the arts and sciences, advancing knowledge, and increasing the flow of capital to entities with a public benefit purpose. The Maryland law allows businesses to commit to a specific public good; and that the specific public benefits in Maryland can encompass the following: 1) providing individuals and communities with beneficial products and services; 2) providing economic opportunity for individuals or communities beyond the creation of jobs; 3) preserving the environment; 4) improving human health; 5) promoting the arts, sciences, or the advancement of knowledge; 6) increasing the flow of capital to entities with a public benefit purpose; and 7) accomplishing any other particular benefit for society or the environment. However, there are concerns as to the lack of clarity in not only the definition of benefits but also the ranking of benefits, perhaps engendering intra-corporate disagreements or conflict between the B-corporation and its stakeholders. The social benefit corporation statutes require the directors of the corporation to consider the impact of their decision-making not "merely" on the shareholders, but also other corporate stakeholders, such as the employees of the corporation, subsidiaries, suppliers, distributors, customers, the local community, society, and the environment, whether local or global. The social benefit report corporation also must publish an annual "benefit report" to disclose the level of performance in attaining those goals as well as any circumstances the corporation's ability to achieve its beneficial purposes. The report must be delivered to shareholders, posted on the company's website, and, in some case, delivered to the state's Secretary of State (who is typically the state cabinet level official who typically is in charge of corporate affairs).

One very serious concern with the creation of a social benefit corporation is that the law is still developing for this new form of doing business; and consequently the major risk of this new corporate entity is the still un-chartered legal liability of the directors, who not only may be sued by shareholders for not achieving social responsibility goals, but who also may be sued by other stakeholders who are adversely affected by a corporation action which they contend is socially irresponsible to a discrete stakeholder group or injurious to the societal good. This new legal cause of action against directors in the U.S. typically is called a "benefit enforcement proceeding." It is quite possible that in the U.S., shareholders, directors, employees, and any other persons or groups that may be specified in the articles of incorporation of the benefit corporation to bring an action against the corporation. The causes of action available to these parties in the benefit enforcement proceedings may include a failure to pursue the general public benefit or any specific public benefit set forth in its articles of incorporation. Consequently, serious question exist about the full legal implications of the B-corporation form. The main legal concern is that unlike other types of corporations or business associations, where executives and managers are merely permitted to consider stakeholder interests, in the benefit corporation there is a clear affirmative legal duty to do so. Furthermore, as emphasized, the state social benefit statutes in the U.S. provide scant guidance as to the scope of the expanded legal duties of the directors, particularly whether the social benefit duties are separate and distinct from traditional corporate duties, as well as to what the relationship is between the two sets of duties. One point is evident, though, and that is shareholder primacy among stakeholders cannot be the motivation behind corporate decision-making. Consequently, a paradoxical situation well could arise because the directors of B-corporations would be legally required to disregard the traditional notion of shareholder primacy and thus take other stakeholder values and interests into account, but they would not be legally entitled to completely ignore shareholder interests. Moreover, to further complicate matters, some of the state statutes also decline to address the key issue as to what non-shareholder stakeholder groups have legal standing to sue to enforce the expanded legal duties of the directors. Now the shareholders of a social benefit corporation may have expanded rights to bring derivative lawsuits (that is, suits pursuant to traditional corporate law against the directors on behalf of the corporation when the directors fail to act) on behalf of other stakeholders. Accordingly, shareholders now may be able to bring a lawsuit against the corporation because its directors failed to consider or adequately consider the values and interests of other non-shareholder stakeholder groups. The social benefit corporate way of doing business in the United States is thus today a vague one, and also one that engenders conflict between pursuing desirable social objectives and striving to maximum profits. As such, there will be inescapable legal conflicts as the courts attempt to define and to reconcile the principles of the legal and fiduciary duty in the context of corporate directors seeking to achieve business objectives and also to fulfill social obligations. So, based on the current state of the law and the legal commentary examined for this chapter, the logical conclusion from the authors' perspective is that the new way of doing business in the U.S. as a social benefit corporation, though well-intended, should be abjured, at least for the present, until the attendant legal rights and responsibilities can be explicated by the courts. Yet social responsibility pursuant to corporate constituency statutes can be a viable legal activity for a company as well as a smart, sustainable, and socially beneficial one, of course.

Social Responsibility, Stakeholders, and Corporate Governance

Corporate governance today has emerged as significant subject for business; and the topic of social responsibility also arises in the context of corporate governance. Initially, one may think of "corporate governance" as having strictly legal components, especially business law and regulatory law. In the traditional governance models, the corporation's primary focus is on shareholder rights, and the primary governance rule is based on maximizing shareholder value. Directors, therefore, have a duty to ensure that companies fulfill their legal obligations, protect shareholder interests, and provide accurate and timely information to investors, markets, and government regulators. Yet corporate governance also has social responsibility as well as ethical ramifications. That is, corporate governance, in the expansive meaning that the authors wish to give to this concept, means the legal, ethical/moral, and social responsibility considerations for regulating business today. Business decision-making cannot be decoupled from the responsibility—legal, ethical, and social—of business leaders for their own risk-taking; otherwise, the whole business and entrepreneurial system will be undermined.

The idea is not "just" to maximize profits by "merely" obeying the law, for example, SEC regulations, but rather to also include ethical, moral, and social responsibility concerns into corporate decision-making. Making profits in a legal manner is obviously an essential component to corporate governance; but the focus on "just" the law is too narrow, the authors contend. To illustrate a more expansive meaning of corporate governance, the American Law Institute in its Principles of Corporate Governance sets forth fundamental principles of corporate governance. The primary principle is for the corporation to conduct the business with an objective of enhancing corporate profit and shareholder gain. However, the corporation may take into account ethical considerations that are reasonably regarded as appropriate to the responsible conduct of business; and also the corporation may devote a reasonable amount of resources to charitable, philanthropic, humanitarian, and educational purposes; and the corporation may do so in both situations even if shareholder profit and shareholder gain are not thereby enhanced. So, although the primary focus is on the monetary value, this objective is moderated by ethical and social responsibility values. The idea is that the corporation will engage in self-governance; and thus regulate, not only by the strictures of the law, but also by morality and ethics, as well as stakeholder and societal concerns, the manner by which it generates profits. In essence, corporations will act legally, morally, and in a socially responsible manner only if those people who exercise control over the corporation, whether directly or indirectly; that is, the directors, officers, and shareholders together, have the vision to see that the collective future of the business, its stakeholders, and society as a whole is inextricably tied to the sustainability of the entity and the society in which it operates and flourishes, as well as the strength of character and leadership ability to implement and act on that vision.

For the traditional corporation some suggestions on how to structure corporate governance to maximize long-term shareholder, stakeholder, and societal value creation are as follows: empower and motivate business leaders to manage for the long-term by using incentive and compensation systems. That is, compensation should be aligned with long-term objectives, and financial rewards should be linked to the period over which results are realized. Incentive structures should also reflect a more full measure of socially responsible performance, for example, by including environmental sustainability, in these incentive programs. The companies it to make these social responsibility considerations contribute to long-term, successful, financial performance. Business leaders, therefore, must exert—leadership—to improve incentive and compensation systems as well as other aspects of corporate governance to enhance sustainability.

Corporate governance guidelines for social responsibility should be premised on fundamental principles. First the company should formulate a corporate social responsibility policy to guide its strategic planning and provide a roadmap for its CSR initiatives. Second, that policy should be an integral part of the organization's overall business policy and aligned with the company's business goals. Third, the policy should be created and framed with the participation of various level executives as well as representatives of other stakeholder groups, and the policy must be approved and overseen by the board and implemented by top management. The corporate social responsibility policy should cover the following core elements: (1) adherence to the law; (2) acting in an ethical, honest, and transparent; (3) consideration of the values and interests of all stakeholders, including shareholders, employees, customers, suppliers, local communities, society at large, and the environment; (4) treating all stakeholders with dignity and respect and as worthwhile means and not as mere means; (5) charitable and philanthropic activities; and (6) activities that promote social and economic development.

A socially responsible firm, however, must also be a realistic one; that is, socially responsible, stakeholder considerations, and environmental efforts must be sustainable economically and should have some relationship to the firm's business. These prudential considerations should be reflected in the company's corporate governance polices. Employees, for example, should also be engaged directly in the company's social responsibility activities so as to engage them, inspire them, motivate them, and thereby enhance morale and productivity. Moreover, a firm's social responsibility program does not have to be a multi-million dollar effort; rather, something as simple as an employee social responsibility "suggestion box," or as straightforward as a recycling or energy saving program, will do to promote employee involvement as well as to promote and give credence to employee social values. Nonetheless, despite the size, a firm's social responsibility efforts should be publicized widely within the company, for example, in company newsletters, as well as externally, for example in company annual "social responsibility" reports and on its website. Being socially responsible, therefore, is a smart and sustainable business strategy the company's corporate governance policies must be tailored to promote this type of social responsibility.

Corporate governance emerges as a particularly challenging endeavor in the social benefit corporation considering its dual mission of profit-making and societal betterment, the concomitant trade-offs among competing stakeholders, including shareholders, of course, the ensuing competition for corporate resources, the lack of a specific B-Corp government regulator, and the absence in the state legislation as to how the conflicting stakeholder demands should be balanced. To solve this corporate governance dilemma, the management of the social benefit company can refer to the standards set forth by the third party evaluator to whom the B-Corp must report. Yet since the social benefit corporation legislation provides no concrete guidance, the legislation envisions that the top management team will weigh the company's social responsibility goals in light of their business objectives, and then arrive some reasonable determination that advances profit and all stakeholder values. Moreover, to advance social responsibility accountability, it will be important that the views of top management team should be balanced within the company by using participatory mechanisms that allow for stakeholder representation, invite stakeholder participation, and keep internal channels of communication open and flowing. At the very least, due to the mixed mission, vague corporate socially responsible standards, conflicting stakeholder demands, as well as citizen and interest group pressure, the activities of the corporation will be, and should be, carefully monitored—principally by its management as part of their governance function, but also by company stakeholders, government legislators and regulators, and citizens.

Implications and Recommendations for Business Leaders

The new corporation structure of the social benefit corporation is a clearly meritorious way of doing business, indeed. Yet the authors believe that at this time it also is plainly a problematic one for business people, directors, and entrepreneurs, even very socially responsible ones. The law is just too new and unsettled as to nature of the public benefit and especially as to the legal risks of being a director of a "B-corp." As such, no corporate board of directors wants to be the "test case" in determining the parameters of legal liability under a social benefit corporation model. Nonetheless, socially responsible people who plan to incorporate can always include social responsibility goals in the articles and bylaws and corporate governance policies of a traditional corporation; and the typical state's constituency statute expressly allows the consideration of other stakeholder groups. So, the legal latitude exists to be socially responsible, yet without mandating a legal duty on the board to be socially responsible. Moreover, the authors assert that it is in the long-term, egoistic, self-interest of the corporation to be a socially responsible one and thus to be active and engaged in community, civic, and charitable activities.

Accordingly, it is the job of the business leader to educate the shareholders, and perhaps corporate management as well, of the benefits that will accrue to the company and the shareholders by the company acting in a smart, shrewd, and strategic socially responsible manner. Corporate social responsibility, as such, should be treated as an investment, not a cost, comparable to quality improvement and employee training. Business leaders, executives, and managers, therefore, must be cognizant of and appreciate the instrumental strategic value of social responsibility in its constituency and sustainability formulations. Business leaders, executives, and managers today surely are well aware of societal expectations regarding the social responsibility of their companies. Business leaders want their businesses to be successful and to sustain that success on a long-term basis.

Figure 6.1 – The Business Sustainability Continuum

Economic	Legal	Ethical	Social Responsibility
Have a viable business model to fill a need while earning a profit. Filling an existing need is the goal and profit is the consequence of doing it well.	Align behavior with applicable local, national and international laws that apply to your business employees, associates, partners, clients, and customers	Act morally and according to your universal values, promises, and obligations. The business must do what it says it will do.	Focus on community, philanthropy, and charity as a strategic part of the business. Successful firms operate on this ultimate end of the continuum.
New Business		*Leading and Established Businesses*	

Business Sustainability Continuum

The term "*sustainability*" also has emerged, along with social responsibility and corporate governance, as important subject matters for business today. A sustainable business is one that is governs itself in a long-term, stakeholder centered, and environmentally conscious manner. To be a sustainable one, the business must be concerned not "merely" with profits, but also must pay attention to, and seek to balance, stakeholder interests and environmental concerns. Sustainability has legal and ethical predicates too; and as such will result in legal and moral decision-making by companies. In order to better illustrate as well as explicate the values of practicality, legality, morality, social responsibility, and stakeholder interests, and their relationship to sustainability, the authors have developed the model presented in Figure 6.1 (Mujtaba and Cavico, 2013), called The Business Sustainability Continuum (BSC).

The BSC illustrates that the continual success and "sustainability" of the business can only be achieved by an adherence to four core values (Mujtaba, Cavico and Plangmarn, 2012): *Economic*, indicating that a business obviously must have a viable business model which fulfills a need and enables the business to make a profit; *Legal*, indicating that this profit must be achieved in legal manner by aligning the conduct of the business with all applicable local, national, and international law; *Ethical*, indicating that since there may be no law or "gaps" in the law nonetheless the business must act in a moral manner and also must act in conformity with its values, promises, and obligations; and *Social Responsibility*, indicating that the business must focus on the community and engage in civic, philanthropic, and charitable endeavors as part of the business' overall strategic plan. Sustainability will help the business; but also help the business help governments solve pressing social problems; and, as such, sustainability provides a means to rebuild trust in the economic and political systems, which naturally is good for business and good for society. Accordingly, corporate governance policies must be devised to give credence and implementation to these "sustainable" values; and thereby will enable the business to achieve success and to sustain that success in a continual manner, thus benefiting the business, its shareholders, communities where it does business, and all the stakeholders affected by the business, including society as a whole. To do so is to act in a truly socially responsible and sustainable manner.

Conclusion to Part II

This chapter has sought to build on the previous chapters' legal materials by introducing the readers to and examining the fields of ethics and social responsibility and showing how, and why, ethics and social responsibility can, and should, be applied to business today. Legality, ethics, and morality are very important values; and today social responsibility is such a value too. Business leaders must be cognizant of these values. Furthermore, the emphasis on stakeholders or constituency groups is an essential component of business leadership and corporate governance today too. The business leader must take an enlightened approach to satisfying the values of stakeholders in order to achieve long-term sustainable success. As emphasized, the ultimate goal is to attain "win-win" resolutions where all the company's stakeholders receive value. Social responsibility emerges as a key element in achieving stakeholder symmetry and success and business sustainability. Furthermore, given the apparent positive relationship between successful financial performance and social responsibility, and the critical need of both these values for society and the economic system, corporate social responsibility, stakeholder analysis, and corporate governance have emerged as most relevant and profound topics for business today.

Social responsibility, moreover, is now not only an "academic" matter for business school students and academics, or "merely" an issue for social activists; rather, social responsibility is also a very real and practical concern for the global business leader, executive, manager, and entrepreneur. Admittedly, in certain cases, social responsibility concerns may be more difficult for business people, who are primarily focused on economic and legal issues, to discern and to handle. Moreover, there may be conflict as various constituencies make conflicting demands. Nonetheless, business leaders in fulfilling their corporate governance functions are expected to recognize competing stakeholder interests, to provide balance among legitimate competing claims, and, as emphasized, to devise practical, legal, ethical, socially responsible, and mutually beneficial solutions. Business leaders very well may have to convince certain stakeholders, such as the shareholders, that it is in their long-term self-interest to accept some short-term financial sacrifice, say in the form of company socially responsible efforts in the local community, in order to produce longer-term greater financial gains. Fundamentally, therefore, business leaders are expected to lead and to lead by values, encompassing legal values, moral values, and now today socially responsible values too. Consequently, cognizance of, adherence to, and successfully dealing with the value of social responsibility have become imperatives for business leaders today. Business leaders must recognize that social responsibility and sustainability are now essential aspects of business; and thus these values must have a prominent place on the corporate vision, mission, and agenda. The view today is that business should pursue profits, of course, but also that business should strive to achieve social objectives too in a sustainable manner. Business leaders should, and actually are expected to, know and understand the rationales for corporate social responsibility and business sustainability as well as to create and implement corporate governance policies and business strategies to be a socially responsible and sustainable business. Social responsibility as well as sustainability, therefore, should now be incorporated into business values, missions, and models along with legal and ethical values. Social responsibility is the now the modern way, and truly the only sustainable way, to do business. However, as the authors have emphasized throughout this work, social responsibility clearly possesses instrumental value because it can be used in a smart, shrewd, and strategic sense to help the business achieve and sustain successful performance. Social responsibility, therefore, is more than just "mere" "pure" charity; rather, in modern business sense social responsibility is an integral strategic component in a company's endeavor to achieve larger "pure" business objectives; and concomitantly, and also propitiously, society as whole is benefitted too by these social responsibility activities. Business, therefore, needs a formal, coherent, transparent, strategic, stakeholder-based, and sustainable policy to social responsibility. The goal is to make a positive, beneficial, and sustainable contribution to the company's growth, economic growth, societal growth, and the betterment of the environment. So, corporate social responsibility and sustainability, together with morality and ethics, are "smart business" and "good business"—for business and society. The old maxim is true: one can do well by doing "good"!

The authors, accordingly, firmly believe that business leaders—whether entrepreneur, CEO, executive, officer, or manager- must act in a legal, ethical, and socially responsible manner. As such, business leaders in pursing profits must obey the law, act for the greater good, treat all stakeholders with dignity and respect, and in a prudent manner be socially responsible by contributing to charities and participating in and supporting community and civic activities. Acting in such a responsible way will require business leaders being cognizant of various stakeholder interests as well as seeking to balance these at times conflicting constituencies in a fair and efficacious manner. This objective is a challenging one, indeed, but also a noble one. Yet the result will be the creation of long-term, sustainable value, not "merely" for the shareholders but for the employees, customers, communities, and all the stakeholders of the organization, including society as a whole.

The recent real estate/mortgage/banking crisis in the United States, resulting in the recessionary U.S. as well as global economy, was in main part created by so-called business "leaders" abandoning common sense, good sense, and ethics, as well as abdicating their corporate governance obligations; and consequently acting in a short-term, solely profit-centered, immoral, if not downright illegal, manner. Instead of earning rewards fairly, the prevailing mentality was a "get-rich-quick" one exacerbated by the false belief that price of real estate would go up—forever! Consequently, people with "NINJA" loans, that is, with no jobs, assets, or income, were borrowing money that they realistically could never repay to buy over-appraised houses. Then, the so-called, though accurately called, "sub-prime" mortgages, guaranteed in main part by the U.S. government, were "securitized" into basically fraudulent securities, though securities rated as "safe" ones. Next, this essentially worthless paper was sold to many, many unsuspecting buyers, all the way to Iceland. This series of events resulted in a financial disaster and economic "meltdown." Throughout the political, economic, business, banking, real estate, and mortgage fields, short-sighted, if not immoral, business people tolerated undue risks, illegal, "borderline" illegal, and clearly unethical conduct. Individualistic, risky, short-term, profit seeking—from real estate agents, mortgage brokers, and bankers—was the "moral" norm; and the deleterious effect on society of this misbehavior did not even register. The result was a massive destruction of value—short- and long-term—the ruination of businesses, business and personal assets, and people's lives, necessitating massive taxpayer "bailouts," and engendering a serious undermining of confidence in economic and political systems.

Capitalism and free markets are built on, as Adam Smith wisely stated long ago, a foundation of morality. The economy needs to be free to function, but the economy also needs rules to function correctly and effectively. And when the legal rules are not present or they are not clear, there is all the more need for ethics and socially responsible behavior. The idea is to create a sustainable form of capitalism, whereby acting in a legal, ethical, and socially responsible manner, as well as taking a long-term perspective, will produce profits for the shareholders but long-term value for all the other stakeholders of the company. The task of business leaders, therefore, is to incorporate not only legal rules but also ethical, social responsibility, and stakeholder considerations into corporate values, mission statements, governance policy, and strategy, and to do so not "just" nationally but globally. Transparency, truthfulness, and trustworthiness have been, are, should be, and must be the hallmarks of successful business; business managers have a moral obligation to be trustees of all the stakeholders of the organization; yet, sadly, these moral lessons now must be learned once again. A true business leader must be keenly aware and engaged, must look ahead, and must foresee the consequences of his or her company's actions on all the firm's stakeholders, including society as a whole. Business leaders must be aware that law, ethics, and social responsibility are all interconnected and underpin the economy and the free market system. The authors hope that their chapter to this book supplies a reminder, a rationale, and a guide for legal, ethical, and socially responsible behavior, as well as a warning of the "fruits from the poisonous tree"; and thus the authors hope that their contribution to this book serves as a tool for true business success, stakeholder responsibility, and organizational and societal sustainability. Capitalism, yes; but a capitalism "regulated" and tempered by law, ethics, morality, and social responsibility, and thus a capitalism with a "communitarian spirit" or, in the words of the Venetians long-ago (yet still quite true), a "communally controlled" capitalism.

Leadership and Mission

The global business leader's principal duty is to create and to articulate a great vision for the enterprise or company and its constituent groups. The vision must be important, noble, engrossing, and achievable. It must highlight an idea or image of what the organization should do in the future as well as display the manner in which the organization will realize its vision. The leader also must fulfill the concomitant responsibility of forming the firm's mission and core values, which, of course, must cohere with the company's vision. This vision, together with the firm's mission and values, will supply the basis for a strong and effective enterprise.

Vision, mission, and values clearly must tell the organization's constituent groups what the organization represents and what principles govern it. The vision, mission, and values, moreover, will furnish agreed-upon standards for evaluating the firm's operations and practices as well as a standard for bringing such standards into alignment with the expressed purposes and direction of the enterprise. Finally, vision, mission, and values will serve as a motivating, concentrating, coordinating, integrating, and governing force for the individual employees of the company. The natural result will be a highly vitalized enterprise.

Another key dimension to business leadership is the communication and explanation to the firm's stakeholders of the vision, mission, and values. Business leadership, in this dimension, is viewed as taking up an educational function, especially considering that some stakeholder groups may not initially or directly comprehend the necessity for change, a longer-term viewpoint, or a more expansive perspective. In addition, global business leaders not only must communicate and explain the vision, mission, and values, but he or she also must impart the firm's commitment to its vision, mission, and values.

The business leader not only must get people to pay attention to the firm's vision, mission, and values, but he or she also must secure, especially on the part of the firm's employees, their acceptance and adoption of the firm's ideology. Such acceptance and adoption can be best obtained on a voluntary basis when the company's vision, mission, and values are in accord with the personal plans, aspirations, and principles of the employees and other constituent groups. The company stakeholders then can see clearly that their own personal growth and success are very closely connected to—and perhaps, to a degree, dependent upon—the firm's development and prosperity.

If a company's vision, mission, and values which are in alignment with those of the employees, the firm's employees in essence elect to adopt and be bound by the firm's ideology. The employees' self-interest will drive them to thus activate the vision, implement the mission, and articulate and act in accordance with the firm's values. Therefore, the vision, mission, and values of the company will emerge as the true source of organizational power as well as a key criterion for decision making within the organization, thereby informing the company's strategy, policy, and methods. Furthermore, the organization's values will ensure the propriety and consistency of its tactics and actions.

It is necessary, of course, for the global business leader to manifest enthusiasm, positive energy, and passion, as well to exhibit confidence, conviction, and determination. The leader's role requires that he or she focus, channel, and motivate the energies, knowledge, and talents of the employees, as well as other relevant constituents, so that the firm's vision, mission, and values become paramount. One assured way to animate employees to achieve the vision, accomplish the mission, and comport themselves with the company values, shared goals, beliefs, and principles, is to set lofty yet achievable goals. Also, managers should believe in and trust the employees to carry out their projects and reward them for their success and accomplishments. At the same time, employees should be challenged and encouraged to reach such objectives.

The challenge for the business leader, therefore, is to create an organizational environment of opportunity, endeavor, and growth. At the same time, the business leader's job is not necessarily to command, but rather to set elevated standards and then to expect and insist on high levels of performance from the employees. Such a demanding attitude on the part of a business leader will produce superior performance as well as a sense of personal fulfillment on the part of the employees. This strategy will make the long-term success of the organization more achievable.

Truly great global business leaders not only induce and motivate their employees to perform, they also inspire people to work together, sacrifice, persevere, dedicate themselves, overcome resistance, and in turn become leaders themselves in order to realize the vision and accomplish the mission. Inspiration is predicated on trust, a commitment to fundamental, shared values, and a belief in people's worth, potential, and dignity. Inspiration is fostered by providing hope and meaning to people, principally by demonstrating that the goals of the individual can be realized at the same time as the business organization's objectives. Such inspired, vision-focused, mission-centered, and values-based business leadership surely will effectuate positive, beneficial, and necessary change.

Ethical global business leaders value themselves and value personal as well as organizational success. At the same time, they must be altogether morally astute and enlightened so as to subordinate themselves to noble purposes, ethical principles, rightful conduct, as well as the shared aspirations, communal values, and manifold contributions of the greater organization. The challenge for a global business leader is to align his or her personal goals with the organization's objectives and also with the needs and aspirations of one's subordinates and employees, and then to ensure that this alignment is centered on a crux of morality and legitimacy. Only then can a leader truly lead and thereby achieve permanent positive transformation for the organization.

Global Legal Perspectives

Social Responsibility: Canada, Mexico, and the United States[23]

Social Responsibility refers to the actions of an individual or firm benefiting society beyond ethics, the direct interests of the firm, institution, or organization, as well as the requirements of the law. When applied with regard to an entire firm, this concept is generally referred to as Corporate Social Responsibility (CSR).

The social responsibility of the Canadian or U.S. manager in Mexico is very complex due to the vast cultural and social differences as well as values differences existing both in business and social life. According to Professor Ilya Adler (2006), doing business in Mexico is very different than in Canada and the U.S. Adler is an expert on Canadian-U.S.-Mexico relations, especially when it comes to the socio-cultural differences and expectations, interactions, commercial relationships and communications within business. Because the values, social practices, managerial methods, and belief systems of the Mexican worker and Mexican manager are so different, there is fertile ground for cultural and social misunderstanding. Invariably, the level and progress of social responsibility for U.S. and Canadian counterpart managers will be affected. In fact, cultural values are so different in certain areas that the Canadian or U.S. manager or businessperson who does not take the time to understand such differences and adjust his or her behavior and expectations will end up frustrated and disappointed. In addition, his or her Mexican business associates may also feel the same.

Working in Mexico can be very shocking and difficult for both Canadian and U.S. managers as the approach to business there is vastly different due to the "fluid" nature of law and the underdevelopment of a strong information system and ethical culture that is comparable to the home countries. Thus, the social responsibility and burden which accompanies it increases for a U.S. or Canadian manager working in Mexico for the following reasons:

---

[23] Contributed by Anthony McFarlane, Nova Southeastern University.

1. These managers have to adapt to vastly different cultural and social values.
2. Adaptation to a society where ethics and social responsibility hold differing perspectives and regard as well as reward makes for much misunderstanding, dilemma, and constraints.
3. Cross-border business relationships always involve international laws as well as domestic national laws.
4. The values and attitudes of resistance to U.S. or Canadian managers can be overwhelming.
5. Bribes and other factors which become part of doing business are taken in different lights.
6. These managers must still abide by their countries' own laws and policies concerning business operations, and the laws of international and multinational entities; and
7. Social responsibility becomes strained due to racial and socioeconomic tensions and expectations from Mexican business partners and subordinates, and from the society in general.

The social responsibility of U.S. or Canadian managers and entrepreneurs working in Mexico involves adhering to the laws of their home country and the expatriate country as well as the internal "laws" of organizations in which they are working, thereby applying fairness from the viewpoint of both cultures and maintaining home standards and policies while not ignoring Mexican laws and social customs. Regardless of the ethics and social responsibility inherent in Canada or in the United States, managers and entrepreneurs must remember that when it is necessary to enter the "world of the Mexican," one must be open to the fact that his/her assumptions about how things are done often are not necessarily going to be true of the new environment. What this means is that a certain compromise of perspectives on the part of U.S. and Canadian managers may be necessary. In extreme cases, a compromise of values which might not necessarily be embraced in their home nations may also become a necessity.

Furthermore, racism and social injustices also seem to be normalized by certain feudal aspects of some Mexican cities. By not heeding such knowledge and proceeding without caution, U.S.-Canada-Mexico managers can become caught in a vice in attempting to apply outside social standards, ethical values, and social justices in business decision making, negotiations, and trade. Organizations with clearly defined ethical and social standards that embrace diversity and cultural differences can achieve a higher level of success by paying attention to social responsibility in the context of U.S.-Canada-Mexico relations.

If a certain course of action was illegal in a manager's own country—say the United States or Canada—but lawful and accepted in Mexico, the standards the manager should follow will depend on several factors, including: 1) the nature of the action required; 2) the particular case or circumstances; 3) the applicability of U.S. and Mexican or international laws; 4) the parties involved and their various claims; 5) the scope of the issue as it relates to individual and firm rights, policies, and rules; 6) the existence or inexistence of agencies and their applicable procedures for dealing with such issues; 7) the definitions of what constitutes legality and what binds the manager's company and his/her responsibilities in Mexican society; 8) the severity of the issue or action in terms of its consequences in Mexico and any forms of "backlash" from the manager's home country; 9) the cost of the action to oneself and the reputation and success of the firm, mostly in the model of costs versus benefits of doing business; and most importantly 10) the particular jurisdiction under which the manager and his/her firm will be held accountable: Mexico, the U.S., or Canada.

Even though all of the above factors will affect the action the manager or entrepreneur decides to take, given that the action is legal under Mexican law, such legality may very well resolve the situation of the immediate environment, especially when it comes to the expectations of Mexican subordinates and business partners. However, complicating matters is the fact that the standards the manager is following in making such a choice essentially run against those of his/her country, in which the action could very well be illegal. Thus, a subsidiary of a U.S.-owned company operating in any foreign country may still be subject to U.S. laws and regulations. If the intended action is completely business-oriented, the manager must first reference United States laws. Laws such as the Foreign Corrupt Practices Act make it illegal for U.S. companies and their managers to attempt to improperly influence foreign officials through personal payments or gifts. So in the example concerning a U.S. manager and his/her firm's business in Mexico, even if it were not illegal under Mexican law, it would still be illegal by United States standards.

On the other hand, the manager could choose to follow the Mexican perspective, believing that the action is not illegal in that country and is therefore permissible. However, various cases and data show that managers can be subjected to "double jeopardy" consequences, as what might be legal in one nation is illegal under another's laws: One law might exonerate, but the other might penalize.

One of the major problems for the global manager, therefore, is the application of laws in Third World countries. The situation will vary depending on what circumstances and acts are involved. However, most recent laws are cross-national or cross-border in their applications when it comes to multinational businesses and their foreign subsidiaries.

Turning again to social responsibility, such responsibility of firms operating in Mexico, for instance, is basically the same as of firms operating elsewhere. While Mexico, as a nation, has many grave social problems and challenges, business firms must ensure that they are contributing to the betterment of the nation and its citizens and not increasing social problems. The accounting firm, Deloitte Mexico, for example, is a company that understands the full spectrum of social responsibility: environmental protection, worker health and safety, corrupt practices, among others. For 2005, Deloitte was named Socially Responsible Enterprise for the fifth consecutive year. According to Ernesto González, Deloitte's CEO in Mexico, a primary objective of the firm is to help in the formation of better citizens who take on more social and civic responsibility and the company considers the company-community relationship a critical factor in building a better country. This philosophy accurately describes the expectations that society and stakeholders have about the social responsibility of firms operating in Mexico. Thus, organizations that fulfill their obligations as "good corporate citizens" will sustain leadership because they will have a strong and positive impact on their people and their community.

To illustrate global social responsibility, there are currently agreements among Canada, Mexico, and the United States regarding environmental protection. The Commission for Environmental Cooperation (CEC) represents the three countries working together to protect their "shared environment." As such, firms operating within these territories are subject to the environmental laws and those rules and policies set forth by the CEC to protect each country's environment from destructive business activities. The environment ministers of Canada, Mexico, and the United States, members of the Council of the Commission for Environmental Cooperation (CEC or "the Commission"), met for the annual Regular Session in June 2006 to reaffirm their commitment to the North American Agreement on Environmental Cooperation, working for a healthier environment in the region. This agency, along with the environmental laws of each nation, provide guidelines and standards by which firms operating in countries, including Mexico, can ensure that their activities are not damaging to the environment.

Mexico's environmental enforcement agency, Procuraduría Federal de Protección al Ambiente, or Profepa, is taking a new look at how it will go about encouraging small business environmental compliance. Moreover, Fernando Montes de Oca Domínguez, of the public interest institute Instituto Mexicano de Derecho Forestal-Ambiental (Mexican Institute of Forest-Environmental Right—Imdefac), stresses the need for citizens to be better informed as a first step toward environmental reform in his country. One way to reach this goal of improved public awareness is through educational conferences (Orol, 2006).

Individual firms are responsible for ensuring that each worker is free from health and bodily injuries within company confines as worker health and safety are paramount in maintaining and carrying out corporate social responsibility.

Firms operating in Mexico are usually aware of this. The Mexican government, along with the United States and Canada, has applied rigorous standards for worker health and safety. The Mexican government is working with the United States and Canada on improving worker safety, and the CEC has become active in examining the effects of environmental degradation on worker health and safety, especially within manufacturing companies, which contribute most to environmental and health problems. The Foreign Corrupt Practices Act (FCPA) applies to all United States and Canadian firms operating in Mexico, and the Mexican government has joined the effort with its trading partners to lessen the occurrence of corruption in business practices. While the Mexican government has yet to devise any significant law on this issue, the application of FCPA by the United States to expatriate businesspeople and firms has been a good deterrent in preventing corrupt practices in many cases.

Therefore, the social responsibility of firms operating in Mexico includes conformance to quality standards and agency and administrative rules regarding worker safety and health issues and environmental protection. Canadian and United States foreign subsidiaries may be subject to home-country rules in addition to Mexican laws regarding these issues despite the "loopholes" that facilitate "bad" practices and corruption. Global managers and entrepreneurs should recognize that as global legal challenges increase, so too will the ethical and social responsibilities they must take on in conducting business activities in a diverse and highly competitive environment.

Management Strategies

The global manager and entrepreneur must utilize ethical and legal strategies to achieve his or her personal and professional goals. This requires that the global manager become familiar with local laws, customs, and practices. The local manager must also become aware of, and fully familiar with, the local culture's definition of business ethics, business mores, and their expectations for socially responsible behaviors from the global corporation.

Every global manager in a legal, ethical, and socially responsible organization should estimate, weigh, and balance all considerations when deliberating over decisions and actions. Specifically, the manager first must ensure that the values of legality, morality, and social responsibility are attained. Then, one must ascertain what facets are most important to analyze in order to determine value maximization over time for a particular situation. In so doing, for each pertinent facet, one must predict and enumerate both the positive and negative consequences of a decision or action as well as its short-term versus long-term effects. Next, one must determine the eventual resultant impact that all these consequences will have on value maximization over time. Finally, for any negative or unintended consequences that possibly may occur, one must resolve how exactly such consequences could be eliminated or at least mitigated.

The Utilitarian model and method emerges as an initial philosophical as well as a practical approach. It is simple to state in its basic form, but arduous to implement. Implementation is difficult because organizations and people are complex, values are diverse and subjective, values of constituent groups are hard to comprehend, and harder to balance, and calculating consequences and their long-range impact on value maximization are very challenging tasks. Nonetheless, if Utilitarianism is learned well, administered thoughtfully and consistently, checked and balanced by Kantian ethics, as well as complemented by social responsibility, the ultimate goals of achieving, creating, and sustaining long-term growth, surplus, wealth, and value maximization will be attained and attained in a legal, moral, and socially responsible manner.

Summary

In addition to the legal ramifications of business decision-making, business today is being called upon to act not "merely" legally, but also in a moral, ethical, and socially responsible manner. Accordingly, this chapter had two components. Part I of this chapter examined ethics, which is a branch of philosophy; and the authors demonstrated how ethics can be applied to business decision-making to determine if business is acting in a moral manner. Moreover, Part II of this chapter examined the related, but distinct, concept of corporate social responsibility; and accordingly the authors discussed and illustrated what it means in a modern-day business context for a business, particularly a corporation, to be a "socially responsible" one.

SEVEN

CONSTITUTIONAL LAW AND BUSINESS

The United States Constitution is the supreme law of the United States. The Constitution serves two general purposes in the United States. First, it establishes the structure of government and allocates power among the various branches of government. Second, it prevents the very government it established from taking certain actions that may infringe upon the liberties of the people it governs, especially with regard to particular actions that restrict the people's individual rights.

Of course, throughout U.S. history, there have been many changes to the Constitution as a result of the way the Supreme Court has interpreted it. Because the Constitution is a relatively short text—with certain key provisions such as "due process" of law and "equal protection" under the law quite vaguely stated—it is a rather flexible document. Many Constitutional provisions now have far different practical meanings versus when they were first enacted. There also has been a perceived need to adapt the Constitution to changing social conditions. Effectively, the hoary maxim in the U.S. is that the "Supreme Court follows the election returns." Even if it is an overstatement, it is a fact that the Supreme Court's decisions do at times reflect the changing social conditions of the country, the same country in which the court operates.

U.S. constitutional law is an evolving field of law. There is an explicit amendment process to the U.S. Constitution. In theory, at least, constitutional change can be accomplished through the formal amendment process, yet the amendment process is difficult to use and, consequently, amendments to the Constitution are relatively infrequent. Neither the U.S. Congress nor any state may promulgate a law that directly conflicts with the U.S. Constitution.

The Supreme Court is the Constitution's main "amender." Thus, the Court has the final authority to determine the Constitution's meaning. In particular, the U.S. Supreme Court has the power of judicial review, which means the Court can declare actions of other government bodies unconstitutional, thereby affording the Justices of the Supreme Court policymaking powers in the U.S. governmental system. However, there are certain limits to the Supreme Court's power to shape the Constitution. First, the Constitution's language is not completely open-ended. Actually, certain provisions are quite clear. Second, based on the old common law precedent system, past constitutional decisions bind the Court, at least to a certain degree. Third, the Supreme Court is dependent on the other branches of government to make its decisions effective. Finally, the Court ultimately is dependent on the public's belief in the Court's fairness, integrity, and fidelity to the rule of law.

The Constitution is also the source of lawmaking authority for the vast amount of laws that govern business in the United States. This chapter examines fundamental constitutional concepts and provisions, paying particular attention to their ramifications for business. This chapter predominantly focuses on the U.S., but also covers constitutional principles and developments in selected international jurisdictions.

Foundational United States Constitutional Concepts

The United States, like many other countries (such as Mexico), is a federal system of government and indeed federalism is one of the most fundamental Constitutional concepts. Federalism is recognized in the Constitution as the premise for the structure of government in the United States as well as the basis for the relations between the national government—called the "federal" government—and the constituent government entities—called "states" in the United States and called "provinces" in other federal systems. In the United States, the states form the union, but power is divided by the Constitution between the national government and its constituent states.

The rationale for federalism is that society is best served by a distribution of powers and functions among a central government, constituent government entities, the states, and local government components of the states, such as counties and municipalities. Clearly, particular levels of government are better equipped to deal with certain problems, such as the national government's ability to wage war and therefore, federalism is the doctrine of delegated powers.

Thus, the U.S. Constitution grants certain specific powers to the national government, most notably in Article I, which grants powers to Congress. The states, as the original sovereign entities, retain the powers not granted to the national government. As a matter of fact, the Tenth Amendment to the Constitution explicitly states that the powers not expressly given to the national government or explicitly denied to the states are therefore reserved for the states or the people.

Historically in the United States, the states, as the original sovereign entities, delegated or transferred certain enumerated powers to the national government while reserving all other powers to the states. The very significant consequence is that in the United States, the national government possesses no powers apart from those delegated to it by the states. Accordingly, the national government can only exercise those enumerated powers expressly granted to it. However, these enumerated powers are very broad, but the national government can exercise power "necessary and proper" to carrying out such enumerated powers. Because there are two main levels of government within the United States, the principle of federal supremacy is of monumental consequence. The Supremacy Clause of Article IV of the Constitution holds that the Constitution and laws and treaties of the United States—that is, the national government—supersede state law. As a result, if there is a conflict between federal and state law, the federal law will invalidate an inconsistent state law, even a provision within a state constitution.

Another critical constitutional concept is the "separation of powers" doctrine. The U.S. Constitution divides the federal government into three branches: legislative, executive, and judicial. Article I establishes the legislative branch, called a Congress, which is composed of a Senate and a House of Representatives. The legislative branch is accorded the sole power to make laws at the federal level. Section 8 of Article I describes the specific areas in which Congress can legislate, which include commerce and taxation. Article I also sets forth rules for the promulgation of legislation. Article II establishes the executive branch of government and places the executive power on the President. The President is empowered by the Constitution to "take care that the laws be faithfully executed." Accordingly, the President has the power to enforce the laws passed by Congress. The President is also designated as the commander in chief in Article II. Finally, Article II sets forth the procedure for electing the President. Article III of the Constitution grants the judicial power to the Supreme Court and other federal courts that were later established by Congress. Article III defines the scope of federal judicial power. Each branch of government, therefore, performs a separate function, and no branch may exercise the authority of another branch.

Closely allied with the separation of powers doctrine is the system of "checks and balances," the objective of which is to ensure that no one branch of government accumulates too much power. In addition to separating the government into three distinct branches, the Constitution creates a system of checks and balances between Congress, the President, and the courts: Each branch of government has certain powers to limit the actions of the other branches. For example, Congress can declare war, but the President is the commander in chief. Congress can make laws, the President can veto laws, but Congress can then override a Presidential veto. The President makes appointments to the Supreme Court, but the Senate must confirm such appointments. Finally, the Supreme Court has the power to declare actions of the other two branches unconstitutional.

Powers of the Federal Government and the States

Federal Legislative Powers

The legislative power at the federal level, as mentioned, is vested in Congress. Legislative power encompasses not only the power to make laws, but also the power to investigate, to hold hearings, and to consider matters upon which legislation may be enacted. The source of this power is Article I, Section 1, which states that "All legislative powers…shall be vested in a Congress." The scope of the federal legislative power is based on the enumerated powers specifically granted to Congress; the powers not delegated to Congress are reserved to the states by virtue of the Tenth Amendment.

However, in addition to the enumerated powers, Congress also has implied powers. Implied powers stem from the "necessary and proper" clause found in Section 8, Clause 18, of Article I. This momentous provision holds that in addition to the enumerated powers, Congress shall have the power to make all laws which shall be necessary and proper for carrying into execution the enumerated powers and all other powers vested by the Constitution in the government of the United States. As a result, Congress can legislate any appropriate "means," such as a draft, to accomplish "ends," such as declaring war and raising an army, as specified in its enumerated powers. Consequently, as will be seen, certain broad federal powers have been implied from the "necessary and proper" clause.

The taxing power of Congress stems from Article I, Section 8, Clause 1, which states that Congress has the power to lay and collect taxes, duties, imposts, and excises. The main purpose of this power is, of course, to raise revenues for the federal government. Yet taxation also has been employed by Congress as a regulatory device because the act of taxation can encourage or even discourage certain activities. Due to the broad scope of taxation powers in conjunction with the equally broad powers of Congress to regulate commerce, the taxing power of Congress has few limits. In fact, many methods of taxation have been upheld by the courts even though their primary purpose is regulatory as opposed to revenue-raising.

The spending power of Congress also comes from Clause 1 of Article 8, which states that Congress has the power to pay debts, and provide for the common defense and general welfare of the United States. It is also a broad power because it is based on any subject matter or activity that Congress can legislate or regulate. In the course of such spending, Congress disposes of revenues accumulated from its taxing power. However, there are certain limitations on the spending power of Congress. Spending, first of all, must be in the interests of the "general welfare": that is, it must be for a truly public purpose, (even though the determination of which is left up to Congress). Finally, another limitation to spending is that Congress cannot exercise this power in derogation of any other independent Constitutional right, such as conditioning the receipt of money or censoring certain content of speech. Naturally, exercising this spending power involves policy choices and political issues, which are beyond the scope of this book.

The commerce power is the preeminent and authoritative power of Congress under Article I, Section 8, Clause 3, to regulate commerce with foreign nations and among the states. This all-important power will be discussed in detail in the next major section of this chapter.

As mentioned, Congress is granted the power in Article I to declare war as well as to raise and support armies and navies. Congress is also empowered in Article I to make uniform laws regarding naturalization and citizenship, which encompasses the power to make rules for the exclusion, admission, and deportation of aliens, as well as the power to make uniform bankruptcy laws, to coin money, and to establish post offices.

Federal Executive Powers

The source of the executive power of the U.S. government is found in Section 1 of Article II of the Constitution, which confers the entire executive power to the President. The essence of the President's executive power comes from the aforementioned "take care" clause, wherein the President is empowered to "take care that the laws be faithfully executed." This power also comes from the President's designation as commander in chief. The President has certain other specific powers, for example, the powers of appointment, pardon, veto, and treaty. Regarding the status of this last power, it is important to note that pursuant to the Supremacy Clause of Section 2 of Article VI, treaties confirmed by the Senate are regarded as the "supreme law of the land." It is also noteworthy that the President does not possess an express right to executive privilege. Rather, it is a privilege that has been recognized by the courts as a means to protect the confidentiality of certain presidential communications.

Federal Judicial Powers

The source of federal judicial power is Article III of the Constitution. In Section 1 of that Article, the federal judicial power is vested in a Supreme Court and in such "inferior" federal courts as Congress deems necessary to establish. Section 2 of Article III deals with the scope of federal judicial power and limits the jurisdiction of the federal courts to four types of cases: 1) cases arising under the Constitution, an act of Congress, or a federal treaty, usually called "federal question" cases; 2) cases in which the United States is a party; 3) cases in which a state and citizens of another state are litigants; and 4) cases in which the parties are citizens of different states, usually called "diversity" cases.

There is, however, an important limitation on the scope of federal judicial power, and that is the 11th Amendment to the U.S. Constitution. As interpreted by the courts, this amendment holds that a citizen of one state cannot sue another state in federal court without that state's consent. Moreover, this amendment has been construed as preventing citizens of the states being sued from bringing suits into federal courts. Yet despite the 11th Amendment, there remain permissible federal lawsuits, such as suits against the political subdivisions of a state, like a county, or suits of states against state officials for violating constitutionally protected rights.

According to the Constitution, the U.S. Supreme Court has both original—trial—and appellate jurisdictions. The Court's original jurisdiction extends to cases involving ambassadors and consuls, as well as legal controversies between two or more states. Meanwhile, the Court's appellate jurisdiction is based on the Court's power of "judicial review," which gives the Court power to declare acts by the other branches of government, as well as state statutes and court decisions, unconstitutional.

There are certain limitations on the jurisdiction of the federal courts. First, the federal courts' jurisdiction extends to a "case or controversy," which means that a legal matter must be definite and concrete, the litigants must have adverse legal interests, and these interests must be factual, adverse, and substantial. As such, the federal courts will not issue "advisory," or hypothetical, opinions. There are no "moot" cases before the federal courts: All matters must be real, and must be resolved. Moreover, in order for the federal courts to assume jurisdiction, the parties before the court must have "standing," which means they must be personally, imminently, and directly harmed by the action or law being challenged. Parties are not allowed to litigate in the abstract; they must be injured in fact. The full meaning of the "standing" doctrine will be covered in the Administrative Law chapter.

The federal courts, as noted, will resolve federal questions: cases with a substantial federal constitutional or statutory question. But the courts will not entertain mere "political questions": that is, questions of foreign relations and military affairs, which the courts deem more appropriately left to the other political branches of the government to resolve. These types of issues include the "burning" issue as to the legality of the "undeclared" U.S. war in Vietnam in the 1970s.

Federal v. State Powers

The Constitution of the United States, as previously mentioned, forms a federal system of government. The Tenth Amendment reserves to the states all powers not specifically delegated by the Constitution to the federal government. However, in the realm of exclusive federal powers, state action is prohibited due to the express provisions of the Constitution. For example, due to Article 1, Section 10, and the powers given expressly to the federal government, no state can itself form a treaty or coin money.

However, there are powers known as "concurrent" powers, powers that can be exercised by both the federal and state governments. These include the power to regulate commerce. The states, moreover, possess what are known as "police powers," but this term is a misnomer as the power of the states to enact laws is considerably more extensive than the criminal law connotation of the word "police." Rather, the states have the inherent sovereign power to enact any law that furthers the health, safety, and welfare of the citizens and residents of the state.

But due to the Supremacy Clause, if the federal government has expressly "spoken" on a matter, any inconsistent state law will be deemed unconstitutional and thereby prohibited. Moreover, if Congress has "preempted" a certain field of law, usually as the result of the existence of detailed and pervasive federal regulation, no state legislation at all will be allowed to intervene. A prime example of this is the area of airline safety regulations.

Preemption—Supreme Court FDA Preemption Decision

The U.S. Supreme Court, in 2009, issued a major decision on the preemption doctrine, ruling that the federal approval of a prescription drug, including the warnings, does not preempt, or provide a defense, to state products liability lawsuits by injured consumers. The decision emerges as a significant victory for plaintiff consumers and a concomitant defeat for the pharmaceutical industry, business in the general, and the former Bush Administration, which had championed the preemption doctrine as a defense to products liability lawsuits. The Court decision was a 6-3 one. The decision upholds the rights of injured consumers to sue the manufacturers of products pursuant to state products liability laws when they are harmed by defective products. The decision was also a major legal defeat for the Bush Administration which had argued that the preemption doctrine applies when there is federal regulation of a product and thus state juries should be prohibited from deciding whether a product is defective under state product liability law. The Bush Administration at the time had argued as a matter of policy and in court, including this case, that federal approval of a drug by the Federal Drug Administration should bar or preempt state court lawsuits. Companies, especially the drug industry, have also long attempted to establish federal regulatory rules as a single standard superseding state law. Justice John Paul Stevens, writing for the majority, said that the former Bush Administration's view did not merit deference. Justice Stevens also explained that the majority interpreted federal regulation as bolstering, not undercutting, the FDA's mission of ensuring drug safety.

Regulation of Commerce and Taxation

The rule pertaining to the regulation of foreign commerce is simple and straightforward when it comes to trade inside a state itself. However, the issue of regulation of interstate commerce is a considerably more problematic matter indeed. The regulation of interstate commerce is construed as a concurrent power; that is, the federal power to regulate interstate commerce is deemed to be concurrent with the states' power to regulate transactions that occur within the states themselves.

The source of this federal power stems from Article I, Section 8, Clause 3, of the Constitution, which states that Congress has the power to regulate commerce among the states. This power encompasses the authority of Congress to regulate the channels and facilities of interstate commerce, such as common carriers, highways, and communication transmission facilities, as well as activities that affect interstate commerce, such as commercial or non-commercial activities, that have national economic effect and even if such activities are wholly intrastate in origin. Moreover, a single business or individual seeking to be regulated has only a small impact on the overall issue of interstate commerce. The actual legal test for the exercise of federal power is whether or not there is an aggregate effect on other states as the result of the class of activities being regulated.

The legal result of the Commerce Clause is to grant to Congress almost unlimited power to regulate commerce, because virtually every business engages in some activity that affects more than one state. Actually, one is hard-pressed to find in modern times a business activity that does not have a sufficient "national" economic effect for Congress not to regulate. The critical legal issue is not how much commerce is involved, but rather how the commerce activity itself affects interstate commerce. In one classic example of commerce and Civil Rights, the Supreme Court upheld the Civil Rights Act over the objections of a local motel owner who discriminated against African-American travelers. The motel owner argued that his business was strictly intrastate and local, and thus beyond the reach of the Civil Rights Act (enacted by virtue of the Commerce Clause). The Court explained that because the motel was accessible to interstate traffic, was advertised nationally, and that a majority of its guests were from other states, the motel was therefore engaged in interstate commerce and thus subject to the Civil Rights Act and its non-discrimination public accommodations provisions.

Another exceptional commerce case occurred in 1995, when the Supreme Court ruled that Congress exceeded its regulatory power under the Commerce Clause when Congress attempted to ban the possession of guns near schools. The Court struck down this law as unconstitutional because the attempted area of regulation had an insufficient connection with interstate commerce.

The states do possess the concurrent power to regulate interstate commerce. The federal power, although potentially all-pervasive, is nonetheless not entirely exclusive. Accordingly, an issue exists as to the extent to which the states can regulate commerce. Congress can expressly authorize the states to regulate interstate commerce. Conversely, Congress may also prohibit state regulations that otherwise might be permissible. However, if there is no express Congressional authorization or prohibition of state laws, then the aforementioned "preemption" doctrine is used to resolve the regulatory question.

The preemption doctrine in essence asks that when there is relevant federal legislation but no express prohibition of state law, the federal intent, as divined by the Supreme Court, is to forbid any state legislation. If the federal courts, and ultimately the Supreme Court, believe that the federal government has preempted, or occupied, the entire regulatory field, then no state legislation will be allowed, even if there is no direct conflict with federal law. The critical preemption decision will be left up to the federal courts, but the more complete the federal regulatory scheme is, and the more the subject matter has been historically regarded as a matter of federal concern as opposed to local concern (such as licensing of nuclear reactors versus highway safety), the more likely are the courts to say that Congress has expressed its intent to occupy the entire field. The idea here is that once Congress is said to have preempted a particular field, thereafter only uniform national regulation will be permitted.

If there is no preemption, no prohibition, and no direct conflict, the states are allowed to regulate local transactions and activities, even though they may affect interstate commerce. However, certain requirements must first be met. First, there can be no discrimination against interstate commerce. Thus, a state regulation that discriminates against interstate commerce will be struck down as invalid. "Discrimination," in this legal context, means that a state is singling out interstate commerce for regulation and/or imposing more burdensome regulations on interstate commerce by, for example, excluding incoming trade, requiring a higher price for incoming trade, requiring the performance of business operations locally, or restricting outgoing trade even if the state's purpose is meritorious in that it seeks to protect local business or to protect local natural resources and preserve the local environment. A good example of this is a state statute, which prohibited the importation into the state of waste material in order to conserve the state's remaining landfill space and reduce pollution, being deemed unconstitutional because it impermissibly discriminated against interstate commerce.

Conversely, if the state regulation does not discriminate against interstate commerce, the regulation may be valid if it passes the "balancing" test. That is, the federal courts will balance the burden on interstate commerce imposed by the state regulation by, for example, weighing the difficulties and costs of compliance against the strength of the state interest in order to determine if the state regulation itself imposes an unreasonable burden on interstate commerce.

One key factor for the courts to consider here is whether or not the state regulation furthers local health, safety, and welfare interests as opposed to merely protecting local economic interests. Yet even a health and safety state regulation will be deemed invalid if it substantially, and thus unreasonably, burdens interstate commerce. For example, state laws regulating the length of trucks on state highways as well as the type of mudguards on trucks have been struck down because of their substantial inconveniencing of interstate commerce as well as their minimal local safety benefit.

In a very significant interstate commerce case in 2005, the U.S. Supreme Court struck down as unconstitutional several states' laws that restricted direct sales by out-of-state wineries to consumers, thereby affording a substantial opportunity to smaller vineyards and other retailers desiring to sell to the consumer over the Internet. The Court's 5–4 decision rejected such state laws as those on the books in New York, Michigan, Florida, and five other states. The majority decision, written by Justice Anthony Kennedy, declared that because the affected states do permit direct-to-consumer sales from in-state wineries, the state laws were discriminatory and thus violated the interstate commerce clause of the Constitution. In ruling against the states, the Court did not seem overly influenced by the concerns of local government authorities regarding the loss of local taxation as the result of an increase in Internet sales. For consumers, the obvious direct benefit is the availability of a greater variety of wines, but it is important to note that the Court's ruling does not open the door to unrestricted Internet wine sales across the board. Rather, states still have the power to prohibit such sales and to prohibit the sale of liquor entirely. The Court's ruling merely upholds that the states cannot set such rules in a discriminatory manner that favors the in-state producers. Consequently, it is conceivable that certain states could respond to the decision by tightening their rules rather than lessening them. The head of the Liquor Control Commission in Michigan, for example, stated that she would urge state lawmakers to expand the ban on direct shipments to cover both local and out-of-state sellers. Meanwhile, the states seeking to uphold their laws stated that their laws were an additional means to stop minors from drinking.

But overall, one point is clear from the decision, and that is that out-of-state wineries will no longer be required, as they were under the former Michigan law, to distribute their products through a licensed in-state wholesaler while in-state producers could simultaneously sell directly to the state's residents. Moreover, the out-of-state wineries will no longer be required, as they were under the former New York law, to open up an office or storeroom or a factory in the state in order to sell their wine to state consumers.

In another important preemption decision with national business ramifications, a U.S. federal district court judge in July of 2006 struck down, on constitutional grounds, a Maryland state law that would have required Wal-Mart, the largest retailer in the U.S., to spend more on health care benefits for its employees. The Maryland law would have required employers with more than 10,000 workers in the state to spend at least 8% of their payroll on employee health benefits or to pay into a fund for the uninsured. The judge ruled that the state law was preempted by the relevant federal pension law, which limits the ability of the states to regulate benefits offered by large, multi-state employers. In this instance, Wal-Mart was the only employer affected.

Interstate commerce must effectively "pay its way," and is not immune from state taxation. This means that such taxation must be fair, and thus there must be a just apportionment of the tax to the "contacts" or physical presence that the interstate commerce has with the "tax situs." A tax situs means the taxing state and the benefits and protection that the interstate commerce receives from the taxing state.

Regarding the power of the states to tax interstate commerce, there are two basic rules. First, premised on the Supremacy Clause and the Interstate Commerce Clause, Congress has the complete power to authorize or to forbid state taxation that affects interstate commerce. Second, when Congress has not "spoken," the states may be able to tax interstate commerce if, in order to satisfy the Interstate Commerce Clause, the tax is not discriminatory and does not put an unreasonable burden on interstate commerce. And in order to satisfy the Due Process Clause, there must be a sufficient connection, or "nexus," between the taxing state and the subject matter or activity being taxed.

A 2005 decision by the U.S. Supreme Court could potentially result in tele-commuting employees facing eventual higher tax bills. The Court declined to hear an appeal by a Tennessee man, Thomas Huckaby, a computer specialist who lived in Nashville and telecommuted to New York. His case involved a New York law that affects people who live in another state but work for a New York employer. Early in 2005, the New York high court, in a 4–3 decision, said that he owed taxes on all of his income from the New York employer, even though he spent only about 25% of his time in New York and the other 75% in Tennessee. The law states that work performed out of state is nonetheless taxable in New York unless it is done for the employer's "necessity." Mr. Huckaby acknowledged working in Tennessee for personal reasons, not because he was required to do so by his employer. However, he argued that the New York "convenience" test violated the U.S. Constitution. Because the U.S. Supreme Court decided not to review his appeal, the New York state decision will stand.

New York state adopted its rule many years ago, due to concerns about commuters who took work home to their homes in neighboring states, such as Connecticut, on weekends, worked on Saturdays and Sundays, and then claimed to owe the state of New York only a part of their income, instead of 100%. The New York state rule stands to affect other commuters who do some of their work from home. For example, in a separate case involving a professor who commuted to New York but who also worked part of the time at his Connecticut home, the U.S. Supreme Court similarly refused to review a lower court ruling, and the professor lost his appeal.

Currently, although only a few states have laws similar to New York's, other states may opt to enforce similar laws, putting in place more hurdles for telecommuters. Thus, many other telecommuters consequently could face higher state income tax bills if other states are motivated by the New York legal success, and thus enact similar laws that tax out-of-state telecommuters.

As a result of such action at the state level, some members of Congress have introduced legislation to protect telecommuters from extra taxes. Telecommuters might get a reprieve if the U.S. Congress passes proposed legislation, called the Telecommuter Tax Fairness Act. The bill, which seeks to prevent states from collecting taxes from employers for work performed outside that state, was sponsored by a Connecticut senator and a Connecticut representative. Pursuant to the bill, employees would have to be physically present and working in a state for a state to be allowed to collect income tax from employees.

Supreme Court Commerce Clause and Tax Decisions

One "exceptional" and leading Commerce case occurred in 1995 when the Supreme Court in *United States v. Lopez* ruled that Congress exceeded its regulatory power under the Commerce Clause when Congress attempted to ban the possession of guns near schools. The Court struck down the Gun-Free School Zones Act as unconstitutional since the attempted area of regulation had an insufficient connection with interstate commerce. However, in a counterbalancing commerce clause case, the Supreme Court in 2005 in *Gonzales v. Reich* deemed that the federal government could regulate predominantly noncommercial activities that took place entirely within a state's border. The case dealt with California's medical marijuana law, which is a law that many states have today, though with differing requirements. Even though marijuana is legal in these states for medicinal purposes, the drug is still illegal under the federal Controlled Substances Act. The law was challenged by two women in California, who were using medical marijuana pursuant to their doctors' advice, and who contended that the federal government could not regulate an activity that was legal in a state; and thus the Controlled Substances Act was unconstitutional. The Supreme Court, however, disagreed, ruling that Congress has the power to prohibit the possession and non-commercial cultivation of marijuana even if wholly within a state as part of a larger regulatory drug scheme as represented by the statute. Consequently, even though legal in a state, medical marijuana users nonetheless can be prosecuted by the federal government. What is even more interesting is that today, as of the writing of this latest edition, two states, Colorado and Washington, have legalized the recreational use of marijuana, yet which cultivation, sale, or use is still presumably a federal offense (though likely a low criminal priority for the Obama Administration).

A momentous and most interesting Commerce Clause as well as taxation power case, dealt with the constitutional validity of President Obama's health care program. The case was decided in 2012 by the Supreme Court. The Court, in a 5-4 decision, upheld President Obama's healthcare law, the Affordable Care Act, also popularly known as "Obama Care," which was the most significant legislative achievement in the President's first term. The decision means that Obama Care will be fully implemented in 2014, with provisions extending coverage to more of the uninsured, providing coverage for pre-existing medical conditions, and, significantly, imposing new taxes to finance the health care expansion. The Supreme Court, in upholding Obama Care, said that Congress acted properly and constitutionally based on its power to tax when it mandated that people buy health insurance or pay a penalty (interpreted as a tax). Chief Justice John Roberts, who wrote the majority opinion, said it was reasonable to construe what Congress has done as increasing taxes on people who choose not to buy health insurance; and Congress clearly has the constitutional power to tax. Roberts reasoned that the financial penalty for not having insurance possessed the essential feature of a tax, which is to produce revenue for the government. Furthermore, Justice Roberts stated that the label of a "penalty" in the law as well as the fact that the law was intended to influence behavior did not matter. Roberts reasoned that the penalty functioned like a tax, just like other taxes, such as on cigarettes, which were enacted principally to create incentives for behavior rather than to raise revenue. Therefore, it seemed that the Chief Justice was seeking to uphold the law, but under the most narrow legal interpretation possible. The use of the Commerce Clause of the Constitution to sustain the law was denied by Roberts and the Court's four "conservative" justices, Justices Antonin Scalia, Samuel Alito, Clarence Thomas, and Anthony Kennedy. The Commerce Clause gives Congress the power to regulate commerce "among the several states." However, Roberts stated that Congress has never attempted to rely on the Commerce power to force people not engaged in commerce to purchase a product they did not want. Rather, Roberts relied on the power of Congress to "lay and collect taxes" to save the insurance mandate and thus to save Obama Care. The Supreme Court decision, therefore, in the long-run may set a new limit on Congress' power under the Commerce Clause to regulate interstate commerce. However, the dissent authored by Justice Ruth

Bader Ginsburg, and joined by Justices Stephen Breyer, Sonia Sotomayor, and Elena Kagan, the "liberal" wing of the Court, said the Commerce Clause was sufficient to justify upholding Obama Care, principally because it addresses a significant interstate problem, that is, access to health care.

Privileges and Immunities

The "privileges and immunities" afforded by the Constitution are divided into two main categories, those of national citizenship and those of state citizenship. Concerning the first type, the 14th Amendment holds that no state shall enact a law which shall abridge the privileges and immunities of citizens of the United States. For example, state laws that restrict the right of the people of the U.S. to move and pass freely from state to state or owning property or commencing a business in a state would be struck down as unconstitutional. However, as construed by the Supreme Court, the Bill of Rights is not a list of privileges and immunities of national citizenship. Thusly, as will be seen, the 14th Amendment's Due Process and Equal Protection clauses must be used to provide protection of individual rights from state action.

Concerning the privileges and immunities of state citizenship, Article IV, Section 2, of the Constitution holds that the citizens of each state are entitled to all the privileges and immunities of citizens of the several states. As a result, a state cannot discriminate against non-citizens and non-residents unless the state regulation is very closely related to a substantial state interest. For example, state laws requiring hiring preferences have been struck down, but state laws charging higher state university tuition for out-of-state students as well as higher fees for hunting and fishing licenses for out-of-state residents have been upheld as reasonable and not unduly burdensome regulations.

A major privileges and immunities case is expected to arise from the contemporary issue of gay marriage, prompted by the Massachusetts State Supreme Court decision holding that same-sex couples from states where gay marriage is banned cannot legally marry in Massachusetts. The state court's decision was premised on 1913 state law that prohibits non-residents from marrying in Massachusetts if their marriage would not be recognized in their home states. The statute, most interestingly, was promulgated at a time when Massachusetts permitted racially mixed couples to marry while many other states did not. Regarding the more recent decision, the Governor of Massachusetts applauded the court's ruling, saying that he did not want to see his state become "the Las Vegas of same-sex marriages." Nonetheless, the gay marriage issue, in addition to the privileges and immunities question, is expected to raise other fundamental constitutional issues, such as equal protection of the law and "comity," which refers to the Full Faith and Credit Clause of Article IV, Section 1, of the U.S.

Constitution, which holds that the states must give "Full Faith and Credit" to the public acts and judicial proceedings of every other state.

The Bill of Rights, Constitutional Guarantees, and Business

Introduction

The first ten amendments to the Constitution are collectively known as the Bill of Rights. The purpose of the Bill of Rights is to protect the citizens of the United States from the very government created by the Constitution. Accordingly, the Bill of Rights embodies a series of protections for the individual against various types of infringement by the federal government. Thus, the Bill of Rights effectively serves as a limitation against government power.

The First Amendment protects freedom of speech, association, religion, and assembly. The Second Amendment holds that the right of the people to "keep and bear arms" shall not be infringed. The Fourth Amendment, which will be covered in the Administrative Law and Business chapter, contains provisions regarding warrants and searches and seizures. The Fifth Amendment contains provisions regarding the privilege against self-incrimination—which also will be covered in the Administrative Law and Business chapter—as well as a prohibition against "double jeopardy," which is being subject to the same offense twice. The Sixth Amendment provides for a speedy and public trial, the rights to counsel, confrontation of witnesses, and cross-examination in criminal cases. The Seventh Amendment provides for the right to a jury trial in certain cases. The Eighth Amendment forbids the infliction of "cruel and unusual" punishment and also forbids excessive bail.

The Bill of Rights originally was a limitation only against federal power and thus only protected against actions by the federal government and not by the states. Of course, in addition to the Bill of Rights, other amendments have since been added to the Constitution. By means of the Due Process clause of the 14th Amendment—which protects against state action, and a process called the "incorporation" doctrine—almost all the protections of the Bill of Rights now have been deemed applicable to the states as well. These rights, moreover, protect not only natural people but also, though to a lesser degree, artificial legal "persons," such as the corporation and other business entities, as will be seen in the Administrative Law chapter and the Business Organizations chapter.

It must be underscored that these rights, as well as other constitutional rights, are not absolute. The Supreme Court, as final interpreter of the Constitution, thereby gives meaning to these rights and determines the boundaries of these freedoms. For example, freedom of speech, although extremely important in the U.S. legal and political system, is not absolute: Speech can be restrained and even punished when it becomes fraudulent, defamatory, or obscene. The paramount example is that one does not have the freedom "to yell 'fire' in a crowded theatre," as the famous old saying holds.

"State Action"

"State action" encompasses the actions of the legislative, executive, and judicial branches as well as administrative agencies at the federal, state, and local government levels or the subdivisions thereof. The language of the Fifth and 14th Amendments, as well as the Bill of Rights, is applicable only to state action, which means that these core federal constitutional provisions only protect against and restrict government action but not the acts of private parties and businesses. In effect, one can assert constitutional rights against government entities, but not against private sector entities. Even if a private entity is substantially funded by the government, even if it is very heavily regulated by the government, and even if it is a government-granted monopoly, it characteristically will be deemed as being mere private.

For example, a government employee may be able to argue that his/her discharge from public sector employment was unconstitutional if the discharge was premised on an impermissible restriction on free speech or association, a wrongful infringement on privacy, or an unreasonable search and seizure. However, a private-sector employee cannot ordinarily utilize these constitutional concepts against his or her private sector employer. There is a monumental difference between a government employee criticizing his or her "boss," and a private-sector employee so doing, as the former may lead to a literal "federal case" for the employee to protect his or her job, whereas the private sector employee may find himself summarily discharged without legal recourse.

It should be noted that some state constitutions afford constitutional rights to employees in the private sector. For example, the California state constitution provides for a right to privacy for all employees in the state. The rights, or lack thereof, of private-sector employees will be covered in the Employment Law chapter.

Due Process

The Fifth and 14th Amendments protect against government deprivation of life, liberty, or property without due process of law. These amendments are most often used to provide procedural safeguards, notably adequate notice and a fair hearing, before the government can take any action against a person or a business. (It is critical to note that a corporation is considered a "person" in cases of due process protections.) In addition to procedural due process, there is a body of law called "substantive due process," which the courts theoretically can use to review the substance of legislation. But the modern legal approach of the courts has been to defer to the legislative branches of government and thus to presume that legislation of an economic or social nature—especially government regulation of business—is valid. A discussion of substantive due process, therefore, is beyond the purpose of this book. Procedural due process, however, is an extremely important legal concept which protects "liberty" and "property" interests from being impaired by the government. Procedural due process will be covered in detail in the Administrative Law and Business chapter of this book.

Due Process: Substantive v. Procedural Due Process

The 5th and 14th Amendments protect against government deprivation of life, liberty, or property without *due process of law*. These amendments are most often used to provide procedural safeguards, notably adequate notice and a fair hearing, before government can take any action against a person or a business. It is critical to note that a corporation is considered a "person" for due process protections. In addition to procedural due process, there is a body of law called "substantive due process," which the courts theoretically can use to review the substance of legislation, but the modern legal approach of the courts has been to defer to the legislative branches of government, and thus to presume that legislation of an economic or social nature, especially government regulation of business, is valid so long as the legislation rationally relates to a legitimate government purpose. However, if government legislation infringes a "fundamental right," such as the voting, interstate travel, marriage, family, and/or First Amendment rights, then substantive due process would require that government have a "compelling government interest" to infringe on such rights. Yet in modern times most situations involving fundamental rights have been handled by the courts using the Equal Protection clause.

Procedural due process is an extremely important legal concept which protects "life," "liberty," and "property" interests from being impaired by the government. Due process in essence means that the process which the government uses to deprive a person (including a corporate "person") of life, liberty, or property (for example, in the latter corporate situation, to fine the business for violating a regulatory law), must be a fair process. Fairness entails the government giving adequate notice to a person that it is going to take some adverse action and then providing a person with a fair hearing before an objective decision-maker. At the hearing the government must demonstrate that it has sufficient reasons—constitutionally, legally, and factually—to deprive a person of a liberty or property interest. The Due Process clause, moreover, has also been interpreted by the courts to require that statutes be reasonably definite and precise and not vague or overbroad. The Due Process clause, finally, has been interpreted to put limits on punitive damage awards (designed to punish and deter wrongdoing, such as an intentional tort or deceit). To illustrate, in one case, *BMW of North America v. Gore* (1996), the Supreme Court overturned a $4 million dollar punitive damage, premised on a $4000 compensatory award judgment, in a civil case for the fraudulent repainting of a car due to some minor pre-delivery damage. Later, the Supreme Court provided some guidance as to what Due Process permits for punitive damage awards. In the case of *State Farm v. Campbell* (2003), the Court indicated that a 4 to 1 ratio between punitive and compensatory damages, though not "binding," was nonetheless "instructive" for Due Process limitations.

Equal Protection

The 14th Amendment to the Constitution holds that no state can deny a person equal protection of the laws. "Person," for equal protection purposes, also includes the artificial legal person—that is, the corporation. Initially, it must be pointed out that the Equal Protection clause in the 14th Amendment only limits the actions of the states; there surprisingly is no similar provision in the U.S. Constitution applicable to the federal government. However, the Due Process clause in the Fifth Amendment, which does apply to the federal government, has been interpreted by the courts as including an "equal protection" guarantee from federal government interference.

To classify is to discriminate, though in a more euphemistic sense. But all statutes and regulations to some degree classify people and businesses. For example, in the tax code there are different rates for different incomes. However, in order to pass the equal protection test, such classifications must be legally permissible. For most laws that regulate business, the courts use a "rational basis" standard to determine the constitutionality of a regulatory law. That is, a government classification need only have a reasonable and rational relationship to the achievement of a legitimate and proper government interest or purpose in order to pass equal protection assessment. For certain other classifications, such as gender, age, and legitimacy, there is an intermediate standard of review, and thus these types of classifications will be upheld if they are substantially related to important government interests. However, certain other government classifications involving "suspect categories"—such as classifications based on race, color, or national origin, or those that burden "fundamental rights," such as freedom of speech and the right to privacy—must pass a much more rigid legal test, called "strict scrutiny." Pursuant to this demanding legal test, such a government classification would violate the equal protection guarantee unless the classification is found to be necessary to a compelling government interest.

Recently, the U.S. Supreme Court made two very important equal protection decisions dealing with the race-based affirmative action programs at the University of Michigan undergraduate and law schools. Although these decisions are based on "state action" and involve the educational sector, they are predicted to cause material consequences to private-sector affirmative action programs in employment.

Equal Protection and Gay Marriage

The 14th Amendment to the Constitutional also holds that no state can deny a person *equal protection of the laws*. "Person" for equal protection purposes also includes the artificial legal person, that is, the corporation. Initially, it must be pointed out that the Equal Protection clause in the 14th amendment only limits the actions of the states; there surprisingly is no similar provision in the U.S. Constitution applicable to the federal government. However, the Due Process clause in the 5th Amendment, which does apply to the federal government, has been interpreted by the courts as including an "equal protection" guarantee from federal government interference.

All statutes and regulations to some degree classify people and businesses, for example, in the tax code there are different rates for different incomes. To classify is to discriminate, though in a more euphemistic sense. However, in order to pass the equal protection test, these classifications must be legally permissible. For most laws that regulate business, the courts use a "rational basis" standard to determine the constitutionality of a regulatory law. That is, a government classification need only have a reasonable and rational relationship to the achievement of a legitimate and proper government interest or purpose in order to pass equal protection assessment. For certain other classifications, such as gender, age, and legitimacy, there is an intermediate standard of review, and thus these types of classifications will be upheld if they are substantially related to important government interests. However, certain other government classifications involving "suspect categories," such as classifications based on race, color, or national origin, or those that burden "fundamental rights," such as freedom of speech and the right to privacy, must pass a much more rigid legal test, called "strict scrutiny." Pursuant to this demanding legal test, such a government classification will violate the equal protection guarantee unless the classification is found to be necessary to a compelling government interest.

In 2013, the Supreme Court enunciated two major decisions dealing with gay marriage. In the first, *United States v. Windsor* (2013), the Court struck down on 5th Amendment Due Process and Equal Protection grounds the key provision in the federal Defense of Marriage Act (DOMA) which recognized marriage as solely between a man and a woman and consequently denied federal benefits to married gay couples who were validly married in states which recognize gay marriage (12 states as of the writing of this latest Edition). Justice Anthony Kennedy, writing for a 5-4 majority, stated that DOMA infringed on gay married couples' "liberty" interest protected by the Due Process clause as well as disparaged, demeaned, and harmed them for no legitimate purpose in contravention of the Equal Protection clause. The decision means that as far as federal rights and benefits (for example, tax, social security, and immigration) are concerned, federal law must treat same-sex marriages the same as traditional marriages, assuming, of course, a gay couple has a valid marriage in a state that recognizes gay marriage. The case was a major victor for gay rights. However, the second Supreme Court holding, in *Hollingsworth v. Perry* (2013), was a much more narrow one, decided on procedural grounds; and was not the sweeping decision outlawing bans on gay marriage that gay rights advocates had wanted and hoped for. In the case, the Supreme Court dismissed an appeal on technical "standing" grounds challenging a lower federal court decision that invalidated on constitutional grounds a California law, in the form of a voter referendum, which banned gay marriage in the state. By dismissing the appeal, the Court let stand the decision of the federal district court which struck down the law. The result means that gay couples can now be legally married in California; but the Court decision just affected that one state. The decision did not adversely affect bans on gay marriage in other states; and thus the result will be to expect more challenges on federal constitutional grounds to other states' bans on gay marriage.

Equal Protection and Affirmative Action

The term "affirmative action" represents a wide variety of programs, from one extreme of setting rigid, fixed job quotas that must be filled by women and minority group members, to the other most "mild" extreme of taking special proactive efforts to ensure that women and minority group members are included in the pool of applicants for hiring or promotion. Almost everyone morally condemns the former and morally approves the latter. In the middle, however, is the type of affirmative action plan that takes race, ethnic heritage, or sex into account when selecting among qualified candidates and that gives such individuals a preference over equally or more qualified white men. Such a preference plan raises a loud emotional outcry, from those who praise it as just redress for past discrimination and stereotyping, to those who condemn it as immoral "reverse discrimination."

The United States Supreme Court, in a very significant affirmative action decision in 2003, permitted the use of race as a preference factor in the college admissions process; but the court also issued a stern warning that colleges cannot use rigid affirmative action systems that resemble quotas, and that they also must adopt race neutral policies as soon as practicable. Justice Sandra Day O'Connor, writing for a 5-4 court majority, stated that the University of Michigan Law

School did not violate the "equal protection" guarantee of the 14th Amendment to the Constitution. Significantly, Justice Sandra Day O'Connor stated that the goal of creating a diverse student body was a sufficiently "compelling government interest" to justify the law school's consideration of race as a "beneficial" admissions factor. She added, however, that race-conscious admissions policies should not go on forever. Twenty-five years from now, Justice O'Connor stated, the court would expect that racial preferences will no longer be necessary.

The University of Michigan's undergraduate admissions policy—a point system that quantified the importance of race—did not survive the Court's scrutiny in another companion case. In that case, Chief Justice William Rehnquist, writing for a 6-3 majority, stated the numerical policy made race the decisive factor in admissions decisions, and thus was unconstitutional. Justice Clarence Thomas, the court's only black member, issued a bitter condemnation of affirmative action as a well-intended but patronizing and ultimately discriminatory attempt by whites to help African Americans. Thomas' dissent began with a quote from an address by Frederick Douglas criticizing abolitionists in 1865 for interfering with blacks' efforts to help themselves. Thomas stated that he believes that blacks can achieve success "without the meddling of university administrators." He declared that a state's use of racial discrimination in higher education admissions is categorically prohibited by the Equal Protection Clause of the Constitution.

In the majority opinion in the law school case, Justice O'Connor rejected the argument of the Bush administration that race-neutral alternatives could be as effective in creating diversity as affirmative action. The Constitution, said Justice O'Connor, does not prevent the law school's "narrowly tailored" use of race in admission decisions in order to achieve a compelling interest in obtaining educational benefits that are produced from a diverse student body. The Michigan law school uses race as a potential "plus" factor to promote diversity, stated Justice O'Connor. The goal of the law school's affirmative action policy was to produce a "critical mass" of minority students on campus. She supported the decision by citing studies showing that diversity promotes learning outcomes and better prepares students for an increasingly diverse workforce, for society, and for the legal professions. Diversity is necessary, she maintained, for developing leaders with "legitimacy" in the judgment of the people. Moreover, she stated that effective participation by members of all racial and ethnic groups in the civic life of the nation is critical if the U.S. truly will achieve the goal of being one "indivisible" nation. She emphasized, in addition, that businesses have made it clear that the skills and knowledge essential in today's increasingly global marketplace can only be created through contact and experience with widely diverse peoples, cultures, ideas, and views.

U.S. Solicitor General Theodore Olsen, however, condemned the Michigan policies as a "thinly disguised quota." Some critics contended that the decisions mean that universities can still racially discriminate so long as they are not obvious about it. Civil rights advocates, however, hailed the decision as a major victory and claimed it not only strengthened affirmative action in a college setting, but also gives added impetus to the use of race in pursuit of diversity elsewhere, especially in employment.

The University of Michigan's president, Mary Sue Coleman, said she was delighted by the decision because the principle of diversity was upheld, and she stated the school would fix its undergraduate policy so that it is not construed as a mechanical quota-based system. Unlike the law school, the undergraduate school awards a specific, predetermined number of points to applicants whose ethnicity or race is underrepresented on campus, specifically a 20-point bonus on a 150-point scale where 100 points guaranteed an admission. The majority of the Court found that this resembled a quota system, a practice previously struck down as unconstitutional. The undergraduate decision also could cause employers to rethink their reliance on quantitative evaluations of job applicants and employees. While the law school decision does allow colleges to consider race as a preferential factor in making decisions, the court made clear that diversity should not be defined solely in terms of race and ethnicity. Universities, therefore, will have to look more broadly at socio-economic factors, special talents and life circumstances, such as family background and income and education levels, in searching for a diverse student body. Justice O'Connor required that universities now must give applicants a personal "holistic" look. The Supreme Court's University of Michigan affirmative action cases in 2003, therefore, emerge as landmark decisions with wide-ranging implications not only for education but also for business and for society as a whole, especially so because the use of race has been upheld legally as a permissible component to an affirmative action preference plan.

The very difficult and contentious issue of affirmative action again reached the U.S. Supreme Court, and also once again in the context of education. In 2006, the Supreme Court heard arguments in a secondary school desegregation case in which two school boards, one in Seattle, Washington, and the other in Louisville, Kentucky, were attempting to preserve voluntarily imposed race-based integration plans. The school board plans were controversial because race was used as a factor to assign students to schools in order to achieve more racially diverse schools. The school districts contended that racial integration is an essential component to a public school education; and that such an objective is a compelling government interest so as to justify a limited use of race in implementing policies that produce integrated schools. The parents that challenged the race-based school assignment plans contended that the Equal Protection clause of the 14th Amendment to the U.S. Constitution as interpreted by the Court forbids any consideration of race in school enrollment decisions. However, proponents of the plan said that the limited use of race is necessary to redress the legacy of racism and school segregation in the United States. Moreover, proponents argued that there are positive benefits for the students and ultimately for society as a whole for students to attend racially diverse schools. Achieving a diverse student body, one recalls, was deemed to be a sufficiently "compelling" interest for the Court to uphold the University of Michigan's law school's affirmative action policy in which race was allowed to be used as one "plus" factor in an otherwise "holistic" evaluation of a candidate for admission. In the Seattle case, involving a city, it is important to note, which never imposed official segregation, students are allowed to enroll in any of ten high schools. However, if a particular high school has more applicants than seats, school official are empowered to use several tie-breaking factors, including race, in order to achieve an enrollment that approximately reflects the city-wide student population. In Seattle, whites account for 40% of the population, with blacks, Hispanics, Asians, and Native Americans accounting for the other 60%. In the Louisville case, the city once had a legally imposed dual, "separate but equal," school system, in which certain schools were reserved for whites and others for blacks. As a result of civil rights litigation, a federal court in 1975 imposed the remedy of mandatory busing in order to achieve integration of the schools. However, in 2000, a federal judge dissolved the desegregation order, finding that the schools had been successfully integrated. In order to maintain integrated schools, school officials in Louisville decided to continue the desegregation policy, which seeks to keep black enrollment in each school between 15% and 50%. A parent whose child was denied admission to neighborhood schools because the child's enrollment would have an adverse effect on desegregation sued because her child was assigned to a school impermissibly due to the child's race.

Even the initial questions and comments by the Justices of the Supreme Court reflected the conservative-liberal dichotomy to the Court. For example, the "liberal" members talked in terms of the benefits of diversity and emphasized the need and desirability of local school officials to develop policies that use race to achieve diversity in school composition. Whereas the "conservative" members asserted that despite the laudable benefits of integration and diversity, the means used to attain these "good" ends must be race neutral, non-discriminatory, and thus moral ones. Of course, the key vote in, as well as author of, the Michigan law school, 5-4, decision, Justice Sandra Day O'Connor, was no longer on the

Court. The key vote, according to legal experts, was Justice Anthony Kennedy, who appears to be very reticent about using race as the classifying factor in admissions decisions. Although it is always difficult to predict the Court, many legal experts nonetheless expected that the Court would enunciate a "split decision" as in the precedent Michigan case. That is, the Court would most likely strike down the Louisville plan since race is the sole factor in assigning students; but uphold the Seattle plan where race is used as "merely" one factor, granted a potential "tipping" one, among a variety of criteria employed to determine school assignments. However, in 2007, the Supreme Court, in a surprising, momentous, landmark, and very close 5-4 decision, struck down *both* the Louisville and Seattle affirmative plans as unconstitutional. Chief Justice John G. Roberts, Jr., writing for the majority, declared that the two school districts had failed to meet their "heavy burden" of justifying the "extreme means" the districts had chosen to classify children by means of their race when making school assignments. Chief Justice Roberts very succinctly explained the Court's reasoning: "The way to stop discrimination on the basis of race is to stop discriminating on the basis of race." Yet the decision may not entirely eliminate the use of race as a factor in making educational decisions. Justice Kennedy, joining the majority, but also writing a concurring opinion, opined that there might be some "narrow circumstances" that would allow the use of race as a criterion in education. Justice Kennedy also declared that "This nation has a moral and ethical obligation to fulfill its historic commitment to creating an integrated society that ensures equal opportunity for all of its children." Nevertheless, the decision very likely will force educational institutions to devise race-neutral criteria, such as socio-economic factors, in designing affirmative policies and plans. As a matter of fact, in the majority opinion, Chief Justice Roberts stated that other means aside from race should be used to promote diversity in schools. Everyone seems to agree that classroom diversity is a very important educational objective, but how to achieve it fairly and constitutionally is emerging as a daunting challenge—legally, morally, and practically.

In 2013, the Supreme Court again tackled the difficult and contentious issue of affirmative action—and again in the context of education. The case, *Fisher v. University of Texas* (2013), dealt with the Texas affirmative action policy of offering admission to the "flagship" Austin campus of the University of Texas to any high school graduate in the top ten percent of his or her high school graduating class in the state. One high school student, a white female, who was not in the top ten percent in her school, was denied admission to the University of Texas at Austin. She claimed that she had higher SAT and GRE scores than black students admitted pursuant to the "ten percent" rule, and thus she contended that she had been discriminated against because of her race in violation of the 14th Amendment to the United States Constitution. The Supreme Court was expected to enunciate a "sweeping" decision, either upholding or striking down affirmative action. However, the Court enunciated a compromise decision. The Court in a 7-1 decision did not invalidate affirmative action. But the Court, with Justice Anthony Kennedy writing for the majority, made it much more difficult for a university (and other entities) to legally sustain an affirmative action program. The Court held that affirmative action programs that have a race component must undergo the rigid legal test of "strict scrutiny." Strict scrutiny, in essence, in the context of affirmative action in education, has three main components: first, the university must demonstrate that having a diverse student body is a "compelling government interest" for an affirmative action admissions program with a race factor; second, the university must show that its admissions program is tailored narrowly to obtain the educational benefits of diversity; and third, the university must show that there is no other practical race-neutral alternative that would produce the same educational benefits of diversity. The Supreme Court then sent the case back to the lower federal courts to determine if the University of Texas "passed" this "strict scrutiny" test. Supporters of affirmative action in education and other areas were naturally pleased the Supreme Court did not totally invalidate affirmative action, but were concerned that the practical result of such a demanding legal standard would jeopardize affirmative action programs. One thing is sure, though, and that is to expect more affirmative action lawsuits in education and other areas.

Freedom of Speech, Press, and Association

The First Amendment to the U.S. Constitution states that "Congress shall make no law…abridging the freedom of speech, or of the press, or of the right of the people to peaceably assemble, and to petition the government for a redress of grievances." The First Amendment has been interpreted to encompass the freedom to associate and not to associate and also to protect the privacy of one's associations. Actions taken to communicate an idea, designated as "symbolic conduct," are also afforded protection. Free speech rights, in addition, have been extended to the Internet by the U.S. Supreme Court. These rights, one will recall, are also applicable to the states by means of the 14th Amendment Due Process clause.

Yet these First Amendment freedoms are not absolute. As a general rule, the government may prohibit and punish speech that produces such negative consequences for society as to outweigh the value of the speech. These include obscene speech, child pornography, or defamatory speech. Regarding the last example, when the "victim" of the defamation is a public official and the defamation regards his or her public duties or official conduct, the courts require as part of "free speech" protections that a showing of "malice" be made. That is, the public official suing for defamation is required to show, by clear and convincing evidence, that the defendant published the defamatory statement knowing it to be false or with reckless disregard of its truth or falsity. This burdensome malice requirement also applies to public figures—famous people in the community—who also seek to sue for defamation.

The courts, therefore, are very protective of speech and plainly recognize the importance of free speech rights in a democracy such as the United States. Nonetheless, if the government interest in restricting speech is sufficiently strong and the restriction on speech is narrowly tailored so as not to "chill" permissible speech, then the courts will uphold the infringement on speech.

Freedom of Speech—Symbolic Speech

Actions, gestures, expressions, as well as articles of apparel, taken or used to communicate an idea, which are designated as "symbolic conduct" or "symbolic speech," are also afforded protection under the 1st Amendment, including the burning of the U.S. flag. Moreover, even offensive, vile, and hateful speech is protected. To illustrate, the Supreme Court ruled in 2011 in *Synder v. Phelps* that a Baptist church had the free speech right to picket and protest against homosexuality and other American "sins," including displaying posters that stated "Thank God for dead soldiers" and "God hates fags," at the funeral of a soldier killed in the Iraq war. It is important to point out that the Court underscored that the protest addressed matters of public concern, the protest was peaceful, and the protest occurred in a public place, on a public street, at a distance from the funeral (approximately 1000 feet as specified by the police). Moreover, the protest did not interfere with the funeral; and the fact that the content of the message was very distressing and caused emotional distress was irrelevant—at least for 1st Amendment purposes. The *Synder* case also illustrates the critical distinction the courts make between the "content" versus the "context" of speech. As emphasized, the content can be hateful; but the government cannot punish people for what they say; yet the government can control in the interests of public safety and welfare the "context" of speech, that is, where, when, and how people exercise their free speech rights.

Freedom of Speech—Supreme Court Corporate Free Speech Decision

The U.S. Supreme Court in 2010 made a very significant decision regarding free speech and business in the case of Citizens *United v. Federal Election Commission.*

The court, in a 5-4 determination, substantially overturned campaign finance laws to the benefit of corporations. The ruling reverses a long-standing limitation on corporate money into federal elections by allowing businesses as well as labor unions to spend money—and as much as they want—directly to support a candidate or to oppose a candidate on television or by means of other media or literature, so long as the contribution is independent of the candidate and the campaign. That is, the decision, though broad in scope, leaves in place the prohibition on direct contributions to candidates from corporations and unions. A corporation long as been considered a "person" under the law for many rights, including most constitutional rights; but there had been restrictions on a corporations' exercise of political free speech rights. Supporters of the decision long have argued that the prohibitions were an unconstitutional infringement on free speech; and accordingly they claim the court's decision is a major victory for First Amendment free speech rights. The decision even allows union and corporation political advertisements in the closing days of an election. Critics countered by saying the decision will give "big business" too much power and influence in political campaigns. Justice Anthony M. Kennedy, writing for the majority, stated that the First Amendment prohibits Congress from punishing citizens or associations of citizens from engaging in political speech. The decision could result in millions of dollars flowing into elections now in the United States from corporations and labor unions, especially for television advertising. Candidates also will not be able to stop corporations and unions from running ads. Yet, a candidate who is short on money may appreciate corporate or union support. Corporations and unions now can spend as much as they want to advance or defeat political candidates, and they can do so by name, in advertising, commercials, and literature; but there can be no coordination with the candidates or their campaigns. One thing for sure, and that is that voters will now be getting a lot more information about candidates on which to base a voting decision. The "marketplace for ideas" created and sustained by the First Amendment has certainly been broadened and increased. Of course, more campaign ads also may mean more "negative ads" as well as a greater potential for more "voter burn-out" over ads. Regardless, the media, especially television and radio stations, should see substantial financial gains as a result of the court's decision. Furthermore, shareholders of corporations as well as members of labor unions should now pay much closer attention as to how these entities spend their money on political campaigns and candidates.

Freedom of Speech—Supreme Court Violent Video Games Decision
Violent video games have given rise to a major legal and ethical controversy between supporters of First Amendment rights to free speech and free

expression and government efforts to protect young people from the alleged harmful effects of violent video games. Critics of violent video games contend that they appeal to the deviant interests of children, but the key legal question is whether these games are protected by the First Amendment to the Constitution. In California, in 2005, the legislature promulgated a law that bans people under the age of 18 from buying or renting violent video games that appeal to "a deviant or morbid interest in minors." The California legislature based the law on findings that violent video games stimulate "feelings of aggression" and promote "anti-social or aggressive behavior." Yet, in 2011, the U.S. Supreme Court in a 7-2 decision, in the case of *Brown v. Entertainment Merchants Association*, struck down the California law as an unconstitutional infringement on the First Amendment to the U.S. Constitution. Justice Scalia, who wrote the majority opinion, stated that even when the objective of government is to protect children, the protections of the First Amendment still are applicable. He explained that the viewing of videogames is essentially the same as reading books or viewing plays and movies. Games, he said, like books, communicate ideas and social messages, and they have many familiar literary devices, such as characters, dialogue, plot, and music, in addition to features that are distinct to the game medium, such as the player's interaction with the "virtual" world. Justice Scalia also added that depictions of violence have never been subject to government regulation. He mentioned Grimm's fairy tales and Saturday morning cartoons as examples of violence depicted in the media. The Supreme Court, as well as other federal courts, have not treated violent content the same as sexual material, which government can restrict or punish notwithstanding the First Amendment if the material is obscene. Justice Scalia explicitly stated that speech about violence is not obscene.

Freedom of Speech—Political Speech v. Commercial Speech

The First Amendment grants the most extensive protection to "political speech," which is speech regarding politics, political candidates, elections, and public affairs issues such as immigration reform. For example, one federal court of appeals ruled that doctors have the First Amendment right to recommend marijuana to sick patients, and the patients have the equivalent right to receive such information. Thus, the federal government's attempt to revoke the doctors' prescription licenses was unconstitutional.

Moreover, even if hateful and false, political speech is protected. The "antidote" for false political speech is true political speech, and thus emerges the "battle of ideas" in a democracy such as the United States, where rational and free debate on the issues serves the public interest. The motivation behind political speech thus is to advance a particular political or public affairs agenda. Even if the political speech is advocated by a corporation—which, although an artificial legal person, is nonetheless a constitutional "person"—the political corporate speech is fully protected. So this type of speech is regarded as a fundamental right, and as such can only be restricted or punished if the government has a compelling government interest such as, for example, to prevent an imminent riot or violence.

"Commercial speech" consists of business marketing and advertising activities. The motivation behind commercial speech is monetary and economic with the primary objective being to propose and consummate a commercial transaction. Yet commercial speech is still speech and, accordingly, is also protected by the First Amendment.

Because the public does have a "right to know," consumers do have a legitimate interest in the free flow of commercial information, which is deemed necessary for the consumer to make a well-informed economic decision. For example, statutes prohibiting licensed pharmacists from advertising, preventing attorneys from advertising (even for lawsuits), or prohibiting ads for birth control and abortion have all been struck down as violating free "commercial" speech rights. Even local prohibitions against "for sale" signs on property in residential areas have been struck down. Accordingly, the Supreme Court has given a very high degree of protection to safeguarding "mere" commercial speech.

Pursuant to the Do-Not-Call Implementation Act passed by Congress in 2003, the Federal Trade Commission created a Do-Not-Call List which is a registry of names of persons not wanting to receive telemarketing calls. Companies cannot make unsolicited phone calls to consumers hoe place their names on the registry unless the companies have done business with the consumer in the recent past. This law was challenged on constitutional grounds as an infringement of the companies' First Amendment commercial speech rights. However, the federal courts have ruled that the FTC's regulations were not unconstitutional restrictions on commercial speech because they furthered substantial government interests by protecting personal privacy and reducing the amount of telemarketing abuse.

The line between political speech and commercial speech, however, is at times very difficult to discern. In one recent case, Nike Corporation was sued under a California consumer-protection statute for its allegedly deceptive advertising. In defending itself against accusations of exploiting its workers in Asia, the company's representatives were not entirely accurate as to the benefits the company provided to its workers. The consumer group thus sued the company for its misleading defense, which it claimed violated the state truth-in-advertising law. Because its speech dealt with a topic of global business concern, Nike defended itself by contending that its speech was in fact "political," and thus it did not have to be entirely accurate or, for that matter, could even be outright false. The California consumer group argued that the speech was "only" commercial in nature since the motivation behind Nike's defensive commentary was purely from an economic standpoint. The case went to the California supreme court which ruled, in a split 4–3 decision, that Nike's efforts to defend itself before critics of its labor practices overseas amounted to commercial speech and thus the company could in fact be sued for its deceptive advertising under California law. (In other words, in order to be constitutionally protected, commercial speech must be true and nondeceptive.) The case was appealed by Nike to the U.S. Supreme Court which granted a hearing and then, while oral arguments were in process, unexpectedly and very surprisingly decided not to decide the case. The decision of the state court was thus left standing and, as a result, Nike eventually settled with the consumer group for $1.5 million. Many people in the legal and business communities were very disappointed in the Supreme Court's action, or lack thereof, as the court was expected to use the case to more clearly define the line between political and commercial speech.

Nevertheless, once commercial speech is established, it plainly can be regulated more extensively than can "pure" political speech. There are two basic requirements in order for commercial speech to be constitutionally protected: First, the speech must concern a legal transaction and legal subject matter; and second, the speech cannot be false, deceptive, or misleading. However, even if lawful and true, commercial speech can still be regulated by government if: 1) government has a rational and substantial interest in restricting the speech; 2) the restriction directly advances the government interest; and 3) the restriction is narrowly tailored and thus is not more extensive than necessary to serve the government's interest.

The key component to the preceding legal tests is what exactly constitutes a "substantial" government interest. In the past, the Supreme Court had upheld a Puerto Rican law prohibiting any advertising of casino gambling aimed at residents, as opposed to tourists, due to a substantial (and paternalistic) government interest in protecting the residents of the Commonwealth from the "evils" and "vice" of gambling. However, the U.S. Supreme Court, in a series of recent commercial speech cases, has abandoned its paternalistic approach to formulating a substantial government interest, and has thereby greatly increased the type and content of mere commercial speech protected by the First Amendment.

The leading Supreme Court commercial speech case was the seminal 1996 unanimous decision of *44 Liquormart*, Inc. v. Rhode Island. In the *Liquormart* case, the Court struck down a state ban on advertising the prices for liquor and alcoholic beverages. The rationale of the Rhode Island legislature was paternalistic and benevolent: the protection of the "good people" of the state of

Rhode Island from the "evils" of "demon rum." The idea was that price advertising would lead to competitive price wars, thereby lowering the price of liquor and alcoholic beverages and thus making them more affordable to the citizens and residents of that state. This reasoning is called the "vice doctrine," which had also been used as an adequate rationale in the Puerto Rican gambling case.

The decision in Rhode Island severely curtailed the government's power to restrict truthful and nondeceptive advertising and marketing. Now, according to the U.S. Supreme Court, government no longer has the broad discretion to suppress truthful and nondeceptive commercial speech, even for paternalistic purposes. Adults now must have the ability to receive information on legal products and services, even if traditionally they are branded as vices and have a high potential for abuse. Thanks to the Court, this effectively means that, to coin a phrase, an individual can "find one's way to heaven, or one can find one's way to hell." Government is no longer responsible for acting as the consumer's mother, father, or big brother.

Restricting speech about vice is thus viewed as being more dangerous than actually restricting the vice activity itself. Obviously, it is now much more difficult for the government to set limits on how business markets, promotes, and advertises its products. The *44 Liquormart* case definitely set a precedent because soon thereafter, in 1999, the U.S. Supreme Court ruled unanimously in Greater *New Orleans Broadcasting Association v. United States* that private casinos now are legally entitled to advertise gambling activities on television and radio. The court declared that advertising of the lawful service of gambling—or "gaming," as its supporters prefer—is constitutionally protected commercial speech even if it is regarded by many as a vice.

Despite this wider scope that the Court has granted to the meaning of commercial speech, it must be emphasized that if the marketing of an adult "vice" product or activity is aimed at children, then government legitimately can act as the "parent" and thereby protect children from these adult activities and products. Protecting the child thus emerges as a substantial government interest, which will allow government to prohibit and punish certain types of commercial speech, which is why the Joe Camel cartoon-like cigarette advertising campaign has become part of advertising history. However, the once voluntary advertising ban of liquor advertising on television is also history as a result of the *44 Liquormart* case.

Both Supreme Court commercial speech "vice" decisions also have enormous implications for the regulation of tobacco, a legal product which is even more controversial than consuming liquor and gambling. And it remains to be seen what will happen, commercially as well as legally, to such new and novel products as "sweet cigarettes," beer-flavored ice cream, and beer-flavored popsicles.

Freedom of Religion

In the First Amendment, there actually are two separate and distinct religion clauses. One is called the Establishment Clause, which prevents the government from establishing a "state religion" or from preferring one religion over another. The second is called the Free Exercise Clause, which prevents the government from interfering with the free exercise of religion.

The government in the United States is supposed to be neutral towards religion, though there are many ways in which government can indirectly, and thus legally, support religion. This includes such seemingly innocuous actions as providing health tests and vaccinations to parochial school children. Awarding monetary vouchers to the parents of children to be used for tuition in any local school, including religious schools, is another matter, and that contentious issue is still a matter of legal controversy. (However, there is a leading Supreme Court decision upholding a voucher program for inner-city residents.) The explication of the "establishment" legal area, however, is beyond the purpose of this book.

Finally, as with free speech, freedom of religion is not an absolute right. For instance, the Mormons in Utah cannot legally practice polygamy, even if it is sanctioned by their religious beliefs, just as Cubans in Miami legally *cannot* sacrifice chickens and goats as part of their Afro-Caribbean Santeria religion. Freedom of religion also emerges as an important and at times perplexing legal issue in an employment setting. An employer legally cannot discriminate against an employee based on the employee's religion and the employer also must make a reasonable accommodation for the employee's religious beliefs. This significant legal area and its applications to business are premised not on the federal constitution but rather on the federal Civil Rights Act. Therefore, it will be covered in the Employment Law chapter.

The Second Amendment and the Right to Bear Arms

The 2nd Amendment to the Constitution guarantees the right to bear arms. However, the specific wording of the amendment has caused controversy as to whether this right is an individual or collective right. The 2nd amendment specifically says: "A well-regulated Militia, being necessary to the security of a free State, the right of the people to keep and bear Arms, shall not be infringed." A "liberal" reading of this language would construe the right to bear arms as a collective one, that is, done through and by means of a government created and controlled militia. However, a "conservative" reading of the 2nd Amendment would construe the right as an individual one, that is, every individual American has the fundamental right to own a gun. To date, in a recent series of cases, the U.S. Supreme Court has tended to the conservative interpretation. In the 2008 case of *District of Columbia v. Dick Anthony Heller*, the Court struck down a Washington, D.C. gun ban that effectively prohibited handgun possession, ruling that individuals have a constitutional right to keep loaded arms for their self-defense, at least in their homes; and then in the 2010 case of *McDonald v. Chicago*, the Court extended its ruling to all states and municipalities. However, in the *Heller* case the Court also said that "reasonable" gun regulations could be constitutionally permissible, that is, regulations designed to prohibit the possession of firearms by felons or the mentally ill, as well as laws forbidding the carrying of firearms in sensitive places, such as schools and government buildings, and regulations imposing conditions and qualifications on the commercial sale of guns, for example, expanded background checks which the U.S. Congress is debating at the writing of this book. The Supreme Court is also expected to decide whether to take up another important 2nd Amendment case, dealing with the right to carry arms beyond the home. New York and other states have laws that impose stringent conditions on obtaining licenses to carry concealed weapons in public. The New York law, for example, requires people who want a permit to carry a gun in public to show that they have a special need for self-protection. The high court in New York has upheld the state law; and New York gun owners have appealed to the U.S. Supreme Court. Similarly, Maryland will not issue concealed-carry permits unless a person can show a "good or substantial reason" why he or she needs to carry a gun in public. These laws are being challenged as contravening the 2nd Amendment. Consequently, if the Court decides to take the New York case, the Supreme Court's decision will emerge as another landmark 2nd Amendment decision since the Court would rule on how far the constitutional right to gun possession extends beyond one's home.

The Fourth Amendment and Business Searches

The 4th Amendment in the Bill of Rights prohibits "unreasonable searches and seizures" by government; and also requires that for a valid search a warrant must be issued based on "probable cause." For example, in 2013 the Supreme Court ruled that the 4th Amendment requires that the police in most circumstances must obtain a warrant before requiring a suspected drunken driver to have blood drawn by means of needle stick. Related to the 4th Amendment is the judicially created *"exclusionary rule,"* which holds that as a matter of due process of law any evidence obtained in violation of the 4th amendment cannot be used against a criminal defendant at trial. As a general rule, a search warrant, issued by a neutral judge or magistrate and not by the police or law enforcement officials, is required in order to have a lawful search by the police; and this warrant must be based on a probable cause, supported by an oath or affirmation. Probable cause means that the law enforcement authorities have sufficient reliable evidence that a reasonable person would be persuaded that a search is justified. The warrant also must be specific, that is, describe in particular what is to be searched and/ or seized; and the search cannot extend beyond the parameters of the warrant, though items in "plain view" can be seized. Whenever a person has a reasonable expectation of privacy as to a place, a warrant will be required. Clearly, searches of homes are protected by the 4th amendment; but what about businesses?

The courts have held that the protections of the 4th amendment also protect places of business from warrantless searches; but also the courts have ruled that the standards for government regulators to inspect a business, for example, to comply with pollution, workplace safety, and zoning laws, are much less stringent than the typical criminal law search warrant that a police or other law enforcement officer needs. The rationale for a lesser standard for business is that government has legitimate regulatory functions to enforce a variety of health, safety, and welfare laws and regulations. To do so means that government regulators need information; and information can be obtained by inspections of businesses among other ways. These agency inspections are governed by the 4th amendment. However, the requirements for obtaining an agency warrant to inspect under the 4th amendment are lenient compared to the criminal law standards. The agency inspector still must get a warrant to inspect a business, but the inspector does not have to point to evidence of a violation or even cite specific reasons. "Probable cause" need not be demonstrated; not even a "reasonable suspicion" of a violation need be shown. All the government agency has to demonstrate is that the its inspections of businesses pertain to the agency's regulatory functions, are necessary to protect the public health, safety, welfare, or morals, and that a period of time has lapsed since the agency's last inspection. Thus, typically, the agency must proceed with a warrant, but the warrant is an administrative law warrant, at times called a *blanket warrant*," under which, for example, certain neighborhoods can be inspected for zoning code violations, or certain types of business can be inspected for worker safety violations. It is thus important to note that people's homes can be inspected by government inspectors, but the purpose is not a criminal law one, but "merely" a regulatory one. There are also exceptional cases where an agency is allowed to inspect without a warrant, such as in the case of a health emergency, or if a business is a "pervasively regulated" one, such as a liquor store, auto reclamation center, gun dealer, or mining business.

The Fifth Amendment and Eminent Domain

The Fifth Amendment to the U.S. Constitution states that private property cannot be taken for public use without just compensation. (This legal protection applies to the states by means of the 14th Amendment and the "incorporation" doctrine.) "Property" is broadly defined to include real or personal property as well as tangible or intangible property. The precise definition of "public use," however, has been so problematic that very recently, the Supreme Court has enunciated a decision that markedly expands its definition. One point that is evident and agreed upon, however, is that the "taking" must be for a "public use." If property is not taken for such a use, it cannot constitutionally be appropriated by the government, even if just compensation is paid. A use is considered public if it is rationally related to some conceivable public purpose; that is, the taking itself serves some social, economic, health, safety, welfare, moral, or aesthetic ends.

A large problem under eminent domain law is to ascertain whether a government action is a taking for which compensation must be paid, or merely a "regulation" pursuant to the state's "police power," for which compensation does not have to be paid. Obviously, if there is a physical appropriation of property—by means of a formal "condemnation" proceeding or permanent physical invasion by imposing a right-of-way easement on private property to benefit the public—then typically there will be a taking. Yet if there is a regulation that forbids any more development of private property—such as an environmental regulation in the vicinity of wetlands—but that same regulation has an adverse economic impact on the value of the property to its owner, has there been a taking? A reduction in the economic value of a property is inherent in any government regulatory scheme: For example zoning ordinances, which typically are upheld. Yet if the government regulation puts an unduly harsh burden on an individual property owner, thereby frustrating his or her reasonable investment expectations for the property and leaving him or her with no realistic economic alternatives and without corresponding widespread public benefit, the courts may say that a taking has occurred. Of course, government can still achieve its regulatory aims, but it will now have to pay for them. But what should be paid? "Just compensation" must be paid if there is a taking, and this is defined as the fair market value of the property without considering any unique value of the property to its owner.

Due Process, naturally, requires adequate notice, a fair hearing, a decision, and an opportunity to appeal that decision when the power of eminent domain is exercised by government. In 2005, a divided U.S. Supreme Court, in the very significant property rights decision of *Kelo v. City of New London, Connecticut*, ruled that local governments can exercise constitutional power of eminent domain to take private property and turn the property over to private developers for economic development, thereby increasing the tax base and/or creating jobs. The decision, though predicated on a Connecticut municipal seizure, has nationwide implications, as will be presented below. Specifically, the Fifth Amendment states that private property shall not be taken for *public use* without just compensation. This case considerably expanded the scope of the

Fifth Amendment, which grants government the power, via eminent domain, to seize property for "public use." Furthermore, the case is significant because historically, government used the power of eminent domain for projects that were clearly "public" in nature: roads, schools, and airports.

All state constitutions have a "public use" requirement for eminent domain. Previously, this public use requirement had been thought to restrict eminent domain to the government taking private property only to create things directly owned or primarily used by the general public, such as bridges, parks, and public buildings. Presently, however, many state and local governments have been using the eminent domain power to take property that was "blighted" or located in a blighted area which a local government wished to redevelop.

In the case of *Kelo v. City of New London, Connecticut*, Susette Kelo and several other homeowners from a New London neighborhood considered to be working class but not blighted, decided to fight eviction from their homes, filing suit after city officials announced plans to raze their homes in favor of a riverfront hotel, condominiums, health club, offices, as well as a pedestrian river walk, all to be developed by a private entity, called the New London Development Corporation. City officials contended that the private developer's plans served a public purpose by increasing economic development, and that the economic growth outweighed the homeowners' private property rights despite the fact that the area to be condemned was not considered a slum. The decision is especially important for areas in which there is little vacant land and where local governments are seeking to redevelop urban areas.

In ruling on the case, the Court, however, emphasized that the states—either via judges or legislatures—can provide as much protection to property owners as they choose and thus put tighter restrictions on politicians who seek to transfer private property from one owner to another. In order to avoid such perceived abuses of private property rights that the Supreme Court may have unleashed in the very significant *Kelo* decision, many state legislatures have taken the initiative to protect private property rights. For example, the Michigan Supreme Court recently decided that economic development is not a valid reason to take property from owners who do not want to sell. Florida is one of more than a dozen states that so far have reformed eminent domain laws as a result of the Supreme Court's momentous decision. In 2006, the Florida legislature passed a bill as well as a constitutional amendment that effectively would prohibit government agencies from using eminent domain to transfer private property from one individual to another (in this case, to private developers). The bill also would make it illegal for government agencies to condemn property merely because it is blighted or slum-ridden. A three-fifths majority vote in both the state Senate and House of Representatives would be required to grant an exemption to this law.

In another state restriction on the expanded local government power of eminent domain, the Ohio Supreme Court ruled unanimously in July of 2006 that a Cincinnati suburb could not constitutionally take private property for a large redevelopment project. The Ohio case involved a city called Norwood, which wanted to seize about 70 homes for a $125-million redevelopment project to build offices, shops, and restaurants in a neighborhood that was regarded as "deteriorating." Though the state court did say that economic factors could be taken into consideration in determining whether a seizure of private property was legal, the economic benefit to government as well as to the local community could not be the only factors to be used to justify the use of eminent domain. Furthermore, the court found that the critical term "deteriorating" was unconstitutionally vague. The state court's opinion, premised on the state constitution, was then diametrically opposed to the federal Supreme Court's decision, which was considered permissible since the federal high court stated that state constitutions could set different (or even higher) standards for property rights.

One point is clear, and that is that the *Kelo* decision will further embolden local governments and private developers to take property for purposes of economic development. As a matter of fact, there has commenced an attempt by a small and very wealthy municipality on Long Island, New York, to seize, by eminent domain, a privately owned golf course to turn into an exclusive "high-end" golf course for people who live within that community and are able to pay the very, very expensive yearly membership fees. The mayor of the community claims that this use of eminent domain would raise the property values in the community, but is such a seizure truly for public use and public benefit?

Impairment of Contractual Obligations

Article I, Section 10, of the U.S. Constitution, called the Contract Clause, provides that no state shall pass any law impairing the obligation of contracts. "Impairment" in this sense means any termination or limitation on the rights and duties to the parties to the contract. It must be emphasized, however, that this impairment provision is only applicable to state legislation and not to decisions by the state courts. Consequently, a state court's overruling of a decision by an earlier state court is permissible even though there may be an adverse effect on either public or private contracts. Moreover, the courts have allowed for contracts to be modified by legislation if to do so is considered to be in the public interest and if the impairment is reasonable. But because the Contract Clause does not apply at the federal level, Congress may enact legislation that adjusts economic interests, including contracts, and may do so retroactively, as long as Congress has a rational public purpose to do so.

Privacy Rights

Significantly, there is no specific guarantee to a right of privacy in the U.S. Constitution. (However, such a right is found in several state constitutions including, for example, the California Constitution.) Nonetheless, at the federal level, a right to privacy has been found by the federal courts derived from the guarantees of principally the First, Fourth, Fifth, and Ninth Amendments to the U.S. Constitution. For example, the U.S. Supreme Court, in a seminal privacy decision, invalidated a Connecticut state law that in essence prohibited the use of contraceptives.

As previously emphasized, the privacy protections in the federal constitution protect against incursions of privacy not only by the government (including government as an employer), but also incursions by the private sector, including private-sector employers. The protection of employees' privacy rights, especially private-sector employees, pursuant to federal and state statutes as well as the common law, will be covered in the Employment Law chapter.

Global Legal Perspectives

The Constitution of the People's Republic of China has a provision stating that the citizens of that country enjoy freedom of speech and press. However, the Chinese government requires that all newspapers and magazines be published by government-owned entities. As of the writing of this book, the Chinese government was investigating the legal relationship between *Rolling Stone* magazine and its local Chinese partner. It is suspected that the Chinese government's investigation was prompted by the cover of the first Chinese issue, which featured the picture of a popular Chinese rock singer whose most famous song is an anthem to the students of the 1989 Tiananmen Square democracy protests. If the relationship with the Chinese partner is deemed illegal, the Hong Kong publisher of *Rolling Stone* could be compelled to stop publishing the magazine altogether.

Mexico and Jamaica: Constitutional Developments

Mexican constitutional law is based on the famous Mexican Constitution of 1917, which is still in effect today. However, certain very important constitutional reforms occurred in 1994, which in particular enhanced the role of the Mexican Supreme Court in the Mexican constitutional order, granting it a new and more powerful role as an arbiter between the Congress and the Presidency.[24] In the past, the Mexican judicial branch, including the Supreme

---

[24] See Zamora and Cossio (2006).

Court, had been, according to two commentators, "captive" to the control of the President. Consequently, the judicial branch never really challenged the President on significant constitutional or legal issues.

In an effort to increase the power and stature of the judiciary, especially the Supreme Court, and to make the judiciary a major player in the development of law and policy in Mexico, significant judicial reforms were adopted in 1994 during the administration of President Ernesto Zedillo. Accordingly, the Supreme Court was restructured, with the bulk of its administrative and disciplinary duties shifting to a new judicial institution called (in English) the Federal Judicial Council. Moreover, and most significantly, the Supreme Court's jurisdiction was modified, enabling it to focus more on constitutional issues. Concomitantly, a new procedural mechanism, called an "action of constitutionality," was created to provide for meaningful legal challenges of government abuses.

These reforms were designed to make the Mexican judiciary more efficient and also to assure the independence of the judicial branch, especially the Supreme Court, from political pressures, thereby bolstering the independence of the courts. The reforms also granted the Supreme Court enhanced powers to arbitrate disputes between the other branches of government and government authorities. An important illustration of the newly enhanced powers of the Supreme Court can be seen in the Court's 2005 decision, which held that former President Luis Echeverria Alvarez, as well as the former Interior Minister and several other government officials, could be tried criminally for the alleged 1971 massacre of dissident protesting students in Mexico City.

In Jamaica,[25] the Rastafarian religion emerged among working-class and peasant black people in the early 1930s, and it has consequently spread worldwide. Jamaica is a parliamentary democracy and is governed under the Constitution of 1962. As a result, the country's people are free to observe their own respective religions, express their views, opinions, and concerns, similar to the privileges people in the United States enjoy. However, Rastafarians and other religious groups continue to face injustices and challenges in the global work environment, even in countries that claim to be "open-minded" or described as "land of the free." Some organizations in Jamaica do not accept Rastafarian employees or, if hired, they tend to be discriminated against for promotions or certain job titles, laregly because most companies do not appreciate the manner in which Rastafarian hair is kept (cutting of hair is prohibited in the Rastafarian religion). Their headwear also is considered inappropriate in certain work settings, notably banks, hotels, and general business offices.

---

[25] Contributed by Simone Maxwell, Nova Southeastern University.

Therefore, are Rastafarians able to truly enjoy freedom of religion in its entirety? Should it be legal for organizations to inhibit their employees from certain hairstyles, dress codes, etc., thus contravening their religious beliefs? These are some of the many factors that should be carefully considered when focusing on business practices from a global legal standpoint.

Italian and Russian Constitutional Reforms

In Italy,[26] significant constitutional reform was effectuated in 2001. The 2001 constitutional reform represented the first major constitutional reform since 1948, the year in which the Italian Constitution was adopted. The Italian Constitution of 1948 established a form of government referred to as the "regional state," which was neither a unitary state nor a federation of component states, but rather a loose federation of autonomous regions. The reforms reshaped the Italian regional state by expanding the powers of the regions and changing the way powers are distributed among the different levels of government. Another rather significant aspect of this reform concerned the legislative power. Pursuant to this reform, the national Parliament can now only legislate on subjects enumerated in the Constitution whereas all remaining topics are within the jurisdiction of the regional parliaments themselves. (There are also concurrent legislative powers among the national government, regions, and states.)

This reform was quite momentous because prior to 2001, the regions were only authorized to approve laws on subjects enumerated in the Constitution. Now the Italian federalist model more closely resembles that of the U.S., where the national (federal) government can only legislate based on its constitutionally granted enumerated powers with the states otherwise possessing the sovereign power to legislate based on their broad, inherent policing power.

In 2006, further potentially momentous constitutional reform was proposed to the Italian citizens. The purposes of the reform now were to strengthen the executive branch, reduce the political instability for which Italy is infamous, and to make the government bureaucracy more responsive. Because centralized powers are more limited than in other Western governments, reforms would have strengthened the premier's powers while also transferring some authority away from Rome to the country's regions and speeding up the legislative process. For example, the reforms would have allowed the premier to dissolve parliament as well as to appoint and fire cabinet members. Other reforms would have transferred health and education functions from the central government to the regions themselves. However, Italian voters, by a 65.5% to 38.5% margin, overwhelmingly rejected the constitutional reforms. One reason for this was

---

[26] See Groppi, Tania, and Scattone, Nicoletta (2006).

perhaps the still-lingering fear of an executive that was too strong, perhaps harkening back to the dictatorship of Benito Mussolini and his World War II-era Fascist regime. This fear is manifested in the fact that Italy has had 61 different governments since World War II.

By contrast, the Russian[27] Constitution of 1993 clearly defined Russia as a federal state, yet one in which the national, central, federal government now is considered the "senior partner" while the country itself is composed of 89 federal components, described in the Constitution as "subjects" of the Russian Federation. The fact that the federal components are called subjects and not "constituent units" of the Federation is quite important. Most of the components are named after a specific geographic territory, while the remaining territories are named after an ethnic group living in certain discrete geographic areas. (The Russian Federation is a very multinational, multiethnic, and multilingual country.) These federal units each offer their own citizenship to Russians, but they have no right of succession. The units vary widely in terms of size and population. The Constitution divides these subjects into six categories: republics, national territories—autonomous and non-autonomous areas—administrative territorial units—regions and territories—and two federal cities, Moscow and St. Petersburg. Moreover, as opposed to the U.S., where all the constituent federal units—in this case, the states—are equal, in Russia, the subjects have varying political statuses.

The Constitution created a very powerful presidential form of government. The President of Russia appoints the Prime Minister, is the head of state, and also represents the Federation, both within the country and in international affairs. The President is also proclaimed as the "guarantor" of the Constitution and of the rights and freedoms of Russian citizens. The President has the right to introduce legislation as well as the power to veto legislation. The President is elected for a four-year term on the basis of universal, equal, and direct voting, which is done by secret ballot. The President can also be re-elected for a second consecutive term. A majority of the electorate must take part in the election and the winner is determined by a simple majority of the votes, which is a requirement the U.S. does not have. Failure to attract the initial majority means a new election must be held and if a candidate does not receive a majority, then there will be a second election between the two candidates who receive the most votes.

The Constitution defines the areas of exclusive federal control, which include the traditional federal powers that the U.S. federal government possesses: national security and defense, foreign policy and foreign relations, and postal service. However, as opposed to the U.S., the exclusive federal powers in Russia also include legislative codes such as the civil and criminal codes as well

---

[27] See Domrin, Alexander N. (2006).

as almost all commercial law. There are also spheres of joint federal-regional jurisdiction, such as control over land and natural resources, public health, social services, listed in the Constitution education, environmental protection, housing, and law enforcement. The Russian Parliament is called the Federal Assembly, which is bicameral and composed of two houses, the State Duma and the Federation Council. The Duma consists of 450 deputies and the Federation Council is composed of 178 members—two from each of the 89 subjects of the Russian Federation—who at times refer to themselves as "senators." The Duma deputies are each elected for a four-year term. The federal units are represented in the Federation Council by two persons, one appointed by the governor and the other elected by the regional legislature. The State Duma must consent to the President's appointment of the Prime Minister, but the Council does not play any role in this process. Also, neither chamber plays any role in presidential appointment of other federal ministers.

Despite the sweeping powers given to the President, there are, as in the U.S., certain checks and balances in place. For example, the Duma and the Council can override a Presidential veto of legislation by a two-thirds vote of both houses. The President can fire the Council of Ministers at his (or her) pleasure. The President also nominates judges for the Supreme Court, the Constitutional Court, as well as the Prosecutor General, but these appointments must be confirmed by the Federation Council.

The subjects of the Russian Federation have complete power in all areas that have not expressly been granted to the federal government. Thus, the subjects have the power to adopt legislation in their areas of exclusive and concurrent jurisdiction, although in the latter case, the legislation cannot contravene federal law—the same federal supremacy principle as in the United States. Ethnic republics, moreover, can adopt their own constitutions. While the Russian language is designated the "official" language of the Russian Federation, each federal unit, a Russian republic, can also adopt its own additional official language alongside Russian. Moreover, the individual republic also can declare itself bilingual or multilingual, and some have already done so. In the U.S., there is no federal official designation of English as the official language, though some states have attempted by referendum to have English declared as the official language for conducting state business.

Constitutional Rights in Turkey[28]

Since the Turkish Republic became a member of the European Human Rights Court (EHRC) in 1952, the EHRC has heard some of the most political and

---

[28] Contributed by Cuneyt Oskal, Nova Southeastern University.

controversial cases involving alleged human right violations by the Turkish Republic. But in 1982, the Turkish Constitution recognized basic human rights, such as the freedom of speech, freedom of the press, religious freedom, freedom of association, the right of assembly, the right to travel, the right to due process of law, privacy, and protection from unwarranted searches and seizures and arbitrary arrests. If an individual claims that his or her human rights have been violated and feels that a Turkish court's decision in the matter is unjust, he or she has two opportunities to challenge the decision. First, that individual may request that the Turkish court reopen and rehear the case. If the victim is still in disagreement with the Turkish court's ruling, the individual can then submit the case to the EHRC for further review. If the EHRC finds that the Turkish Republic violated the individual's human rights, it can then impose pecuniary sanctions on the Turkish Republic.

Management Strategies

Each country is governed by some form of laws, rules, or formal constitution. Therefore, it is important that global business managers and entrepreneurs remain cognizant of the wide variety of regulations in order to remain on favorable terms with the respective governments while at the same time avoiding illegal activities. The following are some suggestions for the global manager and entrepreneur to follow from a legal and practical perspective:[29]

1. *Be open-minded.* As discussed in an article by the Global News Wire, ASIMCO Technologies, a global company, was founded by an American and has subsequently evolved an international business network. The CEO claimed that he initially brought managers from the United States, but the management strategy did not work because they could not really understand China, the Chinese market, or the cultural differences. Hence, managers must be willing to understand all aspects of the country's culture and market in order to be effective.

2. *Keep abreast of relevant updates or changes to the relevant laws, legislations, rules, and especially constitutions.* Laws are constantly being changed or revised, so in order for managers and entrepreneurs to be successful, they have to keep informed as well as develop an inquisitive nature so as to fully comprehend the market in which they operate.

3. *Be socially responsible.* In the instance of managing a company in Jamaica, one would have to be aware that Jamaicans come from various cultures and, as such, encompass different religious groups. Accordingly, management must

---

[29] Contributed by Simone Maxwell, Nova Southeastern University.

be aware that supporting and being respectful of religious groups would give the company a more favorably impression in the public eye. In addition, managers would have to be careful not to out-rightly discriminate against their employees based on religion, as that would negatively affect their business performance.

4. *Possess high integrity*. The global manager and entrepreneur must conduct him/herself with high ethical demeanor, as this will gain them the trust of their employees in addition to making them locally adaptable. Also, a strong sense of integrity inhibits employees from committing legal as well as ethical misdemeanors, such as disobeying the governing body of the host country.

5. *Understand the respective country's constitution and judicial system.* For example, the Constitution of Jamaica guarantees freedom of conscience and expression—including freedom of speech and press—peaceful assembly and association—including the right to join a trade union—freedom of movement and residence within the country and of foreign travel, emigration, and repatriation. It also provides due process of law, including protection against double jeopardy or retroactive punishment. However, there are still companies in Jamaica that do not allow their employees to join trade unions, and if one of their employees becomes a member of such an organization, he or she will be terminated upon the employer's knowledge of such activity. (Such termination would be clearly illegal in the U.S.) Generally, it is advisable that the global manager or entrepreneur stay within the relevant governing codes of conduct—constitutional, statutory, or otherwise—of the country in which he or she operates.

Summary

This chapter first focused on the impact of United States constitutional law on businesses. It examined specific areas that can affect businesses, such as the regulation of commerce and taxation. Additionally, the first ten amendments to the U.S. Constitution, known as the Bill of Rights, have had a strong influence on arbitrary practices in that the Bill or Rights serves as a limitation against abusive government power. These laws are important to business managers and leaders because neglecting them can lead to serious consequences. Some of the U.S. Constitutional rights that were covered in-depth are equal protection, freedom of speech, press, and association. Special attention was given to freedom of religion, the Fifth Amendment, Eminent Domain, and the critical difference between political speech and commercial speech. Constitutional reforms in Italy and Russia were also briefly covered.

EIGHT

ADMINISTRATIVE LAW AND BUSINESS

The term "administrative law" in the U.S. legal system is defined as the powers and procedures of administrative agencies, including the law governing judicial review of agency decisions. Administrative law consists not only of the law promulgated by the large independent federal regulatory agencies, but also the law of other federal agencies as well as the state and local administrative agencies. Administrative law consists of the agency's own laws in the form of "rules and regulations" as well as statutory law, case law, and constitutional law.

An administrative agency can be defined as a government authority other than a court or legislative entity that has the legal power to make and/ or implement law and thereby affect the rights of private parties, businesses, and organizations. While the word agency is the typical designation for such a government authority, an agency can also mean a commission, board, authority, bureau, department, division, or office, to name just a few prominent designations. Administrative agencies, especially at the federal level, have the power to make law, which is a point that must be boldly underscored because by means of lawmaking, agencies make policy. However, as will be seen later in this chapter, agencies can affect policy by other more informal means besides lawmaking.

The legal laws that federal agencies enact are published and codified in a voluminous work called the Code of Federal Regulations while proposed federal agency rules are published in a work called the Federal Register. It is incumbent on any regulated business to be keenly aware of these volumes (which are available online). The Code of Federal Regulations, which is the legislative output of federal administrative agencies, should not be confused with the United States Code, which is the legislative output of the U.S. Congress.

The focus of this chapter will be on the federal or national level in the United States and, in particular, the large independent federal regulatory agencies that are at times called the "fourth branch of government" in the United States. Administrative agencies, laws, and processes in certain international jurisdictions also will be briefly covered.

A significant part of the laws that regulate business in the U.S. stems from these independent regulatory agencies, which are created and empowered by Congress, and whose members are removable only for cause. By contrast, executive administrative agencies are found in the executive branches of government, such as the President of the United States' cabinet. (The heads of executive agencies serve at the pleasure of the President.) The focal point of the administrative law discussion will be at the federal level. It is beyond the scope of this book to examine administrative law and the administrative process in the United States on a state and local level, however, it should be noted that there exist comparable agencies and administrative processes at these lower levels of governance.

Administrative agencies are typically created by legislative bodies. In the U.S., at the federal level, Congress does this by means of enacting legislation which specifies the name, composition, powers, and functions of each agency. It is very important to note that usually agencies are granted a combination of functions: the legislation function to make law by means of rulemaking; the executive power to implement the law, investigate, and take legal action to enforce law; and the judicial power to adjudicate violations of the law and to impose sanctions. The result is that a great deal of power—combined sovereign power—is vested in administrative agencies. Nevertheless, the U.S. Supreme Court has frequently ruled that the existence of administrative agencies possessing combined government powers does not violate the separation of powers doctrine as embodied in the Constitution, which disperses power and accordingly divides the federal government's power into three distinct branches of government, and which also sets up a system of checks and balances among the branches of government. However, the U.S. Constitution, as will be seen, does provide certain legal protections to individuals and regulated businesses against the exercise of agency powers. Moreover, as also will be seen, the courts in the U.S. can exercise their power of judicial review to appraise agency determinations and actions.

At the federal level, the most recent new agency to be created was the Department of Homeland Security, which represented the largest reorganization of the federal government in several decades. The new agency combines under one governmental administrative entity the powers and functions of 22 agencies, including the Secret Service, the Federal Emergency Management Agency (FEMA), Immigration, Customs, the Coast Guard, the Bureau of Alcohol, Tobacco, and Firearms (ATF), and the Drug Enforcement Agency (DEA).

United States Administrative Law

The Delegation Doctrine

When the U.S. Congress initially creates an administrative agency, it ordinarily delegates, or transfers, to the agency certain sovereign powers—specifically legislative power to make laws in the form of rules and regulations pursuant to the agency's rulemaking powers. In the American legal system, the courts have allowed Congress to delegate to administrative agencies very broad powers to make laws and adjudicate cases. Moreover, typically, such delegations have been upheld without Congress providing any significant guidance to the agency as to the substantive nature of the law to be promulgated.

Very vague delegations of power have been upheld by the courts, thereby vesting in the agency a great deal of discretionary power. For example, the Federal Communications Commission has the power to grant broadcast licenses as the "public interest, convenience, or necessity" requires. Conversely, there exist certain limitations on even the very broad grants of discretionary power to federal agencies. For example, agencies cannot tax; rather they can charge fees for services. Moreover, agencies cannot impose criminal sanctions, which is the purveyance of the traditional courts to impress. Of course, the violation of an agency rule can be converted into a crime by Congress—such as, for example, the Security and Commission rule prohibiting trading on inside information—but the prosecution for such a violation is usually left up to the Justice Department and the courts. Agencies can assess and impose civil fines and render other civil redress and can do so without a jury trial, as will be seen. Finally, agencies cannot imprison, which is a function of the traditional court system, but agencies can temporarily detain and confine people, for example, for immigration reasons or in order to effectuate a quarantine.

Making and Changing Administrative Law and Policy

Administrative agencies make policy in three major ways: rulemaking, adjudication, and informally. The first two methods produce administrative law, but agencies are usually accorded the discretion as to how the agency shall proceed to make such law and policy. Rulemaking and adjudication are at times referred to as formal methods of agency policymaking because they are governed by the Administrative Procedure Act, which is an extensive, federal, procedural statute of Congress which tells agencies how they must make law but not what the substantive nature of the law shall be. It is beyond the scope of this book to examine administrative law and the administrative process from a detailed procedural perspective.

Rulemaking is the quasi-legislative power exercised at the agency level, the result of which is a legally enforceable law, termed a "rule" or a "regulation." A rule is defined as an agency statement of general applicability designed to prescribe, interpret, or implement law or policy. Rules are prospective and general; they are addressed to future situations as well as to classes or categories of people or businesses.

Adjudication is the process of making law and policy on a case-by-case basis after a formal, judicial-like hearing before an agency hearings officer at the federal level called an Administrative Law Judge (ALJ). Adjudication is retroactive, and thus may affect, perhaps even adversely, the private parties or businesses appearing before the agency. Federal agency adjudications by ALJs result in decisions and orders that serve as case precedents for future controversies with the same or similar facts. Ordinarily, the agency will utilize the adjudication method to resolve disputes that are specialized and varied or otherwise highly factual-dependent.

One feature to emphasize regarding agency adjudication is that it is quasi-judicial. A jury will not be present at an agency adjudication; rather the ALJ decides the facts as well as laws in the case. Moreover, the traditional rules of evidence, such as the hearsay rule, as well as the right to cross-examine witnesses, ordinarily will not have to be as strictly followed in an agency adjudication as they would be in a more traditional court case. A party is allowed to orally argue a case before the ALJ, and can utilize the services of an attorney, but unless the matter is somehow criminal-related, the government will not provide an attorney. Nonetheless, agency adjudications must be fair to comply with the U.S. Constitution guarantees of due process of law. Moreover, a party is entitled to a decision from the ALJ, with a written statement regarding the pertinent law, factual findings, and reasons for the decision, as well as a record of the hearing. Finally, the losing party is entitled to appeal the agency's ALJ's decision within the agency first and then into the traditional court system, presuming first that a private party has the time, expertise, and money to do this.

As a general rule, agencies are allowed to change existing law and policy as well as render inconsistent decisions. Of course, the agency is expected to enunciate intelligible reasons for an inconsistent determination. The traditional common law rules of res judicata (meaning "the matter is decided") and estoppel (that is, prevention) definitely are not as strictly adhered to in an agency setting, especially when the agency seeks to re-litigate the same issue against other parties. Moreover, agencies are allowed to make erroneous decisions as well as to give erroneous advice. Yet, the more incorrect or inconsistent an agency is, the greater the likelihood that the agency will lose the respect of the traditional court system and any deference that judges may give to agency decisions. Furthermore, consistently changing policies may adversely affect the rights of private parties and businesses, who may have relied on previous agency determinations. However, if a party is seriously and substantially harmed or greatly inconvenienced by a reversal of an agency decision or an erroneous agency decision, then the courts may step in to prevent injustice. For example, this can be done if the agency's wrong advice results in a criminal prosecution or an immigration deportation.

The Informal Administrative Process

In addition to making administrative policy formally by means of rulemaking and adjudication, agencies also can make policy informally. Of course, the term "informal" may not quite be accurate as many of the agency's informal methods of making policy are quite regularized as well as legally constrained. Good examples of agencies acting informally include the agency rendering advice or opinions, engaging in negotiation and settlement procedures, processing contracts and grants and applications and claims, engaging in testing and inspections, and holding public relations events. Any person or business that is regulated by an agency must not only be aware of the agency's formally made policy in the form of rules and regulations and adjudicated cases, but also the agency's informal policy. The latter not only may have legal consequence—especially if a party makes an admission during an informal process—but the agency's informal actions certainly provide a very good clue as to how the agency intends to act formally. For example, even if the Federal Drug Administration does not have a formal policy specifically branding cloning as illegal, the advice, opinions, and speeches by high-level agency personnel surely indicate what the agency's position will be.

Enforcement of Agency Policy

Administrative agencies in the United States can utilize a variety of enforcement techniques in order to ensure compliance with agency law and policy. Formal examples of agency sanctions include the imposition of fines and penalties, the imposition of "cease and desist" and corrective orders (for example, corrective advertising), the assessment of damages and the ordering of restitution, the seizure and destruction of property, the assessment of costs, charges, and fees, and the suspension and revocation of licenses and certificates. Criminal penalties, as noted, are not an authorized sanction for an agency to impose, but an agency may be able to seek criminal penalties in court or transfer the case to the Department of Justice for criminal prosecution. Informal agency enforcement techniques include settling cases, issuing industry guidelines—which may not have the force of law but are persuasive—and the major economic sanction of cutting off funding or other financial aid for noncompliance with agency law or policy.

Agency Obtaining of Information

Agencies cannot perform their executive function of implementation and enforcement without first acquiring information. Of course, most information that agencies secure is obtained voluntarily. For example, the agency may make a "request" to a tobacco company and its advertiser to provide the agency with information regarding product placement in movies. Yet if the requested information is not provided voluntarily, then the agency can compel disclosure by means of subpoena power, which the agency possesses as a result of express Congressional authorization, or by means of the agency's own rulemaking power. Agencies can also obtain information by requiring reports and records from regulated businesses and individuals, by making physical inspections, and by holding hearings. For example, the federal Fair Labor Standards Act empowers the Secretary of Labor to require federal minimum wage and labor hour law reports from businesses that fall under the Department of Labor's jurisdiction. However, if Congress did not explicitly authorize an agency to obtain required reports, the agency itself can do so pursuant to its delegated rulemaking authority.

The subpoena power is a very important agency informational tool. The prevailing legal view is that agencies have very broad power to subpoena testimony and information. Nonetheless, an agency must state the purpose for the subpoena so that a court can determine whether the agency is engaged in a lawful inquiry pertaining to a matter within its jurisdiction. There are, however, certain Constitutional limitations on an agency's power to subpoena. The Fourth Amendment to the Constitution does not require that an agency have "probable cause" or even "reasonable suspicion" to subpoena, yet it does require that the agency must be "reasonable" as to what it is seeking. The object of the subpoena must be specific and not overly broad; thus "fishing expeditions" are prohibited. Moreover, the object of the subpoena must be relevant to the subject matter which the agency is authorized to investigate. (An example of a "reasonable" subpoena was one in which the banks were required by federal banking agencies to report all depositor transactions involving more than $10,000 in currency.) It is important to point out that usually the burden and expense of complying with a subpoena is not a defense. But a court does have the power to scale down an agency request and compel the agency to make it more specific.

There is one major problem, at least as far as the agency is concerned, regarding the subpoena tool. This is the fact that even though an agency has issued a subpoena does not mean that the requested testimony or documents will be forthcoming. In fact, agency subpoenas in the U.S., as opposed to court-issued subpoenas, are not self-enforcing. As a result, if a party refuses to comply with an agency subpoena, the agency must go to a traditional court to secure an order from the court for the party to comply with the subpoena. Court orders can be enforced by means of the court's inherent contempt powers, which include imposing imprisonment. Yet the problem for the agency is that it takes time, effort, and money to first seek the court order, and then wait for the court's decision and subsequent decision as to whether or not the issue is appealable to a higher court. Therefore, the practical result is that the "target" of a subpoena, who has the necessary legal and monetary resources, can effectively tie up the agency for years. Such a course of action is an example of "hard-ball" legal tactics.

In order to enforce a variety of health, safety, and welfare laws and regulations, agency officials can make physical inspections, which is the next important means of information gathering. It must be emphasized that agencies can inspect not only regulated businesses, but also, in certain contexts, private homes. These inspections are regarded as "searches" and thus the agency inspections are governed by the Fourth Amendment. However, the requirements for obtaining an agency warrant to inspect under the Fourth Amendment are very lenient. The general rule for agency inspections is that the agency must obtain a warrant, but it is not necessary for the agency to cite specific reasons. The traditional law enforcement search warrant standard of "probable cause," and even the showing of "reasonable suspicion" are not required. Rather, the agency merely has to demonstrate that its inspections pertain to the agency's functions, are necessary to protect the public's health, welfare, safety, or morals, and that a period of time has elapsed since the agency's last inspection. Thus, ordinarily the agency must proceed with a warrant, but the warrant is a "blanket" warrant under which certain neighborhoods may be inspected, for example, for zoning code violations, or certain types of business are inspected for worker safety violations. Furthermore, there are exceptional cases where the agency is allowed to inspect without a warrant, such as in the case of a health emergency, welfare inspection, or if the scenario is "pervasively regulated," such as auto reclamation centers and gun and liquor stores. Finally, it should be noted that drug testing of employees in "sensitive" positions, such as railroad engineers and U.S. Customs employees, has been upheld despite Fourth Amendment challenges since the government's and public's interest in safety and integrity override privacy interests.

Constitutional Law Protections from Agency Information Collection

Although administrative investigations are not criminal proceedings, they often can result in the imposition of criminal sanctions. Accordingly, there are certain constitutional protections that are applicable in agency investigations and hearings. As noted, the Fourth Amendment applies to administrative inspections while the Fifth Amendment's privilege against self-incrimination can provide a person with legal grounds to refuse to furnish information to an agency if subpoenaed. This privilege arises when the information requested by the agency could provide a "link in a chain" leading to one's criminal prosecution. The Fifth Amendment privilege also will protect a person's personal papers and documents if they are the equivalent to incriminating personal testimony and if they are in one's personal possession as opposed to, for example, in his or her accountant's possession. Moreover, it is critical to point out that the privilege extends only to real—that is, natural persons—and consequently corporations ("artificial" legal persons) as well as partnerships and other business entities cannot avail themselves of the privilege. Of course, while a corporate "person" cannot speak, the custodian of corporate records cannot refuse to produce corporate documents even though he or she may in fact have a personal privilege to refuse to answer specific questions or produce personal papers.

The case of Enron and its former chairman and CEO, Ken Lay (who died of a heart attack in July of 2006), will illustrate the distinction between personal and corporate records. During the course of its stock fraud and insider trading investigation, the Securities and Exchange Commission (SEC) demanded certain documents from Ken Lay, including Enron memoranda and papers, copies of letters and position papers, and drafts of speeches, some of which were in Lay's handwriting. Lay refused, contending that the documents were not Enron documents but rather his own personal papers and that surrendering them would violate his Fifth Amendment privilege against self-incrimination. The SEC argued that the documents were merely Enron corporate records and therefore must be turned over if they incriminated Lay personally. Lay resisted surrendering the documents for over a year until the SEC asked a federal district court judge to make the determination as to the nature of the records. Lay eventually turned over the records. As already noted, agencies such as the SEC cannot prosecute, but they can certainly turn over information they find in business records or any leads therein to law enforcement officials and the Justice Department to pursue possible criminal violations.

The next and very significant constitutional protection to examine is Due Process of Law. In the United States, due process legal protections are premised on the Fifth and 14th Amendments to the Constitution. Due process in essence requires that government not deprive a person of life, liberty, or property without "due process of law." Due process means that before government can take an adverse action against a person, it must provide adequate notice and a fair hearing. Moreover, the government must establish at the hearing that it has permissible reasons—factually and legally—for taking such an action. Thus, a party is entitled to a decision from the government with the reasons stated as well as a record of the hearing in case of an appeal. Moreover, a party is allowed to be represented by an attorney at the hearing, though the government will not provide an attorney unless the matter is criminal in nature. It is important to note here that artificial legal persons, such as a corporation, are considered to be "persons" for purposes of due process protections.

The purposes of due process of law—which originally stems from the English Magna Carta of 1215—are to protect against arbitrary government action and to help ensure fair treatment by government. It is of extreme importance to note that in the United States legal system, due process protects against arbitrary and unfair actions by government—federal, state, or local—but not by the private sector. Consequently, as a general rule, a private sector employer can arbitrarily, capriciously, and unfairly discharge an employee (as will be seen in the Employment Law chapter), whereas a government employer must provide due process in order to effectuate a legal and constitutional discharge. It is also important to note that due process protections do not mean that the government cannot act; rather the government must provide the notice and fair hearing before acting.

Due process protections are effected when the government intentionally deprives a person of life, liberty, or property. For this discussion, please note that the terms "liberty" and "property" are very broadly construed. For example, liberty means more than the freedom from imprisonment or confinement; rather, liberty also encompasses the interests of freedom to contract, the right to engage in employment or occupation, the freedom to marry and to raise children, to worship freely, to exercise free speech, to reside and travel in the U.S., and to acquire knowledge and skills. Similarly, property means more than just the actual ownership of real estate, personal property, or money. Property also encompasses legally protected employment relationships, such as civil service-protected government employment, public school teachers with tenure, benefits under government programs, government-granted professional licenses, and even driver's licenses.

The problem with due process, and the reason it is such a large area in the law, is that the determination of what is sufficient notice as well as what is a fair hearing is very case- and fact-specific, depending on the due process interest at stake. Thus, it is beyond the purpose of this type of book to address all such discrete and detailed due process decisions because this field is more appropriately explicated in a more traditional administrative law text. Suffice to say there is a large expanse in due process protections when the government conduct ranges from a public high school suspending a student for misconduct to a federal or state regulatory agency fining a corporation for violating one of its rules to a federal or state criminal law agency prosecuting an alleged criminal law violator. The hearings in each case will vary from a hearing conducted before the principal of the school to a quasi-judicial hearing before a federal administrative law judge or state hearings officer to a very formal conventional court trial in a federal or state court. What type of hearing is required by due process? As Judge Henry Friendly has stated: "Some type of hearing is required," meaning that the due process explanation is the nature of, problem with, and challenge of this rather important area of U.S. Constitutional and administrative law.

Judicial Review of Agency Determinations

If a private person or business is dissatisfied with a government decision, one can appeal it to the traditional court system, presuming of course one has the time, money, and stamina to undergo an appeal. The topic of judicial review of agency decisions encompasses the availability and means of obtaining judicial review, the impediments or "roadblocks" to judicial review, and the scope of judicial review. While a detailed explication of these topics, though weighty, is beyond the scope of this book, nonetheless the authors would like to make some important fundamental points.

First, as a general rule, all agency determinations are ultimately reviewable by the traditional courts of the United States. Second, generally, the means for securing judicial review will be explicitly set forth in the statute which creates the agency; if not, there are traditional Anglo-American non-statutory procedures for obtaining judicial review, such as a writ of habeas corpus (an order by a court to an agency to provide sufficient reasons for holding or detaining a person), a writ of mandamus (an order by a court to compel an agency to perform a ministerial function), or a petition for an injunction and declaratory judgment (an order by a court declaring an action illegal and commanding the agency to cease).

Even assuming the availability and means of judicial review, a party adversely impacted by an agency decision still must overcome certain impediments to judicial review, colloquially called "roadblocks," which may impede or completely prevent judicial review. Some of these legal hindrances are imposed by the Constitution while others have been created by the judiciary for judicial convenience. The requirement that an appealing party has "standing" to sue is a constitutionally based, absolutely essential, requirement to obtaining judicial review. Because judicial review power granted by the Constitution extends only to "cases and controversies," the "standing" requirement means that an appealing party must demonstrate to the courts that the party has suffered by means of the agency action, an "injury in fact,"—an actual, concrete, personal, particularized, and demonstrable injury or harm to one's person, property, property rights, property interests, economic interests, environmental interests, or legal or constitutional rights.

Another legal impediment to judicial review is the "ripeness" requirement, which is pertinent when an agency has a formal policy in place (for example, a rule branding certain conduct as illegal), but has not yet applied it to any regulated parties. Because courts do not like to litigate in the abstract, a court may say that the agency rule is not yet "ripe" for review, and thus will tell the appealing private party to wait until the agency actually seeks to enforce its policy in a concrete manner before entertaining such a judicial review. The thought process of the judiciary here is that the agency may never actually enforce its own policy—thereby never actually harming anyone—thus making judicial review effectively avoidable.

The next major roadblock to judicial review is called the exhaustion doctrine. "Exhaustion" means that a party appealing an agency decision must first exhaust all administrative remedies before a court will hear the case. That is, the appealing party must first appeal his or her case through the agency itself in an attempt to get a decision rendered at the highest level of the agency (usually the agency commissioners or board members). If that decision is still adverse to the petitioner, he or she can then appeal to the traditional court system. Once again, as far as the judiciary is concerned, an appealing party may theoretically prevail in the agency, thus obviating any judicial review.

A party that wishes to challenge an agency decision in court must be careful because the application of the "exhaustion" rule may essentially preclude judicial review. For example, if a party can no longer return to the agency—perhaps because of the party's own failure to comply with the agency's appeal procedural requirements—then the party may be totally precluded from seeking judicial review. Furthermore, the exhaustion doctrine is a rule of judicial convenience and its application is one of judicial discretion. Accordingly, there are exceptions, such as if there would be irreparable injury in the form of extreme economic burden if judicial review is not immediately granted versus the mere inconvenience and costs relevant to exhausting the agency's avenues of appeal first. Moreover, if it appears that it would be futile for a party to appeal within the agency and obtain relief because the heads of the agency have already firmly held to their policy, then a party need not exhaust his or her remedies within the agency itself. Finally, if the question is constitutional in nature, a court may decide to hear the issue immediately because, ultimately, it is the court that can grant relief for constitutional claims, especially if a party claims that the agency's appeal processes are constitutionally defective.

The final area to examine is the scope of judicial review. That is, when a court finally does receive an appeal from an agency decision, what exactly will the court review and what legal tests will the courts apply to the agency decision to make sure it is a legal one? To what extent does a reviewing court have the power to set aside an agency decision? There are three components to an agency decision that a court will review: 1) questions of law; 2) questions of fact; and 3) any discretionary component in the agency's determination.

Regarding questions of law, the rule is rather straightforward: A reviewing court can completely and totally substitute its own interpretation and opinion of the law in favor of that of the agency. The court thus can substitute its own judgment, and does not have to defer at all to the agency's legal determination. This "substitution" test, it is important to underscore, solely applies to the part of the agency determination involving questions of law: jurisdictional issues, the meaning of the Constitution, a statute, a case, or even an agency regulation.

Regarding questions of fact, the rule as well as result is different as the courts are constrained by a significant administrative law doctrine, called the "substantial evidence" doctrine. This test states that if an agency's factual determination is supported by "substantial evidence," a court must defer to the agency and cannot set aside the agency decision based on a factual issue alone. The substantial evidence test asks that based on the entire record, is there relevant evidence that a reasonable mind would accept as adequate to support a conclusion? If so, then the agency's factual determination must be upheld on appeal. It must be emphasized that this test only applies to questions of fact, such as what events occurred, a party's state of mind, and the credibility of witnesses. Of course, what is the most interesting and thought-provoking aspect of administrative law in the United States is that the courts determine not only if the substantial evidence test is met, but also if the issue, on appeal, is legal or factual in nature. However, that type of judicial power, and how it is exercised, is beyond the purpose of this book.

Finally, if there is a discretionary element to the agency decision—that is, if the agency has exercised independent thought and judgment in making a decision, which is characteristically the case—a reviewing court will not overturn an agency decision unless it is an abuse of discretion. An abuse of discretion means that the agency has acted in an arbitrary or capricious manner or made a clear error in judgment. "Abuse" can be premised on the agency considering inappropriate factors in making a decision or not considering appropriate ones. This standard plainly presents a steep hurdle for a party to overcome in petitioning a court to overturn an agency decision.

Sovereign Immunity

"The King can do no wrong!" That ancient maxim still has considerable importance to modern-day administrative law because it forms the basis for the doctrine of sovereign immunity. This doctrine holds that government action is not subject to judicial review by individual lawsuit except insofar as government has consented to be sued. The modern rationale for sovereign immunity is that individual lawsuits would impose an intolerable burden on government's ability to function for the greater public benefit, thereby outweighing any contemplation of private harm caused by the government.

There are two important exceptions to sovereign immunity. One is the waiver doctrine, whereby both the federal government and also the state governments in the United States have waived their immunity to a limited degree, thereby allowing certain types of lawsuits against government and government officials and employees to proceed, but only, in most instances, for limited amounts of monetary recovery. At the federal level, this waiver statute is called the Federal Torts Claim Act. The second exception is called the "Constitutional Torts" doctrine, which is premised on the Civil Rights Act of 1871. This legal precept holds that lawsuits for money damages are allowed against certain levels of government and government officials and officers who intentionally deprive people of their rights protected by the U.S. Constitution.

Both of these exceptions to sovereign immunity are very detailed, and thus their explication is more appropriately handled in an administrative law text and not in this type of work. Yet as an illustration, it should be noted that in 2006, the U.S. Supreme Court ruled that the Postal Service did not possess sovereign immunity to avert a lawsuit by a woman who allegedly tripped and fell over packages and mail that letter carriers carelessly left on the porch of her home. Accordingly, her negligence cause of action claiming $200,000 in injuries to her wrists, chest, and spine will be allowed to proceed in the courts.

This succinct exposition of U.S. administrative law and the administrative process has attempted to portray as well as explain the fundamental nature, functions, and authority of the so-called "fourth branch" of the U.S. government. This branch, although led and managed by unelected bureaucrats, nonetheless possesses a great deal of discretionary power to make laws in the form of rules and regulations—laws that extensively and specifically regulate business and which must be obeyed.

Global Legal Perspectives

Italy and Jamaica: Administrative Law Developments

Italian[30] administrative procedure is premised on the Administrative Procedure Law, adopted in 1990. The purpose of that law was to set forth the minimum principles that apply to the relationship between government authorities and Italian citizens. Two important parts of the Italian law are the right of access to information and the right of participation. Participation consists of the right to enter an administrative procedure by requesting the disclosure of administrative documents as well as the right to submit written opinions and comments. In addition, the pertinent results of public participation must be taken into account by government authorities. These rights are granted to members of the public

---

[30] See Fracchia, Fabrizio (2005).

who are affected, or are likely to be affected, by government decision as well as to those members of the public who have an interest in the decision.

One benefit of the 1990 law is that, if requested documents are denied by the agency, a party can appeal the decision during the administrative proceeding before an administrative tribunal, even before the agency makes a final decision. Another important part of the law is that it strengthened the position of the ombudsman. In Italy, the ombudsman is conferred with the power to assist people and to facilitate their interaction with government authorities. The rationale behind the ombudsman is that he or she will help ensure that government bodies and agencies will actually listen to people and take their interests into account in government decision making.

An important component of Italian administrative law and procedure is the principle of "subsidiarity," which means that administrative powers should be conferred to the public body which is closest to the people, typically the municipality and municipal agencies. Similar to the United States, delegation is a prominent feature of Italian administrative law and practice. Moreover, as in the U.S., the Italians confront the problems inherent in the extensive delegation of sovereign lawmaking powers to independent agencies—the diminishment of representative democracy and a concomitant weakening of political control. One solution for the Italians has been to open up the administrative process to public participation, particularly by allowing and facilitating private comments and opinions.

However, there is a material exception to participation in Italian law regarding administrative rulemaking proceedings where the purpose of the rulemaking is to issue rules of general application. In such a situation, the provisions in the law regarding public participation are disallowed because the rules would have a wider application involving a great many interests and thus, according to the Italians, public participation could interfere with efficient public administration. As noted, the U.S. also has exceptions to the public notice and participation aspects of certain types of rulemaking, but the U.S. certainly does not have a "blanket" prohibition of public participation for what appear to be "public" rules.

There is also an aspect of Italian law that is especially beneficial to those applying for government licenses, grants, etc., and that is the "silence" principle, whereby the final act of an agency—such as the awarding of a license— will be deemed to be granted if the application has not been rejected within a specific deadline.

In Jamaica,[31] an administrative agency is referred to as an executive agency, and it is set up to reduce central control and delegate authority to the Chief

---

[31] Contributed by Simone Maxwell, Nova Southeastern University

Executive Officers in the various government institutions. Another aim of executive agencies is to substantially improve the quality and quantity of services provided by government agencies. As is the case in the United States, the functioning of the executive agencies in Jamaica is also dictated by set procedures, and they have to abide by laws set up within the context of the constitution. Some of the major executive agencies in Jamaica are the Registrar General Department (RGD), Companies Office of Jamaica, Management Institute for National Development (MIND), and Administrator General Department (AGD). The RGD, for example, was established to monitor the tax department by such means as regulating the amount of taxes that businesses pay to government.

According to the cabinet office in Jamaica, the executive agencies established may be considered "The Way Forward," in order to incorporate the values and ethics of the "old" public service. But some businesses that operate in the public sector are displeased with the executive agencies as they tend to be too thorough in administering their laws. However, the major difference between an administrative agency in the United States and an executive agency in Jamaica is that the executive agency in Jamaica is designed exclusively to govern the public sector while the administrative agency in the U.S. has the legal authority to make or implement laws that affect the rights of private organizations and private parties. Therefore, private businesses in the United States, as opposed to those in Jamaica, must be much more aware and conscious of the role of administrative agencies.

Management Strategies

The global business manager and entrepreneur must be keenly aware of the existence of this administrative "fourth branch of government" in the United States as well as internationally, and also be cognizant of its effect not only at the federal level, but also at the state, province, and local levels. The point that administrative agencies characteristically have the power to make law—law that must be obeyed—is one that cannot be over emphasized as the typical business will be more directly and frequently affected by the administrative law process than by the judicial process. While the more traditional type of lawsuit will hopefully be a rarity for the average business, administrative agencies and administrative law nonetheless affect all business every day and everywhere and in many different ways.

Global business managers and entrepreneurs should consider that they are in a very dynamic business world and they must be able to cope with and adapt to whatever challenges may be posed by administrative agencies. Because each agency is unique in its respective roles—for example, the Securities and

Exchange Commission in the U.S. having powers similar to all three branches of the government—as a result, if the global manager is conducting business in the United States of America, it is essential that he/she become aware of the role of various agencies, especially in the case of permits, certificates, and other types of permissions. Additionally, if he/she is conducting business in, for example, Jamaica, especially in the public sector, it would be imperative for the manager to note factors such as the high level of taxes that the Registrar General Department (RGD) imposes as well as the penalties that will result if the agency's requirements are not met.

Summary

An administrative agency is a government authority other than a court or legislative entity that has the legal power to make and/or implement law and thereby affect the rights of private parties, businesses, and organizations. This chapter concentrated on the large, independent, U.S. federal regulatory agencies that are at times collectively known as the "fourth branch of government." Additionally, administrative agencies have various laws and policies in place, which were examined. The functions, roles, and rights of the administrative agencies were also analyzed in order to show the importance of administrative agencies in relation to global business practices. Administrative practices in Italy and Jamaica were also discussed briefly.

PART II

THE LEGAL ENVIRONMENT OF GLOBAL BUSINESS

NINE

The term "tort" is very old, harkening back to the early common law in England and, even before that, to the Norman-French conquest of England. In United States law, a tort is defined as a wrongful act against a person or property for which a legal cause of action may be brought for the harm sustained. A tort can mean a private wrong, the violation of private duty created by the law, and the violation of which results in a private injury. To compare, a crime is a public wrong, the violation of a publicly created duty, and the violation of which results in harm to the state. Yet it is important to note initially that the same act may constitute both a tort and a crime, for example, an assault and battery, which the state can prosecute as a crime while the victim can also sue for intentional tort damages. A breach of contract is a private wrong also, resulting in a private injury, but the breach arises from the violation of a duty created consensually by the parties. Torts can be personal torts, arising from an injury to a person's body, feelings, or reputation. Torts also can be about property, arising from harm to land, real estate, or personal property. The three major categories of torts in the United States are intentional torts, the tort of negligence, and the doctrine of strict tort liability.

Speaking very generally, people are free to act as they please in the United States as long as their actions do not infringe on or invade the interests of others. But the purposes of tort law are to provide protection to certain legally recognizable interests, to afford a remedy if these interests are wrongfully harmed, and to allocate the risk and cost of injury on a just basis. In a civilized society, a person cannot intentionally injure another person or harm his or her property and each person is entitled to have certain interests, such as freedom from bodily injury, protected. Therefore, if another person intentionally invades such a protected interest, the perpetrator violates a legal duty to the injured person who, as a result, has the legal right to sue for damages for the intentional wrong. Moreover, in a civilized society, everyone is held to a legal duty to exercise reasonable care when one acts. Thus, the victim of one who acts in a careless manner can then bring a lawsuit for damages as a way to compensate for the injury caused by the violation of the duty to exercise reasonable care. (Such a lawsuit is premised on the tort of negligence.) Finally, society, by means of the legal system, may create doctrines that impose liability without fault for types of activities that the law brands as "ultra-hazardous." In such a case, the person so acting is held accountable, even without any intentional wrongdoing or even negligent conduct, for any resultant harm. This type of tort liability without fault is called "strict liability" and is premised on utilitarian rationales.

This chapter examines intentional torts and the tort of negligence in the United States, and then compares certain aspects of U.S. tort laws with the laws of the selected international jurisdiction.

Intentional Torts in the United States

Introduction and Elements

Intentional torts provide a legal remedy for those people whose protected personal or property interests are purposefully invaded or harmed by another. The required elements, or components, to an intentional tort lawsuit generally are: 1) a wrongful act by another; 2) requisite intent; 3) causation; and 4) damages. The victim, as the plaintiff, must establish all these elements to the tort in order to have a *prima facie*, or initial case against the defendant actor.

A purposeful act that is committed volitionally—that is, voluntarily—by the defendant is first required. This act, of course, must intentionally invade a legally protected interest and consequently be a wrongful act. Accordingly, if one person strikes another during the throes of a medical seizure or is pushed by a wrongdoer into a third party who then suffers harm, one has not committed a volitional act.

The requisite intent can be specific or general. Specific intent exists when a person's objective is to cause a certain result or consequences whereas general intent exists when a person does not have a specific goal or result, but acts knowing with substantial certainty that certain consequences will ensue. An example of the latter intent would occur when a person does intend to push another person, who falls and injures himself or herself. The actor may not have intended that specific harm, but is liable nonetheless due to the substantial certainty of the victim falling and injuring himself or herself. An interesting old common law doctrine concerning intent and intentional torts is called the "transferred intent" doctrine, usually found in assault and battery cases. Transferred intent is a legal device that is used when a defendant intends to cause harm to one person but actually injures another person. The defendant's intent to commit the wrongful act is transferred from the intended "target" to the actual victim, who then can sue for the appropriate intentional tort.

The causation requirement means that the harmful result that gives rise to liability must have been caused by the defendant's wrongful act itself. The causation test will be met when the conduct of the defendant is a substantial factor in bringing about the plaintiff's injury.

Finally, there must be some type of injury or harm, which can be minor, but nevertheless will support an award of damages, including punitive damages.

Intentional Torts Against the Person

The first intentional tort against a person is a "battery." A battery is a purposeful, intentional act by the defendant that causes a harmful or offensive contact to the person of plaintiff. "Harmful" or "offensive" conduct is measured by the standard of a reasonably prudent person, that is, a person or ordinary sensibilities and not someone who is overly sensitive. The "person of the plaintiff" refers to not only the physical body of the plaintiff, but his or her clothes, of such items as a purse or laptop that are suspended from the body. It is noteworthy that there is no apprehension requirement for a battery and thus, a plaintiff may recover for a battery even though he or she was not even conscious of the harmful or offensive conduct. There is no requirement of an actual injury, and the plaintiff can recover nominal damages even though there are no material damages sustained. Moreover, nominal damages can serve in many jurisdictions as a predicate for a punitive damage recovery. For example, a male co-worker deliberately patting a female colleague on the rear may not cause her actual physical harm, but it certainly is "offensive" conduct by any ordinary standard of reasonableness and is thus grounds for a battery as well as being the basis for a sexual harassment lawsuit.

Closely related to a battery is its cousin, the "assault." An assault is an act by a defendant which causes a reasonable apprehension of fear in the victim of an immediate harmful or offensive contact to the victim's person—i.e., the fear of a battery. "Apprehension" is measured by the "reasonableness" test: As such, the fear of harm must be a reasonable expectation and not an exaggerated one. Moreover, as opposed to a battery, in order to have this fearful apprehension or expectation, the plaintiff must have been aware of the defendant's action.

However, a person may be placed in a situation of reasonable apprehension of immediate harmful or offensive conduct even though the defendant is not actually capable of committing a battery upon the plaintiff. This circumstance is called the "apparent ability" doctrine. The classic example arises when the wrongdoer points an unloaded gun at the victim who does not know that the gun is unloaded. Legally, it is sufficient grounds if the defendant had the apparent ability to bring about the contact. Words alone, as a general rule, no matter how violent, do not constitute an assault. Some overt act is necessary, such as raising one's arm as if to strike or making a fist. Words alone, however, may form the basis of another independent intentional tort. Finally with assault, there is a requirement of immediacy. That is, the apprehension must be of immediate harmful or offensive conduct. Consequently, neither the threat of future harmful contact nor a conditional threat is sufficient for an assault.

The next intentional tort to the person is "false imprisonment." This tort occurs when a defendant acts or fails to act and thereby confines or restrains the plaintiff to a bounded area. Confinement or restraint can be effectuated by physical barriers or by physical force directed at the plaintiff or a member of his or her family as well as physical force being directed at the plaintiff's property. Threats of physical force to oneself, one's family, or one's property will be sufficient grounds, as will be the failure to provide a means of escape or egress even when the plaintiff originally has come under the defendant's control. Generally, moral pressures and conditional threats will be insufficient means of confinement or restraint. There is, however, no need to resist the physical force used to confine or restrain the plaintiff. Moreover, the time of confinement and restraint is immaterial for the cause of action, though it is material as to the amount of damages. There is no requirement that the plaintiff be aware of the confinement. For an area to be considered "bounded," the plaintiff's freedom of movement must be limited in all directions. Merely blocking one of many exits is insufficient as there is still a reasonable means of escape which the plaintiff was aware of; the area is not bounded, and there is no tort liability.

One important business ramification of the false imprisonment tort occurs in shoplifting cases, where a merchant suspects a person of shoplifting and detains that person to make an investigation. What exactly is the merchant's liability for false imprisonment? Under the common law, as well as pursuant to several state statutes, merchants have been accorded a "privilege" to detain a suspected shoplifter for an investigation. There typically are three basic elements to this merchant's privilege: 1) the merchant must have a reasonable belief as to the occurrence of a theft; 2) the detention must be conducted in a reasonable manner and, concomitantly, only non-deadly force can be used; and 3) the detention must be for a reasonable period of time and only for the purposes of making an investigation as to the suspected theft. Under the common law, this privilege was referred to as the merchant's "shoplifter detention" privilege, but today, pursuant to modern state statutes, the privilege is more euphemistically referred to as a "merchant's protection" privilege.

The tort of intentional infliction of emotional distress[32] arises when the defendant purposefully acts in an extreme, outrageous, or atrocious manner and thereby causes the plaintiff to suffer severe emotional distress. The wrongful conduct itself must be conduct that goes beyond all bounds of decency tolerated by a civilized society. Such conduct is again measured by a "reasonableness"

---

[32] For more details of this tort in the private employment context, see Cavico, F. J. (2003).

test. Mere indignities and annoyances are insufficient, however, if the defendant knows that the victim is more sensitive and thus more susceptible to emotional distress than an ordinary person, then the defendant's conduct will be measured by that "sensitivity" standard. Children and the elderly are good examples of people who are usually more sensitive. Although business examples of such intentional tort are rare, they do occur, usually in a situation where an employee is discharged in an abusive, threatening, humiliating, mocking, and disrespectful manner in full view of his or her co-workers. Although the employer may have the legal right to discharge the employee, especially if the employee is an employee working at-will, the outrageous manner of the discharge may give rise to a separate independent tort.

A major intentional tort with widespread business ramifications is "defamation."[33] The elements needed for a cause of action for defamation that the plaintiff must prove are as follows: 1) false and defamatory language by the defendant; 2) "of or concerning" the plaintiff, that is, identifying the plaintiff to a reasonable reader, listener, or viewer; 3) "publication" of the defamatory language to a third party; and 4) resulting injury to the reputation of the plaintiff. As a basic component of the tort, the false statements must be defamatory; the defendant's language must adversely affect the victim's honesty, integrity, virtue, or reputation within the community. For example, declaring to a discharged employee that he or she is a criminal, a thief, a cheat, and a liar would suffice.

The "of or concerning" plaintiff requirement means that a reasonably prudent person would understand that the defamatory statement referred to the plaintiff him/herself.

The "publication" requirement mandates that the defamatory statement must be communicated to a third party who understands it as such. For example, if the employer in the preceding example did make such defamatory accusations of criminality and immorality but only to the employee, with no one else present, then publication is lacking. Similarly, if the defamatory statement is made in a letter, memo, or e-mail which only the employee sees, then there is no publication. Conversely, if the employer makes the false accusations of employee criminality publicly—over a loudspeaker, employee bulletin board or "virtual" discussion board, or in a "global" email—then there is publication. Regarding the intent requirement, defamation is at times called a "quasi-intentional tort" because even though intent is required, it is merely the intent to publish and not the intent to defame. As such, once purposeful publication is established, it is not a defense that the defendant did not know that the statements were defamatory. Furthermore, it is not a defense that the defendant did not intend to

---

[33] For more details on this tort, see Cavico, F. J. (1999).

defame the plaintiff. Also, anyone who repeats or republishes defamatory material is liable just the same as the original publisher. This rule is called the "repetition" rule and holds that each repetition is a separate publication for which the victim can recover damages.

The "injury to the reputation" requirement of defamation presents a problem, because now one must carefully distinguish between two types of defamation—libel and slander—because the plaintiff's burden of proof as to damage to the plaintiff's reputation may differ depending on the nature of the defamation.

Libel is a defamatory statement recorded in writing or some other permanent form, such as a picture, statue, movie, or on television or radio. There are two important kinds of libel. The first is called "libel per se," which occurs when a statement is defamatory and libelous on its face; no extrinsic facts or explanation are needed. The rule of law is that in such a case, damage to the plaintiff's reputation is presumed by the law and, accordingly, the plaintiff can recover damages without the necessity of proving damages. The second kind of libel is called "libel per quod." This form of libel is not defamatory on its face and, as a result, requires reference to additional facts in order to establish its defamatory nature. In such a case, most courts will not presume damage to the plaintiff's reputation, and thus the plaintiff will be required, as a general rule, to plead and prove special damages, for example, if the defamation itself caused the loss of employment or a business opportunity.

Slander is spoken defamation. It is oral and heard and entails less permanent and less broad areas of dissemination. As a general rule, damage to the plaintiff's reputation is not presumed, and thus the plaintiff has to plead and prove special damages. However, there are four categories of slander that are considered so harmful they are called "slander per se." (The legal consequence of uttering a slander per se is that damage to the plaintiff's reputation is presumed.) The four slander per se categories involving defamatory statements are: 1) holding that a person is guilty of a serious crime of moral turpitude (and not a minor offense); 2) adversely affecting a person's profession, business, or trade; 3) imputing a loathsome disease to a person; and 4) historically, imputing that an unmarried woman is unchaste.

There are four chief defenses to counter defamation: 1) consent; 2) truth; 3) absolute privilege; and 4) qualified or conditional privilege. "Consent" by the plaintiff to the publication of the defamatory statement will be a defense. Consent will be discussed in a forthcoming section of this chapter in conjunction with other intentional torts. "Truth" is a total defense to a lawsuit for defamation: No matter how defamatory the statement is, if it is true, the truth will be a complete defense to a cause of action for defamation, though not necessarily for other intentional torts. An "absolute privilege" arises in court trials and other government proceedings and protects litigants, witnesses, attorneys, judges, and other government personnel. A qualified or conditional privilege will operate as a complete defense, but it may be forfeited by the presence of malice, in the sense of spite or ill-will, or abuse. This means that the publishing of the defamatory statement occurred with an improper motive or for an improper purpose. The "qualified privilege" can be used to protect not only the public interest, but also the private interest—for example, to protect a statement by a former employer to a prospective employer regarding a job applicant. In the absence of malice or abuse, the qualified privilege will even protect defamatory and false statements by the former employer concerning the former employee. However, regardless of the existence of such a common law privilege to defame, which some states have formalized in statutory form, most employers are very fearful of being sued for defamation by former employees and thus are very reticent to be expressive, let alone expansive, in communications regarding former employees.

When defamation occurs on the Internet, unique problems emerge, especially with the repetition rule and the liability of re-publishers of defamatory statements. In particular, the legal issue encompasses whether or not an Internet service provider (ISP) could be construed as a "re-publisher" and thus be potentially liable for defamatory statements made by users of their online services. This perplexing question was resolved by a federal statute in the United States, The Communications Decency Act of 1996, which holds that the provider as well as the user of an "interactive" computer service shall not be liable as a publisher or speaker for information provided by another content supplier. Moreover, the courts have ruled that even when an ISP becomes aware of the defamatory statements on its online system but fails to promptly remove them, the ISP is still not legally liable even though one would assume that ethically, the ISP would feel duty-bound to remove the offensive material as soon as possible.

Defamation can also occur against one's property, at which times the tort is referred to as "disparagement of property" and can include a variety of legal wrongs such as slander of quality, trade libel, or slander of title. The essence of this type of defamation is that the defendant makes an intentional, false accusation impugning the quality or ownership of another person's goods or property. Ordinarily, the standard defamation rules apply to this variant of the tort, but with one major exception. In the "property" form of defamation, in order to recover damages, the aggrieved party will not have any damages presumed. Rather, the plaintiff will have to prove that the disparagement to his or her property or ownership rights caused an actual property loss.

The intentional tort of invasion of privacy protects the right to maintain one's private life free from unwanted intrusion and unwarranted publicity.

Invasion of privacy is a broad legal doctrine as it consists of not one, but rather four distinct invasions of a person's privacy and personality. These four "privacy" torts, succinctly stated are: 1) appropriation; 2) intrusion; 3) "false light"; and 4) public disclosure.

The "appropriation" tort occurs when the defendant appropriates, without permission, the plaintiff's name or picture for the defendant's commercial advantage, typically for the advertisement, marketing, and promotion of the defendant's products or services.

"Intrusion" occurs when the defendant intrudes on the plaintiff's private life, private affairs, or seclusion. It is absolutely essential for intrusion tort liability that the intrusion invades a person's private domain, not a public domain. For example, taking a picture of a celebrity in a public place is not legally actionable. Moreover, the aggrieved party is held to a reasonableness standard; only a reasonable expectation of privacy is protected by the tort. In an employment setting, for example, an employer must be careful when conducting surveillance of employees, monitoring employees, and searching employees, even in the workplace, as the employee is still entitled to some "private space" therein. Moreover, when conducting surveillance off-the-job to, for example, enforce an employer's policies of no-dating of co-workers or no-smoking anytime (on company time or not), the employer must be extremely careful not to contravene the employee's privacy rights protected by the "intrusion" tort. Of course, an astute employer will give the employee notice that certain types of surveillance, monitoring, and searches will be conducted as it will then be more difficult for an employee to claim a reasonable expectation of privacy if he or she is informed in advance that an intrusion (such as drug-testing) will be conducted under certain circumstances. Finally, as will be discussed in the Internet Regulation chapter, a U.S. federal statute allows the employer to monitor the employee's use of the employer's e-mail system.

Also actionable as a privacy tort is the publication of facts by the defendant which places the plaintiff in a "false light." False light means the public disclosure attributing to a person a view or opinion which he or she does not possess or actions which he or she did not take.

Finally, "public disclosure" of private facts about the plaintiff by the defendant is actionable as a privacy tort. It must be emphasized that even if the facts about a person are true, the tort may still lie. Furthermore, the facts themselves must be private and not in the public record.

The legal wrong of fraud also encompasses a very broad formulation under the common law. While fraud is covered in detail in the chapter on Contract Law, certain fundamental points should be expounded upon now. First, one must be cognizant that the most serious type of fraud is intentional fraud, also known as intentional misrepresentation, but known in the old common law days as "deceit." Deceit, as will be shown, provides a defense to a breach of contract suit, a legal means to rescind or cancel a contract and, most importantly, for the purposes of this chapter, the grounds for an intentional tort lawsuit. There are, however, as also will be seen, many difficult hurdles in pleading and proving a "deceit" lawsuit, in particular, the necessity of showing that the defendant knowingly and purposefully lied and intended to lie in order to induce the victim to do or not to do a particular act or transaction.

The next intentional tort, which also has significant business ramifications, is the tort of intentional interference with contractual or business relations.[34] This tort requires the presence of a contact, a business relationship, or the expectancy of a business relationship, of which the defendant is aware and which the defendant interferes with by improper means in order to advance his/her/its own business interests. An example would arise when one competing company wrongfully induces a key employee at another firm to break his contract with his employer to work for the competitor. Intent is required, of course, and is required in the sense that evidence is necessary to show that the defendant intentionally induced the former employee to break his/her contract with the former employer—not merely that the employee breached it—and then went to work for the defendant competitor. One other major problem with this tort is that the laws governing wrongful interference tort are not clear as to what are legitimate and proper competitive actions in seeking new personnel and new business as opposed to wrongful "pirating," which includes predatory, abusive, and malicious tactics. The line between illegal predatory and abusive competition and "mere" aggressive, "tough," "hard-hitting," and otherwise legal competition is not an easy one to draw, not only for this intentional tort, but also under antitrust law, particularly for monopolization analysis, as will be seen in the Antitrust Law chapter.

The final intentional tort to the person is the wrongful institution of legal proceedings, often called "malicious prosecution." This tort is premised on a private defendant (and not a government prosecutor) wrongfully instituting criminal (but not civil) proceedings against a party, and which proceedings terminate in that party's innocence. Furthermore, the defendant must have lacked probable cause to prosecute and possessed an improper motive for instituting the criminal action.

The next major category of intentional torts deals with intentional torts to one's property.

---

[34] For a detailed explication of this tort, see Cavico, F. J., (2002).

Intentional Torts Against Property

The law recognizes that there are protected interests regarding not only one's person but also one's property. Accordingly, there are four main types of intentional torts to property: 1) trespass to land; 2) trespass to chattels; 3) conversion; and 4) defamation to property. This last tort was previously covered in the defamation section.

A "trespass to land" happens when a person purposefully and physically invades another's land or real property. The interest protected by this tort is the interest of exclusive possession of real property. Some physical invasion of the land is required, though it is not necessary that the defendant actually come on the premises. For example, a defendant can be liable for a trespass by intentionally causing objects or third parties to come upon the plaintiff's land. A trespass can exist, moreover, when a defendant remains on a plaintiff's land after the defendant's original lawful right of entry has ended. However, if no physical object or person enters the land, then there is no "invasion" and thus no trespass. The defendant may still be liable under nuisance law if the plaintiff's use and enjoyment of the premises is materially and unreasonably impeded, for example, by noise or odors. The one caveat regarding the intent requirement to trespass to land is that although intent is required, the intent to trespass is not required; only the intent to do the act that constitutes the trespass is sufficient. A mistake, therefore, as to the lawfulness of the defendant's entry on the land is not a defense. Finally, there is no requirement of actual damages in order to have a cause of action in trespass; actual injury to the land or real estate is not required and damages, at least nominal damages, are presumed. In addition, if the trespass continues, it may evoke an equity lawsuit by the landowner for an injunction.

The next type of intentional tort to property is "trespass to chattels" or, in more modern parlance, trespass to personal property (as opposed to real property). This tort requires a purposeful act by the defendant which interferes with the plaintiff's right of, and interest in, possession of a chattel (or thing). This type of trespass can arise by intermeddling, which is conduct which directly damages the personal property, such as intentionally "keying" another's automobile. Intermeddling can also mean dispossession, which is temporarily depriving a person of his or her right to possession of a chattel, and includes such instances as "borrowing" another's bicycle for a ride. As with trespass to land, mistake is not defense. But contrary to the "land" tort, trespass to chattels requires some actual damage to the property or a dispossession for an appreciable length of time. (Nominal damages are not presumed for a trespass to chattels.) Note that if the interference with or dispossession of the chattel is so serious or for so long, the tort may be "upgraded" to the intentional property tort of conversion, which may require the defendant to pay the full value of the property as damages.

Before the important property tort of conversion can be examined, one problem area in the law, caused by the advent of the Internet, must be addressed, and that is whether "spam" and "spamming" can be perceived as a trespass to property. Spam is bulk, unsolicited, and mass e-mail. Because of the burden in time, effort, and money that "spamming" may inflict on an online user or an ISP, some courts in the United States have stated a willingness to accept "spam as trespass" lawsuits. In addition to presenting annoyance, the courts typically will require a showing of material economic harm produced by voluminous spamming before issuing an injunction or imposing tort damage liability under a trespass to chattels theory.

Moreover, due to the uncertainty of tort law as well as the many, and at times conflicting, state statutes regulating spam, the U.S. Congress, in 2003, enacted the CAN-SPAM Act, fully known as the Controlling the Assault of Non-Solicited Pornography and Marketing Act, which went into effect on January 1, 2004. This federal statute applies to any electronic and commercial mail messages and, furthermore, preempts any state anti-spam laws (except state laws prohibiting false and deceptive e-mail practices). It is essential to underscore that initially, the CAN-SPAM Act did not prohibit spam. Rather, the federal law prohibits certain types of spamming practices, such as the offending message not having a return address or having a false return address on the e-mail, "harvesting" e-mail addresses from other Web sites, as well as sending mass e-mails to randomly generated e-mail addresses. The Act also requires an "opt-out" provision, thereby enabling a recipient to block further emails from the same source, as well as the appropriate labeling of any sexually oriented materials appearing in the e-mail message. While the federal statute certainly will preempt conflicting state anti-spam statutes, it remains to be seen whether CAN-SPAM will also override the old common law of torts, especially the "virtual" use of the trespass to chattels intentional tort doctrine.

Continuing with the types of intentional torts, the "cousin" to trespass to chattels is the tort of "conversion." The essence of conversion is a purposeful act by the defendant which amounts to an exercise of dominion and control over a chattel of the plaintiff's, which is so long or serious in nature that the defendant must pay the full value of the chattel as damages. Conversion may be effectuated by a variety of methods: 1) wrongfully acquiring the property (for example, by theft or embezzlement, which also makes the civil wrong of conversion a crime); 2) wrongfully transferring the property, such as by selling or mis-delivering it; 3) wrongfully detaining the property, such as refusing to return it to its rightful owner; 4) substantially changing the property; 5) destroying or severely damaging the property; or 6) misusing the property. The property converted must be tangible personal property, and not land or real property. Recall also that conversion is an intentional tort and thus "merely" causing accidental damage to or loss of the property is not sufficient for the tort of conversion, though, as will be seen in this chapter, it may be grounds for the tort of negligence. At times, it is difficult to draw the line between "mere" trespass to chattels and the more serious legal wrong of conversion. The more serious the damage to the property, the longer the time that the defendant holds the property, and the more extensively the defendant uses the property, the more likely that a jury will find that the conversion tort has been committed. Assuming a conversion, the aggrieved party gets as damages, the fair market value of the property at the time and place of conversion. This means redress can in essence be a "forced sale" even if the defendant offers to return the property; a plaintiff is not obligated to take an item back. Finally, the plaintiff, if he or she does want the item back, can seek a writ of "replevin" from the court, ordering the defendant to return the item.

Defenses

Although the discussion of the intentional torts to persons and property in this chapter has touched on several defenses germane to specific torts, we must make mention of three general categories of defenses: 1) consent; 2) self-defense; and 3) defense of property.

The consent defense holds that as a general rule, a defendant is not liable for a wrongful act if the plaintiff has consented to that act. Consent may be given expressly or impliedly. Implied consent is often referred to as "apparent consent," that is, the consent that a reasonably prudent person would give in such circumstances, such as, for example, when engaging in a bodily contact sport or shopping on "sale day" in a crowded shopping mall. Consent, moreover, will also be implied by the law in an emergency situation where some type of action, such as medical care, is necessary to save an unconscious person's life. Similarly, pursuant to many states' Good Samaritan statutes, a rescuer who voluntarily assists at the scene of an emergency may be absolved from intentional tort liability by statute, though typically the rescuer is still obligated to effectuate the rescue or render aid in a careful and non-negligent manner.

Self-defense is an ancient legal doctrine, and one that still affords a viable defense to intentional tort liability. When a person possesses reasonable grounds to believe that he or she is being attacked, or about to be attacked, that person may use such force as reasonably necessary to protect against the potential harm. This defense is available when one has a reasonable belief as to another party's hostile actions or intentions. The "apparent necessity" of defending oneself is all that is required, not actual necessity and, therefore, a reasonable mistake as to the existence of the danger does not negate the defense: The "classic" example being the "unloaded gun" scenario. Moreover, under the old common law, there is no duty to retreat, though there are certain differences among the states today. Thus, most courts would hold that there is no duty to try to escape; a person may "stand ground," and thereby defend oneself.

Yet how much force may be used in this self-defense? As a general rule, only that force which reasonably appears necessary to prevent the harm will be authorized. Consequently, one may not use force likely to cause death or serious bodily injury unless one reasonably believes that he or she is in danger of serious bodily injury. If more force than necessary is employed, the actor will lose his or her legal right to self-defense. As a result, he or she becomes the potentially tortious aggressor. Finally, it is important to note that if properly used, the right to self-defense extends to third party injuries. That is, if in the course of reasonably defending oneself, one accidentally injures a bystander, the actor is still protected by the defense.

The common law right to self-defense encompasses one's right to defend his or her property. Accordingly, one may use reasonable force to prevent the commission of a tort against his or her property. There are material limitations, however. First, a request to desist must precede the use of force, unless it appears futile or dangerous to do so. Second, this type of defense is limited to preventing the commission of a tort against the property. As such, once the tort is complete or the plaintiff is permanently dispossessed of his or her property, he or she may not use force to recapture or avenge the tort. Yet there is a "hot pursuit" exception, which arises when a person is in "hot pursuit" of someone who wrongfully dispossessed him or her of the property. Once again, only reasonable force can be used, but for defending property, "reasonable" does not include force which will cause death or serious bodily injury.

Conclusion

These common law intentional torts protect against intentional infringements of legally protected interests. When injury to a person or harm to property occurs not through intentional or purposeful conduct, but rather by means of unintentional and careless conduct, another vital area of the law is brought forth—the tort of negligence.

The Tort of Negligence in the United States

Introduction

The legal wrong of negligence is an unintentional tort. In such a case, the actor does not wish to bring about the injurious consequences of his or her act, but the conduct nevertheless creates a risk of harmful consequences. This tort derives from very old common law, with recorded decisions dating back to the 1300s in England, although the tort is even older than that. The overall purpose of this body of the law is to protect a person's interest in being free from harm carelessly caused by another party's conduct. As one "price" for living in a civilized "kingdom," a person is held to a fundamental duty: When one decides to affirmatively act, regardless of the activity, one owes an obligation to others to act in a reasonable, prudent, and careful manner. The failure to exercise this requisite degree of care will subject the careless actor to legal liability for the tort of negligence.

The term "negligence," moreover, is a legal term that is used in two ways. First, it is the name given to the civil wrong tort lawsuit applied for acting unreasonably. Second, it is a type of wrongful conduct which is itself a component of the tort cause of action. In the latter sense, negligence is the conduct that falls below the standard of care imposed by the law for the protection of others from the risk of harm. Intent is not an issue in a negligence case. Even though an actor does not intend a harmful outcome, even though he or she may be morally blameless, nonetheless he or she may be liable civilly for committing a legal wrong. Thus, the common law will not allow a person to defend his or her behavior on the ground that his or her subjective person or frame of mind was to act in a non-negligent manner. The ultimate issue, therefore, is not the reasonableness of the defendant's state of mind, but the reasonableness of his or her conduct.

Negligence, however, is not absolute liability or even liability without fault. In every case, it must be demonstrated that the defendant was at fault by failing to comply with the legal duty to conduct himself or herself in a reasonably prudent manner under the circumstances. Intent is immaterial; conduct is critical. The duty of due care—and thus, potential negligence liability—applies to anyone who acts: driving a car, operating as a surgeon (in which case negligence is treated as malpractice doctrine with certain specialized rules, as will be seen), manufacturing or selling goods, providing services, or hiring, retaining, supervising, disciplining, and discharging employees.

Elements of the Negligence Cause of Action

In order to prevail in a negligence lawsuit, a plaintiff must establish the four key elements to the cause of action: 1) duty of care, 2) breach of duty, 3) causation, and 4) damages.

The first component of negligence is the "duty of care." When a person engages in an activity, he or she is held to a duty of due care to act as a reasonably prudent person. As such, the "actor" must take precautions against creating unreasonable risks of injury to other people or their property. However, there is no legal duty imposed upon a person to take precautions against events which cannot be reasonably foreseen. The plaintiff must show the existence of a duty, recognized by the law, requiring the defendant conform his or her conduct to a legally established standard in order to protect the plaintiff from an unreasonable risk of harm. This standard of care comes from the old common law days and has often been characterized as the "reasonably prudent man" precept (in modern times, it is often referred to as the "reasonably prudent person" standard). This mythical legal person is an average person in the community acting under circumstances surrounding the defendant. It is important to note that the defendant's individual characteristics are not considered. Such considerations include whether or not the defendant is stupid or excitable; rather, the defendant's conduct is measured against this "reasonable prudent person." For example, in the case of a manufacturer of goods, generally, a manufacturer will be held to a standard of care to see that a consumer is not harmed by the goods sold. Consequently, there may be liability imposed against the manufacturer for failing to inspect and/or test the goods and to maintain suitable quality control, for failing to disclose and to warn of known defects in the goods, and for failing to use due care in the design, manufacture, and sale of the goods. This duty of due care extends to all people who might foreseeably be injured by the goods, not just the buyer of the goods. Also, it is important to point out that there are particular standards of conduct for some people that are different from the normal reasonable person standard. For example, members of a profession, such as doctors and lawyers, are deemed to hold and to exercise the knowledge and skills of a typical member of that profession. Such a specialized standard of care brings the negligence doctrine into the realm of malpractice law, which essentially is based on common law negligence principles, but which usually requires expert witnesses to educate the jury as to the particular standard of care in that particular profession.

The second element to a lawsuit for negligence is the "breach of the duty" of due care. Breach of duty occurs when the defendant's conduct fails to conform to the required standard of care. That is, when the defendant's conduct falls below the level required by the applicable standard of care owed to the plaintiff, the defendant has breached his or her duty. This breach can be triggered by an act or by a failure to act when the law imposes an affirmative obligation to act. This key negligence question is regarded as a "question of fact" and thus, is for the jury to decide. Such discovery is usually guided by expert witnesses, most notably in cases of malpractice.

The third requirement to a negligence cause of action is "causation." The law requires a sufficient causal connection between the defendant's careless conduct and the resulting harm. The causation element is satisfied by a showing of two elements: 1) the existence of actual causation, called "cause in fact," and 2) the presence of legal causation, called "proximate cause." It is very important to note that the common law not only requires causation, but also makes a critical distinction between these two types of causation. In fact, causation is really a matter of physics: Causation is a series or chain of events, with one event leading to another and ultimately producing a final conclusion. Therefore, before legal liability can be imposed upon a defendant, there must be sufficient evidence that the defendant's careless action was in fact a cause of the plaintiff's injuries. The standard legal test for establishing causation is called the "but for" test. This legal test holds that an act is the cause, in fact, of an eventual consequence if the latter would not have occurred "but for" the first act. However, when there are several forces that combine and bring about the plaintiff's injuries, and any one of them would have been sufficient to cause the plaintiff's injuries, a special causation test is used, called the "substantial factor" test. This test holds that causation is established in a multiple causation situation when the defendant's conduct was a substantial factor in causing the plaintiff's injuries.

In addition to demonstrating causation in fact, the plaintiff also must show, as part of his or her negligence lawsuit, that the defendant's careless conduct was also a proximate cause of the plaintiff's injury. Whereas causation in fact is a matter of physics, the doctrine of proximate cause is more a question of policy. Proximate cause is a most interesting common law formulation because it is a doctrine that protects careless people. So, even if one acts carelessly, the doctrine of proximate cause maintains that not all of a plaintiff's injuries and harms in fact will be proximately caused by a carelessly acting defendant. Rather, the doctrine holds that a careless defendant is not legally responsible for the unforeseeable, remote, or unusual consequences of his or her own careless act. Accordingly, proximate cause serves as a limitation on the defendant's liability.

It is the function of the jury in a common law system to determine whether proximate cause and causation in fact are present. For example, in a case being litigated as of this writing, there is a negligence lawsuit being asserted by the District of Columbia against certain gun manufacturers, contending that the manufacturers carelessly "over-supplied" guns to the state of Virginia—a state that has liberal gun laws—and that these guns have been purchased legally in Virginia, but then illegally brought into the District, where they have been used illegally to commit crimes and to harm people. These injured District residents, who for the most part have no health insurance, have been treated and cared for by District public hospitals, thereby costing the District a great deal of money for health care expenditures. Assuming that the District can adequately establish the duty and breach of duty elements with its novel "over-supply" theory, it is perhaps provable that these guns in fact caused the injuries. The question then is was it foreseeable that the guns would end up in the District and be used criminally to create harm and injury? All such questions are for the jury to resolve, but how exactly should such a juror decide?

The fourth and final element to a cause of action for negligence is the requirement of damages: The plaintiff must prove some type of actual loss or damage. Damages are not assumed outright in a negligence case and nominal damages are not awarded; rather, some type of actual harm or injury to a legally protected interest is necessary. The objective of damages is compensatory: to restore the plaintiff insofar as possible to his or her condition before the injury or harm occurred. Damages themselves may include special damages, such as economic losses, lost wages, medical expenses, business profits, and future expenses. Moreover, additional damages for "pain and suffering" or emotional distress are recoverable, as are damages for disability and disfigurement. Finally, if the defendant's careless conduct is grossly negligent or reckless in nature, then the plaintiff can recover an extra award of damages, called punitive damages, at the discretion of the jury as a way to punish the defendant and deter others from engaging in such grossly negligent behavior in the future.

It is necessary to point out that several states in the United States have, by statute, curtailed the jury's power to award unlimited punitive damages by, for example, requiring that punitive damages not exceed five times the amount of the compensatory award itself. It is also necessary to point out that the United States Supreme Court has ruled that punitive damages cannot be extreme or excessive—they must bear some reasonable relationship to the harm done, otherwise they will be unconstitutional as violating the Due Process clause of the Constitution.

An important negligence lawsuit occurred in Ft. Lauderdale, Florida, in 2006. Although a local case, it has national implications. The jury in the case decided that the health club chain, LA Fitness, was negligent in operating its facilities and, consequently must pay over $600,000 in damages to the family of a Ft. Lauderdale man who died of sudden cardiac arrest while working out at a local club. The specific negligence that contributed to the patron's death, the jury decided, was that no one attempted to perform CPR on the dying 49-year-old man, and also that the club did not have an automated external defibrillator that could have saved his life. This case emerges as especially noteworthy because it appears to be the first in the United States wherein a health club has been found liable for failing to have a defibrillator on the premises and the fact that it was not a common practice, at the time, to have defibrillators at health clubs did not sway the jury. Now, according to a spokesperson, all LA Fitness facilities have defibrillators.

Generally speaking, damage liability for the tort of negligence is deemed by the common law to be "joint and several." That means that when there is more than one defendant who has caused the plaintiff's damages, they are all equally responsible for paying the judgment, regardless of the percentage of fault attributed to each individual defendant. The policy behind this old common law rule is that it is preferable for a party who is at least partially at fault to pay for all damages as opposed to the innocent, injured plaintiff only receiving partial compensation. (Accordingly, the so-called "deep pocket" defendant can always proceed legally, at least theoretically, against his or her co-defendants.) An example of this is a defendant who is accorded only 20% of the fault but may nonetheless have to pay 100% of the damages if the other, more culpable co-defendant cannot pay. In such a case, the first defendant becomes the proverbial "deep pocket."

However, it must be noted that several states in the United States have now, by statute, changed this common law rule. As a result, such states hold that a defendant only has to pay his/her apportioned share of the damages regardless of the ability of his or her co-defendants to pay the plaintiff fully.

Special Negligence Doctrines

There are a variety of special negligence doctrines, each with its own peculiar rules and far-reaching consequences, that must be briefly addressed. The first is called the doctrine of *res ipsa loquitur,* which comes from Latin meaning "the thing speaks for itself." In essence, *res ipsa loquitur* maintains that the fact that a particular injury occurred may in and of itself establish a breach of the duty owed to the plaintiff.

The rationale behind the doctrine, which is a very old common law one, is that it may be very difficult in certain circumstances for a plaintiff to acquire sufficient evidence to show a breach of the duty of due care, for example, when the plaintiff is injured by a poorly made product but the plaintiff cannot show the careless situation that existed at the defendant's manufacturing facility. This doctrine also acts as a legal device that a plaintiff may be able to use to permit a jury to consider the issue as to whether the defendant was negligent, i.e., that when the facts of the case indicate that the plaintiff's injuries resulted from the defendant's negligence, the jury may be able to infer the defendant's liability. Furthermore, this doctrine may emerge as being very critical for a plaintiff seeking to establish the breach of duty component of negligence.

There are two critical components that a plaintiff must be able to demonstrate in order to take advantage of the *res ipsa loquitur* doctrine: 1) that the accident causing the plaintiff's injury is not the type that ordinarily would occur unless someone was negligent, such as, for example, when an automobile abruptly swerves off the road in "good" driving conditions or a bottle or can of soda sitting on a supermarket shelf suddenly explodes; and 2) evidence must exist showing that the instrumentality which caused the injury was in the sole control of the defendant, such as in the case of the defendant driving the erratic car or the defendant having the power and opportunity to exercise control, such as in the exploding bottle scenario. If these two requirements are present, the legal effect of the doctrine is that the plaintiff has thereby established an initial case for negligence and accordingly, the judge will send the case to the jury, presuming the causation and damages elements are present, of course. However, if the defendant can submit evidence of due care, the jury has the power to reject the plaintiff's res ipsa loquitur inference of negligence and, as such, ultimately find in favor for the defendant.

The second special type of negligence doctrine is called the "negligence per se" doctrine. The premise behind this is that, at times, the standard of care in a negligence case may be established by proving that the applicable statute provides for a criminal penalty in a particular case. The legal result is that the duty enumerated in the statute will replace the more general common law duty of due care. In such a case, the plaintiff must prove that he or she (the plaintiff) is in a class intended to be protected by the statute and that the purpose of the statute was to prevent the type of harm which the plaintiff suffered. So, generally speaking, the statute must pertain to the plaintiff's injury. Examples include when a consumer is injured by an inadequate warning label on a drug when a statute or regulation sets forth the warning, or when an automobile driver is injured by another driver who has violated traffic control laws. The notable effect of establishing the violation of a statute is the occurrence of the "negligence per se" dimension. That is, the plaintiff will have established a conclusive presumption of the duty and breach of duty elements in a negligence lawsuit. Meanwhile, the plaintiff still has to plead and prove the remaining elements of the cause of action.

The next special negligence area is the doctrine of negligent infliction of emotional distress. The question of when a victimized plaintiff can recover mental anguish damages is always a key issue in negligence. There are four key precepts to this legal doctrine. First, if there is a physical injury, then damages for the attendant's emotional distress are recoverable as part of the physical injury. This rule is the traditional "pain and suffering" rule. Second, if there is a physical impact to the plaintiff, which in itself causes no actual physical injury but which is nevertheless accompanied or followed by emotional distress, then damages are permitted for such emotional distress. An example would be when a defendant negligently drives his/her car into the plaintiff, who is not physically injured in any way but who still suffers fright and shock. This rule typically is designated as the "impact rule." Third, the more modern rule that even if there is no physical impact but the plaintiff nonetheless suffers physical disorders, such as shock to the nervous system, then damages are permissible for the emotional and mental suffering. Finally, if there is no impact and the plaintiff does not suffer any physical disorders but the plaintiff does suffer emotional distress, then there is no recovery permitted. An example of this last rule would arise when the defendant negligently "sideswipes" the plaintiff's automobile, which causes the plaintiff to be very frightened and upset, but who even then does not suffer any physical disorder or illness, which means the plaintiff in fact has no cause of action. As noted previously, the rule itself is different when it comes to the intentional infliction of emotional distress. In such a circumstance, no "impact" at all is necessary, but the wrongful conduct must be severe and cause actual and severe emotional distress.

The principles of negligence have long been applied to the owners of land ascertain the duties of landowners to those people who come upon their land. This area of law is also called *"premises liability."* The fundamental principle is that an owner of land owes a duty to exercise reasonable care to safeguard people who come upon the land. This duty extends to land owners who are also landlords and thus have a legal duty to exercise reasonable care to safeguard their tenants and their tenants' guests in the common areas of the leasehold, such as entrance ways, parking areas, laundry rooms, pools, and clubhouses. Under the common law, the basic duty of the landowner was more precisely defined by the status of the person who came upon his or her land. The first category is called "business invitees." These are people who are invited to come upon the land for the benefit of the landowner. The landowner has a duty to protect invitees from dangers that the landowner knew of or should have known by means of a reasonable inspection. That is, for a business invitee there is an affirmative duty to discover and remedy or at least warn of any hidden dangers that might harm the business invitee. So, a supermarket is continually inspecting its premises for wet spots on the floor or banana peels or broken glass or any other hazardous conditions that could cause injury. The supermarket would put up warning signs, cones, or tape until the dangerous condition is corrected. The second category of people that can come upon the land is called "guests." These are people who come upon the land with the owner's permission for the primary benefit of themselves and not the landowner. Examples would include social guests of the landowner as well as sales people who solicit the landowner on their own motivation. The landowner owes a duty to warn guests of dangers that the landowner is aware of or should be aware of, but there is no affirmative duty to inspect for hazards. Finally, the third category is "trespassers." These are people who come on the land without the landowner's knowledge and/or consent. In most states, based on the old common law, the landowner does not owe the trespasser any duty except not to intentionally harm the trespasser, for example, by means of hidden devices or traps, such as "spring guns." However, in some states, even the trespasser has the right to be warned of hidden or latent dangers which could not be readily seen on the surface. However, if a risk or hazard is so obvious, such as a pond or big pit or construction site on the property, then the landowner need not as a general rule warn of the dangerous condition (though the landowner may have liability to children injured based on the "attractive nuisance" theory).

Finally, there is a distinction of great consequence that the common law makes between nonfeasance and misfeasance. Nonfeasance means not acting and, most significantly, as a general rule, there is no legal duty imposed on a person to affirmatively act to aid, rescue, or benefit another person. As a result, nonfeasance is not legally actionable as a tort of negligence. The "classic" case is the drowning example, where the expert swimmer in a boat with a rope and life preserver does nothing and watches the victim drown. Legally, there is no liability; morally, however, is another question. There are many exceptions to nonfeasance. Even if one does not have a duty to act, once one decides to act and affirmatively undertakes to do so for the assistance or benefit of another, one then has a duty to act carefully. Consequently, if the careless "rescuing" causes injury, tort liability for negligence may in fact exist. Similarly, if the defendant's own negligence places another in danger, the defendant is now under an obligation to use reasonable care to aid or rescue that person. Another example stems from the old common law whereby common carriers and innkeepers are under an affirmative legal duty to warn and aid and assist passengers and guests as well as prevent injuries to them and to third parties. Finally, members of a profession may be obligated—not by the law, but rather by the codes of ethics of their profession—to affirmatively act to aid people. Examples include a registered nurse who is morally bound by the code of ethics of the nursing profession and the Florence Nightingale Oath to provide medical assistance.

Defenses

There are three main defenses to a lawsuit for negligence: 1) contributory negligence; 2) comparative negligence; and 3) assumption of the risk. "Contributory negligence" is careless conduct on the plaintiff's part that is a contributing cause to his or her own injury. Contributory negligence is a very harsh common law doctrine because it acts as a complete bar to recovery regardless of how slight the plaintiff's own negligence. However, in most states in the United States today, by statute, the defense of contributory negligence has been abolished and replaced by the doctrine of comparative negligence. "Comparative negligence" is not a complete defense; rather, the plaintiff's damages are determined, the jury makes a finding on each party's fault, and the plaintiff's damages are accordingly reduced by the proportion which the plaintiff's own fault bears on the total amount of the plaintiff's harm.

"Assumption" of risk arises when the plaintiff encounters a known risk voluntarily, for example, by going on stairs that are visibly being repaired. When the plaintiff thereby in essence consents to assuming the risk of injury from a particular hazard, this assumption thereby acts as a complete defense for the defendant.

The Doctrine of Strict Tort Liability in the United States

Strict liability, or liability without fault, is a special type of liability imposed by the common law. Although an actor may not only have not intended any harm, and even though he or she acted in a careful and prudent manner, the actor is nevertheless legally responsible for any injuries caused by his or her conduct.

Strict liability is imposed in three types of situations. One instance involves activities that the law regards as "ultra-hazardous," such as construction blasting, crop-dusting, fumigation, and the construction and maintenance of reservoirs and dams. These activities and conditions are potentially so highly dangerous and threaten substantial injury to the public—regardless of how much care is exercised—that the duty of safety is considered to be one that is absolute, i.e., that insurance is the only "answer" in such a case. Another category of strict liability case deals with the liability of the owners and possessors of dangerous animals, which as a topic is interesting but beyond the purposes of this book. The final category of strict liability is the highly significant and consequential business law and consumer protection doctrine of strict tort liability for the manufacturers and sellers of defective products. This important area will be covered in detail in the following chapter on Products Liability as well as in the chapter dealing with Sales Law.

Global Legal Perspectives

The French Intentional Tort of Emotional Distress[35]

The French Labor Code (Code du Travail) provides for establishing a legal wrong that is comparable in definition to the common law tort of intentional infliction of emotional distress. The French legal wrong is called "psychological harassment." For example, pursuant to the Labor Code and pertinent case law, as analyzed by one legal commentator, an employee is not allowed to suffer repeated acts of psychological harassment where the purpose or effect is the deterioration of working conditions that may violate the employee's rights or dignity, impair the employee's physical or mental health, or compromise the employee's professional future. Similar to the U.S. tort of intentional infliction of emotional distress, the victim in France must demonstrate that the harasser

---

[35] See Yuen, Rachel A. (2005).

intentionally or deliberately harassed him or her. However, the punishment for this type of harassment in France, as opposed to the U.S., is not only a civil wrong—for which the victim or a trade union, with the victim's permission, can institute against the harasser—but also a criminal wrong punishable by a fine and imprisonment of up to one year. The employer is also under certain legal obligations, most importantly to promptly investigate complaints of harassment and to take steps to remedy the harassment as well as to display, in writing, workplace rules prohibiting harassment. If the employer fails to do so, or disagrees factually with the employee asserting harassment, then the matter is referred to an adjudicative panel of the industrial tribunal, which will take proper measures to stop any harassment.

Colombia Negligence Law[36]

As is the case for most Latin American countries, Colombia's jurisprudence, including its tort law, is based largely upon its civil code.

According to two legal commentators whose analysis of Colombian negligence law is based on an analysis of that country's legal scholars, negligence liability specifically entails a link between individuals: one who causes the harm and the other who suffers it. The term liability here encompasses the duty to assume the responsibility for the consequences of one's act or conduct.

Also for the purposes of Colombian law, non-contractual duty is the term that refers to when a person wrongs or harms another or his or her belongings: This form of liability emerges where there is no contractual connection between the two. Non-contractual civil liability is divided into direct or "personal" liability and indirect or "complex" liability. Indirect liability includes vicarious liability as well as acts made with the aid of instrumentalities that are used in dangerous activities. Both forms of liability are codified in the Colombian Civil Code. The Colombian legislature, therefore, maintains a division in the treatment of contractual versus non-contractual liability and this differential treatment is manifested in the separate codification of these two forms of liability in the Colombian Civil Code.

The act that causes the harm or injury does not have to be an illicit act. Rather, under certain provisions of the Civil Code, "culpa," or culpability or fault on the part of the actor, must be demonstrated. But in cases of "dangerous" activities, the aggrieved party only has to prove that the occurrence caused by the defendant was in fact the causation of his or her injuries and harm. Legislators in Colombia thus have attempted to free the plaintiff victim from the burdens of proof and persuasion produced by introducing the element of fault into the

---

[36] See Bartels, Natalia M, and Madden, M. Stuart (Spring 2001).

equation for sustaining a negligence liability cause of action. Accordingly, a victim of a civil non-contractual wrongdoing should prevail if he or she can establish that his or her harm and injuries arose out of the defendant's conducting a dangerous activity as defined by the Civil Code. If the plaintiff is successful in establishing the claim, the breach of due care, as well as the concomitant liability, is presumed by law. This feature of Colombia negligence law clearly provides an important advantage for an aggrieved party who does not have to prove a defendant's fault.

Dangerous activities ("actividades peligrosas") refer to human pursuits that create a high and unavoidable risk of great harm. A defendant can only be exonerated by a break in the causation chain, such as an act of *force majeure.* One important point remains consistent pursuant to Colombia law: The person engaging in the dangerous activity bears the burden of exonerating himself or herself or itself from liability. Otherwise, for negligence liability, there must be demonstrated malice or negligence on the part of the allegedly responsible party and this negligence requirement is founded on the notion of fault. In certain circumstances, fault can be presumed, however, the fact that fault is presumed or proved is a matter of legal interpretation.

The Civil Code, as noted, defines what Colombian law refers to as dangerous activities. Significantly, to drive an automobile is considered a form of dangerous activity as automobile accidents, not unexpectedly, have constituted one of the most abundant sources of Colombian personal injury lawsuits. The elements necessary for negligence for this type of activity are as follows: 1) there must be an accident; 2) the accident must be occasioned by the dangerous activity; 3) the victim is not obligated to demonstrate the culpability of the actor of the injurious act; 4) the person liable must be responsible for the dangerous activity; and 5) the accident cannot be the result of force majeure, the fault of a third party, or the fault of the victim. Examples of such accidents include running a red light and speeding, both situations potentially contain both a criminal act and a civil wrong. Colombian accident law, therefore, is plainly different from the U.S., where driving an automobile is definitely factually dangerous, but nonetheless, U.S. law does not regard driving an automobile as a "dangerous" activity for U.S. "strict liability," which means liability without fault.

Management Strategies

Solicitation of one's co-workers to leave their employment and work for a new firm, especially one to be established by a fellow employee, is a very problematical area legally. In particular, the tort of intentional interference of contract can arise when an employee of a firm plans to leave and start his or her own business and then commences to solicit key employees of the employer during or after employment. If such solicitation occurs during current employment, particularly when the employee has an employment contract for a certain term, the prospective entrepreneur risks a lawsuit based on the old common law's duty of loyalty to one's employer. And in either case, the entrepreneur risks a tort lawsuit for the intentional interference of contract. Both can result in an injunction and the latter can result in tort damages. So, to be safe, the entrepreneurial employee should merely tell his or her co-workers that he or she is leaving or has left, and then if the employees ask why, the entrepreneur can state that he or she plans to, or has started, a new business, and give them a phone number and email where the entrepreneur can be reached. Telling one's co-workers about one's future plans is permissible, but "raiding" them may be a violation of tort and contract law (if there is an "anti-piracy" clause in a contract).

The negligence doctrine certainly can be applied to the employer's hiring of employees, and consequently the employer can be deemed negligent if it does not use due care in the hiring of its employees, for example, choosing the wrong person for a specific job. The rationale is that the employer has a duty to customers, clients, and the general public to act with due care and as a reasonably prudent employer when it comes to hiring the employees to staff its business. For example, if the employer is contemplating hiring a person for a position that requires driving a vehicle, the prudent employer would ask about driving accidents, tickets, and driver license status and any license suspensions, as well as drug or alcohol use; and the employer also should check with the Department of Motor Vehicles for the pertinent jurisdiction. If the employer breaches this duty, and harm is caused to customer or other third party, he or she can sue the employer for negligence. This lawsuit, it should be noted, is one directly against the employer for its own negligence; it is not a vicarious or imputed liability lawsuit (though there may be such a lawsuit if the carelessly selected employee carelessly injures a third party in the course of employment). Negligent hiring typically is based on the employer failing to investigate or failing to do a careful investigation on the background –work, professional, personality – of the employee, and a proper investigation would have discovered some troublesome or problematical fact about the employee. Recall, however, that the employer, as does any person or business that acts, does not have to act perfectly. Negligence law does not require that a party be, in effect, an insurer against harm. The fundamental legal duty is "merely" to act carefully. So, regarding hiring, if the employer does conduct an investigation, and it is a reasonable one, the employer would not be liable even if a more thorough or different type of investigation would have discovered a problem regarding the employee.

Managers must devise strategies and adapt tactics to avoid lawsuits, especially those pertaining to torts and products liability. For example, toys, drugs, and other products vary in their shape, size, use, etc., and it is for this reason that governments of countries are forced to enact laws that protect the general populace from their potential dangers.[37] Global managers who work in manufacturing companies are thus compelled to understand the laws surrounding product safety. Therefore, it becomes a firm's responsibility to provide proper training courses for their international employees, including managers, on how to understand and abide by the various product liability and safety laws that exist globally. Communication becomes a very important tool, especially when companies are trying to sell their products overseas. They must first "win over" the consumers by advertising how safe and user-friendly their products are. This approach is one of the most popular ways of selling products.

Also, communication is only effective when the proper meaning of a law is understood, especially to "everyday" consumers who do not keep up with such laws. Therefore, when trying to sell products, firms are often forced to send out messages to not only protect their image, but also to inform consumers. For example, in the United States, Philip Morris creates several advertisements showing how harmful cigarette smoking can be. These advertisements are done to not only protect and warn consumers from harm that comes from cigarettes, but also to provide a "safety net" from tort and product liability lawsuits. The same situation holds true for drug companies. Warnings and studies are conducted to help consumers but also to protect the firms from lawsuits. Accordingly, management must establish such proactive strategies to prevent future suits that may not only cause a loss in profits, but also lead the firm financially downhill.

Summary

This chapter described the tort law of the United States, including several subcategories. The tort law itself was originally created to protect victims faced with physical harm as well as to deter future injurious cases. The law's initial purpose continues to be relevant today, but it is also expanding globally into several other arenas, including the manufacturing business. Countries around the world have followed in the footsteps of the United States by developing product liability laws and tort laws in order to protect consumers, citizens, and residents. In addition, the laws are also created to protect businesses and manufacturers from consumers who are willing to take advantage of products and laws. It is for this reason that international managers and entrepreneurs are often forced to develop strategies to avoid legal problems with tort law.

---

[37] Contributed by Bina Patel, Nova Southeastern University.

International firms should provide thorough training programs for their global staff, especially management, to understand and review all laws, and especially those pertaining to their type of business. This effort should be made to not only protect the image and the financial well-being of the firm, but also to protect and educate the consumer. In essence, international managers are obligated to acknowledge, understand, and abide by the various tort laws that exist in countries around the world in order to achieve their goals in a legal manner.

TEN

PRODUCTS LIABILITY

The corpus of law dealing with product safety typically is designated as "products liability" law. Product safety emerges as a very important legal challenge for the manager of a global manufacturing, distribution, and sales company. What is the extent of a company's legal obligation to consumer safety? What is a firm's legal responsibility for the products it produces, distributes, and/or sells? Should a company legally guarantee the safety of those who buy and use its products? This chapter examines various legal views in the U.S. and in other selected international legal jurisdictions regarding the legal duties of business to consumers. The chapter also seeks to ascertain the legal responsibilities of various entities on the product manufacturing and marketing chain as they relate to the consumer.

There are a variety of product liability legal theories in U.S. law, and there are also bodies of products liability law in an international setting. Where does a company's duty to protect consumers begin, and where does it end—legally and in a global marketing and legal environment?

U.S. Legal Doctrines

Introduction

Several legal theories in the U.S. impact product safety and, to wit, contract law, the tort of negligence, the tort of fraud, warranty law based on the Uniform Commercial Code and federal statute, and a relatively new and very significant legal doctrine—strict liability in tort. Some of these theories are common-law—based and others are statutory in nature. There are also federal and state agencies that deal with product safety, particularly the federal Consumer Products Safety Commission.

Contract Law

Contract law will be covered extensively in Chapter 12, but it is important to note now that there may be a contractual relationship between the consumer and the seller of the product. And if so, the seller will be obligated by virtue of contract law to fulfill the duties and promises created by the contract as to the nature, characteristic, and quality of the product.

Tort Law—Negligence and Fraud

The tort of fraud—or the intentional "deceit" formulation, as it was called in the old, common law—which was mentioned in the previous chapter, requires, in addition to an express purposeful misrepresentation about a product by the wrongdoer and reasonable reliance by the deceived and aggrieved party on the misrepresentation, a finding supported by sufficient evidence that the wrongdoer made the misrepresentation intentionally and with *scienter*—that is, an "evil mind"—intent on purposefully causing and inducing the innocent party to make an erroneous conclusion. That old, Anglo-American common law "intent" requirement makes the utilization of the tort of intentional fraud a very problematic one in a products liability case. Lying about the quality or characteristics of a product or, for that matter, anything, is not automatically illegal. However, fraudulently and deceitfully lying is!

The tort of negligence, also covered in the previous chapter, requires that the manufacturer, wholesaler, distributor, and retailer of the product exercise reasonable and ordinary care in the manufacture, distribution, and sale of the product. These entities on the marketing chain all have a duty to exercise due care not to harm the consumer or user of the product. As such, the failure to comply with this legally imposed duty of due care may subject an entity on the marketing chain to legal liability based on the Anglo-American common law of negligence. For example, if a product has a warning thereon that it can cause burns, a prudent retailer will store and display it on an upper shelf where young children cannot get their hands on it. By the same token, the prudent manufacturer should also have a child-proof cap thereon.

One point regarding negligence is critical to make, and that is that negligence law definitely is not a scheme of insurance or guaranty law. That is, if a party, say the manufacturer, acted carefully in the production of the product, took all reasonable steps to protect the consumer, and informed the consumer of any "irremovable" risks, then the manufacturer acted reasonably and carefully and thereby fulfilled its legal obligation pursuant to negligence law. The fact that the consumer was still injured is an unfortunate "accident," and a non-compensable one, at least under negligence principles. Because negligence does not exactly equate with an insurance scheme, consequently, a manufacturer is not acting illegally if the consumer was harmed by an unavoidable risk or one that could not have reasonably been foreseen or prevented.

Warranty Law

Warranty law, which is based predominantly in the United States on the Uniform Commercial Code (UCC), requires that the seller of the product "live up to" the claims that are expressly made about the product as well as comply with any warranties that are implied in the transaction and are otherwise imposed by the law. Warranty law will be covered in detail in the chapter discussing Sales Law and the Uniform Commercial Code. However, it is important to note for the purposes of this chapter that the injured consumer may confront certain major obstacles when pursuing legal rights under UCC warranty law. First, there is no legal obligation that the manufacturer or seller make any express warranties at all. Yet some warranties, as will be seen in Chapter 12, are implied by the law, and thus are automatically imposed on certain manufacturers and sellers of goods. Nonetheless, these implications may be legally disclaimed by the manufacturer and seller, thereby rendering the implied warranties legally moot. Moreover, as also will be seen, there are notice and common law privity requirements in attempting to hold certain parties on the marketing chain liable for breach of warranty. Therefore, establishing warranty liability emerges as a difficult task for the injured consumer.

There also is a body of warranty law in the United States based on a federal statute, the Magnuson-Moss Warranty Act, enacted by Congress in 1975. This Act is discussed in the Consumer Protection chapter, but it is appropriate to point out here that there are two major problems with the Act as far as an aggrieved product consumer is concerned. First, the Act does not require a manufacturer or seller to make any express warranties at all; and second, the Act does not create any implied warranties for the consumer. However, if a manufacturer or seller does provide an express warranty, the Act requires that the product be labeled with a "full warranty," which guarantees the repair or replacement of the defective product, or a "limited" warranty, which limits the scope of the full warranty in some manner. This important distinction will be explained in the Consumer Protection chapter.

Strict Liability in Tort

Strict liability in tort is a relatively new legal cause of action for the aggrieved consumer, at least when compared negligence and fraud tort law. But strict liability is a very important and far-reaching legal doctrine, one created to promote consumer safety and to protect the consumer. Thus, strict liability is a doctrine that is very frequently asserted by the consumers who are harmed by products.

The doctrine of strict liability is a common law formulation. It was first promulgated by the Supreme Court of California in 1963, in the seminal case of *Greenman v. Yuba Power Products, Inc.* As an additional time frame point of reference, the doctrine itself was adopted in Florida by that state's Supreme Court in 1976. All states in the U.S. now have adopted strict liability, though in varying formulations. The doctrine was first enunciated in the Restatement (Second) of Torts: a compendium of existing law as well as recommendations of what the law should be, drafted by legal experts, and published by the American Law Institute. Restatements of the Law are not law per se, but they are very persuasive legal authority. This Restatement formulation for strict liability has been adopted in varying forms by virtually all U.S. states.

Strict liability in tort holds that one who sells any product in a defective condition, making it unreasonably dangerous to the user, the consumer, or his or her property, is liable to the ultimate user or consumer if: 1) the seller is engaged in the business of selling such a product, that is, the seller is an entity of the marketing chain; and 2) the product is expected to, and in fact does, reach the user or consumer without substantial change in the condition in which it was sold. Moreover, the doctrine of strict liability in tort applies if: 1) the seller has exercised all possible care in the preparation, distribution, and sale of the product, thereby clearly distinguishing strict liability from the tort of negligence; and 2) the user or consumer has not purchased the product from, or entered into any contractual relationship with, the seller of the product, thereby obviating the old contract "privity" requirement. Strict liability regarding products has been applied to manufacturers, wholesalers and distributors, retailers, as well as to commercial *lessors* of products. Damage to property is a recoverable element of damages in a strict liability lawsuit, but not, however, purely economic losses, meaning lost income, at least in the majority of the states.

One procedural legal problem will arise when a U.S. consumer seeks to bring a products liability action against a manufacturer in a foreign country. While a substantive legal discussion of obtaining jurisdiction over a foreign manufacturer is beyond the purposes of this book, the authors must point out that the U.S. consumer harmed by the foreign product will have to satisfy either state or federal jurisdictional requirements in securing jurisdiction as well as to satisfy the Due Process requirements of the U.S. Constitution, which require, according to the U.S. Supreme Court, a showing of "minimum contacts" between the foreign manufacturer and the United States. If the foreign manufacturer regularly sells, markets, advertises, services, or directly or indirectly distributes goods in the U.S. or even through a U.S. distributor (which the foreign manufacturer plainly cannot hide behind), then that type of presence will demonstrate a sufficient connection to the U.S. consumer market for the aggrieved consumer to not only sue the foreign manufacturer, but also to sue the manufacturer in the U.S. courts.

The essence of strict liability in tort for products is the finding of a "defect" in the product. Accordingly, in most jurisdictions, if a product is defective, it is presumed also to be "unreasonably dangerous" to the user or consumer. Products can be deemed "defective" in three ways: 1) the product contains a "flaw"; 2) the product lacks a warning; or 3) the product is defectively designed.

First, regarding flawed products, the main consideration is to measure the product in its manufactured state with the manufacturer's own specifications and standards for that type of product and then, if the product does not even meet the manufacturer's own "specs," the product is considered legally flawed, defective, unreasonably dangerous. The manufacturer (as well as distributors and retailers of the flawed product) is then strictly liable, in tort, for the flawed product when it causes harm. But it is important to note that evidence of how the product became flawed is not an issue in a strict liability "defect" lawsuit because strict liability is not a negligence lawsuit. Consequently, the fact that the manufacturer demonstrated that it had even an elaborate inspection, testing, and quality-control scheme (which obviously failed!) is irrelevant in a strict liability lawsuit. (Contrarily, such evidence would be critical to the disposition of a negligence lawsuit.)

In the U.S., the term "flaw" is used as one of the criteria for "defectiveness." But in Germany, the term "runaway" product is commonly used, and this latter term more accurately "captures" the usual situation: The manufacturer, though truly striving for that "zero-defect" objective (and award) somehow allowed the product to "runaway" from all the manufacturer's quality control and safety checks. It is interesting to note that one ordinarily does not see "flaw cases" reported in the law reports because typically, the cases are settled before an official and recorded legal disposition. So what real defense does the manufacturer have if the evidence indicates that its product, which caused harm, does not even conform to the manufacturer's own product standards?

The second way a product can be deemed defective is if it lacks a warning or the warning itself is inadequate. To be legally sufficient, the warning must address the nature and severity of the risk, how the consumer should handle the risk, as well as indicate any reasonable alternatives. The warnings, as well as labels and instructions, must clearly, simply, and prominently warn the consumer of the dangers involved in using the product. However, it is not necessary for the manufacturer to warn of risks which the reasonable and rational person should be aware of. Nevertheless, after such "classic" lawsuits as the McDonald's hot coffee case—in which the product was construed as defective due to the lack of a warning that the coffee was hot (actually, very, very hot!)—manufacturers now "err on the side of caution" and warn of risks that one might think an otherwise reasonable person should or would be cognizant of. Examples include warnings: not to use a snow-blower on the roof, not to use a CD rack as a ladder, not to allow children to play in a dishwasher, and not to fold a baby carriage with the baby in it. On the surface, these all seem rather obvious, and one would think this all falls within the purview of common sense and rationality. But nonetheless, the nature of a warning "defect," under strict liability, motivates manufacturers to issue such warnings.

A general warning will not protect a manufacturer from liability for a defectively designed or manufactured product. For example, an automobile manufacturer will not be able to obviate its liability under strict liability law for defectively designed or flawed brakes merely by stating that the brakes may fail under certain conditions. Note, though, that the obverse is not true; that is, an injured consumer can proceed with a failure to warn strict liability lawsuit even if there was neither a design nor manufacturing defect. An example of an obvious risk that a manufacturer would not have to warn could be in the case of a cigarette lighter which typically would ignite and cause a fire when applied to flammable material. Another would be a knife or an axe which might strike one's hand when cutting or chopping.

The manufacturer or seller of a product is allowed to assume the product will be used in a normal fashion. Accordingly, the manufacturer or seller generally will not be held liable for harm or injuries resulting from the abnormal use of the product. There is an exception, however, that may arise when the abnormal or unusual use of the product is deemed to be foreseeable. For example, using a lawnmower with the grass bag removed could be deemed to be a foreseeable misuse of the product, thereby resulting in the manufacturer's or seller's liability when a bystander is injured by a projectile that is shot through the unguarded lawnmower. There also might be a concomitant duty to warn of the foreseeable risk.

There is one legal precedent that does clearly state that the risk of harm from a product can be so evident that the product itself does not require a warning. The case involved a New Jersey college student who fell off a loft bed and then sued and recovered a $170,000 award from a local jury. The student claimed that his fall and injuries, mainly a dislocated shoulder, were caused by the lack of a warning label on the loft bed, which was about six feet off the floor. However, in August of 2006, a three-judge panel of the state court of appeals unanimously overturned the ruling, stating that the obviousness of the danger was an absolute defense. The appeals court explained that warnings would lose their efficacy and meaning if they were placed on every product that is known to be dangerous or would pose a generally known risk of injury if abused, misused, dropped, or fallen from, such as a knife or scissors, glass, a bat or ball, or bicycle. Nonetheless, the injured student's attorney stated that the case would be appealed to the New Jersey Supreme Court. So, the definitive legal pronouncement as to obviousness of the risk and the concomitant need for a warning, at least in New Jersey, has yet to be determined.

Third, a product can be defective because it is defectively designed. But is this nothing but a tautology: that a product is defective because it is defective? Such a legal standard brings U.S. products liability law closer to the old socialist, European, insurance scheme—product-causation-harm equals manufacturer-pay.

There is a test, though an imprecise one, for determining whether a product is defectively designed and which was first enunciated by the California Supreme Court. There are three parts to the test, all of which must be applied to the product to ascertain if it is defectively designed. First, does the product meet the "state-of-the-art"? That is, going back in time to when the product was made (and not at the "present" time, perhaps many years later during a lawsuit), and given the level of science, engineering, and technology available at that time, could anything more have been done to make the product safer? If so, the next part of the test is to factor in two constraints, practicality of use and economic feasibilities. That is, could the product have been made safer and still function as a product of that type? For example, a knife can be designed to be perfectly safe, but then it would not cut. Similarly, a car could be designed to be totally safe to its occupants, but it would look like a tank. As to the economic variable, a similar question is posed: Could the product be designed to be safer, and still be affordable? Exactly how much does a tank cost and what is its fuel mileage? This is not to be facetious because the technology does exist to put crash air bags throughout a vehicle, but then how much would that safety feature add to the cost of a car, especially an "economy" vehicle? If the product is rendered unaffordable by the additional safety features, the manufacturer is not legally obligated to adopt it.

However, this test for a "design defect," it must be underscored, is very vague. Moreover, the application and ultimate decision regarding this legal theory is typically, at least in the U.S., in the hands of a lay jury—a jury guided by experts. But it is never certain what a jury will do in a given situation, especially when faced with an injured, and perhaps very sympathetic, plaintiff. It is also important to note that the Restatement of Torts was again amended, and in 1997, the Restatement (Third) of Torts was approved. Regarding design defects, this newest Restatement keeps the emphasis on an alternative design that was available, reasonable, and practical, but was nonetheless not incorporated into the product as the essence of "defectiveness."

The classic design defect case was the series of Ford Pinto cases commencing in the late 1970s. It was determined that the costs of incorporating the available design improvement (structural alteration of the car) were minimal ($11.00 per vehicle) compared with the risks (ruptured fuel tanks and car fires at collisions over twenty-five miles per hour). Consequently, Ford was found to be legally liable on strict liability as well as negligence grounds and was subsequently subject to considerable punitive damage liability. The amount that Ford had to pay in damages and settlements exceeded $50 million, which was more than double what the alternative design implementation would have cost the company.

In other automobile design defect cases, Daimler-Chrysler, in 1999, was ordered to pay a $60-million judgment in a class action suit in which a jury in Pennsylvania determined that the air bags in certain models of the company's vehicles were defectively designed because they could in fact burn a driver's hands or wrists when deployed due to the venting of hot gases used to inflate the bags. The jury determined that the air bag was defective because it could have been designed differently and more safely by incorporating "smart" air bag technology, such as the use of sensors, which can reduce the force at which air bags are deployed. In another case, General Motors, in 1999, was ordered by a California jury to pay $4.9 billion to six people who were severely burned when their Chevrolet Malibu exploded in flames in a rear-end collision (The gas tanks were mounted 11 inches from the rear bumper.) The jury determined the vehicle to be defective in design because the gas tank was placed too close to the rear bumper and, furthermore, that an alternative design would have placed it over the axle or incorporated a shield. The cost of changing the placement of the tank would have been $8.59 per vehicle.

There are decided advantages to the consumer with the strict liability doctrine. Strict liability, in tort for products, is not negligence law. Thus, evidence of a lack of due care is not required. Also, strict liability is not warranty law and thus, disclaimers as well as notice and privity requirements are not applicable. The injured consumer or user must only establish that the product was defective when it left the seller's hands and that the defect itself caused the injury. By the same token, there are some defenses that a defendant manufacturer (or wholesaler or retailer) can interpose, to wit: 1) assumption of the risk, that is, the user of the product assumed the risk of its use by being aware of the defect or danger and nonetheless used the goods anyway; 2) misuse or abuse of the product; or 3) disregarding the manufacturer's instructions as to proper and safe use.

The justification for the doctrine of strict liability in tort was originally asserted by the California Supreme Court in the name of consumer safety. Accordingly, the doctrine is supported on utilitarian "greater good" grounds that it will not only maintain consumer safety but also advance consumer safety since a manufacturer now will be legally obligated to "keep up" with the "state-of-the-art." There is also a "risk distribution" rationale behind strict liability law. That is, the costs of injuries for defective products should be borne by the manufacturer or seller, who placed the product on the market, rather than by the injured consumer. In essence, the manufacturer can "spread" the risk by factoring it into the price of the product itself. Moreover, the manufacturer, as well as other entities on the marketing chain, can obtain insurance to protect themselves. Once again, the additional cost of the coverage can be factored into the price of the product.

Products liability litigation in the United States also has dealt with tobacco, guns, and fast food, and, in particular, the relationship these products have to the design defect component in strict tort liability doctrine. The tobacco cases are most interesting because they reveal the uncertainties and risks of the U.S. jury system for the litigants, especially two Florida cases. In a 1999 class action lawsuit, a jury in Miami-Dade County found against several tobacco companies, saying that the cigarettes they manufactured and sold to Florida smokers were defective and therefore unreasonably dangerous because they caused a variety of fatal illnesses. Yet earlier, in 1997, another Florida jury, this time in Jacksonville, found that R.J. Reynolds, the maker of Salem cigarettes, which the plaintiff smoked, was neither negligent in the plaintiff smoker's death nor did the tobacco company, ruled the jury, make an unreasonably dangerous and defective product.

Why the disparity in outcomes? The Florida tobacco cases reveal the distinction between the roles of the judge and the jury in the United States. The judge determines questions of law and instructs the jury as to the law and the meaning of the law, such as the design defect test part of the strict liability doctrine. But then the jury, as the "trier of fact" applies the law to the facts of the cases and renders a verdict.

As is the case with many legal precepts in a common law system in the U.S., the design defect test is not a precise formulation, which consequently accords the jury a great deal of discretion. Cigarettes certainly are not technically flawed, but are the warnings adequate? Moreover, most importantly, can a plaintiff sustain his or her burden of proof in convincing a jury that a tobacco company can make a safer cigarette? Also, can the company do so in a practical, feasible, and economic manner? These are difficult burdens to overcome, though not insurmountable ones.

The strict liability doctrine also has spawned a series of gun suits, in which injured plaintiffs argue that guns are defective products. The lawsuits typically are not based on the contention that guns are flawed products (rather, they seem to work very well) or even the assertion that warnings are inadequate (since ordinarily there are many warnings as to their proper transportation, use, cleaning, and storing). Rather, the products liability lawsuits involving guns are based on the premise that guns are defectively designed products. Specifically, the charge is made that the design of guns should incorporate modern "smart gun" technology designed to prevent unauthorized users from firing the weapons. One example of smart gun technology would be a feature, such as a fingerprint code or some type of sensor on the handle or trigger, which would recognize the unique characteristics of someone's grip. The gun industry, in defending product liability suits, argues that such smart gun technology is still in the developmental stage, and has not, as of yet, reached the scientific or legally binding level of state-of-the-art technology.

Certain other issues involve the practicality of adopting such technology and still having a gun that can be used efficaciously for legitimate purposes such as target shooting, hunting, and especially self-defense. There is also the economic feasibility issue of incorporating such safety features into a gun and still having the gun remain as an affordable product. One very noteworthy, tragic, and very revealing gun products liability case, called the Grunow case, occurred in Florida in 2002. In that case, the widow of a teacher, who was slain in 2000 by one of his students—an irate 13-year-old forbidden by the teacher from seeing his girl-friend in class and who used his grandfather's pistol to kill the teacher—sued the distributor of the weapon. But the manufacturer of the gun was bankrupt, and the plaintiff claimed that the weapon was defective in design because it did not have better safety features, such as an internal locking system. The jury in West Palm Beach awarded the widow $1.2 million but also stated on the verdict form that the gun was not defective. The judge was obligated to throw out the jury's verdict since the jury, apparently very sympathetic to the widow, nonetheless found in favor of the defendant distributor on the critical design defect question.

It is also interesting to note that in 2002, former New Jersey Governor Jim McGreevy signed into law the first "smart gun law," mandating that all new handguns that are sold in the state be equipped with safety features that would allow only the owner of the weapon to fire it. While New Jersey was the first state to enact such legislation, the law itself does not specify what smart gun technology must be used. Rather, the law only says that the weapon must recognize the owner as well as be both commercially available and feasible.

The emerging area of products liability lawsuits in the U.S. deals with food, specifically "fast food," and the allegation that such food causes obesity and related health problems. Several lawsuits alleging that fast food violates the strict liability doctrine have been filed, but none, as of this writing, have been successful. Yet perhaps as a result, many companies are placing calorie and nutritional information prominently on the food labels or cartons as well as displaying such information in the restaurants at the food counters. Such meritorious behavior is not only "socially responsible" conduct, but also activity that will go a long way toward complying with the "warning" element to strict liability.

Meanwhile, the much more interesting, as well as perplexing, question is whether fast food is in fact defectively designed. Could a cheeseburger and large fries be made safer and still have the same appetizing taste? Are there alternatives to certain ingredients of the food or product substances or manner in which it is cooked that will emerge as reasonable alternatives? Are these alternatives presently available, and are they practical and feasible? These are issues that will have to be addressed and answered in this growing new field of products liability litigation.

Finally, two other legal doctrines that impact strict liability law are *market share liability* and *statutes of repose*. The former benefits plaintiffs and the latter benefits defendants. Normally, an injured plaintiff has to demonstrate that the defective product that caused the plaintiff harm was produced by a particular defendant manufacturer. However, in some instances, it may be very difficult if not impossible for a defendant to pinpoint which manufacturer out of the many that produced the product, or perhaps which one of the many distributors of the product, made or supplied it to the plaintiff. Accordingly, in some states a court may interpose the doctrine of *market share liability*. This legal principle holds that manufacturers who sold a defective produce, or distributors who supplied it, such as lead-based paint, will be compelled to share to burden of damages based on the percentage each holds of the pertinent product or distribution market. A statute of repose is similar to a statute of limitations. A *statute of repose* is a state statute (and most states have such a statute) that holds that the manufacturer or seller of a product cannot be sued for producing or selling a product that caused harm unless the lawsuit is brought within 10 or 12 years, depending on the state statute, from the date the product was made.

The Consumer Products Safety Commission

The Consumer Products Safety Commission (CPSC) is an American federal and independent regulatory agency, created by Congress in the Consumer Product Safety Act (CPSA) of 1972. The CPSC will be discussed in the chapter dealing with Consumer Protection law. However, it is important to note for the purposes of products liability that the CPSA does not create an additional private lawsuit for damages for consumers injured by dangerous products. Rather, the CPSA affords the consumer, as a private party, the right to sue for an injunction to prevent violations of either the Act or of the rules and regulations promulgated by the CPSC.

Conclusion

The use of any product involves some degree of risk and, accordingly, a key legal question under U.S. common law, statutory law, as well as regulatory principles, is to ascertain the acceptable level of known risk. No one reasonably expects a manufacturer to make a product completely safe or to reduce the risk of harm to zero. Generally speaking then, a product will be considered legally safe if it complies with the applicable legal standards for product safety. And if there are still risks attendant to the use of the product, it nevertheless will be deemed to be legally safe if the risks are known and judged acceptable and reasonable to a rational person in view of the benefits to be derived from the use of such a "risky" product.

Global Legal Perspectives

Global managers are often forced to work with various types of laws in countries throughout the world.[38] Therefore, it is their responsibility to understand how the laws differ in each country, especially if the laws pertain to their type of business. In addition, when promoting products in different countries, managers are able to use each country's law concerning product liability as a way to guarantee the consumers of the importance of safety in their product, particularly when compared with their competitors' products. It is for this purpose that international managers are compelled to keep up with the different laws.

In toy manufacturing companies, for example, global managers usually abide by a safe and user-friendly good in order to promote their products to different cultures and then alter this approach to the various environments. This method also holds true for pharmaceutical companies. In another example, in the pharmaceutical business, managers must be aware of which medications are to be promoted, the manner in which they must be promoted, and other factors that must be taken into consideration, especially legally required warnings because abiding by this strategy will prevent them from facing major lawsuits.

Furthermore, international managers must be aware of the international product liability laws that exist in over 50 countries around the world. It is, however, important to note that there is no single international law concerning product liability, but there do exist several laws pertaining to the same topic. It is, therefore, the responsibility of these managers, promoters, and other managerial personnel to be fully aware of these laws, especially in countries where they conduct business.

For instance, in 1995, Japan's Diet Party introduced the first ever Product Liability Law in order to prevent injuries to consumers. Since Japan is a "hot spot" for businesses all over the world, it would be expected that business companies, including managers, be educated to avoid liability. Furthermore, the procedures pertaining to this topic also vary according to each country. In certain countries such as Japan, product liability law makes it very difficult for the

---

[38] Coauthored with Bina Patel, Nova Southeastern University.

consumer to successfully sue a manufacturer as the consumer typically must prove the existence of the product's defect, the manner it caused injury, etc. In Japan, nevertheless, product liability lawsuits now have been filed over computer software, "konnyaku" jelly, low-fat milk, automobiles, trucks, electronic wheelchairs, instant noodles, artificial breathing devices, surgical devices, electric hotpots, school lunches, imported bottled olives served at a restaurant, and even cigarettes. Yet, most Japanese courts do not favor liability lawsuits being taken to court. In fact, most cases traditionally have been settled out of the court.

Product liability laws have been established to benefit both the consumer and the manufacturer in countries throughout the world. Such law has forced manufacturing firms to develop products that are safe and user-friendly, and to warn the consumer of unavoidable dangers. The laws have also been created to protect manufacturing firms from consumers who seek ways to sue manufacturing firms for non-defective products. However, the law's main goal is still to protect consumers. With product liability law and its variants, countries worldwide are still able to gradually achieve this primary goal.

Chinese Products Liability Law and the "Fairness Principle"

As part of an effort of continuing legal reform, China has adopted a body of products law that imposes liability on manufacturers and sellers of defective products. One interesting and very revealing, Chinese products liability case dealt with a lawsuit in China instituted by an injured high-level Chinese general who claimed that a U.S. company, Medtronic, Inc., manufactured a defective pacemaker that caused him harm, including pain and suffering. The general demanded almost $3 million in damages. As part of the lawsuit, the general's family mounted a very aggressive as well as intensely nationalistic media campaign targeting the United States' company. Moreover, pursuant to Chinese law, press reports can be introduced into evidence to prove the merits of a case. Nonetheless, despite the media campaign, the Chinese court ascertained that the general was injured not by Medtronic's product, but rather due to the fact that the pacemaker had been improperly inserted due to the malpractice of a Chinese doctor. The company was thereby exonerated from products liability culpability.

However, as part of the Chinese legal system, there exists a superseding legal precept, called the "fairness principle," which maintains that even if a plaintiff loses a case, the exonerated defendant nevertheless may have to pay a sum of money to the plaintiff as determined by the Chinese court—in essence, the rich forcibly contributing to the poor. In Medronic's case, the vindicated, though perhaps surprised, company had to pay $2,400 to the apparently "poor" (though obviously not that impoverished) Chinese general. Because what is considered "fair" is a vague notion, consequently, a great deal of discretionary power is afforded to the Chinese courts in order to "right" perceived financial inequities, a fact that the global manager of even a "winning" defendant firm doing business in China should be keenly aware of encountering.

The European Community and Products Liability Law[39]

In the European Community, product liability law, as analyzed by one commentator, imposes strict liability on manufacturers of defective products, very comparable to the U.S. doctrine. A product is deemed to be "defective" in Europe if it does not provide an adequate level of safety that a reasonable consumer could expect from such a product. The age of the product is an additional factor. The fact that a better product is subsequently introduced into the market does not automatically make a product defective. A manufacturer can avoid liability pursuant to an exception called the "developmental risk" exception, wherein a manufacturer can show that the defect was undiscoverable given the state of scientific and technical knowledge at the time the product was put into circulation. In the U.S., this limitation on legal liability is phrased as the "state-of-the-art" test for defectiveness.

Product liability law in the European Community is premised on the 1985 Product Liability Directive, which established the policy on product liability, but which also left specific implementation thereof to the Community's Member States. Member States, moreover, are still permitted by the Directive to regulate contractual or fault-based claims regarding products. The Preamble to the Directive sets forth the two basic objectives of European products liability law: 1) to promote the free movement of goods by harmonizing national legal approaches among Member States; and 2) to protect consumers by establishing a strict liability system for products. As in the U.S., the injured consumer is required to prove that he or she was harmed by a defective product and that there existed a causal relationship between the defective product and the damage. However, contrary to the U.S. strict liability doctrine, in Europe, other persons or entities involved in the production, marketing, and sales process, such as suppliers and retailers, are not liable if they can identify a producer of the defective product. In Germany, as noted by one commentator,[40] the European Directive was "transposed" into national law by the German Product Safety Act of 1990. However, no greater protection is afforded the injured consumer in Germany versus that provided by the Directive.

---

[39] See Liu, Josephine (2004).
[40] See Mollers, Thomas M. (2003).

Management Strategies

Determining the extent and nature of a company's legal obligation to consumer safety is a daunting task. The global manager is confronted with not only U.S. law, but also the law of other jurisdictions which govern product safety and protect the consumer. The United States has a very developed body of consumer protection law, with a major component thereof, strict liability, premised on state-by-state interpretations and standards that are not always precise. Legally, a company is neither expected to guarantee the consumer's safety, nor to bankrupt itself to ensure complete safety. Legally then, the prudent approach for a manager to take is to comply with its contractual obligations, comply with any express implied warranties, be truthful regarding product representations, and be careful regarding the manufacture of its product. Naturally, the manufacturer should strive to eliminate any flawed or "runaway" products by identifying any weaknesses in product production, testing, and inspection, and by having adequate quality controls over processes and, ultimately, over the products themselves.

Second, regarding the design of the product, the manufacturer must be keenly aware of the state-of-the-art, particularly whether there exists some type of safety feature or modification that can be practically and economically incorporated into the product. This is, in essence, a technological concern. The duty to take the latest technological advances into account in designing a product cannot be emphasized enough.

Finally, if no reasonable alternative exists, and there is still a risk to using the product, the global manager must make sure that the product includes a warning concerning the risk. Furthermore, the firm must carry product liability insurance in case the product causes legally compensable harm.

Summary

Products are made for the purposes of fulfilling consumers' needs and desires as well as creating profits for businesses. However, the liability that comes with the development of new products can be very high, depending upon the product itself and the relevant laws in place. Therefore, businesses are forced to seek ways to develop better and safer products as they are likely to face major lawsuits should their products cause harm to the consumers.

In the previous chapter, torts and business were discussed, where the term "tort" was defined as a wrongful act against a person or his or her property that may cause a legal action. The term itself is applicable to the production of products as they too can be harmful, even if used in the correct manner. Accordingly, tort laws were initially established in the products field to give consumers some semblance of justice when faced with harm caused by products. Laws were also developed in order to put pressure on manufacturers to develop safer products. In essence, tort laws, lawsuits, and other legal mechanisms have allowed manufacturing firms to create efficient and effective products that are beneficial to all while at the same time protecting consumers from defective products that cause harm.

ELEVEN

Criminal law is the field of the law that deals with crimes and the punishment of wrongdoers. A crime is an offense that harms society as a whole and, consequently, is punished as an offense against the "state," that is, the government. In the United States, crimes are classified according to their severity. Felonies are more serious crimes—usually punished by imprisonment in a state or federal penitentiary or death—whereas misdemeanors are crimes of a less serious nature, punishable by fines or imprisonment in a local or county jail. The purpose of this chapter is to briefly examine crimes and the criminal process in the United States, paying close attention to business and "cyber" crimes as well as the criminal liability of the corporate entity. This chapter also will examine the international jurisdictional reach of U.S. criminal laws, especially the Foreign Corrupt Practices Act. Finally, the nature of crimes and the criminal process in other legal systems will be examined.

Crimes in the United States—Definition, Classification, Elements, and Defenses

A crime is a legal wrong against the public as a whole. It is an offense which violates the duties owed to society. It is, in the old English sense, a "breach of the King's peace." Accordingly, the offender must make restitution to the public, typically in the payment of a fine or imprisonment or both. An act is a criminal act only if it is defined as such in a federal or state statute or county or municipal ordinance. There are two elements that are required for criminal liability: 1) There must be a wrongful, overt act (in Latin, the *actus reus*) that has been defined as criminal; and 2) This wrongful act must be performed with the requisite state of mind (in Latin, the *mens rea*).

There are certain criminal law statutes, typically involving the public health and safety, which are deemed to be strict liability criminal statutes because one can be guilty regardless of his or her intent or state of mind. Characteristic examples would be statutes that make it a crime to sell tobacco products or alcoholic beverages to minors. For such offenses, a criminal charge can be brought by either the federal or state government. In the former case, the prosecuting agency would be the U.S. Department of Justice while in the latter, the state agency would be a State Attorney or Prosecutor's Office.

Crimes in the U.S. are typically divided into two major categories: 1) felony, which is a serious crime punishable by death or imprisonment for more than one year; and 2) misdemeanor, which is a lesser crime, punishable by a fine and/ or imprisonment for less than one year. Imprisonment for a felony is usually in a federal or state penitentiary whereas imprisonment for a misdemeanor is usually in a county or municipal jail. An important distinction between the criminal and civil law in the U.S. is that criminal law requires a much heavier burden of proof. As noted, the usual standard of proof in a civil case for the plaintiff to prevail is a "preponderance of the evidence," though in some civil lawsuits—for example, fraud—the standard is a higher "clear and convincing" evidence standard. But by the same token, in a criminal case, the accused person is presumed innocent unless the government can prove to a jury that the defendant is guilty "beyond a reasonable doubt."

Crimes against business and business property are, regrettably, rather common. Although it is beyond the purposes of this book to discuss in detail all of the various business crimes, mention must be made of some of the major ones.

The first basic category is theft crimes, which can consist of the following: 1) robbery, which is the taking of a person's personal property from the person by force or threats of force; 2) burglary, which is the taking of one's personal property from one's home or business by an unauthorized entry thereto; 3) larceny, which is the wrongful, intentional, and fraudulent taking of one's personal property, including intangible property, such as trade secrets, as well as tangible property; 4) receiving stolen property (with the knowledge that it is stolen and with the intent to deprive the true owner of possession); 5) forgery (which is intentionally or fraudulently creating a fake document or altering a document with the intent of adversely affecting the legal rights or liability of another person, and which also may encompass, in some states, the unauthorized use of another person's credit card); and 6) issuing a "bad check"—making, issuing, or delivering a check knowing that there are insufficient funds in the bank to cover the check, and, in most states, with the intent to defraud another person. Some of these theft crimes are misdemeanors and others are felonies, depending on the amounts of money or property involved or whether a weapon was used or carried during the crime. Some states have general theft criminal statutes, whereas others have criminal statutes for each individual type of offense. In some states, the categories of theft offenses are even further divided. Examples include larceny, which is sometimes divided into larceny by trick and larceny by false pretenses.

Arson is purposefully and maliciously burning a home, business, or public building. One can commit arson by burning one's own home or business (for example in a fraudulent scheme to collect on the insurance proceeds). Arson, obviously, is a very serious crime and a felony.

Extortion is also a very serious felony. Extortion is the wrongful obtaining of property from another as the result of threats of force or violence or due to the threat of exposing something about a person. In the latter case, the crime usually is referred to as blackmail.

Certain other crimes involving business will be discussed in more detail later in the specific chapter sections.

There are a variety of defenses to criminal law behavior, but again, any detailed explication thereof is beyond the scope of this book. Nonetheless, succinct mention should be made of some of the major defenses, to wit:

1. *infancy*—that is, the juvenile status of the defendant
2. *insanity*—which is a very complicated legal defense, but which in most states means that the defendant did not know the nature or quality of the act or did not know that the act was wrong
3. *mistake of fact*—which may negate a person's requisite state of mind for committing a crime
4. *duress*—which also may negate the requisite state of mind
5. *justifiable* use of force (known traditionally as "self-defense" of person, family, or property);
6. *entrapment*—where the police suggest, pressure, induce, and facilitate the commission of a crime by the defendant
7. *statutes of limitation*—that is, mandatory time periods for the government to bring a prosecution for a crime—however, no limitations period exists for murder
8. *immunity*—where the government has granted an immunity from prosecution usually in exchange for information; and
9. *involuntary* intoxication—though not voluntary unless one was extremely intoxicated while committing a crime

It is again important to underscore that while a mistake as to facts may be a valid defense to criminal liability, a mistake as to the law is not. This is based on the old and very familiar Latin saying, *Ignorancia lex no est excusa* (Ignorance of the law is no excuse). Effectively, not knowing of the law's existence or applicability is not a valid legal defense to the commission of a crime.

Criminal Law Process and Procedure in the United States

Criminal law procedure in the U.S. consists typically of four stages: 1) the arrest, 2) the plea, 3) plea bargaining, and 4) the trial.

An arrest occurs when a person is taken into custody by law enforcement for prosecution or interrogation. The arrested person is informed of the charges against him or her, the police make a report to the prosecutors, and the prosecutors determine whether charges should be filed. If charges are to be filed, in most states, the person, now a criminal defendant, must be taken before a judge or other magistrate to be formally informed of the charges. The judge or magistrate then sets bail.

The next stage, the plea stage, arises when the defendant makes an appearance before a judge to again be formally informed of the charges and to enter a plea of guilty or not guilty (or perhaps *nolo contendere,* which means that the defendant is not pleading guilt or innocence, but is merely not contesting the charges). This stage is ordinarily called the arraignment. If the case is one that entails a felony, many states will require an additional procedural element, a preliminary hearing, in which the prosecution must convince the judge that it has probable cause that the defendant committed the crime. If probable cause is present, the prosecution files formal charges by means of a document filed with the court, which is called the "information." However, if the crime to be charged is a very serious one, the prosecution can present the charges to a grand jury in the form of an indictment, and the grand jury can then issue the formal charges against a defendant. A grand jury is composed of citizens in the community; and is usually larger than the standard criminal trial jury, but the grand jury does not determine guilt or innocence, only whether probable cause exists for believing that a crime has been committed.

The next stage is, practically speaking, very important, and this is the plea bargaining stage. Most criminal law cases do not proceed to a trial but rather are resolved during this stage, wherein the defendant typically agrees to a lesser charge in return for the prosecution dropping or reducing certain other charges.

Finally, there comes a trial. A criminal trial parallels the civil law process in the U.S. legal system as covered in the Chapter 3 discussion. However, at the end of the criminal law trial, the jury determines criminal guilt (or non-guilt) and not "mere" civil liability. It is important to note that a jury finding of "not guilty" does not necessarily mean that a criminal defendant is innocent; rather it means that the government was unable to convince a jury "beyond a reasonable doubt" that the defendant was guilty. Also, very significantly, at a criminal law trial, the defendant does not have to prove anything. Rather, he or she can remain completely silent and has the right to do so, throughout the whole trial. Moreover, the government cannot comment to the jury on the defendant's silence.

United States Constitutional Protections

The Constitution of the United States provides several very important legal protections to criminal defendants, some of which have already been discussed in the Constitutional Law and Administrative Law chapters. However, other very important protections must be mentioned.

The *ex post facto* clause of the Constitution—found in Article 1, Section 10—provides that a person can only be convicted of a crime if that person's actions constituted a crime at the time those actions occurred. This means that retroactively making certain conduct criminal, or retroactively increasing the punishment for a crime, is constitutionally forbidden.

The Fourth Amendment to the Constitution was covered in the context of "administrative searches" by government regulatory agencies. In the "pure" criminal law context, the Fourth Amendment prohibits "unreasonable" searches and seizures. Searches and seizures, however, are permitted if a warrant is issued, based on "probable cause," supported by an oath or affirmation, and the warrant "particularly" describes the place to be searched or the persons or things to be seized. Any search that is deemed "unreasonable" thus generally requires a warrant based on probable cause.

Probable cause for an arrest warrant is based on a reasonable belief that a suspect has committed a crime. In a search context, the key test is whether a person has a reasonable expectation of privacy under the circumstances. Clearly, one would have a very reasonable and legitimate expectation of privacy in one's own home, and thus, a warrant based on probable cause is almost always required for the search of a home. The determination of whether probable cause is present to issue a warrant must be determined by a neutral magistrate and not by the police or law enforcement officials. However, if the place to be searched is open to the public (such as a business), then the courts have allowed warrantless searches if the police entered the business during regular business hours and observed what was visible to the public or visible to customers from the public areas of the premises or business. If evidence was secured in violation of the Fourth Amendment, the search or seizure is considered illegal, and the U.S. "exclusionary rule" applies, which forbids the government from introducing the "tainted" evidence in trial as proof of guilt. Moreover, any evidence obtained from the illegally seized evidence (called the "fruits of the poisonous tree" doctrine) is similarly prohibited in trial.

However, there is an important exception to the "exclusionary rule," called the "good faith" exception. This exception applies when there is an illegal search or seizure that occurs when the police acted in good faith. An example of this is making a mistake or relying on erroneous information from third parties. In such a case, the evidence is admissible, but the police themselves may be sanctioned for their carelessness.

The Fifth Amendment privilege against self-incrimination was covered also in the Administrative Law and Business chapter. But nevertheless, an important criminal law procedural rule, called the Miranda Rule, must be mentioned. This rule is based on a famous U.S. Supreme Court interpretation of the Fifth

Amendment in a case from 1966, *Miranda v. Arizona*. The Miranda Rule extends the privilege against self-incrimination to the early stages of a criminal investigation. The rule holds that a statement made by a person in custody is only admissible in court if the person was informed prior to making the statement of his or her right to remain silent and to have legal counsel present during the questioning.

The Fifth Amendment also contains a Double Jeopardy clause, which forbids a person from being tried multiple times for the same offense. Thus, if a criminal defendant is exonerated, the government cannot appeal the case and thus retry the defendant again at a later time. (A defendant who is found guilty can still appeal his or her case.) However, if the jury cannot reach a verdict (which is called a "hung jury"), the government can still prosecute the case again before a new jury. There are two important exceptions to the Double Jeopardy rule. First, since the U.S. is a federal system, with different levels of government, the federal government and the states are allowed to prosecute the same case based on the same facts. Second, the Double Jeopardy rule is a criminal law rule and thus will not preclude a civil trial (with a lesser standard of proof) based on the same facts.

The Sixth Amendment provides that a criminal defendant has the right to a jury trial (which of course can be waived) for offenses punishable by six months imprisonment or more as well as the right to assistance and representation by an attorney (and to have one provided by the government if the defendant cannot afford an attorney). The right of legal counsel is another right of which a person must be notified due to the *Miranda* case. The Sixth Amendment also provides that a criminal defendant has the right to confront, in open court, the witnesses against him or her.

"White-Collar" Crimes

The term "white-collar" crime refers to crimes committed by businesspeople during the course of their otherwise legitimate occupations. This may include using deceit and fraud as opposed to violence and force to commit crimes against other people or other businesses. The three main types of white-collar crimes are embezzlement, mail and wire fraud, and bribery.

Embezzlement is the wrongful appropriation of another's funds or property by a person to whom the property was entrusted. Embezzlement typically is committed by a company's (or a bank's) executives, officers, employees, agents, accountants, or lawyers.

Mail and wire fraud is a federal crime, based on the Mail Fraud Act of 1990, and premised on using the mail or "wires" (telephone or telegraph as well as radio or television transmissions) in a scheme to defraud another person.

Bribery, including "kickbacks" and "payoffs," is also a white-collar crime. Bribery against foreign public officials is covered by the Foreign Corrupt Practices Act and this aspect of bribery was generally discussed in the International and Comparative Law chapter and will be examined in greater detail in the Global Legal Perspectives section of this chapter. However, it should be noted now that there are other federal and state anti-bribery statutes in place that make bribing "domestic" public officials in the U.S. a crime as well as making bribery in a "pure" commercial context a crime. It is also important to note that the crime of bribery occurs in most cases when the bribe is "merely" offered; the acceptance of the bribe is most likely another crime.

Other white-collar crimes are the theft of trade secrets and insider trading, which will be covered respectively in the Internet Regulation and Securities Regulation chapters of this book.

The Sarbanes-Oxley Act, Securities Fraud, and Trading on Inside Information

In 2002, the U.S Congress, as a response to an eruption of accounting and business scandals, enacted the Sarbanes-Oxley Act which, among several regulatory provisions, materially increased the severity of criminal penalties for securities law violations. The Sarbanes-Oxley Act, as well as the securities law violations—both civil and criminal—under the Securities Act of 1933 and the Securities Exchange Act of 1934—especially pursuant to Securities and Exchange Commission Rule 10b-5, prohibiting against insider trading—will be covered in detail in the Securities Regulation chapter.

"Organized Crime"

The term "organized crime" has come to refer to business crime of an illegitimate nature that entails the providing, in an organized and "businesslike" manner, illegal goods and services such as illegal gambling, narcotics, and prostitutes. A discussion of organized crime is beyond the scope of this book, but two types of such crimes should be mentioned: 1) "money laundering," which is the storage and transmission of "dirty" money through legitimate businesses and banks (the latter of which are now required to report currency transactions involving more than $10,000); and 2) "loan sharking," which is the lending of money at more than the legal interest rates. Finally, it is important to note that the U.S. Congress enacted a very significant anti-organized crime statute in 1970, called the Racketeer Influenced and Corrupt Organizations Act (RICO), which was part of the Organized Crime Control Act. RICO makes it a federal crime to use income obtained from any racketeering activity to purchase an interest in an enterprise, to acquire or maintain an interest in an enterprise through racketeering activity, or to conduct or participate in the affairs of an enterprise through racketeering activity. Racketeering is broadly defined as encompassing not only a wide range of federal or state crimes—such as the conventional organized crimes of gambling, prostitution, narcotics, and counterfeiting—but also business-related crimes, such as mail and wire fraud, embezzlement, and bribery. Thus, RICO has been used not only for its originally intended "organized crime" component, but also to punish and deter white-collar crimes.

In a very novel use of federal racketeering law, the U.S. Justice Department had brought a civil racketeering lawsuit against the big tobacco companies for conspiring for years to deceive the public about the dangers of smoking. While the government did win the lawsuit, the victory itself could be seen as a "hollow" one because the federal district court judge did not impose any financial penalties. The judge, however, did order the companies to admit they lied about the dangers of smoking, forced them to pay for corrective advertising, and banned the use of the terms "light," "mild," "low tar," and "natural" from the marketing of their tobacco products as the judge deemed these terms to be misleading to consumers. It should be noted that the European Union also has specifically banned the tobacco product descriptors of "light" and "mild" as misleading, as have an additional eight countries that have ratified the World Health Organization's tobacco treaty. (The U.S. has not ratified the treaty as of this writing.)

"Cyber" Crimes

"Cyber" crimes are broadly defined as crimes using or directed against a computer or using the Internet as a means to commit the crime. Four major types of "cyber" crimes are: 1) identity theft, 2) "cyberstalking," 3) "hacking," and 4) "spamming." Identity theft occurs when a person steals another person's identification and financial information in order to access and steal that person's financial resources. "Cyberstalking" is the crime of stalking (that is, following and harassing a person) by means of or on the Internet. "Hacking" is the breaking into a computer or computer system without authorization, usually for the purposes of theft, but also, sadly, "merely" for the "fun" of sabotage. "Spamming" is the mass sending of unsolicited bulk e-mail to all people on an email mailing list. Spam has been found to be both a trespass as well as a crime in and of itself, as discussed in the Torts and Business and Internet Regulation chapters and also covered in a spam case in the Cases section of this book.

Corporate Criminal Liability and Federal Sentencing Guidelines

The United States Sentencing Commission is the independent federal agency created by Congress but located in the judicial branch of government and empowered by Congress to establish fair, effective, and consistent sentences for the violation of various criminal offenses and to monitor the sentencing practices of the federal courts. For individuals, the Sentencing Commission has established sentencing guidelines based on categories of "offense behavior" and "offender characteristics." A sentencing judge must select a sentence within the Commission's specified guideline ranges, but a judge may also depart from the guidelines. However, if a judge does this, he or she must provide the reasons for his or her sentencing departure. It must be noted that the U.S. Congress has ended federal parole, meaning that now a federal offender must serve his or her full sentence, but with the possibility of a 15% reduction of the sentence for good behavior.

In 2003, the U.S. Sentencing Commission significantly increased the potential prison time for corporate wrongdoers, meaning that corporate executives now face much greater criminal penalties in the United States. For example, an officer of a publicly traded company who defrauds more than 250 employees or investors of more than $1 million now can receive a sentence of more than 10 years in prison, which is almost double the previous penalty. Moreover, there are longer sentences that can be imposed for larger dollar amounts. And because major corporate frauds typically involve millions of dollars and thousands of employees and investors, corporate executives in the U.S. are now confronting the reality of, in essence, a "life sentence" for criminal wrongdoing.

To illustrate, back in the early 1990s, Wall Street "junk bond king" Michael Milken was convicted and sentenced to 10 years in prison for his role in the financial scandal of his day. However, he served less than two years and emerged with most of his fortune still intact. Conversely, in 2005, former WorldCom CEO Bernard Ebbers was sentenced to 25 years for fraud and related crimes after he had surrendered most of his millions of dollars. Moreover, Adelphia Communications founder John Rigas was sentenced to 15 years in prison for his role in that company's fraud. But because Rigas was 80 years old at the time of sentencing, the probable result will be that Rigas will die in prison, even considering that federal prisoners in the U.S. usually serve "only" 85% of their terms.

Clearly, in the post-Enron environment, the Federal Sentencing Guidelines and concomitant prison sentences have grown considerably more draconian in the United States for what not too long ago was considered "mere" white-collar crime. Moreover, as will be seen in the Securities Regulation chapter, the penalties for securities fraud have been markedly raised by the Sarbanes-Oxley Act of 2002. Penalties for corporations have also been increased.

The penalties for corporations and other organizations are found in the Federal Sentencing Guidelines for Organizations, which were enacted in 1991. The Guidelines provide for severe fines for companies convicted of criminal fraud, antitrust violations, securities fraud, and other types of business wrongdoing. Fines are determined by a "base fine" for a variety of offenses, and then this "base fine" is increased if the company's gain exceeds the fine or if the loss to private parties exceeds the base amount. Moreover, the "base fine" can be increased or decreased based on the culpability of the organization.

Key fine sentencing factors are: whether the organization itself was convicted of a crime, whether executives, officers, and managers knew of and condoned criminal conduct or were purposefully ignorant of criminal conduct, whether executives, officers, and managers cooperated with and assisted government investigators and prosecutors in the investigation of a case and the institution of a criminal proceeding, and whether or not the company had an effective compliance program in existence at the time of the wrongdoing so as to communicate standards of lawful behavior to the employees, monitor the employees' conduct, detect infractions, report them to the government, correct the wrongdoing, and discipline errant employees. The idea is to set severe fine penalties, but then give companies a significant incentive in the form of substantial fine reduction so that they establish compliance programs, self-report wrongdoing, and cooperate with the government in investigating organizational criminal wrongdoing.

Global Legal Perspectives

Brazil and Money Laundering[41]

The internationalization of the world economy and world finances has naturally had many positive consequences but also one very negative ramification: the growth of organized crime globally and a concomitant rise in money laundering. The latter, of course, is a crime, and the purpose of this brief discussion is to point out some of the international regulatory standards dealing with money laundering, specifically examining the legal response of one nation, Brazil, to the problem of money laundering.

The international legal framework in place to deter money laundering is based on the 1988 United Nations Convention against Illicit Traffic in Narcotic Drugs and Psychotropic Substances (called the Vienna Convention). In response to the growth of money laundering as well as the illicit concealment of money and assets, and in order to comply with the Convention, Brazil, in 1998, enacted its first anti-money laundering legislation. In particular, the law seeks to prevent the misuse of the country's financial system. The law imposes a penalty of imprisonment from three to ten years and a fine as well as forfeiture of assets that resulted from illegal practices. The law also created a new administrative agency, called the Council for Financial Activities Control (COAF), to implement the law. The main purposes of this Council, which is located in the Ministry of Finance, are to coordinate policies and propose mechanisms for

---

[41] See Roza, Edni (2005).

cooperation and information exchange. Moreover, to strengthen the country's efforts to combat money laundering, in 2001, Brazil enacted an additional law, called the Complementary Law, which allows disclosure by financial institutions to the government and official government entities when there is a suspicion of a money laundering or concealment of assets crime. The new law also protects financial institutions against any action for breaching the duties of privacy and confidentiality. Most significantly, the 2001 law grants the government—specifically the Federal Revenue and Customs Secretariat—the power to access bank records of financial institutions without needing prior authorization of the judicial branch.

Russian Criminal Law Reforms[42]

The Russian Constitution of 1993 granted a much more powerful role to the courts in adjudicating criminal matters. The enhanced role of the courts and the renewed emphasis on the "rule of law" have been endorsed by Russian President Vladimir Putin as one of his government's highest priorities. The rationale is that the Russian people will be more supportive of the government, especially in criminal matters, if the courts, as opposed to the executive bureaucracy, establish citizen rights and obligations. The goal of the Putin government is to have an independent and transparent judiciary by which civil disputes and allegations of criminal wrongdoing are resolved by courts which the people deem to be objective and fair.

The fact that the judicial tribunals are open and highly visible is important, especially compared with the "bad old days" of secret Soviet tribunals. Moreover, Russian prosecutors no longer have the right to unilaterally arrest people and conduct searches, another marked difference from the Soviet model. Rather, prosecutors must now apply to the courts for permission to arrest and search. Also, there is now a system of public defenders in Russia in place, at least for defendants charged with serious crimes, who now must be provided with a right to counsel. Jury trials, furthermore, are now mandated in every Russian jurisdiction, except for Chechnya. This concept of a jury was taken from the Anglo-American judicial system. Furthermore, today, Russian juries are no longer so easily persuaded by Russian prosecutors as in the Soviet days, when the key "player" in the justice system was the prosecutor and the judge served merely as a functionary.

However, because of this spotted past, contemporary Russian juries may still distrust the once all-powerful Russian prosecutors.

One difference of the Russian judicial system from the Anglo-American model is that the Russians do not have, as of yet, the concept of stare decisis.

---

[42] See LaVelle, Michael J. (2006).

However, there are today three Russian legal organizations that are collecting and publishing judicial decisions on the Internet. (This should have, at the very least, a psychological precedent-like effect.) Another difference is that judges in Russia, after passing a test and being approved by the Chief Judge, President, and legislature, are, after a three-year probationary period, appointed for life but still subject to removal for misconduct. (In the West, only federal judges in the United States have such potential lifetime tenure.) Another difference from the Anglo-American system is that Russian judges are allowed to apply international law, not just treaties to which Russia is a signatory. One interesting Russian criminal law constitutional provision concerns the privilege against self-incrimination and which is far broader than in the U.S. This privilege can be invoked in Russia not only by a defendant but by his or her spouse and "close relatives," which can refer to the children and even the extended family members that have historically shared living quarters in the typically very-cramped Russian apartment buildings.

The United States legal system differs in many important respects from other legal systems internationally. Of great consequence is the fact that in the United States, a person is presumed innocent of a crime until proven guilty. The burden of persuasion and proof, therefore, is on the government prosecuting the case. To compare, in some countries, an accused person must prove that he or she is innocent. Moreover, fundamentally important is the fact that this determination of guilt is typically made in the United States by a lay jury composed of citizens in the community, which is obligated to find the defendant guilty only based on "proof beyond a reasonable doubt." Finally, a person charged with a crime in the United States has the right to many procedural and substantive legal safeguards, some of which are constitutionally imposed, such as the right to be represented by legal counsel and the right to be provided with legal counsel by the government.

The U.S. Foreign Corrupt Practices Act and Bribery

Many U.S. businesses today operate extensively in more than one country, typically through subsidiaries, divisions, or agents involved in manufacturing, marketing, and sales. As such, a U.S. business will operate in a foreign host country where the laws, customs, and practices may be markedly different than those of the United States. In particular, a U.S. businessperson may encounter abroad a practice such as making a questionable payment to a foreign government official, which in fact may be legal as well as socially acceptable in the host country. Nevertheless, the U.S. businessperson must be very cognizant of an important federal statute, the Foreign Corrupt Practices Act (FCPA), which makes certain types of payments a federal crime.

The FCPA was originally passed by the U.S. Congress in 1977 and then materially amended in 1988. The purpose of the Act is to prohibit U.S. firms and businesspeople from bribing foreign officials when seeking overseas business, making illegal certain foreign payments or "payoffs" to foreign officials. A "payment," however is more than the "mere" payment of money; rather, the legal wrong encompasses the transfer of money or anything of value, directly or indirectly, by a U.S. businessperson or firm to a foreign official in order to wrongfully secure business or to maintain business. The usual "payment" situation is the classic "purchase" bribe case, wherein money is paid outright to a foreign official for the purpose of acquiring new business. The FPCA also covers "defensive" bribes, which are used to protect existing business from competition or threatened adverse sanctions. Furthermore, the Act covers "variance" bribes, used to secure improper exemptions from the host country's law—typically environmental or labor laws.

Even though this procedure of "favors" has not been extensively used by businesspeople, it is interesting to relate that the U.S. Justice Department does have a specific office or a process in place for the pre-approval of payments to foreign officials. Yet it might be prudent to ask the government if a political contribution to a foreign candidate or foreign political party, or a payment to an executive or major shareholder of a foreign company owned in whole or in part or controlled by a foreign government, is a proper payment.

There is liability under the statute not only for those business officials who pay or participate in the payment of the illegal bribes, but also for those who know of the payment or are aware of a high probability of the existence of an illegal payment. The FCPA also imposes strict controls over internal accountants, requires that companies keep detailed records and have reasonable accounting control systems, and, in particular, the Act prohibits making false statements to accountants or false entries in books and records in order to conceal suspect accounts and questionable dealings. Sanctions include business fines of up to $2 million, individual fines of up to $100,000, and imprisonment of up to five years.

It is most consequential to underscore the word "corrupt" as it appears in the Foreign Corrupt Practices Act. That critical word has been interpreted by the courts as imposing a requirement upon the Justice Department prosecuting a case to show that the motive of the person making the payment was "corrupt"; that is, the payor had the requisite "evil mind" (or "scienter," to use the old common law language) to wrongfully direct business to oneself or one's own firm. The intent must be shown on the payor's part to induce the foreign official to misuse his or her official position to wrongfully direct business to the payor. (Note, however, that there is no requirement that the payment violate the law of the host country for it to be branded as "corrupt.") Furthermore, if the government is criminally prosecuting the case against a U.S. businessperson, the government will be required to convince a jury "beyond a reasonable doubt" and to a moral certainty that all the elements of the crime are present including, and especially, the evidence of "corrupt" intent.

In the Salt Lake City Olympic bribery case, the FCPA criminal charges against the two principal members of the Salt Lake Organizing Committee (SLOC) were ultimately dismissed by a federal judge—and with prejudice, thereby disallowing the case to ever go to a federal jury—on grounds that the government would never be able to demonstrate that the payments made to the voting officials of the International Olympic Committee (IOC) were made with the requisite "corrupt" motive for an FCPA conviction. The payments, including expensive gifts—such as antique shotguns and pure-breed puppies—the proceeds from fast, turnaround, real estate investments, college tuition for the delegates' children, and knee and cosmetic surgery for delegates' spouses, as well as fees for "escort services," were argued by the SLOC principals as being merely educational, humanitarian, and socially responsible payments in keeping with the "business as usual" bidding and voting practices and traditions of Olympic venue selection.

The Salt Lake City case illustrated well the evidentiary burdens of securing sufficient evidence in the United States. Although the FCPA does have extra-territorial effect covering transactions that occur abroad, getting sufficient evidence for the government to sustain its burden of persuasion and proof will be exceedingly difficult in most cases. One such example dealt with a government investigation against two IBM executives who were thought to have known of bribes that were allegedly paid by an IBM subcontractor in Argentina in order to secure a $250-million government contract. The IBM executives admitted that they had closely supervised the general aspects of the contract, but they said that they were not aware of the existence of an IBM subcontractor for the government project, which was later found out to be a "shell company" that never performed any real work other than allegedly paying the bribes to the Argentine government officials. The investigation, however, came to a close when a key witness, the executive of the "shell company," was found dead, hanging from an electricity pole, with a newspaper clipping of the IBM case sticking from his mouth. The Argentine police concluded (perhaps suspiciously) that the death was a suicide.

The FCPA makes bribery in international business illegal for the U.S. businessperson, but only as a general rule. Accordingly, there are three types of bribes that are legal pursuant to the statute: 1) legal "bribes," 2) "grease" payments, and 3) "good will" payments.

The first type of legal bribe is rather straightforward, as the rule of law holds that if the payment is lawful pursuant to the express written laws of the foreign official's country, then the payment can legally be made.

The second category deals with payments, pejoratively called "grease" or "grease money," but more legally referred to as "facilitating and expediting" payments. The purpose of these kind of payments is to secure the performance of or expedite the performance of routine and clerk-like government actions: processing visas and other paperwork, obtaining permits and licenses, providing mail pickup and delivery, securing telephone, power, and water service, loading and unloading cargo, and protecting perishable goods from deterioration. The intent behind "grease" is to persuade these foreign officials to perform more quickly and more smoothly these customary government services that one is legally entitled to but for which one may have to wait a long time in the absence of a little "grease."

Actual examples of such "grease"—as related to one of the co-authors of this book by his MBA students—include the payment of $2,500 to an official to get his telephone and utility service promptly turned on in a Caribbean country, the attachment of an American $100-bill to each application for the expeditious processing of firearms permits for private security personnel in a South American country, and the transfer of a certain quantity of bathroom and kitchen tile to a lower level military official for the quick processing of a supply convoy through a military checkpoint on the way to an oil installation in another South American country. This last example is important because it must be stressed that "grease" payments are intended for lower level foreign officials: clerks and lower level bureaucrats who have ministerial as opposed to discretionary power. The higher the level of the foreign official is, and the more discretionary authority he or she has, the greater the risk of the legal "grease" payment being challenged as an illegal "purchase" bribe. Also, the "grease" exception is based on the payment of small or relatively small sums of money of things of value. So again, the greater the amount is, the greater the likelihood of the legal exception being superseded by the illegal general rule.

The third type of legal bribe to foreign officials involves payments, characteristically called "good will" payments, that are reasonable, legitimate, and bona fide and which are directly related to the promotion, demonstration, and explanation of a firm's products or services. Examples would include travel, lodging, and meal expenses, as well as entertainment and gifts. The key test is the "reasonableness" of the payment or gift. For example, the Salt Lake City case illustrates the point that the government felt the SLOC "crossed the line" with the nature and degree of "gifts" to the IOC delegates.

Bribery prosecutions are expected to increase in the United States with the passage of the federal Dodd-Frank financial law in 2010. A major purpose of the law is to uncover corporate fraud and wrongdoing, including bribery in violations the Foreign Corrupt Practices Act. Accordingly, the Dodd-Frank law provides financial rewards in the form of monetary payments to whistleblowers who disclose wrongdoing to the SEC. Whistleblowers are guaranteed an award of at least 10% and up to 30% of the sums collected by the SEC provided that the whistleblowers supply original information that leads to at least $1 million in sanctions.

In 2010, Royal Dutch Shell and six other companies settled a lawsuit with the U.S. government in which they agreed to pay a combined $236 million to settle allegations that they bribed government officials in several countries, including Russia, Nigeria, Angola, and Brazil, to smooth the way for importing equipment and materials into the countries as well as to expedite government services, such as approving imports of drilling and other equipment. What is interesting about the case is that Shell and the other companies were entitled to these services; and thus they could argue that the "facilitating and expediting exception to the FCPA applied, but the very large amounts of payments (for example, one company admitted it paid $27 million to foreign government officials over a five year period) militated against the use of the aforementioned FCPA exception. In 2011, IBM settled charges that more than 100 employees of its subsidiaries and joint venture partners paid bribes and arranged junkets for foreign government officials in China and South Korea in order to obtain government contracts. The company paid more than $10 million in fines and penalties, though it did not admit or deny any charges. For example, the SEC charged that an IBM subsidiary in South Korea paid over $200,000 in cash bribes to government officials to secure the sale of mainframe and personal computers to the government. And in China, IBM subsidiaries were alleged to have engaged in a travel scam, using fake invoices, to pay for sightseeing trips and personal vacations for government officials.

Violations of the FCPA can also result in criminal convictions for corporate executives. For example, in 2011, Frederic Bourke, the founder of the Dooney & Bourke accessories company, was sentenced to a one year jail term, as well as a $1 million fine, for violating the FCPA. A jury convicted him of paying bribes in the form of cash and jewelry as well as future promise of payment to obtain government contracts for oil deals in Azerbaijan. He could have been sentenced to a maximum of ten years, however. Another recent example involves former Halliburton executive Jack Stanley who was sentenced in 2011 after pleading guilty to two and one-half years in prison for overseeing and orchestrating the payment of $180 in bribes to Nigerian government officials in order to win construction contracts in that county. His key role in the bribery scheme was to make several trips to Nigeria, meet with senior government officials, and, according to the government, figure out exactly whom to bribe. Mr. Stanley blamed his actions on ambition, greed, and alcohol.

As of the writing of the second edition of this book, some recent investigations of bribery in international business involve some major corporations. JPMorgan is being investigated by the Securities and Exchange Commission for allegedly violating the FCPA by bribing (indirectly) Chinese government officials of state-owned companies by hiring their children and other relatives in order to secure lucrative consulting and other contracts. The company denied any corrupt intent since it claimed it was merely engaged in proper networking activities in a good faith attempt to curry favor with the officials and that the people hired were otherwise qualified for the jobs, which were legitimate positions. The government, of course, will need proof of corrupt intent, which will be difficult to establish as merely seeking to create good will with foreign officials is not a crime if the hiring of their relatives is otherwise appropriate. Nepotism, though carrying a negative connotation, is not in and of itself a crime; and also may be a "good" business tactic. Another case involved the pharmaceutical company GlaxoSmithKline, which is being investigated by the U.S. as well as Chinese government for allegedly bribing Chinese doctors, who are considered civil servants, for prescribing (and purportedly over-prescribing) the company's drugs. The company is accused of taking the Chinese doctors and their families on junkets to prime tourist attractions in China and elsewhere as well as paying them money to prescribe the company's drug in violation of the FCPA. The company, however, insists that the trips were not illegal bribes but in addition to the tourism element had educational and training components. Moreover, the company contends that the monies paid to some of the doctors were merely "honorariums" and speaking fees for their legitimate educational services. And the "rewards" that the company gave to certain doctors, who prescribed the largest amounts of the company's drugs, were not illegal bribes, the company asserted, but merely "continuing education" credits or money to obtain such credits, which the doctors needed to fulfill hospital requirements. Consequently, as with the Salt Lake City case, the intent is claimed to be not "corrupt" but "good," as evidenced by the providing and enhancing of education and training. Also, a "junket," though too carrying a negative connotation, is not necessarily a crime in and of itself; and it also may be another "good" business practice. Time, and government investigations, will tell!

The U.S. business community has long and vociferously argued that the FCPA places it in a distinctly disadvantageous position when competing for business in international markets where business bribery may be a common and accepted practice, legal not only in the host country, but also in the countries of the competitors of the U.S. business community—competitors that are not hindered by a law that makes bribery in international business a serious criminal wrong. For example, in Germany, bribery is not even a criminal law violation, but rather a contravention of the civil law code on unfair competition. Moreover, German law allowed German companies to pay bribes abroad. In France, there is no law explicitly outlawing bribery, but there is a law against the "misuse of corporate funds." Thus, if a French businessperson bribes, and the bribe works, and the company thereby benefits, there is no "misuse," and therefore no legal violation. Therefore, in France, a businessperson who seeks to bribe must be very astute and bribe an honest, corrupt, foreign official, who will take the bribe money, and then do what he or she has promised to do.

These aforementioned German and French bribery laws are just two examples of the types of practices that the U.S. businessperson has had to deal with when competing internationally. Accordingly, in order to create a "level playing field" for all businesspeople, in 1997, the Organization for Economic Cooperation and Development produced a treaty (technically called a "convention") patterned after the FCPA, which makes the bribery of foreign officials a serious crime. As of this writing, many countries, including the major trading partners (and foreign business competitors) of the U.S., have signed the treaty. Of course, because the treaty is patterned after the FCPA, that statute's exception for legal "bribes" naturally applies, and now at the treaty legal level as well. But it is not a defense under the treaty that a businessperson bribe a government official in order to comply with "local customs."

The Organization for Economic Cooperation and Development Anti-Bribery Convention of 1997 made bribery illegal throughout the European Union. Before the Convention, paying bribes abroad was not only legal in Germany, but also a tax-deductible expense for business. The German parliament ratified the Convention in 1999. However, the company said that in order to prevent a recurrence of bribery, it would sanction any wrongfully acting employees as well as implement a business practices review by a global compliance organization.

The United Kingdom passed a new anti-bribery law in 2010, which was implemented in 2011. The new law resembles the U.S. FCPA, for example, allowing "reasonable" and "proportionate" hospitality towards foreign government officials, as well as increasing the criminal imprisonment sanction from 10 years to seven. However, there is one major difference between the two anti-bribery laws. The U.K. law prohibits facilitating and expediting payments, that is, "grease," which are permitted under the U.S. law under certain circumstances. The *Wall Street Journal* (Searcey, 2010) reported that the U.S.

Chamber of Commerce called the British law's criminalization of "grease" payments "troubling."

The U.S. business community also has long argued that the FCPA is a very vague statute, for example, lacking a precise definition of a foreign government official as well as a standard as to where to draw the line between illegal bribes and ordinary gifts, courtesies, hospitality, and acts of kindness. In essence, the business community has been saying it is confused as to exactly what is legal versus illegal pursuant to the FCPA and consequently the statute has a "chilling" effect on U.S. international business operations. Accordingly, the Justice Department in 2012 issued a 130 page document to provide guidance to the business community. Though it is beyond the scope of this book to go over all aspects of this comprehensive document, a few illustrations will be provided. To wit, the government advised that the following would be construed as illegal bribes: 1) The expenditure of $10,000 on dinners, drinks, and entertainment for a foreign government official; 2) The providing of a trip to Italy for eight foreign government officials that consisted primarily in sightseeing and which included $1000 in "pocket money" for each official; 3) The providing of a $12,000 birthday trip for a foreign government official that included visits to wineries and dinners; and 4) The providing of a trip to Paris for a foreign government official and his/her spouse that consisted primarily of touring activities in a chauffeur-driven vehicle. The Justice Department guidance document also states that employees of state-owned companies count as foreign government officials. Whether the new guidance document will provide the legal and practical clarity that the business community is looking for remains to be seen.

The U.S. Economic Espionage Act and Stealing Trade Secrets

In 1966, the U.S. Congress enacted the Economic Espionage Act, which made the theft of a trade secret a federal crime, with very severe penalties imposed, particularly for people who steal trade secrets at the behest of a foreign government or an entity dominated or controlled by a foreign entity. This very important federal statute will be covered in the chapter dealing with Intellectual Property Protection, where state and common law protections for information designated as a "trade secret" will be examined together with other legal doctrines protecting intellectual property.

Management Strategies

Regarding the Foreign Corrupt Practices Act, the U.S. businessperson conducting business abroad must be prepared to encounter the fact that bribery is a common way of doing business in many countries and cultures. Such a norm is exacerbated by the degree to which foreign officials perceive themselves immune to any sanctions for demanding and receiving questionable payments, whether "commission fees" or outright bribes. As previously mentioned, there are exceptions in which it is legal to make payments to foreign officials, but at times it will be difficult to ascertain whether a payment is a "grease" payment or a gift or a bribe.

One approach for the U.S. businessperson to take is to "let the locals deal with it" and "stay out of the loop" by letting the firm's local subcontractors and agents interface with the local government officials who know the system. Asking the Justice Department or the embassy or consulate for assistance could be problematic because these U.S. government officials must strictly adhere to the official "legal line." One very good, practical, and discreet resource will be the U.S. Chamber of Commerce present in the country where one is doing business. Here, the U.S. businessperson will find fellow Americans who live in the country, do business there, and know both the "system" and the "players."

Today, in the post-Enron, post-Sarbanes-Oxley, legal environment in the U.S., not only corporate executives, but also corporate entities are at greater risk of criminal indictment and criminal conviction. The threat of a criminal prosecution of the corporation, which was once rare, is becoming far more common. The U.S. Department of Justice now uses a legal device, called a "deferred prosecution agreement" to proceed against corporations. Under such an arrangement, the government charges the company with criminal behavior, but puts the prosecution on hold in return for a promise to reform. If the company presents compliance and behavior to the satisfaction of government prosecutors, then at an agreed-upon date, the charges expire. An independent monitor, picked by the prosecutors and paid for by the company, is appointed to report compliance and to report any problems to the government. At the same time, the company, however has to agree with a list of alleged violations and also agree not to contest them—otherwise, swift prosecution and conviction are threatened. Faced with this new legal reality, companies which once may have resisted threats of prosecution now are more willing to cooperate with the government.

Corporate criminality in the United States, as noted, is determined primarily by the federal Organizational Sentencing Guidelines, as applied and interpreted by the Department of Justice. If convicted, the size of the corporation's crime is the key factor, but other pertinent considerations are how thoroughly the corporation monitored the behavior of its employees through its compliance program and whether or not the corporation was willing to cooperate with the government. Cooperation is defined as demonstrating willingness to identify the culprits within the corporation, to make witnesses available, to disclose the complete results of internal investigations, and to waive attorney-client and "work product" legal privileges. Consequently, retaining suspected employees without sanction, paying their legal fees, and entering into joint defense agreements with them may be construed as evidence of a lack of cooperation.

Company executives now are leery of even appearing to defend any type of impropriety. The perhaps unpleasant and certainly awkward result for the corporate entity is that the corporation, in order to avoid an indictment and a possible conviction—entailing substantial fines, but also which could be the equivalent to a corporate "death sentence," as it was for the former Arthur Andersen accounting company—may have to help the government prosecute its own employees. Such "help" may consist of breaking promises of confidentiality made to employees as well as overriding privacy concerns.

So, not monitoring employees adequately in order to detect criminal conduct, and thereby, in effect, "pleading ignorance," is not a viable management strategy. The failure to have an effective compliance program would increase the firm's chances of being indicted and, if convicted, would enhance the applicable penalties. Most significantly, in order to "help" and to fulfill the legal duty to cooperate with the government, companies may have to declare to the government that certain employees (a small group of "fall guys," perhaps) of the firm violated the law.

How much "due process" a company would give to such an employee before declaring him or her a "guilty" employee is one problem area that a company will have to address. Because a company wants to be helpful and cooperative with the government, it certainly is in the company's interest to provide "guilty" parties, but a company, at least an ethical one, still wants to treat its employees fairly. Accordingly, a small amount of help to such companies who want to pay the legal bills of their indicted employees was given in 2006 by a federal district court judge in New York, who ruled in the KPMG accounting fraud case that the government cannot discourage companies from paying such legal fees. An important factor in the case was that the company had a standard practice of paying the legal fees of employees who faced legal charges stemming from their work with the company. The company also capped pay of legal fees at $400,000 for the affected individuals before they were indicted. The company then threatened to fire anyone who did not cooperate with the government. Nonetheless, the government is expected to appeal the judge's decision.

Summary

Crime is a major factor that adversely affects people in countries throughout the world. Therefore, society is faced with overcoming such a challenge through the establishment of laws that are applicable both nationally and internationally. It is for this reason that managers from countries are forced to adopt certain aspects of other countries' legal systems in order to combat crimes while conducting business.

The criminal process itself varies in specific areas, including jurisdiction, jury trails, the process of evidence, and so forth. However, the similarity across all countries is that crime is immoral, and justice is the solution. Global managers must be keenly aware of the criminal laws that exist in every country in which they conduct business, as crime is defined in different ways in various regions.

Criminal behavior exists in all sectors, including multinational business. It is for this reason that legal "audits" are conducted on a regular basis to ensure or prevent illegal behavior by corporations. Even in the United States, criminal behavior not only exists "on the streets," but also in the corporate world, where executive and managers are oftentimes engaging in illegal efforts for personal gain. Accepting "gifts" in return for favors is a very common type of crime, as it is practiced in all areas of the world and among all types of businesses.

Global managers and entrepreneurs must be very careful to abide by all laws in whichever countries they conduct business, especially since some countries' laws are considerably more harsh than others regarding criminal acts and their punishment.

TWELVE

CONTRACT LAW

A contract is an agreement between two or more persons that is enforceable as law. Business transactions are based on such agreements, wherein each party to the agreement obtains certain rights and assumes certain obligations. When an agreement between the parties meets all the requirements of a contract, the law makes the agreement binding on the parties thereto. As a result, if one party fails or refuses to perform (that is, "breaches" the contract), the other aggrieved party now has a legal action for damages or enforcement of performance. Contracts, accordingly, are the foundation of all business—locally, nationally, and globally. Businesspeople rely on agreements and the promises of contracts being fulfilled because they are legally binding obligations.

It is very important to note that a contract is an agreement, but an agreement is not necessarily a contract. A "mere" agreement arises when the minds of two or more persons meet on any subject, regardless of how trivial. By contrast, a contract emerges only when the parties intend to be legally bound by the terms of their agreement. The purpose of this chapter, therefore, is to ascertain when agreements rise to the level of legally enforceable agreements (meaning contracts), first pursuant to U.S. law and then under selected global legal systems.

In the U.S., contract law is based primarily on the common law, that is, judge-made law stemming from old English traditions. However, the common law of contracts has been modified significantly in the U.S. by the promulgation of the statutory law of contracts, called Sales law and based on the Uniform Commercial Code (which is covered in the next chapter). Moreover, with the advent of the Internet, several statutes have been passed in order to bring the old common law of contracts into conformity with modern technology. Accordingly, this chapter will examine, in detail, contract law in the U.S. and then focus on certain aspects of contract law in an international context.

Contract Law in the United States

Classification of Contracts

The initial order of business is to define the types of contracts that are possible under Anglo-American common law. The first classification is between express and implied and quasi-contract contracts.

An express contract is one based on words—oral or written—in which the parties signify their intention to enter into a contract as well as the terms of the contract by words expressed at the time of the agreement.

An implied contract, however, is one in which the duties and obligations the parties assume are not spelled out quite so expressly, but rather are implied by their acts and conduct or deduced from the circumstances. That is, the parties indicate, by their conduct, what their intentions are. A very basic though typical example would occur when one person asks another to perform a service, but nothing is said by either party as to compensation. In such a case, the law will imply a promise to pay a reasonable compensation, presuming naturally that the expectation of compensation is itself reasonable. Another classic example occurs when a bidder raises his or her hand at an auction, thereby indicating an acceptance, a contract, and a sale.

The implied contract theory may be used to protect an employee at-will by limiting the employer's right to discharge without just, good, or reasonable cause, even in the absence of an express written employment contract. Some key factors to establish an implied contract case are: (1) the employee was a long-term employee; (2) the employee received raises, promotions, and bonuses throughout his or her career; (3) the employee was given assurances that he or she would remain in the employer's employ if the employee did a good job; (4) the employer had stated that it would not terminate employees unless the employer had good cause; (5) the employee had not been formally counseled, criticized, or warned about his or her performance; and (6) the employer had employment manuals or codes of conduct that gave assurances of discharge for cause only.

The quasi-contract (also called *Quantum Meruit)* is a very unique feature of the old common law as it is not a "real" contract like the express and implied models are. Rather, a quasi-contract is a legal fiction created by the law in order to prevent the unjust enrichment of one person at the expense of another. In essence, the courts "pretend" that a contract has been formed, and thereby impose an obligation on a person receiving a benefit or service, even though that person had no intention of entering into a contract. The objective of this fictitious legal device is to prevent this person from being unfairly and unjustly enriched. The classic common law example would be when a doctor renders emergency services to a victim lying unconscious on the street, and, when the person recovers, he or she may be liable for the reasonable value of the doctor's services. There is one major limitation on the quasi-contract doctrine, however, and that is the benefit conferred cannot have been granted unnecessarily, negligently, or through misconduct. If this happens, the contact will not be imposed by the law.

The next classification of contracts examines the distinction among valid, void, voidable, and unenforceable contracts.

A valid contract is one that is enforceable by the courts and contains the following elements, all of which will be addressed in detail in this chapter:

1. A mutual agreement between the parties to do or not do a certain thing, and this agreement must be genuine.
2. The parties must be competent to contract.
3. The promises and obligations of each party to the contract must be supported by the common law requirement of "consideration."
4. The subject matter and purposes of the contract must be legal and lawful.
5. In some cases, the contract must be evidenced by a writing.

A void contract is a legal nullity; it has no legal effect and is not enforceable in court. The usual example of a "void contract" is an agreement between two parties to commit an illegal act.

A voidable contract is an enforceable contract, but one which a party thereto has the choice to perform or reject the contract and withdraw without liability. However, until that one party decides to avoid the contract and does so, the contract remains in full force. One classic example is a contract between an adult and a minor, which is voidable at the option of the minor though enforceable against the adult. Another is an agreement induced by fraud, which is voidable at the option of the defrauded party.

Finally, an unenforceable contract is a valid contract, but the courts will not enforce it because a party has an affirmative and superseding defense, such as the "running" of the Statute of Limitations (the legally prescribed time within which to bring a lawsuit) or the Statute of Frauds (which may require a writing for a contract to be enforceable).

As can be surmised from the preceding discussion, contracts can be oral or written. Some types of contracts, such as a contract to sell real property, must be evidenced by an order in writing for it to be enforceable pursuant to Anglo-American law. However, there is nothing inherently wrong with an oral contract, which is enforceable as a general rule, though certainly not advisable as a written contract due to the fact that there will likely be later disputes as to the oral agreement's exact terms.

Contracts also can be executed and executory. An executed contract is one in which the terms have been fully performed by all the contract parties, whereas an executory contract is one in which the terms of the contract have not yet been fully carried out by all the contract parties. Thus, if one purchases merchandise, pays for it, and receives it, that contract is now executed, but if one agrees to work for someone for a year and the other party promises to pay a monthly salary, that contract is executory as both parties still owe performance: to wit, the work performance and the pay performance.

The final classification of contracts in the common law system is the important differentiation between unilateral and bilateral contracts.

In a unilateral contract, an act is done in consideration of a promise; an agreed-upon exchange for one party's promise is not another party's return promise, but rather the performance of some act by the other party. For example, when a homeowner says to a roofer, "If you repair my roof, I promise to pay you $1,000," a unilateral contract is contemplated. But the critical as well as problematical point for contract law is that a unilateral contract can only be accepted as the actual full performance of the requested act.

In a bilateral contract situation, there is a mutual exchange of promises to perform some future act; one promise is made in consideration for the promise of the other contract promise. In a bilateral contract, one party wants not the immediate performance of an act, but rather the making of a return promise. For example, one party promises to sell his/her vehicle to another party for a price and the other party in return promises to purchase the vehicle at that price. The most efficacious way to spot a bilateral contract is to look for the parties exchanging promises—a promise for a promise is bilateral.

The unilateral vs. bilateral distinction is a significant one under the common law because in a bilateral situation, if either party refuses to perform the promise, there is liability for breach of contract. But in a unilateral situation, there is no promise made by one party to the contract, and thus that party is not liable for breach of contract if he or she fails to perform. Yet when he or she does perform the requested act, that party can still enforce the contract. The promise is thus only binding on one contract party.

Remedies for Breach of Contract

Assuming that a contract is valid, what remedies are available to the aggrieved party when the other contract party fails to live up to his or her part of the bargain (i.e., that party has breached the contract)? The basic types of relief available are damages, rescission, specific performance, an injunction, and reformation.

Damages are regarded as a legal remedy—a remedy at law as opposed to one based in equity. There are several types of damages that may be awarded for a breach of contract. Damages may be nominal, which means that in such a case, the plaintiff can prove that the defendant did breach the contract, but the plaintiff is unable to establish any loss. Nevertheless, the court can award a nominal sum to the plaintiff, which may be sufficient to impose the court costs, as well as perhaps attorneys' fees, on the defendant. Nominal damages also may serve in some jurisdictions as a predicate for punitive damages. Finally, the fact that the plaintiff went through the time, effort, and expense of suing the defendant, even though the plaintiff did not sustain any real loss, certainly indicates to the community—particularly the business community—that the plaintiff is not a person to be trifled with and that the plaintiff will insist on contractual obligations being fulfilled.

Second, damages may be compensatory. Compensatory damages arise when the plaintiff can prove a breach of contract and also can prove an actual injury. In such a case, the plaintiff is entitled to monetary compensation for the exact amount of his or her loss. The objective is to place the aggrieved party in the financial position he or she would have occupied if there had been no contract breach by the defendant. In a breach of an employment contract situation, the wrongfully discharged and vindicated employee would be entitled to reinstatement as well as a back pay award, and also reinstatement of seniority and other benefits.

Compensatory damages for breach of contract also encompass expectation damages and reliance damages. Expectation damages are those which compensate the aggrieved contract party for the amount lost as a result of the other contract party's breach of contract; that is, the damages are the amount required to place the aggrieved party in the position he or she would have been in if the contract had been performed. This form of compensatory damages is also called the "benefit of the bargain" standard for damages. Reliance damages compensate the aggrieved party for any expenditure made in reliance on a contract that was subsequently breached. The purpose is to return the aggrieved party to the position he or she was in before the contract was formed.

However, there is an important principle that constrains the conferring of compensatory damages, which is called the Mitigation Rule. This is a rule of contract law that benefits defendants who wrongfully breach contracts. Pursuant to the Mitigation Rule, even if the defendant purposefully breaches the contract, the plaintiff, although the injured party, has a legal duty to make a reasonable and good faith effort to minimize his or her own damages. So, in the employment scenario where the employer has breached the contract, the employee is under a legal duty to make a reasonable and good faith effort to find suitable alternative employment. Further pursuant to the Mitigation Rule, a plaintiff will not be allowed to let his or her losses mount up when they could be reasonably avoided.

A third component related to compensatory damages is consequential damages. Consequential damages are damages above and beyond compensatory damages which resulted from the breach of contract and which the parties to the contract should have foreseen as being likely at the time the contract was made. It is imperative to note that in order to recover consequential damages, there must be a showing that the breaching party was aware, or should have been aware, of the special circumstances at the time of contracting. A generalized knowledge of the other party's business affairs ordinarily will not be sufficient.

The preeminent illustrations of consequential damages are loss of profits and loss of good stemming from the original breach of contract. There is, however, a limitation on consequential damages, called the Speculative Damage rule. This restraining precept holds that in order to recover consequential damages, the plaintiff's loss must be reasonably certain of computation; if not, the damages may be deemed "speculative" and consequently not recoverable. A typical "speculative" example would be a plaintiff who is seeking lost profits from a new business that never turned any profits. The speculative damage limitation on consequential damages may pose a problem for an entrepreneur seeking lost future profit damages. Since an aggrieved contract party must show the profit that he or she would have received if the other party had not breached the contract, it could be very difficult for an entrepreneur to recover lost future profits if the business never started or has just commenced or has been in operation for merely a short period of time.

The fourth type of damages is called "liquidated" damages. Liquidated damages arise when the parties to a contract include an explicit provision in the contract that fixes the amount of damages to be recovered if one party breaches the contract. It must be emphasized that the liquidated damage clause in the contract will govern the award of damages, and therefore will be the only recoverable damages, even if the actual loss is more or, the obverse, if there is no actual loss. Before enforcing such a provision, the courts usually will require that the liquidated damage amount be reasonable and also that the actual damages themselves would have been difficult to ascertain. If the liquidated damage amount is construed to be unreasonable or excessive, it will be deemed a "penalty" and stricken from the contract, and the plaintiff will get actual damages only.

Finally, at least theoretically, a breach of contract plaintiff can recover damages for emotional distress as well as punitive damages for a breach of contract. But such awards are rare in breach of contract cases as they require some element of a very personal subject matter to the contract in the case of emotional distress or some evidence of bad faith, recklessness, maliciousness, or fraudulent conduct in the case of punitive damages.

As opposed to the "legal" relief of monetary damages, other types of relief in a contract law setting are termed "equitable" remedies since they originated in Anglo-American law in Courts of Equity. The main equitable remedies are: rescission, specific performance, the injunction, and reformation.

A rescission is an order from a court that cancels a contract and releases the injured party from all contractual obligations. For example, if a party is fraudulently induced into entering into a contract, that victimized party can immediately bring suit requesting rescission rather than waiting to be sued by the other party in order to enforce the contract. Yet if neither damages nor rescission are adequate remedies, a court may then compel the defendant contract party to carry out the terms of the contract. While this remedy is limited, it is nonetheless available for a breach of a real estate contract or a contract where the subject matter is deemed unique personal property. Another example is perhaps pursuant to the Uniform Commercial Code, when goods, though not unique, are in very short supply.

It must be underscored that the remedy of specific performance cannot be utilized to enforce an employment contract or a contract for personal services due to U.S. Constitutional constraints as well as very serious practical ramifications.

An injunction is a court order forbidding a defendant from performing a particular act. Injunctions are thus granted when there is a showing by the aggrieved of the inadequacy of money damages as a remedy as well as a demonstration of irreparable harm if the injunctive relief is not granted. A typical use of an injunction would arise in an employment situation where the employee quits the employer's employment and then, in violation of the terms of a legal covenant-not-to-compete, seeks to work for a competitor of his or her former employer. In such a case, especially if the former employee had access to confidential and proprietary information, the former employer can seek an injunction and a court order mandating that the former employee not work for the new employer and continue to obey the terms of the non-competition clause in his contract. Violations of injunctions are punishable by a court's contempt powers.

The final major equitable remedy is reformation, which in essence is an order by a court rewriting the terms of an agreement to conform to the actual intent of the parties. This is to correct what was not reflected in the contract due to some type of error or mistake.

The Requirements of a Valid Contract

In order to attain the legal status of a binding and enforceable contract under Anglo-American common law principles, five requirements ordinarily must be present: mutual agreement (which must be genuine), consideration, capacity, legality, and in some instances, a writing. It is of great consequence to relate that under the common law, these requirements are measured by an objective test: Whether the requirements for a contract are present is determined by a "reasonable person" standard and not by the subjective intentions of the parties.

Determining "reasonableness" is ordinarily regarded as a question of fact for the jury to resolve under an Anglo-American legal scheme.

A. Mutual Agreement

1. The Offer The first element to a valid contract is the presence of mutual agreement between the parties. Mutual agreement can be broken down into two essential components: an offer and an acceptance. Accordingly, the initial question one asks to determine if a contract exists is whether an offer has been made and was this offer followed by an acceptance. The offer is the legally recognized beginning to the contract, the proposal to actually enter into a contract. The offeror is the person who makes the offer and the offeree is the person to whom the offer is made. The offer is the proposal made by the offeror to the offeree indicating what the offeror will give in return for a specified return promise or act by the offeree.

There are several requirements necessary to have a valid offer. First, the offer must manifest a definite intent on the offeror's part to enter into a contract. Consequently, communications by one person in which the language is merely tentative, exploratory, or requests additional information, is not "offer language." Such language does not manifest a sufficient intent to enter into a contract. Rather, such language is merely preliminary negotiations language. To illustrate, the fact that a statement looks toward a contract in the future does not make the statement an offer if it merely shows the intent to begin negotiations. For example, phrases suggesting only preliminary negotiations include: "Are you interested...?" "I would like to get...," or "Would you give...?"

Similarly, if a person's language is construed as merely an "invitation to make an offer," then no offer has been made. Invitations to make offers may look like offers, but in actuality, they are invitations to the public to make offers at certain times and places. The classic examples of mere "invitations" are advertisements, catalogs, price lists, and window displays. They are merely invitations to the public to make offers to merchants which the merchants can either accept or reject. The "invitation to make an offer" doctrine thus illustrates the protection that the old common law gave to merchants: If invitations were construed as offers, a merchant might find himself over-accepted when his stock of goods is oversold. Accordingly, the over-accepted merchant would be subject to lawsuits for breach of contract.

There are, however, two exceptions to the "invitation" rule. The first arises when the "invitation" is clearly phrased as an offer, invites those to whom it has been addressed to take a specific action, and, most importantly, limits the quantities involved so as to protect the merchant from being over-accepted. The second exception involves "rewards," which are announcements to the public that a reward will be paid for the return of lost property or the capture of a criminal.

The second element needed to be in place for an offer to be valid is that it must be reasonably definite, a factor which is measured by an objective, reasonable person test. While the offer and the material terms therein must be reasonably definite, the omission of minor terms should not affect the offer's validity. Accordingly, pursuant to the common law, the offer must make clear the subject matter of the proposed contract, the quantity, the time of performance, and the price, as well as other material terms. As will be seen later in the next chapter, the Uniform Commercial Code (UCC) makes some important modifications as to the necessary ingredients to an offer, especially pertaining to the price term.

The third element for a valid offer is that it be seriously intended. Accordingly, an offer made in jest, in a joking manner, in fear, anger, or spite is not a valid offer. However, becuase the test for determining the validity of a contract is one of "reasonableness," there may be times when an offer is not seriously intended by the offeror, but the offeree had no way of knowing the secret thoughts and feelings of the offeror. Accordingly, if the offeree is reasonably certain that the offer was made in earnest and accepts, there very well may be a binding contract, even though the offeror did not intend that the offer was serious. Again, and this cannot be emphasized enough, the test for a contract under the common law is objective and not subjective.

The fourth and final requirement for a valid offer is that the offer be communicated to the offeree. The rule of law is that an offer cannot be accepted by the offeree until the offeror has communicated it to the offeree. Furthermore, an offer is not considered to be legally "communicated" until the offeree has knowledge of it. Consequently, if the offeror's offer falls into the hands of the offeree without the knowledge and consent of the offeror, it cannot be accepted. Similarly, if an offer is directed to a specific individual or business, it cannot be accepted by anyone else. There is one exception to this rule based on public policy rationales, at least in some states in the United States. This exception pertains to reward offers that may be "accepted" even if the person doing the requested act was not even aware of the reward offer.

Once a legally recognized offer has been made, the next area to examine is termination of offers. Regarding termination, it is critical to distinguish between revocation and rejection of offers.

Revocation is the retraction or withdrawal of the offer by the offeror, and such a revocation ends the offer and terminates the offeree's power of acceptance. There are several important common law rules that apply to revocation. First, an offeror may revoke the offer at any time prior to the acceptance. Second, the revocation is effective when it is actually received by the offeree. Revocation can also be implied, for example, when the offeror sells the subject matter of the offer to another and the offeree knows of this. Finally, a revocation of an offer to the public must be accomplished in substantially the same manner as its announcement. Accordingly, the fact that the offeree did not hear or read of the withdrawal is irrelevant.

It is important here to differentiate "firm offers" from options. A firm offer is an offer that includes a statement maintaining that the offer will be held open for a particular period of time. Under the common law, even a firm offer can be revoked prior to the expiration of the stated term, but this rule has been changed under the UCC, as will be seen in the next chapter when the subject of a UCC merchant's firm offer is discussed. But what is an option or an option contract? Very simply, an option is a firm offer in which the offeror has received something of value from the offeree in order to keep the offer open. When a firm offer rises to the level of an option, it neither can be revoked during its specified period of time nor can it be terminated by the purported rejection of the option by the offeree, at least in some states, since the offeree has "paid" for the right to change his or her mind as to accepting the option during the time period. Offers can also be revoked due to a lapse of time. The basic rule of law is that the offer is revoked by the lapse of time specified in the offer. Yet what if the offer does not state a time period? If no time is specified, then the offer is revoked by the passage of a reasonable period of time. "Reasonable," of course, depends on the facts and circumstances of a particular case, and is thus for the jury to decide. But certain key factors would be the presence of language by the offeror asking for an immediate reply, the means of communication used, whether the subject matter of the offer fluctuates in price, or whether the subject matter of the offer is perishable goods.

As opposed to revocation, a rejection of the offer is a statement by the offeree to the offeror that the offeree does not accept the offer. The basic rule of law is that a rejection terminates the offer, even though the offer may not have otherwise elapsed. Rejections are effective only when they are actually received by the offeror.

Finally, offers can be terminated by operation of the law, meaning that if the offeror dies or goes insane, the subject matter is automatically destroyed. Also, intervening illegality of the subject matter of the offer or some aspect of the intended contract can lead to termination. This automatic termination occurs even if the offeree was not aware of the changed circumstances at the time that he or she "accepts."

2. The Acceptance An offer can become a contract only if it is accepted by the offeree. Acceptance is the expression of assent by the offeree to the terms of the offer, by which the offeree exercises the power conferred upon him/her by the offeror to create a legally binding agreement. There are five requirements to have a valid acceptance: 1) the offeree must know of the offer; 2) the offeree must manifest an intention to accept; 3) the acceptance must be unqualified and unconditional; 4) the acceptance must be made in a manner requested or authorized by the offeror; and 5) the acceptance must be communicated to the offeror.

There are four major problems inherent in the common law's acceptance doctrine. First is the effect of silence. The general rule of law is that silence by the offeree does not constitute an acceptance. That is, the offeror cannot state in the offer that if the offeror does not hear from the offeree within a period of time, the offeror will conclude that the offeree has accepted. The exception to this rule, though, occurs if the offeree has led the offeror to believe that the offeree's silence will constitute an acceptance. So, if the offeree responds to the offeror by stating that if the offeror does not hear from the offeree within a stated period of time, then acceptance will be effectuated. This marks a permissible and legal means of "silence" as an acceptance. Similarly, if the parties, in their past dealings, have used silence as a means of acceptance, then the offeree's silence may be construed as an acceptance, at least for the transaction presently under contention.

The second problem area deals with the legal concept of a counteroffer. The conventional, Anglo-American common law precept holds that an offer must be accepted without any deviation in the terms of the offer. As a result, if the purported acceptance varies, qualifies, conditions, adds to or subtracts from the offer, then the communication is viewed as a counteroffer. Moreover, the effect of a counteroffer, pursuant to the common law, is to serve as a rejection of the offeror's offer, which thus ends the offeror's offer forever, even if the offeree also states that he or she is "accepting" the offer. This old common law is at times called the "Mirror Image" rule, which means that the acceptance must be a "mirror image" of the offer.

Counteroffers, however, must be distinguished from mere inquiries, in which the offeree is not rejecting the offer but is merely seeking more information about the offer. For example, if the inquiry about lowering the price of the offered goods is answered in the negative by the offeror, then the original offer can still be accepted, presuming it is not revoked. But how exactly does one differentiate a counteroffer/rejection from a mere inquiry? A reasonableness test applies, utilized by a jury to resolve a question of fact in order to ask whether a reasonable person in the "shoes" of the offeror would have construed the communication from the offeree as an offer itself, as opposed to merely a request for more information.

It is very important to note that material changes in the old common law counteroffer rules have been made that apply to contracts for the sale of goods under the UCC (which will be discussed in the next chapter) as well as for when a party attempts a counteroffer against an electronic offeror on the Web due to The Uniform Computer Information Transactions Act (as will be examined in the chapter on Internet Regulation).

The third problem area regarding acceptance deals with the legally required means that the offeree must use in order to communicate the acceptance to the offeror. The initial common law rule holds that when the offeror clearly states the medium of communication that the offeree must use, then that method must in fact be used or else the offeree's intended "acceptance" will be construed as a counteroffer. Presuming that a particular means of acceptance has not been specifically demanded by the offeror, the prevailing and newer common law rule is that an acceptance can be communicated by any means reasonable under the circumstances.

"Reasonable" in this context means that if the offeree uses the same means of communication in accepting the offer that the offeror used in making the offer, such means will ordinarily be deemed as being reasonable. Prevailing customs of the industry or trade as well as the past practices of the parties themselves are important factors in deciding "reasonableness." While such a "reasonable" acceptance, as a general rule, will be legally effective upon dispatch, one exception pertains to acceptances made by fax, and that is that they are only effective upon receipt. But it is further important to note that the offeror can negate the rule holding that an acceptance is effective upon dispatch merely by stating in his or her offer that the *acceptance* of the offer will be effective only upon receipt by the offeror.

The final problem with acceptance deals with the acceptance of unilateral offers. In a unilateral offer situation, the offer, which calls for the performance of an act, can only be accepted by the performance of the act—full and complete performance. Thus, the offeror technically, but still legally, can revoke his or her unilateral offer before full performance even though the offeree has already started to perform, perhaps even substantially so. How does the law protect the partially performing offeree in such a situation? There is always the quasi-contract doctrine. In some jurisdictions, the offeror's right to revoke is suspended for a reasonable period of time so as to give the partially performing offeree an opportunity to complete performance and thus accept the unilateral offer and turn it into a legally binding contract. In other jurisdictions, as well as under the UCC, the beginning of performance by the offeree is construed as an acceptance, thereby turning the performance of the unilateral action into an implied bilateral promise to complete performance.

B. Consideration

The term "consideration," in its Anglo-American, common law contract meaning, may not be familiar to many businesspeople, but this requirement is indispensable to the formation of a legally binding contract. The general rule of law maintains that a contract will not be enforced unless it is supported by "consideration." Thus, if there is no consideration present, then ordinarily, an agreement is not enforceable even if the promises thereto are in writing. For example, if an employer promises an employee a bonus, and the employee, of course, agrees, the employee nonetheless is well advised to ensure that the employer's promise is supported by consideration. Similarly, if the employee promises the employer that the employee will not compete against the employer upon leaving the employer's employ, the employer is well counseled to ensure that the employee's promise is supported by consideration. Promises not supported by consideration are generally not legally binding, and thus it is quite legal to break them, though usually not ethical to do so.

In determining exactly what consideration is, the first step is to define the two crucial parties in the contract scenario. The "promisor" is the party who makes a promise and the "promisee" is the party to whom the promise is made. Consideration is viewed as whatever the promisor demands in return for his or her promise.

The test for consideration, under Anglo-American common law, is called the "legal detriment" test. The first step in applying this test is to focus on the promisee, the person to whom the promise is made, and to ask oneself the following question: Has the promisee incurred a legal detriment under the contract? If so, then consideration is present and, accordingly, the promisor's promise is enforceable. Detriment can be based on the promisee performing any one of four actions as a result of the promisor's promise: 1) the promisee can make a return promise to do something which he or she is not otherwise legally obligated to do; 2) the promisee can make a return promise not to do something which he or she has a legal right to do (called "forebearance"); 3) the promisee can do something that he or she is not otherwise legally obligated to do; or 4) the promisee can refrain from doing something that he or she has a legal right to do (again, called "forebearance"). It is important to note that for a promise or an act to refrain from doing something deemed to be detrimental, the activity the promisee is promising to give up or giving up must be one that is lawful.

There are several problem areas with the old common law construct of consideration. The first involves the mutuality requirement. Pursuant to the mutuality of obligation rule, in order for a promise to be construed as detriment, it must impose a real obligation on a party. If a party's promise does not in fact impose such an obligation, it will be branded as fake or illusory and thus cannot serve as consideration. For example, if there is a cancellation clause in a contract in which one party reserves an unlimited and unrestricted right to cancel, then that party has a "free" way out of the contract and the promises that he or she made therein are considered merely fake or illusory. However, if the cancellation clause is somehow limited by requiring that the contract be in effect for a stipulated period of time before any cancellation thereof, basing cancellation on a specified event, or having a notice requirement followed by a time period, then the promises in the contract will be real and thus will be able to serve as detriment and consideration.

The second problem area under consideration deals with the adequacy of consideration. Pursuant to the common law precept, the law is not concerned with the adequacy or sufficiency of consideration, merely that there exists the presence of technical legal detriment. Thus, as a general rule, the adequacy of consideration—the relative value or worth of the two promises or the promise for the act—is irrelevant. The common law does not prohibit "bad" bargains, nor will a common law court "police," fix, or readjust the monetary values of the respective promises and acts. However, when a judge is asked to issue an equitable remedy, such as a specific performance, or when the contract is deemed as "unconscionable" under the UCC, then a judge will consider the adequacy of consideration.

The third problem area of consideration, which already has been alluded to, deals with insufficient consideration. The general rule of law is that performing or promising to perform an action that one is already legally obligated to do is insufficient consideration. One can be under a preexisting public duty to perform an act and, as a result, if one's performance falls within the scope of one's public duties, neither one's promise to perform nor actual performance will serve as legal detriment. For example, if in return for a promise of money, a police officer promises to watch a certain business, a witness promises to tell the truth, or an employee promises to perform his or her job carefully, all of those promises are insufficient consideration to support the promisor's promise of a money payment because the parties are already legally obligated to do those duties. The same situation arises when the preexisting duties are contract-based. If one party is already obligated by a prior contract to perform an act for another party, then neither a new promise to perform the same act—typically for more money—nor the actual performance of the act will be consideration for the promisor's promise to pay more money.

This common law can be succinctly stated as follows: Modification of a contract requires new consideration. So, for example, if a repairperson demands additional money from a homeowner for doing the same repair work that was originally contracted for outright, the homeowner's promise to pay more is not enforceable because the repairperson "suffered" no real detriment in doing the already contractually obligated action. However, as will be seen later in this chapter, the UCC makes a material change to this modification rule.

Even under the old common law, there are exceptions to the "modification" rule. Therefore, if there is an agreed-upon subsequent promise of different performance than originally contacted for, even if slightly different, then there will be sufficient consideration to support a promise to pay more money for what is substantially the same act. Similarly, if there are unforeseen and extreme difficulties in the performance of the contract, then a new promise to pay more money for the same act is enforceable, presuming, of course, there is agreement between the parties. Finally, there is nothing to prevent the parties from mutually rescinding their first contract, thereby canceling it, and then substituting a brand new contract for the same act for more money.

These common law rules are very important when it comes to the payment of debts. For example, the common law holds that the partial payment of a past-due debt is insufficient to support the creditor's promise to cancel the remainder of the obligation. The reason for this is that the creditor is already entitled to the remaining payment, and thus the debtor is not promising anything new or different to the creditor. Even in most states in the United States, this applies if the creditor accepts a partial payment in the form of a check from the debtor which is endorsed "payment in full" and which is then cashed or deposited by the creditor. Yet if the debtor pays the debt early or performs some service, in addition to paying the lesser sum, then the creditor's promise to discharge the debt will be enforceable. Moreover, if a debt is legitimately deemed "unliquidated,"—that is, genuinely in dispute as to the existence or amount of the debt—then the cancellation of the honestly disputed debt for a lesser amount than the creditor initially claimed will be enforceable. In essence, both the creditor and the debtor undergo detriment by forgoing their right to institute a lawsuit in order to get a court to rule on the existence or amount of the obligation.

The next problem area pertaining to consideration deals with past performance, meaning that a contract party is motivated by a past event when promising to make a current payment. Characteristically, the past event was some transaction between the parties in which one party benefited, and now that same party feels morally obligated to the other. Yet under the common law, past performance or moral consideration is not consideration and consequently, any promises based thereon are unenforceable. Sometimes this "past performance" rule is phrased as the "bargained for exchange" requirement of consideration, meaning that the promise must cause the detriment and the detriment cannot come first and thereafter motivate a "moral" promise.

The final problem area regarding consideration concerns the exceptions to consideration. For example, the promise to pay a debt barred by the Statute of Limitations (which sets forth time periods in which to institute a lawsuit) is ordinarily enforceable even without new consideration and even though something in writing may be required. Promises to charities also are enforceable without consideration based on grounds of public policy. Finally, the doctrine of *promissory estoppel* may serve as a substitute for consideration. This common law doctrine maintains that even if there is no technical legal detriment present, if one party makes a promise to another, and the person to whom it has been made reasonably relies on it and then acts on it and, in so doing, substantially changes his or her position or suffers great inconvenience, then the original promising party will be estopped (that is, legally prevented) from even raising the issue of a lack of consideration.

C. Capacity

The third requirement for a valid contract is the element of contract capacity. Capacity means that the parties must be fully *legally competent* to contract, but it does not mean that a party must be *intellectually competent* to contract. So effectively, under the common law, a person is free to make all the "stupid" contracts he or she is capable of!

If a party lacks totally the legal capacity to contract, such as a person adjudged to be insane, the resulting contract is a legal nullity, meaning void. However, many people can have partial capacity to contract. This includes minors, in whose cases the contract is deemed to be voidable and can be disaffirmed (that is, set aside) by the party with partial capacity. But until that party specifically disaffirms, the contract is considered valid and binding on both parties.

Minors, those people under the state's age of majority for contracting (usually 18 years), are the best example of contract parties with partial contract capacity. The general rule in the United States is that all minors' contracts are voidable at their option. To disaffirm, the minor must merely indicate to the other party his or her intention not to be bound. Disaffirmance can be expressed by words or implied by actions. This right to disaffirm continues until the minor reaches the age of majority or until a reasonable time thereafter. It is important to note that this right to disaffirm is one-sided, as it inures only to the benefit of the minor. Even if a contract is executed (meaning fully performed) by the minor and an adult, the minor can still disaffirm. The minor thus receives his or her consideration back, and the minor's only obligation is to return the consideration he or she received back to the adult if the minor is able. As a result of this rule, which is called the majority rule in the United States, the minor is not liable for any damage, depreciation, or use of the property.

The rationale for this rule is to protect minors from mistakes of youth and lack of judgment, regardless of any hardship incurred by the adult contracting parties. So, in order to avoid the potential problems of contracting with minors, an adult such as a merchant may opt to not deal with them directly, to contract with the minor's parents, or have the minor certify in writing that he or she is 18 years of age.

There are three exceptions to the general rule of the voidability of a minor's contracts. One exception involves a significant canon in the common law, called the doctrine of ratification. In the context of a minor's contracts, the ratification doctrine maintains that once a minor reaches 18 years of age, he or she can ratify contracts made earlier. Ratification occurs when the minor indicates to the other party his or her intent to be bound by the earlier contract. Ratification can be express, such as, for example, when the minor, upon reaching 18 years, promises to abide by the agreement. Or ratification can be implied, such as when the minor reaches 18 years and continues to use goods or services, for more than a reasonable time, that the minor received and is receiving under an earlier contract.

The second exception concerns the minor's liability on the contract when the subject matter of the contract is deemed to be a "necessity," such as food, clothing, shelter, or medical care. If the contract to purchase a necessity is still executory, then the minor is still allowed to disaffirm. However, if the contract is executed, then the minor will be liable for the contract—not necessarily for the contract price of the necessity, but for the reasonable value as set by a court.

The final exception governs those situations where the minor misrepresents his or her age. Again, if the contract is executory, the minor can still disaffirm, even if he or she lied. However, if the contract is executed, the minor will only be permitted to disaffirm if there is no loss to the other party. As a result, the minor in such a case must restore the consideration received as well as account for any loss, damage, depreciation, or use. Clearly, the minor who lies will receive less legal protection from the law.

D. Legality

Legality is a required element of a valid contract as the contract's purpose, subject matter, and means of performance must all be legal. The contract cannot be for the attainment of any objective that is prohibited by any law as a contract that runs contrary to a statute or regulation is considered illegal and void. For example, many counties in the state of Florida, in the aftermath of hurricanes, enacted laws that prohibit "price-gouging," specifically by prohibiting the sale of essential commodities at "unconscionable" prices during the time of a declared emergency. Moreover, a contract which is contrary to the public policy of a particular jurisdiction—that is, one determined by the high court in that jurisdiction to be adverse to public health, safety, and welfare—is considered illegal and void.

Contracts running contrary to statute are illegal, for example, gambling contracts in most U.S. jurisdictions. Such a contract is illegal and void and thus neither party to the illegal agreement can use the court system to sue the other for the breach of the gambling debt. However, the advent of Internet gambling has created major problems—both legal as well as practical—for U.S. government authorities, primarily due to the fact that the locations where the Internet gambling companies are located do in fact legalize that type of Web gaming. Thus, when the consumer-gambler located in the U.S. makes a wager, he or she is in fact engaging in a lawful activity. Of course, if and when the U.S. consumer does not pay his or her gambling obligations and the foreign firm attempts to sue in the U.S. courts, the U.S. consumer very well might interpose a defense of illegality.

Another problem area concerning legality of contracts arises when a licensing statute is contained in the contracting. In the United States, there are laws at all levels of government, primarily in statute form, that make it illegal to operate certain types of businesses, trades, or professions without a license. Accordingly, the issue arises as to whether an unlicensed person or business can recover for services rendered under such a contract.

The critical point for contract analysis is to distinguish between two types of licensing statutes: regulatory and revenue-raising. The former is a statute designed to protect the public from incompetent and/or unethical people or businesses. Therefore, if the applicable licensing statute is regulatory, then the rule of law states that the unlicensed person or business cannot recover compensation as the contract is essentially illegal and void. An example would be a contract by a lawyer who is not licensed to practice law within that particular jurisdiction. Of course, the lawyer, as well as any unlicensed person under a regulatory scheme, could confront very serious criminal sanctions for not having a license. However, if the licensing statute is "merely" revenue-raising, i.e., one that is designed primarily to raise money from licensing fees, then the contract by the unlicensed business or person is considered valid and he or she can recover compensation. However, that person or business might be subject to civil or even criminal punishment for violating the law. An example would be a corporation that fails to pay its charter fees or annual license fees. Its contracts would still be valid, though it might lose its charter if the licensee fees are not paid. Another similar revenue-raising example would be an occupational license that a municipality typically requires for a person or a business to conduct business within that local jurisdiction.

Usury is an ancient term, but one that nevertheless has meaning for modern-day contract law. In some U.S. states, there will be statutes in place establishing the maximum rate of interest that can be charged on ordinary (that is, non-corporate) loans. The typical usury interest rates are 15–18% per year for obligations up to $500,000, and rates up to 25% for obligations over $500,000. Charging interest in excess of the state's permitted interest rates is deemed to be usury, and is illegal. The result of usury is that the lender is prohibited from collecting the excess interest, but the lender still can recover the principal and the interest at the lawful rate, though in some jurisdictions, the lender cannot recover any interest at all.

Two chief circumstances will be examined regarding contracts that are illegal because they run counter to public policy. These two circumstances involve contracts with covenants-not-to-compete and contracts with exculpatory clauses. The topic of covenants-not-to-compete will be covered in detail in the chapter on Intellectual Property Protection, but a contract explication of the topic is required herein. First and foremost, a fundamental general rule of law is that a contract in restraint of trade or commerce is illegal and void. Consequently, if a person contracts and thereby agrees not to engage in a particular business, trade, or profession, that contract is illegal and void as it runs counter to public policy. However, if that promise not to do business is in the form of a non-compete agreement, which is an ancillary part of a larger contract such as a contract for the sale of a business or an employment contract, then that non-compete promise may be enforceable.

In order to resolve the legality of non-competition agreements, it is initially necessary to ask whether the non-competition agreement appears in a contract for the sale of a business or an employment contract. In the contract for the sale of a business, the covenant must be reasonable in its time (duration) and place (geographic trade territory). If the covenant is reasonable in both time and place, the seller of the business will be prohibited from entering the designated business area for the specified period of time. Even though there is some restraint on trade and competition, the covenant is justified as a reasonable means to prevent the seller of a business from in essence "retaking" the goodwill asset by engaging in the same or similar business again in the same area, thereby seeking to patronize his or her old customers.

Covenants not to compete also arise in employment contracts, whereby typically the employee promises not to work for a competitor of the employer or to engage in a similar business for a specified period of time. In most U.S. jurisdictions, such a covenant is legal and enforceable, regardless if it produces a harsh effect on the employee, so long as the covenant is reasonable as to time and place and the employer can demonstrate a legitimate business interest to justify the covenant. Covenants in employment contracts, especially the critical "legitimate business interest" of the employer factor, will be covered in more detail in the Intellectual Property Protection chapter.

One final covenant point, however, must be covered, and that is what happens when the covenant is unreasonable. The majority rule means that if a covenant is unreasonable in any one of its core legal requirements, then the whole covenant is illegal and void and stricken from the contract, which is still otherwise valid. In such a case, the buyer of the business or the former employer gets no legal protection against competition. The minority rule means that a judge will reform a covenant to make it both reasonable and enforceable.

The other circumstance under which a contract can be deemed illegal because it runs counter to public policy is that the contract has an exculpatory clause. This means that one of the parties to the contract agrees to free the other party of all liability for physical injury or monetary harm negligently caused by the other party. This is the type of clause that is usually found on valet parking and dry cleaning tickets.

As a general rule, the courts will strike down an exculpatory clause as illegal and void, though some courts may desire a showing that the clause affected a large segment of the public and involved a quasi-public business, such as a communications company, or that the party inserting the exculpatory clause had superior bargaining power over the other party, such as at an auto dealership.

The final area to examine under the legality requirement to contracts is the effect of illegal contracts. As noted, illegal contracts are void and unenforceable, so consequently, neither party to the illegal agreement can be assisted by courts in any way, regardless of the consequences to the parties. There are two exceptions, however. The first is called the "protected parties" exception, which arises when there is a statute designed to protect a certain class of people. Accordingly, any contract made in violation of the statute is enforceable by persons within that class despite the technical illegality of the agreement. For example, a member of the public can sue an unlicensed member of a profession, such as the legal profession, for breach of contract as well as for legal malpractice since the purpose of the statute licensing attorneys is to protect the public from incompetent and/or unethical lawyers. The second exception to the general effect of illegality is called the "divisibility" or "severability" doctrine. The rule of law here is that if a contract is severable into separate agreements and the parts that are legal can be performed separately, then the contract is enforceable as to the legal parts. But if the contract is indivisible—that is, the promises therein are so interdependent that the contract can only be performed as a single entity—then the illegality in any one part will effectively "contaminate" the entire contact and render the whole contract illegal and therefore unenforceable. For example, as mentioned, a contract with an illegal covenant-not-to-compete will generally be upheld, though the illegal covenant component will be stricken from the contract. To compare, a contract in which a landlord's rental payment is derived from the legal sale of food and beverages and the illegal proceeds from gambling most likely will be struck down in its entirely.

E. Writing

As a general rule, oral contracts are just as enforceable as written contracts, yet only if the terms can be proved in court. However, there are certain classes of contracts that will not be enforced unless their terms are evidenced specifically by a writing. This rule is commonly known in Anglo-American law as the Statute of Frauds. The reason for the Statute of Frauds—not to be confused with the separate and distinct legal wrong of fraud—is to prevent the use of perjury and false testimony in proving the existence and terms of an oral contract. Accordingly, if a writing is required and not present, then the contract is deemed unenforceable, even though the defendant has an affirmative obligation to assert the Statute of Frauds as an affirmative defense or else see it waived. It is also very important to underscore that the Statute of Frauds only applies to executory contracts. As such, if the parties enter into an oral agreement that should have been written, but both parties have still fully performed the terms of the contract, then the law will not allow the transaction to be set aside due to the lack of a writing.

Pursuant to the Statute of Frauds, there are six categories of contracts that must be evidenced by a writing. The first is a contract to sell land, including structures permanently attached to the land, or any interest in a land, such as a mortgage or easement. Of course, in the usual situation, there will be a formal written contract to expressly reflect the parties' agreement. But this real estate contract is different from the deed, which is the legal instrument later executed by the seller in order to officially transfer legal title of the real estate to the buyer (as will be seen in the chapter on Real Property Law). There are two exceptions to this first rule. One pertains to real estate leases for a year or less, which ordinarily are enforceable even if oral in nature (though certainly not advisable). The second exception is called the doctrine of Part Performance, which holds that an oral contract for the sale of a land is enforceable if the buyer has paid part of the purchase price, taken possession of the property, and made substantial improvements to the property itself.

The second category of contracts that must be evidenced by a writing deals with executory, bilateral contracts that are, based on their own terms, incapable of being performed within a year from the date which the contract was formed. The reason for this rule is that disputes over the provisions of an oral contract are even more likely to occur when the oral contract is one that is long term. For example, a contract to manage a business for five years, or a three-year employment contract, must be evidenced by a writing in order to be enforceable. Further complicating matters is that witnesses die and their memories fade with time. There is, however, one interesting, though perhaps a bit convoluted, exception to this rule. The exception holds that if there is any possibility, regardless of how remote and unlikely, under the terms of the contract, for the contract to be fully performed within one year from the time the contract was made, then no writing is required, even though actual performance actually took longer than one year. An example would be an agreement by a caretaker to take care of a person for his or her lifetime. This type of contract can be oral in nature because there is a possibility that the person cared for will die within the year of contract formation.

The third category of contracts that must be evidenced by a writing is a contract of guaranty. The first and foremost point here is to distinguish guaranty contracts from suretyship contracts. A suretyship contract involves a promise made by a party, called a surety, to a third person, typically a creditor or merchant, to be responsible for the debts or obligations of a third person. Accordingly, the contract is between the surety and the creditor or merchant. The surety is primarily liable for the debt, and the creditor can demand payment directly from the surety the moment that the debt is due—the creditor does not have to exhaust any legal remedies against the debtor first. In layperson terms, the surety is regarded as a "co-signer" on the original obligation, thereby becoming jointly liable for the payment thereof together with the original debtor. It must be emphasized that surety agreements do not have to be in writing.

To compare, a guaranty contract is one in which a party, the guarantor, makes a secondary (sometimes called a "collateral") promise to pay the debt or obligation of another. The guarantor is secondarily liable on the obligation, and thus the guarantor can be legally required to pay the obligation only after the principal and primary debtor defaults and after the creditor has made a good faith attempt to collect from the debtor. The Statute of Frauds requires these secondary guarantee promises to be in writing in order to be enforceable. There is an exception, however, called the "Benefit to the Promisor" exception, which holds that if the promisor's main purpose in guaranteeing the debt or obligation of another was to gain some advantage or benefit for himself or herself, then the oral guarantee promise will be enforceable. (The UCC's Statute of Frauds will be covered in the next chapter.) One point should be very clear, and that is when one is "backing" or co-signing an obligation, one should be absolutely sure as to whether one is a surety or "merely" a guarantor.

The fourth category of contracts that must be evidenced by a writing is an agreement by an executor, administrator, or personal representative to pay the debts of an estate from his or her own personal funds.

The fifth category involves contracts made in consideration of marriage, such as prenuptial agreements, which must be evidenced by a writing.

The last category of contracts that must be evidenced by a writing is a contract under the UCC for the sale of goods worth $500 or more.

Now that one is cognizant of the classes of contracts that must be evidenced by a writing, the next issue to examine is the type of writing required. The Statute of Frauds, it is important to note, does not require a formal written contract prepared by an attorney, even though such a practice is surely advisable in the business realm. Rather, all that is required is some type of note, memo, letter, paper, sales slip, invoice, or even a check which, in written form, contains the essential terms of the agreement and which also is signed by at least one key party, such as the "party to be charged" (the party against whom the claim for breach of agreement is made). It is significant legally to relate that the memo need not be in existence at the time the agreement was made. Rather, it need only be in existence when the lawsuit is brought. In addition, there is no requirement that the person who ultimately signs the memo do so with the intention of binding himself or herself. Finally, it is important to mention that a statute governing Internet transactions, the Uniform Electronic Transactions Act (UETA), holds that an electronic signature is equal to a written signature on a paper contract, and that an electronic record satisfies the writing requirement for a contract pursuant to the Statute of Frauds. UETA will be covered in detail in the Internet Regulation chapter.

The final area to cover in the general area of the "writing" requirement is a rule, called the Parole Evidence rule, which is an evidentiary principle as well as a contract law precept. The Parole Evidence rule maintains that when the agreement between the parties is reduced to a writing which is intended as the complete and final expression of the parties' agreement, then no modification or contradiction of that agreement will be allowed by oral testimony or by other writings made prior to or at the same time as the parties' "final" agreement. This rule does not apply to subsequent transactions. Rather, the parties can later modify or, for that matter, completely rescind their prior agreement. In addition, the parties are allowed to use either oral or written evidence to help explain or interpret their agreement as well as to show that the assent to the agreement is not genuine. The Parole Evidence rule only applies when the parties intend their written agreement to be final and complete, one reason why, in business contracts, one characteristically sees an "integration" clause explicitly stating that all prior written and oral agreements have been incorporated into the "final and complete" contract.

1. Genuineness of the Agreement Although a contract may appear to be genuine and valid in all respects, it nevertheless may be unenforceable because the consent of one of both parties thereto was lacking. There are four major doctrines in Anglo-American law which render consent to the agreement invalid: mistake, fraud, duress, or undue influence. A contract obtained under any of these circumstances is voidable and can be set aside at the option of the innocent and aggrieved party.

It is critical when examining the mistake doctrine to first differentiate two types of mistake, unilateral mistakes and mutual (or bilateral) mistakes. A unilateral mistake is made by one party to the contract without the knowledge of the other party. The unilateral mistake rule maintains that such a mistake has no effect on the validity of a contract. As a general rule, no relief exists for the mistaken party and he or she must perform the contract or be sued for breach. Unilateral mistakes ordinarily arise in four ways: 1) errors in computation, such as in a bid, where one's party offer is mistakenly low; 2) mistakes in word processing or transcription; 3) errors in transmission by an intermediary, such as an interpreter, translator, or telegraph service; and 4) mistakes in judgment as to the value, quality, or worth of the subject matter of the contract. In all of the aforementioned situations, the contract is binding regardless of the mistake made by any one of the contract parties.

The reason for this common law is that the parties to a contract typically deal at "arms length," and unless there is affirmative fraud or a duty to disclose, a unilateral error is not a defense to performance. This means that one should be very careful in putting forth construction bids or when selling "junk" or a "cheap" stone that turns out to be a priceless antique or precious jewel.

However, there is an exception to the general common law rule of no relief for unilateral mistake. This exception is called the "palpable mistake" rule, and it holds that if the mistake is so obvious and patent that the non-mistaken party is, or should have been, aware of the mistake, then the contract is voidable by the mistaken party. The reasoning for this exception is that it would be unfair for the non-mistaken party to in effect "snap up" the contract with the obvious mistake therein.

The mutual mistake rules are different. The general rule is that if a mistake is made by both parties to the contract, then the contract is voidable by the party adversely affected, though either party can technically rescind the agreement.

For example, mutual mistakes as to the existence, nature, character, or identity of the subject matter of the contract, the quantity thereof, or the means of performance will provide relief to the performance of the contract. The rationale for this rule is that the parties' minds never truly meet and thus any "agreement" is considered to be not genuine. There is, however, an interesting exception to the general mutual mistake rule, which holds that when both parties know the identity and nature of the subject matter but are mistaken as to the future value of the subject matter, then there is no relief for the party adversely affected, and the contract must be performed.

Duress is the forcing of a person to enter into a contract by means of threats to the person, his or her family, or his or her property. Such compulsion in essence "robs" a person of free will, thereby invalidating consent, rendering the contract voidable at the option of the aggrieved party. One distinction that the law draws is important for the duress doctrine, and that is the difference between threatening someone with a criminal action or regulatory proceeding and merely threatening a civil suit. The former threat is regarded as duress and will invalidate the consent to any contract secured by such a threat. Conversely, the threat of a civil suit, presuming it is made in good faith, is not duress, even if one is mistaken as to his or her right to sue.

Furthermore, one should be aware of the concepts of economic duress or business compulsion, whereby one party in an inferior bargaining position becomes the victim of a wrongful threat by a party in a superior bargaining position designed to cause financial ruin or to put someone out of business. As a result of such a threat, the victim "agrees" to enter into a contract with very unfavorable terms. Such economic duress will render the contract voidable and thus will serve as a contract defense. Moreover, in some jurisdictions, economic duress will give rise to a separate tort cause of action for money damages and other tort relief.

The last area to address concerning the genuineness of the agreement is the significant doctrine of fraud.[43] Fraud is a very general legal formulation which covers a wide variety of legal wrongs premised on the misrepresenting of facts. The first important point is to recognize that if fraud is in fact committed in the contract inducement or performance, that induced legal wrong can be used in four main ways: 1) the victim of the fraud can interpose the fraud as an affirmative defense in a breach of contract lawsuit for non-performance; 2) the victim of fraud, instead of waiting to be sued for breach of contract, can proceed to a court and ask the court to rescind the contract on grounds of fraud; 3) if the contract is executed, the victim can

---

[43] For a detailed examination of fraud in the employment context, see Cavico, F. J. (1997).

sue to recover money or goods turned over to the wrongdoer as well as sue for contract damages; and 4) the fraud may rise to the level of the legally actionable tort of fraud and the victim thereof can sue the perpetrator of the fraud for the intentional tort of fraud.

The second important point about fraud is to recognize that there are three types of misrepresentation wrongs: 1) fraud in the old common law sense of deceit; 2) negligent misrepresentation; and 3) innocent misrepresentation.

Fraud in the sense of deceit is more accurately referred to as intentional fraudulent misrepresentation which requires, as will be seen, evidence of an intent to deceive. The remedies for deceit encompass the full range of contract remedies and defenses, equitable rescission, and tort relief and tort damages, including punitive damages.

Fraud in the sense of negligent misrepresentation is premised on a misrepresentation made, not intentionally, but by carelessness. The party making the misrepresentation does not do so purposefully, but rather because of a failure to exercise reasonable care before making the misrepresentation, such as not uncovering crucial underlying facts.

Negligent misrepresentation provides contract remedies and rescission and also tort damages, but not punitive damages.

The last "generic" fraud category is called innocent misrepresentation, and it is a most interesting legal notion. In this situation, a party does make a misrepresentation, but that party honestly believes that the statement is true and there is in fact no negligence in having made the misstatement. In such a case, the aggrieved party can rescind the contract and receive restitution, even though there is no damage recovery.

The fraud of greatest consequence is fraud in the sense of an intentional misrepresentation, that is, deceit. This type of fraud is in essence lying, but "legally recognized lying." Not every lie is illegal in the "eyes" of the law, only fraudulent lying. Fraud in this sense can thus be defined as knowingly and purposefully inducing a person to enter into a contract as a result of an intentionally or recklessly made false statement of material fact. Accordingly, fraud makes the resulting contract voidable, thus affording the victim restitutory and damage remedies, and also serving as the basis for a weighty intentional tort lawsuit. However, there are many elements to the legal wrong of fraud-deceit-lying that first must be satisfied before the aggrieved party can begin to interpose or sue based on the appropriate doctrine.

Fraud is premised on a false statement of material fact: any words or conduct that likely would cause an innocent party to reach an erroneous conclusion. Actively concealing material facts and thereby preventing the other party from discovering the truth is treated as fraud, even though there are no express misrepresentations. It is critical here to note that the misrepresentation must concern "fact," that is, actual historical events, circumstances, or occurrences, and not mere opinions or predictions, which are not legally actionable unless perhaps made by an "expert."

The person making the false statement must know that it was false at the time made or that he or she made the statement in reckless disregard of its truth or falsity. Deceit therefore is an intentional legal wrong, and accordingly, there must be evidence that the wrongdoer possessed an "evil mind" (called the scienter requirement). That is, there must be evidence of a purposeful intent or design to deceive and to induce the innocent party to act in a certain way.

Even if these requirements are met, there still must be a showing that the aggrieved party reasonably relied on the misrepresentation. Consequently, if the party making the misrepresentation can show that the other party knew of the true facts before taking the action—for example, entering into a contract—then there is no reasonable reliance present and thus, no deceit. Similarly, if a buyer is given an opportunity to view and inspect goods, the buyer is presumed to then be cognizant about any obvious or patent defects. As a result, the buyer cannot accept "blindly" whatever the seller misrepresents.

Moreover, if a non-lawyer misrepresents the law, as a general rule, this is not considered grounds for fraud. The perhaps "twisted" logic for this rule is that because "ignorance of the law is no excuse," ergo everyone is presumed to know the law, and thus reliance on a lie about the law is not considered reasonable.

Finally, if the person bringing the fraud lawsuit seeks to recover monetary damages based on the fraud, he or she must show some type of financial harm or physical injury as a result of such misrepresentation.

One major problem with fraud is the general rule that silence is not fraud. The rationale for this old common law rule goes back even further to Roman times and the Roman saying *caveat emptor*, "Let the buyer beware." Under the common law, there is no duty to volunteer information, so consequently, refraining from disclosing pertinent facts unknown to the other party is not fraud. Another reason given for this rule is that the essence of fraud is the affirmative misleading of one person by another. For example, there is no duty for a seller of a pre-owned car to tell a prospective buyer that the car was previously in an accident.

There are many exceptions to this rule. One common law exception arises if one is deemed to be a fiduciary, meaning that one is in a relationship of trust and confidence with another party, such as the attorney-client relationship, a relationship between partners, or the principal-agent relationship. In such a case, there is a duty to speak and silence will equate to fraud. In addition, several states, by statutes, have modified the old common law and now hold, for example, that the seller of real property has an affirmative duty to disclose latent and hidden defects that a basic inspection would not disclose, such as subsoil conditions or termite infestation. There are also applicable federal statutes such as those pertaining to securities fraud (as will be seen in the Securities Regulation chapter), under which the old common law "silence" rule has been changed by legislative pronouncement and thus where silence can be considered fraud.

The penalties for a fraud lawsuit can be severe. A very vivid example of a punitive damage award for fraud was demonstrated by the Oregon Supreme Court, which upheld a $79.5-million punitive damage award against Philip Morris USA in favor of the widow of a smoker who lost his life due to lung cancer. The widow sued the company for negligence and fraud, contending that it waged a 40-year publicity campaign to undercut published concerns about the dangers of smoking, but the punitive damage award was based on the fraud claim only. It is interesting to note here that the state supreme court rejected the argument of Philip Morris that the punitive damage award was excessive and thus violated the Due Process clause of the 14th Amendment to the U.S. Constitution, which has been interpreted by the U.S. Supreme Court as forbidding grossly excessive or arbitrary punishment. Instead, the state supreme court stated the company's conduct was "extraordinarily reprehensible."

In Florida, in July of 2006, the state supreme court overturned a jury determination in a big tobacco lawsuit that awarded $145 *billion* in punitive damages to approximately 700,000 smokers who filed a class action suit against the large tobacco companies for deceiving smokers about the addictive nature and harmful effects of smoking. The Florida Supreme Court stated the punitive award was "excessive" as a matter of law because it was unreasonably high and would have bankrupted the five tobacco company defendants. To make matters worse for the smoker plaintiffs, the court decertified their class, thereby forcing each individual smoker to institute his or her own fraud suit against the tobacco companies as well as necessitating each to prove that smoking caused his/her illnesses.

2. Third Party Rights and Obligations in Contracts A contract creates both rights and obligations. As a general rule, a person, not a party, to the contract neither has any right to the benefits derived from the contract nor any obligation to discharge the duties therein. There are, however, three chief exceptions to this rule: 1) third party beneficiary contracts, where the parties to the contract intend that a third party will benefit from the contract; 2) assignments of contract rights, where one contract party transfers his or her contract rights to a third party; and 3) delegation of contract duties, where one contract party delegates his or her contract duties to a third party. These three exceptions will be briefly addressed and compared and contrasted.

The essential *third party beneficiary* rule is that the parties to a contract may contract to have a performance or benefit rendered to a third party. The third party's rights are set at the time the contract is made and, moreover, this third party, who is to benefit by the contract, can sue to enforce it. But the third party can sue only if the third party is a "donee" or "creditor" beneficiary and not merely an "incidental" beneficiary.

It is important to to point out here that the first two categories of third parties are regarded as intended beneficiaries whereas the latter is a beneficiary who is only incidentally or indirectly affected by the contract. As a consequence, the incidental beneficiary cannot sue to enforce the agreement. An example would be a home supply "superstore," which would only incidentally benefit from all of the home improvement contracts between homeowners and contractors in the local community. In a creditor beneficiary situation, rather, the creditor is considered a creditor of one of the original contract parties, and that specific contract party's intent is to discharge a debt owed to the creditor. Typically, the original contract party performs some service for the other contract party who in turn pays off the debt to the performing party's creditor. In a donee beneficiary situation, the original contract party does not owe any duty or obligation, but wants to make a gift to the third party. The classic donee example is a life insurance contract, wherein the insured designates a beneficiary, who is regarded by the law as a donee beneficiary and, accordingly, can enforce the contract against the life insurance company.

An *assignment* arises in the law when one of the original contract parties later transfers his or her contract rights to a third party who was not a party to the original contract. An assignment extinguishes the contract rights (but not duties) in the transferring party and sets those rights up in the third party. No special formalities are necessary for an assignment; any words that show an intent to transfer will suffice. The assignment itself can be oral unless the original contract or the subject matter of the assignment is governed by the Statute of Frauds or the original contract requires any assignment to be written. Consideration is not required either. Thus, even a "gratuitous" transferee of contract rights can enforce those rights. However, if there is no consideration, the assignment can then be rescinded by the original contract party at any time before the contract has been performed.

Three key "players" emerge in this assignment "drama": 1) the assignor, who is the original contract party transferring his or her rights; 2) the assignee, the new third party to whom the rights are transferred: and 3) the obligor, the other original contract party who now owes performance to the assignee. As a general rule, because the law favors the free transfer of contract rights as being "good" for business transactions, all contract rights are assignable. Nonetheless, there are four situations where an assignment would be deemed as being impermissible: 1) when the assigned right is the right to receive unique personal services, such as an executive administrative assistant; 2) where the assignment would materially affect the duties of the obligor, such as, for example, when the obligor's duty to deliver goods would be significantly expanded; 3) when there is a prohibition against assignment in the original contract, which the courts will enforce unless the assigned right is the right to receive money, which can be freely assigned despite a purported restriction in the original contract; or 4) where a federal or state statute prohibits the assignment, such as a wage assignment. As noted, the effect of the assignment is to set up the assignee as the "real party in interest," which means that the assignee can sue directly on the contract, and in his or her own name, and as a result, without the assignor being joined as a party. As a result, the rights transferred to the assignee by the assignment are not lost or modified by the assignment.

However, and this next rule is critical, the non-assigning party—that is, the obligor—retains all defenses as though there was no assignment and, consequently, the obligor can interpose any defense, such as fraud or failure of consideration, that the obligor had against the assignor or against the assignee. This contract law assignment defense situation is very different from the transfer of rights under commercial paper law, wherein the party obligated to pay on paper—such as a negotiable promissory note—may not be able to interpose certain contract defenses if the paper is negotiated by a Holder in Due Course, who is an elevated and special person in the eyes of the law.

One last problem area regarding assignments is whether notice of the assignment is required. The technical legal rule is that no such notice to the other original contract party, the obligor, is required. However, as a matter of the utmost practicality, the assignee should promptly notify the obligor of the assignment because, absent notice, the obligor has the right to assume that the contract's rights have not been assigned. Consequently, if the obligor performs those rights for the assignor and not the assignee, then the obligor is not liable to the assignee.

The final third party area to examine is the *delegation of duties* doctrine, which is comparable to assignment law except that in a delegation situation, one of the original contract parties, called the delegator, is transferring his or her contract duties and obligations to a new third party, called the delegatee, who is now responsible for performing those duties for the other original contract party, called the obligee. As a general rule, all contract duties are delegable, unless performance by the delegatee would vary materially from that of the delegator, or where the duties involved are personal ones, such as legal representation. But if the duties are merely standard, routine, and non-personal—such as in the typical general contractor–sub-contractor scenario—the transfer of the duties will be upheld, even over the objections of the obligee. Consideration is not required for a delegation even though in the "real world," one party would not agree to assume contract duties without being paid.

There is another important difference between assignment and delegation. A delegation does not excuse the duty of the original contract party, the delegator, to perform. Rather, with a delegation, the primary duty to perform is placed on the delegatee even though the delegator is still secondarily liable for performance of the contract duties. (In an assignment, one will recall, the assignment extinguishes all rights for the assignor and sets up the rights entirely for the assignee.)

Finally, a delegation must be distinguished from a novation, where the original contract party transfers duties to a new party, at which point that original contract party is completely released from the contract by the other original contract party, who also agrees to accept the new third party as a substitute contract party. This will be covered in the next section of this chapter.

3. Performance and Discharge of Contracts The fundamental contract law concept of "discharge" basically means that contract obligations have come to an end and, as such, the duties of the parties have been terminated.

Contract discharge can occur in an assortment of ways. The most prevalent method is for the contract to be performed by the parties. That is, each party completely fulfills his or her promises and all terms of the contract are carried out, meaning that the contract is effectively discharged by performance. This is how the vast majority of contracts come to an end and, naturally, there are no legal problems in such a situation.

The other side of the spectrum will be a discharge resulting from one party's breach of the contract, meaning one party refuses or fails to perform contract duties to a minimum required by the law. In such a case, there is a breach of contract, which can trigger a potential lawsuit, but also discharging the other party's duties and thereby terminating the contract.

A contract also can be anticipatorily breached, meaning that one party, prior to the time set for performance, clearly and unambiguously announces his or her intention not to perform. In such an anticipatory breach situation, the innocent party can sue immediately for breach of contract.

There are three major potential problem areas when it comes to a party's performance: 1) the time of performance; 2) satisfactory performance; and 3) substantial performance. Regarding time of performance, the general common law rule maintains that if a contract does not provide the time by which performance is to be completed, each party has a "reasonable time" to perform. Moreover, even if the contract does state when performance is to be rendered, performance ordinarily must occur on that date or a reasonable time thereafter. Therefore, let's assume that a certain party wants to ensure performance on a certain date. Under the common law, a party can make performance mandatory on an exact date by inserting in the contract an express "time is of the essence" clause, requiring performance on a set date. With such a clause, performance must occur on that exact date, or otherwise, there is a breach of contract. Moreover, a related "essence" rule which maintains that "time is of the essence" may be implied from the subject matter of the contract, such as the purchase of fireworks for a Chinese New Year's celebration.

Second, the question of a satisfactory performance may arise in a contract when there is a clause stating that a party's performance must be "satisfactory" to the other party. Such a clause will be upheld, as long as the performance is such to satisfy a "reasonable" person, not merely the subjective desires of the other contract party. Yet if the satisfaction clause in the contract involves the personal taste of one party—such as in a contract to paint one's picture—then a party can reject on grounds of personal dissatisfaction, even if not reasonable, as long as that party is acting honestly and in good faith.

The final performance problem area concerns the substantial performance doctrine. Problems frequently arise in situations such as construction contracts, where the promisor's performance is to some degree defective or deviates from the terms of the contract. What are the rights of the substantially performing party? The modern common law rule is that the substantially performing party may demand his or her rights under the contract, thereby allowing him/her to recover the contract price but minus the amount necessary to correct the defect or deviation in performance. Significantly, note that the substantially but not fully performing party has not breached the contract.

There are two requirements for a party to take advantage of the substantial performance doctrine. First, there must be, in fact, substantial performance, meaning that the performance must be near complete and the missing or defective part must be minor and not material. Second, the defects and deviations could not have been intentionally or willfully caused or be the result of bad faith (even though carelessness is permissible). If either of these two requirements is missing, then the performing party cannot rely on the substantial performance doctrine, and, moreover, will be in breach of contract.

Contracts can be discharged by the occurrence or failure of a "condition" in a contract. A condition typically is an express conditional clause in a contract that states that some event must occur before one party has a duty to perform or refrain from performing. There are two main types of condition clauses, condition precedent and condition subsequent.

In a condition precedent situation, the duty of performance of a promise in a contract will not become operative until a specified act or event takes place. That is, the contract formed is valid, but if the event does not occur, the condition is said to have "failed," and the contract is discharged and, consequently, the obligations of the parties come to an end. Examples would be a contract with a promise to purchase real property, "subject to," "on condition," or "provided" that financing can be obtained and/or zoning approval can be secured.

The result with a condition subsequent can be the same, the discharge of the contract. In a "subsequent" situation, there is a contract, and usually some performance, but there is also a clause in the contract that states that if a specified future event occurs, the contract is cancelled, inoperative, or void. Any remaining contract duties are thereby discharged by the occurrence of the specified condition, and the contract comes to an end. An example would be a long-term lease to rent property for a fast food restaurant located near a school with a provision in the contract that if the school is permanently closed, the contract becomes void.

Examples of conditions precedent are the prior approval of a loan application by bank and the Procuring of flood insurance before a mortgage is obtained. There is a restriction in condition law, to wit: a condition of a party's obligation cannot be made conditional on some occurrence or event exclusively within the control of that party (otherwise, that party's obligation would not be a real one, and the conditional promise would be fake or illusory one).

The next area of discharge of contracts deals with the doctrine of discharge caused by impossibility of performance. The general rule here is that a party's duty to perform is discharged when, after the contract is made, the promised performance has become, without that party's fault, impossible to perform. "Impossibility" in this sense can be present when either the subject matter of the contract, the source of supply, or the means of performance is destroyed. However, in the latter two cases, there should be an express designation of the intended supply source or performance means. A contract also will be discharged by impossibility when, after the contract is made, new laws are effected which make the contract illegal. Finally, in a personal services or employment contract, the death or physical incapacity of the performing party discharges the contract via impossibility.

The impossibility of performance doctrine must be compared and contrasted with two related doctrines, the common law's "frustration of purpose" doctrine and the UCC's "commercial impracticality" rule. Frustration of purpose is a minority-held view in the United States and means that if the purpose or value of the contract has been destroyed, then the contract is discharged, even though technical performance is still possible. The courts will insist that the purpose of the contract be known and recognized by both contract parties, and that the party must not have assumed the risk of the contract becoming worthless. An example would be a contract by an auto dealer with a contractor to build a showroom for the new Chinese car imports, but the U.S. government in effect bans the importation of such cars by putting extremely high tariffs thereon.

Pursuant to the UCC, a seller's duty to deliver goods pursuant to a UCC sales contract will be discharged when performance becomes "commercially impractical." Such a duty is discharged even though performance is still technically possible, but as long as the seller promptly notifies the buyer of the problem. Classic examples of impracticality would be severe shortages of supplies or raw materials or a drastic increase in prices caused by unforeseen circumstances, such as a war or embargo or local crop failure. A mere increase in cost to the seller or change in market price will ordinarily be inadequate for a seller to take advantage of this UCC precept.

Finally, discharge can be caused by an agreement of the relevant parties. The parties may mutually agree to rescind—that is, cancel—their contract, thereby terminating it and discharging both parties' obligations. Contracts can be discharged by an accord and satisfaction as well as by a novation, which are both similar though not identical legal doctrines. In an accord and satisfaction, the contract parties agree that one contract party will accept and the other will render a performance that is different from the original contract. This agreement is called the accord, and when this accord is performed, the original contract is discharged along with the accord agreement. In a novation, the contract party entitled to receive performance under the contract agrees to release the party who is bound to perform and also agrees to substitute another party to perform in the original contract party's place. A novation is more than a delegation of duties situation because the released party is completely discharged, and the new party alone is responsible for performance.

Effect of Bankruptcy on Contracts

The automatic stay that occurs when a person goes into bankruptcy has a significant effect on contracts. The legal effect of the stay means that creditors, including contract claimants, are prohibited from instituting any legal action to enforce a contract or to obtain any money owed pursuant to a contract. Moreover, a party that has a contract with the bankrupt party (now called the debtor in bankruptcy) can neither seize, attach, or foreclose on any collateral or property nor cease performing any promised obligation under a contract without first receiving the permission of the bankruptcy court Furthermore, a conditional provision in a contract that attempts to give one contract party the right to cancel the contract if the other contract party goes into bankruptcy is not enforceable as it violates public policy as well as the primacy of federal bankruptcy law over state contract law.

Global Legal Perspectives

Argentina v. United States[44]

There has been a great deal of convergence in the area of contract law in civil and common law jurisdictions in recent years. One example concerns Argentina, which has a civil law system, but whose fundamental contract law provisions pertaining to the formation of contracts closely resemble those of the United States.

As in common law systems, in civil law systems, the formation of a contract is based on the agreement between the parties. The agreement must encompass all essential terms of the contract and, in order to be valid, the agreement must be entered into by competent parties who have the capacity to contract. The contract must have a definite subject matter and a legal objective and purpose.

Regarding formation, it is interesting to note that in Argentina, the civil code expressly states that consent must be given in the form of offers or proposals from one party to the other, which must then be accepted by the other contract party. The Argentinian code also states that an offer may be revoked as long as it has not been accepted, which is the common law rule as well. Also, regarding the acceptance of the offer, Argentina follows the old common law "mailbox" rule, whereby a contract is formed once the offeree sends the acceptance of the offer to the offeror. However, unlike the U.S. and its adherence to the traditional common law rule, in Argentina, an offeree may revoke his or her acceptance before it is received by the offeror even if it has already been dispatched. In the U.S., if the acceptance is sent before the revocation, it is too late as a contract has already been formed and the purported revocation is a legal nullity. Thus, in the U.S., the offeror can revoke offers. In Argentina, the offeror can revoke his or her offer, while the offeree can revoke his or her acceptance *before* the offeror receives the acceptance. This latter Argentinian rule marks a major distinction in the otherwise converged contract law systems.

---

[44] See Hermida, Julian (2006).

A Korean Contracting Experience[45]

It can be said that a contract in the United States spells out the business relationship in detail: "a meeting of the minds" on what is expected by each party to the contract. Any change of performance or product "specs" requires (in most cases) an addendum to the contract.

But in some cultures, such as Japan and South Korea, while the contract establishes a relationship, the terms are "set in clay" rather than "cement," i.e., there is some "wiggle room". Changes can be made to accommodate changing conditions by mutual agreement. As an example, a Korean firm (D) contracted with an American hotel (H) to design and supervise construction of a five-star hotel. Subsequent to the start of construction, the contractee sought some changes: to increase its size because its restaurants had become big earners at the other hotel, with some earning more from restaurants than rooms and to increase the size of the exercise facility, because health club membership became popular and a good income earner. The U.S. firm balked at these changes since such requests were not in the original contract, and construction had already begun. Stalemate ensued, and work was brought to halt, which was further exacerbated by communication difficulties. Dr. Glick was asked to mediate so the antagonists could avoid "losing face" in any concessions. The renegotiations worked out only after the president of the U.S. company came to Korea to finalize the negotiation.

Generally speaking, Koreans in business and government admit they often favor U.S. contractors as being honest, doing what they say they will do, "not playing games," and not trying to "squeeze" more money. Yet Koreans also feel frustrated by the rigidity of U.S. contracting and having to deal continually with legal counsel. To illustrate, a U.S. firm that had won a telecommunications project was not invited to bid on a subsequent and larger telecommunication contract because of frustration with the U.S. project engineer who "stuck to" the contract and showed no flexibility. Therefore, flexibility is an important strategy in working with global partners.

Management Strategies

U.S. firms will often go the "extra mile" for customer good will. Some foreign government personnel assume Americans are rich and can therefore afford to pay a "little extra" to the "poor" client. Consequently, it is not uncommon for a government agency to withhold the performance bond to serve as an additional price discount. The government agent will, if the firm persists,

---

[45] Personal Communication with Dr. Norman Glick, July 2006.

negotiate a partial return. The judicial route is usually a "non-starter," as it would cost more than the bond value, and in most "poor" countries, there is an ingrained prejudice against the "rich Americans."

There are certain contracting techniques that can be used with global partners. On government contracts, when buyers want to change "specs" to add something to a project that involves increased costs but not increased payments, the buyer may make adjustments in certain other areas, such as training or supervision so as to increase the level (on paper at least) to cover the increased costs of the addition. Of course, there are problems inherent when contracting with government agencies. For example, a U.S. firm provided large container-lifting cranes for a port (to Country X). The firm provides a performance bond that is returned upon successful completion of the project. The agency, however, withheld the bond, claiming a failure to satisfactorily complete the job. Dr. Glick interceded, and after some negotiation, got the bond returned when it became clear that the firm lived up to the contract and "then some."

A global businessperson must be aware that the creation and validity of a contract pursuant to the common law is determined by the law of the place where the agreement was entered into. For instance, contract law is at times "loose" in the United States because there are few "formal" requirements, such as a writing (as a general rule), a seal, or the document needing to be notarized. Furthermore, in certain states, there is the possibility of an oral contract, or an objectively real, and thus valid, contract that nonetheless does not reflect the subjective desires of the parties.

"Reasonableness," in contract terms, may be both imprecise as well as a concept foreign to a businessperson from a legal system with highly detailed legal codes, but the term "reasonableness" is a critical one in ascertaining not only whether a contract was legally formed, but how the agreement is to be performed. Furthermore, a global businessperson, especially one not familiar with the Anglo-American common law, must be keenly aware of the old, but still prevalent, requirement of consideration. Most people might think that a promise to perform, and the agreement and acceptance thereof, will be sufficient to make the promise enforceable. However, if the promise is not supported by consideration, then this is not the case, as has been seen and underscored in this chapter.

For instance, a common "trap" for an unwary employer would arise when, after the initial employment contract with an employee is signed, the employer asks the employee to sign a covenant-not-to-compete, effectively a non-competition agreement. The employee accedes to this request and signs an agreement, thereby promising not to compete against the employer when the employee leaves the employer's employment. The validity of covenants-not-to-compete will be covered in the Intellectual Property Protection chapter, but as a matter of contract law, the issue emerges as to whether the employee's promise not to compete is enforceable. What did the employer give in return for the promise not to compete by the employee? What technical legal detriment did the employer "suffer"? If none, then the employee's promise is unenforceable, notwithstanding agreement or even a written agreement. Such a result is why the astute employer will include the covenant as part of the original employment contract—where there are mutual promises and performances—or will have the employee sign the covenant later as part of and in exchange for a promotion and/or salary increase.

Contract Negotiations and Clauses[46]

When contract negotiations have been lengthy and complicated, the parties can avoid disputes about what they finally agreed to in the contract by including a clause, called an integration or merger clause, which states that the contractual agreement embodies the entire agreement of the parties and prevails over all prior as well as contemporaneous agreements, promises, and/or representations of the parties. Furthermore, the contract parties can reduce disputes by including a non-reliance clause in the contract, which states that the parties attest that they have not relied on any representations or promises that may have been made during the course of contract negotiations and drafting that are not explicitly set forth in the written contract. Such a clause should help to ward off claims by one party that he or she was fraudulently or negligently induced to enter into the contract.

Choice of Law and Forum Provisions[47]

As a fundamental principle of contract law, the contract should specify where disputes are to be adjudicated and which jurisdiction's law will be applied to any dispute. The contract thus should expressly and clearly state that all the parties to the contract agree to submit to the jurisdiction of the courts in the designated locale. However, it must be pointed out that a court may refuse to enforce a choice of law provision in a contract if the law selected contravenes a fundamental public policy of the state where the court that is deciding the dispute is located. Each individual country as well as each state within the United States has its own body of contract law that will be used to determine

---

[46] See Bgley and Dauchy (2008) and Davidson and Forsythe (2011).
[47] See Bgley and Dauchy (2008) and Davidson and Forsythe (2011).

if a contract is valid, if it has been breached, and what the remedies for breach of contract are. These laws may be dissimilar; yet the choice of one country's or one state's laws may be dispositive of the contractual dispute. Therefore, a contract should also include a choice-of-law provision that states which country's law or state's law will govern the contract. Closely related to the choice-of-law provision is the "forum selection" provision. By means of a forum selection the parties promise to litigate any disputes in a specifically designated jurisdiction pursuant to that jurisdiction's law. Otherwise, if there are no such provisions and the laws are dissimilar, a "conflicts of law" situation will emerge, and a legal determination will first have to be made to determine which jurisdiction's law will apply to the transaction. Typically, the country or state with the most significant relationship to the contract will have its body of law applied to the controversy. Although the two types of contract provisions are closely related, the "choice-of-law" provision may be more specific and will be most useful if there is uncertainty about the exact nature of the law in a specific jurisdiction. For example, an employment contract may state in a forum selection clause that the law of the employer's state will apply, which state law recognizes the validity of covenants not to compete; yet if the covenant is arguably breached in a state, such as California, that does not recognize the validity of non-competition agreements, then an argument can be made that the contract dispute is a performance one and thus the state where the breach occurred, that is, California, has the most significant relationship with the contract. In the latter case, the employee would prevail. So, to be safe, the employer should stipulate a "choice of law" clause in the contract specifying that its state's law, which recognizes, covenants not to compete, will apply to any contract dispute.

Summary

This chapter provided an in-depth analysis of contract law and its associated elements: legal issues, classifications, remedies for breach of contract, the requirements of a valid contract, the rights and obligations of all parties, as well as global legal perspectives and management strategies. The popular use of contracts is mostly seen in the international business arena, specifically by Western nations, such as the United States. However, as industrialized nations continue to work with developing countries in terms of exporting and importing and the manufacturing of goods, contracts are highly recommended.

Variations in laws and regulations allow for diversification among contract laws. The International Court of Justice, for example, provides penalties for countries that breach agreed-upon contracts. This regulatory role is also filled by other organizations, such as the EU, NAFTA, CARICOM, and so on, which also penalize firms that breach contracts and violate contractual laws. Because of the possibility of penalty, the vitality of contract law has become a significant factor for all global businesses.

Thus, international managers, entrepreneurs, and employees working abroad are now encouraged, and expected, to understand the variations in laws that exist among different countries when entering into an agreement. As the world continues to "turn global," managers, entrepreneurs, employees, international organizations, and countries are dependent upon contracts in order to ensure successful business negotiations, stable business dealings, and mutually profitable relationships.

THIRTEEN

SALES LAW AND THE UNIFORM
COMMERCIAL CODE

In addition to being aware of the common law of contracts, a global business manager or entrepreneur doing business in the United States must be aware of a new and relatively recent body of law governing contracts—the Uniform Commercial Code (UCC), which governs contracts for the sale of goods and which makes some major changes to the old common law of contracts. The UCC is designed to change the common law to reflect modern commercial practices, particularly the mass distribution of goods to consumers.

The UCC was first introduced in the U.S. in 1951 as a proposed uniform sales law by a group of legal and commercial experts. It was thereafter offered to the state legislatures and has now been adopted by virtually every state in the United States. However, although the Code is supposed to be consistent and uniform among the states, which the UCC usually is, there may be material differences that have been made to the Code upon its adoption by a particular state. Thus, the prudent businessperson in the U.S. is well-advised to carefully check his or her own state's version of the UCC, which is found in the state's commercial statutes, rather than to definitely rely on the generic version of the UCC or, for that matter, this book or any book pertaining to the UCC.

In addition to the UCC, this chapter will cover the United Nations Convention on Contracts for the International Sales of Goods (CISG), as well as the terms of sale in international trade.

The UCC has several major sections, called Articles, which seek to extensively regulate commercial transactions. For example, Article 3 deals with commercial paper transactions and Article 4 deals with banking transactions. While an examination of the entire UCC is beyond the scope of this book, the authors will concentrate on Article 2, which deals with the sales of good, and especially those sections of Article 2 that make material changes in the common law of contracts. It should also be mentioned initially that the UCC's Article 2A applies to the commercial lease of goods, which in fact will be very important when examining UCC warranty law later in this chapter.

The UCC's Article 2 only applies to the "sale of goods." Accordingly, the old common law still governs service contracts, including employment agreements, as well as real estate sales contracts. First and foremost, it is critical to define the UCC's indispensable term, "good." A "good" is a moveable, tangible, personal property, that is, a thing. Land, structures and buildings attached to the land, as well as fixtures—things which are so attached to the real estate that their removal would cause material harm to the real estate—are not considered goods as they are not "personal" but "real" property. "Tangible" means a physical existence is required in order to be a "good." Hence, patents, copyrights, trademarks, investment securities, and contract rights are not "goods."

As mentioned, the UCC applies to the sale of goods, not services. Yet a major problem arises when there is a mixed transaction, that is, the same transaction involves the sale of goods and also the provision of some services. By legislative or judicial decree, some of these "mixed" cases have been settled. For example, anything specially manufactured for a buyer is now considered a good, as is computer software. Similarly, a meal in a restaurant is deemed to be the sale of a good, and not a service. However, a blood transfusion usually is regarded as a service and not a sale of the blood.

The test the courts will apply to determine the nature of the subject matter of the contract is called the "predominant feature" test, in which the major aspect of the contract will determine its nature as a sale of goods or service contract. For example, in a construction contract, the predominant feature is the building and not purchase of the building supplies. As such, the common law will govern the contract. This distinction between sales and service is crucial to the law of contracts because the UCC makes some very significant changes to the old common law of contracts and, in addition, the UCC's body of warranty law applies only to the sale of goods (and the commercial lease of goods). For example, the courts have ruled in the case of combined medical sales of goods and service contracts that the implantation of medical devices, as well as the transfusion of blood, are predominantly medical services and not sales of goods; consequently, a patient will not be able to sue a hospital for breach of the UCC's implied warranty of merchantability since the patient is predominant purchasing implantation and transfusion services and not purchasing good in the form of devices or blood. The patient, of course, can still sue for any negligence in the performance of the service, but the plaintiff patient will have to prove the elements of the tort of negligence.

It is further necessary to define another key term in the UCC, "merchant." It must be underscored immediately that the UCC's Article 2 applies to the sale of goods by anyone, but there are certain special provisions of the UCC, and with some uniquely harsh effects, that apply only to merchants. Therefore, who is a "merchant"? A merchant is a person or business that regularly deals in goods of a particular kind as a retailer, wholesaler, distributor, or manufacturer. A merchant also can be a person who holds himself or herself out as having knowledge and/or skills peculiar to the goods and commercial practices involved in the transaction. (There obviously can be overlap between the first and second categories.)

Finally, one can be deemed a merchant by employing a merchant for a particular transaction, such as an agent or broker.

Finally, it is of great consequence that the UCC states that a covenant of good faith and fair dealing is implied in every UCC contract in which the parties are deemed to promise not to do anything to hinder, impair, frustrate, or destroy the reasonable expectations and legitimate rights of the other contract party to enjoy the "fruits" of the contract.

Formation of the Sales Contract

As previously emphasized, certain UCC provisions make for some very material changes in the old common law of contracts, notably when the contract is for the sale of goods. Moreover, many of these changes have "relaxed" the old common law rules pertaining to the formation of a binding contract. Thus, the UCC reflects a rationale to make it easier to enter into commercial contracts, especially for merchants.

The first noteworthy UCC alteration deals with the offer, specifically the irrevocability of the offer. The common law states that an offer to make a contract can be revoked by the offeror at any time before acceptance. Even a "firm offer"—that is, one with a promise not to revoke—is attached, it is nevertheless still revocable by the offeror under the common law. Also, the offeree, who is paying the offeror something of value to keep the offer open—that is, consideration—converts the offer into an irrevocable one, meaning an "option."

The UCC has a unique option dealing with the revocability of offers, called a "merchant's firm offer." If a UCC offer is made by a merchant, written and signed by the merchant, and explicitly states that it is a "firm offer" or at the least that it will be held open, then the merchant's firm offer will be deemed irrevocable, even without consideration. The merchant's firm offer will be irrevocable for the time specified therein, but if there is no specified amount of "reasonable" time, it may not be longer than three months.

The second area is the formation of the sales contract to address deals with the definiteness of the agreement. Generally speaking, as opposed to a common law contract, a sales contract will be enforceable even if one or more terms is left open, presuming a court believes that the parties intended to make a binding contract. Of course, the larger the number of undecided terms, the less likely a court will find that the parties intended to be legally bound.

The first contract term to examine is the price provision. Under the common law, the courts ordinarily will refuse to enforce a contract without a fixed price term as the agreement would then be branded as being too indefinite. The UCC rule is quite the opposite, meaning that a fixed price is not essential to a valid UCC sales contract. Rather, while the purchase price can of course be specified, significantly, it can be left open or completely omitted. The UCC contract is thereby valid, but what is the price of the goods? The UCC holds that if the contract is silent as to the price, then the courts should assume that the price is reasonable at the time and place of delivery of the goods. Also permissible in UCC contracts are "agreements to agree" by the parties to set the price of the goods in the future, agreements to refer the pricing of the goods to a third party, and even a contract provision in which one of the contract parties reserves to himself or herself the right to fix the price in the future, even though the party with the reserved right must do so in good faith.

The quantity provision in a contract is one term on which both the common law and the UCC concur. Both bodies of law require that there be a quantity term, and that the quantity of the subject matter be set forth explicitly, specifically, and definitely. Otherwise, the contract will be deemed invalid and void for indefiniteness. There is one exception in the UCC for requirements and "output contracts," those contracts where a buyer promises to buy all of his/her requirements from a seller and/or where a seller promises to sell all of its output to a certain buyer. These types of contracts, so critical to commerce, usually have been upheld as valid contracts, despite charges of an absence of definitiveness as well as a lack of consideration.

To a certain degree, the UCC modifies the time provision for performance of a contract. If no time for performance is stated in the UCC contract, then the rule is the same as the common law: One can perform the contact within a reasonable time period. However, if the UCC contract does specify a time for performance, then the UCC contract must be performed on that date and no "time is of the essence" clause is required. This UCC alteration of the common law is premised on the UCC's "perfect tender" rule, which will be discussed later in this chapter.

It is also quite permissible under the UCC, and perhaps under the common law as well, to have a valid contract with an open delivery provision. In the case of the UCC, if no place for delivery is specified in the contract, then the place of delivery is deemed to be the seller's place of business or, if none exists, then the seller's residence. However, if both parties know that the goods are at a location other than the seller's business or residence, then that place where the goods are located is considered the place of delivery.

Similar to the offer component to mutual agreement, the UCC makes certain major changes regarding the offeree's acceptance. Two principal alterations will be addressed—acceptance by shipment and an acceptance with additional terms, popularly known as the "battle of the forms" because a great deal of modern business is conducted by standard forms prepared by commercial buyers and sellers of goods. Concerning the first topic, acceptance by shipment, the problem arises when a buyer offers to purchase goods from a seller for "prompt" or "immediate" shipment. The question is then what exactly must the seller do to form a binding contract. Under the common law, this type of offer was regarded as an offer to form a unilateral contract and, as a result, the actual and complete shipment by the seller was the only way to accept. However, pursuant to the UCC, a seller can accept by either promptly shipping the goods or by promising to ship the goods, thereby blurring the distinction that the common law drew between unilateral and bilateral contracts.

Another related and perplexing issue emerges if the seller promptly and immediately ships nonconforming goods. Under the common law, such a shipment would most likely be construed as a counteroffer, but pursuant to the UCC, the shipment of conforming goods by the seller is both an acceptance of the contract as well as a breach of the contract. However, the UCC does allow the seller to ship the nonconforming goods to the buyer as merely an "accommodation," which the Code construes as a counteroffer, presuming the seller promptly notifies the buyer in writing that the seller is shipping as a courtesy and is *not* accepting the offer.

The second UCC acceptance alteration to relate is one of great consequence. This change deals with purported acceptances that contain more terms than in the original offer. Recall the common law's "mirror image" rule, whereby the offeree's acceptance must be identical to the offeror's offer, and consequently, any additions or variations in the "acceptance" will render it a counteroffer, and thereby a rejection of the original offer. While the UCC makes a very dramatic change to the common law counteroffer rule, it is first necessary to point out that even under the UCC, if the offeree clearly states that there can be no contract formed unless the offeree's exact set of terms is accepted by the original offeror, then the offeree's response is treated as a counteroffer. In essence, the offeree is saying "take it or leave it" on the offeree's terms. However, when the offeree "merely" sets forth additional terms in the acceptance than contained in the offeror's proposal, the UCC holds that a contract nonetheless exists.

The next issue to resolve is what exactly happens to the additional terms. The general rule is that the additional terms are only construed as being proposals for additions to the contract, which the parties can negotiate over. Yet if the dealings are between two merchants, then the additional terms automatically become part of the contract unless: 1) the offeror's original offer expressly limited acceptance to the offered terms (that is, the offeror has in essence said "take it or leave it"); 2) the additional terms are regarded as "material" alterations to the contract, such as an arbitration clause or a disclaimer of warranties; or 3) the original offeror, within a reasonable time, notifies the offeree proposing the additional terms that the offeror objects to them.

The UCC also makes a change in the old common law consideration requirement when a UCC contract is modified. Under the common law, modification of a contract requires new or different consideration. But pursuant to the UCC, modification of a sales contract is valid even without new or different consideration, presuming, of course, that the parties have mutually agreed to the rescission. Therefore, an agreement between the parties to extend the time of delivery of the goods, or for the buyer to pay more money for the same goods, is enforceable.

Also, even though consideration is not required, a writing may be necessary if the original contract is within the UCC's Statute of Frauds, the modification brings the contract within the scope of the Statute of Frauds, or the original contract requires any modification to be in writing.

The UCC's Statute of Frauds becomes operative when the price for the goods is $500 or more. Accordingly, it will apply when a sufficient writing is necessary to have a valid contract. Yet the lack of a writing does not make a UCC contract void, merely unenforceable, which means the lack of a writing must be pled as an affirmative defense. It also means that one may waive the writing requirement by making an admission in one's pleading or testimony as to the existence of the sales contract.

There are four chief exceptions to the UCC's Statute of Frauds writing requirement. The first is called a "written confirmation" by a merchant doctrine. When both parties to the transaction are merchants, and one merchant receives a confirmation of an oral sales agreement in writing, and the writing is adequate to bind the sender merchant, then the writing will also bind the recipient merchant unless he or she objects in writing within 10 days. This rule is a very novel UCC proposition because the recipient merchant is bound even though he or she did not actually sign anything.

The second exception deals with partial acceptance of goods and holds that a UCC oral agreement is enforceable by the receipt and acceptance of goods, but only to the extent that the goods are received and accepted.

Similarly, the third exception deals with the partial payment of goods, maintaining that an oral agreement is enforceable with respect to goods for which payment has been received and accepted.

The final exception governs the situation where goods are specially manufactured by the seller for the buyer. Specially manufactured goods are defined as goods not suitable for resale to others in the ordinary course of the seller's business. In such a circumstance, an oral agreement is enforceable against the buyer if the seller has made a substantial beginning on the manufacture of the goods or has made commitments for the procurement of raw materials.

The last UCC doctrine that brings about a material change in the old common law of contracts is the UCC's "unconscionability" doctrine. One recalls the common law precept that a court will not be concerned with the adequacy of consideration—the relative worth of the promises and/or acts in the contract—only the presence of consideration. Yet the UCC brings into the law of sales the equitable concept of fairness in the guise of "unconscionability." Accordingly, a court will not enforce a UCC contract if it is unconscionable.

The UCC deliberately refrains from defining what constitutes an "unconscionable" contract. The courts, meanwhile, have attempted to define this central term, for example, by stating that it means a contract that is so unfair it "shocks the conscience" of the courts or a contract that has terms extremely and unreasonably favorable to one party and unfavorable to the other party. While the meanings are not clear, one fact is, and that is that the courts will not be receptive to "unconscionability" allegations by one merchant against another or claims of unfairness by a sophisticated businessperson against the other contract party.

Title and Risk of Loss

The ultimate goal of a sale of goods contract is to transfer the ownership of the goods and all rights and responsibilities thereto from the seller to the buyer. One major problem arises if there is a passing of time after the formation of the sales contract and the eventual transfer of ownership to the buyer. Events can occur during this lapse of time—the goods can be damaged, destroyed, lost, or stolen. Thus, the key legal issue arises as to which contract party bears the responsibilities for the goods. Prior to the UCC, this question was resolved by ascertaining who had title to the goods. Although title is still important for taxation issues, the UCC has abandoned the concept of title as the determining factor of who is responsible for the goods. Rather, the UCC has established specific rules, called risk of loss rules, to determine responsibilities for the goods.

The UCC rules specify exactly when the risk of loss passes from the seller to the buyer. Furthermore, these risk of loss rules determine which party, the buyer or the seller, bears the loss when, without the fault of either party, some harm comes to the goods prior to or during their delivery to the buyer. Accordingly, there are three important general rules. First, if there is a risk of loss provision in the sales contract which specifies at what point the risk of loss shifts from the seller to the buyer, the provision effectively controls the risk question.

Second, presuming no such contract provision exists and if the goods are shipped by a carrier from the seller to a buyer, it is essential to determine the type of carrier contract. If the carrier contract is a shipment contract, which requires the seller to place the goods in the hands of the carrier and not to deliver them to a particular destination, the risk of loss passes to the buyer, upon delivery of the goods, by way of the seller to the carrier. But if the carrier contract is a destination contract, which requires the seller to deliver the goods to a particular destination, the risk passes to the buyer only when the goods arrive at the destination and the buyer is so notified. It should be noted that in the sale and delivery of goods, there are a variety of specialized destination and shipment contracts, each with their own unique risk of loss provisions. These specialized contract provisions will be covered in detail in the Management Strategies section of this chapter.

Third, in most other risk of loss situations, the key factor is whether or not the seller is a merchant. If the seller is a merchant, the risk passes to the buyer only when the buyer actually receives the goods. But if the seller is not a merchant, the risk passes to the buyer when the seller has placed the goods at the buyer's disposal and so notified the buyer.

Warranties

In making a sale of goods, the seller often warrants or guarantees the title to the goods or that the goods conform to a certain standard or operate in a certain way. By making such a guarantee, the seller thereby agrees to redress any loss or damages that the buyer may suffer if the title to the goods or the goods themselves are not as represented. Warranties can concern the title to goods or the quality of the goods. Warranties can be express—that is, created by the words or actions of the seller—or implied—that is, imposed automatically by the law.

Regarding the title to goods, two important implied warranties must be mentioned. One is the implied warranty of good title, wherein the seller is deemed to guarantee the title to the goods and that the transfer is itself rightful. Note that the seller does not have to be a merchant to have this warranty imposed and also that ignorance of a defect in the title is not an excuse. The second implied title warranty is a warranty that the goods are free from any liens or encumbrances, of which the buyer, at the time of sale, had no knowledge thereof.

It is necessary to differentiate express warranties of quality from implied warranties of quality regarding the quality of the goods. *Express warranties* of quality come from the express words or actions of the seller. The seller need not use the exact words "warranty" or "guaranty" and the buyer need not demonstrate that the seller intended to make such a warranty. There are three types of express warranties: 1) affirmation of fact or promise; 2) conformity to description; and 3) conformity to model or sample.

An express warranty by "affirmation of fact" or promise occurs when the seller makes a statement of fact or promise to the buyer in the course of negotiations which relates to the goods and which is part of the "basis of the bargain."

The factual statement or promise creates an express warranty that the goods conform to the statement or promise made about them. No technical words are necessary to create an express warranty, which may be oral or written. "Basis of the bargain" here means that the buyer has in part relied on the warranty in making his or her decision to buy the goods. Comparable to fraud law, warranty law holds that mere opinions or predictions cannot form the basis of an express warranty unless perhaps made by an expert, i.e., there is a major distinction between saying that the car is a "great car" and a "good buy" versus that the car has a "200-horsepower engine" and "only 75,000 miles," as the latter are factual statements and the former merely opinionated utterances.

Another example of "puffing" would be "this car is a top-notch car"; whereas the statement "this car gets 28 miles per gallon" would be a factual statement and the basis of an express warranty.

The second type of express warranty, "conformity to description," is similar to and overlaps the first type. Accordingly, any description of the goods by the seller that is part of the basis of the bargain creates an express warranty that the goods conform to the description. A description can encompass any descriptive name or words, such as "seedless grapes," "pitted prunes," or "boneless chicken," or a trade term, such as "Post-It" notes or "Granny Smith" apples.

Finally, the third type of express warranty arises when a model or sample is used to sell the goods. In such a case, the goods must conform to the model of the sample. A "sample" is a part of the actual goods taken from the whole whereas a "model" is a scale representation of the goods but is not taken therefrom.

One last express warranty issue to address is to determine who on the marketing chain is legally responsible for an express warranty. A manufacturer or wholesaler is only liable for the warranties made by the retailer at the time of sale if the retailer had the legal authority to make such warranties. However, a retailer will be held to adopt any express warranties made by the manufacturer or wholesaler and will be equally liable thereon.

In addition to the express warranties, which are explicitly made by the seller of goods, the UCC implies certain other warranties simply because a sale of goods is made in a certain manner. These *implied warranties* are imposed regardless of the seller's intentions and despite the fact that the seller has made no statements or promises regarding the goods. Unless these warranties are expressly disclaimed by the seller (as will be seen shortly), the implied warranties arise by operation of law in every sale of goods—used as well as new—although some states, by statute, have curtailed implied warranty liability for certain very old used goods.

There are three very important implied warranties created by the UCC: merchantability, fitness for a particular purpose, and wholesomeness. The first to examine is the implied warranty of "merchantability." The rule of law is that in every merchant's contract of sale, the UCC will imply a warranty that the goods are of "merchantable" quality. It is critical to point out that only a seller who is a merchant (with respect to the type of goods sold by the merchant) is deemed to make this warranty. Neither a sale by a private individual nor an occasional sale by a merchant who regularly deals in other goods will trigger this warranty.

What does the key term "merchantability" mean? The standard for merchantability includes several criteria: 1) the goods must be fit for the ordinary purposes for which the goods are used; 2) the goods must meet normal commercial standards for goods of that type; 3) the goods must do their intended job safely; 4) the goods must be around the middle range of quality (and not the highest); and 5) the goods must be adequately packaged and labeled. For example, a shoe should have its heel well enough attached so that it does not break off during normal walking (as opposed to, say, mountain climbing). Similarly, a refrigerator that keeps food cold but then shorts out and causes a fire is not doing its intended job safely.

The second implied warranty is called the fitness for a particular purpose warranty. If a seller is aware of a particular use of goods by a buyer and the buyer has relied on the seller's judgment in order to select suitable goods, an implied warranty of fitness for that particular use is thereby created by the law. Accordingly, it is essential that the seller has knowledge of the buyer's intended use, meaning that the seller should know what the buyer's special requirements are and also understand that the buyer is relying on the seller to fulfill those special requirements. For example, when a buyer goes to a sporting goods and camping store and asks the seller for hiking shoes capable of hiking on a mountain trail, a "fitness" warranty likely will be imposed. It must be underscored that this implied warranty applies to both merchants and non-merchants alike, as long as the knowledge and reliance factors are present. By contrast, the merchantability warranty applies solely to merchants.

The third and final type of implied warranty is wholesomeness. For example, when the goods sold are food or beverages, a warranty automatically arises that the goods be fit for human consumption. A retailer grocer, it is important to note, is deemed to make this warranty regardless of whether the grocer or the customer selects the goods and notwithstanding whether or not the goods came to the grocer prepackaged and in sealed containers. Restaurants are also deemed to make this warranty because they sell goods primarily and service secondarily, regardless of whether the food is sold in or off the premises.

There is one troubling issue with the wholesomeness warranty. Just how "wholesome" does the food have to be? How fit must the food be for human consumption? Obviously, if the food is contaminated, it is unfit. Likewise, if there is a foreign object in the food, such as metal, glass, or a rodent, the food is contaminated. The problem occurs when there is a natural object in the food, such as a chicken or fish bone in a can of tuna or chicken. In most states throughout the United States, the food is not considered unwholesome, and thus the implied warranty is not breached because the object in the food is a natural one. Yet some states, instead of the "foreign v. natural" test, use a "reasonable expectation" test, and thus would ask whether a reasonable person would expect to encounter a fish bone in a can of tuna versus say in a fresh-grilled grouper sandwich prepared in the Florida Keys.

Although warranty law can provide the consumer a great deal of legal protection, there is one very serious problem with warranties, especially implied ones, and that is that they can be, in certain circumstances, disclaimed by the seller and thereby excluded from the sales transaction. As to the disclaimer of warranties, as a general rule, the seller can disclaim and exclude warranties, but any disclaimer must be "conspicuous," meaning that a reasonable person should be aware of the disclaimer (meaning that "fine-print" disclaimers will not be effective). Furthermore, a disclaimer protects only the person or business that inserts it, not any other seller in the marketing chain.

The first disclaimer area to examine is the disclaimer of express warranties. While the disclaimer of an express warranty is theoretically possible, the UCC states that any such disclaimer will be "disregarded" if it is considered unreasonable. The courts have construed this UCC provision by maintaining that if an express warranty formed part of the basis of the bargain, any attempted disclaimer thereof is unreasonable, thereby in effect meaning that express warranties, as a practical matter, can rarely be disclaimed.

Sellers, however, have much greater freedom under the UCC to disclaim implied warranties. The first method is by a "catch-all" disclaimer, meaning that the buyer buys the goods "as is," "with all faults," "as they stand," or "in their present condition." Such language, if conspicuous, ordinarily will exclude all implied warranties of quality. The second way pertains to disclaiming the implied warranty of merchantability, meaning that the merchantability warranty can be disclaimed; the disclaimer can even be oral, but the word "merchantability" must be specifically mentioned. The third way concerns disclaiming the "fitness" warranty. In this situation, the warranty can be disclaimed and the word "fitness" need not be mentioned, but this disclaimer must be in writing. Finally, in some jurisdictions, a seller can effectively disclaim the merchantability and fitness warranties by limiting the seller's liability solely to the "repair or replacement of defective parts."

Warranties can also be waived by the buyer. In the typical waiver situation, the buyer has inspected the goods prior to the sale, and consequently, the buyer is not allowed to bring a lawsuit for breach of warranty as to any obvious or patent defect or any defects which a reasonable inspection should have revealed. In addition, if the seller insists on or demands an inspection, and the buyer refuses, the buyer is not permitted to bring a breach of warranty claim for defects to the goods which a reasonable inspection should have revealed.

In order to prove a breach of warranty, a plaintiff must show the following: 1) a sale of goods; 2) a warranty was made and not disclaimed; 3) the goods did not conform to the warranty; 4) the plaintiff was injured; and 5) that the plaintiff's injuries were factually and proximately caused by the non-conforming goods. If the plaintiff can do so, he or she may be able to recover damages as the following: 1) any loss of value in the goods or the fair market value of the goods; 2) consequential damages, such as loss of goodwill and lost profits; 3) property damages; 4) personal injury damages; and 5) incidental damages, such as storage and inspection fees and return freight charges.

There are, however, two serious obstacles to a plaintiff's recovery for breach of warranty. One is the old common law "privity" doctrine, which meant that there had to be a contractual relationship between the parties in order for one to maintain a lawsuit against the other. Thus, only the actual buyer of the goods could sue for breach of warranty, and he or she could only sue his or her immediate party in the marketing chain, usually the retailer. The UCC has liberalized the old common law privity rule to a degree by allowing lawsuits not only by the immediate buyer but also by the buyer's family, household, and guests. However, these parties still only could sue their immediate party in the marketing chain.

In some jurisdictions, the privity rule has been abolished for breach of warranty lawsuits, meaning that anyone who could reasonably be expected to use, consume, or be affected by the goods could sue and could sue anyone on the marketing chain. An example of this latter point of view would be a lawsuit against a manufacturer by an innocent bystander who was injured by a homeowner's use of a lawnmower produced by the manufacturer considered not "merchantable."

Another problem with a breach of warranty lawsuit is notice requirement. The rule of law is that in order to recover for breach of warranty, the buyer must give notice of the breach within a reasonable time after the breach is discovered. The notice can be oral or written, and should attempt to identify the breach or at the least indicate that there is a problem with the goods. If there is no notice, the buyer's cause of action is totally barred.

While the breach of warranty law provision provided by the UCC does in fact afford some legal redress to the consumer, there are, as has been seen, many difficulties with a breach of warranty lawsuit.

Performance and Remedies

The final two related areas to cover in the law of sales are the performance of the sales contract—that is, the obligations of both the seller and buyer that are necessary to fulfill their agreement—and the remedies available to the buyer or the seller if either party fails to live up to the sales contract obligations.

Performance of the sales contract can be divided into two basic areas: the seller's obligation, which is to deliver conforming goods; and the buyer's obligation, which is to accept and pay for the goods. Taking the seller's obligation first, how exactly does a seller deliver goods? The rule of law is that a seller fully performs his or her delivery obligation by making a "tender" of delivery. That is, the seller is required to place and hold conforming goods at the buyer's disposition and also give the buyer notification necessary in order to take delivery. The seller, in addition, must keep the goods available for a reasonable period of time and must make the "tender" at a reasonable hour.

Of great consequence to the parties is the UCC's "perfect tender" rule, which holds that if the goods or the tender of delivery fail in any respect to conform to the contract, the buyer is not obligated to accept them. This means that the goods and their tender must conform in every detail to the terms of the contract. The old common law "substantial performance" doctrine, therefore, does not apply to UCC contracts, which represents a noteworthy change the Code makes to the common law.

While the "perfect tender" rule may seem harsh, there are some exceptions to the doctrine. The first is called the Cure Doctrine. If the seller makes a tender of delivery which is deficient, but the time of performance has not yet expired, the seller can cure any defects by promptly notifying the seller of his or her intention to cure and then make a conforming delivery before expiration of the time for performance. The second exception deals with installment contracts and holds that when goods are required or authorized to be delivered in separate lots, the buyer can reject a particular installment only if the defect substantially impairs the value of the installment. Because the defect in a particular installment is considered a breach of the sales contract only if it impairs the value of the whole contract, the UCC applies the doctrine of substantial performance to installment goods contracts. The third exception is the aforementioned doctrine of commercial impracticality, which not only may discharge performance but also may excuse a delay in performance. Finally, if the seller makes improper shipping arrangements, the buyer can reject delivery only if material loss or delay results.

The buyer's fundamental obligations under the sales contract are to first provide facilities to receive the goods and then to actually accept the goods. (Note, however, that before acceptance can occur, the buyer is permitted to inspect the goods.) "Acceptance" means that the buyer takes the goods as his or her own and then pays for the goods. Acceptance can occur in three ways: 1) the buyer expressly indicates acceptance by words; 2) the buyer has had a reasonable opportunity to accept the goods and fails to reject them in a reasonable time; or 3) the buyer performs any act inconsistent with the seller's ownership of the goods, such as using, consuming, or reselling the goods. The buyer is also allowed to make a partial acceptance, meaning that when part of the goods is defective, the buyer can accept the conforming part and reject the non-conforming part. The buyer is allowed to pay for the goods with a check, but the seller can demand payment in legal tender—that is, currency—but then the seller must afford the buyer a reasonable time in which to secure the currency.

The UCC provides corresponding *remedies* for the breach of the sales contract. The buyer's remedies are divided into two categories: 1) when the seller fails to deliver the goods and; 2) where the seller delivers non-conforming goods.

In the first instance, the buyer can cancel the contract, recover any prepayments made, and "cover." Cover entails the buyer purchasing goods elsewhere in a commercially reasonable manner and receiving damages, measured as the difference between the cover price and the contract price. However, if the buyer does not wish to cover, the buyer can obtain the difference between the market price and the contract price.

Where the seller delivers non-conforming goods, the buyer can cancel the contract, recover any prepayments made, and, pursuant to the "perfect tender" rule, reject the delivery, as long as it is done within a reasonable time and with notification to the seller. However, if the buyer has already accepted the goods, it is generally too late for the buyer to reject; rather, the buyer must revoke his or her acceptance.

It is very important to emphasize that a revocation of an acceptance must be premised on a defect in the goods that substantially impairs the value of the goods. Significantly, the "perfect tender" rule applies only to a buyer's rejections and not to revocations. A revocation, moreover, must occur within a reasonable period of time after the buyer discovers the defect in the goods but before any substantial change in the condition of the goods. The effect of a rejection or revocation is that the buyer does not have to pay for the goods, the seller has the responsibility of taking the goods back, and the buyer can cover and receive damages. The buyer can also accept the goods despite the non-conformity and recover damages, the measure of which is the difference between the actual value of the goods and the value if the goods had conformed to the contract.

The seller's remedies for breach of sales contract are likewise divided into two categories: 1) when the buyer breaches before receiving the goods; and 2) where the buyer breaches after receiving the goods.

In the first case, the seller can cancel the contract, withhold or stop delivery of the goods, or resell the goods in a commercially reasonable manner and recover damages, the measure of which is the difference between the contract price and the resale price. However, if the seller chooses not to resell the goods, the measure of damages is the difference between the contract price and the market value of the goods.

When the buyer breaches after receiving the goods, the seller can recover the purchase price as damages. Damages also can encompass consequential damages—for example, lost profits and damage to goodwill and business reputation, as well as incidental damages, such as inspection and storage fees and return freight charges.

Global Legal Perspectives

The United Nations Convention on Contracts for the International Sale of Goods[48]

There is no worldwide court in which to resolve the disagreement whenever a contract dispute arises from doing business with two or more countries. However, the United Nations Convention on Contracts for the International Sale of Goods (CISG) creates a mechanism to solve this problem. As of 2006, thirty-seven nations have ratified this treaty, which provides a uniform text of law for the international sale of goods. The CISG is given automatic application to all contracts for the sale of goods between traders from all countries that have adopted it. Furthermore, the CISG establishes uniform legal rules to govern the formation of international sales contracts as well as the rights and obligations of the buyer and seller.

The CISG only applies to international commercial sale of goods. Accordingly, the sale itself must be international in character, meaning that it involves parties whose places of business are in different nations. Second, the CISG covers the sale of goods; it may not apply to contracts that include services. But where a contract includes both goods and service elements, the CISG *will* apply unless the preponderant part of the obligations of the party who furnishes the goods consists in the supply of labor or other services. Finally, the CISG only applies to commercial transactions, not to sales of goods that are bought for personal, family, or household use unless the seller, at any time before or at the conclusion of the contract, either knew not or ought to have known that the goods involved were bought for such use. Additionally, the CISG does not apply to the following types of sales: by auction; on execution or otherwise by authority of law; of stocks, shares, investment securities, negotiable instruments or money; of ships, vessels, hovercraft or aircraft; or of electricity. Each of these elements constitutes an important limitation on the scope of the CISG applicability.

---

[48] Contributed by Miguel Orta, Nova Southeastern University.

The CISG's rules closely follow Article 2 of the UCC, which is fully enforced in 49 of the 50 American states. Under the CISG, a proposal to create a contract is not sufficiently definite as an offer unless it indicates the goods and either expressly or implicitly fixes or makes provisions for determining the quantity and the price. By contrast, the UCC is more flexible in contract formation. The UCC will hold an agreement to be valid, despite missing terms such as performance and price, if the parties intended to be bound by the agreement and a reasonably certain basis exists for granting a remedy.

Under the CISG, an offer becomes irrevocable if it indicates, through either a fixed time for acceptance or otherwise, that it is irrevocable. An offer also becomes irrevocable if the offeree reasonably relies on the offer as being irrevocable and acts in reliance upon it. Furthermore, under the UCC, an irrevocable offer must exist in a signed writing that, by its terms, assures that the offer will be held open. Contract acceptance then occurs upon receipt thereof by the offeror under the CISG.

Many UCC jurisdictions hold that acceptance occurs when it is mailed, dispatched, or transmitted by the offeree to the offeror.

The CISG does not require that a sales contract be reduced to a writing. Accordingly, under the UCC's Statute of Frauds, oral contracts for the selling of goods for a price of $500 or more are generally not enforceable unless, for example, the existence of a contract is conceded to, or payment or both delivery and acceptance have occurred.

The CISG generally leaves questions relating to the validity of a contract, and the effect that the contract may have on the goods sold, to be determined by applicable domestic law.

Management Strategies

A global businessperson must be aware that there are two bodies of contract law in the United States: 1) the older common law of contract, based predominantly on judicial decisions and applicable to contracts of employment and service and the purchase and sale of real estate and; 2) newer statutory-based sales laws of the UCC, which apply to the purchase and sale of "goods." Thus, it is critical to determine the exact subject matter of the contract so as to precisely determine one's rights and responsibilities. And it is again very important to emphasize that many provisions in the UCC change the old common law, in particular, making it easier for the parties to enter into a contract.

Therefore, once it is ascertained that the UCC does in fact apply to the contract, the next step is to check the applicable state's version of the UCC, which can be found in its state statutory law. The global businessperson also must be aware of the CISG, and especially the changes the CISG makes to the UCC.

Terms of Sale in International Trade[49]

Despite wide differences among national laws, there is a high degree of uniformity in contract practices for the export and import of goods. This universality of trade practices (including terms of sale) is due to the development of the concept of "law merchant" by international mercantile custom. The law merchant refers to the body of commercial law that developed for merchants and their merchandise in Europe during the medieval period. Today, this body of law is known as "Sales Law" and, in the U.S., is based on the UCC.

Trade terms are intended to define the method of delivery of the goods sold and the attendant responsibilities of the parties, which include carriage of goods from seller to buyer, export/import clearance, division of costs/risks, etc. Such terms also help the seller in the calculation of the purchase price. For example, a seller quoting the term of sale as FOB will evidently charge a lower price versus quoting CIF because the latter includes not only the cost of goods but also expenses incurred by the seller for insurance and freight in order to ship the goods to the port of destination.

The national laws of each country often determine the rights and duties of parties with respect to terms of sale. In the U.S., the Revised American Foreign Trade Definitions (1941) and the UCC govern terms of sale. Since 1980, the sponsors of the revised U.S. foreign trade definitions have also recommend the use of Incoterms. Parties to terms of sale could also agree to be governed by Incoterms, which were published by the International Chamber of Commerce (ICC) in 1953 (latest revision, 2000). These guidelines now enjoy almost universal acceptance.

The ICC is a non-governmental entity, meaning that Incoterms are neither considered national legislation nor an international treaty. Effectively, Incoterms apply when the parties expressly indicate their intentions to incorporate these terms into their export sales contract. Even if the parties do not explicitly agree to be governed by Incoterms, they could be made an implicit term of the contract as part of international custom. Incoterms are revised every ten years so as to better represent contemporary commercial practice (Incoterms, 1980, 1990, 2000). In order to avoid any misunderstandings, parties to export contracts should always state the application of the current version of Incoterms.

While the UCC and Incoterms complement each other in many areas, trade terms are not understood in the same manner in every country, therefore, it is important to explicitly state the relevant law that governs the contract at hand. For example, a contract should state "FOB New York (Incoterms)" or "CIF Liverpool (UCC)."

---

[49] Contributed by Belay Seyoum, Nova Southeastern University.

All trade terms are classified into four groups based on the point of transfer of risk (delivery) from seller to buyer:

1. *Group E terms (Ex-Works):* This grouping has only one term, and it represents the seller's minimum obligation. Effectively, it places the goods at the disposal of the buyer. There are no contractual arrangements between seller and buyer with regard to insurance, transportation or export.

2. *Group F terms (FCA, FAS, FOB):* The seller is expected to bear the risk and expense of delivery to a nominated carrier. It is the buyer's responsibility to arrange and pay for the main carriage to the point of destination.

3. *Group C terms (CRF, CIF, CPT, CIP):* C terms establish the point of delivery (transfer of risk) from seller to buyer at the point of shipment. However, it also extends the seller's obligation with regard to the costs of carriage and insurance up to the point of destination. This means that the seller bears certain costs even after the critical point for the division of the risk or damage to the goods has been reached. These are often referred to as "shipment terms."

4. *Group D terms (DAF, DES, DEQ, DDU, DDP):* The seller's delivery obligation extends to the country of destination, meaning that the seller could be held liable for breach of contract if the goods are lost/damaged after shipment but *before* arrival at the agreed upon point of destination. The seller may therefore be required to provide substitute goods or other forms of restitution to the buyer. These are often referred to as "arrival terms."

Each Group, and the shipping terms therein, is further explained in the following passages.

Group E (Ex Works, Ex Warehouse, Ex Store)

Ex Works, Ex Warehouse, Ex Store (named place): Under this term, the buyer or agent must collect the goods at the seller's works, warehouse, or store. The seller bears all risk and expenses until the goods are placed at the disposal of the buyer at the time and place agreed upon for delivery—normally the seller's premises, warehouse, or factory. The purchase price becomes payable at the time of delivery. Risk is not transferred to the buyer if damage or loss is attributed to the failure on the part of the seller to deliver the goods in conformity with the contract (for example: damage due to inadequate packing of goods). Also, the buyer bears all risk and charges pertaining to pre-shipment inspection, export/import licenses, and customs duties/taxes needed for exportation. The buyer is also responsible for the clearance of goods for export, transit, and import because the seller makes the goods available to the buyer in the country of export. This term of sale is similar to a domestic sales transaction even though the product is destined for export.

Group F (FCA, FAS, and FOB)

Free Carrier (FCA), named place: The seller bears the risk and costs relating to the goods until delivery to the carrier or any other person nominated by the buyer. The place of delivery could be the carrier's cargo terminal or a vehicle sent to pick up the goods at the seller's premises. The seller is responsible for loading the goods onto the buyer's collecting vehicle, but if the place of delivery is the carrier's cargo terminal, the seller is only required to bring the goods to the terminal but is not obligated to unload them. (What is hoped for is that the carrier is more likely to have the necessary personnel and equipment in place to unload the goods at its own terminal, rather than the seller.) Upon delivery of the goods to the carrier, the seller receives (from the carrier) a receipt which serves as evidence of delivery and contract of carriage made on behalf of the buyer.

Neither party is required to insure under FCA. However, the seller must provide the buyer (upon request) with the necessary information for procuring insurance. Besides payment of the purchase price as provided in the contract, the buyer has the following obligations: 1) obtain at his/her own risk and expense any import license and other official authorization necessary for importation of the goods as well as for their transit through another country; 2) contract at his/her own expense for carriage of the goods from the named place of delivery; and 3) pay the costs of any pre-shipment inspection except when such inspection is mandated by the exporting country.

Free Alongside Ship (FAS), named port of shipment: This term requires the seller to deliver the goods to a named port alongside a vessel to be designated by the buyer. "Alongside the vessel" has been understood to mean that the goods be within reach of a ship's lifting tackle. In this situation, the risks to the goods pass to the buyer upon the seller's delivery alongside the ship. This implies that all charges and risks for the goods are borne by the buyer from the time they have been effectively delivered alongside the vessel. But the seller must obtain, at his own risk and expense, any export license and other official authorizations, including customs formalities, that are necessary for the export of the goods.

The seller's obligation to clear the goods for export is similar to that of FOB contracts. There is an implied duty on the part of the seller to cooperate in arranging a loading and shipping schedule, render at the buyer's request and expense every assistance in obtaining necessary documents for the import of the goods and their transit through another country. The seller must provide the buyer (at his/her own expense) with the usual proof of delivery and must also contract (again at his/her own expense) for the carriage of goods from the port of shipment. Because the buyer has to nominate the ship, he/she has to pay any additional costs incurred if 1) the named vessel fails to arrive on time, or 2) the vessel is unable to take the goods. In such cases, a premature passing of risk will occur. Costs of any pre-shipment inspection are borne by the buyer except when such inspection is mandated by the exporting country.

The use of FAS is appropriate in cases where sellers take their shipments to the pier and deposit them close enough for loading. However, presently, most of the outbound cargo is delivered to the ship lines days before actual placement alongside the vessel. It is also not applicable in cases of "rolling cargo" (which includes cars and trucks) that can be driven aboard a vessel or into ports with shallow harbors (i.e., those ports that do not allow for vessels to come alongside the pier).

Free On Board (FOB), named port of shipment: The central feature of FOB contracts is the notion that the seller undertakes to place the goods onboard the ship designated by the buyer. This includes responsibility for all charges incurred up to and including delivery of the goods over the ship's rail at the named port of shipment. The buyer must nominate a suitable ship and inform the seller of its name, loading point, and delivery time. If the ship originally nominated is unable or unavailable to receive the cargo at the agreed-upon time for loading, the buyer then must nominate a substitute ship and pay any and all additional charges. Once the seller delivers the goods onboard the ship, the buyer is responsible for all subsequent charges, such as freight, marine insurance, unloading charges, import duties, and other expenses due on arrival at the port of destination. Unless otherwise stated in the contract of sale, it is customary in FOB contracts for the seller to procure the export license and other formalities necessary for the export of the goods. This is because the seller, as opposed to the buyer, is more familiar with licensing practices and procedures in the exporting country.

Transfer of risk occurs upon the seller's delivery of the goods onboard the vessel. The seller's responsibility for loss or damage to the goods terminates upon delivery to the carrier. The ship's rail is thus considered the dividing line between the seller's and buyer's responsibility in terms of transfer of risk. In this dimension, FOB does not appear to be consistent with current practices except for shipments of non-containerized or bulk cargo or shipments made by a chartered vessel. But in many other cases, sellers are required to deliver their outbound cargo to ship lines days before the actual loading of the cargo. The seller, however, remains responsible for the goods until the actual delivery onboard the vessel.

Group C (CIF, CFR, CPT, CIP)

Cost, insurance, and freight (CIF), named port of destination: The CIF contract places upon the seller the obligation to arrange for shipment of the goods. The seller must ship the goods described under the contract at the destination and also arrange for insurance to be available for the benefit of the buyer or any other person with insurable interest in the goods. In the absence of express agreement, the insurance shall be in accordance with the minimum of cover provided under the Institute of Cargo Clauses or any similar set of guidelines.

The cost of freight is borne by the seller, and the buyer undertakes to pay upon arrival of the merchandise. The seller must notify the buyer that the goods have been delivered onboard the vessel to enable the buyer to receive the goods. The seller must tender the necessary documents: commercial invoice, bill of lading, and policy of insurance to the buyer so that the latter could obtain delivery upon arrival of the goods or recover for their loss. The buyer must accept the documents when tendered by the seller when they are in conformity with the contract of sale and pay the necessary purchase price. Import duties/licenses, consular fees, and charges to procure a certificate of origin are the responsibility of the buyer while export licenses and other customs formalities necessary for the export of the goods have to be obtained by the seller.

The CIF contract may provide certain advantages to the overseas customer because the seller often possesses expert knowledge and experience to make favorable arrangements with respect to freight, insurance, and other charges. This could be reflected in terms of reduced import prices for the overseas customer. Under a CIF contract, risk passes to the buyer upon delivery, i.e., when the goods are put onboard the ship at the port of departure.

Rejection of documents versus rejection of goods: When proper shipping documents, which are in conformity with the contract, are tendered, the buyer must accept them and pay the purchase price. The right to reject the goods arises if, after the goods are landed and an examination has taken place, the goods are found not to be in conformity with the contract. It may also happen that while the goods conform to the contract, the documents themselves are not in accordance with the contract of sale. Discrepancies may arise between documents, such as bills of lading, commercial invoices, draft and the letters of credit, or the contract of sale. In this case, the buyer could accept the goods but reject the documents and claim damages for a breach of condition relating to the goods.

Thus, under a CIF contract, the right to reject the documents is separate and distinct from the right to reject the goods and payment is often made *against* documents. The buyer's acceptance of conforming documents does not impair subsequent rejection of the goods and recovery of the purchase price if, upon arrival, the goods are not in accordance with the terms of sale. Tender of the goods cannot be an alternative to tender of the documents in CIF contracts.

Loss of Goods: If the goods shipped under a CIF contract are destroyed or lost during transit, the seller is entitled to claim the purchase price against presentation of proper shipping documents to the buyer. Because insurance is taken for the benefit of the buyer, the buyer can claim against the insurer insofar as the risk is covered by the policy. If the loss is due to some misconduct on the part of the carrier and is not covered by the policy, the buyer could then recover from the carrier. The only difference between CIF and CFR term is that the latter does not require the seller to obtain and pay for cargo insurance.

Carriage Paid to (CPT), named place of destination: This is similar to the CFR term except that it may be used for any other type of transportation. Even though the seller is obligated to arrange and pay for the transportation to a named place of destination, he/she completes delivery obligations and thus transfers the risk of loss/damage to the buyer when the goods are delivered to the carrier at the place of shipment. The seller must notify the buyer that the goods have been delivered to the carrier (the "first carrier" in the case of multimodal transportation) and also give any other notice required to enable the buyer to take receipt of the goods. The term "carrier," in this sense, is appropriate for multimodal transportation.

When several carriers are involved (pre-carriage by road or rail from the seller's warehouse for further carriage by sea to the destination) and the goods have been handed over for carriage to the first carrier, the seller has fulfilled his/her delivery obligation under CPT terms. By contrast, in CFR and CIF contracts, delivery is not completed until the goods have reached a vessel at the port of shipment. In the absence of an explicit agreement between the parties, there is no requirement to provide a negotiable bill of lading (to enable the buyer to sell the goods in transit). In this case, the buyer must pay the costs of any pre-shipment inspection unless such inspection is mandated by the exporting country. Given the absence of post-inspection provisions in the Incoterms, the CPT does not appear to restrict inspection before payment. Rather, the CPT term is similar to the CIP term except in that the seller is not required to arrange or pay for insurance coverage of the goods during transportation.

Group D (DAF, DES, DEQ, DDU, DDP)

All D terms share certain common features, including arrival/destination terms. The seller is required to arrange for transportation, pay freight, and bear the risk of loss to a named point of destination. The seller must place the goods at the disposal of the buyer (though this varies according to term). There is no requirement for use of a negotiable bill of lading and delivery is considered as having occurred only after arrival of the goods. Incoterms do not require insurance during transportation. Also, the seller may have to arrange and pay for insurance or act as self-insurer during transportation. The buyer must pay the costs of any pre-shipment inspection except when such inspection is mandated by the exporting country. There are no provisions for post-shipment inspection.

Among the Group D terms, delivery Ex Quay (DEQ) and delivery Ex Ship (DES) are used for waterborne transportation while the other three can be used for any type of transportation, including multimodal transport.

Delivery at frontier (DAF), named place: DAF is frequently used in continental export trade (USA-Canada) where rail or road transportation is involved. This should specify not only the frontier, but also the place of delivery (for example, "Delivered at U.S.-Canada frontier, Vancouver"). The "frontier" refers to a geographical or customs frontier and can be that of the country of export, import, or some intermediate frontier.

The seller's obligations under DAF term have been defined as follows: to obtain at his/her own expense any export license and other documents necessary for placing the goods at the buyer's disposal; to contract, at his/her own expense, for the carriage of the goods to the named point at the place of delivery at the frontier and; to place the goods at the disposal of the buyer on the arriving means of transport not unloaded at the named place of delivery. The risk of loss is upon the seller until the goods reach the place of delivery at the frontier, but then passes to the buyer upon arrival, without unloading. If there is not a designated place of delivery, it may be determined, by custom, to provide the buyer (at the seller's expense) with the necessary documents (invoice, export license, transport document) in order to enable the latter to take delivery of the goods. The seller must also provide customary packaging, which is required for the delivery of the goods at the frontier.

The buyer must bear all risk of loss or damage to the goods from the time they have been delivered at the frontier.

Delivery Ex Ship (DES), named port of destination: The DES term is applied only for waterborne transportation and almost always used with charter vessels. The seller is responsible for the carriage of the goods to the named port of destination. Transfer of risk from seller to buyer occurs when the goods are placed at the buyer's disposal onboard a ship at the named port of destination.

The seller "delivers" when the goods are placed at the disposal of the buyer onboard the vessel not cleared for import at the named port of destination. This means that the seller bears all the risk and expense involved in bringing the goods to the named port of destination (before discharging), i.e., the goods should be made available to the buyer onboard the vessel at the unloading point in such a way as to enable the goods to be removed from the vessel by unloading equipment. The seller is also obligated to notify the buyer of the estimated time of arrival of the vessel, provide the necessary documents—such as invoice and bill of lading—as well as procure export licenses and other customs familiarities necessary for the export of the goods and their transit through another country.

The buyer is responsible for unloading the goods and import clearance.

Delivered Ex Quay (DEQ), named port of destination: The DEQ term is used for waterborne transportation. A central feature of this term is that the seller arranges and pays for transportation to the named port of destination. Delivery is considered to have occurred when the goods are placed at the buyer's disposal on the quay or wharf at the named port of destination, i.e., when the seller discharges the goods on the quay or wharf.

The buyer is required to clear the goods for import and handle other formalities and charges necessary for importation. With regard to other issues, such as notice to buyer, provision of documents, packing, etc, it is similar to the DES term. However, if the parties wish to extend the seller's obligations to the handling of the goods from the quay to a warehouse or terminal in or outside the port of destination (risk and expense to be incurred by the seller), it is then appropriate to use delivery duty paid (DDP) or delivery duty unpaid (DDU) term.

In DDP, delivery occurs when the goods are placed at the buyer's disposal on any means of transport not unloaded at the named port of destination. Unlike DDU, the seller pays for import duties and other charges necessary for importation at the port of destination. But in certain other areas, such as notice to buyer, provision of documents, or packing, the DEQ term is very similar to DDU and DDP terms.

There are certain major differences between arrival contracts and a CIF contract. In arrival contracts, delivery is effected when the goods are placed at the disposal of the buyer. But in a CIF term, delivery is effected upon the loading of the goods onboard the vessel at the port of departure. In arrival contracts, the buyer is under no obligation to pay the purchase price if the goods are lost in transit, but for CIF contracts, the buyer is required to pay against documents. However, in such a case, the loss of goods gives the buyer the right of claim from the carrier or the insurance company, depending on the circumstances.

So which Incoterms are appropriate? Simply put, the choice is dependent upon the type of cargo and the buyer's intention to sell the goods in transit. It also depends on the ability of the parties to obtain the most favorable contract of carriage.

The appropriateness of C vs. F terms is an important issue. In cases where the seller can procure maritime insurance at a competitive price and where government regulations exist to use national shipping line, it may be appropriate to use CFR and CIF. But if the parties prefer the seller to procure carriage (CPT) and insurance, then CIP may be appropriate. When the buyer can procure insurance at a competitive rate, the parties may prefer to use FAS or FOB. The status of manufactured goods is also an important factor as exporters of manufactured goods often sell on extended terms using DDU and DDP (where the seller makes goods available to the buyer at the cargo terminal) in order to remain competitive. But because such goods are normally containerized, the parties can also use FCA, CPT or CIP. For large buyers, such as wholesalers and department stores, it will be advantageous to use Ex Works or FCA because they may find it auspicious to arrange for transportation in order to ensure just-in-time deliveries.

Incoterms only deal with matters pertaining to the interpretation of the terms of delivery. The rules do not deal with the transfer of property rights to the goods, exemptions from liability, or consequences in cases of breach of contract. They do, however, deal with obligations in connection with delivery, the provision of documents, insurance, clearance of goods for export/import, and so on. Incoterms attempt to reflect contemporary commercial practice. Accordingly, they offer a variety of terms ranging from Ex Works, which entails minimal obligation for the seller, to extended obligations (FCA, FAS, FOB). It also provides for maximum obligations for the seller (DAF, DES, DEQ, DDU, DDP). Incoterms are often used in contracts of sale and contracts of carriage, but the seller's obligation to take out insurance for the benefit of the buyer applies only under CIP and CIF terms. The parties must individually arrange insurance as they see fit under all other terms.

Summary

Contract laws, as discussed in the previous chapters, illustrate the major elements associated with agreements that are legally binding. This chapter continued with the same topic, but provided further in-depth analysis of the pertinent legal issues.

The advancement in technology has forced governments to modernize their laws, at least in terms of protecting domestic firms, specifically those firms that have grown to become international (i.e., those that will continuously enter into contracts). As discussed in this chapter, the sales contract and its vital components—including title and risk of loss, warranties, performance, and remedies, as well as global legal perspectives, and management strategies, particularly terms of sale in international trade—are all to be conducted in accordance with the guidelines provided by the UCC and the CISG. The UCC and the CISG are thus very important legal tools for international managers to understand, specifically when designing contracts with their global partners. Therefore, it is important for all managers, firms, and employees to fully understand the laws, regulations, and concepts associated with contracts and the sales of goods.

FOURTEEN

The essence of agency law is to effect legally binding results by utilizing the services of others. The term "agency," however, is very broad as it concerns the rights and liabilities created in one person by the acts of another. Because a great deal of the world's work is performed by agents, agency law is a very important commercial law subject matter.

Agency is one of the most common, basic, and pervasive legal relationships in global business. Nearly everyone will come into contact with the agency relationship, usually in the form of a sales agent or employee. The usefulness to business everywhere is obvious, because no single person can perform all of the actions required to conduct a business. Moreover, the business owner can conduct multiple business operations simultaneously and on a worldwide basis by means of agency. The corporate entity, furthermore, as an artificial though legal, "person," can act only through agents and employees and, consequently, can then only enter into contracts by means of agents and employees.

Agency law encompasses three fundamental and distinct legal fields: 1) contract rights and liabilities of third persons created by parties who use agents and employees; 2) tort liability of persons for the wrongful acts of their agents and employees; and 3) contract and tort duties which the parties to an agency relationship owe to one another.

This chapter accordingly will examine agency law in the United States, and then compare U.S. agency law to the laws of certain other international legal jurisdictions.

Agency Law in the United States

Definition of Key Terms

There are three critical and foundational classifications made in agency law: 1) the employer-employee relationship, called "master and servant" in the old English common law; 2) the principal-agent relationship; and 3) the employer-independent contractor relationship. It must be emphasized that these legal categories are not mutually exclusive. Thus one person, for example, a salesperson, can be both an agent and employee.

The first classification is of the *employer-employee relationship*. An employee is a person who is employed to render services of any type and who remains under the control of another in performing these services. The essential characteristic of the employer-employee relationship is the power and right to control. The employer—that is, the "master"—must at all times control or have the right to control the physical conduct of the employee—that is, the "servant"—in the performance of his or her duties. There is either no or very little discretion in the sense of independent thought and judgment exercised by one regarded as a conventional "employee."

The second relationship is the *principal-agent relationship*. An "agent" is a person who works for another (called the "principal") but who also acts for and in the place of the principal in order to effectuate legal relations with third parties. The essence of the principal-agent relationship is that the agent transacts business for the principal, represents and negotiates for the principal, and, most significantly, enters into contracts on the principal's behalf. The agent, moreover, can bind the principal to contracts with third parties. In essence then, an employee "merely" works for another whereas the agent represents another and thus ordinarily possesses a great deal of discretion in carrying out the purposes of the agency. An agent can be a "special agent"—that is, authorized to bring about a particular undertaking for the principal—or the agent can be a "general agent"—that is, authorized to represent the principal in any and all authorized dealings.

Finally, an *independent contractor* is a person who renders services in the course of an independent occupation. The independent contractor contracts with the employer only as results to themselves, not on how the work itself is to be done. Accordingly, the primary feature of this relationship is that the employer has no right of control as to how the work is executed.

As noted earlier, a person may fulfill both roles. For example, an architect may also be empowered to make certain contracts on behalf of a property owner. Therefore, determining if a person is working for an employer or an independent contractor is a crucial legal decision because many bodies of law, such as tort liability principles as well as federal and state employment, tax, safety, and Workers' Compensation laws will all apply to "employees" but not to independent contractors.

Creation of the Agency Relationship

The agency relationship can be created in four ways: 1) by agreement of the parties; 2) ratification; 3) estoppel; and 4) operation of the law.

An agency relationship is consensual in nature and thus usually arises by an *agreement between the parties*. Accordingly, contract law principles form an important component to agency law. A manifestation of mutual agreement by the parties is required, meaning that the principal indicates that he or she consents to having the agent act on his or her behalf and, conversely, the agent indicates his or her consent to act for the principal. This mutual agreement can be expressed by oral or written words, or implied by conduct.

In order to be a principal, one must have the legal capacity to enter into a contract. That is, only a person having contract capacity can appoint another as his or her agent. Yet any person may be an agent regardless of contract capacity, including a minor being designated as an agent. Consideration is not a requirement to the agency relationship, thus one can be a "gratuitous agent."

Regarding the purposes of an agency relationship, any legal purposes that do not contravene public policy are permitted. For example, appointing someone as one's agent to vote in a public election will be deemed contrary to public policy and thus prohibited.

As to other formalities, there generally are none except for one notable exception. If the Statute of Frauds requires that the contract the agent makes with a third party be in writing, then concomitantly, the agent's original authority from the principal must be in writing. This requirement is called the "Equal Dignity" rule. For example, if one intends to appoint another as his or her agent to sell real estate, two writings will be required: the real estate contract the agent enters into in order to sell the property to a third party, and also the agent's authority from the principal to act as his or her agent.

What if there is a failure to comply with the Equal Dignity rule? If the agent's original authority is not in writing, any contracts governed by the Statute of Frauds and executed by the agent will not be enforceable against the principal. Rather, the contract, even though in writing, will be deemed voidable by the principal.

The term "power of attorney" frequently is used to designate an express agency relationship. A power of attorney is an express written instrument that confers authority on an agent. Powers can be "special"—authorizing the agent to do certain acts only—or "general"—authorizing the agent to do all business for the principal. Both should be witnessed and acknowledged by a notary public and in either case, the agent is at times called an "attorney in fact," which appellation should not be confused with an "attorney at law," as the latter is an attorney admitted to state bar associations and who is thus licensed to practice law in certain jurisdictions.

The second method in which the agency relationship can come into existence is by means of the *ratification* doctrine. Ratification occurs when a person who is not an agent or an agent who exceeds his or her authority makes a contract for a purported principal. The principal then accepts the benefits of the unauthorized contract or affirms the conduct of his or her alleged "agent." In such a case, the principal is bound to the agreement by his or her ratification thereof, even though there may never have been an agency agreement. Ratification can be express, meaning that the principal gives his or her express approval, or implied, which means that the principal accepts the benefits or gains certain advantages from the unauthorized agreement.

There are two important limitations on the ratification doctrine. First, there can be no partial ratification, meaning that the principal cannot ratify the beneficial aspects of the agent's unauthorized behavior and refuse to affirm the rest. Second, before ratification by the principal, the third party can rescind the unauthorized transaction. Ratification will be discussed further in the section dealing with liability of the parties.

An agency by *estoppel* arises when a principal either intentionally or carelessly creates the appearance of an agency relationship. That is, the principal, by his or her conduct, has misled a third party to reasonably believe that he or she is dealing with a real agent of the principal, thereby relying on the "agent" and consummating some transaction with the "principal." In such a case, the principal will be estopped—that is, prevented—from denying the existence of the agency relationship.

Agency by estoppel typically arises when a merchant-employer, by words or conduct directed to a third party customer, leads the customer to believe that a mere sales employee is an agent who is empowered to conduct more business besides merely selling items at a certain price. That is, the principal has in effect "cloaked" a certain person with the attributes of agency. It must be stressed that the two critical requirements of such an estoppel are that the words and conduct come from the principal and not from the agent, and that the third party reasonably relied on the manifestations of agency.

Finally, the agency relationship can take place by *operation of the law*. In this, the law will impose an agency relationship even in the absence of a formal agreement. This includes, for example, family situations where one spouse purchases necessities and charges the other spouse's account. In such a case, the latter spouse is liable as a principal on public policy grounds.

Duties of the Principal and Agent

This area of agency law can be logically divided into two categories: 1) the principal's duties to the agent; and 2) the agent's duties to the principal. In both cases, these obligations can arise by the agency agreement or automatically by the operation of the law.

The principal owes three basic duties to the agent: 1) compensation, 2) reimbursement, and 3) cooperation. The principal, as the party employing the agent, must pay the agent the agreed-upon value for the agent's services unless the agent's services are to be rendered gratuitously. The principal also must reimburse the agent for all expenses and losses reasonably incurred by the agent in discharging his or her duties for the principal. Finally, the principal must assist the agent and cooperate with the agent and do nothing to hinder the agent's performance of his or her duties. For example, if a sales agent is given an exclusive territory, the principal is not allowed to "invade" the territory and make sales; if so, the agent can recover the profits that he or she would have made.

The agent owes four basic duties to the principal: 1) obedience, 2) due care, 3) accounting, and 4) the fiduciary duty. The agent's first duty, "obedience," means to obey the clear and legal instructions of his or her own principal. If the instructions are ambiguous, the agent is obligated to interpret them in a reasonable manner. Of course, if there is an emergency, the agent can deviate from the instructions in order to protect the principal's property and effectuate the purposes of the agency.

The agent is under a duty to use reasonable "due care" in performing the work of the agency. If the agent fails to perform at all, the agent is liable for breach of contract and if the agent performs but performs carelessly, the agent is also liable for the tort of negligence. Even if an agency is gratuitous in nature, the agent nonetheless owes the principal this duty of due care.

The agent, in addition, has a duty to render an "accounting" to the principal. That is, the agent must keep and make available to the principal an accounting of all property and moneys received and paid out for the principal. The agent cannot mix his or her property and money with that of the principal, but if an agent does commingle property and money, or the distinct ownership thereof cannot be ascertained, the principal can then legally claim all the property and money.

Finally, and most importantly, the agent owes the principal the "duties of a fiduciary." Because the agency relationship is one of special and lofty legal relationships which the law deems to be fiduciary in character, the parties to the fiduciary relationship are considered to be in a relationship of trust and confidence. Accordingly, they owe each other the duties of loyalty, faithfulness, honesty, integrity, and full disclosure. The agent, therefore, is under a duty of faithful service. Moreover, the agent is obligated to notify the principal of all matters that come to the agent's attention and which might affect the subject matter of the purposes of the agency.

Furthermore, an agent cannot directly compete nor act for persons who compete with the agent's principal, nor can the agent acquire an interest in a business that competes with the principal unless the principal consents. For that matter, absent consent, an agent is not allowed to take up a position that is adverse to his or her own principal. Thus, any secret profits, rebates, commissions, advantages, or benefits that an agent obtains by virtue of his or her employment rightfully belong to the principal. Specifically, if an agent is a purchasing agent authorized to purchase certain property for the principal, the agent cannot, without permission, purchase that property for himself or herself. Similarly, if an agent is a sales agent, authorized to sell property for the principal, he or she cannot buy that property for himself or herself, even if the price paid is a fair one.

A dual agency—an agent acting for more than one principal—is not permitted unless, of course, both principals are fully informed and give their consent. An agent who acts in such a dual capacity, for example, representing both a selling and a buying principal, cannot recover any commissions even if the transaction is a fair one. In addition, an agent, even a former agent, cannot disclose confidential or proprietary information (including customer lists and trade secrets) of his or her principal.

When the agent violates his or her fiduciary duty, the principal can sue for breach of contract. However, because under the common law the breach of a fiduciary relationship is considered to most serious, the principal is allowed to sue for the intentional tort of fraud, which includes the possibility of a punitive damage recovery. Moreover, any transaction undertaken by the agent who breached the fiduciary duty is considered to be voidable at the option of the principal. Finally, any profits or advantages gained by the wrongfully acting agent are deemed to be held in a constructive trust for the benefit of the principal.

Termination of the Agent's Authority

Agency relationships come to an end, thereby terminating the agent's authority, in two main ways: 1) termination by the acts of the parties themselves, and 2) termination automatically by operation of the law.

An agency relationship can be terminated by the acts of the parties in any one of five ways: 1) lapse of time, 2) accomplishment of the purposes of the agency, 3) occurrence of a condition, 4) mutual agreement, and 5) by the act of only one party. Regarding the "time" method, if an agency is created for a specific period of time, it terminates at the expiration of that period of time. If no time period is stated, the agency expires upon the passing of a reasonable period of time. If the purpose of the agency is accomplished, even if by the efforts of another agent or the principal, the agency is terminated, presuming of course that the agent has knowledge of this key fact. Moreover, the occurrence of a specified event or condition will terminate the agency, presuming that the principal and agent had agreed to the condition. Mutual agreement can cancel an agency, just as it can cancel a contract. The principal and agent can always agree to cancel their agency, regardless of a previously existing contract or specified time period.

However, a problem in agency law arises when one party unilaterally seeks to end the agency relationship. The common law rule is that because an agency relationship is one that is consensual, it is terminated whenever either party acts to end the relationship. Even though such a termination contravenes a binding agency agreement, a party can nonetheless cancel it as the parties have the "power" to do so, though not necessarily the "right." When the agent terminates, that action is called "renunciation," and when the principal terminates, the action is called "revocation." It is critical to observe that if either the renunciation or revocation breaches a valid agency agreement, the parties can be sued for breach of the agreement and may have to pay money damages as a result thereof (however, the agency relationship still comes to an end).

There is one important exception constraining the principal's power to revoke, called the "agency coupled with an interest" rule. Pursuant to this precept, if an agency is created for the benefit of the agent, and the agent has been given some type of legal interest in the subject matter of the agency, the principal is not allowed to revoke the agency. The classic example of "interest agency" is when a debtor borrows money from a creditor and as security turns over the title to a certain property to the creditor, the creditor is then appointed by the debtor/principal as the creditor/agent with the power to sell the property if the debtor defaults on the obligation. Note, however, that the mere expectancy of an agent to make commissions, profits, or fees is not sufficient to create an "agency coupled with an interest."

Agencies are also terminated by the operation of the law. First, this can happen if either the principal or agent dies or becomes insane, and this termination does not depend on either the agent or a third party acquiring knowledge of the principal's death. Thus, any transaction by an "agent" after his or her principal's death is not considered binding on the principal's estate. Yet again, the exception here is an "agency coupled with an interest."

Second, the loss or destruction of the subject matter of the agency may result in the relationship's termination. If the destruction or loss is total, the agent's authority is terminated; but if the loss is partial, the rule is that the agency relationship is terminated if further actions by the agent will not be in the best interests of the principal.

Third, a change in circumstances affecting the value of the subject matter of the agency may result in its termination. Specifically, if there are unforeseen and substantial changes which materially affect the value of the subject matter of the agency, and it is reasonable to assume that the principal would not want the agent to proceed, then the agency is terminated. An example would be when an agent is authorized to sell "scrub land," and then oil is surprisingly discovered thereon.

Fourth, bankruptcy of the parties may result in a termination by operation of the law. If the agent goes bankrupt, there is a termination when the agent's ability to act for the principal is impaired, for example, when the agent is the principal's investment broker. If the principal goes bankrupt, the agency relationship is terminated when there is a reasonable presumption that the principal would not want the agent to act.

Finally, a change in the law, which makes the subject matter or the performance of the agency illegal, renders the agency terminated.

Liability of the Parties

The major categories of agency liability are 1) the liability of the principal to third parties, and 2) the liability of the agent.

Regarding the *liability of the principal,* the key initial consideration is to ascertain if the agent was authorized and was acting within the scope of his or her authority when making a contract with a third party. It is a fundamental rule of agency law that a principal is only legally responsible when his or her agent is authorized to act on behalf of the principal. Accordingly, it is critical to determine the source of the agent's authority. There are two general sources of agent authority, actual authority and apparent authority. Moreover, actual authority includes four types of authority: express, implied, incidental, or emergency.

Actual authority is the power to carry out whatever the principal has expressly implied the agent to accomplish as well as any authority incidental thereto, including emergency authority. "Express authority" is the authority specifically and explicitly accorded to the agent by the words, oral or written, of the principal whereas "implied authority" is the authority impliedly granted by the principal to the agent by the conduct of the principal manifested to the agent. Implied authority also encompasses the types of authority that an agent in a similar position reasonably would possess. "Incidental authority" is that authority which is granted to the agent that is necessary to accomplish the purposes of the agency. Finally, if there is an emergency or some unforeseen contingency, and the agent cannot contact the principal for further instructions, the agent is deemed to have the authority to perform those acts necessary to protect and preserve the property, rights, and interests of the principal.

Actual authority must be differentiated clearly from the next important type of agent authority, *apparent authority.* Apparent authority arises when the principal, by his or her own words or conduct manifested to third parties, has reasonably misled third persons to believe that an "agent" has authority to act on a "principal's" behalf.

The critical distinction between the two types of authority is that "actual" is based on an expression of authority made by the principal directly to the agent whereas "apparent" authority is premised on the principal's expression of authority to third parties. As the old common law maxim states, "an agent cannot create his own apparent authority." Therefore, one important factor in determining the existence of apparent authority is whether or not the third party reasonably believes and relies on the principal's assertions. The principal's manifestation of agency authority can be expressed by words: for example, by saying that a "mere" clerk employee is "my sales agent." Or it can be by conduct: for example, by cloaking the "agent" with possession and thus apparent ownership of goods.

As mentioned briefly earlier in the chapter, the ratification doctrine is a method by which authority can be created in an agent. Ratification in essence is the affirming by the principal of a prior act supposedly done on the principal's behalf, but one that was not authorized. The legal result is that the prior unauthorized act is now treated as if it had been authorized by the principal from the outset. Ratification can be express, such as the principal notifying the agent or the third party that the principal wishes to be bound, or implied, such as by conduct of the principal, like retaining the benefits of an unauthorized transaction, bringing suit to enforce an unauthorized agreement made by the agent, or by failing to act when a reasonable principal would have objected to the agent's unauthorized course of conduct so as not to cause a third party unnecessary effort or expense.

There are several other requirements to ratification. First, an act must be capable of ratification; a principal can only ratify acts which the principal could have authorized at the time the act was done. Second, the agent must have indicated to the third party that the agent was acting for a principal and not just for the agent. Consequently, an undisclosed principal cannot ratify. Third, in order to ratify, the principal must be aware of all material facts, or have reason to know such facts as they pertain to the transaction. When the principal learns of the material facts, such as the discovery of valuable minerals on land the principal's unauthorized agent sold to a third party and which transaction the principal ratified, the principal can rescind his or her ratification. However, if the principal is ignorant of material facts, but this ignorance stems from the principal's failure to investigate or make inquiry when the "reasonable person" would do so, then the ratification will be ineffective. Fourth, the ratification must occur within a reasonable time period after the principal learned of the transaction. Fifth, the entire transaction must be ratified; the principal cannot only ratify the beneficial parts. Finally, the formalities for the ratification must be the same as necessary for the original transaction. Thus, if the original transaction must have been in writing, then the ratification also must be in writing.

The key legal effect of ratification is aptly described by the "relation back" rule, which holds that once the agent's act is ratified, it is treated as authorized from the outset. However, until the principal does ratify, the third party can treat the contract with the unauthorized agent as an offer which, until ratification, the third party can revoke. Moreover, if there has been a change of circumstances and, as a result, it would be unfair to the third party for the principal to ratify, then ratification will be ineffective. For example, this occurs when the principal attempts to ratify an unauthorized contract by the "agent" to sell property, which subsequently has been damaged or destroyed, to the third party.

One very important consequence of the principal-agent relationship is the notion of "imputed knowledge and notice." Accordingly, as a result of the agency relationship, the principal may be charged with the knowledge of facts that have been disclosed to the principal's agent. The rule of law here is that notice to an agent equals notice to an agent when the receipt of notice is within the scope of the agent's actual or apparent authority.

The next question is what is the *liability of the agent* in an agent-principal-third party relationship? The first and foremost rule of law is that when an agent acts properly for his or her principal, there is no personal liability on the agent's part. However, when the agent acts without authority or exceeds his or her authority, the agent is personally liable to the third party unless the principal ratifies the transaction. There are three major problem areas when attempting to ascertain the liability of the agent when the agent acts on another's behalf: 1) nonexistent principals, 2) undisclosed principals, and 3) partially disclosed principals.

In a situation of "nonexistent principals," the problem is handled legally in a straightforward manner, meaning that an agent who purports to act for a nonexistent principal is personally liable for that transaction. For example, a corporate promoter who negotiates and then contracts on behalf of a corporation which has not yet received its corporate charter (and thus, a legal existence) from the state, takes upon himself or herself a very great legal risk. This area will be covered more in the Business Organizations chapter.

The "undisclosed principal" case is most interesting. In this situation, the agent deals with the third party but makes no statement regarding the agency or the name of the principal, and the agent's name alone appears on the contract.

There are several legal rules that govern the legal rights and duties among the agent, the principal, and the third party. First, the agent is personally liable on the contract. However, if the agent is held liable to the third party, the agent, presuming he or she was acting within the scope of his or her authority, may effect an indemnification action against the principal. Second, once the principal's identity is made known, the principal is also considered liable on the transaction, again assuming the agent's acts were authorized. In such a case, while the third party can either elect to sue the principal or the agent, he or she is only entitled to one recovery. Third, and most importantly, the principal is allowed to enforce the contract against the third party even though the third party believed that he or she was only dealing with the agent. However, if the agent fraudulently misrepresented to the third party that he or she was acting alone and in a nonrepresentational capacity, then the third party is permitted to rescind the contract. Fourth, where the performance by the principal would impose a greater burden on the third party versus performance by the agent (such as in a requirements contract) or where the performance involved a personal element (such as a services contract), the third party similarly will be allowed to rescind. Finally, once the third party has paid or performed for the agent but before the third party has become aware of the principal's identity, the third party can rescind. Yet once the third party becomes aware that the agent has been acting for a principal, the third party must then perform for the principal.

The "partially disclosed principal" situation is the most interesting. In such a case, the third party knows the agent is acting as an agent, but does not know the identity of the principal. Typically, the agent will sign the contract in his or her own name, but also will indicate that he or she is signing as an agent. Accordingly, there are three concise rules that govern this situation. First, the agent is still personally liable on the contract. Second, the principal is liable. Third, the principal is entitled to all the rights and benefits of the contract, but with the same limitations as the undisclosed principal scenario.

Tort Liability for the Acts of Others

The first category of relationships to examine in order to ascertain tort liability is the "master-servant" (to use the old common law term) relationship, which is today called the employer-employee relationship.

The key issue at hand is to determine the legal liability of the master/employer for the torts of his or her or its servant/employee. The governing rule, which goes back to Roman times, is called the doctrine of *respondeat superior*, which in essence means "let the master answer" for the wrongs of his or her servant. This seminal legal doctrine thus holds that the master/employer is legally liable for all torts committed by the servant/employee acting within the scope of employment. As a result, a third party injured by an employee's tort can proceed against both the employee and the employer even though the employee is directly liable and the employer is "merely" vicariously liable. The nature of the employer's vicarious liability is "strict," meaning the employer is responsible even though the employer has exercised due care in the hiring and supervising of the employee. This liability is also considered "joint and several," which means that the employer can be sued alone or together with the employee. The employer, however, has the right, at least theoretically, of indemnification from the wrongdoing employee.

In order for the doctrines of *respondeat superior* and vicarious liability to apply, two essential elements must be established. First, was there a master-servant relationship, as opposed to a principal-agent or employer-independent contractor one? And second, was the servant's wrongful act committed within the course or scope of his or her employment? In order to have a master-servant relationship, the employer must have the power and right to control the physical manner in which the employee performs his or her job. In neither the principal-agent nor the employer-independent contractor relationship is this physical control element present.

It also must be noted that there is a legal doctrine, called "employment by estoppel," which is created when one person intentionally or carelessly creates the appearance that another person is in his or her employ and a third party reasonably relies on that "appearance" to his or her detriment. In such an "estoppel" situation, the "employer" is now legally prevented (or estopped) from denying the employment relationship and is thus liable to the third person as if he were effectively a "master." For example, if a health club advertises that it employs skilled "trainers," who wear the logo of the health club on their exercise clothes, and relying on the advertising and name recognition, a person engages the services of such a trainer and is thereby negligently injured, the defendant health club may be estopped from denying that the trainer is its "servant."

One of the most difficult questions in agency law is to determine the status of a person employed as either a servant/employee or an independent contractor. Answering this question is crucial not only for tort liability but also for tax and Workers' Compensation liability (the latter two fields are beyond the scope of this book). Regarding tort liability, one recalls the seminal doctrine of *respondeat superior*, which is limited to wrongful acts committed only by a servant/employee and not by an independent contractor. As a consequence of this doctrine, vicarious liability does not apply when the tortious acts are committed by a person's independent contractor. Therefore, as a general rule, the employer is not liable for injuries and harms caused by the employer's independent contractor even though the independent contractor was acting for the employer's benefit.

As previously mentioned, the key test in determining whether a person is an employee or an independent contractor is the "right to control." That is, does the employer have the right to control the employing party's conduct in the actual performance of the work? In the master-servant relationship, the master has the right to control whereas in the employer-independent contractor relationship, the employer is only bargaining for results and retains no control. The classic and clear case is when a homeowner hires an electrician or plumber to do repairs, meaning that the home owner is hiring an independent contractor. Some other typical examples of independent contractors would be legal and accounting professionals hired by an employer, as well as medical professionals the employer retains to treat its employees. Also, general building contractors that a property owner hires to do work and the sub-contractors retained by the general contractor usually will be regarded as independent contractors because they own their own businesses and are not controlled by the property owner.

However, if the nature of the relationship is not clear, there are several pertinent factors that the law will apply: 1) the actual extent of control over the details of the work; 2) whether the person employed has an occupation or business of his or her own which is distinct from the employer; 3) whether the type of work done is usually done under direction or independently by a specialist; 4) whether the employer provides the place of work and supplies the instrumentalities and tools for the work; 5) the method of payment—whether by time or by completed project; and 6) the level of skill, knowledge, and expertise required for the work. Making this critical determination is regarded as a question of fact for the jury in a common law system to decide.

There are, however, exceptional situations, based on grounds of public policy and utility, when an employer will be liable for the torts of his or her independent contractor. One exception arises when the nature of the work is highly dangerous or ultra-hazardous. The other concerns nondelegable duties: when an employer is under a duty by law or public policy which is not delegable, and thus where the employer will be liable for the wrongful conduct of its independent contractor. Examples of nondelegable duties are: an employer's duty to provide and maintain a safe place of employment for his/her employees; a landlord's duty to provide and maintain safe rental premises and to make proper repairs; and the duty of an owner of a business to keep open to the public the premises so that they remain safe for the public.

Once the nature of the person employed has been established as being a servant/employee relationship, the second critical issue to resolve before imposing vicarious liability on the employer is the "scope of employment" question. That is, did the employee commit the wrongful act within the course or scope of his or her employment? In answering this question, which again is viewed by the common law as a question of fact for the jury to decide, several rules of law must be addressed.

First, in order to be within the scope of employment, express authorization by the master is not necessary; it is not a requirement to show that the master explicitly authorized or permitted the particular act, as long as the act occurred within the normal course of the employee's duties. For example, if the employee is hired to make deliveries using the employer's vehicles, but instead the employee uses his or her own vehicle and negligently causes an accident, the employer is nonetheless still liable even though the act was not authorized because it was still within the scope of the employee's duties.

Moreover, even if certain acts are specifically forbidden by the employer, the acts nevertheless still may be within the scope of employment. For example, if the owner/employer of an automobile service franchise tells an employee not to do certain types of precision mechanical work but the employee nonetheless does so and thereby causes harm, the employer may still be liable if that type of mechanical work is within the scope of employment for that employee. The rationale for this rule is that by merely instructing one's employees never to do certain activities, the employer could unfairly absolve himself/herself of vicarious liability.

The doctrine of *respondeat superior* also can apply to intentional torts committed by the servant/employee. The rule of law holds that if the intentional tort occurs within the scope of the employee's employment and is intended to further the employer's business interests, then the employer is liable. However, if the employee, in committing the intentional tort, is motivated to further his or her own personal interests, then the employer is not vicariously liable. Therefore, there is a major difference legally between a "bouncer" at a bar ejecting a loud and abusive patron with excessive force and thereby committing a battery versus a delivery employee who, upon delivering a package to a person, recognizes this person as a "long-lost enemy" and strikes this person, thereby committing a battery. The employer in the first case will be vicariously liable for the intentional tort, but not the employer in the second scenario.

One important intersection of agency law and vicariously liability law deals with a principal's tort liability for his or her agent's misrepresentations. The essence of the agency relationship, one recalls, is representational: The agent "stands in the shoes" of the principal, negotiates for, and enters into contracts on the principal's behalf. Therefore, the agent will be making representations to a third party on behalf of the principal, and accordingly, the principal is exposed to tort liability when the third party enters into a contract and thereby sustains a loss due to the agent's misrepresentations. Again, the essential vicarious liability requirements have to be shown: Was the agent actually or apparently authorized to make representations? If so, was the alleged misrepresentation made within the scope of the agent's authority? If these requirements are present, the principal will be liable for the agent's misrepresentations, even intentionally fraudulent ones. The rationale for holding the principal liable for such an intentional tort is that the principal, by using and empowering an agent, has thereby placed the agent in a position to make representations and, by so doing, has given an aggrieved third party the impression that the agent has such authority.

The doctrine of *respondeat superior* generally is a rule imposing civil liability and thus is not applicable to the criminal law. Therefore, ordinarily a master is not criminally liable for the acts of his or her servant. Yet there are exceptions such as those regulatory laws governing the sale of alcohol and tobacco to minors as well as the sale of adulterated drugs and impure food. Also, the corporate entity, as "master," can be deemed vicariously liable for the criminal acts of its officers, agents, and employees, as will be seen in the chapter on Business Organizations.

The "scope of employment" requirement to vicarious liability also presents some interesting legal and factual questions. One concerns the employee's use of the employer's vehicle or equipment outside the scope of employment. The general rule of law here is that the mere fact that the employer allowed the employee to use its vehicle or equipment is not sufficient to impose liability on the employer if the use is outside the scope of employment. The employer thus will only be deemed liable when the vehicle or equipment is used for advancing the employer's own business rather than furthering the employee's personal interests. In the classic example, the employee uses the employer's vehicle and has permission to take the employer's vehicle home. But the employee uses the vehicle for his or her own recreational use and, in so doing, negligently causes an injury. As such, the employer will not be deemed vicariously liable.

Another "scope" issue concerns employees who commute to and from work. In traveling to and from work situations, the employee will be deemed to be outside the scope of employment unless the employee, in addition to his or her standard commute, will also be doing a special errand for his or her employer. Traveling salespersons, furthermore, are always deemed to be within the scope while traveling, even while not technically working.

The departure by an employee from authorized activity has always presented a problem for the common law. The problem arises when the employee temporarily departs from his or her instructed duties and undertakes some personal business. Under the old common law, this situation was called—most quaintly though quite accurately—"detour and frolic." The classic case occurs when the employee, while delivering goods for the employer, goes out of his or her way to visit a "friend," and while so doing, injures a third party. The deciding legal issue here is whether the employee was acting within the scope of his or her employment when the actual harm occurred.

There are two main rules governing "detour and frolic." First, only a "substantial departure" will take the employee outside the scope of his or her employment, meaning that if the deviation from the direct route is only a minor one—that the employee undertakes an incidental personal chore or act, causing just a slight delay, and that it happens while the employee's principal purpose is still to serve the employer's business—then the employee is still within the scope. Second, presuming a substantial departure, when exactly is there sufficient re-entry into the "scope" for there to be vicarious liability for the employer? For there to be a sufficient scope reentry, the common law requires that the employee resume the intent to further the employer's business, physically turn back to the departure point, and come reasonably close to the departure point.

Also related to the "scope" issue is the unauthorized guest problem—when the employee, without authority, invites third persons to join the employee in the employer's vehicle, and the third party is injured due to the employee's negligence. The majority rule under the common law is that the employer is not liable because such an invitation is construed to be outside the scope of employment, even when the employee's conduct, which caused the harm, is within the scope. But it should be noted that there is a distinct minority view that would hold that the employer is vicariously liable in the latter case.

Finally, vicarious liability, pursuant to the doctrine of *respondeat superior*, must be distinguished from the employer's liability based on the employer's own personal breach of a legal duty. That is, the employer or the employee will be liable for tortious acts of a person when the employer is directly and personally at fault, even if the harm itself is caused through an employee. For example, if the employer directed or authorized the wrongful act, the employer will be liable as if the employer himself/herself had committed the legal wrong. Similarly, if the employer knows that his or her employee is acting in a reckless or careless manner yet still allows the employee to continue performing, then the employer, together with the employee, will be held liable for careless retention and supervision.

Initially, the employer could even be considered negligent in hiring the employee if the employer or a "reasonable, prudent person" knew that the employee was not qualified or capable of executing the work in a careful manner. In such a case, the employer also may be liable for acts normally outside the scope of employment. Such types of liability are regarded as "direct" as opposed to vicarious.

All of these key issues are deemed to be questions of fact for a jury to decide in a common law system.

Global Legal Perspectives

Mexico: Real Estate Agents and Notaries[50]

In Mexico, unlicensed real estate agents are allowed to show property to potential buyers and explain the real estate purchase and transfer process to them. Because Mexico does not license real estate agents, consequently, any person can form a real estate company. Also in Mexico, there is no real estate commissioner or regulatory agency or department at any governmental level.

Although many Mexican attorneys and real estate agents speak English and will communicate with the client in English, the law requires that all documents governing the transaction be written in Spanish. Accordingly, a certified translator should prepare copies of all documents. This translation effort will increase translation costs but will ensure that the buyer knows precisely the content of the documents. If a dispute regarding the contract arises, however, the translated versions will not be admissible in court.

Surprisingly, it is not common in Mexico for both parties to a real estate sale and purchase to have legal counsel. In every sale and purchase transaction, however, a notary public ("notario") will be involved. A Mexican notary is an attorney who, after passing several examinations that concentrate on different subjects of Mexican law, secures an authorization (called a "patent") granted by the government of each state of Mexico. Notaries perform quasi-public functions delegated by state governments and hold office for life unless removed for cause. The notary is empowered with the authority to attest documents, draft documents, verify the acts therein, and record documents before the Public Registry. Any transfer of ownership document must be formalized by a notary, who is responsible for ensuring the transaction is documented and effectuated in the form required by law. The documents issued by the notary are valid public documents whose legitimacy cannot generally be objected to. The documents thus will be considered as true and legal in any controversy brought before a Mexican court.

The notary will investigate different aspects of the transaction, including the underlying facts, supporting documents, and accompanying instruments. Once the legal validity of the transaction has been ascertained, the notary will create a deed (or "escritura"). The deed is then registered with the Public Registry of Property, and the transaction is complete. The ownership of real estate is recorded in the Public Registry, depending on the type of property.

---

[50] See Angeleynn Meya (2004).

Because all Registries are public, third parties are able to research Registry files and know all the transactions that have been made in connection with a specific property.

Every notary is also responsible for calculating taxes and requesting his or her clients to pay these amounts. The notary then pays the tax authorities.

The legal restrictions that U.S. citizens as well as other foreigners confront in purchasing certain real property in Mexico will be covered in the Real Estate chapter.

Agents and Employees in International Business

In the global arena, joint venture and ownership of foreign subsidiaries are naturally going to involve expatriate agents and employees and, thus, personnel training.[51] The expatriate manager draws on the host country national (HCN) subordinate's understanding of local business practices and regulations, particularly at the beginning of the assignment. The expatriate relies on HCN subordinates to initially help bridge the culture gap, provide intelligence on local business practices and host government policies, and support their supervisor's activities involving host country contacts in the private and public sectors, particularly where a language barrier is an issue.

The greater the cultural differences between home and host countries, the more expatriate managers must rely on local subordinates. Considering the relatively high turnover among expatriates, the HCN provides the "institutional memory" and continuity regarding local operations. Effectively, the local subordinate may be the critical link in a smooth and successful transition for the expatriate manager.

Empirical studies on sales force management found culture a critical factor affecting the management of a transnational sales force. Accordingly, cultural differences account for the largest percentage of U.S. expatriates who fail to complete their overseas assignments as well as for the low level of effectiveness of those who remain. Furthermore, lack of training to prepare employees for foreign assignments may, in part, explain the high failure rate among U.S. firms when compared with firms in other industrialized countries as fewer U.S. firms reported their company had formalized training versus West European and Japanese firms. In addition, the inability of a spouse to adjust to different physical or cultural environments is given as the main reason for U.S. expatriate managers curtailing their overseas assignment.

---

[51] Contributed by Norman D. Glick, Montgomery College.

There is a high cost associated with cutting short an expatriate manager's assignment, beyond the transportation and "settling in" costs. The expatriate personifies the firm and affects the firm's reputation regardless of the positive reputation the firm may have in its home country. Management thus needs to give more attention to the selection and training of those assigned to supervisory positions in foreign markets and to provide cross-cultural training for the spouses of global managers.

Culture moderates the behavior of a leader and a follower within organizations as well as the greater functioning of organizations as a whole. Accordingly, a management system needs to be suited to its cultural context. A study of two U.S.-owned plants producing the same product in the United States and Mexico—each managed by local nationals—found productivity at the two facilities was equal even though there were significant differences in management style.

The following generalizations comparing U.S. and Japanese salespersons show how different cultural values can influence job performance. First, the U.S. salesperson would be comfortable making "cold calls" to the top management of a potential account and be more concerned with closing a sale versus establishing a long-term relationship. The U.S. salesperson would accept a mixed compensation package with a significant portion involving commission and bonus, which reflects his or her individual accomplishments in surpassing sales targets. By comparison, a Japanese salesperson may not be comfortable making "cold calls" or calling on senior executives without an introduction, and may be more focused on establishing or reinforcing the relationship versus "closing." The Japanese salesperson, like his or her U.S. counterpart, would have sales quotas, but the Japanese salesperson prefers a straight salary rather than salary and commission, and he or she would expect group rather than individual rewards.

Gert Hofstede, in his seminal study using data collected from IBM employees in 40 countries ranging across occupations from unskilled workers to research Ph.D.s, identified those dimensions upon which country cultures differ regarding work-related values. His study provided a basis for identifying countries where work-related values generally differ from those of the United States. He found that individualism vs. collectivism, or how society values the individual's acts vs. the collective group, may be the most important dimension of cultural variation. The autocratic/paternalistic leader is the preferred leadership behavior in collectivist countries compared with the consultative style in individualistic countries like the United States. This suggests that U.S. managers, raised in an individualistic culture, will have to alter their leadership style to be effective in a collectivist setting. There is, however, some evidence that a leadership style consistent with U.S. cultural values could be effective in some collectivist countries, including Japan, Taiwan, India, and Brazil. There is also evidence that local employees in collectivist cultures where the autocratic leadership style is the accepted norm prefer supervisors who are more relationship-oriented versus task-oriented.

Apparently, relationship-oriented leadership may be an effective leadership style in the workplace. It transcends cultural differences, suggesting a certain universality of human behavior. While local employees working in a culture characterized by paternalism accept the autocratic leadership style, they nevertheless respond favorably to relationship-oriented leaders. These local employees respond well to those who are considerate. Therefore, cross-cultural training will give the expatriate leader the tools to be able to better evaluate the situation. The effective leader will then have both the skills needed to evaluate the situation as well as the ability to adapt his or her leadership behavior to the host-country's culture.

Effective leaders recognize that overseas operations have become an increasingly important part of a firm's operations, involving considerable start-up as well as ongoing operations costs. Firms operating in disparate market environments quickly learn that, as in marketing, there is no single approach that will work in all or even most markets. Accordingly, the same level of attention given to the product "launch" in these markets needs to be given to preparing agents and employees for overseas assignments.

Management Strategies

Employment At-Will and Disclaimers

Assuming the employer wants to preserve the at-will employment status of its employees, the employer should insert disclaimers in its handbooks and codes of conduct for its employees. The disclaimer should state that nothing in the handbook and code should be construed to create an express or implied employment contract, that the employee's status with the company is as an employee at-will and that nothing can change the at-will employment status of the employee except an express written contract signed by the CEO or high level executive of the firm, and that the employer reserves the right to change, modify, revise, add to, subtract from, suspend, or discontinue employment policies and practices at any time. However, for certain employees, the employer may want to consider binding these employees contractually to the firm. Such employees would be very qualified and capable ones who would be difficult to replace, especially in a "tight" job market, highly trained employees, particularly when the employer has invested the time and effort in the training, or the employees have access to confidential information and trade secrets.

The implied contract theory may be used to protect an employee at-will by limiting the employer's right to discharge without just, good, or reasonable cause, even in the absence of an express written employment contract. Some key factors to establish an implied contract case are: (1) the employee was a long-term employee; (2) the employee received raises, promotions, and bonuses throughout his or her career; (3) the employee was given assurances that he or she would remain in the employer's employ if the employee did a good job; (4) the employer had stated that it would not terminate employees unless the employer had good cause; (5) the employee had not been formally counseled, criticized, or warned about his or her performance; and (6) the employer had employment manuals or codes of conduct that gave assurances of discharge for cause only.

Independent Contractor Status

There are several advantages to the employer for using independent contractors as opposed to employees, to wit: the employer is generally not liable for the torts committed by the independent contract in performing the employer's work; the employer does not have to hold and pay Social Security and Medicare taxes; the independent contractor is not entitled to unemployment compensation and usually, depending on the state, not entitled to worker's compensation; the independent contractor is not entitled to minimum wage and overtime pay requirements of federal and state labor law; the employer need not withhold income tax from the pay of the independent contract (but may have to file an informational return with the IRS or other tax agency); and the employer will not be providing such employment benefits as health and life insurance, paid holidays and vacations, and retirement plans. From the employer's perspective, therefore, it may be financially advantageous to classify a worker as an independent contractor as opposed to an employee. An employer does not have to provide the following to an independent contractor: workers' compensation insurance, unemployment compensation, health insurance benefits, Social Security taxes, Medicare taxes, as well as tax withholding.

What steps can an employer take to ensure that a worker is classified as an independent contractor as opposed to an employee? First, a written contract explicitly designating the worker's status as an independent contractor and spelling out his or her services and the conditions of employment is critical. However, merely calling an employment relationship an "independent" one is certainly evidentiary, but not dispositive of the issue. Other factors, which should be spelled out in the contract, include the responsibilities of the contractor, the time frame for their performance, that payment will be in a lump or divided sum for the performance of those services, and that the contractor will supply all the necessary tools, supplies, and equipment. If any other workers are to be hired, the responsibility to do so, as well as any insurance (liability and workers' compensation), benefits, and taxes must be the responsibility of the contractor. Even if an employer calls and names a party doing work for the employer as an "independent contractor," merely using that label is not dispositive of the issue of the status of the party. Rather, the courts will examine the actual working relationship between the parties to determine if the party is truly an independent contractor or really is an employee. Of course, though not controlling on the issue of status, the fact that a party is called an independent contractor certainly is evidence of that status.

Agent's Authority for Contracts for Business Entities

When a contract is entered into with a business entity, whether corporation, partnership, or limited liability company (LLC), it is critical to ensure that the person signing the contract on behalf of the entity has the legal authority to do so. Typically, any general partner in a partnership or the managing member of an LLC will have such authority to bind the business. However, for an LLC as well as a partnership situation, it is important to be aware of the fact that state LLC and partnership statutes may require that some major transactions have to be approved by all the LLC members or all the partners in the partnership. Regarding the corporation, the contract with the corporation must be signed by an appropriate corporate officer. The CEO thus generally has the authority to enter into most contracts on behalf of the corporation. However, pursuant to state corporation laws, some types of contracts must be first authorized by the board of directors, such as agreements for the issuance of stock or to sell most of the corporation's assets. Consequently, the prudent person will first seek evidence, characteristically in the form of a board resolution, or perhaps in the corporation's articles of incorporation or bylaws, that specifies that the corporate officer in fact has the appropriate contract authority. Because agents are fiduciaries in a relationship of trust and confidence with their principals and since they "stand in the shoes" of their principals, the business officer, manager, and entrepreneur must be very careful in selecting agents. Agents can bind the business contractually as well as adversely affect it by means of tort law by their actions or inactions; and thus agents can affect the finances and reputation of the business—for good and for bad.

Sales Agent Authority

When goods or services are purchased on credit through a sales agent, the seller-principal may afford itself some flexibility by including in the contract a conditional clause, specifically an approval clause stating that the buyer's sales order, although signed by the principal's agent and normally binding on the seller-principal, nonetheless is not a valid contract unless and until it has been approved by the seller-principal. Using such a conditional contract clause will enable the sales agent to take orders, embody them in a contract, yet not without unknowingly binding the seller-principal to an unauthorized buyer or order.

Summary

Because "commerciality" has become a well-known concept in the global business industry, governments (and specifically the U.S. government) have established commercial and agency laws. Agency law, its development, the duties of agents and principles, the termination of an agent's authority, the liability of parties, torts, global legal perspectives, and management strategies are all elements that pertain to agency law. These elements have all been thoroughly discussed in this chapter.

As multinational firms continue to conduct business practices with their global partners, they are obliged to abide by both the host and home country's laws. In most Eastern countries, for example, business is normally conducted through a local agent, who often helps to "smooth" business negotiations and deals. Therefore, the agent/principal relationship is a vital tool for global firms, as well as for managers and entrepreneurs, who are focused on achieving successful results.

FIFTEEN

Because the establishment of a business can be complex, there is a necessary understanding of relevant national and local laws. Entrepreneurs that want to establish a business must become aware of the laws that apply to each specific type of business prior to deciding whether to have a sole proprietorship, a partnership, a corporation, a limited liability company, or a joint venture with another national or international organization. This chapter outlines some of the information that business owners, academic scholars, and entrepreneurs need to know about the various types of business organizations in the United States. The chapter outlines some of the risks and benefits associated with each type of organization so that the entrepreneur can better decide which format best fits his/her business purpose. The chapter also examines certain aspects of international and comparative business organization law. Furthermore, the advantages and disadvantages of each way of doing business will be examined later in the chapter.

Business Organizations in the United States

Choosing the Business Form

Choosing the right form of doing business is a critical determination for the business person and entrepreneur. The main consideration in choosing a business form to do business will be the extent to which the entrepreneur's personal assets will be protected from the obligations and liabilities of the business. Other factors typically will be the type of tax treatment for the business, particularly avoiding double taxation, as well as converting ordinary income into lower long-term capital gains, the attractiveness of the entity to potential investors and lenders, the potential for attractive incentives for employees, and the costs and effort to start, form, and maintain the business. Regardless of the legal nature of the proposed business, certain key questions must be resolved initially, to wit: Who are the key "players" and what percentages of the business will they own? Who will be controlling the business? How, and by whom, will the business be managed? Who is contributing capital, property, and services to the business, and to what extent? How are property and service contributions to be valued? How much time will the participants be required to spend on business matters? What happens if a key "player" dies or become incapacitated or his otherwise unable or willing to stay with the business? How will the participants' tenure with the business be maintained; that is, what protections are there regarding the expulsion of a participant? Answering the ownership issue is, of course, critical, since that arrangement will determine who and to what extent the participants will share in the financial success of the business. The objective is to answer these preceding questions in a clear, precise, and also fair manner, since the success of the business will depend on everyone knowing their rights and responsibilities as well as knowing that they have a fair share in the "fruits" of the business to be "harvested" by their hard work.

Sole Proprietorship

The sole proprietorship is the most basic form of business organization, with the owner of the business in essence being the business. Any person who does business individually without utilizing any of the other forms of business organization is doing business as a sole proprietorship.

Partnership

Partnership law in the United States was originally dictated by the common law—that is, case law. But due to a lack of legal consistency among the many states, a proposed statute, called the Uniform Partnership Act (UPA), was drafted in 1914. The UPA was inspired by and borrowed from the English Partnership Act of 1890. Pennsylvania was the first state to adopt the UPA in 1915, and today, virtually all of the American states have adopted it. The UPA is a fairly comprehensive statute, but it does not cover every conceivable case or prescribe every rule of law. Therefore, it may be necessary to examine other bodies of law—in particular, contract and agency law—in order to resolve partnership disputes.

It is important to point out initially that there is no federal partnership law per se in the U.S., but rather a series of state partnership statutes based on, though not necessarily identical to, the UPA. Accordingly, partnership law in the U.S. is consistent to a degree, but it is not absolutely uniform, despite the title to the UPA. Therefore, the prudent businessperson is well-advised to check the individual state version of the UPA where he or she is contemplating doing business as a partnership.

The basic scheme of the UPA is to regulate, with great precision, the rights of the partners against third parties while permitting great flexibility among the partners in their relations with one another. For example, Section 18 of the UPA states that the rights and duties of partners are determined by the rules in the UPA, but are *subject* to any agreement between or among them. Therefore, the UPA rules apply in the absence of contrary agreement, but with one important exception regarding the fiduciary duties of the partners, which cannot be varied or delimited by the partnership agreement.

The core definitions of partnership law and practice are found in Section 6 of the UPA. A partnership is an association of two or more persons to carry on as co-owners in a business for profit. "Business" includes every trade, occupation, or profession, and thus the object of a partnership can literally be any and all business transactions. Moreover, "person" includes individuals, partnerships, corporations, and other associations. The name of a partnership can be any name, even if distinct from the persons composing the partnership, or it may have no name. However, states in the U.S. all have "fictitious name" statutes for businesses that require the filing of a fictitious name with a state or local government entity and also usually requiring the publishing of the fictitious name in a newspaper in general circulation where the partnership does business. The penalty for noncompliance is that the partnership will not be allowed to bring a lawsuit or defend itself from a lawsuit. The duration of a partnership can be for a fixed term, or the completion of an objective or set of objectives. Furthermore, a partnership need not have a fixed term, in which case it is called a "partnership at will," which means that it can be dissolved at any time by any partner without violating the partnership agreement.

The ownership element to a partnership is critical. Ownership entails the power of ultimate control and the concomitant right to make management decisions. "Control" is thus a very important factor in determining whether a partnership exists. A problem arises if partnership management is centralized in one partner—the classic "managing partner"—in that co-ownership (and thus a partnership) can still be found if the other partners have a right to control.

Another problem in partnership is determining if a partnership is a legal entity separate and distinct from its members, such as a corporation or a limited liability company, or "merely" an aggregate or association of individuals. Generally, the UPA follows the "aggregate" view of the partnership. For example, partners have unlimited personal liability for partnership debts, contracts, and torts. As such, the partnership is not a legal entity shielding the partners from personal liability like a corporation would do. Also, for U.S. federal income tax purposes, a partnership does not pay taxes; it files an "information return" with partnership income and losses being taxed to the individual partners.

A partnership is treated as an entity for certain purposes. For example, the partnership can acquire real and personal property in its own name. Also, a partnership can sue or be sued in its own name. However, a judgment against a partnership can only be enforced against partnership assets, but not against the personal assets of the partners (in a lawsuit, the plaintiff will name and serve the individual partners also). Finally, federal bankruptcy law in the U.S. treats the partnership as an entity.

The concept of a "partnership by estoppel" is an important one in the UPA. Section 16 of the UPA states that one, who by words or conduct, represents himself or herself as a partner or consents to another person representing him or her as a partner, may be deemed liable as a partner, regardless of intent, because that "partner" is estopped (prevented) from even raising the issue of lack of technical partner status. Section 16 is designed to be used by third parties who have extended credit to the partnership or who have entered into contracts with the partnership based on good faith and reasonable reliance on representations of partnership status.

Typically, however, a partnership is premised on a contract, and thus is considered a consensual relationship. The general rule is that a partnership is formed by an agreement, and thus the consent of the parties and their intention to become partners are indispensable elements to the formation of a partnership. However, it is not necessary that the agreement and consent be manifested by an express contract. Rather, they may be implied from the representations and conduct of the parties.

As to the formalities of any partnership agreement, there really are none and the agreement, as a general rule, does not have to be in writing. However, there are two important "writing" exceptions. First, if the partnership is for an express period of more than a year, a written agreement is necessary. And second, a writing may be required for the partnership agreement, depending on the particular state exercising jurisdiction, if the main purpose of the partnership is to buy and sell and invest in real estate. Regardless, a writing spelling out the rights and duties of the partners is always strongly advisable in any and every case.

Together with the "intention" and "control" factors, the sharing of profits and losses of a business is an essential element of every partnership. The sharing of profits and losses indicates that there is a "community of interest" between or among the partners as co-owners of a business. It is important to note that profits and losses need not be shared equally. Rather, the division may be left to the parties in their agreement. Section 7(4) of the UPA contains a significant provision pertaining to profits and losses, stating that the receipt by one person of the share of profits of a business makes a *prima facie* case (that is, presumed to be true unless contradicted by other evidence) that a person is a partner in a business. However, Section 7(4) continues by stating that no such inference of a partnership may be drawn if the profits are received in payment of a debt, as wages for an employee or agent, as rent to a landlord, as an annuity to a surviving spouse of a deceased partner, on interest on a loan, or as consideration for the sale of goodwill or a business or other property. Furthermore, Section 7(3) of the UPA holds that merely sharing the gross receipts of a business does not of itself establish a partnership. Finally, joint ownership of property does not of itself establish a partnership, as a business enterprise is required for a partnership.

Partnership property can consist of any property—real or personal, tangible or intangible—that be privately owned. At times, it is necessary to clearly differentiate between partnership property, the partner's interest in the partnership, and the property of individual partners as there may be different creditors, tax considerations, and inheritance ramifications. Section 8(1) of the UPA defines partnership property as all property originally brought into the partnership or subsequently acquired by the partnership by purchase or otherwise on account of the partnership.

The problem of determining the exact ownership of property can be a problem when property is used in the partnership business but the title to the property resides in an individual partner. The controlling factor in ascertaining the ownership of property is the intent of the partners, as manifested by their partnership agreement, records, and "books." However, if that intent is not clear, the courts will apply certain criteria to determine ownership. If the property was acquired with partnership funds or assets, Section 8(2) of the UPA states that such property is partnership property unless a contrary intention appears. This section will create a presumption, though a rebuttable one, that the property so acquired belongs to the partnership even if the title to the property is in a partner's name or even several or all of the partners' names. The fact that property was purchased with the personal funds of an individual partner is merely evidence that the property belongs to the partner, because it may be that the partner contributed that property to the partnership or purchased the property for the partnership. However, if the property was purchased with the personal funds of an individual partner, the title to the property resides with that partner, and the property is real estate, the courts very likely will demand a clear showing of intent for the real estate to be treated as partnership property.

Other criteria for determining ownership of property include whether the property was used for partnership purposes, whether the partnership paid for repairs and improvements to the property, whether the partnership paid insurance premiums on the property, and whether the partnership paid taxes on the property. These factors, however, are not conclusive, but are merely evidentiary factors in determining intent.

In addition to the right to manage the business, the property rights of a partner are designated in Section 24 of the UPA as the rights in specific partnership property as well as the partner's interest in the partnership. Section 25 of the UPA explains the partner's rights in specific partnership property. The partner is treated as a co-owner with his or her other partners of a specific partnership property, holding such property as "tenants in partnership." Tenants in partnership means that a partner has the equal right to possess specific partnership property for partnership purposes, subject to the agreement. Moreover, no partner has the right to possess partnership property for any other purpose without the consent of the other partners.

As to the nature of the individual partner's interest in the partnership, Section 26 of the UPA states that such an interest is the partner's share of partnership profits and any surplus after a final settlement of all accounts. Also, most significantly, this interest is deemed to be personal property. Consequently, even if the partnership holds real estate and is in the real estate business, the partner's interest in the partnership is personal (not real) property, which means that for inheritance purposes, the property passes to the personal property beneficiaries in the deceased partner's Will and Testament.

Section 27 of the UPA states that a partner can assign his or her interest in the partnership, but that such an assignment does not make the assignee a partner; rather, the assignee is entitled to receive the share of any profits that the assigning partner would have received.

Finally, regarding property, Section 28 of the UPA deals with the rights of creditors of the individual partners. These creditors do not have the right to attach, seize, or execute on partnership property; the creditor of an individual partner must first obtain a judgment against the partner and then secure a "charging order" against the partner-debtor's interest in the partnership. The effect of such an order will be that the creditor will be entitled to receive all profits and any surplus that would have gone to the partner-debtor until the debt is satisfied.

The contract of partnership usually (and most advisedly) will specify the rights, duties, and liabilities of the parties between or among themselves. Thus, any questions pertaining to the governance of the partnership should be able to be resolved by reference to the terms of the agreement. Section 18 of the APA does provide important rules for determining rights and duties of the partners, but that section also states that the APA rules are subject to any partnership agreement. As a result, the partners are free to vary many aspects of the relationship between or among themselves. Yet, there is one significant exception: The partners cannot, by their agreement, vitiate the fiduciary nature of the partnership relationship. Also, any limitations on the authority of a partner or partners to bind the partnership legally on contracts and other obligations, although effective between or among the partners themselves, may not be effective to bind third parties who have no knowledge of these limitations.

The basic principles for managing the partnership business are found in Section 18(e) of the UPA. This section states that all partners have equal rights in the management of the partnership and the conduct of partnership business. If there is a disagreement, a majority vote rules. However, the following actions require the unanimous consent of the partners: 1) deciding extraordinary matters; 2) determining fundamental changes in the partnership business; 3) admitting new partner(s); 4) deciding to do acts in contravention of the partnership agreement; and 5) doing acts enumerated in Section 9(3), such as disposing partnership goodwill, submitting a partnership claim or liability to arbitrations, confessing a judgment against the partnership, assigning partnership property in trust for creditors, or doing any act that would make it impossible to carry on partnership business, such as selling all assets or an essential asset of the partnership. Voting by majority rule is, of course, just one option and thus the partners, in their agreement, can specify other voting arrangements such as voting by a partner's interest in profits or other schemes for weighted voting, or by having high voting requirements for defined types of actions, such as a three-quarters vote for expelling a partner.

The UPA certainly allows one partner to be the "managing partner." Actually, it is quite common in partnership practice to concentrate all management authority in one partner or into a small committee. This is more efficient, but it surely increases the workload as well as intensifies the fiduciary duty of the managing partner.

Section 18(f) of the UPA deals with the compensation of partners. This section holds that a partner is not entitled to remuneration for acting in the partnership's business. Rather, the partner is only entitled to his or her share of the profits. This rule holds even if one partner has greater skill and knowledge, one partner is the managing partner, one partner devotes more time and effort to the partnership, or even if the creation of the profits can be attributed to one specific partner's efforts.

The courts will not rewrite the partners' agreement for them. Accordingly, if the partners desire that a salary be paid to a partner—typically the managing partner—all the partners must agree and an explicit salary provision in the initial partnership agreement would most surely be advisable. Not even the illness or disability of a partner will be grounds to impose salaries or to adjust salaries or the share of profits, so again, this unfortunate contingency should be provided for expressly in the agreement. Furthermore, there is no express duty for a partner to work at all for the partnership as some partners will only contribute capital and others, services. There is also no restriction on a partner having other business interests or taking other employment, as long as there is no competition with the partnership. Once again, the partnership agreement should expressly treat all these issues.

The sharing of profits and losses in the partnership is governed by UPA Section 18(a), which has three important rules. First, each partner must be repaid for his or her contributions to the partnership, whether by way of capital or advances. Second, the partners share equally in the profits and surplus remaining after all liabilities, including those to the partners, are satisfied. And third, if there are losses, each partner must contribute to those losses—whether via capital, advances, or otherwise—according to the partner's share of the profits. But the fact that the capital contributions of the partners are unequal, or that one partner has put in all capital while the others have contributed only services and skills, does not change the UPA rule on equal sharing. Of course, the partnership agreement can specify how profits are to be divided if not equally, and such an agreement will also bind the partners as to the sharing of losses in the absence of a special agreement.

Related to Section 18(a) is Section 18(b), dealing with indemnity and contribution. Section 18(b) states that the partnership must indemnify every partner with respect to payments made and personal liabilities reasonably incurred in the order and proper course of partnership business or for the preservation of partnership property. If the partnership does not have sufficient funds to indemnify a partner, he or she is entitled to ratable contributions from co-partners.

Sections 18(c) and (d) deal with the interest a partner is entitled to for making a loan, advance, or capital contribution to the partnership.

Section 21 of the UPA is a very important section because it firmly establishes the fiduciary nature of the partnership relationship. The relationship of the partners to each other and to the partnership is fiduciary in nature, just like the relationship between principals and agents (as was discussed in the Agency Law chapter). This means that the relationship is one of trust and confidence, good faith, loyalty, full disclosure, and fairness. Competing against the partnership by, for example, making secret profits or commissions, or personally taking advantage of a business opportunity that is within the scope of the partnership's business would be examples of a breach of the fiduciary duty. One recalls from the Torts and Business chapter that the violation of a fiduciary is the equivalent of fraud.

Section 22 grants each partner the right to a formal accounting of all partnership affairs when there is a violation of the fiduciary duty as well as when the partner is wrongfully excluded from either partnership business, the possession of partnership property, and also under other circumstances when it is just and reasonable to have a formal accounting. Section 19 requires that the partnership books be kept at the principal place of business and that every partner have access thereto for inspection and copying. Section 20 states that a partner must render, on demand, true and full information on all matters relating to the partnership to an inquiring partner or his or her legal representative.

The tort liability of the partnership and partners is addressed by the UPA in Sections 13 and 15. Section 13 deals with the liability of the partnership, holding that the partnership is bound by any wrongful act or omission of any partner, acting in the ordinary course of business of the partnership, which causes injury or loss to a third party. This liability encompasses liability for negligent acts, willful and malicious acts, and intentional torts such as fraud, assuming that they are committed within the scope of partnership business. Meanwhile, Section 15, specifically 15(a), deals with the nature of the individual partners' liability. This section maintains that the partners are jointly and severally liable for everything chargeable to the partnership under Section 13.

The effect of these two sections is that the UPA dictates that a partner assumes liability for the torts of his or her co-partners. The effect of "joint and several" liability, as noted in the Torts and Business chapter, is that a cause of action can be legally instituted against a single partner without joining the others. Moreover, a judgment against a single partner does not definitely dispose of the liability of the other partners in lawsuits against them. The matter is not *res judicata* because the liability is "several." Also, based on agency and vicarious liability principles (as discussed in the Agency Law chapter), the partnership and partners are liable as principals for the acts of their agents as well as employers for the acts of their employees (presuming that the agents and employees were acting within the scope of their authority).

The UPA does not deal specifically with the criminal liability of the partnership. But based on old common law principles, the partnership ordinarily is not recognized as a separate and distinct entity for criminal law purposes, as a corporation is. The result is that technically, a partnership cannot commit a crime. However, the individual members of the partnership may still be criminally responsible as individuals for unlawful acts committed by the partnership. However, if a crime requires specific intent, only the partner(s) who possesses such intent may be charged criminally. However, there are certain criminal statutes, such as selling alcohol or tobacco to minors, that impose absolute liability, including criminal liability, on the partners even if the unlawful act was done without the knowledge or consent of the other partner(s).

The contract liability of the partnership and partners is governed by Section 9 of the UPA. Section 9(1) affirms the old common law rule that a partner is considered to be an agent of the partnership for the purpose of partnership business. The result of this section is that the principles of agency law regarding an agent's authority to contractually bind his or her principal are incorporated into partnership law. There is, however, also an express "apparent authority" doctrine in Section 9(1), holding that an act of a partner for apparently carrying on in the usual way the business of the partnership binds the partnership unless the partner has no authority and the third party, who dealt with the partner, had knowledge of the lack of the partner's authority. This means that the right of a partner to contractually bind the partnership can be restricted by the partnership agreement. However, any secret limitations by the partners as to one or more partners' limited contract authority will not be binding on the third party who lacked knowledge of the limitations. Of course, the partner who exceeds his or her limited authority has committed a violation of the partnership agreement, but that fact is considered moot to the third party who lacks knowledge. Section 9(2) further elaborates on the "apparent authority" doctrine by holding that an act of a partner, who is not apparently carrying on the business of the partnership in the usual manner, does not bind the partnership unless the act is authorized by all the other partners.

As to the nature of a partner's contract liability, Section 15(b) states that the partners are only "jointly" liable for the contract obligations as well as debts of the partnership. Thus, a contract claimant or creditor must sue *all* of the partners. If a lawsuit is brought against less than all, any subsequent legal action will not be able to be maintained against a partner who was not joined as an original defendant. Significantly, "joint liability" means that each partner is still liable for the whole amount of the contract obligation or debt. Moreover, the release of one "joint" partner releases all. A partnership can be sued alone, without the necessity of joining the other partners, but in such a case, a judgment against the partnership is only binding on partnership property and not on the individual property of the partners. Thus, plainly, a plaintiff will sue and serve not only the partnership but also the individual partners. A plaintiff who does so and recovers a judgment will then be able to "execute" the judgment against either the partnership property or the individual personal property of the partner. Although in some states, a judgment creditor will have to proceed against partnership property first.

There are four categories of liability, ranked in order of payment and regarding liabilities owed to: 1) creditors other than partners; 2) partners other than for capital and profits (for example, loans or advances by partners); 3) partners with respect to capital contributions; and 4) partners with respect to profits. If there are losses, meaning that the partnership liabilities exceed its assets, each partner must contribute to making good the losses in accordance with his or her share of the profits. If a partner is insolvent or refuses to contribute his or her share, the remaining partners must make up that share proportionately to their share of the profits.

The final area of partnership law to cover is at times confusing dissolution and termination of the partnership. There are four key concepts that must be learned. The first is "dissolution" itself, which is a technical UPA term defined in Section 29 as the change in the relation of the partners caused by any partner ceasing to be associated in carrying on the business of the firm. That is, dissolution is the point of time when the partners cease to carry on business together as partners. Yet dissolution may not necessarily cause the termination of the partnership. Thus, the second concept is a dissolution which leads to the continuation of the business in an altered form. Conversely, the third concept is a dissolution which leads to the "winding up"—that is, the liquidation—of the partnership when all partnership affairs are settled, and which ultimately leads to its termination, which is the fourth concept.

There are two general categories of dissolution: 1) dissolution caused by certain events that automatically dissolve the partnership by the operation of the law (but which may not necessarily result in the partnership's termination), and 2) situations in which a court, upon application, may decree dissolution. Moreover, the first category of dissolutions can be further subdivided into dissolutions caused without any violation of the partnership agreement and dissolutions in contravention of the partnership agreement.

Section 31 of the UPA enumerates the causes for automatic dissolution. Section 31(1) states that dissolution can be caused without any violation of the agreement between the partners by the expiration of the term or particular undertaking of the partnership, or when there is no definite term or undertaking. This is done by the express will of any partner merely by an expression of an intent to dissolve. When there is no definite term or undertaking, a partner can dissolve even though dissolving the partnership results in losses to the other partners. However, because partners are fiduciaries, the right to dissolve cannot be exercised in bad faith, for example by a partner dissolving so as to arrogate to himself or herself a profitable partnership business opportunity.

A partnership can also be dissolved without violating any partnership agreement when a partner is expelled from the partnership pursuant to an expulsion provision in the partnership agreement. In such a case, the remaining partners are allowed to carry on the business, and the expelled partner cannot compel a liquidation and termination of the partnership even though the expelled partner is both entitled to be paid the net amount due from the partnership and to be discharged from all partnership liabilities.

Section 31(2) of the UPA states when a partnership can be dissolved in contravention of the initial partnership agreement. The rule is that any partner at any time may effectuate a dissolution of the partnership by merely expressing his or her will to do so even though such dissolution is in contravention of the agreement. The rationale of the UPA is that a partner has the power, though not necessarily the right, to dissolve the partnership and this right is emphasized by the consensual nature of the relationship. However, the wrongfully dissolving partner may be liable for breach of the partnership agreement and thus for damages, with the remaining partners allowed to continue the business.

Section 31(4) deals with the death of a partner. The rule of law is that the death of any partner results in a dissolution of the partnership unless otherwise stated in the partnership agreement. Moreover, absent an agreement, the personal representative of the deceased partner can force a liquidation and termination of the partnership or can agree with the remaining partners to continue the business.

Section 32 of the UPA deals with judicial dissolution of the partnership and specifies those events that may lead to a dissolution provided there is an appropriate judicial declaration. For example, the death or disability of a partner, misconduct, gross negligence or neglect, or breach of the partnership agreement by a partner, as well as the fact that the business can only be carried on with substantial losses are all grounds for judicial dissolution upon proper application to a court. Note that mere quarrels, disagreements, minor differences, and friction, as well as ordinary or developmental business losses ordinarily will not be grounds for judicial dissolution.

The astute reader can see that a partnership is a very fragile way of doing business since so many things can cause its dissolution. For example the withdrawal, retirement, or admission of a new partner is a very common event in the life of any partnership, but none of these contingencies are mentioned in the UPA. Consequently, unless there is an explicit provision in the partnership agreement, any of these events will cause a dissolution of the partnership. Dissolution, however, does not automatically terminate the partnership as it may continue on in an altered form.

However, dissolution may lead to the next stage of the partnership, the winding up or liquidation stage wherein the business continues but only so far as to conclude preexisting partnership affairs. Neither existing contracts are discharged nor are creditors' rights impaired. The partnership continues to have legal existence for the purpose of fulfilling outstanding agreements, settling accounts, and converting assets into cash and the partners are still liable for existing partnership debts. Section 41 holds that if the dissolved partnership is continued instead of being liquidated, the new partnership remains liable for the debts of the previous partnership and, as such, the creditors of the first or dissolved partnership effectively become creditors of the partnership that is continuing business.

Whether a dissolved partnership is continued or liquidated and terminated depends primarily on the terms of the agreement. Therefore, it is imperative to have a well and thoroughly drafted partnership agreement specifying causes for dissolution and then clearly stating that such a dissolution will result in the continuation of the business in an altered form and not the liquidation and termination of the business. Section 40 of the UPA provides the rules for distribution of partnership assets upon a dissolution that has led to a liquidation and winding up of the partnership.

Joint Venture

A joint venture is a type of business relationship where two or more persons combine their knowledge, labor, and property to achieve a single undertaking. A joint venture is very similar to a partnership in many ways such as in the absence of an agreement to the contrary, members to the joint venture share profits and losses equally. The major difference between the joint venture and the partnership is that the former is for a single transaction or undertaking whereas a partnership is for a continuing business relationship. The precise point of division between a partnership and a joint venture is very blurred, however. In most states, the courts will apply the UPA to resolve joint venture disputes.

Today, the joint venture is primarily used in transnational business alliances in order to achieve some specific purpose. An interesting and very socially responsible use of the joint venture method of doing business is manifested by the American ex-basketball star, Earvin "Magic" Johnson, who is "teaming up" with major travel businesses to bring more minorities into the rapidly growing business of selling travel "packages" from home. The name of the joint venture is the Magic Johnson Travel Group, and it will supply the computer software and training to sell cruises from home. Partners in the joint venture include Royal Caribbean Cruises and GoGo Worldwide Vacations. As a matter of fact, Johnson, a leading advocate of developing urban areas, has formed joint ventures with several other businesses, including Burger King, Starbucks, and AMC Theatres, to develop inner-city locations.

Another example of a joint venture in the international arena is the venture formed by the European firm Marinvest and the U.S. Carnival Cruise Corporation's Italian cruise company, Costa Crociere, to build and operate a cruise terminal north of Rome. The European Union's antitrust regulator, the European Commission in Brussels, approved the project in 2006.

Limited Partnership

The limited partnership is a business entity that did not exist in the old common law. Rather, it was created by statute, specifically the Uniform Limited Partnership Act (ULPA), which most states in the United States have adopted. The goals of the ULPA were to allow small businesses to compete for capital and to afford investors the opportunity to obtain a commercial interest in a business but without the personal liability of partners. The ULPA follows the pattern and rules of a general partnership in many respects but imposes extensive formalities as well as restrictions on the activities of certain partners in return for their release from personal liability.

A limited partnership is defined by the ULPA as one formed by two or more persons and having as its members one or more general partners and one or more limited partners. The general partner(s) undertakes the management and assumes the personal liability of the business whereas the limited partners make a financial or property contribution to the business and thereby obtain a property interest therein. The limited partner is precluded from undertaking any management responsibilities. The formation of a limited partnership is patterned after the ULPA, but with one important exception: The limited partnership requires the filing of a detailed registration statement, called a certificate, which contains many formalities, and this must be filed with the appropriate state authority.

There are two major drawbacks to a limited partnership. First, there are many complicated and very rigid formalities to its creation. Second, it was not clear under the ULPA, how much review, advisory, or veto power a limited partner could exercise before he or she was deemed to participate in management, thereby suffering the very harsh penalty of effectively forfeiting the protection from personal liability. Because of these difficulties, the limited partnership was never developed to the extent initially predicted, especially now with the creation and growth of the Limited Liability Company. But the limited partnership still exists as a very specialized business structure: In the tax fields, it is often utilized in the creation of a tax shelter. However, use of the limited partnership is beyond the scope of this book.

It should be noted that in 1976, the ULPA was revised through the Revised Uniform Limited Partnership Act (RULPA) in an attempt to further encourage its use as a business form. The RULPA allows for greater participation by a limited partner and tries to establish some clear and permissible boundaries for limited partners to get involved in the business. While a limited partner exercising "control" over the business is still prohibited, the RULPA nonetheless enumerates certain "safe acts" that a limited partner can perform, such as consulting or advising the general partner, approving or disapproving amendments, being an agent or employee of the business, acting as a surety of the business, as well as voting on certain matters (including dissolution, removal of the general partner, selling all the assets of the business, incurring extraordinary indebtedness, and changing the nature of the business), all without being deemed to "control" the business. Yet this revision of the ULPA has not increased the use of the limited partnership which basically, except for the aforementioned specialized uses, has been superseded by the Limited Liability Company method of doing business.

Limited Liability Partnership

In yet another new form of doing business, limited liability partnerships (LLPs) have come into existence pursuant to state statutory law as many states have enacted very similar legislation in order to permit the creation of LLPs. Today, LLPs are designed primarily to be used by attorneys, accountants, and other professionals as a way of doing business. Therefore, any detailed explication of the LLP form is beyond the scope of this book.

However, certain fundamental LLP points must be made. One key aspect of the LLP way of doing business is that there does not need to be a general partner who is personally liable for the debts and obligations of the partnership. Instead, all partners are limited partners and thus, they can lose only their capital contribution should the partnership fail or be sued. Most significantly, there is no personal liability beyond the partner's capital contribution. The tax benefits of the LLP form are obvious: LLPs enjoy "flow-through" tax advantages very similar to other types of partnerships. This means that no tax is paid at the partnership level and all profits and losses are reported on the individual partner's income tax returns.

The LLP is created formally by the filing of an "articles of partnership" with the relevant state's secretary of state's office, and this filing is a public document. Note that a "domestic" LLP is one formed in the state of organization. Such an LLP may do business in other states, but must accordingly register as a "foreign" LLP. In some states, any partnership may register with the Secretary of State's office as an LLP. The registration fee initially was $100 for each partner who is a state resident. Usually, an LLP must maintain $100,000 per partner in liability insurance coverage. These amounts were pursuant to the original statute, and one can naturally expect them to increase.

The name of a registered limited liability partnership must contain the words "limited liability" or the specific designation "LLP." A partner in an LLP is not individually liable for the obligations or liabilities of the partnership, whether in tort or contract, that may arise from errors, omissions, negligence, malpractice, or wrongful acts committed by another partner or by an employee or agent of the partnership. However, each partner remains liable, individually and jointly and severally, for all other debts and obligations of the partnership, including his or her own errors, omissions, negligence, malpractice, or wrongful acts as well as those acts committed by any person under his or her direct supervision or control. Partnership assets are subject to all partnership liabilities, including malpractice claims.

There are two important points regarding LLP law: 1) In most states, LLPs are restricted to certain types of professionals, such as accountants and lawyers; and 2) Most states require LLPs to carry a minimum of $1 million in liability insurance to cover negligence, wrongful acts, and misconduct by partners or employees of the LLP, with the rationale being that third parties will have a compensation source to recover for their injuries.

Corporation: Introduction, Nature, Formation, and Powers

The corporate way of doing business in the United States is a creation of the states themselves. A corporate charter is given by the state, granting the ability to conduct business as a corporation. The states can regulate the incorporation of a business as well as the activities of the corporation and state statutes can vary, as the discerning reader is aware. Furthermore, there is no federal or uniform corporate statute, though there is a "model" act that has been offered to the states for official legislative enactment, called the Revised Model Business Corporation Act.

A corporation is defined as an artificial legal entity, independent of its owners-investors, and created by the state pursuant to a corporate charter with powers conferred upon it by the state. A "domestic" corporation is one formed under the laws of the particular state and a "foreign" corporation refers to all other corporations, either from "sister" states or international jurisdictions. In most states, a corporation is formed by the filing of an appropriate document with the appropriate state official, usually the Secretary of State, who is charged with the primary responsibility of administering corporate laws and the paying of a specified fee. Corporate existence begins on the date of filing as endorsed on the charter.

Most states have four types of corporate statutes: 1) general business corporate statutes, which will be the focus of this book; 2) nonprofit corporation statutes; 3) professional corporation statutes designed for attorneys, physicians, and accountants; and 4) small, "close," or "closely held" corporation statutes. This last example, for all practical purposes, has been superseded by the Limited Liability Company form of doing business, as will be shown.

State corporate laws have special provisions to enable a foreign corporation to transact intrastate business. A distinction is at times made between "publicly held" corporations and "closely held" corporations. The former are corporations whose outstanding shares are held by a large number of people, whose shares are traded on national or international security exchanges, whose stock prices are published, or whose activities are regulated by the Securities and Exchange Commission (SEC). A "closely held" corporation, however, is one with relatively few shareholders (usually less than 35), all or most of whom participate in management. Because there is no real outside market for shares of a closely held corporation, they are not regulated by the SEC. In fact, some states even have special statutes or special statutory provisions in place for close corporations. One such characteristic provision is that the free transferability of shares of the close corporation may be restricted.

The corporation, it must be stressed, is a separate legal entity, distinct from its shareholders; it is an artificial legal person. The corporation is owned by its shareholders and managed by a board of directors chosen by the shareholders. The corporation as a legal "person" can conduct business in its own name, much in the same way a "real" person can. Therefore, business can be done, assets acquired, contracts entered into, and liabilities incurred, all in the name of the corporation. Moreover, the corporation can sue or be sued much as a living person, pay taxes, obtain business licenses and permits, and own bank accounts. Of course, as an artificial person, the corporate entity acts exclusively by and through officers, employees, and agents. For Constitutional law purposes in the U.S., the corporation is treated as a "person" for "due process" and "equal protection" purposes, as well as for the Fourth and First Amendments but not for the Fifth Amendment privilege against self-incrimination.

There are certain distinct advantages to the corporate form of doing business. First and foremost is limited liability. Corporate obligations and debts are separate and distinct from those of the shareholders, even if one shareholder owns all the shares. The corporation, of course, is unlimitedly liable, but the shareholders are not personally liable for the debts of the corporation. (The shareholder's liability is limited to the amount of his or her own investment.)

Another positive feature of the corporation is centralized management in a board of directors and officers being selected by the board. Directors and officers may be shareholders, but it is not technically required that they have any ownership interest in the corporation.

Continuity of existence is another advantage. Theoretically, corporate existence can be perpetual. As opposed to a partnership, which has been shows as being a very fragile way of doing business, the existence of a corporation is not dependent on who its owners and investors as well as its directors and officers are at a particular time. If a shareholder or director dies, or if a shareholder sells or transfers his or her shares, the corporation continues to exist as a separate entity. Furthermore, if it is necessary to raise additional capital, new shareholders may be brought in without changing or disturbing the corporate form.

Other advantages of a corporation are the ease of transferability of ownership, shares being freely transferable, access to capital markets by means of issuance of stocks and bonds to the public, and the attractiveness of the corporate form of doing business to investors.

The major disadvantage of the corporation in the U.S. is double taxation. The corporation is taxed as a separate entity with its own tax rates for corporate earnings, but then, if the corporation pays these now diminished earnings as dividends to the shareholders, the dividends are treated as income to the shareholders and taxed again. (In a partnership, one recalls, total income is taxed only once, directly to the partners.) However, there is a specialized corporate form, called a "sub-chapter S" (S) corporation form for the pertinent section in the Internal Revenue Code, whereby the corporation can be taxed as a partnership. Thus there will be only a single tax on corporate income at the shareholder level, meaning that corporate income is not taxed separately and if the S corporation has losses, a shareholder can use the losses to offset other income. However, there are numerous requirements for an S corporation, the most notable of which are: only a domestic corporation with 100 or less shareholders can be an S corporation; the S corporation can only have one class of stock; resident aliens cannot be shareholders; and there are limits to the amount of money that can be placed in pension funds.

An S Corporation is one that was in essence created by federal tax law in the United States. The Internal Revenue Code allows certain shareholders to have a corporate business while being taxed as individuals. "S" refers to the pertinent section in the tax code. The S corporation entity does not pay income taxes; rather, the profits (or losses) of the entity are "passed through" to the individual shareholders who report them on their individual tax returns. These profits and losses must be allocated based on the share ownership in the corporation. The advantage to the S corporation is thus clear: there is no "double taxation"; profits earned by the S corporation are only taxed once. The S corporation, therefore, would be a very attractive investment vehicle for investors who do not work for the company. However, if the shareholders in the S corporation are also employees who receive salary and bonuses, which are deductible, then the rationale for forming an S corporation is not as strong. There are certain requirements to forming an S corporation. An S corporation can have no more than 100 shareholders; almost all of whom must be individuals; none of whom can be non-resident aliens; and the S corporation can only have one class of stock. These requirements mean that the S corporation will not be able to have access to a wide capital pool due to the shareholder limitations as well as the fact that international and institutional investors, such as other corporations, are prevented from being shareholders. Also, because of the one class of stock requirement, the S corporation cannot issue inexpensively priced stock to promoters and organizers, and must issue stock to employees at the same price paid by investors (assuming during the same time period).

The formation of a corporation is a fairly straightforward process. First, a state of incorporation must be selected. A small corporation that intends to do business in just one jurisdiction will obviously choose that state to incorporate, but if a corporation plans to conduct business in other states, the corporation will need a certificate of authority. While this is usually considered only a formality, the states will naturally require a fee as well as an official registered corporate agent in the state. As to the "mechanics," of filing, one must check (or have one's attorney check) the specific state statute as to details. The filing of a document with the appropriate state official, usually the secretary of state, is mandatory along with the payment of a filing fee and the document, in many states, must be notarized. The document is most typically called an "articles of incorporation," though in some states it is called a "certificate of incorporation" or a charter. Also, some states may require local filing of the document and others may require a newspaper notice of the filing. If the document conforms to the laws of the state, it is approved, and corporate existence is deemed to begin at the date and time of filing as determined by the secretary of state.

Incorporators are the person(s) who execute and sign the articles of incorporation. Three is the traditional number required, but today many states require only one. Generally, incorporators must be over 18 years of age if the incorporators are natural people, as opposed to another corporation or a partnership, which also can be incorporators. Moreover, there are no citizenship or residency requirements. The functions of the incorporator(s) are to execute and deliver the articles to the secretary of state, receive the signed charter back from the secretary of state, and finally call the first meeting of the initial board of directors (which is named in the articles) when the organization of the corporation is completed. Because the role of the incorporator is merely ministerial (typically with ceremonial overtones), serving as an incorporator generally will not give rise to any personal liability on the incorporator's part. Also, an incorporator should not be confused with a "subscriber," who is a person who agrees to buy shares in the corporation and, upon so doing, becomes both an investor and participant.

The "articles of incorporation" is an agreement among the incorporators concerning the organizational details of the corporation. It is also deemed to be an agreement between the corporation and the state, between the corporation and the shareholders, and an agreement among the shareholders themselves. The exact requirements for the document are ascertained by reference to a particular state's corporate law, but generally speaking, there are just a few uniform requirements for a valid "articles of incorporation."

First, it must be in writing. Second, the document must name the corporation. Most states will require that the name be distinct or distinguishable from all other corporate names or not be the same or deceptively or confusingly similar. The secretary of state will already have a registry of corporate names, and the states have procedures in place to check names as well as to register for a brief—usually six months—period. Also, a prospective corporate name can be gained for a nominal fee while the corporate papers are being prepared for actual filing. In addition, the name must have attached to it some words indicating "corporateness," such as "Incorporated," "Inc.," "Company," or "Co." There also may be a requirement for the corporation to comply with a local "fictitious name" statute (which would apply to any business form), whereby the principals behind the fictitiously named business must register with the state.

The entrepreneur contemplating forming a corporation (or an LLC, a Limited Liability Company) should first conduct a name search in order to ascertain if the desired name (and website) is available. There are state and local registries for fictitious names as well as domain name registries and federal and state trademark and service-mark registries. The entrepreneur should register not only the company name and website but also the trademark and service-mark. Note that many state corporation statutes allow a person to reserve a name for a fee for a certain time period, for example, six months, while the entity is being formed with that name.

The duration of the corporation can be perpetual. In some states, the articles must state the time period for duration, whereas others just presume that the existence will be perpetual unless a shorter period is explicitly stated.

Usually a provision for the purposes of the corporation must be included, although a "general purposes" provision is acceptable. A "general purposes" provision means the corporation seeks to do "any and all lawful business." Of course, specific purposes can be stated, but then, if the corporation seeks to do business beyond these limited purposes, it must amend its articles.

As to corporate powers, it ordinarily is not necessary to state them because most states either have very long and broad lists of corporate powers that every corporation automatically possesses, or the states simply state that a corporation has all the powers a natural person has for the carrying on of business. Thus, it is not necessary to recite powers in the articles. However, the articles can preclude the corporation from exercising certain powers, such as making loans to directors or officers.

An act beyond the powers or purposes of the corporation is known as an *ultra vires* act, which can be enjoined by the state or by a shareholder lawsuit and also which can be the basis of a corporate action to recover damages against the directors and/or officers who committed the *ultra vires* act. In most states, the *ultra vires* doctrine has been abolished as a defense against or by third parties; no executed act of the corporation with a third party can be deemed invalid as *ultra vires*.

Most states will also require a capitalization provision in the articles, usually that the type, number, and price of shares the corporation is authorized to issue must be stated. However, there is no requirement that any shares authorized actually be issued. Also, some states may have minimum capital requirements, for example, that the corporation receives $500 or $1,000 before commencing business. If this is so, usually an affidavit to that effect will be sufficient to satisfy the appropriate state official.

Directors are required for a corporation and must be named in the articles. Some states require three, unless there are only one or two shareholders; but in most states a corporation need only have one director. Often, there are residency and shareholder requirements in order to be a director.

The function of the initial board (or sole director) named in the articles is to complete the organization of the corporation, with the initial board serving until the first annual meeting of shareholders, when the shareholders elect the new board. The purposes of such a meeting are to accept share subscriptions, accept contracts, leases, and loans, issue shares of stock and set the consideration for shares, select officers, and adopt bylaws. Even if a corporation is a very small or "closely held" one, such a meeting should occur, though it could be informally conducted, and there should be minutes kept for the meeting.

Every corporation is also required to have a registered office and a registered agent at that office. The registered office characteristically is the corporate attorney's office, and that attorney is designated as the registered agent. Of course, the registered office can be the corporation's business office, and the registered agent can be a corporate employee so designated. The purpose of the registered office and agent is to provide a place and a person to receive service of process, tax notices, and other official communications, from the state or otherwise. The articles must also have the names and addresses of the incorporators.

Finally, the articles can include other provisions for the regulation of business, such as preemptive rights and cumulative voting, which will be explained in due course. They can also include changing quorums, such as from one-third to three-quarters, or mete out larger voting proportions for certain actions.

The "articles of incorporation" must be distinguished from the "bylaws," which are the private rules and regulations for governing and managing the internal affairs of the corporation. The bylaws are not filed as they are not part of the public record. The bylaws may need to be approved by all the original incorporators prior to the election of directors, or may have to be approved by the board of directors, by the shareholders, or by a combination thereof depending on the particular state statute. Any very important internal provision or perhaps a very unusual one should be included in the articles and not the bylaws.

The bylaws of a corporation can focus on a variety of subject matters dealing with corporate governance. For example, the bylaws can include provisions dealing with the number of directors (though note that some state laws may require the number to be stated in the Articles of Incorporation), the calling of board of directors meetings, the voting rights of directors, how board vacancy are to be filled, the removal of directors, and the term for the directors are to serve. Bylaws can also have provisions for restricting the transferability of shares as well as for granting a "right of first refusal" for the corporation or its assignees to purchase shares at the time of a transfer by a third party. These latter bylaw provisions can be very important to a new, small, and closely-held corporation since it is critical that the stock be owned by the people who commenced the business and who are directly and substantially involved with its success.

A corporate seal is no longer required in most states, though it is desirable to have such a seal as it differentiates corporate transactions from the transactions of its individual members.

A potential problem area in corporate law and practice concerns pre-incorporation transactions. A "pre-incorporation transaction" is one done on behalf of the corporation or in the corporation's name and which occurs before the articles are filed. Thus, it occurs before there is any official corporate status. There are two main types of pre-incorporation transactions: 1) subscriptions for shares and 2) contracts by promoters.

A "share subscription" is an offer to purchase and pay for a specified number of unissued shares of the corporation. In a pre-incorporation subscription, the corporation is legally not yet formed (and thus a contract offeree does not technically exist). A post-incorporation share subscription is a subscription for unissued shares of an already existing corporation. Corporate statutes in most states typically make pre-incorporation subscriptions enforceable by the corporation for a limited period (usually six months) after the formation of the corporation. In such a case, the subscription is irrevocable by the subscriber and consideration is irrelevant. Of course, the person who subscribes does not become a shareholder until the subscription price is fully paid.

A "promoter" is a person who develops and organizes a corporation. That is, he or she procures the capital, assets, personnel, and facilities, and secures the subscriptions for shares. Then, usually as a last step, the promoter arranges for the corporation to be formed. The objective of the promoter is to take these actions only in the corporation's name because a third person, especially a creditor, may want the personal liability of the promoter.

The critical question is whether or not the promoter is personally liable for contracts made on behalf of the corporation. In a majority of states, the answer is yes, even if the promoter signs the contract in the corporation's name and signs in a representative capacity. Because the promoter is construed in the majority of cases to be an agent for a non-existent principal—meaning the corporation has not yet been legally formed—the promoter is considered to be personally liable. In order to avoid liability, the promoter is advised to obtain a continuing offer or an option on behalf of the corporation.

After the corporation is formed, it is not automatically bound on pre-incorporation contracts entered into on its own behalf because, once again, it did not exist and thus the promoter was not its agent. A corporation, however, may become liable for a promoter's contract by expressly or impliedly adopting it or by accepting the continuing offer or option which the promoter made on the corporation's behalf.

It must be emphasized that promoters are also regarded as fiduciaries and owe duties of trust, confidence, good faith, full disclosure, fairness, and honesty to the corporation and its shareholders (prospective as well as present). For example, if the promoter sells property to the corporation, the promoter must make full disclosure to the board of directors and to the shareholders, and the contract for sale must be a fair one. The promoter, however, is not automatically entitled to reimbursement for expenses incurred in promoting or for any salary during the pre-incorporation period. Furthermore, if there is a failure to incorporate, the promoter must return all money to the subscribers and he or she cannot deduct anything for expenses or salary.

Another major problem area in corporate law and practice concerns the defective formation of a corporation. That is, there are mistakes and delays in the filing of the articles. The mistakes can be minor, such as having an incorrect address, or major, such as an attorney preparing but then forgetting to file the articles. Delays naturally can result, for example, because the Secretary of State may decline to accept the first filing because of a minor defect that must be, and which is, corrected. The problem is that in the meantime the "corporation" has commenced business and the overriding issue, at least for the "shareholders," is what exactly is their liability for the obligations of this "corporation"? There are three legal doctrines that apply to this "defective" situation: 1) *de jure* corporate status, 2) *de facto* corporate statue, and 3) corporation by estoppel.

First, a *de jure* corporation is one in which the Secretary of State has accepted the articles and issued a certificate of incorporation, a charter, or a copy of the articles duly certified. Such a status is conclusive evidence that the corporation is validly incorporated, even if there are mistakes and omissions. Still, the state can bring a legal action, called a *quo warranto* (by whose authority), which compels the corporation to correct any deficiencies or cancel its charter.

A *de facto* corporation is a most interesting concept. In such a case, even though there is no *de jure* status, the corporation nonetheless will be recognized as a valid corporation for all purposes except as against the state. Accordingly, this doctrine can be used to "clothe" the "shareholders" of a defectively formed "corporation" with corporate attributes, in particular, limited liability, as opposed to holding the "shareholders" to partner status. Generally speaking, most states would mandate the following three requirements for a *de facto* corporation: 1) a law under which such a corporation might be lawfully organized; 2) a good faith and *bona fide* attempt to organize and incorporate under the law (for example, a director's meeting, shares being issued, bylaws adopted, an attempt at filing of articles); and 3) an actual use and exercise of corporate powers (for example, some business being transacted as a corporation).

A corporation by estoppel is a legal doctrine that may be used by the "shareholders" even when there is neither *de jure* nor *de facto* status. There is no real corporation or even a *de facto* one. Rather, there is an estoppel (a preclusion) from denying corporate existence. Such an estoppel arises when a third party has dealt with the business as a corporation, for example, by contracting with or extending credit to the "corporation." In such a circumstance, the third party is estopped (prevented) from even asserting that the corporation does not legally exist.

The limited liability that the corporate form of business organization provides to investors is naturally a very attractive feature of doing business this way. However, there is legal doctrine that maintains that even if a corporation has *de jure* status, a court may be able to disregard the corporate entity. This doctrine characteristically is called "piercing the corporate veil." Note, however, that the corporate "fiction" is a basic legal assumption, and there usually must be compelling evidence for a court to ignore the separate "corporateness" of the entity. Most often, this "piercing" legal doctrine comes into play when the corporation has sustained some type of liability and the corporation is insolvent, and a third party seeks to recover against the shareholders in their personal capacity. Based on this legal doctrine, the court may look through the fiction of the corporate entity and hold the persons doing business in the name of the corporation personally liable for corporate debts. However, this "piercing" doctrine can only be applied, if at all, against the shareholders of the corporation.

There are two general requirements for a court to disregard the corporate entity. First, there must be a unity of interest and ownership demonstrated to the extent that the separate personalities of the corporation and its individual human components no longer exist. Second, there must be a showing that if the corporate entity is not disregarded, and the acts are treated as those of the corporation alone, the law will be violated or public policy circumvented, or an unfair or unjust result will ensue. The "classic" example is when the sole shareholder sets fire to corporate property and the corporation sues to recover on the fire insurance policy.

It is important to note that it is not sufficient to simply "pierce the veil" because the primary motive for incorporating was to achieve limited liability. Rather, the lack of unity requirement means that the corporation is so organized and controlled as to make the corporation merely an instrumentality, conduit, "shell," "dummy," or "alter ego" through which the individual shareholder(s)— often a single shareholder— conducts business activities for convenience.

There is no precise test to determine whether a corporation is a "dummy." A variety of factors are used, to wit: 1) the fact that all the shares are owned and controlled by a single shareholder or a small number of shareholders (note that this fact in and of itself will be inadequate to disregard the corporate entity); 2) the fact that a single person governed or influenced the corporation (again this factor alone is insufficient); 3) the business commenced without completing the organization of the corporation, i.e., no shares were issued, no shareholders meetings were held, no directors were chosen or elected, and no officers were selected; 4) the corporate formalities and "routine" were not adhered to, i.e., no dividends were issued, no meetings of shareholders and/or directors were held, no corporate records were kept, and no minute entries were made; 5) corporate property and funds were not kept separate, rather, they were commingled with the shareholders' personal property and funds; 6) corporate affairs are not distinct from the shareholders' personal affairs, i.e., the execution of corporate contracts not in the corporate name or the use of the same office, attorney, letterhead, mailbox, website; and 7) if the corporate capitalization is regarded as "thin."

Regarding the final "thin" factor, the law expects a corporation to commence and carry on business with adequate capital and assets so as to meet reasonably foreseeable business needs, obligations, and risks. Unavoidable losses are permissible to suffer; capital is not necessary to cover every conceivable contingency. Yet not having adequate insurance, especially liability insurance to make a tort claimant "whole," as well as siphoning off funds to the shareholders, are both consequential "piercing" factors. The rationale of this "unity" requirement is that it is inequitable for the shareholders to ignore the forms and rules of corporate organization and behavior but then to later claim the advantage of the corporate limited liability "shield."

The burden of showing that the corporation is a mere "dummy" is on the party alleging the doctrine, and this legal issue is regarded as a question of fact for a jury to decide. Of course, if a third party potential contract or creditor claimant against the corporation is concerned that the corporation may not be able to fulfill its contract or debt obligation, the third party can insist on the personal guarantee of the principal shareholders.

Finally, it should be noted that the "piercing the corporate veil" doctrine also may apply in the case of a parent and subsidiary corporation. A subsidiary corporation is a separate and distinct corporation, though its "parent" is usually the sole or majority shareholder. There is nothing inherently wrong with a parent-subsidiary relationship, and the law does permit some commonality in boards, officers, employees, and shareholders, as well as a close functional working relationship. But when the subsidiary is a mere "conduit" for the parent, akin to a department or division, the subsidiary is "thinly" capitalized, the operations and assets are too commingled, or the representations or advertising confuses the identities of the two, the corporate entity of the subsidiary can then be disregarded. Of course, in such a case, the ultimate defendant is still a corporation, i.e., the parent.

Rights and Responsibilities of Corporate Directors and Officers

The rights and responsibilities of directors and officers as well as shareholders are very important areas of corporate law and practice. The first task is to distinguish between directors and officers and then to describe their roles in corporate governance and management.

A director is a natural person designated in the articles, selected by the incorporators, or elected by the shareholders to act as director whereas an officer is a person in a position of authority and trust in regular and continuing employment at the corporation. Directors are the governing body of the corporation, while officers are administrative and executive officials. As such, directors may delegate management of the day-to-day business of the corporation to executive officials as long as they remain under the ultimate direction and control of the board.

Another difference between directors and officers is that individual directors are not regarded as agents of the corporation, while an officer is so regarded. However, as will be shown, when the directors collectively act as a board, the directors are then regarded as agents of the corporation.

In most states, a corporation must have the following personnel: 1) a chairperson of the board; 2) a president or chief executive officer who is the general business manager of the corporation subject to the ultimate control by the board; 3) a chief financial officer; and 4) a secretary. These positions are provided for by the articles or bylaws. Agency law principles cover the authority of these corporate officers as well as agents and employees of the corporation. The same person may hold any number of offices in most states. The duty of selecting officers falls on the director(s). Directors are elected annually whereas officers serve at the "pleasure" of the board. Consequently, officers can be removed with or without cause by the board at any time (subject to any binding employment contract, of course).

Although the president of the corporation is the principal executive officer, the general manager, and an agent of the corporation, the president nonetheless "only" has the authority pursuant to agency law principles to make contracts and to perform actions appropriate to the ordinary course of business. For example, the president has the authority, even by means of "incidental" agency authority, to make usual and regular hiring and firing decisions and to adjust the compensation of employees. However, it is the board of directors that has the authority, the sole authority, to perform extraordinary or unusual transactions, for example, long-term employment contracts, real estate contracts (unless that is the regular business of the corporation), surety and guaranty contracts, employing legal counsel, making litigation decisions, negotiating loans, and incurring debts.

The distinction, therefore, between presidential "ordinary" decisions and board "extraordinary" ones emerges as critical and problematic in corporate law and practice as well as a "trap for the unwary." That is, a third party dealing with or contracting with the corporation must ensure that the corporation (the principal) is bound by the contract of the president (the officer-agent) of the corporation. If the president lacks agency authority to bind the corporation because the contract is deemed "extraordinary" for the board, then the corporation is not bound even though the president-officer-agent who exceeded his or her authority is bound. The third party, of course, wants the corporation-principal to be bound, so what is the solution? If there is any doubt as to the nature of the contract or transaction, the third party must insist on a certified copy of the board resolution that authorized the contract or transaction, thereby empowering the president-officer-agent with actual agency authority.

The officer of a corporation or the manager of a limited liability company is not personally responsible for the obligations of the entity so long as the officer or manager clearly indicates that he or she is signing in a representational capacity by naming the entity and indicating one's status as an officer or manager after one's signature. When a contract is entered into with a business entity, whether corporation, partnership, or limited liability company (LLC), it is critical to ensure that the person signing the contract on behalf of the entity has the legal authority to do so. Typically, any general partner in a partnership or the managing member of an LLC will have such authority to bind the business. However, for an LLC as well as a partnership situation, it is important to be aware of the fact that state LLC and partnership statutes may require that some major transactions have to be approved by all the LLC members or all the partners in the partnership. Regarding the corporation, the contract with the corporation must be signed by an appropriate corporate officer. The CEO thus generally has the authority to enter into most contracts on behalf of the corporation. However, pursuant to state corporation laws, some types of contracts must be first authorized by the board of directors, such as agreements for the issuance of stock or to sell most of the corporation's assets. Consequently, the prudent person will first seek evidence, characteristically in the form of a board resolution, or perhaps in the corporation's articles of incorporation or bylaws, that specifies that the corporate officer in fact has the appropriate contract authority.

The election, resignation, and removal of directors are regulated in detail by state corporate law, but some general observations must be offered. First, as to the qualifications for serving as a director, most states have an age requirement of 18 years of age, and some states require that the director must be a resident of the state and/or a shareholder of the corporation. Additional requirements can be specified in the bylaws, including for example, the posting of a bond. Second, as to the number of directors, most states require that the number be stated in the articles. In some states, however, naming the number of directors in the articles is optional, and if the number is not provided in the articles, it usually must be stated in the bylaws.

In some states, there is a minimum number of directors, typically three. However, currently in most states, a corporation can have only one director. Yet even those states that require three will permit one or two if there are only one or two shareholders in the corporation. Subsequent to the initial board's service, directors are elected by the shareholders at their annual meeting to hold office, and the directors serve until the next annual meeting. Interim vacancies can be filled by either the board or the shareholders, depending on the state statute, and usually require a majority vote. Staggered terms for directors are permissible and are in fact a common practice. Designed to ensure management continuity, one-third of the board is elected each year for a three-year period.

Directors, any or all, can be removed by the shareholders at any time with or without cause in most states, though some states will require a reason to be specified. Directors can also be removed by a court pursuant to a shareholder suit. However, a certain percentage of shareholders, usually 10%, will be required to commerce the lawsuit. In addition, the shareholders will have to convince a judge that the director(s) engaged in dishonest or fraudulent acts or committed a gross abuse of authority or discretion.

A fundamental principle of corporate law is that for the directors to act and to legally bind the corporation, the directors must act collectively as a board. Most state statutes, however, do not require regular meetings of the board to be held at stated times. Rather, the time and place of the meetings are addressed in the articles or bylaws. Regular meetings of the board do not require any notice as long as the time and place are fixed by the articles or bylaws. Furthermore, special meetings of the board *do* require notice even though, generally, a notice of a special meeting does not need to include its purpose. However, notice can be waived if the directors all meet as a board or a director without notice attends a meeting and does not object to the lack of notice. Furthermore, in some states, any board action may be taken without any meeting if all the members of the board consent in writing to the action. Finally, meetings are now allowed to be conducted by conference telephone or other telecommunications equipment. The traditional requirement of the directors physically meeting has been dispensed with in virtually all states.

A *quorum* for a board meeting is a majority of all directors—a majority of the entire board without vacancies—though the articles or bylaws may provide for a lesser or greater quorum number. When a quorum is present, a majority vote of the board of directors present constitutes a binding act or resolution of the board of directors of the corporation. Again, the articles or bylaws may require a larger voting percentage generally or for certain types of actions by the directors.

The board of directors is the governing body of the corporation. Directors have the power to govern, control, and manage the corporation collectively, subject to any restrictions in state statutes, the articles, or bylaws. It is a fundamental principle of corporate law that collective action by the board is required, meaning that the powers vested in the directors can be exercised only in a collective capacity. As a result, no act is a valid corporate act unless, generally, it is done by the directors duly assembled as a board. The realities of everyday business practice, however, especially for a large corporation, mean that the directors' primary role is to formulate major policies rather than to be directly involved in the daily management of the corporation. This includes rolling out a new product line, deciding on extraordinary transactions—such as selling or leasing corporate assets out of the ordinary course of business—and to work out very important contracts—such as major labor-management collective bargaining agreements. Accordingly, the board of directors can delegate the daily and ordinary management and business affairs to officers, employees, agents, and others, as long as these individuals are under the ultimate control and direction of the board. However, directors have certain statutory duties—such as declaring dividends and proposing, changing, and adopting bylaws—which cannot be delegated.

The board of directors of a corporation has the authority and responsibility to oversee the CEO of the company and to make sure that his or her performance is sufficient. Accordingly, it is essential that the board members have point of views that are independent of those of the CEO and that may be at variance with the view of the CEO. That is, boards of directors are not there to merely "rubber-stamp" the CEO's decisions. Important functions of the board of directors regarding the CEO are to review the performance of the CEO each year and to set the CEO's compensation for the next year. Of course, in discharging the latter responsibility, the board can consult with specially formed consultation committees.

The primary functions of the board of directors include: establishing long-term corporate objectives and the policies and strategies to achieve these objectives; hiring and firing a chief executive officer (CEO) as well as other officers to implement policies and to operate the corporation on a daily basis; determining the contract and salaries for the CEO and other officers; declaring dividends and the nature and amount of dividends; deciding and approving fundamental corporate change, such mergers, consolidations, acquisitions, and amending the articles (with shareholder approval also in certain cases); determining new types of business for the corporation as well as exiting types of business; deciding whether to borrow money or to extend credit on behalf of the corporation; determining whether to issue new classes of stock or whether to buy back stock; and instituting litigation and hiring attorneys to represent the company. The board of directors of the corporation, as emphasized, does not exist to merely "rubberstamp" decisions of the CEO, but rather must be ready and prepared to have a perspective of the firm and to make decisions contrary to that of the CEO. The board thus should review the performance of the CEO each year and set the CEO's compensation for the next year.

Corporate directors and officers are regarded by the law as fiduciaries; that is, they owe fiduciary duties to the corporation and the shareholders as a whole. A fiduciary duty encompasses acting in good faith and with integrity, honesty, trust, and confidence as well as acting in the best interest of the other party or entity.

The standard corporate board consists of 7 to 11 directors. A state corporation statute may specify a certain minimum number of directors; conversely, in some states a corporation may be allowed to have just one director. Directors as a general rule need not be shareholders of the corporation; but the state corporation statute, the articles of incorporation, or bylaws may impose this requirement.

A board of directors, furthermore, is allowed to create board committees. That is, a board may appoint specific directors—with two being the standard minimum number—to executive committees in order to perform certain routine and ordinary board functions, such as the compensation of officers, and such a committee has the full authority of the board. However, the board cannot delegate total control and management to a committee. Again, state statutes will deem certain matters to require full board approval, including, for example, any matter that requires shareholder approval, filling vacancies on the board, fixing the compensation of directors, amending, repealing, or adopting bylaws, or any other extraordinary matter.

Because of the many functions of a board of directors as well as the heightened risk of legal liability, the board is allowed to create specialized committees composed of board members. Typical committees would be an executive committee, a compensation committee, an audit committee, a litigation committee, and a nominating committee. The board is as a general rule is allowed to delegate to these board committees the power to act on behalf of the entire board. However, the usual state corporation statute would mandate that certain board powers must be exercised by the whole board and thus cannot be delegated to committees, for example, the power to declare dividends and authorize the issuance of stock, approve fundamental corporate change, such as a merger, appointing replacements for board vacancies, and amending the bylaws.

Regarding the compensation of directors, in the past, directors normally were not compensated for their service to the corporation. However, in modern times, due to the increase in the amount of work and supervision required as a director as well as a marked increase in the legal liability for serving, most corporations in the U.S. today now compensate directors. Directors also may be shareholders of the corporation and thus may have an additional motive to serve, and to serve well, that is, to protect their investment. It is important to note that in many states directors are allowed by a state corporation statute to set their own compensation but those statutes also allow for the negation of that power if there is a specific contrary provision in the articles of incorporation. In addition to compensation, many companies also pay directors for the expenses of attending meetings.

Compensation of directors always seems to emerge as a problematic corporate issue. The first compensation rule is that the articles or bylaws can fix the compensation of directors. The second rule is that absent any internal corporate rule, the directors have the power to fix their own compensation unless specifically negated in the articles or bylaws. Directors, however, are regarded as fiduciaries and thus owe duties of trust and confidence to the corporation (though not directly to the shareholders).

In most states, corporations are allowed to indemnify directors for expenses incurred in conducting corporate business, including payments to reimburse the director for legal costs, fees, and judgments sustained as a result of lawsuits against the director for his or her position or actions as a director. Moreover, most states permit the corporation to obtain insurance, called Directors and Officers Insurance (or "D&O Insurance") to protect directors and to cover indemnification. In some states, a court may also order that a director be indemnified if the director acted in a fair and reasonable manner and in the best interests of the corporation.

The fiduciary status and duties of directors are very important corporate law principles. Directors are regarded as fiduciaries of the corporation and serve in a relationship of trust, confidence, honesty, and loyalty. However, directors at times serve on more than one corporate board, but the fact that a director has many business affiliations is not in and of itself a violation of the fiduciary duty. A conflict of interest is forbidden, such as serving on the boards of competing companies. Full disclosure of any potential conflict of interest must of course be made, as well as the disclosure of any transaction or contract in which the director has a material interest.

Directors are also under a duty of due care, meaning they have a legal obligation to use reasonable and prudent business judgment in conducting corporate affairs. They are expected to attend board meetings and presentations, ask questions (and not sit silently, as the Enron board did), be informed, review reports and other materials, seek professional advice from lawyers, accountants and others, study options and alternatives, and make decisions based on information received from officers, professionals, and others. Nevertheless, directors are neither guarantors nor insurers of the corporation's business success.

Directors are protected from "bad" decisions by a significant corporate rule called the "Business Judgment Rule." This rule holds that if a director acts in a reasonable, prudent, good faith, and informed manner, but still nonetheless makes an honest mistake in judgment or a poor business decision causing the corporation to suffer, the director is not liable to the corporation for damages. The "bad" director, of course, may be removed or not re-elected by the shareholders.

Furthermore, several states now, by statute, permit directors to consider the consequences of a particular corporate course of conduct not just on the company and the shareholders (the primary stakeholder group), but also on the company's broader stakeholders, such as the employees, local communities, and society as a whole. If a director or directors breach the duties of trust and due care owed to the corporation, but the corporation (controlled by the directors) does not bring a cause of action for redress, the shareholders may be able to bring a lawsuit on behalf of the corporation by means of a "shareholder derivative suit." The shareholders must first petition the board of directors to bring the lawsuit, the shareholders typically must post a bond, and any recovery belongs to the corporation.

Rights and Responsibilities of Shareholders

The next important area of corporate law to address is the shareholder, who is in fact the owner of the corporation. The technical legal definition of a "shareholder" is a "holder of record of shares," Meaning that shareholders are the human ownership component of the corporation. Generally, anyone with capacity to contract may be a shareholder, and even a corporation can be a shareholder of another corporation. One may become a shareholder by an original purchase of shares or by transferring another person's shares.

The relationship of the shareholders to the corporation is contractual, defined principally by state statute, the articles, and the bylaws. Evidence of shareholder status usually is ascertained from the certificate for shares and by the corporate records. It must be emphasized that eligibility to vote at corporate elections is determined conclusively in most states by the corporate records, even though a determination as to who possesses title to shares may be later determined judicially. Furthermore, the shareholder retains his or her status and relationship until there is a transfer of shares registered on the corporate books.

Shareholders possess several important rights and interests in the corporation. Generally, a share of stock is regarded as property (of the intangible kind) and gives the shareholder an ownership interest in the corporation. This interest is the right to participate in profits and, upon dissolution and termination, the right to share in any distribution of assets. Shareholders, however, have no right or claim to corporate property in their individual capacities and, as such, shareholders cannot dispose of title to corporate property.

When dealing with the corporation, the shareholder is regarded as a separate entity and distinct from the corporation. As a result, a corporation may enter into a contract with shareholders and may buy and sell property with shareholders. As a general rule, shareholders are not fiduciaries, but a dominant or controlling shareholder may be construed as owing fiduciary duties, not only to the corporation, but also to minority (in number) shareholders. The rule is that such a dominant or controlling shareholder will not be allowed to use his or her power to control the activities of the corporation for only self-benefit and in a manner detrimental to minority shareholders.

Shareholders—individually or collectively—are neither regarded as agents or representatives of the corporation, nor are they authorized to perform any corporate acts. Although shareholders are the ultimate owners of the corporation, they have no power to directly control the corporation as far as the day-to-day management of corporate affairs. Rather, shareholders have several indirect methods of controlling the corporation, such as by electing directors, removing directors, approving amendments to the articles, approving, amending, or repealing bylaws, and approving fundamental change. Shareholders, of course, can always consult with and make recommendations to the board of directors as well as protest to the board. Shareholders also have the right to inspect the corporation's books, records, and properties. Moreover, this right cannot be defeated or unreasonably restricted by the articles or bylaws. The purpose of the inspection must be proper and reasonably related to the shareholder's interest and not for the purposes of harassment or obtaining confidential information. In addition, a written demand is usually necessary and the inspection must occur at a reasonable time. In some states, a shareholder must hold a minimum number of shares (for example, 5%) for a minimum period of time before the shareholder can exercise the right to inspect. However, a court can order an inspection or appoint an accountant for an audit if any shareholder can demonstrate sufficient grounds, such as fraud or waste being committed.

Shareholders meetings are a very critical component of corporate law and practice. Annual meetings must be held, the place is usually fixed in the bylaws (or the place is deemed to be the principal executive office of the corporation), and the time is also usually fixed in the bylaws. The chief purpose of the annual meeting is the election of directors. The power to elect directors is vested in the shareholders at the annual meeting, and the corporation cannot divest shareholders of that vital right and power. At the meetings, any other proper business may be conducted (though there may be notice requirements as to the proposed transactions).

A special meeting is any meeting other than an annual meeting. A special meeting ordinarily is called by the board, its chairperson, the president or CEO, or in most states, by shareholders holding not less than 10% of the voting shares. The purpose of a special meeting can be for any purpose, but only subjects described in the written notice of the special meeting can be acted upon. As a general rule, when the shareholders are required or permitted to take any action at a meeting, written notice of the meeting must be given to each shareholder who is entitled to vote. The notice must specify the date, place, and hour of the meeting, and if the notice is for a special meeting, the nature of the business to be conducted must also be noted. If the purpose of the meeting is to elect directors, the names of the nominees must be stated. In some states, obtaining the written consent of all the shareholders is sufficient to authorize an action, even without a meeting or notice.

For a meeting, either general or special, a quorum is necessary. A quorum is a certain majority of shares needed in order for a holder to vote (in person or by proxy). The articles or bylaws may increase or decrease the quorum requirements in some states, to no less than one third of the shares. The articles or bylaws can increase this amount, but not decrease it in most states. Once a quorum is present, a majority vote of the shareholders present binds the corporation.

A shareholder is entitled to one vote, per share, per subject. A corporation is required to keep a written record—that is, "minutes" —of the meeting. Voting at a meeting need not be done by ballot, unless a shareholder demands it before a vote or the bylaws specifically require a ballot. The record date is the day on which eligibility to vote is determined, a date characteristically set by the directors or bylaws and which is set usually 10 to 50 days before each shareholder meeting.

"Record holders" are holders of voting shares on the record date who are thus eligible to vote at the meeting. A voting list of shareholders eligible to vote at the meeting must be prepared before each shareholder meeting and must be available for inspection.

Shareholders may authorize another person, not necessarily a shareholder, to vote the shareholder's shares as well as to exercise shareholder discretion. Such an arrangement is called a "proxy." The articles cannot deny or unreasonably restrict the proxy rights of shareholders. A proxy must be written but ordinarily there is no required standard form. Usually, the duration of a proxy is eleven months from its date (and thus a new proxy would be necessary for the next meeting) unless stated otherwise. Proxies are revocable by the shareholder, even if a proxy says it is irrevocable and consideration was present. A proxy can be thus revoked by a written revocation delivered to the corporation, a subsequent proxy given by the same shareholder, by a voting in person by the same shareholder, or by the death of the shareholder once the corporation receives notice thereof. The percentage of shareholder vote required is a majority of voting shares present, thereby presuming a quorum. However, the articles or bylaws usually can increase, but not decrease, the percentage of shares required for the election of directors.

An interesting and important shareholder voting right is called "cumulative voting." Cumulative voting means that a shareholder is entitled to cast one vote for each share in the shareholder's name, and at the election for directors, the shareholder may "cumulate" his or her votes. That is, the shareholder's votes equal the number of shares multiplied by the number of directors to be elected; the shareholder can then cast all these votes for one candidate for director (or the shareholder can distribute the votes as he or she sees fit for one or more candidates). Of course, cumulative voting works only if there is plurality voting—meaning that the directors are running "at large" rather than for specific places—and the candidates receiving the highest number of votes up to the number of directors to be chosen are winners.

The purpose of cumulative voting is not to enable certain shareholders to control the board of directors; rather, the objective is to ensure some minority representation on the board. There are several standard requirements for cumulative voting, to wit: 1) the candidates' names must be placed in nomination prior to voting; 2) at least one shareholder has given advance notice prior to the meeting of his or her intent to vote cumulatively; 3) if one shareholder gives notice of intent, all shareholders may accumulate; 4) all directors to be chosen must be voted for at one time; and 5) in most states, the shareholder's right to cumulative voting must be granted by specific provision in the articles of corporation.

Other voting mechanisms for shareholders to exercise their authority (at least indirectly) are the pooling agreement and the voting trust. A "voting trust" arises when shareholders transfer legal title of shares to a trustee, who becomes the recordholder of the shares. The trustee is a fiduciary who, in the usual case, votes the shares in accordance with the terms in the trust even though the trustee can be accorded discretion in voting. The equitable ownership of the shares, and thus the right to receive dividends, remain with the shareholders, who get a voting trust certificate. The standard requirements for a valid voting trust are that it must be written and signed, irrevocable, have a usual statutory maximum period of ten years, and be for a proper purpose, such as maintaining control.

A "pooling agreement" is an agreement between two or more shareholders who agree that their shares will be voted as specifically provided for in the agreement. The result is that shares are voted in a bloc. The standard requirements for a pooling agreement are that it be written, signed, designated for a proper purpose such as to maintain control and to ensure stable management, it be used only for matters within the province of shareholders, and it be for a limited duration in most states. Pooling agreements can be enforced by a decree of specific performance.

Shareholders also can impose restrictions on the transfer of shares. As a general rule, in the absence of any specific agreement, shares of stock are freely transferable. Restrictions on the transfer of shares may be valid and may be very important, especially in a small or closely held corporation. The three most common means of restricting the transferability of shares are the option, the buy-sell agreement, and the right-of-first-refusal. An "option" can be granted to the corporation or to shareholders (usually proportionately) to purchase shares at a designated price. If the corporation or other shareholders refuse to exercise their option, the selling shareholder can then offer shares to an outsider. A "buy-sell agreement" makes it contractually mandatory for the corporation or other shareholders to buy shares. The "right-of-first-refusal" gives the corporation or other shareholders the right to meet the best price that the selling shareholder has been able to obtain from outsiders.

One of the most common forms of share transfer restrictions, typically found in a small, family, or closely held corporation, is the right of first refusal. Pursuant to this legal concept, if a shareholder wants to transfer his or her shares of the company, the company or the shareholders (or whomever is specifically is designated in the agreement) first must be given the opportunity to purchase the stock based on the terms and conditions offered by a third-party purchaser. Usually there is a time period from between 30 to 90 days to purchase the stock which period commences after receiving notice of the proposed sale. Furthermore, if the company or other shareholders are unable or unwilling to purchase the stock the selling shareholder is free to sell to the third party purchaser.

A buy-sell agreement is another legal device used to restrict the transfer of shares of stock and thus to ensure that the ownership of the shares of stock of a company remains with a small group of shareholders. Characteristically, such an agreement allows or even obligates a corporation or other parties named in the agreement to purchase at fair market value another party's stock that a party is obligated to sell when certain events occur, for example, when an employee leaves the corporation.

The reasons for these restrictions on the ordinarily free transfer of shares (which is a traditional positive attribute of a corporation) are to enable the participants in the corporation to decide who will participate, to ensure stable management, to protect against unexpected changes in the corporate ownership interests, and to maintain relative secrecy. The legal validity of such restrictions depends on whether they unreasonably restrain or prohibit the transferability of shares. For example, a total prohibition would usually be struck down, though a longer one may be upheld. In most states, the restrictions must appear in the articles or bylaws or perhaps in an agreement among the shareholders and must be for a lawful purpose, for example preventing outside investors from entering into a family owned corporate business or maintaining proportionate shareholder interests. An indispensable requirement is that the restriction must be noted conspicuously on each share, subject to the restriction. Without such notice, any restriction is unenforceable against a person who lacked prior knowledge.

One problem with all these transfer restrictions is establishing the price for the stock, especially because in small or closely held corporations there is generally no established market for the shares. Presumably in all these agreements, there is a stated price. But if there is no such stated price, the "book value" of shares or the best offer by an outsider may be used. Failing all those methods, arbitration can be utilized.

Stock options must be differentiated from stock warrants. A stock warrant is a right granted to a person for a given period of time to purchase a stated amount of stock at a stated price. The price is usually equal to the fair market value of the stock when the warrant is issued, thereby allowing the holder of the warrant to benefit from any increase in the value of the stock. The stock warrant is different from the stock option in that the latter is granted only to a company's directors, officers, and employees in connection with their services to the company, whereas the former is sold to investors.

How should one compensate employees in a start-up corporation? One effective way is to utilize stock options to attract talented, hard-working, and ambitious employees. Many people may be encouraged to join an entrepreneurial company due to the opportunity to receive equity incentives, in particular stock options. The smart entrepreneur thus can use stock options as a compensation device. Usually, a start-up company will create a group of shares pursuant to a formal stock option plan that has been approved by the board of directors and the shareholders. Then, options to purchase stock can be made from this group of shares. Typically, an entrepreneurial firm will devote about 20% of its shares for issuance to employees as stock options. The price of such stock is usually the fair market price of the stock at the time the option is granted.

Basic Corporate Finance

Dividends are certainly an important part of any corporate legal and practical analysis for the shareholders. "Dividends" are the share of corporate profits to be apportioned among the shareholders as a return on their investment. However, until dividends are declared by the corporation, the profits made by the corporation remain with the corporate entity. Once declared, that portion of the profits declared as dividends becomes the property of the shareholders. Moreover, once declared, dividends represent a debt owed by the corporation to the shareholders that can be enforced legally by the shareholders unless funds are not available to pay the dividends. Shareholders who are "shareholders of record,"—those officially on the corporate books as shareholders—are, on a specific date (the "record date"), entitled to dividends.

Dividends can be paid in cash, property, or stock. A stock dividend is the payment of stock to the shareholder from the corporation's own authorized but unissued stock. A stock "split" is not a dividend; rather, the value of the share of stock is reduced accordingly. All states have rules as to when dividends can be paid and from what corporate accounts. It is beyond the purposes of this book to examine this complex area of state law.

Certain important points must be made. First, the states are consistent in holding that if a corporation is insolvent or would likely be made insolvent, no dividends are permitted. Similarly, if the corporation cannot meet its current obligations, or would be likely, as a result of the payment of dividends, to be unable to meet its obligations, the payment of dividends is not permissible. Second, in all states, dividends can be paid from retained earnings. Third, in some states, dividends can be paid from current net earnings, meaning yearly net profits. However, in most states, dividends cannot be paid from current earnings and these prohibited dividends are at times referred to as "nimble" dividends. If the directors make an improper payment of dividends, they may be held personally liable to the corporation and its creditors for the amount. Also, shareholders who receive the dividends, knowing that they are improper, are also personally liable to the corporation and its creditors for such funds.

As to the payment, amount, and timing of a dividend declaration, state corporate statutes characteristically place a great deal of discretion in the board of directors. As a result, the directors' decision as to dividends ordinarily will not be "second-guessed" by the courts as long as the directors are acting in good faith and with the corporate welfare in mind. Consequently, as a general rule, shareholders cannot compel a corporate board to declare dividends. However, if there is a very large surplus (and not just a "mere" surplus), and the board has no definite plans to use it, the shareholders may be able to convince a court to compel the directors to declare dividends.

The capital structure of the corporation is obviously another central corporate area to examine, though any detailed explanation is more appropriate for a corporate finance text. However, certain critical definitions and salient points must be made.

First, the corporation's debt securities represent creditor interests that must ultimately be repaid. There are two main types of debt: 1) a bond which is a debt obligation secured by a lien or mortgage on corporate property, and 2) a debenture which is an unsecured corporate obligation.

Capital stock consists of 1) authorized capital, 2) common stock, and 3) preferred stock. "Authorized capital" is the total number and kind of shares that the corporation is authorized to use and which ordinarily must be stated in the articles. There is no limit on the number of shares that may be authorized, there is no requirement that all or any specific portion of the authorized shares actually be issued, and a corporation may issue fewer shares than authorized but not more unless the articles are amended. "Common stock" consists of the shares that have no preference over any other class of shares with regard to the payment of dividends or the distribution of assets upon liquidation. The corporation must have at least one class of common stock because common stock represents the residual ownership of the corporation as well as the ultimate claim to profits and assets. Ordinarily, common stock is voting stock, though it is permissible to have a non-voting class of common stock also. Shares of common stock are also known as equity securities. "Preferred stock" consists of the shares of stock that are not common. Preferred stock can be voting stock, though it usually is non-voting stock. A corporation is allowed to have a variety of preferences or priorities as to dividends and asset distribution, but these preferences must be stated in the articles.

Three corporate finance terms are fundamental: 1) par value, 2) stated capital, and 3) capital surplus. "Par value" refers to the amount designated as such by the incorporators and draftsperson of the articles. The articles generally must state the value of par for each class of shares or state that the shares are without par. Note that usually this amount is a nominal amount and not a true indication of the actual price of the shares. The "stated capital" is the par value of shares issued with par value and the entire amount of consideration received for no par shares. Stated capital represents the initial investment money placed at risk of the business by the shareholders. Of course, there is no uniform requirement that any specific amount be placed in stated capital. "Capital surplus" also represents part of the investment capital placed at risk of the business by the shareholders. Capital surplus consists of the consideration paid for par value shares in excess of par as well as that portion of the consideration received for no par shares, which is not allocated to stated capital. The distinction between stated capital and capital surplus is very important because in most jurisdictions, a corporation has greater legal latitude to issue dividends or make distributions from capital surplus.

States also have rules for the quality and amount of consideration to be paid for shares. Generally, shares are issued for consideration as determined by the board of directors. Consideration may consist of money paid, labor done, services rendered, debts or claims cancelled, or tangible or intangible property, such as good will or patent or contract rights. The judgment of directors as to the value of consideration is usually conclusive and binding absent fraud or bad faith, for example a gross estimation of services performed for the corporation resulting in "watered" stock. Note, however, that in the case of labor or service, consideration is legal payment for shares only if the labor and services are performed—future services and labor do not constitute consideration.

"Preemptive rights" are an important corporate concept. The purpose of preemptive rights is to protect shareholders' proportionate interests in the event of issuance of additional shares. Preemptive rights are defined as the right to preempt, or to purchase before others, a new issue of shares in proportion to the shareholder's present interest in the corporation. There is one significant constraint on preemptive rights: Shareholders do not have these rights in most states unless they are explicitly provided for in the articles of incorporation. Also, preemptive rights only apply to shares previously unauthorized, and not to previously authorized but unissued shares. In addition, the preemptive right can be exercised only for the same class of stock. The price for a "preemptive" purchase of a share must be fair, and thus not more than any subsequent offer to others. If a shareholder does not or cannot exercise his or her preemptive rights, the shareholder ordinarily cannot complain, even if he or she was financially unable to purchase the shares.

Fundamental Corporate Change and Corporate Termination

The final area of corporate law concerns fundamental corporate change. The major types of change to consider are as follows: 1) amending the articles of incorporation, 2) merging corporations, 3) consolidating corporations, 4) purchasing corporate assets, 5) purchasing controlling shares of stock of a corporation, and 6) dissolving and terminating corporations.

Regarding "amending the articles," the rule is that a corporation may amend its articles at any time. The amendment may include any provision that would have been lawful to have included in the original articles. The standard amendment procedure is as follows: approval by the board; approval by the shareholders generally by a majority of shareholders entitled to vote (but if any amendment would adversely affect any class or series of stock, those shareholders are entitled to vote separately, even if their shares are non-voting shares); and finally, filing with and approval by the state.

The next type of fundamental change is the "merger." However, it initially is necessary to distinguish between a merger and a consolidation. A merger is a legal combination of two or more corporations and after the merger, only one corporation continues to exist. Thus, the surviving corporation issues shares or pays consideration to the shareholders of the disappearing corporation. By contrast, a "consolidation" is the combination of two or more corporations so that each corporation ceases to exist and a new corporate entity emerges. In a merger, the surviving/absorbing corporation is recognized as a single corporation. As such, it possesses all the rights, privileges, and powers of itself as well as those of the disappearing corporation. It automatically acquires all of the disappearing corporation's property and assets without the necessity of a formal transfer, and it becomes liable for all the disappearing corporation's debts and obligations. The results of a consolidation are essentially the same as a merger. In fact, in some states, the concept of corporate consolidation has been abolished and merger law is used to, in essence, create a new entity.

All states have statutes authorizing mergers under certain conditions and federal and international antitrust may have to be taken into consideration as well. But the basic state requirements for a merger are as follows:

1. The board of directors of each corporation must approve the merger plan.
2. The shareholders of each corporation must approve the plan at a shareholder meeting. In most states, merger approval requires a two-thirds vote. In addition, each class of stock must approve the merger, including the holders of non-voting stock.
3. A merger plan is filed with the state's Secretary of State.
4. When the state merger requirements are deemed to be satisfied, the state issues a certificate of merger to the surviving corporation.

Note of a special type of merger must also be made, called either a "short form" or "parent-subsidiary" merger. Some states allow this type of merger, which is found in the Revised Model Business Corporation Act. Essentially, this type of merger has a simplified procedure when a parent corporation seeks to merge a substantially owned subsidiary corporation into the parent. This "simple" merger can be accomplished without the approval of the shareholders of either corporation—the only approval needed is the approval of the board of directors of the parent. There is one main requirement. The parent must own at least 90% (or 80% in some states) of the outstanding shares of each class of stock of the subsidiary corporation.

What if a shareholder objects to the merger? Such a shareholder possesses dissenting rights, usually called "appraisal rights." The rationale behind this legal doctrine is that a shareholder should not be forced to become an unwilling shareholder in a different corporation. Accordingly, the appraisal right is the right to dissent to certain fundamental change, such as the merger, and to be paid a fair value for the number of shares held on the date of the merger. Generally speaking, appraisal rights apply to mergers, consolidations, and the sales of substantially all corporate assets. They do not, however, apply to shareholders in a short-form merger. Once again, the states have detailed statutory procedures that must be followed exactly for a shareholder to take advantage of his or her appraisal.

In general, the mandatory steps are as follows:

1. A written notice of dissent must be filed by the shareholder prior to the vote.
2. After the merger or other applicable fundamental change is approved, the shareholder must make a written demand for payment.
3. The shareholder is then entitled to "fair value" for his or her shares based on the value on the day of the vote.
4. If the shareholder and the corporation cannot agree, a court will determine the value.

The "purchase and sale of assets" and the "purchase and sale of stock" may both rise to the level of fundamental corporate change. Regarding the purchase of assets, when a corporation acquires all or substantially all of the assets of another corporation by direct purchase, the acquiring corporation simply extends ownership control over those physical assets. Shareholder approval of the shareholders of the acquiring corporation generally is not required, however, for the corporation selling its assets, the board of directors and the shareholders must approve the sale unless the sale occurs in the ordinary course of business.

As an alternative to the purchase of corporate assets, a corporation can purchase a substantial number of voting shares of stock of another corporation.

The effect is that the purchasing corporation can then control the other corporation. In such a case, the purchasing corporation must deal directly with the shareholders in an effort to purchase their shares. Such a public offer to purchase is called a "tender offer" and, as noted, is regulated by state and federal securities laws.

Dissenting and appraisal rights exist for the shareholders of the selling corporation. As a general rule, the acquiring corporation is not liable for the obligations of the selling corporation unless there is an express or implied assumption of the selling corporation's liabilities, the sale is really a merger (a *de facto* merger), or the acquiring corporation continues the selling corporation's business and retains its same personnel.

The final fundamental change is the "dissolution and termination of the corporation." "Dissolution" is the cessation of corporate business—except for winding up—which leads to the termination and legal "death" of the artificial corporate person. "Liquidation" or "winding up" is the process by which corporate assets are converted to cash and distributed among the creditors and shareholders.

Dissolution can occur in a variety of ways, as follows:

1. Dissolution can be voluntary. Usually dissolution must be approved by the board and the shareholders or, in some states, by the written unanimous consent (or a supra majority in some states) of the shareholders.

2. Dissolution can occur involuntarily by the Secretary of State or other equivalent officer when the corporation fails to comply with the state's administrative requirements which can include failing to pay its annual taxes, failing to submit an annual report, or failing to have a registered officer or agent in the state.

3. Finally, dissolution can be effectuated judicially in three main instances: a) The Attorney General of the state or equivalent legal officer can seek a judicial dissolution of the corporation if its articles were procured by fraud, the corporation has exceeded its powers or purposes, or it violated the law. b) The shareholders can seek a judicial dissolution if they have sufficient grounds, for example when the business has been abandoned for a period of time (usually one year) or the directors are deadlocked and the shareholders cannot break the deadlock and irreparable harm is being suffered by, or is threatened to, the corporation. c) A creditor of the corporation can seek judicial dissolution if the creditor possesses an unsatisfied judgment and the corporation is insolvent.

Other grounds for judicial dissolution by shareholders are when the shareholders themselves cannot elect directors, when corporate assets are being misapplied or wasted, or when there is fraud or abuse of authority. Note in some states the "mere" fact that the business is not profitable and is not likely to be profitable or that the company is being mismanaged is insufficient shareholder grounds for dissolution. Moreover, in most states, a designated number of shareholders must join the petition for judicial dissolution (usually one-third of the shareholders), but only in a small, closely held corporation.

The standard dissolution-liquidation-termination procedures in a voluntary action are as follows:

1. The board of directors acts as a trustee for corporate assets.
2. The corporation ceases business except for purposes of winding up.
3. New business is now conducted.
4. The corporation must send a notice to each known creditor and claimant.
5. Current rights and claims are not adversely affected by the dissolution, but the board of directors must put a reasonable fund together to satisfy future claimants, who generally have a three-year period to present any claims.
6. An "articles of dissolution" is filed with the state, usually after liquidation.
7. The date the article was received and approved by the state is the official dissolution date and thereby marks the termination of the corporation.

Note that a state will not approve the dissolution if there are any pending claims or lawsuits against the corporation or if there is no provision for future liability. Shareholders are not liable beyond their initial investment in the corporation or for more than the assets distributed to the shareholder.

Constituency Statutes, Social Benefit Corporations, and Corporate Governance

Many states today now have statutes called either "constituency" or "stakeholder" statutes which permit the board of directors of the corporation to consider the interests and values of other stakeholders or constituency groups, beyond the shareholders, affected by the corporation's actions, such as the employees, suppliers and distributors, consumers and customers, the local community, and society as a whole. These statutes allow the directors to attempt to balance and align the values and interests of at times competing stakeholder groups and even permit the directors to make decisions that favor one or more stakeholder group over the shareholders, who traditionally have been the sole focal point of corporate decision-making. These state statutes vary in scope and application so naturally reference should be made to the pertinent state's corporate constituency statute. The social benefit corporation is a new form of doing business by having a traditional corporation but with an express public purpose stated in the articles of incorporation. The social benefit corporation as well as constituency statutes was discussed more fully in the Business Ethics and Corporate Social Responsibility chapter.

The term corporate governance encompasses the laws, rules, and doctrines that govern a corporation and its operations. The basic model of corporate governance entails the shareholders, the owners of the corporation, electing the board of directors, which sets long-term corporate goals and the policies and strategies to achieve those goals, as well as appointing officers to implement the policies and strategies and run the corporation on a daily basis. Corporate governance in a broader sense includes all the laws and regulations, government and internal corporate rules, that govern the corporation, as well as ethical and social responsibility doctrines that are used today to evaluate corporate activities. Corporate governance was discussed more fully in the Business Ethics and Corporate Social Responsibility chapter.

Limited Liability Company

In recent years, a majority of states in America have approved a new form of doing business. This is the new "hybrid" business entity, called a limited liability company (LLC).

In 1995, in order to promote harmony among the states' LLC laws, a Uniform Limited Liability Company Act was created by the National Conference of Commissioners on Uniform State Laws. However, to date, not all states have adopted the Uniform Act. Thus, in order to precisely ascertain one's state LLC law, one must examine the LLC statutes of that particular state. For the purposes of this chapter, the common elements of the LLC form of doing business will be examined.

There are two principal documents that pertain to the LLC. The first is its charter document. This document is typically a short document called either the articles of organization or a certificate of formation which is filed with the secretary of state. It contains basis information as to the name of the LLC, its address, its agent for service of process, its term (which can be perpetual), and whether the LLC will be a member managed one or a manager managed one (that is, in the latter case the manager is chosen by the members). The other principal LLC document is called its operating agreement, which closely resembles a partnership agreement. This agreement should be detailed, specifying, among other provisions, the LLC's ownership structure, how the LLC will be governed and managed, and how the profits and losses are to be apportioned. As with the partnership, general legal forms should be avoided in creating an operating agreement, and accordingly an attorney should be consulted to draft an agreement tailored to the needs of the LLC members.

The disadvantages of an LLC are: lack of access to capital markets since there is no stock to be offered and sold to the public; ownership interests are not freely transferable (which could be a major problem if a large number of investors is anticipated); and uncertainty due to the vague definition of an "investment security" as to whether the buying and selling of LLC interests is a securities transaction thus governed by federal and state security laws

The LLC is formed pursuant to an "articles of organization," meaning that it is an unincorporated business entity combining the most favorable attributes of a general partnership, limited partnership, and corporation. The LLC may elect to be taxed as a partnership. In some states, the LLC is allowed to have just one member-owner, and while co-owners can co-manage the business, they have limited liability. Accordingly, the foreseeable result is that many entrepreneurs who begin new businesses will choose the LLC as their legal form of conducting business.

The LLC is a "legal person," meaning that it is a separate legal entity distinct from its members. It can sue or be sued, enter into and enforce contracts, hold title to and transfer property, and be found civilly and criminally liable for violations of the law. Effectively, the LLC is a "creature" of state law. As noted, the state's LLC law predominantly is based on the Uniform Limited Liability Company Act. However, if the state's LLC statute is silent on a particular matter, the state's partnership law must be consulted.

The owners of the LLC are called "members" and, most importantly, these members are not personally liable to third parties for debts, obligations, and liabilities of the LLC (beyond their capital contribution). The members thus have limited liability. Yet, if a member agrees—either in the articles of organization or other writing, or if he or she personally guarantees the repayment of LLC obligations—then the member will naturally be held personally liable.

Certain formalities are required by statute to form an LLC. (Again, make sure to consult the relevant state's LLC statute when contemplating the LLC way of doing business.) Generally speaking, an LLC can be organized for any business purpose, as long as it is lawful. However, there are certain regulated industries, such as banking and insurance, which cannot use the LLC form. Moreover, the LLC cannot operate in certain professions, such as accounting, law, and medicine, even though these professionals can use the new LLP form. Even though it can conduct business in all states, the LLC can be organized in any state but only in one state. Note that the LLC's name must include the phrase "limited liability company" or "LLC." In addition, the LLC name cannot violate any trademarked name or be deceptively similar to other trademarked names. Finally, a name for the LLC can be reserved with the appropriate state official, for example the Secretary of State (who is not to be confused with the federal government presidential cabinet position).

Why should one operate a business as an LLC? An "S Corporation" has limits on the number of shareholders and classes of stock (only one). In a general partnership, the partners are personally and unlimitedly liable. In a limited partnership, there must be at least one general partner who is personally liable. Limited partners, moreover, are precluded from participating in management. By contrast, in an LLC, the members can participate in management.

An "articles of organization" (not one of incorporation) must be filed with the appropriate state official. An LLC may be organized by one or more persons, but if there is only one member, a sole proprietor can obtain the LLC benefit of limited liability. The existence of the LLC begins when the articles of organization are filed. (Filing is conclusive proof of LLC status.) The LLC's articles of organization must set forth the name of the LLC, its address, the name and address of its initial legal agent (usually its attorney) for services of legal notices and lawsuits, and the name and address of each organizer. In addition, the articles must include the following: whether the LLC is a term LLC, and if so, the term; whether the LLC is manager-managed, and if so, the name and address of each manager; and whether any member of the LLC is to be personally liable. The articles also may set forth provisions from the members' operating agreement and any other matters not inconsistent with the law. Finally, the articles of organization can be amended at any time by filing an "articles of amendment."

The duration of the LLC is regarded as being at will unless it is designated as a term LLC and the duration is specified in the articles. An at-will LLC, has no fixed term.

A member's capital contribution may be in the form of money, personal property, real property, other tangible and intangible property, services performed, contracts for services to be performed, promissory notes, or other agreements. The LLC's operating agreement may provide that a member's ownership interest may be evidenced by a certificate of interest in and by, the LLC.

A general partnership, limited partnership, as well as a corporation may be converted to an LLC.

A "foreign" limited liability company is a *non-domestic* (that is, not in the specific state of the organization) LLC that wants to do business in all other states. Such a foreign LLC needs a certificate of authority from the appropriate state official in order to do business in that state.

The powers of an LLC are the same powers as for an individual. Members of the LLC may enter into an operating agreement, which regulates the affairs of the company and the conduct of its business, and governs relations among its members, the LLC's manager, and the company. The LLC is liable for any loss or injury caused to anyone as a result of a wrongful act or omission by a member, manager, agent, or employee of the LLC who commits an act within the ordinary course of business of the LLC or with the authority of the LLC.

It is important to note that an LLC can be either member-managed or manager-managed. An LLC is presumed to be member-managed unless designated as a manager-managed LLC. If the LLC is member-managed, all members have agency authority to bind the LLC to contracts. In a manager-managed LLC, it is important to note, only the designated managers have the authority to bind the LLC to contracts (which, of course, are in the ordinary course of the LLC's business or that which the LLC has authorized). In a member-managed LLC, each member has equal rights in the management of the business regardless of the size of his or her capital contribution. The business of the LLC is decided by majority vote.

Note, furthermore, that members' and managers' authority to bind the LLC to contracts may be restricted in either the articles of organization or in the operating agreement. However, the restrictions do not affect the apparent authority to bind the LLC to third parties who do not have notice of the restrictions. Yet if the restrictions are in the articles of organization filed with the secretary of state or appropriate state official, then such filing will be deemed to constitute notice to the public. If the restrictions are merely in the operating agreement, then a third party must have actual notice thereof.

As to the sharing of profits and losses, the general rule is that a member has the right to an equal share in the LLC's profits. The members can amend this in the operating agreement, for example when the members' capital contributions are unequal. In regard to compensation and reimbursement, a non-manager LLC member is not entitled to remuneration for services performed to the LLC—the exception is remuneration for the winding up of the LLC. The manager of an LLC is paid compensation as specified in the employment contract with the LLC. The LLC, in addition, is obligated to reimburse members and managers for payments made on behalf of the LLC and to be indemnified for liabilities incurred in the ordinary course of business.

Pertaining to information, the LLC must give members access to the records at the LLC's principal office. A member, furthermore, has the right, on written demand, to obtain a copy of the LLC's written operating agreement.

Concerning lawsuits by a member, a member of an LLC can bring a direct lawsuit against the LLC to enforce a member's rights under the articles of organization, the operating agreement, state LLC law, and other federal, state, and local laws. For example, such a lawsuit may be used to enforce a member's right to vote, inspect books, and compel dissolution. If the LLC is harmed by a third party, a member/manager has the right to bring a lawsuit on behalf of the LLC against the offending party in order to recover damages. This type of lawsuit is called a "derivative" suit. Note that it is required that a member must have made an effort in order to secure initiation of the lawsuit by the LLC. Note also that a member, if successful, can recover reasonable expenses and attorneys' fees.

A member's ownership interest in the LLC is called a "distributionist interest," which is regarded as personal property and may be transferred. The transfer, however, does not entitle the transferee to be a member of the LLC. Rather, the transferee only receives the transferor's distribution rights.

Significantly, note that there is a limited duty of care owed to the LLC. Accordingly, a member/manager owes a duty of care *to the LLC* not to engage in: 1) known violations of the law, 2) intentional wrongful conduct, 3) reckless conduct, and 4) grossly negligent conduct which harms the LLC. It is essential to emphasize that the preceding rules indicate a limited duty of care *because liability for ordinary negligence is not included.*

The LLC is liable to third parties for injuries caused by a member/manager who is acting on LLC business (including injuries caused by ordinary negligence). A member/manager is also personally liable for injuries caused to third parties by the member/manager's own negligence. As to the duty of good faith and fair dealing, the member/manager owes to the LLC and other members such a duty in discharging responsibilities. Note, however, that there is no fiduciary owed by a non-manager member of the LLC. He or she owes no duty of loyalty and good faith, or of fair dealing, to the LLC and its other members. Rather, the non-manager member is treated as the ordinary shareholder of a corporation.

To complete the LLC examination, it is necessary to state a few rules regarding the always-perplexing area of dissolution and winding up. LLC laws typically (but not exclusively) use the term "disassociation" in place of "dissolution." The first rule is that a member of an LLC always has the *power* to disassociate from the LLC, regardless of whether the LLC is at-will or for a fixed term. However, disassociation from a term LLC before the expiration of the term is deemed to be a wrongful termination, and the member acting so will be liable for any damages caused to the LLC and its members for the wrongful disassociation.

If the LLC is at-will, then the LLC must purchase the disassociating member's distributionist interest. Recall that in the at-will situation, the member has both the *power and the right* to disassociate. As to the amount of the disassociating member's distributionist interest, it is either fixed in the agreement or set forth by the court (with "fair market value" as the standard).

Note that there are some interesting rules regarding notice of disassociation in LLC law. First, for two years after a member disassociates from an LLC, he or she possesses the apparent authority to bind the LLC to contracts in the ordinary course of business. Exceptions arise, however, if the third parties knew previously of the disassociation or were given notice of the disassociation. Furthermore, the LLC can give constructive notice of a member's disassociation with the Secretary of State or appropriate state official. The name of the disassociated member must be included. This notice is effective against any person who deals with the disassociated member, regardless of whether the third party was actually aware of the notice.

The dissolution of an LLC can be effected by: 1) an event specified in the agreement; 2) the consent of the percentage specified in the agreement; 3) the LLC's activity becoming illegal; 4) a court if it becomes impracticable to carry on the business of the LLC or if the economic purpose of the LLC is likely to be unreasonably frustrated; and 5) the Secretary of State, or appropriate state official, for failure to pay taxes and fees or to file an annual report.

At the expiration of the LLC's term, some members may want to continue the LLC. They can do so if: 1) there is a unanimous vote to continue for a specified term, and an amendment to the articles is filed; and 2) there is a majority vote to continue the LLC as an at-will LLC. If the LLC is not continued, it is wound up. "Winding up" is the process of preserving and selling assets of the LLC and distributing the money to creditors and members. Any member other than a wrongfully disassociating member can participate in the winding up of the LLC's business, and the winding-up member can maintain the LLC's business for a reasonable time. The LLC's assets are first applied to paying off creditors and thereafter to members in equal shares unless the operating agreement provides otherwise. After dissolution and winding up, the LLC can terminate its existence by filing an "articles of termination" with the Secretary of State.

Franchise

"Franchising" is a method of continuing a certain business that has existed for many years. However, the growth of the franchising method of doing business in recent years has been dramatic. The use of the franchise format has become pervasive throughout the United States as well as in the global economy. Concomitantly, the franchise way of doing business has become subject to a wide array of laws: international, U.S., federal, state, and local. This discussion will address some of the major aspects of the franchise way of doing business, but will focus on one important legal aspect of the franchise business relationship:

the covenant of good faith and fair dealing pursuant to the law of the United States.

There are many ways for a manufacturer, seller, or supplier to convey its products and services into the marketplace. One principal method of distribution is by means of the legally recognized business relationship of a franchise, the first critical term to define and explicate. While there are various common law and statute definitions—both federal and state—generally speaking, a "franchise" is a method of conducting business that combines the advantages of a recognized, proved, centralized, and unique way of doing business with the capital, initiative, ambition, and "hands-on" management provided by a local and independent business entrepreneur, with the goal of leveraging that businessperson's success far beyond his or her typically limited resource potential. The franchise owner is a legally independent entity, but is economically dependent on the franchisor and is in fact an integral unit of the franchisor's business system.

The benefit to the franchisee is that the franchisor's business system is characteristically already a proved way of doing business, encompassing the provision of uniform products and services, advertising, and computer and reservation systems. Furthermore, the franchisor is available to provide continuing assistance, guidance, and training to the franchisee. Of course, the franchisor usually obtains an initial fee as well as a percentage of the franchisee's gross profits for sales and a percentage for advertising fees for granting to the franchisee the right to use the franchisor's name in the selling of products and services. The consumer also benefits because the consumer can obtain uniform products and services at numerous distribution points. The franchise, therefore, is a very appealing way of doing business, because a businessperson with a small amount of capital can become a true entrepreneur. In addition, the pride of owning one's own business surely will motivate the franchisee to make the business successful.

The key issue is to ascertain when a business relationship rises to the level of a franchise, thus triggering special legal rights and responsibilities regarding the covenant of good faith and fair dealing. The critical franchise factor is the commonality of the economic situations and legal rights the parties have to contend with in their business. Even so, the immediate, as well as foremost, difficulty confronting both franchisees and franchise law analysts regarding the good faith covenant is how the federal and state franchise statutes define the term "franchise" in different ways.

As already mentioned, the term "franchise" is defined by a variety of state laws, some of which require the registration of franchise offerings and/or disclosure to prospective franchises. Other states may not require registration or disclosure, but they do nonetheless regulate the relationship between the franchisor and franchisee. Each state's individual definition does contain certain common definitional components to the term "franchise," to wit: some type of association by the holder of the franchise, the franchisee, with the franchisor's trademarks and service marks; the payment of a fee or consideration for the right to use the franchisor's trademarks and service marks—the franchisee fee; the right to sell goods or services as well as providing for a system for marketing and doing business; the position of the franchisee as an integral component in the franchisor's distribution system; the providing of material assistance by the franchisor to the franchisee in opening, marketing, and managing the business and, concomitantly, a significant degree of control exercised by the franchisor over the franchise business; and, finally, a "community of interest" between the franchisor and franchisee.

At times, the requirement of a "community of interest" is used to describe the relationship between the franchisor and franchisee. Differences in the various states' definitions of key terms—such as "franchise," "good faith," "fair dealing," and also commercial reasonableness—naturally can be crucial in determining whether legal redress is available in a particular case.

Franchise also is defined at the federal level, notably by a Federal Trade Commission Rule, similar to the state definitions. The Federal Trade Commission deems a business arrangement to be a "franchise" if among other factors, the arrangement is a continuing commercial relationship for the right to operate a business pursuant to the franchisor's trade name or to sell the seller's branded goods, the franchisor provides significant assistance to the buyer, and the franchisor can exercise significant control over the buyer's business operations. A business relationship rises to the level of a "franchise," therefore, if it satisfies one of the many legal definitions of the term.

The essence of a franchise is the franchise agreement between the franchisor and franchisee, which means that the franchise relationship is contractual in nature. Each franchise industry, business, and relationship has its own distinct contract, of course, but there are certain common and fundamental provisions that must be addressed.

First, there will always be a provision dealing with the franchisee's payment for the franchise. An initial fee is typically required, usually a lump sum for the franchise license and for the privilege of being part of the franchisor's business system. Moreover, the franchisee will be obligated to pay a certain percentage of weekly, monthly, or annual gross sales to the franchisor for the continuing right to remain a franchisee, as well as another smaller percentage for advertising costs.

412 THE LEGAL ENVIRONMENT OF GLOBAL BUSINESS

Another very important provision in the agreement will be the location of the franchise, which the franchisor must approve. The location will be the franchisee's territory, and it should be an exclusive area that only the designated franchisee can serve. The agreement will also specify the type of premises for the business, whether the premises are to be constructed, purchased, or leased, the kinds of equipment and furnishings (and who supplies them), and the specific standards for the premises.

The agreement will grant the franchisor the right to inspect the premises in order for the franchisor to maintain quality standards and to protect the franchisor's name and reputation. Furthermore, the agreement will specify the form of the business for the franchise—meaning if it is owned by a partnership or a LLC or under some other structure—as well as the capital structure of the business.

There will be provisions in the agreement for standards of operation, for example sales requirements, quality standards, computer software, recordkeeping, as well as standards for the hiring, training, and supervision of personnel. Usually, the franchisor will require the franchisee to purchase certain types of equipment or supplies, but not exclusively from the franchisor as there may be antitrust problems. Typically, the franchisor will give the franchisee a choice of approved suppliers, including perhaps the franchisor itself. Similarly, due to antitrust concerns, the franchisor cannot contractually set the price by which goods are to be sold or services are to be performed. Rather, the franchisor can "suggest" the retail prices of goods or services.

The duration of the franchise is usually set forth in the franchise agreement. The time period is characteristically a relatively short one (from one to three years) so that the parties can ascertain whether they want to continue doing business together. In addition, in the typical franchisee agreement there will be "for cause" termination provision, which specifies certain circumstances, such as death or disability, insolvency, failure to meet sales quotas or to maintain standards, and breach of the franchise agreement, which will operate to end the franchise, presuming some reasonable notice period is given.

One final and important point relating to the agreement must be made, and that is that the franchisee agreement is almost always drafted by the franchisor, the party with superior bargaining power. Naturally, this means the agreement will contain provisions that are favorable to the franchisor. Of course, if either party breaches the agreement, the aggrieved party can sue for breach of the franchise contract, receiving contract damages such as the loss of income, profits, and salaries.

One of the main statutory protections afforded to the franchisee stems from a Federal Trade Commission rule that requires the franchisor to provide sufficient accurate information to a prospective franchisee so that he or she can make an informed business decision. This information includes an "Earnings Claim Document," which enumerates the requirements for the franchisor's claims about existing profits or projected sales income.

Another important document, called a "Basic Disclosure Document," is mandated. This document includes information regarding the business experience, financial picture and history, and backgrounds of the franchisor and its principals. The document also must describe the business of the franchise, the initial funds required to be paid by the franchisee, recurring payments, any personal participation required by the franchisee, site selection, training programs, and a sample franchise agreement. The document must have information concerning the establishment of the franchise and its renewal, cancellation, or termination.

In addition to this federal statute, there also are, in some U.S. states, franchisee protection statutes which, for example, may prohibit the franchisor from making any misrepresentations in the initial sale of the franchise and also which may require the franchisor to terminate the franchisee only for certain specified grounds and/or in "good faith." Otherwise, absent any statutory protection, the main source of redress for the franchisee is the old common law implied covenant of good faith and fair dealing.

The common law covenant of good faith and fair dealing[52] which is implied in contracts, including franchise agreements, has been defined by the courts in a variety of ways. The covenant means that the parties honestly and reasonably carry out their contractual obligations. The covenant implies a reasonableness standard to contract obligations, meaning that neither party to the agreement shall do anything which will have the effect of destroying or injuring the right of the other party to receive the fruits of the contract.

The Restatement (Second) of Contracts maintains that every contract imposes on each party a duty of good faith and fair dealing in its performance and enforcement. The Restatement notes that the phrase "good faith" is used in a variety of contexts, and its meaning varies somewhat according to the context. Nonetheless, the Restatement equates "good faith" enforcement or performance of a contract to faithfulness to an agreed-upon common purpose and consistency with the justified expectations of the other party. The Restatement further defines "good faith" duty by elaborating what is prohibited under a contract: a variety of types of conduct characterized as involving "bad faith" because they

---

[52] For a detailed explanation of the covenant in a franchise business context, see Cavico, F.J. (2006).

violate the community standards of decency, fairness, or reasonableness. The Restatement also identifies several instances of conduct that generally would constitute a violation of the duty of good faith such as: evading the spirit of the bargain; lack of diligence and slacking off; willful rendering of imperfect performance; abuse of power to specify terms; and interference with or failure to cooperate in the other party's performance. Finally, the Restatement notes that a party's conduct can contravene the good faith obligation even if the party believes the conduct to be justified, and also points out that fair dealing may require more than honesty.

The Uniform Commercial Code provides a statutory definition of "good faith" in the case of a merchant: honesty in fact and the observance of reasonable commercial standards of fair dealing. Accordingly, in examining the law, one can discern that the implied covenant of good faith and fair dealing contains both a subjective and objective element: subjective good faith and objective fair dealing and commercial reasonableness. These legal standards are certainly applicable to the franchise relationship and will provide the parties, especially the franchisee—who is typically the weaker party—a degree of protection from abuse and overreaching that is above and beyond statutory law.

For example, even if the franchisee agreement does not specify an exclusive territory for the franchisee, the covenant of good faith and fair dealing may preclude the franchisor from granting additional franchises or from operating itself in an area served by the franchisee. Another illustration would be if the franchisor seeks to terminate a franchise or not renew a specific franchise when the franchisee has spent a considerable amount of time, effort, and money to open or to develop the business. While the franchisor is aware of such expenditures, even if the franchisor has the technical legal right to terminate or to not renew, the covenant of good faith may prevent the franchisor from so acting.

Global Legal Perspectives

Although joint ventures are a very efficacious way for a company to do business overseas, the global manager always must be aware of superseding nationalistic and geopolitical concerns. For example, in 2006, the Russian government announced that it will restrict foreign energy companies to the role of "junior partners" in most of that country's oil and gas fields, thereby keeping the most valuable reserves for growing Russian companies. While a government spokesperson stated that the country is still "open to" and "eager for" foreign investment and the formation of joint ventures, including the development of natural resources, a new Russian law prohibits foreign companies from owning more than 49% of companies that are seeking to develop the rights to certain deposits which the government deems to be "strategic."

International Franchising Laws [53]

Franchising laws exist in many countries and, very generally speaking, are patterned after the equivalent laws of the United States. These laws deal with three major areas: pre-transaction disclosures, franchise registration, and regulation of the business relationship between the franchisor and franchisee, especially in the area of termination. Although it is clearly beyond the scope of this book to examine in detail franchise law on a global basis, the basic franchise laws of a few selected international jurisdictions will be mentioned.

Australia has a franchising Code of Conduct which is included in that nation's Trade Practices Act. The Code requires the preparation and delivery of a disclosure document to the franchisee together with a copy of the Code itself. The law also specifies a "cooling-off" period, includes a provision to provide notice and an opportunity to "cure" breaches in the franchise agreement prior to termination, as well as a statutory mediation procedure to resolve disputes.

China has a Regulation of Commercial Franchises statute that requires pre-sale disclosure to the franchisee and which also mandates that the franchisor make any other disclosures required by the franchisee. The Chinese franchise law also requires that the franchisor register its trademarks pursuant to that country's Trademark Law. Significantly, the Chinese law imposes a duty of good faith, fair dealing, honesty, and credibility on the parties to the franchise relationship. The franchisor also has an obligation to warrant the quality of goods furnished by its designated suppliers as well as a duty to conduct advertising and promotional activities. Interestingly, the Chinese law requires the franchisor to have at least two company-owned franchisees in China for more than one year.

Indonesia has a franchise law called the Provisions and Procedure for the Implementation of Franchised Business Regulation, which also requires pre-contractual disclosure. Other interesting provisions under the Indonesian law mandate that the franchise agreement must not only be in writing but also in the Indonesian language, and must be subject to Indonesian law. Furthermore, in Indonesia, franchisors as well as franchisees must give priority to the maximum use of domestically produced goods and materials (presuming they meet quality standards) as well as to small- and medium-sized businesses.

---

[53] See Mills, Pamela J., and Morris, Duane (2005).

In Italy, franchise law is found in the Rules on the Regulation of Franchising. Italian franchise law does not require registration, but does impose a duty of loyalty, fairness, and good faith on both the franchisor and franchisee. One interesting provision in the Italian law is a requirement that prior to instituting a franchise network, the franchisor must have tested its business concept in the market.

Korea has a very detailed, and significantly titled, franchise statute, called the Act on Fairness in Franchising Transactions, which requires a pre-sale disclosure in accordance with the Act and also which subjects both parties to an obligation of good faith. Furthermore, the Act imposes several material obligations on the franchisor, to wit: notice requirements for non-renewal; notice as well as "cure" requirements for breaches of the agreement; formulation of a business for a successful franchise; continual development and enhancement of sales methods and product and service quality; installation of facilities and the provision of products and services to the franchisee at reasonable prices; education and training of the franchisee and its employees; continual furnishing of support and advice to the franchisee; avoiding encroachment in the franchisee's business region; and using the best efforts to resolve disputes through communication and negotiation.

Russia has a franchise law that requires franchise agreements to be in writing and to be registered by a government agency. Notable franchisor obligations under the Russian law are to provide continual technical and consulting assistance, including training and advance training, to the franchisee and its employees, as well as to supervise the quality of goods, work, and services. Price-fixing and certain "exclusive" practices are prohibited. Furthermore, franchisees who have complied with the franchise agreement are granted the right to renew again on the same terms. An interesting provision in the Russian law deals with a franchisor who does not renew but then enters into a new franchisee agreement for the same territory within a three-year period. In such a case, the franchisor will be required to give the prior franchisee the right to obtain the new franchisee or to pay certain compensation.

Therefore, even a brief comparative summary as attempted herein clearly reveals the scope and complexity of international franchise law. But making international franchising truly challenging for the global entrepreneur and manager is the need to always be cognizant of not only a different legal environment but also a different cultural environment. Thus, the astute businessperson will seek to tailor his or her business format and operations to be in conformity with local cultural and moral norms and customs.

Israel: New Corporate Law[54]

In 2000, Israel adopted a new corporate law called the Companies Law, which covers many of the fundamental aspects of corporate law. The law is based on English common law principles and is also very heavily influenced by U.S. corporate legal doctrines. As in the U.S. law, Israel's law unequivocally states that an Israeli company is a separate legal entity distinct from its owners, the shareholders, and thus the shareholders only have limited liability. For the first time, the law also codifies what previously had been judicial-made law regarding promoters, derivative actions, and the "piercing the corporate veil" doctrine. Undercapitalization of a company now will be grounds to disregard the corporate entity, but only if there is an unreasonable risk of undercapitalization. Also, the new law simplified the rules for incorporating a business in Israel. The law constituted the Israel Securities Authority (ISA), which is the equivalent of the U.S. Securities and Exchange Commission, as an independent regulatory body whose function is to protect the affairs of the security-investing public.

The Companies Law assumes the existence of a free and fair marketplace and thus only interferes with the market when there is perceived to be a specific market failure. However, because many Israeli companies have highly concentrated ownership, the Companies Law has stricter rules to protect minority shareholders versus those in the United States.

Moreover, the law frequently uses such terms as "good faith," "accepted way," and "fairness" and contains more rule-oriented standards than U.S. law. However, the exact application of these terms to particular disputes is left to the Minister of Justice to decide. For example, the Companies Law requires that a shareholder is obligated to act in good faith in a way that is acceptable to the company and its fellow shareholders as well as to not abuse his or her powers. Shareholders who hold decisive positions or who are control holders are also now held to a fairness standard in relationship to their dealings with their company and fellow shareholders. Shareholders who are control-holders also must avoid any conflicts-of-interests. One interesting provision of the new law is that now the bylaws of a corporation can be altered by a simple majority of the company's shareholders.

Another important provision is the prohibition of a board member acting as the CEO of the company, which had been a common practice in Israel prior to the passing of the new law.

---

[54] See Ben-Zion, Yael, T. (2006).

One final noteworthy provision of the new Israeli corporate law is that they now must have independent "outside" directors, who are to be appointed by the shareholders at a general meeting with special rules. Furthermore, the outside directors must possess professional qualifications, and at least one outside director must have financial and accounting expertise.

Management Strategies

Business Organizations—Choosing the Right Form of Doing Business

What type of business form should the entrepreneur choose—a corporation, S corporation, partnership, or limited liability company (LLC)? Usually, the entrepreneur will choose the LLC because the LLC provides the limited liability protection of the corporation as well as the favorable tax treatment of the partnership. The S corporation does have the preceding advantages too, but it has other limitations as pointed out that the LLC does not have, such as the restriction on the number of shareholders in the LLC and the preclusion of corporations as shareholders. If the entrepreneur expects the business to be a widely and publicly held one, then the traditional corporation is the logical choice. Yet many entrepreneurs are "small" business men and woman who do not anticipate an initial need to sell shares of stock to the public to raise capital, and who thus do not want to undergo the expense and effort of forming and operating a traditional corporation, and thus they logically choose the LLC. In the entrepreneur intends to distribute business earnings presently, then with the LLC the earnings can be distributed without incurring a second level of taxation. Distribution of corporate earnings to the company's employees is a tax deductible expense, but distribution of earnings to shareholders are taxed as corporate income first and then taxed again as dividend income to the shareholders. Of course, the gain on the sale of stock held for more than one year is taxed at the more favorable capital gains rate. Since most small businesses distribute earnings on a current basis, the LLC is preferable. Also, if the entrepreneur expects there to be initial business losses, then again the LLC is preferable because the LLC enables its owners to deduct these losses from their personal income. The main consideration in choosing a business form to do business will be the extent to which the entrepreneur's personal assets will be protected from the obligations and liabilities of the business. Other factors typically will be the type of tax treatment for the business, particularly avoiding double taxation as well as converting ordinary income into lower long-term capital gains, the attractiveness of the entity to potential investors and lenders, the potential for attractive incentives for employees, and the costs and effort to start, form, and maintain the business.

Starting a Business in the United States

Starting a business can at times be stressful, time-consuming, and/or a joyful experience when one has the right information and the cooperation of expert colleagues. This chapter has provided a comprehensive coverage of various forms of a business that one might initiate. And while this information provides the foundation of various entities, one must also seek the assistance of professional experts, consultants, and attorneys to successfully move forward in starting a business as the rules and policies of various localities within the United States and countries abroad might vary drastically.

For example, with the right information and the help of an expert, one can easily start a business in the state of Florida by going to the Florida Department of State website (http://www.dos.state.fl.us) and filing the online form for a Limited Liability Company. Once the state registration forms are completed, then one also needs to go to the government website (www.irs.gov) to receive an Employer Identification Number (EIN). The EIN is very similar to a person's Social Security Number (SSN) in the United States.[55]

By filing the forms electronically through the websites, information regarding more assistance is also available. For example, in 2006, for questions about a Limited Liability Company, one could call the suggested telephone number (850-245-6051) to get information from a "live" person. For information regarding an EIN, one could call government officials at the Internal Revenue Service (IRS), United States Department of Treasury (telephone: 800-829-4933 or 800-829-1040) to get more information from "live" operators and experts on this process.

Seeking the help and guidance of a local expert before starting a business is a very important strategy for aspiring managers and entrepreneurs. For example, if a business is being initiated in the South Florida region, then it is important to seek advice from someone who knows the state and local laws of Florida. The consultant or attorney and his/her organization should personally handle your business affairs and legal interests or direct you to an expert who can. He or she should dedicate the time and attention to your specific legal and business needs. For a consultant and attorney, seek the help of someone who is an expert and current in his/her field and who is committed to the success of his or her own firm and organization as well as yours.

An LLC usually will best match the purposes of a small business, and one will be able to get the LLC electronically registered and the EIN secured within a one-hour period. While filling out the electronic forms usually will not take too long, knowing the right information and putting the right names as owners

---

[55] Contributed by Stephen C. Muffler, Nova Southeastern University.

and principals of the new company can be time-consuming. Also, filling out the forms in the right manner with the right names is a very important point. This is where the expert can recommend strategies that will prevent possible challenges and "headaches" from occurring in the future. Utilizing the advice and guidance of a local expert is thus a very beneficial strategy for initiating the start of a small organization in the state of Florida or, for that matter, anywhere.

While there are many strategies that global managers and entrepreneurs must be aware of when initiating and conducting business in today's complex work environment, seeking the advice and guidance of a local legal expert is one of the most important. The authors recommend that aspiring managers and entrepreneurs should: 1) initially understand the nature of their business and industry; 2) clarify their mission and vision for the company; 3) decide which form of a business organization might best fulfill the needs of the company; 4) get the assistance of a local legal expert about the laws and business organizations; and finally 5) get started and initiate the business.

Partnership—Advantages v. Disadvantages

One major advantage to the partnership way of doing business is that the partnership pays no income taxes. It is not considered an entity for tax-paying (as opposed to tax-reporting) purposes. Accordingly, in a partnership the partnership's income or losses "flow through" to each individual partner and thus are reported on the partner's individual tax return. There is, moreover, more flexibility in a partnership, as opposed to a corporation, when it comes to allocating income and losses. For example, in a partnership where on partner contributes services and the other capital, the tax losses generated from the expenditure of the capital contributed by the "cash partner" can be allocated to that partner.

A disadvantage of a partnership is the tax treatment of foreigners (that is, persons who are not citizens or permanent residents of the United States). Investing in a partnership usually would equate to a foreigner being engaged in a trade or business in the U.S., thereby allowing the U.S. to tax the foreign partner's income generated from the partnership. A foreigner partner would also have to file a tax return. However, with a corporate investment in stock or bonds, a foreigner usually would not pay any income tax on the income from a U.S. corporation which the foreigner invests.

Partnership Agreement

Assuming business people are contemplating doing business as a partnership, it is strongly advised that the prospective partners consult with an attorney and have drafted a detailed and specific partnership agreement. As noted, in the absence of an agreement, state partnership law in form of the Uniform Partnership Act (UPA) will govern the relations of the parties, and perhaps not in ways that some of the partners intended. To illustrate, the UPA requires partners to share profits and losses equally regardless of the partners' individual initial capital contributions. The partner contributing a larger capital contribution may want and expect a larger share of the profits. If so, it is incumbent on this partner to have an appropriate partnership provision so as to supersede the UPA sharing equally rule. Another example deals with the paying of salaries to partners. Again, in the absence of an agreement the UPA controls; and the UPA provides no salaries for partners regardless of the time and effort a partner may spend in managing, and making successful, the business. As such, the prospective managing partner should insist on a salary provision in the partnership agreement so as to override the UPA. Of course, drafting a detailed and specific partnership agreement will make the partnership way of doing business more difficult and expensive to form, but nonetheless the formulation of a partnership agreement is essential to regulating the relation of the partners to one another and thus the smooth functioning of the partnership. Finally, there are standard partnership legal forms that one can purchase, and such forms can give the prospective partners an idea as to the provisions they may want, but since a partnership is typically a unique type of business relationship as well as a very personal one, an attorney should be consulted to draft an agreement unique to the incipient partnership.

Business Ownership Structure[56]

The entrepreneur should consider both potential liability and income tax consequences when contemplating a corporate structure for either a new venture or the acquisition of an existing organization. To address liability concerns in today's litigious environment, the entrepreneur should choose a C-corporation, Sub-S Corporation, or a Limited Liability Company. These organizational structures practically eliminate personal liability except in cases of fraud, income tax withholding, tax liability, and hazardous waste liability. Although certain types of partnerships limit the liability of certain partners if all the rules are followed, protection of one's individual assets is still the primary concern.

Before deciding on which organizational structure to choose, one should first consult an attorney. However, as noted, the structure of choice in today's legal environment is the LLC. In the U.S., as long as the state where the LLC is registered treats the LLC like a Sub-S Corporation for tax purposes, then the property valuation benefits ("basis") of the LLC outweigh the benefits of the other two corporate structures.

---

[56] Contributed by Thomas M. Tworoger, Nova Southeastern University.

The property valuation benefits of the LLC become significant if property owned by the LLC is transferred to an entity with the same ownership. The basis or cost that the land was originally purchased for remains the same for the new entity without triggering a "phantom income" gain from an increase in the fair market value of the property. For example, assume one's LLC purchased a building for $500,000 in 2006 and decided to transfer it to another entity with the same ownership in 2016. In 2016, the building may have appreciated and now have a fair market value of $1,500,000. If one transferred the property from the LLC, then one will have maintained the original basis. But if one transferred it from a Sub-S or C-corporation, then one would have a "phantom gain" of $1,000,000. Consequently, there would be income tax on that gain even though no actual money changed hands.

The main difference between Sub-S corporations and C-corporations is the treatment of income tax. Sub-S corporations cannot exceed 75 shareholders and shareholders cannot be non-resident aliens. Besides the "corporate veil" limiting liability, the Sub-S Corporation taxes the shareholders only once. Income and losses, as well as depreciation, flow through the Sub-S directly to the shareholder(s).

In a C-corporation, the shareholder is taxed twice. The corporation pays income tax, and when it declares a dividend, the shareholder must pay taxes on that dividend. Even in cases where dividends are not consistent, the primary shareholder(s) may draw a salary from the corporation, but this salary is subject to income taxes.

Once again, the benefits of an LLC seem to far outweigh the benefits of all of the other corporate structures.

After ascertaining the best way to conduct business, hiring the right employees is a critical aspect of a manager's responsibility, especially for foreign assignments. Hiring employees for international assignments can be a time-consuming task as it requires matching the right persons with the job and the culture. The cost of unsuccessful expatriate employees can be as high as a million dollars for some posts, so managers must make sure that the staff going abroad is ready and prepared to successfully complete its jobs. Furthermore, the family and spouses of expatriate employees must also be a very important part of the equation or decision-making process as the number one reason for most expatriate failures seems to be the spouse's inability to effectively adjust to the new culture.

Global managers and entrepreneurs, regardless of what strategies they choose to use to recruit and prepare employees for international assignments, must recognize that foreign operations have become a very important aspect of an organization's success. Firms operating in disparate market environments must quickly learn that there is no "one-size-fits-all" strategy or a single approach that will work in all or even most regions. Consequently, a high level of attention needs to be given to selecting the right form of business organization to do business, and then to recruiting, hiring, developing, and preparing staff for assignments, especially those overseas.

Summary

Establishing a business can be complex and cumbersome. First and foremost, opening a business requires an understanding of the national and local laws. As discussed in this chapter, entrepreneurs that wish to establish a business must become aware of the laws that apply to each type of business prior to deciding whether to have a sole proprietorship, a partnership, a corporation, a limited liability company, or a joint venture with another national or international organization.

This chapter outlined some of the information that business owners, academic scholars, and entrepreneurs need to know about the various types of business organizations in the United States. The chapter also outlined some of the risks and benefits associated with each type of organization so that the entrepreneur can better decide which format best fits his/her purpose for the business. For example, any person who does business individually, without utilizing any of the other forms of business organization, is conducting business as a sole proprietorship. The sole proprietorship is the most basic form of business organization as the owner of the business is in essence *the* business. The advantages and disadvantages of this way of doing business, as well as those of the other forms of doing business, were examined in this chapter.

Finally, the chapter closed with a global legal perspective as well as presented certain strategies that will be beneficial for global managers and entrepreneurs.

SIXTEEN

REAL PROPERTY LAW AND
LANDLORD-TENANT LAW

Real property law is of extreme importance in today's society as land (and its possession) has been a significant issue since the beginning of history. This chapter will elaborate on fundamental concepts that relate to and affect real estate property law, such as: types and transfer of property, legalities associated with property ownership, and real estate mortgages. Additionally, U.S. property law will be compared with the laws of other countries to demonstrate how laws can impact businesses and individuals in a global real estate context. This chapter also examines landlord and tenant law in the United States.

Real Property Law in the United States

Introduction, Definition, and Nature of Property

Ownership of property and the rights to property are very important and firmly held beliefs in Western civilization law, history, and society, especially in the Anglo-American tradition. Property law in the U.S. is based on the old English common law, and contemporary property law is still predominantly common law, though now there are many statutes that regulate the ownership, transfer, and use of property.

"Property" can be defined generally as anything that can be owned, possessed, used, or disposed of. The two basic types of property are real property, which is not movable, and personal property, which is movable. There is also the concept of a "fixture," which is a piece of personal property that has become so firmly attached to real property that it is considered part of the real property. This chapter examines the nature of property, paying particular attention to real property, and also discusses how ownership rights to property are transferred. Furthermore, property law in the U.S. is contrasted with property law in other countries and other legal systems.

Real v. Personal Property

"Real property" consists of land: the actual soil and attachments to land such as fences, trees, crops, minerals, and waters. (There are certain specialized property rules for trees and perennial crops as well as for rivers and streams, but their explication is beyond the purposes of this book.)

A "fixture" is personal property that has become attached to the land, thereby becoming part of the real estate. There are some basic rules to determine if a piece of personal property has become a fixture. The first and foremost question is how securely attached is it to the property? If the personal property is so securely attached that it cannot be removed without damaging the real property to which it is attached, then it likely will be regarded as a fixture. A secondary question is what was the intention of the person attaching the personal property? If the personal property is merely loosely attached, and the person installing the property has expressed his or her intention clearly, that intention ordinarily will control. However, if the personal property cannot be removed without damaging the property, it will be regarded as a fixture regardless of intention. The final question to ask is who installed the personal property? If the owner of the real property installed it to the real property, that is evidence that it is a fixture. Yet, if a tenant installed the personal property, that fact is evidence that it should remain as personal property. However, the first rule is controlling, meaning that if the tenant so firmly secures the personal property to the real property, it will be regarded as a fixture, which means it passes to the landlord at the termination of the tenancy, and without any compensation to the tenant.

Personal property is any property or property right that cannot be classified as real property. There are two types of personal property: 1) tangible, which is personal property that can be seen, touched, and possessed, such as products or goods; and 2) intangible, which is property whose ownership is manifested in some type of document or writing, for example a contract or stock certificate, patents and copyrights, as well as commercial paper, such as a promissory note, trade draft, or check. While all of the aforementioned types of personal property have been or will be discussed in this book, an explication of commercial paper law is beyond the purposes of this work.

Real property is divided into two major classifications: 1) the fee simple, and 2) the life estate. The "fee simple" or "fee simple estate" is the largest and most complete ownership right that an individual can possess in real estate under U.S. law. Fee simple status gives the owner the right to the surface of the land, the subsoil beneath, and air space above, subject, of course, to certain government regulations. The "life estate" is an estate in which the owner owns the land (and structures and attachments thereto) only for the owner's lifetime, and at the death of the present owner, the title to the land passes as directed by the original owner. A life estate with a "reversion" means the title to the property passes back to the original owner whereas a life estate with a "remainder" means the title does not pass back to the original owner; it "remains" away and passes to some third party. Reversions and remainders are called "future interests."

There are several ways of acquiring ownership to property. Property can be purchased: The buyer pays the seller and the seller conveys title to the property to the buyer. Property can be received by means of a Will and Testament, whereby the owner transfers the property at his or her death by means of a legally recognizable testamentary document. If a person dies "intestate," meaning without a will, the owner's heirs will receive title to the property by means of descent, as a matter of law, and pursuant to a state's laws of descent. Property can also be given as a gift, which is transfer of the property by the owner to another person without any consideration being paid or given. "Accession" is a means of acquiring property by an addition or increase in property already owned, for example the produce of land or the young of animals. "Accretion" occurs when the boundary to property is a river, stream, lake, or ocean, and the land is increased by the shifting flow of the water or the depositing of silt or sand on the bank. "Confusion" is the mixing of goods by different owners so that the parts belonging to each owner cannot be identified and separated. In such a case, if the confusion is willful, title to the entire mass passes to the innocent party, unless the person causing the confusion can clearly prove who exactly owns what. "Adverse possession" is a method of acquiring title to real property by occupying for a period of time fixed by statute, usually 21 years. The occupancy, however, must be continuous, open, visible, exclusive, and "hostile" (that is, asserting ownership of the property). Property ownership can also be premised on creation, such as in cases of inventing or authoring when title to such creations can be made secure through patent and copyright law.

Finally, ownership rights to personal property can be obtained to abandoned, lost, or mislaid property. If property is abandoned, the person who discovers and takes possession of it acquires title thereto. Property is considered abandoned when the owner has actually discarded the property and without any intention of reclaiming it. If property is lost, the finder thereof has the right to possession against everyone but the true owner. Property is lost when the owner, through carelessness or accident, unintentionally and involuntarily leaves the property somewhere, but there is no intention of the owner to part with the title to the property. Typically, there are statutes regarding the finding of lost property and statutory notice and posting procedures. If followed, these statutes will enable the finder to obtain title to the property.

Property is designated as "mislaid" if it is intentionally and voluntarily left in some place by the owner and then forgotten. Again, there are state statutory procedures that deal with converting the possession of mislaid property to title ownership, but most states, if the original owner cannot be found, will grant title to the owner of the "locus in quo," that is, the owner of the place where the property was first mislaid.

Real property can also be owned concurrently, meaning that two or more people can own the property at the same time as co-owners. There are three types of concurrent ownership of property: 1) the tenancy by the entirety, 2) the joint tenancy, and 3) the tenancy in common.

A "tenancy by the entirety" is a method by which married couples can own property.

There are two important features to a "joint tenancy." First is the right of survivorship, which means that when one spouse dies, his or her interest in the property automatically vests in the surviving spouse. Moreover, a spouse cannot unilaterally transfer his or her interest in the tenancy in the entirety without the consent of the other spouse. The married couple must be explicitly and specifically designated as husband and wife in the instrument creating the joint tenancy. Furthermore, a joint tenancy is a form of ownership whereby two or more people who are not married can own property with a similar right of survivorship. Such a right of survivorship will inure to the benefit of the surviving joint tenant, even superseding the other joint tenant's Will and Testament. However, a joint tenant can unilaterally transfer his or her interest without the consent of the other joint tenant, which thus ends the joint tenancy. It is important to note that for the law to recognize a joint tenancy ownership of property, the intention of the parties to create the joint tenancy must be very clear, for example by stating the parties own the property not merely "jointly," or even as "joint tenants," but rather as "joint tenants and not as tenants in common."

Finally, a "tenancy in common" is a way of co-owning property, but with no right of survivorship. The interest of a deceased co-tenant passes according to his or her Will and Testament or a state's laws of intestacy, and the tenancy in common is not destroyed. In addition, a tenant in common can transfer his or her interest without the consent of the other party and also without destroying the tenancy in common.

Transfer of Real Property

The usual method of transferring title to real estate is by means of a sale, in which there are two key components: 1) the contract of sale, and 2) the delivery of the deed. When the deed is executed, that is, delivered, by the *donor*, title vests in the recipient of the gift, the *donee*. Even when title to real property is conveyed as a gift, there must be a deed.

A *deed* is a written legal instrument signed by the seller of property conveying title to the buyer of the real property. The seller is known as the grantor and the buyer is known as the grantee. There are two main types of deeds: 1) quitclaim deeds, and 2) warranty deeds.

In a "quitclaim deed," the grantor gives up any claim which he or she may have to the real property. The grantor neither makes any warranties that the title is good nor even that the grantor has a title claim. The grantor conveys only the interest that the grantor has and no more. Note that in the typical real estate transaction in the United States, a quitclaim deed is not used because the contract specifies a warranty deed.

A "warranty deed" not only conveys the grantor's interest in the real property, but also makes certain warranties or guarantees. There are two types of warranty deeds. The first is a general warranty deed wherein the grantor warrants the following: 1) the grantor has good title to the property; 2) the grantee will have quiet and peaceful possession free from all claims; 3) the grantor will defend the grantee against all claims against the property; 4) all prior grantors had good title; and 5) there are no defects of any prior grantor's title.

The second type of warranty deed is the special warranty deed, wherein the grantor warrants that the grantor has the right to sell the property. The grantor does not warrant the genuineness of any prior grantor's title. In the United States, this type of deed ordinarily is used by executors and personal administrators of estates, trustees, and sheriffs at foreclosure sales. As such, these only warrant that they have the legal right to sell whatever interest the owner of the property has.

A deed possesses certain fundamental characteristics. The parties to the deed are the *grantor* and the *grantee* and they both must be named in the deed. If the grantor is married, the grantor's name and his or her spouse should be named in the deed. If the grantor is unmarried, the deed should indicate such status by using the words "single" or "single person."

Consideration is the amount paid by the grantee to the grantor for the real property. A statement of consideration must be made in the deed although the amount specified need not be the actual price paid for the property.

The covenants in a deed usually refer to promises made by the grantee. Covenants can be affirmative, whereby the grantee promises to do something, such as maintaining a driveway used in common with an adjoining property. Likewise, covenants can be negative, whereby the grantee promises not to do something, for example not using the property for business purposes or not constructing a certain type or size of dwelling.

The description in a deed naturally refers to the description of the property to be conveyed. The property must be correctly described: Any description that identifies the property is sufficient. Typically, the description in a deed is the description by which the present owner acquired title to the property.

The deed requires a signature, specifically the signature of the grantor. If the grantor is married, the spouse also should sign.

Finally, a deed contains an acknowledgment. That means that the deed must be formally acknowledged before a notary public, whereby the grantor acknowledges the instrument as a deed. Typically, states in the U.S. also require that there be two witnesses to the signing of a deed.

Delivery of the deed is an essential requirement to the transfer of title to a real property. The rule of law in the U.S. is that a deed is not effective until it is delivered. "Delivery" from a technical legal standpoint means the grantor gives up possession and control of the deed. Consequently, if the grantor maintains control of the deed or reserves the right to demand its return before the deed is delivered to the grantee, there is no legal delivery. For example, the grantor leaving the deed with his or her own attorney is not a delivery—because the attorney is the agent for the grantor—until the grantor's attorney delivers the deed to the grantee.

Title to the property is complete and vested in the grantee upon delivery. The deed need not be recorded in order to effectuate a title transfer. However, a deed *should* most certainly be recorded. All states in the U.S. have recording statutes, the purposes of which are to establish clarity and certainty to property ownership and to prevent fraud. Copies of deeds or other instruments pertaining to real property can be recorded in government offices, where they become part of the public record. Fees are of course required, but the fees are well worth it because recording gives notice "to the world" that a particular person owns a particular piece of property. Furthermore, recording allows the deed to be used as evidence in court without further proof of its authenticity. Recording also protects the grantee against a second sale of the property by the grantor.

As noted, the grantor in a warranty deed has an obligation to transfer good title. Yet one way for the grantee to ensure that he or she has obtained good title is to purchase title insurance from an insurance company. Then, if there is any loss to the insured grantee caused by undiscovered defects in the title, the grantee will be reimbursed by the insurance company. An abstract of title is usually a component of the title insurance process. The abstract shows the complete history of the real estate, encompassing prior deeds, mortgages, taxes, judgments, and liens, both paid and unpaid.

Real Estate Mortgages

A mortgage is a lien given on real property to secure a debt. The mortgage is not the debt itself, but only the security for the debt. The land, as well as any interest in the land, or improvements thereon, may be mortgaged.

The *mortgagor* is the person who gives the mortgage as security for the loan of money, and the *mortgagee* is the person or business that holds the mortgage as security for the debt. The mortgagor has possession of the property. If the debt is defaulted, the mortgagee takes possession of the property or sells the property at a foreclosure sale.

The mortgage contract is a written instrument, generally in the same form as a deed. It usually is given to raise money for the purchase price of real estate, but one can borrow money for any reason and secure the loan by means of a mortgage. The mortgage lien attaches to the real property described in the mortgage.

A mortgage should not be confused with a "security interest," which is a creditor's or seller's lien on personal property, which is governed extensively by the Uniform Commercial Code. Security interests, as well as other liens on personal property such as artisan's liens, are beyond the scope of this book.

The mortgagor has certain obligations and duties by virtue of granting a mortgage. The mortgagor's first duty is to make all payments of interest and principal when due. The failure to pay either is a default, which gives the mortgagee the right to foreclose on the property. Typically, in a mortgage there will be an acceleration clause which states that if any payment of interest or principal is not made when due, the entire principal automatically becomes due immediately. Conversely, if the mortgagor wishes to pay off the mortgage debt before it is due, thereby saving interest, he or she must have expressly reserved that right at the time the mortgage was given. Otherwise, the mortgagor can still pay off the debt, but must also pay the full interest amount.

A second fundamental obligation of the mortgagor is to pay all taxes, assessments, and insurance premiums on the property. If the mortgagor does not pay them, the mortgagee can pay them, and then seek reimbursement from the mortgagor. Moreover, if the mortgage contract requires the mortgagor to pay, the failure to pay is regarded as a default. As a general rule, the mortgagor does not have to keep the property insured for the benefit of the mortgagee, but the mortgage contract can impose a duty to insure on the part of the mortgagor. The mortgagee can also insure the property.

The third duty of the mortgagor is to not perform any act that materially impairs the security of the mortgage, such as tearing down a structure. Any acts that are deemed to be a "waste" of assets give the mortgagee the right to foreclose.

The mortgagor has certain rights, however. The first and foremost is possession of the property. Of course, upon default, the mortgagee takes possession. Second, if there are any rents or profits that accrue from the property, they belong to the mortgagor. Next, when the mortgagor has made final payment, he or she has the right to have the mortgage lien cancelled. The final right is the mortgagor's right to redemption.

After default and foreclosure, the mortgagor has the right to redeem the property by paying the amount of the mortgage plus all costs. As noted, if the mortgagor fails to pay the mortgage debt when due, there is a default and fore-closure and, consequently, the mortgagee can force a sale of the mortgaged prop-erty. The proceeds from such a sale go first to pay any taxes, then the costs of the foreclosure, next to pay off any mechanic's liens (that is, claims by workers who have performed work on a home or building or who have furnished materials for construction or renovation), and finally the mortgagee is paid. If the proceeds from the sale are greater than the aforementioned debts, the surplus belongs to the mortgagor. But if the proceeds are insufficient, the mortgagee can obtain a judgment against the mortgagor for the remaining balance due.

Finally, if one is contemplating buying mortgaged property, he or she must know the very important distinction between "assuming a mortgage" and buying property "subject to a mortgage." In the former case, the buyer becomes primar-ily liable for the payment: The buyer is liable on the mortgage as fully as the original mortgagor. However, if a buyer takes property "subject to a mortgage," the buyer is not personally liable for the mortgage debt, which still exists on the property. In either case, the original mortgagor is still liable.

Government Regulation of Real Property and Eminent Domain

In the United States, even though the ownership of property is a very impor-tant, indeed sacred right, government can control the use of property. For example, state and local governments, pursuant to their sovereign "police power"—that is, the power to make laws to benefit the health, welfare, and safety of their citizens—enact zoning regulations. Zoning laws are the main type of land use regulation in the United States. Although an explication of zoning laws is beyond the purpose of this type of book, the major purpose of zoning law is to designate certain types of permissible uses for property within a county, municipality, or zoning district. Typical "uses" are residen-tial, commercial, light industrial, heavy industrial, or mixed use. If an owner of a property seeks to use property for a use that is not allowed, he or she must seek a "variance," that is, an exemption, from a government authority, usually a local zoning commission. The owner ordinarily must demonstrate undue hardship if the variance is not granted.

Even more significant than regulation, and as pointed out in the Constitutional Law chapter, government at all U.S. levels—federal, state, and local—possesses the power to seize and to take private property for "public" use or purpose. But the Constitution also requires that government pay the owner of the property "just" compensation for the property. As stressed in that chapter, what exactly constitutes a "public" purpose as well as what is "just" compensation are ongoing and very controversial and contentious issues: legally, morally, and practically.

Land Use Permitting and Entitlements[57]

The key to successful investment in and development of real property is the ability to obtain the requisite permits for development as well as the optimization of the entitlements for the property. The following are the common definitions for the terms "permitting" and "entitlements":

1. Permitting—official government sanction to perform a regulated activity.
2. Entitlement—a right to benefits specified by law, or as some developers view it, a limitation on the use of the land or its improvement.

Multi-jurisdictional Levels. Permits and entitlements typically must be obtained at a number of different levels of government. For example, there are federal permitting requirements, state permitting and growth management regulations, and local and regional authorities to deal with. Each level can prevent a project from going forward. In addition, not all reviewing agencies share the same perspective on approval criteria, thereby resulting in a disjointed and nonlinear process.

Local Government Process. Today, in many jurisdictions where there is any market activity occurring, the result is negative impact on areas such as transportation, emergency services, and school issues. In response to these negative impacts, state and local authorities often create comprehensive growth management plans. These are intended to be primary, long-range, growth management tools to plan for future development in an orderly fashion and to respond to anticipated changing conditions. They usually include both maps and text.

Key elements of the plan include general land use categories as well as goals and objectives. Land development codes and regulations, which are detailed regulations designed for implementing the Comprehensive Plan, typically establish zoning, setbacks, and buffers, among other things. They also typically define approval and administrative processes. Among these are:

- *Zoning (Right-to-Use),* which specify use, density, intensity, height, setbacks, and mid-range issues consistent with the Comprehensive Plan.
- *Planned Development Approvals,* which initially offer a more flexible zoning technique, but usually require another post-approval process to tie down the details. Typical elements include an approved master concept plan and approved resolution by the governing authority.
- *Subdivision/Plat Approvals* set out the requirements for dividing land, as well as for impact fees, exactions, and other government requirements.
- *Development Orders and Engineering Approvals* are the final plans that detail

---

[57] Contributed by John Wayne Falbey, Nova Southeastern University.

civil engineering or related requirements. These are necessary in order to construct horizontal improvements on the property.

- *Temporary Use Permits* govern uses on the property, such as sales or event tents or trailers. (One must plan ahead and consider these for major events held on the property.)
- *Special Exceptions* are intended to govern situations excluded from a specific zoning code or regulation.
- *Zoning Variances,* on the other hand, govern items specifically covered by a regulation. However, they are allowed to vary from the code if a certain approval process is followed.
- *Administrative Variances* differ from special exceptions and variances in that they are approved by administrative staff without a public hearing or legislative body approval.
- *Building Permits* are the official documents or certification that authorizes construction, alteration, enlargement, or the like of a building or structure on the property.
- *Dock and Shoreline Permits* often must be obtained in order to construct structures in or adjacent to water bodies or along shorelines.
- *Vegetation Removal Permits* are required prior to any cutting, trimming, removal, or other impact on vegetation.
- *Consumption on Premises* is governmental permission to consume alcohol on certain premises, such as clubhouses, restaurants, and other uses of the property wherein alcoholic beverages are to be served.

State Environmental Resource Permit Process. Moving up a notch from the local governmental level, the property owner encounters the land use regulations promulgated by the state. These may include:

- *State Wetland Resource Permit Process,* which sets forth areas designated as wetlands.
- *Environmental Resource Permit (ERP),* which regulates both environmental and surface water management. These may exist in two or more varieties, including: 1) Standard General ERPs, which are designed for predetermined impact and are usually easier to obtain due to their standardized nature; 2) Individual ERPs, which are unique and require specialized evaluation.
- *Consumptive Water Use Permit (CUP)* provides official allowance for consumption of water from the aquifers beneath the property's surface.
- *Individual De-Watering Permits* are required in order to remove surface water or groundwater prior to construction in certain areas.
- *Works of the District* are permits that apply to government construction.

- *Sovereign Submerged Lands Authorizations* set out the requirements to be met prior to building upon government-owned submerged lands.
- *Coastal Construction Control Line Permits (CCCL)* usually are required to perform construction along coastlines.
- *Endangered Species Take Permits* apply to habitats of species determined to be endangered by federal law.

State Development of Regional Impact Process. States that have been experiencing rapid growth that previously outstripped the government's ability to control the impacts of development on the lands within its jurisdiction have developed special bodies of regulations to deal with large-scale developments. In Florida, for example, these are known as DRIs (Development Regional Impact statements), while in California they are referred to as CEQA (Comprehensive Environmental Quality Assessment statements). Their purpose is to establish thresholds for larger projects in order to review, in advance of development, what the impacts of these projects will be on the environment and quality of life in the area that will be impacted. (Generally, they relate project scale to population levels of the jurisdiction.) These governmental reviews identify regional issues that impact more than one jurisdiction, for example two or more counties. These issues usually relate to transportation, environment, and affordable housing.

Community Development Districts. These are the creations of state statutes. While they may not exist in every state, generally their purpose is to enable the creation of a special governmental geographic district to finance infrastructure and similar improvements. Generally, the process works as follows:

- *Petition to Create District*—includes identification of geographic boundaries.
- *Assessment Methodology*—to determine how funds raised for development will be repaid, by whom, and in what amounts.
- *Engineer's Report*—an independent engineer's finding that improvements are justified, necessary, and benefit the land.
- A *Preliminary Offering Statement* is prepared and approved.
- *Adoption of Final Assessment* that is to be placed on the land to be improved is approved. This may allow the owner-developer to pass on costs to end-users (i.e., home buyers). This often is critical to the viability of many master-planned communities.
- Bonds are validated.
- The *Issuance of Bonds* is authorized.
- The *Construction Management Agreement* is entered into between the governing authority of the district and the developer.

Federal Permitting. The third major level of land use permitting involves the federal government. Federal regulations apply uniformly in every state.

Oftentimes, the role of a number of federal agencies is that of a commenting agency versus a permitting agency.

Federal requirements frequently are more onerous than those of the primary agency. Among the principal regulations are: 1) Federal Wetland Jurisdictional Determination, which involves a complex review of wetlands areas on the property. Upland areas also are included in the review, although the review is not as complex; 2) Dredge and Fill Permits are required for excavation activities on the property.

Post-Permit Compliance. The owner's or developer's efforts are completed with the issuance of the requisite permits, however, steps must be taken to ensure permit conditions are continuing to be met. This is an often overlooked step as plans must be made to assign permit conditions to another entity, the developer will maintain significant liability. A commonly accepted way of doing this is to assign permit conditions to a continuing entity, such as a homeowners' association or the community development district.

Construction, Mitigation, and Monitoring. The permitting process typically consists of additional steps beyond the planning and pre-construction stages. For example, the following activities often are required:

- *Invasive/Exotic Plant Removal* is a frequent and often expensive step.
- *Environmental Monitoring Guidelines* require careful adherence. Documentation is required at the turnover of the project to the client.
- *Tree Protection* regulations require that clear direction be given to the land-clearing crew, otherwise, the developer or property owner may face consequences such as fines and/or loss of permits.
- *Surface Water Management System* regulations require that both functionality and aesthetics must be considered.
- *Conservation Easements* are often required or offered by the developer or owner as a bargaining chip in the permitting process. Typically, the developer maintains ownership of the land while meeting environmental regulations. The remaining rights may be used to provide amenities to end users.
- *Mitigation Banks* enable the developer to restore off-site areas in exchange for clearing and filling onsite environmental areas impacted by the development activities.

Tactical and Strategic Entitlement Considerations. The owner or developer of real property is not totally adrift in this seeming miasma of onerous, confusing, and often conflicting regulatory schemes. Rather, certain tactical and strategic moves should be considered depending on the nature of the development situation. For example, *tactical* ploys might include any or all of the following:

- Good design components may convince local governments to allow higher density or intensity of use. However, basic changes to allowances for "density" (the number of dwelling units on the site) and "intensity" (the degree of commercial usage on the site) need to be carefully evaluated to determine the overall effects. For example, increased density may trigger certain impacts or exactions because of increased road or school usage.

- On the other hand, careful integration of uses, such as incorporating a public access park in the development, often reduces the impact of exactions.
- Development agreements allow complex terms to maximize benefits to a development.

Strategic Entitlement Considerations might include:

- Planning for large areas, known generally as "sector planning," may be required to make changes for small areas. This occurs when several large-property owners band together to do long-range, overall planning for their combined properties.
- *Specific Plans* are local government plans that might eliminate problems and open up long-range opportunities.
- *Transfer of development rights (TDR)* from one area (the sending area) to another (the receiving area) can increase the density allowances on the receiving area, thereby increasing its value and lowering per unit acquisition and development costs.
- *Smart Growth Initiatives* often are regional in nature and address complex issues such as integrating land uses, transportation systems, and environmental systems into a single comprehensive plan. The objective is to solve regional problems and thus improve the quality of life.
- *Safe Harbor Agreements* are long-range environmental permitting strategies critical for long-range projects dealing with issues such as endangered species that move around on large properties.
- *Habitat Conservation Plans* usually plan for the survival of endangered species and protect a property owner from incremental problems. Examples in the United States include those for the: 1) Fringe-toed lizard (Southwest desert); 2) Red-cockaded woodpecker (East); and 3) Gnatcatcher (West).

Land use permitting and entitlement, therefore, emerge as absolutely critical components to the successful investment in, and development of, real property.

Landlord-Tenant Law[58]

If one does not own the real property but rather occupies it, then most likely one has a tenancy, which thereby has created a leasehold interest. Tenancies come in various forms and often are represented by a written contract known as a lease.

---

[58] This material contributed by Stephen Muffler, Attorney at Law, Nova Southeastern University

This part of the chapter thus will address the following subject matters: types of tenancies; the obligations and covenants between the tenant, also known as the lessee, as well as the landlord, also known as lessor; and the remedies if there is a breach of the lease agreement. Keep in mind that, like all other contracts, the necessary elements identified in the Contracts chapter must exist for a promise to become a lease. If the term of the contract is to be a year or longer, then the Statute of Frauds will require the lease to be in writing.

Types of Tenancies

A *term tenancy*, also referred to as a tenancy-for-years, is an interest in land which a tenant has exclusive rights to the land for a certain time period, which is often for a year or more. These are fixed duration leases; and once they have expired, by operation of law, they become periodic tenancies unless the parties expressly renew them for another defined term. While most residential term leases are for one year, commercial leases can vary in length from a few months to ninety-nine year leases. Most commercial leases range from two to five years, with options to renew and extend the lease for a longer term should the tenant desire to continue a successful business at that particular location. The longer the term of the lease, the more likely that it will contain rental escalation clauses, which provide for a formula to raise the rental so that the lease payments keep pace with inflation, and over-and-above any rental increases the parties contemplate over the term of the lease. Term leases can expire naturally upon completion of the term; and also may terminate early by agreement of the parties; or terminate through a court action. Leases, moreover, can be terminated due to the destruction of the real property or by merger into the freehold estate if the tenant ultimately becomes the owner of the real property, either through a written option to purchase provision within the lease, or if the tenant exercises a written right of first refusal found within the written lease to match a third party's offer to buy the real property.

A *periodic tenancy* is one that continues from a period-to-period. Often this time frame is one month; and unless one of the parties gives proper notice, the period resets after its expiration and continues automatically for another like period of time. This situation could last for many years if the parties continue their landlord/tenant relationship and both voluntarily allow the periodic term to continue. Most state laws require prior notice to the other party should one of the parties to a periodic tenancy wish to end the relationship and tenancy. Depending on the state, the required minimum time period to deliver the termination notice to the other party may be equal to one full term or half of the lease term. It is not unusual for these periodic tenancies to not have a written lease since they are, by their very terms, less than one year in length. However, it is recommended that all periodic tenancies be represented by a written lease so that all parties clearly understand their rights and obligations in regard to the leasehold interest. Periodic tenancies allow the flexibility to both parties to end their contractual relationship at the end of each term, but they do not guarantee any long term tenancy between the parties, for better or worse. Commercial leases tend not to be periodic tenancies since businesses must have stable, predictable, leasehold "duration terms" to build-up and continue a successful commercial venture at the site.

If a lease interest is not a term or periodic tenancy, then it most likely will be considered a *tenancy-at-will*. Tenancy-at-will is a leasehold interest that is terminable at the option of either party for any reason whatsoever. A common state legislative effort to clarify this area of law and distinguish among the types of tenancies is represented by Florida Statute Section 83.01 which provides:

> *Any lease of lands and tenements, or either, made shall be deemed and held to be a tenancy at will unless it shall be in writing signed by the lessor. Such tenancy shall be from year to year, or quarter to quarter, or month to month, or week to week, to be determined by the periods at which the rent is payable. If the rent is payable weekly, then the tenancy shall be from week to week; if payable monthly, then from month to month; if payable quarterly, then from quarter to quarter; if payable yearly, then from year to year.*
>
> Copyright © State of Florida. Reprinted by permission.

A tenancy-at-will is, by its very nature, at the whim of the parties who can cancel the tenancy at any time for, for any reason, or no reason.

Finally, the last type of tenancy is called *tenancy-at-sufferance*. Technically, it is more of a "hold over" of an occupant of property under a lease that has expired without the permission of the landlord. At common law, this type of tenancy was created by operation of law by the continued holding over of a tenant, whose initial possession was lawful but has since expired. A tenancy-at-sufferance, unlike the other aforementioned tenancies, provides no rights to the occupier as a tenant and no estate interest in the land. Consequently, there is a "thin-line" between a trespasser and a tenant-at-sufferance. The former is unlawfully on the property without the permission or consent of the owner, while the latter is a hold-over tenant who once had rights under a valid tenancy, but those rights have now expired and lapsed, leaving the occupier susceptible to immediate removal through proper court process.

Obligations and Covenants between the Parties

Regardless of the type of tenancy, there are some common rights and responsibilities by and between the parties. If there is a written lease, then the terms and conditions of that written agreement will dictate the parties' relationship. Common covenants that are found in all leasehold interests can be classified as landlord duties and tenant duties.

Landlords have duties to deliver the leasehold premises to the tenant, free from other occupants. A landlord also has the obligation to make sure that the premises has no code violations and the walls, roof and concrete slab are in good repair. Further, the landlord in a residential lease warrants that the premises is "habitable," even if the lease does not specifically require the landlord to make repairs. *"Habitability"* is an implied warranty that arises by operation of law in residential leases and generally cannot be waived by the tenant; and accordingly any provision within a residential lease that attempts to do so is often held void or unenforceable as a violation of public policy. Another closely aligned warranty that landlords must provide to tenants is called the *covenant of quiet enjoyment*. Quiet enjoyment is a tenant's right to the undisturbed use and enjoyment of real property without unreasonable disturbance by hostile claimants or neighboring tenants. Finally, landlords are held responsible for unreasonably dangerous conditions, physical or otherwise, on the property or in the common areas of the premises pursuant to a specific negligence theory called "premises liability." What constitutes a breach of habitability, quiet enjoyment, and/or premises liability is often a factual matter, decided on a case-by-case basis by a jury. Generally, many state statutes allow for the landlord to shift the responsibility of some landlord duties upon a commercial tenant, so long as such a shifting of duties will not be a violation of public policy. Conversely, courts often void the shifting of these landlord duties upon a residential tenant's shoulders as such a burden shifting is *per se* (that is, automatically) a violation of public policy. Should the property be sold, then the new owner often "stands-in-the-shoes" of the prior landlord, and as such is under the duty to perform under the lease's terms and the aforementioned obligations.

Tenants likewise owe duties to landlords under a leasehold relationship. The most obvious is to pay the rental. In a residential lease, often this payment is structured on a month-to-month basis due at the beginning of each month. In a commercial lease, this payment may be classified as a "triple net lease," which means the tenant will pay, in addition to rent, some or all of the real property expenses, which can include its pro-rata share of real estate taxes, insurance on the real property, special assessments, and common area expenses shared by other tenants in a multi-use commercial center, and insurance on the real property. A "gross lease" rental rate arises when a commercial tenant is charged on lump-sum per square foot of the premises, which includes all the afore-mentioned related expenses. Sometimes, commercial leases define the rental on a percentage of profits earned by the tenant over a period of time, such as a month or year, and such leases also allow the landlord to audit the tenant's business records to accurately determine the rental payments due under such lease payment provisions. In both commercial and residential leases, often landlords require prepayment of last month's rental and also a security deposit. It is not unusual for commercial leases to require the principal owners and/or officers of the tenant's business entity to personally guarantee the performance under the lease. That is to say, if the tenant's business entity fails to pay rental, or otherwise fails to perform under the lease, the landlord has the ability to sue the personal guarantors for damages which are caused by the tenant's breach of the lease. Tenants also are under a duty not to commit "waste" to the premises, which means they will not physically damage the real property, normal wear-and-tear excepted. Tenants may assign or sublease the premises or property, unless the written lease prevents such actions.

Remedies for Breach of Lease

If one of the parties fails to perform the duties and/or obligations under a lease, then a breach has occurred; and that breach generally relieves the other party from performing under the agreement. Landlord and tenant law is very state-specific, which means each state has a set of statutes that control and govern the parties' relationships and provides for remedies in case of a breach. Often these state statutes require notice of a breach be provided to a party as well as an opportunity to cure said breach prior to the lease being terminated or vesting a party with a legal cause of action. Similarly, it is typical that written leases have detailed notice provisions which require the non-breaching party to notice the breaching party of the breach, prior to exercising a right to terminate and/or seek other remedies.

If a tenant breaches the lease, these statutes or contractual provisions often allow the landlord to seize security deposits, accelerate and recover the remaining rental due under the lease for the remaining balance of the term, terminate the leasehold, evict the tenant from the premises, and also seek re-letting costs and expenses, including real estate commissions incurred in securing a replacement tenant for the premises. One principle common in almost all states is the landlord's inability to use "self-help" evictions, which is a term that describes a landlord taking matters into "their own hands" and physically changing the locks or preventing the tenant from access to the premises or physically removing the tenant from the premises, extra-judicially. Failure of a landlord to seek remedies via the court system and to abstain from using "self-help" can result in a costly separate tort action by the tenant against the landlord, even if the tenant breached the lease first and should have and could have been dispossessed from the premises. Finally, often written leases have indemnification provisions, which require the tenant to reimburse the landlord for any losses suffered by the landlord due directly to the tenant's actions or inactions at the premises.

Tenants are also afforded a number of remedies should the landlord breach the lease. These include withholding of rental, directing rental to pay for expenses to cure a physical defect in the premises, interpleading the rental into the court registry for the judge to decide the proper ownership of the funds in light of a landlord's breach, lease termination, and/or seeking consequential damages. Consequential damages are money damages which flow naturally from the landlord's breach of lease and can include costs of moving the business to a suitable replacement location or loss of business due to the landlord's breach. If a landlord wrongfully evicts a tenant through "self-help," many courts will issue an injunction against the landlord from interfering with the tenant's continued business at the premises, or a court could grant punitive damages payable to the tenant by the landlord to punish the landlord's improper and unacceptable anti-social behavior. In commercial tenancies, sometimes a tenant specifically negotiates a provision within a retail center that exclusively allows that tenant the ability to furnish services or goods to the public from the premises, precluding any other competing tenants in the common shopping center or commercial complex. If such a provision exists, and a landlord breaches this provision by allowing a competing tenant to commence business transactions at the common shopping center or commercial complex, then the tenant may sue the landlord for monetary damages and loss of business. These "use exclusivity" provisions in commercial leases awarded to tenants do not violate anti-trust laws since they cover only the specific shopping center or commercial complex owned by the landlord, so competing businesses can still rent locations outside the property lines on a contiguous parcel of land.

Global Legal Perspectives

Acquiring Real Property in Mexico[59]

The Mexican Constitution prohibits foreigners from owning property in Mexico within 100 kilometers (about 62 miles) of a border or within 50 kilometers (about 31 miles) of a coastline. This prohibited area is known as the "Restricted Zone," and although it is quite large (encompassing over 40% of the total land area in Mexico), foreigners can own property *outside* of this area. However, even within the Restricted Zone, there are different rules regarding the purchase of residential property as compared with non-residential property.

---

[59] See Boreale, Michael (Summer 2005).

For residential property within the Restricted Zone, foreigners must enter into a trust agreement, known as a *fideicomiso*, with a Mexican bank in order to acquire the property. By means of this trust arrangement, a foreign buyer can obtain beneficiary rights to the property and its unrestricted use for a 50-year period. The foreign buyer pays the Mexican seller for these rights to the property while a bank serves as the trustee and as legal titleholder to the property. There are, of course, fees attached to having a Mexican "partner" as trustee. Approval is required as well as a permit from the Mexican Ministry of Foreign Affairs. This arrangement emerges as a "shortcut" to the Constitutional prohibition against foreign property ownership.

The procedure for obtaining non-residential property, however, is more "streamlined." Non-residential property includes property used for, among other uses, commercial, industrial, and agricultural purposes as well as for the providing of services. Foreigners can own such property within the Restricted Zone if foreign purchasers abide by an agreement known as the Calvo Clause, which treats foreigners as Mexican nationals in regard to the property, but only if foreigners abjure from invoking the protections of their home governments regarding the property. The acquisition of such property must be reported to the Ministry of Foreign Affairs, but the purchase does not require express government approval. The rationale for this legal distinction regarding property ownership is the desire by the Mexican government to promote investment in Mexico.

This Mexican legal device of the *fidelcomisco* means that foreigners can obtain the beneficiary rights of ownership to property in Mexico. However, legal title is held by a trustee, which typically is a Mexican bank. For most people, the trust operates as a standard type of family trust, but after the 50-year duration period, it must be renewed. Corporations, however, do not need to work through a trust in order to acquire property. Corporations can buy property outright, provided that it is used for business purposes.

Property Laws in Nigeria[60]

Real property law in Nigeria has undergone a very interesting transition from the ancient customary law to the time of the Land Use Act of 1978, which is a federal statute incorporated into the Nigerian Constitution. Traditionally, Nigerians believed that real property in Nigeria belonged to God, yet land could be held communally in a community-based tenure system administered and managed by village chiefs, headsmen, and elders. Through time, an informal property registry and recording office were created. Property disputes between families were mediated and, if necessary, arbitrated at the village level, with

---

[60] See Boudreaux, Karol C. (2005).

adjudications being rendered by chiefs of different tribes if necessary. Under this customary system, the first person to clear and use unclaimed land established possession and use rights. That first possessor would then distribute the land to family members based on need. Women, however, were not allowed to own property or inherit property, but did have certain rights to possession and use if they lived with their husband's family.

A person who possessed land was required to use it to benefit the family or community group. If he did, then he could keep the property, pass it on to his heirs, pledge it as collateral for the satisfaction of a debt, and exclude strangers from the land. However, generally, people could not sell or mortgage property in Nigeria.

In 1978, however, the customary system of land ownership came to an abrupt end as the result of the Land Use Act, which vested ownership of all land in Nigeria to the government, which is to hold the land in trust and administer its use for the common benefit of the people. Yet even though the government holds title to the property, the government does allow the long-term leasing of property. Furthermore, all land administration functions, such as sale, lease, or inheritance, were taken by the 1978 law from the village chiefs and local communities and thereby granted to government administrative agencies which operate under the office of the state governors. All previous forms of title—official and customary—have been replaced by "certificates of occupancy" issued by the government officials. These government officials, furthermore, have the power to revoke customary land rights if the land is needed for a public purpose.

Acquiring Real Property in Turkey[61]

Since the Turkish Republic was created in 1923, three constitutions have been enacted: 1) the 1924 Constitution, 2) the 1961 Constitution, and 3) the 1982 Constitution, which is currently in place. This section analyzes the rights of foreigners to acquire real property in Turkey under each constitution.

The 1924 Constitution did not provide for foreign investors and foreign individuals, whose nationality is not Turkish, to own or buy property in Turkey. In fact, Article 70 of the 1924 Constitution explicitly stated that only Turkish citizens had the right to own property within Turkish borders.

The 1961 Constitution, however, lifted the prohibition preventing foreigners and legal aliens residing in Turkey from purchasing real property, thereby affecting a shift in favor of foreign investment. This shift notwithstanding, there were still numerous limitations faced by non-Turkish nationals when purchas-

---

[61] Contributed by Cuneyt Oskal, Nova Southeastern University.

ing real property in Turkey. These restrictions were later removed in July, 2003, when Article 35 of the Title Deed Law was amended by way of Law No. 4916.

The 1982 Constitution, albeit replacing the 1961 Constitution, retained many of the laws originally enacted in the 1961 Constitution, and its modifications and improvements were minor. Of importance, the 1982 Constitution provides the same flexibility to international investors with respect to the purchase of real property in Turkey.

However, in March of 2005, there were some setbacks with respect to the purchase of real property by non-Turkish nationals when the Constitutional Court repealed the provision of Law No. 4916. The repeal ensued as a result of the growing fears that selling Turkey's lands was tantamount to selling Turkey to foreigners.

Law No. 4916 originally stated that individuals of non-Turkish nationality could purchase property in Turkey as long as it was used solely for residential or business purposes, the property was within the boundaries of specified areas, the purchaser complied with certain legal restrictions, the foreign purchaser's country allowed Turkish nationals to purchase property in his or her country (this is referred to as the principle of "reciprocity"), and the total area of the land purchased did not exceed 2.5 hectares (or 25,000 m2). It should be noted that provided that a foreign person is granted approval from the Council of Ministers, he or she may purchase an area of land exceeding the statutory limit. By December of 2005, Parliament's General Assembly passed Law No. 5444, which re-enacted Article 35. However, it imposed new limitations that were not present under Law No. 4916.

When Law No. 5444 was promulgated, the additional limitations imposed were as follows:

1. Under the principle of reciprocity, reciprocity has to be both *de facto* and *de jure*. "De jure" means according to law or by right, and "de facto" means in reality, in fact, or in actuality. The distiction lies in the fact that something can be legally permissible (e.g., a law providing that foreigners have the right to purchase property), but in reality, one is not able to do so for whatever reason. In other words, if a law is provided for, but it is not carried out or enforced, the right provided for by law (i.e., *de jure*) is only provided for "on paper" (i.e., *de facto*).

2. Foreign entities, such as corporations, are not authorized to purchase real property unless the entity falls under the certain limited exceptions that are the purview of private laws. The only foreign entities that can purchase property are entities that fall under the purview of the following private laws such as the Tourism Incentive Law, the Law on Industrial Regions, and the Petroleum Law.

3. Real persons, as well as any legal entity, are prohibited from purchasing real property in military zones, special security areas, and other areas designated as prohibited areas by the Land Registry Office.
4. Foreign foundations, associations, cooperatives, communities, and groups are precluded from purchasing property in Turkey.
5. Purchases that are perceived as being against the Turkish Republic's interests can also be forestalled by the Parliament.

In addition to addressing the limitations placed on foreigners purchasing property in Turkey, Law No. 5444 also addresses foreigners' rights to inherit property located in Turkey. Law No. 5444 provides that foreigners have the same inheritance rights as Turkish nationals to inherit property, provided that the foreigner's country also allows Turkish citizens to inherit property in his or her home country. Thus the principle of reciprocity, discussed above, is also applicable in the case of the inheritance of property. For example, if a person whose country does not allow Turkish citizens to inherit property is bequeathed property, then a forced sale is ordered on the property. The proceeds, proportional to the current value of the property, will be given to the foreigner in lieu of the real property.

In contrast with the limitation placed on the amount of real property that can be purchased by foreigners, Law No. 5444 does not place any limitations on the quantity of land that can be inherited by a foreign national. On a more general note, Article 35 safeguards the rights of foreigners, including legal residents of Turkey, to own or inherit irremovable property as long as the usage of such property does not interfere with the public interest. Restrictions on Article 35 can only be placed by way of a constitutional amendment in order to be legally applicable.

Management Strategies

When a person—either individually as a potential home or business owner, or as a representative of his or her company as a purchaser—is contemplating buying property in the United States, he or she should take heed of the following general advice, and our advice should also be well heeded by U.S. citizens who seek to make real estate purchases in other countries.

First, retain a reputable real estate agent to represent your interest and to help negotiate the deal. The real estate agent should not be the agent who listed the property for the seller.

Second, retain a reputable attorney before signing the real estate contract. The attorney will review the contract and any related documents and then will represent a party at the real estate closing. In the U.S., state and local real estate and legal organizations can provide the names of real estate agents and attorneys in good standing. Similarly, for the U.S. citizen considering a foreign purchase, one should contact the local U.S. Consulate to procure a list of real estate agents and attorneys in good standing. Real estate law in the U.S. is complex enough, but in certain other countries, real estate law can be extremely difficult for a foreigner to ascertain.

Third, obtain title insurance, if available. If not, retain an attorney to do a title search and prepare an abstract of title. For example, it should be noted that some U.S. title insurance companies will provide title insurance to U.S. citizens who wish to purchase in other countries, most notably in Mexico, where there is now a very large retirement community of U.S. "retirados."

Real Estate: Leasing v. Owning[62]

"It's all about dirt!"

Contemporary business textbooks typically recommend that "startups" and existing businesses should lease instead of owning their own facilities. The reasons for this range from real estate not being your core competency to depreciation on real estate reducing the profits on your income statement. However, the textbooks are wrong. Reduction in income alone should be enough of a reason to own your own real estate and defer some income tax.

By depreciating the buildings, you can either own the property within your company and defer some income tax, or you can form an LLC, which you own outside the company as a way to defer a portion of your personal income taxes. Although you will have to recapture the depreciated amount at 25% when you sell the property, there is a good chance the property will appreciate and the profits of the sale will be taxed at the lower capital gains rate (currently 15%).

With advice from an attorney and accountant provided, you first need to decide if you should own the property personally (with a separate LLC) and lease it back to the company, or should your company own the property? If you are in the "startup" phase when funds are "tight," you may not want to tie up your capital, or you may not have enough money to start the business and be able to buy the property. If this is the case, then you should try to negotiate an option to buy the property after the first five years of the lease. There is a good chance that the property will appreciate enough to finance the entire option amount, or perhaps the seller may even want to finance the property in order to maintain an "income stream."

Therefore, if you decide to own the property personally, you should first establish an LLC to own the property as this legal entity will limit your

---

[62] Contributed by Thomas Tworoger, Nova Southeastern University.

personal liability in the event of litigation. Each additional location should be a separate LLC so as to avoid any litigation on your property adversely affecting your other properties. Although multiple LLCs will result in a good deal more paper work, bank accounts, and tax returns, the superseding purpose is to limit your liability.

Furthermore, it is imperative to ask your accountant about the favorable real estate treatment that an LLC affords the members (owners) when compared with a corporation.

By owning the property personally, the company will pay rent to the property owner (with the rent amount typically the amount of the mortgage payment). The company will also pay utilities, maintenance, and taxes. This business arrangement is called a "triple net lease" or a "net lease." This arrangement simply means that a person—the landlord—has no expenses in relation to the facility and the land. The company will also pay to insure the premises.

The downside to owning the property outside the company is that you will have to charge the company sales tax for the rental amount. In some states, the company will even have to pay sales tax on the property taxes (that is, "construed rent").

The good news, however, is that if you decide to sell the company someday, you can "sell" the property twice—once in a ten-year lease to the buyer who bought your company, and then once after that lease terminates. The assumption is that the tenant who bought your company will be a good credit risk.

An additional advantage to owning the property is to use it as a "finance platform." As the property appreciates, you can refinance it and borrow more money. You can then either loan the additional proceeds of the mortgage to the company for its cash flow needs or, if the company owns the property, then you can use the additional money for working capital. But do not forget that mortgage rates are considerably cheaper than lines of credit, loans against receivables, or other forms of debt.

Thus, "it's all about dirt," especially because there is a good chance that the property may someday be worth more than your business. In fact, it may eventually become your retirement plan—a plan that keeps on appreciating.

Summary

After reading this chapter, you should be able to understand the definition and nature of real property law, distinguish between real and personal property, and owning versus leasing real property. You should also understand the legal complexities of transferring real property, real estate mortgages, and the regulation of real property, especially in relation to eminent domain. This chapter has also focused on property law in the U.S. compared with other countries and legal systems, discussed in detail land-use permitting in the United States, and provided a basic explanation of landlord and tenant law in the United States.

PART III

THE REGULATORY ENVIRONMENT OF GLOBAL BUSINESS

SEVENTEEN
Intellectual Property Protection

Conceiving, inventing, constructing, and developing useful and creative information and instrumentalities are the hallmarks of the entrepreneur. Such information and devices may have taken considerable effort and expense to create and may be very valuable to the success of a business and a businessperson as they can provide a business with a distinct competitive advantage.

Problems perforce arise when an employee possessing such vital information and knowledge moves from one firm to another in today's highly competitive, knowledge-based global economy. Therefore, the key legal question emerges as to how one can protect such information or inventions from being misappropriated not just in the U.S., but also in the many other legal jurisdictions where the global businessperson works. Knowing how to protect such information is not only important to a company, but also important to an individual entrepreneur, who naturally wants to keep such information confidential while simultaneously perhaps wishing to share this potentially valuable information with venture capitalists and other interested parties. The purpose of this chapter, therefore, is to demonstrate the variety of ways information can be legally protected, first pursuant to U.S. law, and then pursuant to international treaty and the laws of selected foreign jurisdictions.

Intellectual Property Protection in the United States

In the United States, the term "intellectual property law" has come to designate a very broad field of law encompassing several forms of law—international treaty, federal and state statutes, criminal and civil, and state common law—as well as a variety of legal doctrines from federal patent and copyright law. State trade secret law and contract law also will come into play in this important field. All of these legal doctrines combined govern the methods by which a company, inventor, or entrepreneur can safeguard information and inventions and thereby prevent others from wrongfully exploiting such intellectual property.

An important rationale behind intellectual property law in the United States is the desire to motivate the creation, production, use, and proper disclosure of such creative endeavors by granting to the creators of such information specific legal protections against the infringement and misappropriation of such intellectual property. The law in the U.S. also attempts to strike a balance by encouraging the disclosure and use of intellectual property as well as seeking to further creative and entrepreneurial activity. The law also attempts to protect legitimate competitive advantage and to help instill ethical behavior in the marketplace.

However, as the line between physical and intellectual property becomes less clear—especially regarding the distinction between computer hardware and software—the challenges in determining the existence and efficacy of legal protections will become more apparent. Further complicating matters is the fact that none of the important legal doctrines to be covered in this chapter were originated and developed with computers in mind.

Patent Law

A "patent" is an exclusive legal right granted by the federal government to the inventors of new and useful inventions, processes, and improvements. The owner of the patent has the right to exclude others from making, using, or selling the patented invention for up to 17 years. As such, the patent holder has a legally granted monopoly to that invention by virtue of having obtained a patent.

A patent is obtained by the filing of an application with the U.S. Patent and Trademark Office and the receiving of subsequent approval. Once accepted, the patent holder must place the words "patent" or "pat" on the product, object, or design, followed by the patent number, which gives notice to all of the existence of such a patent. Patents last up to 20 years from the date of the application.

In addition to be being both novel and useful, the invention itself must be non-obvious. For example, mimicking a mental process or premising something on a mathematical formula destroys "patentability" because the "laws of nature" are not new. This rationale has presented formidable hurdles to the patenting of computer software. However, in 1981, the United States Supreme Court ruled that it may be possible to obtain a patent for a process that incorporates a computer program but only if the process itself is patentable.

It is also important to note the "reverse engineering" exception to patent law wherein a person can take the basic idea and function of an invention and accomplish the same result through a different series of steps, thereafter legally able to resell the "new" device.

Copyright Law

A "copyright" is another exclusive legal right granted by the federal government to the creators of original works of authorship, such as writings, recordings, works of art, and movies. The copyright gives the author the exclusive right to reproduce, distribute, display, and to perform the work and the expressions found in the work as well as to authorize others to do the same. Copyrights can be registered at the United States Copyright Office in Washington, D.C., and while registration is permissive and voluntary, it is strongly recommended.

For example, for authors, the duration of a copyright is the life of the author plus 70 years; for publishers, 95 years after the date of publication. It is important to note that copyright law, in essence, "only" protects the expression of an idea whereas a patent protects the application of an idea, thereby conveying to the patent-holder a greater degree of protection versus the copyright holder.

Modern copyright law is based principally on the federal Copyright Reform Act of 1976. This statute makes it illegal for a person to duplicate the exact expression, or a substantially similar expression, of a copyrighted work and then use it or resell it without the permission of the copyright holder. But copyright infringement does not have to be of the entire work or a word-for-word theft. Furthermore, copyright infringement can also occur if a person or a business aids or abets copyright violations by others. The leading textbook case is the famous Napster decision, where the U.S. Court of Appeals held that Napster was vicariously liable as a contributor to copyright infringement by assisting others to violate copyright law by means of its file-sharing software, which allowed people to obtain copies of copyrighted music without the permission of the copyright holders.

It is also very important to note that a 1980 Congressional amendment to the Copyright Reform Act of 1976, called the Computer Software Copyright Act, includes computer programs under that legal protection. Specifically, the statute now classifies computer programs and software as literary works.

However, another 1980 amendment, as interpreted by the courts, permits people or businesses who buy copyrighted software to make copies and modifications of the software for their own use and, under certain circumstances, to transfer the software. But the modification and distribution must be for personal use or for internal business purposes and not for unauthorized distribution. Nonetheless, to deter such potentially widespread distribution of software, most software manufactures today market their software through licenses rather than sales.

In 1998, the U.S. Congress enacted the Copyright Term Extension Act, which lengthened the time periods for the protection of copyrighted works, as noted above. As with patent law, an important exception exists under copyright law, stated explicitly in Section 107 of the Copyright Act. This is called the "fair use" exception, which allows the limited use of copyrighted materials, principally for educational use, without the need to pay any royalties to the copyright holder.

It must be emphasized here that copyright law does not prevent a person from taking the basic idea of a copyrighted work and then, by means of different expressions, in essence recreating it as an independent work, then reselling it.

An example of a copyright legal contest arose when one of the creators of the famous Broadway musical *Grease* accused several large cruise lines—including Carnival Cruise Lines and Celebrity Cruises—of copyright infringement by staging his play at sea for years without his permission. Under copyright law, any producer of a show that makes use of the story, dialogue, or lyrics of a musical beyond the singing of a few of its songs is required to purchase a license for what the law calls "grand performing rights." There are two very interesting aspects to this case, one practical and the other legal. The practical issue is how the purported unlicensed use was discovered. In this case, it was discovered when the wife of one of the co-creators told her husband, upon returning from a Hawaiian cruise, that she had seen a "full-blown production" of *Grease* in the ship's theatre. The interesting legal issue is the jurisdictional question. Because many of the cruise line companies are incorporated and registered in foreign locales—principally Liberia and Panama—acquiring jurisdiction in the U.S. represents a major legal challenge. However, U.S. companies would still be bound by the laws, including copyright law, of the nations where their ships are registered, presuming, of course, that certain countries have copyright laws and have signed intellectual property treaties.

Copyright—Fair Use Doctrine

Even if material is protected by federal copyright law in the United States, there is an important exception called the "fair use doctrine." This exception allows people to make limited use of copyrighted materials for "fair use," which includes commenting, criticizing, reporting news, and engaging in scholarship and research. Pursuant to copyright law, there are four criteria to determine "fair use," to wit: (1) the purpose and character of the use, especially whether the use is commercial or not; (2) the nature of the copyrighted work; (3) the amount and substance of the copyrighted work used; and (4) the effect of the use on the value and potential market of the copyrighted work. As a general rule, if the use amounts to a substantial revision or is transformational, that is, the use adds new information, interpretations, or understanding of the copyrighted work, the use is more likely to be deemed to be a "fair use." However, the more commercial the use is and the more it diminishes the value of the copyrighted work, the less likely that a use will be construed as a "fair" one.

Trademark Law

A "trademark" is obtained by registering the mark with the appropriate federal or state government agency. Trademark law at the federal level in the United States is governed by the Lanham Act of 1946 as amended by the Federal Trademark Dilution Act of 1995. At the federal level, the agency in question is again the

U.S. Patent and Trademark Office. Most states have comparable trademark statutes and agencies.

A trademark is a legal right granted by either the federal or state governments to protect names, logos, slogans, images and appearances, and other symbols, as well as combinations thereof, that identify goods and services and that distinguish them from other goods and services. Service marks refer to marks used to distinguish the services of the holder from that of its competitors (e.g., American Airlines). Protection not only is extended to distinctive trademarks but also to famous ones. Trademark protection also extends to the registering of famous names as domain names on the Internet, that is, "cybersquatting." "Trade dress," the design, overall appearance, and image of a product or service is also protected by trademark law.

Trademark law protects the owner of the trademark from others who might use the same trademark or a similar one on their products and services, thereby misleading and confusing the public. In the classic "Coke" case (no pun intended), in 1920 the U.S. Supreme Court gave trademark protection to the Coca-Cola company for its product's "nickname," "Coke," against a company that was attempting to market a rival product called "Koke."

Trade Secret Law

Because of the difficulties involved with securing federal patent, copyright, and trademark laws, the creators of intellectual property can utilize trade secret law, which is based on state statutes or state common law, in order to protect proprietary information. Trade secret law[63] is considered to be complementary to federal patent, copyright, and trademark law, and thus is not preempted by federal laws. Trade secret law is predominantly based on state law, with one very important exception: a federal statute which criminalizes the theft of a trade secret.

One major advantage to trade secret protection as compared with patent and copyright law is that trade secret protection theoretically can be carried out in perpetuity. Every state has a body of trade secret law. Generally speaking, trade secret law will protect information that is valuable and subject to reasonable efforts to maintain its secrecy. The primary state statute on point is the Uniform Trade Secret Act, which many states in the United States have adopted. This statute follows the old common law definitions and rules for acquiring and protecting trade secrets, meaning that there is legal liability, both criminal and civil, for the misappropriation of a trade secret. "Misappropriation" occurs when a person, typically an employee and his or her new employer, acquires another's trade secret, usually the trade secret of the former employer, and the

---

[63] For a detailed examination of trade secret law, see Cavico, F. J. (2001).

acquiring person knows or should know that the trade secret was secured through improper means. The key fact in misappropriation is that the trade secret was obtained, conveyed, or used without the consent of the original owner.

Remedies for a misappropriation of a trade secret can be both criminal and civil. Civil remedies include an injunction against actual or threatened misappropriation, monetary damages for the actual loss as well as for the unjust enrichment of the misappropriating party, and perhaps punitive damages and attorneys' fees. An "injunction" can forever prohibit an employee from disclosing a trade secret to a competitor or using it himself or herself. Many state statutes, as well as a federal statute, make the misappropriation of trade secrets a crime. Even if a state does not have a precise criminal statute on point, a state's civil theft statute should be able to encompass the intentional misappropriation of a trade secret.

The predicate for any type of legal trade secret protection is "information," which obviously is a broad term, but one that is very liberally construed by the courts. Information can consist of devices, designs, patterns, programs (including computer software), processes, procedures, techniques, compilations (such as customer and supplier lists), as well as other valuable proprietary information, such as price markups and profit margins and research results. Information can be "hard," in the sense of a scientific formula, such as the formula for Coca-Cola, which is the "classic" (no pun intended) trade secret example. Information can be "soft" in the sense of plans and strategies, such as an entrepreneur's business plan or a company's marketing strategy.

To illustrate how "soft" information can be, and how "hard" a jury can be, in one notable Florida case involving the Walt Disney company, a state appeals court ruled that the idea and detailed business plan for a sports-themed park could be construed as "information" and remanded the case for trial so that a jury might determine if this idea was a trade secret that Disney had misappropriated from a development company and its two principals. The jury decided in fact that the idea was a trade secret and that the Disney company had misappropriated it. The jury then awarded the plaintiff company $240 million in damages. Now Disney is being sued by the family of a now-deceased relative, who contends that Disney misappropriated the idea for Epcot, which their relative had proposed to Disney many years ago, calling his idea for a theme park "Miniature Worlds." Assuming that the major legal impediment of the Statute of Limitations can be overcome, one wonders what a Florida jury will do with such a case. One can only begin to contemplate the damages that might be awarded for misappropriating the concept of Epcot.

Regarding "value," it should be pointed out that even "dead-ends" reached in research and development can be protected so as to prevent one's competitors from obtaining such knowledge and thereby preventing similar costly and time-consuming fruitless efforts. The requisite "information" must possess economic value, either real or potential, meaning that the information gives a business a commercial, economic, or competitive advantage. In order to have value, this information must have some degree of novelty. Consequently, if the information is generally known or readily ascertainable by competent people, it is not considered trade secret information because of the simple fact that it lacks "value." Trade secret protection does not extend to information that is generally know or readily ascertainable. Therefore, any information deemed to be in the public domain cannot be the basis for a legally protected trade secret. Since such information is public it is available to a firm's competitors and customers. For example, the information contained in a company's own product, service, and promotional materials that are distributed to the public will be deemed "pubic," even if they contain technical information. Similarly, information even if confidential, that is mistakenly disclosed by a company's employees is nevertheless "public." Trade secret protection is also not available for information that is "reverse engineered," that is, taking apart a product, examining its components and internal workings, and then reconstructing the product with a different series of steps. Yet, if this process cannot be readily or easily accomplished, then the trade secret protection for the product is not lost.

The final factor in information achieving trade secret status is the secrecy element. The person or business attempting to convince a court that his or her valuable information is in fact a legal trade secret must demonstrate that reasonable security measures were adopted and continued in order to maintain the secrecy of such information. "Reasonable" means exactly what its name implies, and thus establishing it will depend on the facts and particular circumstances of the case. Obviously, a high-tech firm with a defense contract will have more elaborate secrecy procedures in place versus a small sales firm or an entrepreneur with a business plan in hand. Designating appropriate information as confidential and proprietary is the first step, then protecting it by lock-and-key and passwords is a good start on the road to a trade secret destination.

Furthermore, reasonableness does not mean that the information cannot be disclosed. Rather, certain information must be disclosed, for example to key "need to know" employees and outside sales personnel, vendors, subcontractors, and licensees in order for a company to function. They of course must be clearly, as well as regularly notified only to use the information in the scope of their duties. Yet the more people the information is disclosed to as well as the paucity of precautions regarding the disclosure, the less likely that the information will achieve trade secret status.

Having employees and others who need access to the information sign confidentiality and non-disclosure agreements is an extremely important factor in maintaining "secrecy." When an employee resigns, the employer should discuss the handling of trade secrets as part of the "exit interview" and also communicate with the employee's new employer, informing it that the employee had access to certain trade secrets

Trade secret disputes can arise when an employee leaves one firm and brings confidential information with him or her to a new employer who is a competitor of the former employer. What can the new employer do to protect itself? The new employer must first emphasize that no trade secrets from the former employer can be brought to the firm; and then the new employer should try to make sure that the employee has not brought any computer discs or devices, documents or papers, or other material that can be construed as a trade secret. Moreover, the new employer should require the new employee to sign a statement saying that he or she is not bringing any trade secrets or confidential information to the new employer.

Plainly, information should not be broadcast over the Internet if a court is later to be expected to grant it trade secret status. Trade secret audits—to see what information needs to be protected and how—are naturally advisable.

To further demonstrate reasonable measures, the manufacturers of computer software typically use software licensing agreements to preserve secrecy by means of forbidding the licensee to copy the program and also requiring the licensee to sign a confidentiality agreement. Another more "plebian" example concerns the expiration dates on bottles of beer, which the manufacturers place on the cans by means of unintelligible, cryptic codes that look like hieroglyphics, but which can be deciphered by the manufacturer, of course, as well as by its wholesalers and distributors. Using complex codes is certainly an example of a "reasonable" secrecy measure.

A new form of security measure for trade secret protection is a new computer technology, fingerprint reading sensors that requires a computer user to swipe his or her finger on a sensor in order to gain access to a computer or to certain Web sites. Fingerprints are more difficult to mimic or to copy than passwords, and it is more convenient for a user to merely swipe his or her finger than to remember a bunch of passwords, which often are written down in several places as well as used time and again. But because trade secret law requires that a security measure be "reasonable" under the circumstances, it is still not certain if fingerprint sensors for computers are feasible, practical, and cost-effective security devices.

Whether the secrecy measures adopted are in fact sufficiently reasonable is regarded as a question of fact for a jury to decide. Once information is established as a trade secret, if it is improperly used by a person either individually or in his/her capacity as an employee in a new firm, the person and the new employer can be sued for misappropriating a trade secret.

On the federal level, misappropriating a trade secret can be a very serious legal wrong because the U.S. Congress has converted the misappropriation of a trade secret into a federal crime by means of the federal Economic Espionage Act of 1996. The title to the Act is a bit of a misnomer because the statute criminalizes any theft of a trade secret and not just by "foreign agents," though the federal government usually will leave "minor," "domestic" misappropriations to the states to prosecute.

The definition of a trade secret under this federal statute is essentially the same as under the state statutes and the common law. The statute has two separate provisions that criminalize the theft or misappropriation of a trade secret. One is aimed at foreign industrial or economic espionage and requires that the theft of a trade secret be done to benefit a foreign government or an instrumentality or agent of a foreign government. In the latter case, it must be shown that the foreign government substantially owned, controlled, sponsored, dominated, directed, or managed the entity. The second provision in the Act is directed at the more common business and commercial theft or misappropriation of trade secrets.

The penalties for violating the Economic Espionage Act are very severe, with substantial monetary fines, forfeiture of any property or proceeds made in violation of the Act, and imprisonment of up to twenty-five years. To illustrate, in 2010, a former Goldman Sachs computer programmer received an eight year sentence for theft of trade secrets for stealing the company's confidential source code in an attempt to build a similar trading platform for his new employer, an international technology firm. In 2012, a former software engineer for Motorola was sentenced to four years in prison for stealing Motorola's trade secrets in the form of telecommunications technology and attempting to turn the technology over to a Chinese company. Also, in 2012, a former employee of DuPont pleaded guilty to taking trade secrets dealing with manufacturing processes and selling them to a Chinese government owned firm. He faced 15 years in prison pursuant to the Economic Espionage Act.

In an interesting "domestic" trade secret theft case, in 2006, the U.S. government indicted a former secretary who worked for Coca-Cola and two others for conspiracy, wire fraud, stealing Coke's trade secrets, and attempting to sell them to PepsiCo. The confidential information involved Coke product samples as well as the mysterious "Project N." The alleged crime was revealed when PepsiCo informed Coke and the government that the company had received a letter from a person that offered to sell Coke's trade secrets to "the highest bidder." A lawyer for the secretary stated that part of her defense will be that Coke's alleged "secrets" were really not that secret. However, a jury convicted the secretary of stealing trade secrets; and she received an eight year prison term in 2007.

Finally, in an international context, it should be noted that in 2010 the Chinese government, specifically the Assets Supervision and Administration Commission, promulgated a new trade secret law that also has a very broad definition of a trade secret. In essence, virtually anything that has not been publicly disclosed and could hold economic value for a company will be construed as a trade secret by the Chinese government. Moreover, state owned companies will have to classify commercial trade secrets by level of importance with certain highly confidential information, particularly dealing with technology, being classified as national state secrets. There are civil and criminal sanctions for violating the law with, as expected, the harshest penalties imposed for stealing the latter.

Covenants-Not-To-Compete

Covenants-not-to-compete,[64] also called non-competition clauses, were first addressed in the Contract Law chapter. This important legal concept will be more extensively covered in this chapter, with particular reference to employment relationships.

First, you will recall that a covenant-not-to-compete can be found in a contract for the sale of a business or in an employment contract. Furthermore, the covenant clause must be ancillary, or part of a larger contract, and must also be supported by the common law contract requirement of "consideration." Although covenants-not-to-compete are disfavored in the law because the law favors economic advancement and competition and does not want to restrain people from pursuing their careers and entrepreneurial ambitions, the law will restrain competition in a properly drafted covenant situation. One notable exception is the state of California where covenants-not-to-compete in business are completely illegal.

Covenants-not-to-compete typically are found in two contract situations: the sale of a business and an employment relationship. In the first case, as noted earlier, a business owner is selling his or her business to a buyer, and the buyer wants assurances that the seller will not resume the same or a similar business in the same locale, thereby, in essence, retaking the "good will" that the buyer purchased as part of the purchase of the business. Accordingly, in order to protect himself or herself, the buyer will insist, as part of the sales contract, a non-competition clause, in which the seller promises not to compete, directly

---

[64] For more details on Covenant-not-to-Compete law, see Cavico, F. J. (2001).

or indirectly, in the same or similar business for a period of time designated in a trade territory. Based on the common law, such a non-competition clause will be upheld if it is reasonable as to duration and also to place, i.e., trade territory. Both requirements are necessary, and if one or both are not present, the covenant is considered to be unreasonable, overbroad, invalid, illegal, and stricken from the contract, though ordinarily the remainder of the contract will not be adversely affected (which means the buyer now has a business but no protection against competition).

For example, in the sale of a "high-end" Italian restaurant in Ft. Lauderdale, Florida, a trade territory of a radius of several miles and a time period of two to three years should be deemed reasonable, but a ten-year period would be considered unreasonable. The idea is to give the new buyer, who has purchased a going concern with a good reputation, a reasonable opportunity to demonstrate that he or she can continue the business on a prosperous footing.

As noted, if the covenant is overbroad, the courts usually will not "reform" it, meaning that they will not rewrite covenants or change time periods and territories to make them reasonable and enforceable. However, if the covenant-not-to-compete is found in an employment contract, either by statute or by common law interpretation, most courts *will* impose a third requirement for the validity of the covenant. This can be seen in the employment situation. The employee signs a contract, either initially or as a modification of another contract, in which the employee promises that when he or she leaves the employer's employ for any reason (fired, quits, "down-sized," "right-sized," laid-off, off-shored, out-sourced, etc.), he or she will not compete against the employer, directly or indirectly, as an employee for another firm or in his or her own business capacity for a certain period of time and within a designated trade territory.

In order to have a legally valid and enforceable non-competition agreement in an employment situation, the first two requirements are the same, as in the sale of a business circumstance. However, in most states in the U.S, either by statute or common law, a third, and very significant requirement is necessary. The party seeking to enforce the covenant—that is, the employer—must show that it is not only reasonable in time and place, but also that it is necessary to support a legitimate business interest of the employer. But before this third requirement is explicated, it is interesting to note how the first two compare with the two restrictive covenant situations.

As to the time or duration requirement, the employee is in a more beneficial position compared with the seller of a business because the courts typically will require much shorter time periods for covenants-not-to-compete in an employment situation. If the employment is related to the technology field, the courts will insist that a "reasonable" duration be a short time period.

As one court declared in throwing out a one-year covenant-not-to-compete in an Internet publishing company employment case, one year is an "eternity" in such an on-line technical field due to the very rapidly changing and advancing of technology. To demonstrate, In Florida, by statute, a time period of six months or less in an employment covenant situation is presumed to be reasonable while a time period of two years or more is presumed to be unreasonable. Anything in between carries no presumption, and is left to the discretion of the court.

Presumptions are merely assumptions, of course, and thus can be rebutted, but one will need evidence to do so. The time period interpretation is the "good news" for the employee while the trade territory interpretation is the obverse "bad news." In many companies which are truly global in nature, the trade territory or geographic area for the restrictive covenant may legitimately be the entire world! In such a case, presuming the third covenant requirement is present, the former employee may need to rely on family, spouse, or a sympathetic "significant other" and go back to school to effectively "wait out" the covenant time period.

Therefore, the third requirement for a valid covenant in an employment situation is that the covenant be necessary to further a legitimate business interest of the employer. The burden of proof and persuasion is on the employer to demonstrate not only the reasonableness elements, but also an adequate interest to support the covenant. Examples of a sufficient employer business interest arise when the employee the company wishes to be constrained from competing with has access to confidential, proprietary, or trade secret information of the employer, including business and customer lists and records, has established goodwill with the employer's customers, and when the employer has invested extraordinary, specialized, unique, or valuable training and/or education in the employee.

Regarding the education dimension, a few seminars on hiring and firing skills, diversity training, and ethics courses most likely would not suffice, but enabling the employee to obtain an MBA degree or a license or certification from a government agency (for example to repair planes pursuant to a Federal Aviation Administration certification) most likely would be an adequate interest to protect.

Once these three requirements—time, location, and necessity—are present, the covenant is enforceable, and the employee cannot compete in contravention of the covenant. Covenants can be enforced by means of a lawsuit for breach of contract as well as by an injunction, which can be upheld by a court's traditional "contempt" powers. However, a showing of "irreparable harm" must be shown for an injunction. Moreover, in most states, it is no defense that the enforcement of the covenant would be harsh or oppressive or unduly burdensome to the employee; perhaps an employee whose job was outsourced cannot take advantage of another opportunity locally due to a covenant. The employee signed the covenant as part of his or her contract, which the employee presumably read (and will be deemed to have read in the eyes of the law), and the employee will be so bound.

In one recent and notable covenant employment case, Microsoft sued a former company vice-president, who served seven years with the company, possessed a doctorate degree, and who is an expert in search technology and was one of the architects of the company's China policy. The former employee was hired by Google and named as the head of that company's China operations and placed in charge of establishing a research and development center in China. Microsoft contended that its former employee had breached his employment contract, specifically the covenant-not-to-compete provision, and thereby requested damages and an injunction to prevent the employee from working for Google. A Washington state court judge, however, ruled that the former Microsoft employee could work for Google and could help that firm establish its operations in China, but the judge restricted the former employee from working on projects, products, and services that were directly competitive with those on which he had worked at Microsoft as well as restricted him from making key budgetary and personnel decisions for the China project. Both companies were displeased with the judge's covenant "reform" decision.

Anti-Piracy and Non-Solicitation Agreements

Anti-piracy and non-solicitation agreements are clauses in contracts which bar a departing employee from soliciting or serving the former employer's customers, clients, and employees. These types of provisions typically are enforceable based on the reasonableness and legitimate business interest standards found in restrictive covenant law. Also related to the aforementioned provisions are clauses in contracts which require the departing employee to repay the company's training and education costs if the employee does not stay with the employer for a reasonable period of time after completion of the training or education. Again, this type of provision will be held legally binding and effective if it is considered to be reasonable.

A non-solicitation agreement is typically part of the employer's contract with its employees or independent contractors, for example, an "outside" sales force, which states that when these parties leave the employer's firm they will not solicit the employer's customers, clients, or employees. The non-solicitation agreement also can be used in contracts with the employer's clients and customers by stating that they will not solicit the employer's employees. In the latter case, the employer may be concerned that a client will "hire away" from the employer one of the employer's very good employees who has been serving the client very well, as the client decide it would be less expensive to have the work done "in-house." It also should be noted that non-solicitation agreements are enforceable in all the states, even ones such as California, which do not enforce covenants-not-to-compete.

Anti-piracy agreements (also called "no-raid" agreements) are similar to non-solicitation agreements. Anti-piracy agreements are typically part of the employee's contract with the employer in which the employee promises when he or she leaves the firm for another firm or to embark on an entrepreneurial venture not to solicit other employees to join them or to hire the employees for a stated period of time. However, even if there is such an agreement, the courts usually maintain that the employee who is leaving is allowed to tell his or her fellow employees of his or her plans. Of course, the employees cannot be solicited; but if they on their own wish to join the departing employee, that conduct would generally be permissible. Yet there is, obviously, a "fine-line" between soliciting one's fellow employees and "merely" informing them of one's employment or entrepreneurial plans and aspirations.

Confidentiality and Non-Disclosure Agreements

These types of agreements forbid employees from using confidential, proprietary, and trade secret information that they became cognizant of while working for their former employer. These types of agreements can be used to protect a wide variety of trade secrets and confidential and proprietary information. Such agreements can also be drafted to cover meetings, communications, and even conversations. A single employment contract can of course include non-competition, non-solicitation, and non-disclosure provisions. Often, such provisions are used at the hiring stage when an employer requests executives and managers to sign such agreements.

The first point is that there is neither a standard type of confidentiality or non-disclosure agreement nor a standard set of terms. Generally, the agreement will state that one uses the information only for a specific purpose. In addition, there will usually be a provision that the party receiving the information will use a certain level of care, such as "commercially reasonable efforts," to protect the information. Otherwise, there may be provisions to the effect that the party receiving the information will not disclose it except to people with a "need to know" or perhaps only to certain named individuals. Yet it is possible for the non-disclosure agreement to state that one party is prohibited from even revealing that he or she has any such information. The agreement should be as specific as possible as to exactly what the confidential information is that is protected by the agreement.

Additionally, in such agreements one typically finds a clause dealing with the length of the agreement, usually limiting the time the agreement is in effect. Frequently, one will find in such agreements a clause that confidentiality is waived under certain circumstances such as when a court or government agency requires disclosure.

There should be some type of provision as to what happens to the information, which may include, for example, its return or its destruction for when the agreement ends.

As with any contract agreement, one can and should attempt to negotiate the best agreement possible with the advice of legal counsel.

Employee Inventions

Another perplexing intellectual property problem arises when an employee creates certain knowledge or invents some device that is potentially valuable to the employer as well as to the employee who created it. But who exactly possesses the property rights to such employee creations?

This field of law has always been a problem area. The rules are predominantly common law formulations and they are not precise by any means. The problem—legally, ethically, and practically—is exacerbated when the employee does his or her creating on his or her own time and with no or minimal use of the employer resources but the creation does in fact relate to the employer's job and the employer's business.

The best way to describe the law governing employee inventions is to categorize employee inventions into three main groups: 1) "service" inventions, 2) "shop right" inventions, and 3) "free" inventions.

First, a "service" invention occurs as a product of one's employment. The employer and employee usually have a contractual agreement that states that the employee is hired to make inventions or to create intellectual property. In such a case, the common law holds that the employee is legally obligated to turn over the invention to his or her employer. In this sense, the invention or creation characteristically entails a considerable utilization of the employer's resources. The employee is ordinarily given a fixed amount of money, as per the contract, with characteristically a bonus amount for a valuable invention.

Second, a "shop right" invention materializes when the employee is neither obligated by contract to invent or create nor is there any understanding, explicit or implicit, that the employee is hired in whole or in part to invent or create, but the employee nonetheless invents. However, the employee is inventing or creating utilizing the employer's resources extensively and substantially, for example by using equipment, supply facilities, materials, other employees, and confidential and trade secret information. In such a case, absent a contract provision to the contrary, the employee must give his or her employer the "right of first refusal" to the invention. If the employer decides to use the invention, the employee must share in the royalties and profits therein. But if the employer decides, after a reasonable period of time, not to use the invention, the employee/inventor can use it or take the device and knowledge to a new employer.

The third type of invention, the "free" invention, comes about when there is no contract or understanding of any type between the employer and employee, and the employee does not use or materially utilize the employer's resources. The invention or creation is made on the employee's own time, using wholly or principally his or her own resources, though the invention or creation may create results for the employee's job or the employer's business. In the "free" case, absent any contractual agreement to the contrary, the employee is legally entitled to the profits and royalties of his or her invention.

Global Legal Perspectives

International Intellectual Property Protection Agreements

Taking a global perspective, there are several international agreements in place that protect intellectual property. As such, they must be mentioned, though succinctly. The main agreements are: 1) the Paris Convention of 1883; 2) the Berne Convention of 1886; 3) the TRIPS Agreement of 1994; 4) the GATT Agreement of 1994; 5) the WIPO Treaty of 1996 and; 6) the Madrid Protocol of 2003.

The Paris Convention, known fully as the Convention of the Union of Paris, in which approximately 90 countries adhere to, allows a party in one signatory country to sue for patent and trademark protection in the other member countries.

The Berne Convention is the international copyright treaty, affording legal rights to copyrighted works in all the member countries. Copyright notice on the work itself is not required to secure copyright protection under this treaty for works produced after March 1, 1989, although again, it is strongly recommended that such notice be placed so as to rebut a claim of "innocent" infringement.

TRIPS stands for Trade-Related Intellectual Property Rights. It is an agreement that over 100 nations have signed, granting legal protection to patents, trademarks, and copyrights. The most important part of TRIPS is the provision that each signatory country provide, in its own domestic law, legal protections for intellectual property rights as well as legal mechanisms and sanctions to enforce these rights.

GATT stands for the General Agreement on Tariffs and Trade, which established the World Trade Organization (WTO). (The WTO is an international trade organization of which the U.S. is a member.) GATT's intellectual property provisions, which were ratified by the U.S. Congress, changed U.S. patent law to make patents valid for twenty years, and also changed U.S. law to make the time period run from the date the patent application was filed.

WIPO stands for the World Intellectual Property Organization. The WIPO treaty upgraded intellectual property protection, particularly on the Internet.

The Madrid Protocol is an international treaty dealing with trademark protection that has been signed by over 60 countries, the major purpose of which is to facilitate international trademark registration.

Mention also must be made of the U.S. Digital Millennium Copyright Act of 1998, which, among other copyright provisions, implemented the provisions of the WIPO Treaty as well as established civil and criminal penalties for those who circumvent encryption software and anti-piracy protections for protected digital works. This U.S. statute is supposed to be a model modern intellectual property protection statute for other nations.

Covenants-Not-to-Compete in the Netherlands and Spain[65]

In the Netherlands and Spain, covenants not to compete in employment contracts are valid and enforceable under certain circumstances. Based on 2004 legislation by the Dutch Parliament, in the Netherlands, covenants must contain the following elements in order to be lawful: 1) the duration of the restraint; 2) the geographic scope of the restraint; 3) a clear description of the activities to be restrained; and 4) a provision that reasonable compensation will be paid by the employer if the employer wants to hold the employee to the non-compete clause upon termination of the employment agreement.

Similarly, in Spain, non-competition clauses in employment contracts are valid and enforceable only if adequate compensation is paid to the employee upon termination of the employment relationship. But Spain also requires that the employer have an effective commercial or industrial interest in preventing the employee from competing. In addition, the agreement must be limited in time. Furthermore, the Spanish Supreme Court recently ruled that an "opt-out" clause in an employment contract, whereby an employer can waive the non-competition obligation to pay compensation to the employee merely by giving prior notice, was null and void.

In the U.S., as noted, although there are comparable requirements for a valid covenant in an employment contract, the payment of any consideration to the restricted former employee is definitely not one of them!

---

[65] See Collins, Erika C. (Summer 2005).

Russia: New Trademark Law[66]

In 2002, the Russian legislature amended their 1992 Trademark Law, thereby making substantive changes for the protection of domain names. Pursuant to the 2002 amendment, the commercial use of a trademark or a confusingly similar sign on the territory of the Russian Federation, with respect to goods for which the trademark has been registered or to similar goods, will be regarded as an infringement of the rights of the holder of the mark, and thus an illegal use of the trademark. Furthermore, this prohibition applies to the use of trademarks or confusingly similar signs on the Internet, including domain names.

The amended statute also provides that a trademark will be protected not only on the basis of its registration, but also if the mark is protected by an international treaty, or if the mark can be recognized as a well-known trademark as a result of its extensive use to the extent that it is widely known in the Russian Federation among consumers with respect to goods of the holder of the mark. The amended statute is significant because it provides legal protection to trademarks that are well known though not necessarily registered in Russia.

Of course, the amended statute will not help a company whose trademark is well known in the West but not well known in Russia. In such a case, the company will have to do business there to obtain recognition or to formally register its trademark in Russia.

Management Strategies

The practically-minded global manager, inventor, and entrepreneur must first be keenly aware that obtaining patent protection is not easy, not fast, and definitely not cheap. Moreover, it is still an ongoing legal debate as to whether certain creations, such as computer software, are even patentable. Regardless, the eminently practical constraint is that by the time one secures, if one can, a patent for one's own product—especially if it is computer hardware, or perhaps even software, or technologically-related—the "march" of technology moves so rapidly and is so ever-changing that you may find yourself the owner of a very expensive, and quite useless, patent.

Trade secret protection, in comparison with patent and copyright protection, is very broad and relatively easy to attain. The "information" component to a trade secret can encompass the expression of an idea—as in copyright law—the application of the idea—as in patent law—and the very idea itself. As opposed to patents and copyrights, trade secret law requires no registration, no filing fees, no notice, no disclosure, and no lengthy, expensive, and time-consuming procedures.

---

[66] See Meyers, Mariyetta (2005–2006).

Furthermore, a covenant-not-to-compete and a confidentiality agreement are not required for trade secret protection, though both are certainly advisable. All one needs is "information"—which conceivably can be any concept or notion—some potential value to the information, and the adoption and maintenance of reasonable measures to safeguard the information. For example, an entrepreneur, before showing his or her business plan to potential investors in the business, can prominently indicate on his or her business plan the words "confidential" and "secret" and further indicate that the plan is being disclosed for limited business review purposes and is not to be disclosed to or shared with others.

Customer or client list compilations, as noted, may be protected under trade secret law. However, even if an employee has personally compiled a customer or client list but no considerable effort or expense was involved and the names are readily obtainable from public sources, the employee may be able to take the list with him or her to a new employer or use it entrepreneurially, absent other restrictive contractual provisions.

Covenant-not-to-compete law is a difficult area to deal with practically. Granted, the employer does have legitimate interests to protect in a very competitive global business environment, but the employer does not want to go "overboard" and compel the employee to sign an overbroad, severe, and perhaps even illegal covenant. If so, the employer will get no protection unless the employer can beseech a judge to rewrite (reform) the covenant, which judges characteristically are reluctant to do.

Another legal and practical problem arises when the contract which contains the covenant is drafted in one state, which will enforce covenants (valid ones, of course), but the alleged violation of the covenant takes place in another state, for example, California, which prohibits covenants in employment contracts. Consequently, the determination as to which state's law applies to the agreement will be dispositive of the case. So, if California law applies one can work in that state regardless of a covenant drafted in another state. This determination is based on a body of law called "conflicts of laws," which deals with cases that involve different jurisdictions. An examination of this body of law is beyond the purposes of this book. However, some basic "conflicts" rules are that the validity of a contract (including one with a covenant, of course) is determined by the law of the state where the contract was drafted; whereas if the issue is the performance of a contract the law where performance occurs would control. Accordingly, since the main issue in a covenant case would be whether the covenant itself is legal, valid, and enforceable, the law where the contract containing the covenant should be the controlling law.

Generally speaking, regarding validity, the covenant in an employment scenario should be limited in time to no longer than a year and probably less for anything "high-tech." The employer also should be very specific as to the type of work the employee will be restricted from doing. Furthermore, the covenant must make sure that the geographic area is tied into that specific type of work.

Again, identifying information legitimately to be protected and identifying the pertinent personnel to be restricted are critical legal and practical elements for the prudent employer. If there is a valid covenant in place and a violation thereof, the employer is well advised to act promptly if it intends to seek an injunction because it will be more difficult for the employer to show irreparable harm if an employer waits too long. Of course, probably the best basic and commonsense advice to the employer is to treat your talented employees well, make them part of the "team," empower and reward them appropriately, which will enable the employer to keep its valuable employees and its intellectual property.

As far as the employee is concerned, usually he or she is in a "take-it-or-leave-it" situation regarding the contract with a prospective or current employer. You can refuse to sign on, of course, but then you may be escorted by security to the exit and the street. But depending on the employee's level and knowledge and skill base, it may be possible for the employee to negotiate the "contours" of the covenant, for example by seeking to eliminate a geographic area where the employer does not do business and does not have any plans to do business, or by asking for a "bonus" as an incentive to sign the covenant. If the employee does sign, it is always good advice to gain as much knowledge, skills, and education as possible in the event that he or she is thrust into the marketplace, a marketplace further limited by an enforceable covenant.

Also, upon departing one's former firm, it may be possible to negotiate a "graceful" exit by perhaps asking for a sum of money for the time period the covenant is in place. In England, this type of provision is common, and is called "garden relief" to indicate that one will be at home taking care of the garden, while being paid by the employer, until the covenant time period expires.

Finally, as the famous poem alludes, one can "always go home again," at least, and presumably, temporarily, and "regroup."

Regarding the ownership of employee inventions and creations, such as the development of computer software, the prudent company will have policies and practices in place to govern this issue because it is a difficult area to handle legally, morally, and practically. The contract between the company and the employee should have a provision addressing the property right to employee creations and inventions. Otherwise, the common law rules, which are a bit vague, perforce must be applied. Practically speaking, a contract provision should not be totally one-sided and the employee must be allowed a fair share of the royalties and profits from the invention or creation. To reward and compensate the inventor-employee will encourage employee creativity and justly reward the successful employee for his or her special contribution to the firm's success.

Perhaps a special company committee can be established to determine the employee's involvement and the amount of special compensation to be awarded. The amount should be based on the commercial value of the invention and could be in the form of a bonus. However, in the absence of an explicit contract provision or a pertinent stated policy, the employee who invents a device or creates a program on his or her own time, with no or minimal use of company resources, may reasonably assume that such a creation rightfully belongs to the employee, even if the creation pertains to his or her work. In such an instance, the legal system very well could back up lawfully the legal component to "rightfulness."

Non-Disclosure Agreement Checklist[67]

A non-disclosure agreement as part of the employment contract should be seriously considered by the employer. The non-disclosure agreement will require that the party not disclose confidential information to anyone outside the employer's company unless necessary to conduct the employer's business. Such an agreement will protect trade secrets as well as other confidential and proprietary information. Also, recall that one required element of converting information into a legally protected trade secret is a showing that the employer utilized reasonable methods to maintain the secrecy of the information. Accordingly, one "tried and true" way of demonstrating that "secrecy" requirement is for the employer to have a contractually based non-disclosure agreement with its employees and other parties who have access to confidential information. These parties would include, in addition to the employees, independent contractors, suppliers, vendors, distributors, the "outside" sales force, and even actual and potential investors in an entrepreneurial endeavor. Thus, by means of the non-disclosure agreement, the employees and other parties are put on notice that they will have access to confidential information, that they have an obligation to keep this information secret, even after their relationship with the employer ends, and also that the employer can demonstrate to the court that it took a "reasonable," and required, legal trade secret measure to maintain the secrecy of the information. The importance of a firm having a non-disclosure agreement can-

---

[67] See Bagley and Dauchy (2008) and Davidson and Forsythe (2011).

not be over-emphasized. If trade secrets exist, then a reasonable non-disclosure agreement will be upheld by the courts even in states such as California that will not enforce post-employment covenants not to compete.

Trade Secret Checklist[68]

In order to fully take advantage of trade secret law, the employer or entrepreneur should first determine if the business in fact has trade secrets, and, if so what exactly are they. Next, a determination must be made as to who in the business must have access to this confidential information; then the business must take steps to ensure that all the people that have access to the trade secrets recognize the information as confidential and promise to treat it as such. Recognizing that a non-disclosure agreement is a very efficacious way for the employer or entrepreneur to maintain the secrecy of the information as well as to create the trade secret itself, such an agreement should be required of all employees. Finally, in addition to the non-disclosure agreement, the business must ascertain what other "reasonable" steps it should take to maintain the secrecy of the information.

Covenant Not To Compete Checklist[69]

A covenant not to compete in order to be valid must be a part of or ancillary to or subordinate a larger contract. A restrictive covenant, standing alone, usually will be deemed to be an illegal restraint of trade or a violation of public policy. Examples of the "larger" contract would be an employment contract, a sale of business contract, or a partnership agreement, and in most states even an employment at-will employment relationship.

Regarding the time period, as a general rule, courts will find a period of one year of less to be reasonable in an employment contract, and a period of three of more years to be unreasonable. For the sale of a business, time periods of five years have been deemed reasonable. Regarding the geographic area in order for it to be deemed reasonable some courts will require that the geographic area correlate to the employer's actual trade territory. Legitimate employer interests to support a covenant not to compete include the protection of goodwill, long-term customer relationships, trade secrets, confidential information, and business relationship.

Although some states such as California have statutes prohibiting covenants from restraining a person from engaging in any lawful profession, occupation, trade, or business, there are exceptions, for example, when a person sells all of his or her shares in a corporation and the company is sold as an ongoing business, or when a partnership is dissolved but not terminated and continues in an

---

[68] See Bagley and Dauchy (2008) and Davidson and Forsythe (2011).
[69] See Bagley and Dauchy (2008) and Davidson and Forsythe (2011).

altered form, or when a limited liability company is sold. The prudent approach is naturally to ascertain a state's statutory and common law regarding covenants and their validity, and then to use the aforementioned choice-of-law and forum selection provisions to ensure the desirable legal result.

It is important to note that a court will not enforce a covenant not to compete that is unreasonable in the sense of being overbroad in either duration or territory. Consequently, the employer must avoid a covenant in which the employee promises never to compete or not to compete for an unreasonable amount of time or promises not to compete for an unreasonable trade territory. An employer who is "greedy," and thus who demands too much for an employee, and who gets it, as a consequence may get nothing in the form of legal protection as the entire covenant may be struck down as overbroad, unreasonable, invalid, and illegal. Accordingly, the employer is well advised to think carefully what legitimate business interests it is seeking to protect by means of the covenant and to what degree (in time and place) the employer reasonably needs protection against competition; and then consult with an attorney about the creation of the covenant-not-to-compete, since the attorney will be able to advise the employer if its restrictions will likely be upheld by the courts, or conversely whether they may be struck down as overbroad and unreasonable, thereby affording the employer no covenant protection whatsoever.

Inventions Checklist[70]

If an employee is expressly hired to invent, then clearly as a matter of contract law, any inventions belong to the employer. Also, the employer can have an employee sign an invention assignment agreement whereby the employee agrees to transfer to the employer the rights to any inventions created or developed by the employee during the course of his or her employment and also for a certain time thereafter, usually a one year period. Furthermore, it should be noted that federal copyright law in the U.S. holds that the copyright to any work created by an employee during the scope of his or her employment belongs to the employer, even if the employee has not signed any assignment agreement. In order to avoid patent and copyright problems, the employer and entrepreneur should specify in the employment contract that any work created by the employee during the course of his or her employment, such as an invention subject to patent or a computer program or software subject to copyright, belongs to the employer. The language of such an agreement can extend beyond works that are subject to patent and copyright, of course. Yet, in order to motivate the employer's more creative employees, the language in the agreement can specify that the employer

---

[70] See Bagley and Dauchy (2008) and Davidson and Forsythe (2011).

and the inventing employee jointly share the ownership rights in the invention or work, or that the inventing or creating employee will receive type of recognition and bonus for the idea or invention.

Summary

All of the intellectual property legal protections covered must be of heightened concern to the global businessperson and entrepreneur. Creating and developing intellectual property is characteristically an expensive and time-consuming process. Additional, the advent of the Internet and the relative ease of transmission and duplication of information on a truly global stage means that the gain the creator expects to accrue from his or her creative efforts may be imperiled unless actions are taken to legally safeguard such intellectual property.

EIGHTEEN

Inappropriate use of the Internet can result in criminal and civil liability; therefore, Internet regulation is an extremely vital topic. This chapter examines the governing bodies and laws that control e-contracts, the extent to which e-contracts are valid and enforceable, as well as the privacy issues that businesses have to bear in mind when conducting business via the Internet. Consequently, businesses must be cognizant that the Internet is a global and not merely a nationwide system. Managers must comprehend other nations' Internet policies and rules before they carry out business proposals such as e-contracts. Also, businesses in the United States need to ensure that their Internet practices are in accordance with the respective statutes governing computer transactions.

Online Contracts

The advent, development, and proliferation of the Internet as a global tool not only of communication but also as a means of doing business presented the legal system with a challenge of how to keep pace with the rising and spreading technology. This is especially true concerning electronic or "e-contracts," particularly because contract law is a field of law where many of the common law rules are literally of ancient heritage.

The legal system in the United States, however, has adapted to the new technology of contracting and doing business. Accordingly, the U.S. legal system has promulgated three very important statutes governing e-contracts: the Uniform Electronic Transactions Act (UETA), the Uniform Computer Information Transactions Act (UCITA), and the federal Electronic Signature in Global and National Commerce Act, all of which will be examined. But first it is necessary to point out that UETA and UCITA are "model" acts, prepared by the Conference of Commissioners on Uniform State Laws. These acts provide uniform rules for contracts involving computer transactions and the Internet, but they are not considered laws unless they are adopted by the various state legislatures in the United States.

Uniform Electronic Transaction Act

The objective of the UETA is to place electronic records and signatures on the same level as paper contracts and written signatures, effectively making electronic contracts as enforceable as paper ones. UETA applies only to those transactions between parties or entities that have agreed to conduct their business transactions by electronic means, such as by using the Internet.

There are two major components of UETA. First, an electronic record will satisfy the writing requirement of the Statute of Frauds. Second, an electronic signature is equal to a written signature on a paper contract. Furthermore, UETA maintains that an electronic signature will have the same effect as a notarized signature if the signature includes all of the standard information as required in an oath.

It must be stressed that UETA does not displace existing contract law—common law and statutory—but rather "merely" attempts to ensure that electronic contracts and signatures are treated legally as equivalent to paper contracts and written signatures.

Uniform Computer Information Transaction Act

The UCITA is a model act that establishes a uniform and extensive set of rules that govern computer information transactions. The term "computer information transaction" is broadly defined as an agreement to create, transfer, or license computer information or information rights.

There are several UCITA provisions that have relevance to e-contracts. First, regarding offer and acceptance, if an offer is in an electronic form, thereby evoking an electronic response in order to accept the offer, the contract is effectively formed when the electronic acceptance is received.

Second, regarding counteroffers, UCITA makes a notable change to the old common law, specifically in that counteroffers are not effective against electronic offerors. The rationale for this is that most electronic entities do not have the ability to evaluate or accept counteroffers or to make counteroffers. Thus, a contract is formed if the electronic offeree takes an action in response to the electronic offer that causes the electronic offeror to perform or to promise to perform the agreement, regardless of any additions, conditions, or qualifications being placed in the acceptance. An example would be an acceptance of an offer to purchase software with the proviso stated "but only if I am satisfied with the software."

Third, regarding mistakes, the UCITA rule is that a consumer is not bound by a unilateral electronic error if: 1) there is prompt notification of the error; 2) the consumer has not used or benefited from the information; 3) the consumer delivers all copies of the information or destroys the information at the request of the other party; and 4) the consumer pays all costs for shipping, reshipping, and processing. It must be emphasized that this rule only applies to consumers. However, it is equally important to relate that the consumer will not be entitled to any relief if the other party has provided a reasonable method to detect, avoid, and correct errors, for example an information verification process that must be utilized before an order is processed.

It is also important when discussing acceptance to distinguish between a shrink-wrap agreement and a click-on agreement. A "shrink-wrap agreement," characteristically used in the sale of computer software, is an agreement in which the provisions are expressed inside a box in which the goods are packaged. When the buyer opens the box, he or she is informed that by retaining the goods in the box, he or she thereby agrees to the terms of the shrink-wrap agreement. As a general rule, the courts will enforce shrink-wrap agreements even if the buyer and user of the goods did not read the terms of the agreement.

A "click-on agreement" is an agreement made by a buyer who, after completing a transaction on a computer, frequently for the purchase of software, is required to specify his or her agreement to the terms of the offer by clicking on an "agree" button. (The terms of such an agreement usually are found on the seller's Web site.) Again, as a general rule, the courts will enforce click-on agreements, maintaining that by clicking on "agree," the buyer-offeree has manifested his or her acceptance.

Finally, UCITA has created a novel provision called "authenticating the record." The rule is that if a contract requires a payment of $5,000 or more, the contract is enforceable against a party only if that party has authenticated the record. "Authentication" in essence means electronically signing the contract—wherein the signature becomes part of the record—and then verifying the information a second time before an order is placed. Similar to the Uniform Commercial Code's (UCC) merchant's written confirmation doctrine, UCITA holds that if the parties to a contract are merchants and the contract is for $5,000 or more, the contract may be enforced even without authentication if one party sends a letter or record confirming the contract and the other party does not reject it within ten days of receiving it.

Of course, since UCITA is a model act, a person doing business in a particular state in the U.S. must ascertain whether his or her state has adopted the act and, if so, in what exact form.

Electronic Signature in Global and National Commerce Act

The United States federal law that made electronic signatures equally as valid as written signatures was enacted by Congress in 2000 and is called the Electronic Signature in Global and National Commerce Act, also known as the "E-Sign" law. Before this federal law, electronic signatures were already legal in most of the states in the United States, but there was a problem of lack of uniformity among the states as state statutes differed as to what type of signatures were considered valid. The E-Sign law, therefore, was not only an effort to legalize electronic signatures but also an attempt to standardize the various state laws. The federal law, however, did not specify what type of technology must be used to create a legally binding signature for an Internet transaction.

Another goal of the statute was to place electronic contracts on an equal footing with paper contracts. Accordingly, the statute deems that electronic contracts, in most cases, will meet the requirements of the Statute of Frauds.

The federal statute preempts state laws except if a state has enacted the e-signature provisions of UETA, in which case the state is exempt from the federal statute.

The E-Sign Act as well as UETA, in order to protect people who do not want to, or cannot, do business electronically, stipulates that the use or acceptance of electronic signatures be voluntary. A valid electronic signature can include any mark or process intended to be the signature of an electronic contract, for example, a name typed at the bottom of an email message or a "click-through" process on a computer screen where a person can click on an "I Agree" component of a Web page.

Anti-Spam Statute

An anti-spamming statute was promulgated in 2006, the U.S. Safe Web Act (also known as the Undertaking Spam, Spyware, and Fraud Enforcement with Enforcers Beyond Borders Act), which is designed to prevent spam originating from servers in other countries. The U.S. Safe Web Act enables the U.S. Federal Trade Commission to share information and cooperate with foreign government agencies to investigate and eventually prosecute spamming, spyware, and other instances of fraud and deception on the Internet.

Conclusion

Therefore, are e-mail or e-contracts valid and enforceable? The answer is yes, assuming that all elements to a contract are present. However, certain problems inherent in the technology nonetheless remain.

For example, as to securing evidence of the e-contract, one simple and straightforward solution is to print out all pertinent e-mail communications as well as all "electronic" prior negotiations. Regarding the Statute of Frauds and the "writing" requirement of certain contracts, the practical solution is to print a paper version of the electronic contract, which certainly will comply with the Statute of Frauds.

Finally, regarding the signature requirement of contracts, an e-contract need not have a personal signature in order to be valid and enforceable. Rather, it is now acceptable for an electronic signature to be legally sufficient. But there is one caveat and that is that the Acts discussed herein are only U.S. federal and state statutes, and obviously Internet business and contracting are conducted globally. As of this writing, an international treaty on e-contracts does not yet exist. Thus, one engaging in Internet contracts globally is well advised to be aware of the laws, or lack thereof, of other countries regarding online contracts specifically as well as those pertaining to Internet commerce generally.

Internet Privacy—The Electronic Communications Privacy Act

The Electronic Communications Privacy Act (ECPA) is a federal statute enacted by the U.S. Congress in 1986 that makes it a crime to intercept an electronic communication at the point of transmission, in transit, when stored by a server, or after receipt by the intended recipient. The statute also makes it illegal to access stored e-mail. In addition to criminal penalties, the statute allows an aggrieved party to sue the interceptor for civil damages.

There are, however, two important exceptions whereby stored electronic e-mail communication can be accessed without violating the law. First, access is permitted by a party or entity that in fact provided the electronic communication service. A prime example would be an employer accessing the stored e-mail communications of its employees who utilized the employer's e-mail system. Second, government and law enforcement entities and personnel can access stored communications when investigating suspected illegal activities, though a valid search warrant may first have to be obtained for the ultimate disclosure of such communications.

Internet Domain Names—The Anticybersquatting Consumer Protection Act

In 1999, the United States Congress enacted the Anticybersquatting Consumer Protection Act to protect Internet domain names. A "domain name" is a distinct designation that identifies a Web site. In the past, domain names could be registered for a fee with private organizations that maintain databases of domain names, but legal controversies often resulted from the allegedly deceptive use of certain domain names; "cybersquatting" was the term used to describe such unfair uses of domain names.

Cybersquatting results when a person or business registers a domain name that is the same or very similar to another's domain name or trademark or even a "famous" person's name. The "squatter" then, in the typical case, attempts to sell the domain name back to the original owner. The federal statute now makes this practice illegal if the domain name is identical to or confusingly similar to the name of another and there is evidence of bad faith intent. Examples of bad faith would be the intent to divert the owner's customers, to harm its good will, or "merely" to offer to sell the domain name back to its owner.

The act makes cybersquatting illegal, and accordingly provides civil remedies to the victim of cybersquatting, who can sue for actual damages (including lost profits) or for statutory damages.

Finally, it should be mentioned that a private entity called the Internet Corporation for Assigned Names and Numbers (ICANN), under contract with the U.S. government, now is primarily responsible for regulating the issuance of domain names on the Internet. Futhermore, ICANN has established an arbitration process, called the Uniform Dispute Resolution Policy, to resolve domain name disputes. All users of the ICANN registration process are held to agree to use this dispute resolution procedure.

Global Legal Perspectives

Internet Monitoring in the United Kingdom[71]

Internet monitoring in the United Kingdom is extensively regulated by several statutes. British employers' electronic surveillance of their employees' Internet usage and e-mail also must comply with the United Kingdom's implementation of the European Union Directive on Data Protection.

The major statute in the U.K. is the Data Protection Act (DPA) of 1998. The DPA requires that the "data controller"—the one processing the information, typically the employer—notify the employees about the monitoring system as well as protect the data according to certain data protection standards. There is one exception the DPA, though, and that is where the electronic monitoring is permissible without notification when it is done for the purpose of preventing a specific crime. The DPA also requires that the monitoring be not only lawful, but also, most interestingly, fair to employees and that personally identifiable data be protected. Furthermore, the monitoring program must be reasonably related to achieving a legitimate business purpose and must respect the privacy of individuals.

Another important statute in the U.K. is the Regulation of Investigatory Powers (RIP) Act, which makes it a criminal offense to intentionally intercept, without authorization, any communication in the course of transmission. The RIP Act allows employers to intercept e-mail and monitor Internet access as long as *both* senders and recipients consent.

The Lawful Business Practice Regulations (LBPR) also provides additional exceptions to the RIP Act. The LBPR authorizes the interception of electronic communications without the employees' express consent in five situations: 1) to determine the existence of facts, to establish compliance with regulatory and self-regulatory practices or procedures, such as quality control and training

---

[71] See Rustad, Michael L., and Paulson, Sandra R. (2005).

processes; 2) to prevent or detect crimes; 3) to detect or investigate unauthorized use of electronic communications systems; 4) to secure or maintain effective system operation; and 5) to determine whether or not the communications are business communications. The monitoring of company employees, however, must be limited to their use of the company's computer system within the scope of the employees' work duties.

Argentina and Electronic Contracts[72]

In 2001, Argentina amended its civil code to legalize electronic contracts and signatures in order to reflect the increasing use of electronic contracts and signatures in that country as well as to "stabilize" its contract law. The Argentine law is called the Digital Signature Law (DSL) and it established uniform legal recognition of electronic documents and signatures. Most significantly, the DSL recognized the legal validity of documents constructed and signed electronically. Furthermore, DSL established a rebuttable presumption of validity concerning the identity of parties who sign contracts with "digital" signatures, but not those who use "electronic" signatures. In essence, in Argentina, a digital signature is an electronic one, meaning that the user thereof has a valid digital certificate at the time of formation, which was issued by an authorized certification agent who also must verify the signature contained in the electronic document.

Management Strategies

E-communication[73] has become the "order of the day" in most organizations. As a result, management must keep employees informed that they may encounter the Internet's global and national legislation in their business transactions. E-contracts have become a significant aspect of business partnerships and ventures, aiding in simplifying business processes by saving time and money while decreasing the chances of human error.

However, management must also focus on certain strategies when dealing with e-contracts in order to ensure that the contract process is a smooth and not very nerve-wracking experience for the parties involved. So, a very important consideration is that managers should ensure that online contracts are properly formed and enforceable. If this requirement is not imposed, disputes could occur between both parties, which would hinder the business process or result in serious legal risks if there are doubts about the effective communication of the terms and conditions.

Second, management should keep abreast of innovative technological systems, such as IBM's Contracts Online, which allows clients to review and sign

---

[72] See Hynick, Jeff (2005).
[73] Co-authored with Simone Maxwell, Nova Southeastern University.

a contract, track its status, and see who made alteration to the document online. Such systems will help to improve managers' levels of business performance.

Finally, management should ensure that they keep employees informed of any current updates regarding online laws, statutes, or acts, as well as the elements required for a legally enforceable contract. For instance, if people are conducting an online contract in Jamaica, they should be advised that there is no law enforcing e-signatures in that country, meaning that an e-contract requiring electronic signatures would not be recommended to be used in Jamaica.

Management should realize that Internet regulation is a very sensitive issue that needs to be closely monitored.

E-Mail Monitoring Policies: Avoiding Invasion of Privacy Claims in the Workplace[74]

"It was conceivable that they watched everybody all the time. …You had to live—did live, from habit that became instinct—in the assumption that every sound you made was overheard, and…every moment scrutinized."

Orwell's vision in *1984* may have seemed unreasonably pessimistic, but just how fanciful is this Orwellian premise? Has it in fact become reality in the context of today's ever-watchful work environment? Orwell's prose now appears rather clairvoyant since recent statistics indicate that over half of all large and mid-sized corporations monitor employee e-mail and Internet use. With such increased surveillance by employers, it is conceivable that employees are more inclined to resort to legal recourse in resolving claims based on an invasion of their privacy.

First, it should be noted that the United States Constitution only protects individuals from intrusions by the government, not private-sector employers. As such, employees are relegated to seeking redress under either the ECPA of 1986, state statutes, or state common law. Even then, the ECPA and its numerous exceptions do not provide the employee with much protection, and very few states have enacted privacy statutes. As a result, the only viable alternative remaining will require that the employee bring a claim predicated on state common law under a tort theory of invasion of privacy.

The common law, as noted, has traditionally recognized four torts for invasion of privacy: right of publicity, public disclosure of private facts, false light, and intrusion into seclusion. However, most workplace privacy claims will be governed by the tort of intrusion into an employee's seclusion. To effectively prove an intrusion claim, an employee must establish that he or she has a reasonable expectation of privacy and that the employer's review of the employee's information would be highly offensive to a reasonable person.

---

[74] Contributed by Shakila Faqeeri, Florida State University.

Several courts throughout the United States have expounded upon this legal principle in the context of an employer's use of e-mail monitoring. In one widely noted case, a federal court in Pennsylvania rejected an employee's privacy claims against an employer that had intercepted e-mail messages containing disparaging comments about a supervisor despite the fact that the employer had repeatedly relayed to the employees that all workplace e-mail communications would be confidential. Meanwhile, several California courts have come to the same conclusion in deciding that employees have no expectation of privacy where they had executed a form detailing the use of the company's computers. Other courts have even gone so far as to hold that employer monitoring of employee e-mail in a "personal folder" on a workplace computer is not an invasion of privacy. However, a state trial court in Massachusetts permitted an employee's invasion of privacy claim to proceed where the employer had not previously warned that it would be monitoring e-mail.

Although the case law is still sparse, the courts generally have held that an employer's business interest in monitoring the use of their company's computer systems supersedes the employee's right to privacy in the workplace. Nonetheless, a corporation should take the prudent approach in heading off any potential sources of litigation that may arise in such contexts. In doing so, a corporation's e-mail-monitoring policy should be governed by two overarching principles, notice and reason.

The purpose of giving notice to employees is to clarify the company's legitimate business interests in its use of monitoring. The notice will also serve to diminish the privacy expectations of employees by informing them that monitoring regularly takes place. Such notice can be provided in either company handbooks or policy manuals.

Conversely, an employer should avoid policies or customs that might justify an employee's expectation of privacy. In addition to providing notice, a corporation should establish a rational and logical connection between its legitimate business interest and its use and method of monitoring so that a court will not deem the policy to be an unreasonable invasion.

Summary

Internet regulation is a very pertinent issue in today's global marketplace. Therefore, this chapter has looked at the essential legal systems that govern computer transactions and the Internet. These statutes include the UETA, UCITA and the Electronic Signature in Global and National Commerce Act. Internet privacy and Internet domain were also discussed with regard to the acts by which they are regulated, the ECPA and the Anticybersquatting Consumer Protection Act. This chapter also examined the validity of e-contracts, both nationally as well as globally.

NINETEEN

The purposes of securities regulation laws are twofold. The first objective is to provide potential as well as actual investors with adequate information about a company, its principals, and plans in order to make investors more knowledgeable when making decisions about buying and selling shares of stock. The second purpose of securities laws is to prohibit deceptive and manipulative practices in the securities marketplace.

This area of business is a very complex area of the law, and is very heavily regulated, especially in the United States. The intent of this chapter, therefore, is to provide a basic examination of fundamental securities laws, first in the United States, and then in selected international jurisdictions.

United States Securities Laws

The issuance, sale, and transfer of securities are extensively and exactly regulated in the United Stated by both federal and state statutes as well as by government regulations promulgated by administrative agencies, principally the federal Securities and Exchange Commission (SEC). The most important federal laws are found in three statutes: the Securities Act of 1933, the Securities and Exchange Act of 1934, and the relatively new Sarbanes-Oxley Act of 2002. All of these statutes are administered and enforced by the SEC.

States also have securities laws, called colloquially "blue sky" laws. These regulations characteristically mirror the federal laws but are used for purely intra-state transactions or transactions where the SEC chooses not to exercise federal jurisdiction. It is beyond the purposes of this book to review the securities laws of the states, though a few general comments will be made.

The SEC is an independent regulatory agency, created by the Congressional 1934 Act, and empowered by Congress to administer and enforce all the federal securities law. Congress has allowed the SEC to engage in market surveillance so as to ferret out and regulate undesirable market practices. The SEC also has been delegated by Congress the power to make rules and regulations that have the force of law.

For example, there is the very important Rule 10b-5, prohibiting certain trading on inside information. Another rule, promulgated in 2000, allows corporate executives to sell shares of their firm's stock without facing insider-trading charges. The rule requires that executives create the plan at a time when they do not know of any material "inside" information. They must also fix the dates or the price of the trades in advance.

Recently, the SEC has promulgated a rule requiring certain types of disclosure of executive compensation. The SEC executive compensation rule would require companies to furnish tables in their annual filings that show the total yearly compensation for their chairman or chairwoman, their chief financial officer, and the next three highest-paid executives. Stock options as well as retirement benefits would have to be spelled out as well. Companies would also be required to explain the objectives behind their executives' compensation.

The SEC is also involved with many other activities pertaining to securities, for example requiring the disclosure of facts concerning offerings of securities regulating the trade in securities on national and regional securities exchanges and in the over-the-counter markets, licensing and regulating the activities of brokers, dealers, and investment advisors, investigating securities fraud and insider trading, imposing administrative sanctions and civil fines, and recommending criminal prosecutions against people who violate the securities laws to the Department of Justice. One thing the SEC does not do, however, is guarantee the economic merits or commercial success of any investment opportunity. Thus the SEC will not "stamp" an initial offering or subsequent sale as a "good," "bad," or even a "risky" one. Rather, the agency will strive to ensure the complete disclosure of accurate and material facts as well as protection from deception and fraud.

However, in order for the SEC to acquire jurisdiction of a security matter, a "security" must be involved. The definition of a security can take many forms, the most common of which is a share of stock or a bond issued by a corporation. But the word "security" also encompasses any investment contract in a profit-making plan, funded by shared investments, and where the profits are primarily derived from the efforts of third persons. Accordingly, there are many other potential security interests, such as investments in limited partnerships, franchises, and condominiums.

Perhaps even the purchase of a new type of property investment, called a "condo-hotel room," in which the buyer buys "in fee simple" (as discussed in the Real Estate chapter) a hotel room can also be construed as a security. But is the buyer also purchasing a security? The question is critical to resolve because if the purchase is of a security, then the seller of the condo-hotel room now is obligated to comply with a whole host of detailed and complex securities regulations. As of the writing of this book, the SEC has not yet made a definite ruling, but the developers of condo-hotels, such as Donald Trump, with his huge Ft. Lauderdale beach project, are anxious to know. But for the purposes of this chapter, the authors will presume that a security is present in the form of a traditional share of corporate stock.

The Securities Act of 1933

As emphasized, the Securities Act of 1933 is a type of statute relating to disclosure. It is designed to promote fairness and stability in the securities markets by requiring that certain essential information concerning the issuance of stocks and the principals behind the issuance are made available to the investing public. There are two major sections of the Act: Section 5, which details both the requirements for a registration statement as well as a prospectus; and Section 11, which sets forth the penalties for noncompliance with Section 5 requirements.

The basic principle of Section 5 of the Act is that, unless a security specifically qualifies for an exemption, it must be registered before it is offered to the public through either interstate commerce or via a security exchange. The issuing corporation must file a registration statement with the SEC. Furthermore, investors must be provided with a "prospectus," which is a document that describes the securities to be sold, the issuing corporation and principals behind the sale, material facts concerning the financial operations of the corporation, the nature of the investment, and, most importantly, the risk of the investment. The objective of the prospectus, as well as the registration statement, is to provide adequate information to the investment public to enable the unsophisticated investor to evaluate the financial risk involved, and thereby granting him or her the ability to make an informed investment decision.

As stressed, the SEC does not formally approve or disapprove of the issuance of securities or certify the risk or the degree thereof of a certain security. It is beyond the purpose of this book to cover in detail the registration process or, for that matter, all of the contents of the registration. But regarding the latter, the registration statement must contain certain key information, such as a description of the security offered for sale, the issuing corporation, the principals and management of the business, any current or potential litigation, as well as how the corporation intends to use the proceeds of the sale of the securities. Most importantly, a detailed financial statement certified by an independent Certified Public Accountant (CPA) firm is required.

As noted, there are certain exemptions to the 1933 Act by which a company will not have to comply, either totally or partially, with all the registration requirements of the Act. Again, it is beyond the purpose of this book to cover in detail all the exemptions and the precise nature thereof, but a brief and very general mention should be made of three important exemptions: 1) the "small offering" exemption, which eliminates the complicated and costly registration requirements for offers to sell securities below a specified dollar amount and/

or to a specified number of investors; 2) the "sophisticated investor" exemption, which pertains to offerings made to investors with sufficient knowledge and experience in business and financial matters, who are capable of evaluating the merits and risks of the prospective investment; and 3) the "private offering" exemption, which pertains to non-public offerings to a limited number of people who would have the necessary knowledge to make an informed investment decision, for example management personnel who are offered stock by their corporation.

Section 11 of the Act imposes legal liability when either the registration statement or prospectus contains false material statements and, most notably, material omissions. Pursuant to securities law, as opposed to the common law, "silence" very well can be deemed as fraud. The key qualifier "material" means that the information, if stated accurately or disclosed, would have deterred or tended to deter an average ordinary and prudent investor from purchasing the securities at issue.

Minor errors, minor omissions, and irrelevant information are not grounds for liability. Rather, the thrust of Section 11 is to ensure the disclosure of those facts that would be an important indication of the nature of the investment, its risk, and the condition of the issuing corporation and its business affairs. Examples include an overstatement of sales or profits, an understatement of debts and liabilities, and the criminal records of corporate executives.

There are criminal and civil penalties for violating the provisions of the 1933 Act. The SEC can impose civil fines and is also authorized to bring an injunction to stop an improper offering. Finally, investors are permitted to bring a private cause of action for damages to a federal court for monetary losses caused by the violation of the Act. It is important to note, however, that a private plaintiff bringing a lawsuit does not have to show that he or she relied on the false or misleading statements, which is different from how the reliance element to the lawsuit is presumed.

The Securities and Exchange Act of 1934

The Securities and Exchange Act of 1934 has several purposes. It provides for the registration and regulation of security exchanges, securities brokers and dealers, and national security associations. It also provides for the regulation of proxy solicitation for purposes of voting. Most importantly, the 1934 Act is a very broad anti-fraud statute: It applies to all purchase and sale of securities, and it seeks to police, punish, and deter fraudulent, deceptive, and manipulative practices in the securities marketplace.

It is very important to observe that the Act prohibits affirmatively false, deceptive, and misleading statements and conduct. But it also prohibits the omission of material information in the purchase and sale of securities. Furthermore, the Act also seeks to prevent and punish insider trading, that is the use of material "inside" (non-public) information in the purchase and sale of any security.

There are very serious civil and criminal penalties for violating the 1934 Act, including individual fines of up to $5 million and corporate fines of up to $25 million, and imprisonment for up to 20 years. Private actions for damages are also allowed.

The 1934 Act's anti-fraud and insider trading provisions cover all cases of securities trading, whether on organized exchanges, over-the-counter markets, or in private transactions. The Act covers any form of security regardless of whether a firm's securities are registered under the 1933 or 1934 Act. Of course, federal jurisdiction must be present, which is readily accomplished in any case since virtually no commercial transaction can be effectuated in the U.S. today without some connection to, or use of some instrumentality of, interstate commerce. However, if a particular case is deemed too small for the SEC or the Justice Department to get involved, there are, as will be seen later in this chapter, state security laws and agencies that parallel the federal laws and the SEC.

Section 14(a) of the 1934 Act regulates the solicitation of proxies from shareholders of Section 12 corporations. A Section 12 corporation is one that has assets of more than $10 million and 500 or more shareholders. Among other requirements, such a company must file a registration statement with the SEC for its securities. Section 14(a) authorizes the SEC to regulate the content of proxy statements sent by a corporation to shareholders who are seeking the power to vote on behalf of the shareholders in a particular corporate election. This law requires the proxy solicitation materials to fully and accurately disclose all the facts that are relevant to the matter to be voted on. The law also prohibits false and misleading statements in proxy materials sent to shareholders.

Section 14(a) also regulates "tender offers," which are public invitations to shareholders of a public corporation to sell their shares. If an offeror is seeking 5% or more control of a company, the offeror must disclose sufficient facts about his or her background and intentions. There is also a provision for liability for making false or misleading statements or omissions in the "tender offer."

One major problem that the 1934 Act seeks to remedy is the wrong of insider trading. That is, corporate insiders, such as directors, executives, officers, and managers, due to their position, often have access to nonpublic, confidential, "inside" information that can materially affect the price of their company's stock. The possession of such information very well could provide them with a distinct and unfair advantage over the general public and average shareholder.

Pursuant to the common law, as noted in the Torts and Business chapter of this book, liability for fraud is attached only to intentional, affirmative misrepresentations. Silence, as a general rule was not deemed to be fraud, but there was an exception in the case of silence by a fiduciary, which would be construed as fraud. Yet the problem for insider trading wrongs was that even though corporate directors, executives, and officers were deemed to be fiduciaries, their fiduciary duty was owed only to the corporation and not to the purchasers or sellers of their company's stock.

The 1934 Act attempts to redress this potential flagrant insider trading inequity in two ways. One is in Section 16(b), which regulates "short swing" profits by insiders. The other, which will be covered in the next section of this chapter, is the very significant Section 10(b), as elaborated and implemented by SEC Rule 10b-5.

Section 16(b) makes corporate directors and officers, as well as large shareholders (that is, those holding 10% of more of a company's stock), turn over to the corporation all short-term (or "short-swing") profits: those made from the purchase and sale or sale and repurchase of the company's stock within a six-month period. It must be emphasized that it is irrelevant as to whether the corporate insider actually used such inside information. Regardless of whether or not the information was used, all short-swing profits must be returned to the corporation. This section of the Act in essence presumes, irrebuttably, that such an insider possesses inside information and is taking advantage of such information. Section 16(b) applies not just to the purchase and sale of stock, but also to stock warrants and options. Finally, the section requires directors, officers, and large shareholders to report their ownership interests and stock-trading activities with the SEC.

Section 10(b) of the 1934 Act and SEC Rule 10b-5—Insider Trading v. Trading on Inside Information

Section 10(b) of the 1934 Act is one of the most important anti-fraud provisions in federal securities law. Pursuant to this very broad law and its related SEC Rule 10b-5, it is illegal to make any false, deceptive, or misleading statements regarding the purchase or sale of securities. It is also illegal to fail to state material facts regarding the purchase and sale of securities or to employ any fraudulent, deceptive, or manipulative device or scheme that harms another person who participates in the securities market. The Act and SEC Rule also prohibit insider trading.

It is very important to emphasize that the coverage of these laws is not restricted merely to insiders, as is Section 16(b). Rather, potentially any person having access to or receiving material information of a nonpublic nature and who trades thereon is subject to Section 10(b) and Rule 10b-5.

Securities fraud crimes are specific intent crimes. That is, the government must demonstrate that the alleged wrongdoer acted purposefully, intentionally, and knowingly to misrepresent facts, to deceive or mislead, or to omit facts. This intent requirement is called "scienter," which is an old common law requirement for fraud, though the term is Latin in origin. Basically it means the presence of an "evil mind," meaning that one committed a wrongful act knowingly and purposefully. It also must be stressed that if the U.S. government is prosecuting a person for criminal violations of federal securities laws, the government must convince a jury, "beyond a reasonable doubt," that the defendant possessed scienter, as well as convince it of the other elements of the crime.

A key element to the government's criminal case against former Enron CEO Ken Lay was scienter, because the presence of an "evil mind" is necessary for the specific intent crimes of securities fraud and insider trading. Ken Lay's defense was known in legal circles as the classic "idiot" or "ostrich" defense: that one was unaware of any wrongdoing, that one was a weak and careless manager, that one was deceived and manipulated by other "bad" people, and, critically, that while one did make misstatements, one lacked the specific criminal intent to misrepresent material facts about the company and to trade based on inside information.

Such a defense *did* work for Richard Scrushy, the former CEO of Health SouthCorporation, who was acquitted on similar accounting and securities fraud charges. Of course, legal experts have related that it helped in Scrushy's case that he was tried in Birmingham, Alabama, where he was well known as "Little Richard," the "minister's son," and where he regularly preached in, and contributed to, the African-American churches there, and where the local jury was in part composed of African-Americans.

The "idiot defense," however, *did not* work for Enron's Ken Lay and Jeffrey Skilling. In May of 2006, a "home town" jury in Houston found both former Enron executives guilty of securities and wire fraud and conspiracy and found Skilling also guilty of insider trading. The victory was viewed as a major victory for the government, underscoring corporate accountability. The victory was also seen as the "grand finale" to the era of corporate scandals, culminating in the passage of the very strict Sarbanes-Oxley Act by the U.S. Congress.

Sentencing was expected for the Enron executives in late 2006, but Lay was still declaring his innocence right up until his death in early July 2006. Lay stated to the end that he "firmly believes" in his innocence. Skilling seemed resigned, almost stoical, saying that he was disappointed by the verdict, but "that's how the system works." Skilling was ultimately sentenced to 24 years and four months in prison, which has been the harshest sentence to stem from the Enron scandal and collapse. Not to be disrespectful to the dead or to be overly cynical, but it should be noted that Ken Lay, even in death, is causing major problems in the effort to provide some type of material redress to the former Enron employees and shareholders as well as mutual fund- and pension-holders of the stock. Because Ken Lay died before he was officially sentenced, he was not technically convicted. Actually, Lay's conviction was erased because he died before his appeal was effectuated. In October 2006, a federal judge vacated Lay's conviction, thereby wiping out the jury's verdict. Although it is way beyond the scope of this book to deal with this unusual "twist" in criminal law, it should be mentioned that Lay's death will bring the government's attempts to seize Lay's substantial remaining property to an end since he is *not* considered to be a felon. So, incredibly, instead of the defrauded Enron victims receiving most of the assets, Lay's surviving spouse will be the main beneficiary of his death.

"Materiality" is another requirement to civil and criminal liability under the securities laws. That is, liability attaches only to misrepresentations and omissions of "material" facts in connection with the purchase or sale of a security. A fact will be regarded as being material if it likely would have affected the price of a company's stock. Another definition of materiality is that a reasonably prudent investor would have attached importance to the fact when making his or her investment or sale decision.

For example, changes in a firm's financial position, dividend payments or adjustments, sales and profit information, new discoveries of products, processes, or minerals or oil, the sale or purchase of substantial assets, illegal activity by corporate directors, executives, and officers, as well as an impending merger or takeover all very probably would be deemed "material" facts, and thus legally must be stated accurately and disclosed fully. Furthermore, in a private cause of action for violation of the securities laws, a plaintiff, in addition to scienter and materiality, must prove "reliance," that is that he or she reasonably relied on the false or misleading statement or omission to his or her own detriment.

Section 10(b) and SEC Rule 10b-5 prohibit and punish insider trading. Additionally, as will be seen, the term "insider" is broadly construed by both the SEC and the courts. However, securities law in the U.S. does make a critical distinction between *insider trading*, which is always illegal, and *trading on inside information*, which generally is illegal, though there are two important exceptions. In order to fully explicate this very complex and consequential area of the law, it is first necessary to point out that in the U.S., there historically have been two competing legal theories regarding the use of inside information in the purchase or sale of securities. One of the theories is called the narrow, or insider, or misappropriation theory. The other is called the broad, outsider, or level-laying-field theory.

Under the "narrow" theory, only certain people are liable for trading on inside information, and under the "broad" theory, potentially anyone is liable for trading on inside information. The prevailing legal view in the U.S. is the "narrow" theory. However, even before this legal liability theory can be discussed, it is first necessary to establish certain prerequisites.

For legal liability to be attached to insider trading, one first needs information, second, material information, and third, inside material information. Since "materiality" has been briefly discussed, the crucial terms "information" and "inside" will be examined. The problem with these terms, as well as "materiality," for that matter, is that there are no precise definitions to them. This is perhaps by design as the SEC and the Justice Department very well may want people, particularly insiders, to think very carefully when they start trading and especially when trading in their own company's stock.

"Information" ordinarily means factual information: concrete, actual, historical, or scientific information. Whereas predictions and opinions are ordinarily not regarded as sufficiently factual to be "information," rumors and speculation similarly are not regarded as information. Furthermore, statements in the form of questions are not regarded as sufficiently factual for liability. Of course, it can be a fine line between a mere opinion or rumor and a fact, especially if either is based on some underlying actual facts. For example, if the staff research assistant to a company's high-level executive reports to a friend that his/her "boss" has been asking for a lot of information about a potential merger partner, is that sufficiently factual to be "information"? It is certainly not public, which brings one to the next foundational requirement. Even if this is considered "information," it must be "inside," meaning that it is non-public, confidential, and proprietary.

Many questions come into play here. How is the information characterized? Who knows of the information? How many people? How did they come to know of it? Did the recipients of the information know, or should they have known, that the information was private? Did they know that someone breached a fiduciary relationship or duty of loyalty in obtaining or passing on the information? These are key questions that must be answered, ultimately perhaps by a jury. Such questions also indicate what the wise reader has already discerned: The law is not physics!

So, presuming that information is factual, material, and inside, exactly who is liable under the "narrow" theory? There are three categories of people who can be liable for insider trading under the narrow theory: 1) the one misappropriating, 2) insiders, and 3) "tippees" of insiders.

The first classification, "misappropriators," is rather simple and straightforward. These are people who steal inside information, spy it out, or bribe for it, and then trade on it. In addition to their initial crimes, they are subject to securities law liability.

The second category, "insiders," is the one the government is most concerned with because there exists the greatest chance for abuse. Effectively, if an insider knowingly and purposefully trades in his or her own company's stock based on the possession of material, inside information, the insider commits a very serious legal wrong. The term "insider," it must be emphasized, is broadly construed and covers not only traditional insiders such as directors, executives, officers, managers, employees, and agents of the company, but also people known as "temporary insiders," such as the firm's attorneys, stock brokers, investment bankers, and financial printers.

Of course, what if the insider—either permanent or temporary—does not trade directly, but rather tips off someone else to trade. That circumstance brings the reader to the third classification of liable people, tippees. A "tippee" is a person to whom material inside information is transmitted to from an insider. The "usual suspects" when it comes to "tippees" are the relatives, friends, and business associates of the insider. The foremost tippee case was the famous Supreme Court *U.S. v. Chestman* decision, in which the Court upheld the conviction of a former stockbroker who was deemed to be a tippee and who conspired with a family insider in the trading of company stock before the sale of the company to a large competitor. What makes the case unique is that the stockbroker was a "remote tippee" in the sense that the information was passed on to him from the insider by means of a very attenuated chain of family personal and business conversations.

However, regardless of how remote, tippees are liable only if they were in conspiracy with an insider, meaning that they knew they were acting improperly in concert with the insider to commit a legal wrong. There is, of course, a big difference between being a co-conspirator and acting to trade, and merely hearing a comment from an insider and trading thereon. Yet there is an exceptional form of liability for a special type of tippee, called an inadvertent tippee, who is under some type of recognized fiduciary duty. So, for example, if an ordinary person not connected to an insider hears a comment by an insider at a public place regarding the company, and trades thereon, there is no liability, because there is no conspiracy and no legal tippee status. But if the member of a profession, such as a doctor or lawyer, hears even inadvertently from an insider some private fact pertaining to the company, the doctor or lawyer cannot trade on it due to the obligations of their profession and especially their fiduciary duty to their clients and patients.

The leading inadvertent tippee case was a Supreme Court decision in which the court upheld the insider trading conviction of a psychiatrist who traded on private information obtained from a patient-insider during treatment. The psychiatrist, although not in conspiracy with his patient, was legally liable due to the breach of the fiduciary relationship and the confidential nature of the professional relationship.

The famous "tippee," or alleged tippee case, was the saga of Martha Stewart, whom the SEC is proceeded against civilly for being a tippee of, and in conspiracy with, an insider, her "good friend" Dr. Waksal, the principal shareholder and CEO of ImClone, Inc. Recall that Stewart was convicted of, and served her time for, perjury and obstruction of justice, but the government did not prosecute her for the crime of trading on inside information. As noted, the burden of proof for the government in such a criminal case would be "proof beyond a reasonable doubt," which apparently the government believed it could not adequately demonstrate because the transmission of the clearly insider tip that the Food and Drug Administration (FDA) had rejected ImClone's main cancer-fighting drug did not come directly from Dr. Waksal to Stewart, but rather through an attenuated chain of Dr. Waksal, the senior broker, the junior broker, and *then* to Martha Stewart. Of course, the irony of the situation for Stewart is that she was judged as a felon, went to prison, lost her broker's license, and forfeited any right to serve as an executive of a publicly traded company, including her own, all for lying about and covering up a trade which the government believed it did not have enough evidence to prosecute as a crime. The SEC pursued Martha Stewart only civilly for inside trading, where of course the burden of proof is less; and that civil lawsuit was ultimately settled by her paying a substantial fine.

There is an even greater irony in that the drug that was at the center of all the controversy, upon further testing, actually may have some cancer-fighting properties. As a result the drug was submitted to the FDA again for approval. So Martha Stewart, as well as Dr. Waksal, should have held on to their stock, and thus the "good doctor" would now not be in prison for seven years for the crime of insider trading. He was clearly an insider acting on inside information.

Accordingly, the reader may be thinking that the "narrow" theory of insider trading liability is not that narrow at all. In truth, it is not that narrow, but it is also not the broad theory either, under which anyone who trades on material, nonpublic information, regardless of how acquired, commits a legal wrong. This is a very consequential distinction in securities law because, as interpreted by the courts, there are two types of people who can legally trade even based on the possession of material, inside information. These people are the "lucky" and the "smart."

The "lucky" would be those people who inadvertently or by happenstance come upon information, such as the classic case of the janitor who came upon some abandoned corporate property which contained some very valuable information. Suffice it to say, this fortunate—as well as astute—janitor is no longer working in that occupation. Yet, one should be very careful about appearing too "lucky," especially if one winds up trading in the sector in which one works, let alone in one's own company's stock.

The more realistic exception that allows trading on inside information is for the "smart" person—market professionals and perhaps skillful amateurs too. These are people who discern information, which is in fact inside information, but by legitimate means such as searching public sources of information, extrapolating therefrom, and making deductions, which may be correct. These people are effectively rewarded for their diligence and intelligence.

However, if one does not have the time or skill or inclination to engage in such work, one can always retain the services of a market professional. This exception to the general prohibition against trading on inside information is based on the premise that allowing market professionals to ferret out by legitimate means leads to more accurate and efficient markets, which benefits all investors. Yet again, we offer the same cautionary advice, and please excuse the language, but "Do not be too darn smart."

As noted, manipulation can be grounds for legal liability under the broad anti-fraud provisions of the 1934 Act. A prime example of a manipulative practice would be an Internet "pump and dump" stock scheme. One such case involved a teenager, who had won a stock picking contest on CNBC. The teen entered Internet stock chat rooms as well as placed e-mails praising particular stocks that he owned, i.e., the "pump." His messages were sent by the hundreds and under many aliases, all "hyping" the stock. The interest that the volume of such communication engendered caused the price of the stock to rise, and then the teenager sold the stock, i.e., the "dump." He made several hundred thousand dollars using this scheme, but he was eventually sued by the SEC. His lawyer contended that the teenager's statements were merely opinions and "puffing." The teenager eventually settled the case by "disgorging" almost $300,000 of the $800,000 he had made in profits.

Yet due to the fact that the settlement neither involved any criminal sanctions nor prohibited the teenager from trading stock, and that he was allowed to keep $500,000 in profits, the SEC came under a great deal of criticism, even ridicule, for being "bested" by a teenager. So the next "pump and dump" case that came within the SEC's purview had a dramatically different result. That case involved a 24-year-old UCLA graduate who also sent out hundreds of messages under many aliases "hyping" stock in Internet chat rooms. He made more than $1 million in profits, but was, at the SEC's urging, prosecuted by the Justice Department for manipulating stocks, was convicted, and sentenced to 15 months in federal prison. Some observers thought the penalty was too harsh while others noted that the sentence certainly was a deterrent to "pump and dump" schemes, but no one was laughing at the SEC anymore.

Finally, a brief mention must be made of the Private Securities Litigation Reform Act of 1995. As noted, there is liability under federal securities for misrepresenting as well as omitting material facts, but generally there is no liability for "mere" opinions or predictions because they are not "facts." Nonetheless, companies were reticent to make future projections of financial results, due to the fear of being sued if the projections were not accurately forecast.

Plainly, there is a fine line between an opinion/prediction and a fact, especially when the former is based in part on the latter. Therefore, the U.S. Congress passed the 1995 Act to in essence give companies a "safe harbor" to make such forecasts. Specifically, the Act legally protects "forward-looking" statements if they contain "meaningful cautionary statements" that explain why the projections may not be achieved or if the statements were made without the knowledge that they were in fact misleading.

The Sarbanes-Oxley Act of 2002 and Corporate Governance

The Sarbanes-Oxley Act (SOX) of 2002 was a Congressional response to the spate of corporate scandals exemplified by the infamous Enron collapse. SOX emerged as one of the most important modifications of federal securities laws since the enactment of the 1933 and 1934 acts. The main purposes of SOX are to protect investors by improving the accuracy and reliability of corporate disclosure and to increase and improve corporate accountability and governance.

The Act also imposes very harsh—some would say draconian—penalties for violations of the securities laws and SOX provisions. One of the principal provisions of SOX is to require corporate chief executives to take legal responsibility for the accuracy and completeness of financial statements and reports that are filed with the SEC. Chief Executive Officers (CEOs) and Chief Financial Officers (CFOs) now must *personally* certify that the statements and reports are accurate and complete. This means that the days of Enron CEO Ken Lay claiming "ignorance and innocence" as to the "financials" are long gone!

The Act also created a new federal agency, the Public Accounting Oversight Board, which reports to the SEC. This agency oversees and regulates public accounting firms. Of course, the accounting profession was regarded in the "pre-Enron days" as an independent, autonomous, and self-regulating profession, governed by a code of ethics, much like law and medicine. But the failure of the accounting profession to regulate itself (let alone others) brought down upon itself a new federal regulatory agency to "police" the now delimited "profession."

The certification requirements of SOX are a very important and consequential feature of the statute. Section 906 mandates that CEOs and CFOs of most major companies whose stock is traded on public stock exchanges must now certify the financial statements and reports that are required to be filed with the SEC. These corporate executives must certify that the statements and reports fully comply with SEC requirements and, in addition, that the information therein fairly represents, in all material respects, the financial conditions and operations of the company.

Furthermore, Section 302 requires that CEOs and CFOs of reporting companies certify that they reviewed the reports and then sign them, designating that to the best of their knowledge, the report neither contains any untrue statements nor omits any material facts. Additionally, the signing officers must certify that their firms have established internal control systems to make certain that any relevant material information is ascertained and is placed in the report. Finally, the signing officers must certify that they disclosed to auditors any significant deficiencies in the internal control systems of the firm. Certain reports are required to be filed quarterly as well as annually with the SEC.

In addition to the certification requirements, there are other important corporate governance provisions in SOX. Section 402 prohibits any reporting company or a company filing an initial public stock offering from arranging, extending, renewing, or maintaining a personal loan for a director or executive officer. (Still, there are some exceptions in the Act for consumer and housing loans.) The objective of this provision is to prevent companies from making personal loans to corporate directors and officers and then forgiving the loans to the detriment of shareholders.

Section 806 of SOX provides protections for "whistleblowers." This provision prohibits publicly traded companies from discharging, demoting, suspending, threatening, harassing, or otherwise discriminating against an employee who provides to the government or assists in any government investigation regarding activities that the employee reasonably believes constitute a violation of securities fraud laws. The whistleblowing employee is protected if he or she discloses information internally or to federal regulatory and law enforcement agencies or to a member of Congress or a Congressional committee. But the employee is not protected if he or she makes a report to the media.

It is important to emphasize that the SOX whistleblower protection provisions will protect an employee who has a reasonable belief of wrongdoing, even if that belief later is determined to be unfounded. To compare, some state whistleblower protection statutes, such as the one in Florida, while it allows the employee to report the violation of any law, rule, or regulation, it also will require that the employee report an actual violation of the law. Even if it is reasonable, a belief alone as to a violation will be insufficient for whistleblowing legal protection if the employee is erroneous as to his or her "illegal" conclusion.

SOX also requires that regulated companies set up confidential whistleblowing reporting systems so that employees can express their concerns about illegal accounting and auditing practices and securities fraud. Employees should be able to anonymously contact, electronically or otherwise, an independent ethics center, which will then alert the company directors, officers, executives, and managers as to a possible problem.

Section 406 of SOX deals with codes of ethics. Initially, it must be stressed that the Act neither mandates that SOX-regulated companies adopt codes of ethics, nor that if such codes are in fact in existence, the Act does not make them legally binding. Rather, the Act requires that publicly traded firms report to the SEC as to whether or not the firm has a code of ethics for senior financial officers, and if not, the reasons for the lack thereof. The objective of this provision is to let the potential investor know that he or she may be making an investment in a firm that does not have a code of ethics in place.

Furthermore, SOX also requires that if a regulated company changes its codes of ethics, or makes any exceptions or waives thereto, the company must make an immediate disclosure to the SEC as well as disseminate the information publicly by means of the Internet or other comparable electronic means. Again, the objective is to warn current shareholders and potential investors of possible problems at the firm. This ethics "exception" disclosure provision resulted directly from the Enron disaster, where the company did have a fine-sounding code of ethics, but many exceptions were made thereto by the company executives.

Finally, SOX substantially increases the penalties for securities fraud and related crimes. Specifically, Section 906 holds that a CEO or CFO who certifies a financial report statement to be filed with the SEC while knowing that the report or statement does not fulfill SOX reporting requirements, can be subject to up to $1 million in fines and up to ten years in prison, or both. In addition, if the CEO of CFO willfully certifies a report knowing that it is does not fulfill SOX requirements, the CEO or CFO is subject to a penalty of up to $5 million in fines and 20 years in prison, or both. Section 1106 of the Act increases the penalties for willful securities law violations of the 1934 Act, in particular by increasing the fines up to $5 million and an individual's imprisonment up to 20 years. Section 1107 deals with retaliation against whistleblowing employees, although in the statute Congress (to the dismay of the authors of this book) used the pejorative term "informants" instead of the neutral term "whistleblowers."

Regardless, the penalties are very severe for an employer of a publicly traded firm who retaliates against a whistleblower. The Act decrees a punishment of a fine as well as up to ten years in prison, or both, for knowingly and purposefully taking any adverse action against a person—including interfering with a person's lawful employment or livelihood—for making whistleblowing disclosures or assisting with a government investigation.

State Securities Laws

In the United States today, not only the federal government, but all the states have their own bodies of securities laws, which usually parallel the federal laws. These laws regulate the theoretically purely intrastate purchase or sale of securities. But these laws are characteristically employed in securities cases in which the federal government has declined jurisdiction. Thus, it is quite conceivable for both the federal government and a state government to have concurrent jurisdiction of a securities case. As a matter of fact, the federal securities laws specifically preserve state remedies.

The purposes of the state laws are to prevent the issuance and sale of worthless securities and to protect the investing public from fraudulent and deceptive practices. State securities laws colloquially are referred to as "blue sky" laws, which plainly indicates their main objective of preventing the sale of securities that are as worthless as the blue sky! Although it is beyond the purposes of this book to examine all the states' securities laws, a few common features should be pointed out.

First, as noted, the state statutes usually pattern themselves after the federal statutes, especially as to the anti-fraud and insider trading prohibitions. Second, most states regulate securities brokers and dealers. Third, most states provide for the registration of securities offered or issued within the state with an appropriate state agency or official, together with the filing of detailed background and financial information, unless there is a state exemption. Finally, most states take the approach of the federal government in the U.S. and "merely" mandate that certain disclosures be made before stock is offered for sale. Most states thus will not pass judgment as to the wisdom of a particular stock investment.

However, there are a few states that have fairness standards that a company must meet in order to sell its stock in the state. If these standards are not complied with, the state can forbid, by virtue of its "police power," the issuance of the securities. Similarly, it is possible for a state to provide more securities law protection versus the federal government. Take the case of the State of Ohio and the type of investment known as a "viatical" investment or settlement. Viaticals are life insurance policies sold to investors for a materially lesser amount of the stipulated death benefit. When the policyholder dies, the investor can cash in the policy for its full value. Viatical investments originated in the 1980s to provide cash to AIDS patients, who possessed life insurance and no heirs, and who needed money right away for medical expenses. Viaticals investments, however, became rife with fraud and abuse, but they were not regulated by the SEC. However, some states, such as Ohio, passed legislation to place viaticals under the purview of state securities laws and regulators, which require that such investments must be sold by licensed individuals, be registered with state officials as securities, and that the risks of such an investment be disclosed to investors.

Global Legal Perspectives

Securities laws of the U.S. are not limited to the country's borders—they have extraterritorial effect. In today's global marketplace, false and misleading statements made internationally can harm investors in the U.S., thereby triggering U.S. securities law enforcement.

The leading case arose in 2000, when the SEC filed a securities fraud case against a German company because its executives deliberately misled investors when they denied that the company was in merger negotiations. The case was settled, and the German company did not admit or deny any liability, but agreed that it would not violate U.S. securities laws in the future. The case was the first of its kind regarding a foreign company, and its purpose was to "send a message" to foreign companies and executives who sell securities in U.S. markets that they are subject to U.S. securities laws regardless of where the false or misleading statements, omissions, or manipulation occur, either in the U.S. or internationally.

What is interesting about the case is that the denial of the merger talks was not illegal pursuant to German law, where such denials are common. But in the U.S., corporate executives must say "no comment," and if they instead decide to speak, they must speak truthfully and fully about such potential mergers.

One of the reforms mandated by the SOX was to require that publicly-traded U.S. companies institute whistleblowing "hot lines" for employees to report, confidentially and anonymously, either corporate or fellow employee wrongdoing. However, a serious problem has emerged for those U.S. companies that do business in Europe, specifically where European data protection laws make it difficult for an employee or any person to anonymously accuse someone of wrongdoing. These laws typically provide that a citizen of the European community has the right to know who is collecting information about him or her, and these laws also may include provisions restricting what corporate information can be revealed to outsiders. For example, in France, a government agency ruled that anonymous whistleblower "hot lines" do not provide adequate protection for people accused of wrongdoing. The result is that many U.S. companies are confronted with a legal dilemma. They are required by SOX to establish whistleblowing "hot lines," but if they do so for their European subsidiaries, they may effectively violate European laws. As of the writing of this book, government regulators in the U.S. and Europe are attempting to devise a compromise whistleblowing policy that preserves anonymity but also protects the rights of the accused person to his or her personal information. Businesses are anxiously awaiting the solution, but in the meantime, companies are exposed to significant legal risks.

Japan and Inside Information[75]

Diametrically opposed to the U.S., in Japan, the failure of a director of a corporation to disclose important information that would affect the price of stock is not a criminal or civil wrong. Fraudulently concealing information, however, is an offense. Even more significant, the issue as to whether or not a director in Japan has a duty to inform the other party about inside information when trading in his or her own company's stocks generally has been met with a "negative answer." Unless there is a case of "clear-cut fraud," a director will not be obligated to make redress to a party simply because the director failed to disclose certain inside information about the company that the director came to know in the course of his or her work unless the other party affirmatively asked the director to disclose the information.

However, actively concealing or purposefully delaying the release of information probably will constitute fraud in Japan, with criminal and civil ramifications. Therefore, Japan, even in its securities laws, appears to mirror the old Anglo-American common law general rule that "silence is not fraud." Recall that in the U.S., when it comes to the purchase and sale of securities, silence—i.e., the failure to disclose material information—is considered fraud. Furthermore, the legal wrong of insider trading is a very serious criminal and civil infraction in the United States.

Management Strategies

"Going Public"[76]

When should a company "go public"? That is, when should a company contemplate selling shares of stock to the public? Offering shares of stock to the public will surely result in access to broader financial markets from which to obtain capital. Moreover, once the company goes public, it can use shares of stock as opposed to cash to acquire employees, technology, products and services, as well

---

[75] See Misawa, Mitsuru (2005).
[76] See Bagley and Dauchy (2008) and Davidson and Forsythe (2011).

as other businesses. "Going public" will certainly enhance the visibility of the company, and assuming the company does well, it can return to the public market for additional capital. "Going public" also will typically result in the shares of the company's stock being valued at a much higher price than that originally set by the promoters and organizers of the company, which will afford these original participants as well as early investors, a ready market for the sale of their stock. Yet there are many critical questions to answer in making this determination. First, does the company need significant new amounts of capital that only can be obtained by a public offering of stock? Are the initial investors "tapped out"? That is, are they now unwilling or unable to provide additional capital? Second, can the company make a public offering viable — financially and practically? That is, is the company at the stage where it is ready to expand into new markets, to introduce new products and services, and to engage in sufficient research and development? Does the company have or can it obtain the working capital to sustain the expansion created from initially "going public"? Third, is the company and its principals (directors, officers, major shareholders) prepared — legally, financially, and practically — to assume the extensive legal obligations, particularly in the area of disclosure to government regulators and shareholders, that will now be necessary? Are these principals prepared to reveal substantial information about their experiences, background, financial transactions, business dealings, and legal proceedings? Is the company prepared to provide detailed audited financial statements to government regulators? Is the company prepared to spend the time, effort, and money to comply with federal and state security laws? Can the company afford the attorneys' and accountants' fees, which easily could cost several hundreds of thousands of dollars, for the initial offering and to maintain compliance with the laws, particularly the Sarbanes-Oxley Act which mandates much more strict controls and procedure for corporate governance, disclosure, verification, and internal accounting processes.

The Sarbanes-Oxley Act and Human Resource Management [77]

The SOX, although mainly viewed as a statute that substantially affects a company's finance and accounting departments and personnel, is a law that also has significant ramifications for the firm's human resource management (HRM). It is a misconception to think that SOX affects the accounting departments alone. Rather, the statute has implications for human resource professionals as well as in-house counsel because, as noted, SOX significantly expands not only financial reporting and certification requirements, but also the protection for employees of publicly traded companies who "blow the whistle" on certain allegations of corporate misconduct.

---

[77] See Pohlman and Mujtaba (2007).

Yet few publicly traded companies recognized early enough that human resources (HR) plays a prominent role in SOX compliance. Therefore, emphasis as well as practical information is needed as to the prominent role that HR should be playing in the SOX "drama." The three main areas where SOX and HR intersect are: 1) internal documentation and controls; 2) executive compensation and pension plans; and 3) "whistleblower" provisions. In addition, HR professionals can be involved in other SOX-related issues, such as designing and redesigning executive pension, insurance, and loan programs, developing and implementing corporate governance procedures, training employees regarding new SOX rules and standards, and establishing codes of ethics, conducting ethics education and training, administering ethics codes, as well as creating ethics "hot lines."

SOX, as noted, mandates detailed documentation. Consequently, the task will be shouldered by HR professionals working with CFOs and finance, accounting, and auditing personnel to ensure that documentation systems are in place and the required documentation is produced in a complete and accurate fashion. Of course, it will also fall on HR to test the new documentation systems as well as to conduct the training on the new systems.

The whistleblowing provisions of SOX will definitely involve HR. It will be the duty of HR to initially educate managers and supervisors as well as all personnel as to the need for fair treatment of employees. HR will then need to inculcate that SOX has very severe penalties, both civil and criminal, that will be imposed on managers who retaliate against employees of SOX-regulated firms who blow the whistle on certain securities fraud misconduct.

Establishing this "corporate culture" of legality and morality at the firm will thus materially involve HR. All of these additional SOX-mandated requirements will naturally add extra work and stress to the employees of the firm (especially to HR). Consequently, HR will confront yet another challenge: managing the additional work and coping with the employees' added stress (including their own).

Perhaps the most fundamental responsibility of HR will be in the area of values alignment. It will be incumbent of HR professionals to make sure that the legal values mandated by SOX are aligned with the values of the employees and with corporate goals, including operational efficiency and the observance of high ethical standards. In essence, SOX involves people and values, and anything that impacts people and values has everything to do with HR. Therefore, SOX will present many challenges for HR professionals, but challenges present opportunities and a wonderful opportunity for an HR professional in a SOX-regulated company to demonstrate that he or she can assume a leadership role to help strategically navigate the organization through the shoals and rapids of SOX so as to achieve success and value-maximization for the firm and all its stakeholders.

Insider Trading v. Trading on Inside Information—Risks and Rewards

Clearly, there is substantial legal liability for trading on inside information. In 2013, former hedge-fund manager, Doug Whitman, founder of Whitman Capital, was sentenced to two years in prison for trading on insider information that he received in the form of confidential tips about Google and other technology companies. He made almost $1 million based on the illegal trades; but he was heard on secretly recorded phone calls discussing "moles" and about sending "presents" to sources. The government prosecutors sought a five year prison term, but Mr. Whitman apologized and said he had been punished enough already, including the loss of his livelihood and the disintegration of his marriage. Also in 2013, Anthony Chiasson, co-founder of a hedge-fund firm, received a 6 year sentence for insider trading. The government asserted he was a member of what prosecutors called a "criminal club" of hedge-fund analysts who shared secrets about technology companies, including Dell, which led to about $68 million in profits for Chiasson's firm. A lengthy sentence was necessary, prosecutors said, to deter others from insider trading. And in 2011, in the longest-ever insider trading prison sentence to date, hedge-fund manager, Raj Rajaratnam, received an 11 year term for illegally making more than $50 million in illegal profits by trading on secret information provided by insider contacts at such firms as Goldman Sachs and Google. On the civil side of the law, in 2010, Angelo Mozilo, the former head of Countrywide Financial Corp, and the highest ranking corporate executive to be accused of wrongdoing in the recent housing/mortgage/securities crisis, agreed to pay $67.5 million in penalties to settle civil fraud and insider trading charges. Mr. Mozilo was a strong advocate of home ownership and one of the pioneers of the sub-prime and adjustable rate mortgages that were at the bottom of the real estate "boom," and then "bust." It also should be noted that Mr. Mozilo received almost $250 million in compensation at Countrywide for 1998 through 2007. As of the writing of this updated edition, the Justice Department and the SEC are investigating so-called "expert networks," which are companies that recruit people such as industry specialists, corporate employees, consultants, and doctors and medical professionals, and pay them up to $1000 an hour for their advice. Hedge funds as well as sophisticated investors are willing to pay "big money" for professional advice by knowledgeable and experienced people that will help them make better, as well as more profitable, trading decisions. However, the government is concerned that these expert networks may really be insider trading rings and that the information the experts provide contains secret, confidential, inside information. In one case, in which the government did file insider trading criminal charges against seven consultants and employees at an expert network firm, the consultants received as much as $200,000 each for their information about technology companies, which the government alleges included inside information (apparently valuable enough to merit the consulting fees!).

Moreover, despite the scope and complexity of the securities laws, one fact should be abundantly clear, and that is that the government will very carefully scrutinize a corporate insider's purchase and sale of his or her own company's stock. In its code of ethics, code of conduct, or employee handbook or manual, a company should make it very clear that the employees cannot disclose confidential information about the company to unauthorized people or use the information to buy or sell securities. The company must stress that all material information concerning securities, financial conditions, earnings, acquisitions or divestures, new products or processes, or activities of the firm must remain confidential until fully and properly disclosed to the public. Furthermore, the employees should be firmly advised not to discuss confidential company business with friends or associates, or non-authorized employees. They also should be counseled to refer any calls from security analysts or the financial media to an appropriate corporate officer.

A prudent company should also warn its employees against trading of a competitor's stock based on inside information about their own firm. The trading by a corporate insider of the shares of his or her own company's stock, based on the possession of material inside information, is a very serious legal wrong. Consequently, if a reader of this book "really" wants to go to federal prison, this route would probably be the "best" way to go about it.

So what is an insider to do if he or she knows that something "bad" has happened at the company, but it is not yet public knowledge? Should he or she do nothing, at least until the information becomes public, and then sell, taking a loss but then giving his or her accountant "something to work with"? Or should he or she have faith in the future of his/her firm, perhaps? Or maybe, as the stockbrokers relate, one's short-term investment has now turned into a long-term investment. All of the aforementioned represent options that are better than serving years in a federal prison. And now with the draconian penalties imposed by SOX, the prison terms are meted out in years, no longer in months, for securities fraud and insider trading crimes.

Another "moral" to insider trading law in the U.S. is that even though the legal system adheres to the so-called "narrow" theory of insider trading, this theory is not that narrow at all. In fact, in practice, this theory truly "casts a very wide net" and one never quite knows the extent to which the government will pursue a case. In one classic example, the confirmation by a corporate insider of an article published in *The Wall Street Journal* about a firm's possible acquisition was deemed to be material inside information, resulting in an insider trading conviction and a sentence of 21 months for a corporate executive. Of course, when "inside" information becomes public knowledge, then it is no longer inside information and anyone, including an insider, can trade on it, presuming there are no affirmative misrepresentations, of course.

But how long should an insider wait before trading on his or her own company's stock? Even if the information is now public, the insider should wait a reasonable time before trading. And what is a "reasonable" time period? Basically, the insider should not "jump the gun," and should wait until the information truly is filtered down to (discerned by) and "digested" (evaluated) by the investing public.

Note also that for certain types of companies and securities, the SEC has detailed rules, called open and closed "windows," that pertain to waiting time periods before trading is allowed after a public announcement. As to legally trading with inside information that you have obtained because you are "lucky" or "smart," the best strategy the authors can offer is not to be too lucky or too smart, especially if you are trading in your own company's stock, as you may have to later convince SEC and Justice Department attorneys, as well as the jury, of the propriety of your own luck or smartness. So, for example, if you are in a stock-picking club, the authors would advise the discerning reader to examine companies and businesses in a sector that is definitively not related to your own firm's business activities.

Summary

This securities law chapter, in addition to providing examples of U.S. and selected international securities laws, discussed an important legal exception to the general rule that prohibits trading on inside information: If the information is secured properly, not by bribing for it, stealing it, or by being "tipped off" by an insider, but by such appropriate means as studying public records, obtaining factual information therefrom, and making logical and intelligent deductions therefrom, the practice is legal. It is that exception that makes the activities of market professional sector analysts legal. They can ferret out and discover, by legitimate means, what is truly confidential and private information (inside information), and then trade on it even though others may not have this knowledge. What is the justification for this legal exception? Once again, the justifying rationales are economic: The market is supposed to be more accurate and efficient by allowing these professionals to discover legitimately, and then use, inside information.

In the chapter, the authors briefly provided information on the economic rationales for this exception, and the reader can certainly make use of this "intersection" of law and economics for further reflection and research.

TWENTY

Private concentrations of economic power can pose a serious danger to freedom—political as well as economic. The fundamental purpose of antitrust laws is to prevent "big business" from cornering so much economic, political, and social power that open and free markets, capitalism, and even democratic forms of government are threatened. The purpose of this chapter is to examine antitrust laws, concentrating on federal antitrust laws in the U.S. as well as antitrust laws in the European Union and selected other international jurisdictions.

United States Antitrust Law

Overview and Exemptions

A "trust" is something that was created in England in the 1500s as a means of holding and disposing of property. It must be noted upfront that there is nothing inherently wrong with a trust. In a trust, title to property can in effect be split into "legal" and "equitable" title, with the trustee, such as the trust department of a bank, holding legal title to property and maintaining and investing property as a fiduciary for the benefit of the beneficiaries of the trust, who possess equitable title to the property. Such a legal arrangement is still widely used today as a means of estate planning.

However, in the U.S. certain "greedy capitalists" and "robber barons" got their hands on this nice legal instrument and perverted it to create monopolies and restrain trade. The most famous (or infamous) trust was Rockefeller's, the "original" alleged "Robber Baron." In Rockefeller's Standard Oil Trust, the participants turned over shares of stock (and thus, voting power) to a trustee, who then voted the shares in a uniform manner so as to fix prices and to control production. Thus, if a firm dared to compete against the Standard Oil Trust, the trustee would vote in drastic price decreases so that there would be no way for a competitor to compete at those very low prices. Consequently, when the competitor was eliminated, the trustee would vote in very steep price increases, so that the trust could recoup its losses. (As will be seen, the ability to lower and raise prices at will is the hallmark of possessing monopoly power.)

The result of such trusts was that these companies, whether in oil or other sectors of the economy, accumulated and wielded such power that companies outside the trust could not successfully compete, or, better yet (at least from the perspective of the trust), would not even contemplate competing because to do so would be the equivalent of economic suicide.

The name to the body of law that was developed to curb such unfair business practices was accordingly called "antitrust" law. Antitrust law in the United States came about in the post-Civil War environment. Very large business enterprises, such as the railroads, which were vital to winning the war, were engaging in very anti-competitive and unfair business practices in order to reduce or eliminate competition and to form monopolies, especially in the form of trusts, so these laws became a necessity.

(What is most interesting, as will be seen in the merger discussion in this chapter, as well as in a case study, is the Exxon-Mobil merger, which was approved by the government and which, over the objections of many, had the effect of putting back together two main components of the old Standard Oil Trust—all to Rockefeller's smug satisfaction, to be sure.)

The purposes of U.S. antitrust law are to prevent, punish, and deter anti-competitive conduct and unfair business practices. The overarching objective is to foster competition—which ultimately is good for the consumer—in the form of more, better, and lower-priced goods and services. Competition thus is deemed to be as essential to the protection of a free enterprise economic system as well as to the preservation of a democratic political system.

These antitrust rationales are surely still applicable to business, government, and society today. But one very significant change has occurred, and that is that when U.S. antitrust law was created, the "market" in the U.S. was basically a national market, or even a set of regional markets. However, today, for so many goods and services, the market is truly global. As will be seen and emphasized throughout this chapter, how exactly one defines the relevant market is an absolutely crucial determination under antitrust law. Therefore, U.S. antitrust law must be viewed and applied in a global context, which is probably the most critical point—both legally and practically—that the authors can make in this chapter.

The federal level of the United States will be the focus of this chapter. There are two principal federal statutes: the Sherman Act of 1890 and the Clayton Act of 1914.

The post-Civil War origins of antitrust law can readily be discerned when one realizes that the principal legislative author of the Sherman Act was Senator John Sherman, who was not only a recognized financial authority, but also the brother of renowned Civil War general, William T. Sherman (of the March to the Sea, "war is hell," and burning of Atlanta fame). At that historical juncture, the United States had come a long way from the Jeffersonian ideal of a democratic nation of small farmers and small merchants, and Senator Sherman had spoken for years about the lessening of competition and the formation of huge business entities in the country, a situation exacerbated by the Civil War and concomitant marshalling and consolidation of industrial and transportation resources.

The two principal federal regulating bodies for antitrust laws are the Justice Department (DOJ)—specifically the antitrust division—as well as the Federal Trade Commission, which has certain overlapping jurisdiction with the DOJ, especially regarding merger approvals. For federal laws to apply, there must be some connection to interstate commerce, which is easy to find in today's economy.

The U.S. also has corresponding bodies of antitrust law in place to regulate purely intrastate unfair business practices as well as to assume jurisdiction of cases that the federal government regulators deem too small for the federal government to get involved.

There are criminal and civil penalties, including dissolution and divestment, for the violation of antitrust laws. Moreover, private parties harmed by antitrust violations can bring private lawsuits for damages. If such suits are successful, they can recover treble damages as well as attorneys' fees. The Sherman Act, for example, has penalties in the form of fines for individuals of up to $350,000 per violation and imprisonment of up to three years and corporate fines of up to $10 million per violation.

There are, however, several fields and entities that are exemptions to federal antitrust law: labor unions, banking, insurance, utilities, and professional baseball. Labor unions are regulated by an extensive body of federal and state labor laws and labor regulatory agencies. Insurance and utilities are very heavily regulated and supervised by the states as well as by state insurance and utility commissions. Banking is very heavily regulated by both the states and the federal government. And as for baseball, due to an old Supreme Court decision on technical interstate commerce grounds (but more likely for some other obscure historical reasons), "America's sport" is generally not subject to antitrust law. (However, there are certain exceptions today to benefit players' choice of teams and salaries.) Other professional sports, regarded as mere "big business," are, however, governed by antitrust law.

It is important to note an animating rationale behind U.S. antitrust law, as indicated by the Supreme Court. Antitrust law in the U.S. exists to protect competition, and thus ultimately to benefit consumers, but not necessarily to protect competitors. Accordingly, the government is obligated to demonstrate some type of harm or threat of harm to the consumer in order to prevail in an antitrust case. One recalls that to this day, Bill Gates of Microsoft, even though his company was deemed to be an antitrust violator, nonetheless still contends that overall, his actions and Microsoft's "monopolistic" conduct inured and served to the benefit of the consumer, and very substantially so.

Also, it is important to note that the fundamental rationale of antitrust law in the European Community has been not to protect competition, but rather to protect competitors, such as Airbus, which was deemed too big and important to fail. European Community antitrust law will be covered briefly later in the Global Legal Perspectives section of this chapter.

The Sherman Antitrust Act—Introduction

In 1890, the United States Congress passed the Sherman Antitrust Act. The statute was called "An Act to Protect Trade and Commerce against Unlawful Restraints and Monopolies," which, as a descriptive title, very nicely sums up the major purposes of this seminal antitrust statute. There are two main sections to the Act: Section 1, which deals with restraints of trade; and Section 2, which deals with monopolization.

Section 1 states that every contract, combination—in the form of a trust or otherwise—or a conspiracy—in restraint of trade or commerce—is illegal, and is thereby to be punished civilly and criminally, including punishment as a felony crime. Section 2 states that every person who monopolizes, or attempts to monopolize, or who combines or conspires with another person(s), to monopolize any part of trade or commerce, is similarly guilty of a legal wrong—civilly and criminally and as a felony.

The differences between the two sections are important to observe. Section 1 requires two or more people in order to have a violation. Obviously, a person cannot contract, combine, or conspire by him- or herself. As such, the essence of a Section 1 legal wrong is the act of joining together to restrain trade or commerce. Section 2 of the Sherman Act, however, not only pertains to several people who seek to monopolize trade or commerce, but also applies to an individual person or business because the statute explicitly states "every person" in its wording. Consequently, unilateral conduct (such as in the case of Microsoft, as will be seen later in this chapter) can result in a violation.

These differences in approach also mean that there are differences in the types of cases that are brought under each section. In Section 1 cases, the government (or a private party suing) must be fundamentally concerned with finding some kind of agreement—expressed by written or oral words or implied by conduct—that produces a restraint of trade. For the government to prosecute such a case as a criminal wrong, the government must convince a jury, beyond a reasonable doubt, that an agreement existed to restrain trade.

The presence of an agreement is indispensable to liability. Accordingly, it is not a legal wrong for one business to track, by lawful means, the pricing policies of its competitors and then, by independent judgment, to meet those policies. This practice is called the doctrine of "conscious parallelism," and is permissible under antitrust laws. For example, the authors are sure that some readers may be waiting for the winter tourist season rates of some pleasant beach resort destination to end in favor of the much cheaper summer rates. Is it not a coincidence that the hotels and motels all seem to make the winter/summer rate transition at the same time, or that the winter season rates seem to last longer and longer, and consistently so, for all the tourist businesses? For example is this uniformity caused by agreement, which would potentially be a felony, or is it merely "conscious parallelism" at work, which is quite legal as well as good business practice? The government needs evidence in order to make that critical determination.

It must be stressed that there is nothing inherently legally wrong with having a monopoly. Rather, it is how one achieves a monopoly and what one does with it that can be the legal wrong. The essence of Section 2, therefore, is to find the monopoly, ascertain that monopoly power exists, and then to determine if that power was abused. Section 2 cases first deal with the structure of a business in the marketplace, specifically, whether it is a monopoly. Second, it asks whether that monopoly power was abused to maintain or expand a company's business. Accordingly, both structure and conduct are necessary to prove illegality. The legal wrong of Section 2 is not the "monopoly," but rather the monopolization or monopolizing of commerce which, as noted, is a legal wrong that can be committed by one person or by one business entity.

The Sherman Antitrust Act—Restraints of Trade

Section 1 of the Sherman Act deems "every" contract or combination of contracts that restrain trade or commerce to be an illegal act and potentially a felony. Yet when the Supreme Court was first called upon to interpret the Sherman Act, the Court was not even sure that "every" contract signed in restraint of trade or commerce was meant by Congress to be illegal.

For example, take the case of two people in small business, who are independent contractors in the same business. For our sake, let's say they are in heating and air conditioning installation, service, and repair, and they both practice in the same market. These two businesspeople decide to form a partnership, which is a combination based on a contract. Now, as partners, these small businesspeople are no longer competing against one another. Rather, they have combined and, technically, they have restrained trade and commerce.

But are partners necessarily felons? Let's take another example of an employer and an employee, who sign an employment contract that has a covenant-not-to-compete clause, in which the employee agrees not to compete against the employer upon leaving the employer's employ. That is effectively a restraint of trade, but again, does that restriction necessarily make the employer and employee felons?

When the Supreme Court first interpreted the Sherman Act, it interposed a limitation on the "every" contract language in the statute itself. The limitation, which is extremely important for antitrust restraint of trade law, is called the "Rule of Reason." This rule holds that only those restraints that impose an unreasonable restraint on trade and commerce are illegal. Thus, not all agreements between competitors that restrain trade are illegal, rather only those that unreasonably restrain trade and commerce. Without the "Rule of Reason," conceivably any business agreement could violate the Sherman Act.

How does one determine if an agreement to restrain trade does so restrain it unreasonably? The key test is to determine the consequences of the agreement. If there are more pro-competitive and pro-consumer benefits from the restraint of trade that outweigh any negative consequences, then the restraint of trade will be judged to be legal. In such a case, the restraint of trade restrains trade, but "merely" reasonably so, meaning that the restraint is legal.

The problem with the "Rule of Reason," as can be clearly discerned by the astute reader, is that it opened a gaping "loophole" in antitrust law, in practice vitiating Section 1 of the Sherman Act. As a result, later the Supreme Court created a countervailing doctrine, called the "per se" doctrine, to govern those restraints of trade that were so flagrantly anticompetitive that the Court deemed them to be automatically illegal. "Per se" means "in and of itself," inherently, automatically, or "on its face." Accordingly, if a restraint of trade is deemed to be a "per se" restraint, it is automatically considered illegal (presuming there is evidence, of course). Consequently, a court is precluded from even determining whether the benefits of the agreement outweigh its anticompetitive effects.

In essence, the state of the law as it stands can be summarized as follows: If a restraint of trade is deemed to be governed by the "Rule of Reason," there is a potential defense that one can assert in court, which may render the restraint permissible. But if a restraint of trade is deemed to be governed by the "per se" doctrine, one has no defense, and it now may be time to ask a judge for leniency in sentencing.

Therefore, the critical question emerging in antitrust law in the U.S. today is: What is the nature of the restraint? Unfortunately, the dividing line between restraints is not clear, and both the Supreme Court and the federal courts have not been consistent through the years in categorizing such restraints. Nonetheless, there are two broad kinds of restraints: horizontal restraints and vertical restraints. As a very general rule of law, most horizontal restraints (but not all) are governed by the "per se" doctrine and thus are considered illegal. Most vertical restraints (but not all) are governed by the "Rule of Reason" and thus may be judged to be legal. So, the best way to approach Sherman Act Section 1 is to first ascertain whether the restraint is horizontal or vertical.

"Horizontal restraints" are those that restrain competition by competitors in the same market as well on the same level of the marketing chain. This means that a retailer agrees with another retailer, a wholesaler agrees with a wholesaler, or a manufacturer agrees with a manufacturer to restrain trade. The three main types of horizontal per se restraints are: 1) price-fixing agreements, 2) group boycotts, and 3) market divisions.

A price-fixing agreement is an agreement among competitors to fix prices. This type of collusion is a per se violation of the Sherman Act; reasonableness is never a defense. The illegal agreement can be one among competitors that explicitly sets prices, or an agreement that restricts output or limits supplies, thereby indirectly setting prices. The two premier auction houses in New York City, Sotheby's and Christie's, were found liable for fixing the price of auction commissions, and Sotheby's CEO was convicted of price-fixing and sentenced to a prison term of up to three years. In 2013, the Justice Department settled a price-fixing case with Macmillan Publishers, one of five major book publishers accused of conspiring with Apple to raise the price of e-books for consumers. The Justice Department alleged that the five companies and Apple worked together to raise retail e-book prices and eliminate price competition. Other companies that have settled are Hachette, HarperCollins, Simon & Schuster, and Penguin; but Apple as of the writing of this second edition is still in negotiations with the government.

The second type of horizontal per se agreement is the group boycott, which is an agreement between two or more sellers to refuse to deal with another person or business. The classic example arises when two or more manufacturers agree to "freeze out" a retailer, usually because the retailer is selling the manufacturers' products at too low a perceived price. In 2003, several major music companies settled an antitrust suit with the government in which the government alleged that these music companies engaged in a group boycott to shut out discount retailers such as Target, Wal-Mart, and Best Buy, who allegedly were selling the companies' music CDs at too low a price. The settlement involved the payment of $143 million in cash and CDs, payable to the government, private parties who joined the music antitrust lawsuit (and who received about $13 each), and libraries and schools (who received music CDs). In agreeing to the settlement, the companies denied any wrongdoing.

There is, however, an important exception to the group boycott rule, which occurs when the boycott is organized against a company for political reasons, for example when students at various universities organize to protest against manufacturers who sell clothes at the university book stores, as the clothes are declared to be made under abusive and exploitative labor conditions. In such a case, the First Amendment right to free speech and expression supersedes antitrust law. Another example was the famous California grape boycott organized by Cesar Chavez, the Farm Workers Union, and their allies in the 1970s to protest abusive working conditions.

The third type of illegal per se restraint is the horizontal market division, which occurs when competitors at the same level divide up territories or customers. For example, and purely hypothetically, if McDonald's, Burger King, and Wendy's all agreed to divide up the territory of the Florida Keys—with McDonald's taking from the upper Keys to Key Largo, Burger King taking the middle Keys to Marathon, and Wendy's taking the lower Keys and Key West—such an arrangement would be a violation of antitrust law, potentially punishable as a felony. Once again, reasonableness is no defense for such a restraint of trade. Thus Wendy's could not argue that by having an exclusive "burger" territory in the lower Keys, it would be able to more effectively compete against Kentucky Fried Chicken and Subway, thereby benefiting the consumer. There is no "pro-consumer" defense to a per se restraint.

Certain horizontal restraints, however, are not governed by the per se doctrine, but rather by the Rule of Reason. In addition to covenants-not-to-compete (which were pointed out in the Intellectual Property chapter), there are legal restraints if there is a reasonable element. Two other important examples of legal horizontal restraints are trade associations and their associated activities and joint ventures.

"Trade associations" are organizations within the same business, industry, or profession that are formed for information sharing and educational purposes as well as to defend common interests and to pursue common objectives. Trade associations can engage in joint advertising campaigns as well as representation of their members before government officials and agencies. The approach of the courts to trade associations is to apply the Rule of Reason. Accordingly, even if a trade association agreement or practice restrains trade, but the practice nonetheless is sufficiently beneficial to the public, a court may deem the trade association practice to be legal as a reasonable restraint of trade. For example, joint lobbying efforts by businesses in order to convince legislators or executives to take some action—such as recent efforts by U.S. furniture manufacturers to convince the government to place tariffs of over 100% on furniture imported from China—generally are permissible under the Rule of Reason.

However, if the trade association practice causes substantial anticompetitive—and thus anti-consumer—consequences, then a court will likely strike down the practice as an unreasonable restraint of trade. For example, as of the writing of this book, the U.S. Justice Department has brought an antitrust lawsuit against the National Association of Realtors, accusing it of seeking to illegally restrain competition by restricting access by discount brokers to Internet listings of homes for sale. This practice, states the government, stifles competition, keeps prices artificially high, and thus hurts consumers.

"Joint ventures" are also governed by the Rule of Reason. A joint venture is, in essence, a partnership for a specific purpose or undertaking. Presuming there is no price-fixing or market division, joint ventures are analyzed, and typically upheld, under the Rule of Reason. For example, the government has approved a joint venture between Shell Oil and Texaco to combine their U.S. refinery businesses. Another recent example of an approved joint venture is the agreement between Boeing Co. and Lockheed Martin Corp. to merge their financially troubled government rocket businesses. The combined business will launch government weather, surveillance, and communications satellites. The joint venture was approved by the Justice Department, the Pentagon, and the Federal Trade Commission, but with the stipulation that competitor Northrop Grumman Corp. be protected from potential abuse by the joint venture's much larger market presence, specifically by requiring the new joint venture company to provide Northrop and other satellite makers with equal access to their launchers.

Finally, it must be noted that the Bill of Rights of the U.S. Constitution takes precedence over Congressional antitrust law. Thus it is permissible for companies to jointly petition the government for a redress of grievances. Accordingly, it would be permissible legally for General Motors and Ford jointly to lobby the President and Congress to ban the importation of all foreign-made cars.

The second major category of restraints is vertical restraints, which, as noted, generally are governed by the Rule of Reason but not always. A "vertical restraint" is one that is based on an agreement between people or businesses at different levels in the manufacture, distribution, and sales process. Even though parties to an agreement may be in the same industry, they are at different levels in the "marketing chain" and thus not in direct competition with one another. For example, a vertical agreement would be one between a manufacturer and a wholesaler, between a manufacturer and a retailer, or between a wholesaler and a retailer.

There are three main types of vertical restraints: 1) territorial and customer restrictions, 2) refusals to deal, and 3) price agreements, also called resale price maintenance agreements.

One example of "territorial and customer restrictions" is an arrangement made between a manufacturer and a wholesaler(s) and a retailer(s), by which the latter two entities are given an exclusive geographic territory to distribute and to sell the manufacturer's goods. Another example arises in the case of a franchise, whereby the franchisor grants the franchisee an exclusive territory to sell goods or to perform services. The franchisee, as well as the wholesaler and retailer, must stay in their prescribed territory, while the franchisor and manufacturer agree not to allow any other entities to do business with them in the specific territories. These types of business arrangements have usually been upheld by the courts under the Rule of Reason, because there are benefits that will accrue to the consumer from allowing a manufacturer or franchisor to achieve efficiencies and to maintain certain standards in the distribution and sale of its products or services. Benefits also will accrue by entities that have been approved by the manufacturer or franchisor.

Regarding the second category, "refusals to deal," you will recall that a horizontal group boycott is a per se Sherman Act violation. However, a single entity, usually a manufacturer, unilaterally is able to refuse to deal with a wholesaler or retailer because there is no agreement, only individual action. Presuming there is no violation of any other law, one is free to deal or to not to deal with whomever one wishes.

Vertical price agreements consist of three types of vertical pricing situations, all of which are governed by three distinct and very important rules. The first vertical price arrangement is a vertical price-fixing agreement as to the minimum price of goods. For many, many years, a vertical minimum price agreement, for example, between a manufacturer and a retailer, was governed by the per se doctrine, meaning that such an agreement was automatically illegal. To illustrate, as recently as 2000, the shoe manufacturer, Nine West, the largest seller of women's shoes in the U.S., agreed to pay $34 million to settle antitrust charges that it conspired and agreed with several large retailers to fix the minimum price at which its shoes could be sold. However, in June of 2007, the U.S. Supreme Court, in a very significant antitrust decision, ruled that it is no longer automatically illegal for a manufacturer to collude with a retailer or a distributor to agree to set the minimum retail prices for goods and services. Rather, such an agreement will be governed by the Rule of Reason, which holds that a restraint of trade, such as a vertical minimum price fix, can be valid if it is a "reasonable" one, that is, it produces a preponderance of benefits for competition and thus ultimately the consumer.

The second type of vertical pricing situation deals with a manufacturer's "suggested" retail price for goods. A manufacturer is permitted to merely suggest the prices at which its goods are to be sold. But there is no agreement between the manufacturer and a wholesaler or retailer to sell the goods at any fixed price; it is "merely" a suggestion. However, what if the retailer or wholesaler ignores the manufacturer's suggestion and sells the goods below the suggested price? Then the legal doctrine known as the Colgate Doctrine applies, by which the manufacturer can unilaterally refuse to deal with the vertical entities that ignore its "suggestions." At this juncture, the situation becomes more of a topic for economic analysis versus legal analysis because it needs to be determined who is the predominant economic entity, the manufacturer or the retailer. Who needs whom more? Does Mattel need Toys "R" Us more so that it can sell its Barbie dolls, or does the retailer need the product from the manufacturer more? For example, who "blinks" first? Similarly, in 2009, a dispute arose between Costco and Coca-Cola. Apparently, Coke has a "suggestion" as to the minimum price its beverages can be sold. Yet Costco refused to abide by the suggestion, asserting that it wants to provide its customers with low-prices. Whereupon Coke refused to provide any more products to Costco, causing the former Coke shelves in Costco to be empty. Next, intensifying the dispute, Costco put up signs on the shelves saying that its objective is to provide consumers with products at the best possible prices, but that Coke has not provided Costco with competitive prices. Negotiations ensued and the matter was settled and Coke products are now back on the shelf at Costco (but at what price is for the discerning reader and shopper to see!).

The third vertical pricing situation deals with a vertical price agreement as to the maximum price of goods. For years, this type of agreement was treated the same as a minimum price fix: as being *per se* illegal. However, in 1997, the U.S. Supreme Court, in a very significant case, changed the "rules of the game." The Court upheld that vertical price agreements as to the maximum price of goods are now governed by the Rule of Reason. As such, if such an agreement is ultimately good for consumers, for example by preventing price gouging when supplies are "short," it may be deemed a reasonable and thus legal restraint. However, there is a school of economic thought that says that a legal agreement as to the maximum price of goods will operate in a market, in essence, as the minimum price since the prices will be driven up to the maximum allowed level. Then in 2007, the Supreme Court similarly ruled that a minimum price fix between a manufacturer and a retailer as to the minimum price at which goods could be sold was no longer governed by the *per se* doctrine, but by the Rule of Reason. The rationales given to support this significant legal change were that upholding a minimum agreement as to price could result in more competition and better service by making it easier for new producers to enter the market since the new producers as well as retailers would be assured of recouping their investments in manufacturing, production, and distribution. Another rationale asserted to support the change in the law was that an agreement as to the minimum price of goods would protect the brand image, especially of "high-end" goods, since the goods could not be legally sold below a certain price, thereby benefitting the manufacturer, retailer, and consumer. But it is beyond the purposes of this book to examine all these interesting and thought-provoking economic and marketing assertions.

The Sherman Antitrust Act—Monopolization

Section 2 of the Sherman Act prohibits monopolization and attempted monopolization. The Act says that every person who monopolizes, attempts to monopolize, or combines or conspires to monopolize any part of trade or commerce commits a legal wrong, punishable potentially as a felony. The legal wrong of attempted monopolization is usually based on showing anti-competitive or predatory conduct, in particular predatory pricing, which is an attempt by a company to drive its competitors out of the market by selling goods or services substantially below the normal costs of production and distribution. Once the competition is eliminated, and monopoly power achieved, the monopolizing firm will seek to recapture its losses by setting very high prices for its goods or services.

As emphasized, there is nothing inherently wrong with having a monopoly. Rather, it is the manner in which one achieves the monopoly or the manner in which one exercises monopoly power that is the legal wrong. Predatory practices are evidence that a monopoly is intentionally being sought, or has been wrongfully acquired by improper means. It is also evidence that one is wrongfully using his/her monopoly power, i.e., that he or she is monopolizing trade and commerce, thereby making the actor a legal wrongdoer. It is important to note that for the legal wrong of attempted monopolization, actual monopolization is not technically required, but there must be a showing of a serious purposeful attempt to secure a monopoly together with a strong likelihood of actually succeeding.

In order to fully explicate monopolization law, it is first necessary to define monopoly and to distinguish a monopoly from an oligopoly. A "monopoly" arises when one company holds such dominance in a market that it can control prices and eliminate competitors. An "oligopoly" is a "shared" monopoly where a few companies share monopoly power. As noted, possessing a monopoly, being a monopolist, or for that matter sharing an oligopoly or being an oligopolist is not a legal wrong despite the negative connotation associated with the terms and the public perception (or misperception) of illegality.

One can also achieve a monopoly by natural growth or normal development resulting from superior products and services, customer preferences, business knowledge and skills, visionary leadership and able management, the failure of competition, and even the possession of a patent. In such a case, the monopoly is said to be "thrust upon" the firm.

It is not the intent of the Sherman Act to punish and destroy large and very large companies that legitimately earn and maintain very large market shares which thus may be considered monopolies or oligopolies. It is also certainly not the intent of the Sherman Act to prop up incompetent competitors. Rather, the legal wrong is "monopolization" or monopolizing trade or commerce. Generally speaking, there are two fundamental requirements to the legal wrong of monopolization, the presence of monopoly power in a relevant market and the presence of intentional wrongful conduct in acquiring, maintaining, or expanding that monopoly power. These two general requirements have to be broken down into a series of critical monopolization questions: What is the market? What is the defendant firm's market share? Does the defendant possess a monopoly? Does it exercise monopoly power? Is there evidence of intentional wrongful conduct in acquiring, maintaining, or expanding that monopoly power?

The first issue in any monopolization analysis is to define the relevant product or service market. This is an absolutely critical issue, not only for monopolization law, but also for merger law since the size and scope of the market will determine if a firm has a monopoly or, as will be seen in the next section, whether a merger will be approved by the government. Ascertaining the market entails two analytical steps. First, what is the product or service market? Second, what is the geographic market?

The product or service market consists of the categories of the defendant company's products or services when compared with its competing goods and services. The key test is to determine the interchangeability of the goods or services in question. Interchangeability is based on the price, use, and quality of the product or service in question. If products or services are closely related in price, use, and quality, they are thus deemed to be interchangeable.

The next question then is: Are the competitors in the same market? Let's take a look at the snack industry. What is the product market for snacks? Are peanuts, pretzels, and potato chips in the same market, or are they in separate and distinct markets? Or, just the opposite, are they in a much broader "snack" market? Furthermore, are coffee and tea interchangeable? What about sports drinks and bottled water?

All of these products, at one time, have been the center of "market" debates. The geographic market is, of course, the geographic area where the product or service can be purchased. Specifically, it refers to the area of the world, country, region, or locality where the product or service is sold in commercially significant quantities, as well as the type of stores that sell the product or provide the service. For example, is the geographic market for oil, gas, and petroleum products the entire world? What about the airlines? Is their market their "hubs," a region such as the Caribbean, the nation, or the whole world?

The critical point here is that the broader the market is defined, the less likely that a defendant company will have the requisite market share for a monopoly and thus be able to exercise monopoly power. For example, in the classic aluminum foil case, the government contended that at one time, Alcoa, with its 90% share of the aluminum foil market, possessed a monopoly. But the company countered by asserting that the market it was in was really "flexible wrapping materials." The federal courts agreed with Alcoa, and thus the company's 90% monopoly market share dropped precipitously to only 16% in the more broadly defined market, thereby ending the government's antitrust case.

After determining exactly what the relevant market is, the next step is to ascertain the defendant company's market share. There are no firm tests to establish monopoly-like market share. However, as a general but practical guideline, a percentage of more than 70% is necessary for the finding of a monopoly. Also, control of 90% or more of a market is clear evidence that a company has a monopoly in place. However, "merely" having a monopoly is not sufficient for the legal wrong of monopolization; one also must have concomitant "market power." Market power in essence is the power to raise and to lower prices in the market at will, thereby driving competitors from the market as well as being able to intimidate others from even entering the market as competitors.

What makes monopolization law so interesting, as well as at times perplexing, is that even if a company has a monopoly, it still may not have market power. The classic illustration is the Las Vegas movie chain case, where at one time, one company owned every movie theatre in Las Vegas—a 100% market share and, therefore, a monopoly. However, the company still did not have the requisite market power. So, additional "market power" factors must be examined. In particular, the ease of entry into the market, the current competition in the market, the strength of those competitors and their plans to expand in the market, as well as pricing patterns and other market trends are pertinent. Apparently, in the Las Vegas movie case, the federal court believed it would be relatively easy for other big national movie chains to enter that market.

Another such example dealt with the sports drink market. Presuming sports drinks are in fact a separate and distinct market, at one time Gatorade held 83% of the market which, on its face, is a monopoly-like percentage and an indication of market power. But the other two competitors in the markets were very large and powerful and had the ability to market their own sports drinks very heavily. At the time, those competitors with their small market shares were the Coca-Cola and Pepsi-Cola companies. Therefore, even if Gatorade had a monopoly, it very likely did not have sufficient market power to raise and lower prices at will and also did not have the ability to eliminate Coke and Pepsi from the market entirely. Actually, Coke and Pepsi have dramatically increased their market shares, and Gatorade, the onetime "monopoly" company, has been purchased by a large multinational food and beverage company, of which it is now merely just a division thereof.

Yet another example concerns Microsoft, which at one time possessed a 90%+ share of the market for computer desktop operating systems. Microsoft CEO Bill Gates argued vociferously that Microsoft did not have monopoly power due to the rapidly changing nature of technology, the many new technology companies entering the field, as well as the fact that the government had approved the mergers of competing technology firms. The federal courts agreed with the government that the company was a monopoly possessing market power, but Bill Gates' argument was certainly plausible under current antitrust law interpretation.

To demonstrate further, take the case of Sony, which had a market share of 70% of the video game market. Are video games a separate and distinct market? For example, is a 70% share of that market a monopoly? Even assuming the answer is "yes" to those two key questions, does Sony possess sufficient market power? Who else manufactures and sells video games, to what extent, and what are their plans? Such a line of reasoning is monopolization analysis under antitrust law.

The penultimate legal issue of monopolization is not resolved yet, because one more major requirement is necessary. That is intent. In order for one to be guilty of monopolization, the government needs proof that one possessed the intent to monopolize. That is, the defendant company not only possessed monopoly power in a relevant market, but also willfully and wrongfully acquired, maintained, or expanded such power. Evidence of deliberate wrongful action is necessary.

What makes monopolization law very confusing is that this "evil" intent can not only be established by acts that are illegal (such as price fixing), but also by acts that are legal but are nonetheless regarded as being predatory, abusive, unfair, and unethical because they are done by an entity having monopoly power. For example, lowering the prices for goods and services, providing more goods and services, or providing "free" goods and services to the consumer certainly are ordinarily not illegal activities, but may be evidence of intentional wrongful conduct under monopolization law. Recall the case of Microsoft, where the company's decision to give the consumer its Internet icon on the desktop for "free" was evidence of wrongful conduct because the intent of the company, as evidenced by certain e-mails (such as those titled, "Kill the baby"), was to drive Netscape from the market. Indeed, Microsoft was deemed to be a monopolizing company and consequently was sanctioned, but the sanctions ultimately approved by the U.S. Court of Appeals were considerably more lenient, relatively speaking, than those originally sought by the federal district court judge, who wanted to break up the company into two firms for "hardware" and "software" production.

To further illustrate monopolization, the U.S. government has been investigating certain airlines for monopolizing conduct at their "hubs." Presuming an airline hub is a defined market, and that an airline possesses monopoly power at such a hub, the question arises as to whether or not the airlines engaged in predatory practices to maintain their hub monopolies and to drive out competition. In this instance, one practice the government is taking a very close look at is called "bracketing." Bracketing occurs when a major airline not only reduces its prices to meet the prices of a low-cost carrier and adds additional flights, but it also places these flights right before and right after the flights of the low-cost carrier. So, the flying public now has three choices for an equally priced flight—two from a major carrier and one from an "upstart" carrier. The public typically chooses the "known entity," and the low-cost carrier is driven from the market. Next, as the discerning reader can surmise, what happens is that the additional flights are removed from the schedule and the price is then "jacked" back up, usually exceeding the original price. Is this a monopolistic exercise of monopoly power by an entity possessing a monopoly? Or is this just "tough," aggressive, "hard-hitting" capitalistic competition? There is nothing wrong with giving the consumer lower airline fares and more flight choices, is there?

The Clayton Act—Mergers

The Clayton Act of 1914 is another major piece of federal antitrust law in the United States. This Act regulates mergers and prohibits certain types of business practices and arrangements, in particular, price discrimination and exclusive dealing and tying arrangements, which have a high potential for restraining trade or commerce. The Act is enforced by the Justice Department and the Federal Trade Commission, and its enforcement is similar to the Sherman Act with the exception that criminal penalties are generally not available.

Section 7 of the Clayton Act contains the paramount test for the government approval of mergers. This test states that the government will not approve a merger if there is a reasonable probability of a substantial lessening of competition or the tendency to create a monopoly in a given market. Again, as with Section 2 of the Sherman Act, determining the market is the first key step: The broader one makes the market, the greater the chance of the merger being approved.

Take some examples. First, the Office Depot-Staples merger was disapproved in 1997 by the government mainly because the government contended that the market was defined as "office supply superstores," as opposed to "any and every store," which could potentially include every company from Kinko's to Wal-Mart that sold office supplies, which was the proposed merged company's argument. The federal district court judge agreed with the government as to the market determination as well as to the fact that the merger did not pass the merger "test." Since the market was defined as consisting of three office supply super-stores, the merger of the number 1 and 2 stores at the time would leave, according to the government, a "dwarfish" number 3, Office Max, thereby resulting in a substantial lessening of competition. Thus, the companies had to "un-merge," which is a most interesting process indeed, but beyond the purposes of this book to examine. However, in 2013, the government approved the merger of Office Depot and Office Max. What had changed? The answer is the "market"! The companies successfully argued to the government that the market had changed and now was much broader, including such giant ground and online retailers as Costco, Wal-Mart, and Amazon, and thus the merger would result in more competition, especially against industry leader Staples, and better prices for customers.

Another classic example deals with the Exxon-Mobil merger. Briefly, the government approved that merger mainly due to the oil and gas market being defined globally, which means that not only were British Petroleum and Royal Dutch Shell "players," but the government also contended that the "state-owned" oil companies, such as Pemex and the members of the OPEC, were players in the market as well. All of a sudden, the gigantic merger of two former competitors at the same level of production and distribution did not seem that large at all when compared with the entire worldwide market. Other major horizontal mergers that have been approved by the government in the last few years include Delta and Northwest Airlines, United and Continental Airlines, and most recently American Airlines and US Airways, as well as Live Nation and Ticketmaster Entertainment, and Sirius and XM radio. However, the government is challenging the merger of Anheuser-Busch InBev with Mexico's Group Modelo, maker of Corona and other imported labels, because the government believes that the market is the more narrow one of "trendy" imported beer, where the merged company purportedly would be too dominant, as opposed to the Anheuser-Busch InBev contention that the market is a broad one encompassing beer, wine, and other alcoholic beverages and thus the merger would produce more competition and lower prices.

The term "merger" is simply the union of two or more companies, whereby two previously independent firms are combined. The term is very broadly construed under antitrust law to cover not only traditional corporate mergers, but also consolidations, acquisitions of stock or of assets, or the creation of holding companies. The Justice Department and the Federal Trade Commission have overlapping jurisdiction to approve mergers. And for certain mergers, such as communications and banking, other specialized federal agencies such as the

Federal Communications Commission and the Federal Deposit Insurance Corporation also must approve.

There are three categories of mergers: horizontal, vertical, and conglomerate. A "horizontal merger" is a combination of two companies that were direct competitors in the same product or service and located in the same geographic market. A "vertical merger" is a combination of firms at different levels of production and distribution, such as a manufacturer acquiring a wholesaler. A major vertical merger approved by the government was the purchase by Comcast of Universal/NBC. A "conglomerate merger" is a combination of firms dealing in unrelated products and services.

The horizontal type of merger is the one that is most likely to be challenged by the government, while the conglomerate merger is the one least likely to be challenged. The vertical merger is also not likely to be challenged unless there is a real threat of markets being foreclosed because potential competitors will be too intimidated to enter a market against the newly merged, and thus usually much larger and more formidable, competitor.

Market concentration is the critical consideration in most merger cases. Accordingly, the government's focus has been on horizontal mergers since these mergers, by removing competitors in the same market and on the same level, could engender monopoly power or result in a substantial lessening of competition. Yet, as noted, most horizontal mergers have in fact passed the Section 7 test. Just to name a few more, AOL-Time Warner, Chevron-Texaco, American Airlines-TWA, and Disney-ABC, are all mergers that have been approved. Another recent merger example is the acquisition by U.S. appliance manufacturer Whirlpool Corporation of appliance maker Maytag Corporation, which was approved by the Justice Department too. Although this horizontal merger of two former major competitors resulted in a dominant share of the market for washers and dryers, the U.S. Justice Department approved the merger, citing the efficiencies and cost-savings to be obtained as well as the fact that the companies are now under increasingly intense foreign competition, mainly from China. Thus, the Justice Department believed that competition would not be reduced by the merger and that the merged companies would not be able to raise prices to consumers.

Actually, it is hard to recall more than one or two mergers in recent years that have not passed this test! Broadly defining the market has been the key fact in the government's approval of so many of these horizontal mergers. This has gone on to such an extent that former Senator Arlen Specter, commenting on the Exxon-Mobil company and the very high gas prices and concomitant company profits at the time of the writing of this book, declared that this aspect of U.S. antitrust law was "worthless."

The Clayton Act—Price Discrimination, Exclusive Dealing, Requirements Contracts, and Tying Arrangements

The Clayton Act of 1914 was designed to strengthen antitrust law by making certain anti-competitive and monopolistic practices illegal that were not specifically covered by the Sherman Act itself. Effectively, the Clayton Act forbids price discrimination, exclusive dealing, and tying arrangements. Tying arrangements are governed by Section 3 of the Clayton Act, which makes it unlawful for a company to sell or lease goods or contract for the sale or lease of goods on condition that the buyer or lessee not use or deal in the goods of a competitor of the seller or lessor. However, this can only be effective if the effect of such an arrangement is to substantially lessen competition in any part of trade or commerce.

The usual "tying arrangement" provides that the customer can buy or lease a desired product (the "tying" product), but only if the customer buys or leases another product (the "tied" product). The purpose of Section 3 is to prevent the buyer or lessor, who presumably possesses market power over the tying product, from extending that market power into the tied product, thereby adversely affecting competitors in the tied product as well as, ultimately, affecting the consumer.

Section 3 of the Clayton Act also deals with "exclusive dealing contracts," which are agreements between a buyer and a seller in which the buyer contractually agrees to deal only with a specific seller. These types of agreements are not automatically illegal despite that they eliminate competing sellers from the market. Rather, such agreements are governed by the "substantial lessening of competition" legal standard.

"Requirements contracts" require a buyer to buy all of its requirements from a particular seller or sellers. These contracts are treated by the Clayton Act very similarly to exclusive dealing contracts.

Finally, price discrimination is governed by Section 2 of the Clayton Act, as amended by the Robinson-Patman Act of 1936. Pursuant to Section 2, it is illegal for a seller to discriminate in price between different buyers of goods of similar quality and quantity. But again, this can occur only if there is a substantial lessening of competition. Consequently, it may be illegal for a seller to reduce the price to one buyer below the price charged to that of the buyer's competitors. It is important to note here that Section 2 applies to goods, not services, and that the goods must be substantially the same and sold to different purchasers at contemporaneous times but at different prices. Furthermore, the seller of goods possesses certain defenses, and thus can argue that the price differences were due to cost savings because of sales and bulk discounts as well as lower prices caused by the meeting of the equally low prices of competitors or price changes due to changing market conditions.

Global Legal Perspectives

The Extraterritoriality of U.S. Antitrust Law

United States antitrust law has extra-territorial application in two important respects. First, the law extends to U.S. nationals abroad who are engaged in activities that restrain trade or monopolize commerce in the U.S. or who adversely affect U.S. and foreign commerce. Second, U.S. law applies to the activities of foreigners and foreign companies who conduct activities that illegally restrain trade or monopolize commerce in the United States.

The Sherman Act applies to conduct of U.S. business abroad as well as to foreign businesses that have an adverse effect on U.S. domestic commerce. The Clayton Act is also applicable to acquisitions combining domestic and foreign firms as well as potentially being applicable to combinations involving only foreign firms if there would be a substantial lessening of competition in the U.S. domestic market.

The fact that the business activities are done abroad or by foreign companies will not excuse such firms and their managers from the reach of U.S. law. Of course, the government's ability to secure evidence becomes more difficult as an antitrust case literally moves abroad, especially when it comes to the government obtaining evidence of wrongful conduct by foreign nationals in their own country.

One of the leading U.S. extraterritorial antitrust cases was a federal court of appeals decision in 1997, which upheld a criminal price-fixing case against the Japanese manufacturers of fax paper for conspiring to raise the prices of that product. The Japanese companies contended that U.S. antitrust law did not apply because the alleged criminal activity occurred overseas. The Japanese government also contended that the criminal prosecution of the companies violated international law as well as the sovereignty of Japan. Both contentions were rejected by the court. Another case occurred in 2005 when Samsung Electronics, the largest memory-chip maker in the world (by revenue), pleaded guilty, along with another South Korean firm and a German company, of criminally fixing the prices of chips. The fines paid by the companies amounted to approximately $700 million, and several company executives were sentenced to jail terms. And in 2013, two Chinese vitamin companies were found liable by a jury in a civil trial for fixing the prices of vitamin-C for several years. The case was brought by plaintiffs, who included a Texas animal feed company and a N.J. vitamin distributor. The allegations were that the companies voluntarily formed an illegal price-fixing cartel that increased price significantly. The plaintiffs were awarded $162 million in damages, which sum is triple the amount that the jury awarded due to damages in anti-trust actions being trebled. The companies attempted to defend their actions by blaming directives from the Chinese government for the price-fixing but the Chinese government stated to the U.S. government that it does not compel price-fixing for any exported product.

However, despite the extraterritorial reach of U.S. law, the Act of State doctrine in international law, as noted in the International and Comparative Law chapter, precludes any antitrust legal action against foreign governments or government-owned companies who collude to fix prices and supply, such as the case of the OPEC cartel. For example, in 2006, the U.S. government launched an investigation into the practices of several Chinese manufacturers of vitamins. The U.S. government believes that the Chinese companies have been conspiring to fix the prices of vitamins, especially vitamin C. Currently, Chinese manufacturers supply more than 85% of the vitamin C used in the United States. As of the writing of this book, no criminal charges have been filed, and the Justice Department and the FBI are having a very difficult time obtaining evidence of a conspiracy. And even if criminal charges are filed, the companies are expected to defend against the prosecution by asserting that the companies are merely "agents" of the Chinese government, and thus, like OPEC, they are not subject to U.S. antitrust laws.

Antitrust Law in the European Union

The European community now has an established body of antitrust law, the major purpose of which is to ensure the fairness of the unified European market. Companies thus should be able to compete on equal terms. This focus on competitors, as opposed to competition, means that in Europe, the initial emphasis is on the rival companies instead of on the consumer, as is the case in the United States. The European Union can penalize companies as much as 10% of their annual global sales if the European Commission finds evidence of price fixing or of other antitrust violations.

The Commission has a Merger Task Force that can disapprove a proposed merger even without taking the company to court. The European Community has a unique merger doctrine, called "portfolio power," which refers to a merger that enables two companies to offer a broad portfolio of related products and services. If such a portfolio power merger threatens competitors, the Commission will block it even though the efficiencies and cost savings obtained thereby will help consumers. For example, in 2001, the European Commission did not approve the merger of General Electric Company and Honeywell International, Inc. on grounds that the merger would have harmed competitors in the aviation, avionics, and airplane engine industries, even though the U.S. government had already approved the merger.

In 2005, however, the European Community's antitrust commissioner stated that the Commission intended to evaluate mergers as well as monopolies on the same terms as the United States. The U.S., as has been emphasized, has the consumer's interest as the superseding rationale for antitrust law. Accordingly, such a "philosophic" shift for the Europeans from protecting competitors to protecting competition and thus the consumer would be a dramatic change indeed.

Antitrust Law in China

In 2006, the People's Republic of China promulgated its first piece of antitrust legislation, called the Antimonopoly Law. Under the proposed law, the Chinese government will be empowered to review mergers and acquisitions for their impact on competition in the Chinese domestic market. The law, which has notification and review provisions, applies to both domestic Chinese and foreign firms that do business in China.

In addition to regulating mergers and monopolistic conduct, the law, despite its title, also bars price fixing and other cartel-like behavior that restrains trade and hurts competition. The Chinese government has been concerned that several foreign companies, such as Microsoft and Eastman Kodak, are so large and powerful that they are becoming dominant in large sectors of the Chinese market. Furthermore, the government has been concerned with such monopolistic tactics as predatory pricing and the buying out of smaller Chinese competitors.

Apparently, what is holding up the law, which has been a decade in the making, is the determination of the jurisdictional thresholds. This means the monetary value of the transaction as well as the sales and assets that the firms must have in China before companies will be subject to the notification requirement. Foreign companies naturally are concerned as to the final determination of the threshold amounts and exactly how much impact a deal made in the U.S. or in Europe has to have in China in order to trigger the new law. Also holding up the law is the determination of what specific government agency in China will be the government's antitrust enforcer.

But regardless of the threshold amounts decided, and what government agency is to be the enforcer, because China now has such a central role in the global economy, the new Antimonopoly Law will certainly have global reach. As such, the law will present yet another legal challenge to the global manager.

The government of China's State Council (equivalent to a cabinet), finally gave approval to a new draft of antitrust law. This legislation, the Antimonopoly Law, would produce significant consequences for Chinese and foreign businesses. The legislation would give the government even more substantial powers over the expanding private sector in China. The law is designed to prevent not only illegal monopolies but also price fixing and anticompetitive collusion.

The law, among other provisions, required companies engaging in mergers anywhere to notify the Chinese government and secure its approval if the size of the merger deal or the degree of the companies' operations in China exceeded certain standards. The legislation also gives the government the power to block the merger if the government believes it would reduce competition in relevant markets. The proposed law does not specifically target foreign businesses, but naturally, many businesses are concerned as to the scope and application of the new law since some foreign multinationals have significant market shares in China, to such an extent that they effectively have legal monopolies. Consequently, several large multinationals now are very concerned that they will be the target of antitrust lawsuits in China, from the government as well as from Chinese competitors.

Management Strategies

In its code of ethics, code of conduct, or internal regulations, a company is well advised to have an antitrust compliance policy statement and to make sure that such a policy is communicated to the employees. The policy must make it clear that the company and all its employees will adhere to the "letter and the spirit" of all antitrust laws and that any failure of the employees to comply will be cause for discipline, including termination. The policy should explain in a clear, succinct, yet substantive manner the major types of antitrust violations—such as price fixing and territorial divisions with competitors—as well as spell out that there is no defense for certain automatic antitrust violations, which carry not only civil but also criminal sanctions. The employees further should be warned to be very careful in trade association meetings when discussing business with competitors. The policy must require employees to report antitrust violations or suspected violations to the legal department, ethics department, or other appropriate personnel. The employee should be able to report anonymously, and confidentiality should be maintained to the fullest extent possible. Furthermore, the employees must be assured that they will not be retaliated against in any way for reporting such violations.

Summary

This antitrust chapter, in addition to providing an examination of U.S. and selected international antitrust laws, provided a discussion of a very important Supreme Court case in the United States that changed the rule of law for vertical price fixing. In the past, a vertical price fix between a manufacturer and a retailer as to the minimum and maximum price of goods was a per se (automatic) legal wrong. However, now it is permissible to have a price fix as to the maximum price of goods if there are sufficient pro-consumer benefits therefrom, such as preventing price gouging in times of scarcity (the Supreme Court case dealt with the sale of gasoline by a wholesaler).

Yet some economists say that a legal price fix as to the maximum price of goods will do more harm than good to the consumers in the long run because the prices ultimately will be driven up to the fixed, and legal, set price. Thus the maximum will be, in essence, converted into a minimum fix. The authors attempted to explain this paradox, but we will leave it to the reader to attempt to answer the overriding economic arguments.

TWENTY ONE

Today's employment and labor laws can be very complex and challenging for most professionals. Despite the complexity of local and international laws, managers and global employees are expected to become familiar with "the basics." Thus, global managers and entrepreneurs, at a minimum, should be familiar with the legal, moral, and ethical mores and expectations of each country in which they are operating. This chapter discusses such concerns regarding employment, civil rights, labor, and immigration laws for global managers who are working in the United States as well as in international jurisdictions.

The Employment At-Will Doctrine in the United States

Introduction, General Rule, and Rationales

The starting-off point for any discussion of the employment law and practice in the United States is the employment "at-will" doctrine. This doctrine, originally adopted from English law, is a mainstay of the law of the United States, being the general rule of employment in virtually all the states in America. (What is interesting is that the doctrine has been abrogated in England, but it is still very vital in the United States and emerges as the traditional legal principle governing employee terminations.)

The employment at-will doctrine holds that where an employee is hired for an indefinite period and there is no contract or no contract provision limiting the circumstances by which the employment relationship can be terminated, then the employee can be discharged at any time, with no warning, notice, or explanation, for no reason or cause, or even, according to the old (and still precedent) cases, for a morally wrong reason or cause. The employee, however, also can terminate the employment relationship under the same circumstances. So, theoretically, either party can sever the employment relationship, but in the "real world," it is the employer who possesses the greater economic and bargaining power and thus the party who can inflict the more severe abuse due to the "lawless" nature of this rule. Certainly the vast majority of employees today are surely not quitting their jobs for arbitrary and capricious reasons and telling their bosses, in the words of the famous old Country Western song, to "take this job and shove it"!

Assuming the employer wants to preserve the at-will employment status of its employees, the employer should insert disclaimers in its handbooks and codes of conduct for its employees. The disclaimer should state that nothing in the handbook and code should be construed to create an express or implied employment contract, that the employee's status with the company is as an employee at-will and that nothing can change the at-will employment status of the employee except an express written contract signed by the CEO or high level executive of the firm, and that the employer reserves the right to change, modify, revise, add to, subtract from, suspend, or discontinue employment policies and practices at any time. However, for certain employees, the employer may want to consider binding these employees contractually to the firm. Such employees would be very qualified and capable ones who would be difficult to replace, especially in a "tight" job market, highly trained employees, particularly when the employer has invested the time and effort in the training, or the employees have access to confidential information and trade secrets.

There are many examples of the employment at-will doctrine in operation. There are also concomitant examples of employees' attempts to circumvent the doctrine and thereby to convert their discharges into "wrongful discharges." In one particular Florida case, a female employee of the Florida Marlins baseball franchise was fired allegedly for taking her daughter to work on a national "Take Your Child to Work Day" in violation of company policy and when her employer specifically told her that it did not participate in that program. Assuming the employee was an employee at-will, she could legally be discharged, though whether such a discharge was a moral one is another question. However, the employee in this case is also asserting that a male employee who took his son to work that day was not disciplined at all, and thus the female employee's case of "losing" employment at will could readily be converted into a "winning" Civil Rights sex discrimination case.

The objective for the terminated employee at-will is to convert his or her discharge into a "wrongful discharge." That often used, general term refers to any civil action instituted by an employee against his or her employer for unlawful termination of the employment relationship. While there is no single theory of wrongful discharge in the United States, there exist a wide variety of statutory and common law theories that an employee can try to use in order to challenge his or her discharge.

Statutory Exceptions

Due to the potential for abuse engendered by the traditional employment at will doctrine, many legislative enactments have been promulgated in the U.S.

at the federal and state level to delimit the scope of an employer's legal license to terminate an employee. Three major statutes are state whistleblower protection laws, the federal Civil Rights Act (CRA), and the federal National Labor Relations Act. The first two will be mentioned in a succinct fashion in this section in relation to employment discharge. The latter two statutes together will be fully explicated regarding all the terms and conditions of the employment relationship later in this chapter.

Many states in the U.S. now have whistleblower protection statutes[78] that protect employees in that state. Most significantly, these statutes include private sector employees who disclose wrongdoing by their employer or by fellow employees. Discharging an employee for "blowing the whistle" or threatening to do so is a violation of these statutes, thereby granting the terminated employee, even one who is at-will, a legal cause of action against his or her employer.

Although it is beyond the scope of this book to examine in detail the several state whistleblower protection statutes, certain general observations can be made. First, in order to be protected, the statutes uniformly require that the employee disclose some type of legal wrongdoing, a violation by the employer or fellow employees of an actual "legal" law, rule, or regulation. Furthermore, the statutes are consistent in requiring that the employee report this legal violation to some type of governmental regulatory or law enforcement agency and not to the media or even a public interest group. Similarly, the statutes are fairly consistent in holding that the wrongfully discharged employee receive, as legal redress, the usual employment remedy of "reinstatement and back pay," but neither damages for "pain and suffering" nor punitive damages.

However, the state statutes do diverge in two major respects. Some will allow the whistleblowing employee to report the wrongdoing directly to an appropriate government agency, whereas others will mandate that the employee first bring his or her concerns to the immediate supervisor and then up through the management hierarchy. Second, some statutes, such as Florida's, will require as a legal predicate an actual violation of the law. Others, such as those in place in New Jersey, will protect the good faith whistleblower who makes a report of wrongdoing but who ultimately is erroneous in his or her assertion of illegality. Thus, some states will protect whistleblowing based on an employee's reasonable suspicions of illegal wrongdoing.

Mention also must be made of state so-called Lifestyle Protection Acts, which are statutes that protect the employee from being discharged for engaging in lawful off-hours and off-the-job activities or engaging in off-the-job associations. However, these statutes typically include exceptions whereby the

---

[78] For a detailed comparative analysis, see Cavico, F. J. (2004).

employee nonetheless can be discharged if he or she harms the reputation or the economic interests of the employer by the activities or associations. Colorado has such a statute but a state appeals court ruled in 2013 that the law does not protect a medical marijuana user from being discharged after the employee was fired for testing positive for the drug in violation of company policy. The state appeals court rationalized its decision by stating that marijuana is still illegal pursuant to federal law. The same result and rationale would certainly apply to now legal (but only under Colorado state law as well as Washington state law) recreational marijuana use in the state. However, it also should be pointed out that so far two states, Arizona and Delaware, have restricted the discharge of medical marijuana users unless they have been shown to be impaired on the job. Colorado does not have such a law.

One of the major tenets of the National Labor Relations Act (NLRA) states that an employer cannot terminate an employee as a means of discouraging or encouraging union activity. An employee must make an initial case that his or her discharge was motivated by the employee's pro-union support or activity, but if the employee does make such an initial showing, the employee does not automatically prevail. Rather, in order to defend itself from a charge of an unfair labor practice pursuant to the NLRA, the employer now has to demonstrate a legitimate job-related reason for the employee's discharge. As such, the employee is no longer in the terminable at-will category. However, as will be shown, in order to utilize the NLRA, the affected employee must fall under the Act's coverage. For example, managers and supervisors are excluded from the NLRA's coverage.

Title VII of the CRA prohibits a discriminatory discharge based on certain protected categories. As such, similar to the NLRA, if an employee makes an initial case that his or her discharge was an impermissible, discriminatory discharge, the employer now is compelled to defend itself against discrimination charges by offering a legitimate job-related reason for the discharge. Once again, the employee is "taken out" of the employment at-will doctrine. The CRA also includes a non-retaliatory provision, thereby forbidding the employer from discharging the employee for exercising his or her rights under the Act. As with the NLRA, not all employees are covered by the CRA, and not all discriminatory discharges are prohibited, only those based on certain "protected" categories.

In addition to federal and state statutory exceptions to the employment at-will doctrine, there is a large amalgam of common law theories and causes of action that can be used by a purportedly wrongfully discharged employee.

Common Law Exceptions

There are three general common law legal theories that can be used by the discharged employee to convert his or her case into a wrongful discharge case:

1) contract-based theories, 2) tort-based theories, and 3) the "public policy" doctrine, which can be either a contract- or a tort-based theory, depending on the jurisdiction.

Contract-based theories consist of express contracts, implied contracts, and the covenant of good faith and fair dealing, as applied to terminations. One initial and very fundamental point to make is that if the employee has a contract with the employer and the contract includes a provision that terminations will be based only on "good cause," then the employee clearly is not an employee "at-will." An example would be a college professor at a private university who has "tenure," which is, at times, misconstrued as being lifetime employment. Rather, it is "only" a continued employment subject to a termination for good cause. Whether a private-sector business employee in a global and very fluid economy can negotiate such a contract is another matter.

However, in addition to being express, contracts, as noted in the Contract Law chapter, can also be implied. So, even though there is no express contractual provision regarding termination, the courts may construe the employment relationship and setting, past personnel practices of the employer, and especially the statements, actions, and policies of the employer, in order to require good cause for a discharge. The courts will particularly focus on any express codes of ethics or conduct handbooks or manuals to see if there is language regarding notice and warnings, disciplinary procedures, and rehabilitation steps, or even for language that the employees will be treated fairly and with respect. For example, if there are statements, either oral or written, by the employer that the employee's employment is permanent, that there will be no arbitrary discharges, that the employee will be employed as long as he or she satisfactorily does the job, or that the employee will only be terminated for a good reason, such statements may be enough for a court to say that there is an implied contract that the employee be discharged only on a showing of good cause.

Tort-based theories can be premised on intentional torts as well as the tort of negligence, with the premise being that when the terminated employee sues the employer for the independent tort, the employer, in defending itself against the tort lawsuit, must demonstrate a legitimate reason for the employee's discharge. Accordingly, intentional torts, as well as the tort of negligence, both of which are separate and distinct from the at-will employment relationship but which occur as part of the discharge, can convert the at-will employee's termination into a wrongful discharge action.

Torts were covered in the Torts and Business chapter. For our purposes here, as an example, the intentional torts of assault and battery, defamation, fraud, and invasion of privacy can be used as the predicate for a wrongful discharge suit, presuming the employee possesses sufficient evidence to sustain the tort lawsuit.

The tort of negligence, for example caused by a negligent job evaluation of an employee or negligently not warning the employee of a poor evaluation, can also be utilized as such predicate.

Yet there are problems with using these theories in an at-will employment context. For example, regarding the tort of intentional interference with contractual relations, the courts may take a narrow view of the tort and say that the employee at-will has no valid contract to be interfered with at all. Furthermore, it is a basic premise of the interference tort that a contract party cannot interfere with his or her own contract, but only breach it. Effectively, the interference must be done by a third party.

Similarly, regarding the tort of intentional infliction of emotional distress, one recalls that the requisite conduct must be atrocious and outrageous. Consequently, "merely" firing an at-will employee will be insufficient to trigger tort liability unless there is some attendant outrageous conduct in implementing such a discharge. However, in one case, the terminated employee, a social work manager at a hospital, recovered $105,000 from a jury for being discharged in an abusive manner, which caused her emotional distress. The employee was forced to leave her belongings in a plastic bag and was escorted out the door by security guards in full view of gaping coworkers. Furthermore, a supervisor told her that she would be arrested for trespassing if she returned, even though there were no allegations of criminal wrongdoing or any indication of disloyalty. As one management seminar speaker put it, but "do not laugh at fired workers!"

The "public policy" doctrine is a tort-based, common law doctrine which is adhered to, though in varying degrees, by all the states in the United States. The public policy doctrine maintains that an employee, even an at-will employee, cannot be discharged for engaging in an activity that public policy encourages. Conversely an employee cannot be discharged for *not* engaging in an activity that public policy discourages, such as illegal and immoral conduct. The exact definition of "public policy" is not clear, but generally it concludes activities that promote the health, safety, and welfare of the citizens and residents of a state as well as activities that encourage lawful and ethical conduct. Ultimately, the high court of each state, the state supreme court, will determine what "public policy" means on a case-by-case basis, though the courts are guided by the state's constitution, statutes, and prior judicial decisions.

For example, firing an at-will employee for serving on a jury or grand jury, for filing a Worker's Compensation claim, or for filing a safety report with state regulators are all violations of public policy because the law in fact favors all of those activities. Similarly, firing an employee for refusing to violate a statute or to participate in illegal activity will typically trigger the public policy doctrine.

Additionally, the disclosing of wrongdoing by the employer or fellow employees, even if not protected by a state whistleblower protection statute, may afford the whistleblowing employee at-will the legal recourse to challenge such a discharge.

In one particularly interesting public policy case, an employer fired an armored truck driver who left his vehicle unguarded while he attempted to rescue a woman from a knife-wielding robber. The supreme court of the state of Washington, however, ruled that the defendant company wrongfully terminated the plaintiff employee for violating the company's work rule, which prohibited armored truck drivers from leaving their vehicles unattended. The state supreme court decided that a discharge for saving a woman from a life-threatening situation violated public policy, which encourages such "heroic" conduct. The court emphasized that society values and thus should encourage voluntary rescues in life-threatening circumstances.

In another more mundane U.S. case, an employee was fired from his grocery store job for wearing a Green Bay Packers football T-shirt to work. While this may not seem that dramatic, the store was located in Dallas, and the employee wore the shirt during the weekend of the National Football Conference championship game between the home team, the Dallas Cowboys, and Green Bay. There is no civil right, to the authors' knowledge, that specifically protects Green Bay Packers football fans from discrimination.

In another oft-cited and notorious case, an at-will employee, an engineer in a defense and technology company, was encouraged to "speak his mind" in company employee forums called Dialog, All-Hands, and Straight-Talk. The company even provided a "facilitator" to encourage employees to speak up. The employee did in fact speak up, criticizing his employer's upper-level managers for receiving "enormous" bonuses at a time of poor economic performance, layoffs, and budget reductions, and without regard for the fate of lower-level company employees, the interests of shareholders and the public good. The employee was discharged and sued for a violation of public policy, contending that he was commenting on important public issues. However, the court ruled that the expression of his opinion of his company's management was merely "a matter between him and his employer" and thus not a public policy violation.

In most states, a successful claim of a violation of the "public policy" doctrine is, in fact, a tort violation. This means that the wrongfully discharged employee has a tort lawsuit against his or her employer for tort damages, including damages for "pain and suffering" and punitive damages. For example, in one noteworthy case, an employee, a gastrointestinal research scientist, was fired by his pharmaceutical company employer for protesting the company's alleged failure to disclose the adverse side effects of an anti-ulcer drug it was developing. The employee then complained to the Food and Drug Administration. A California jury found that the scientist had been discharged in violation of the fundamental public policy of the state of California and awarded him $2.5 million for economic loss and emotional distress as well as $15 million in punitive damages.

The covenant of good faith and fair dealing, as noted in the Sales Law chapter, is implied in all contracts, including employment contracts. Most courts would rule that the covenant will not automatically require good cause for all terminations; such a construction is viewed as too unwarranted an interference with the legitimate exercise of managerial discretion. However, a court may construe that this covenant prohibits an employer from discharging an employee in bad faith or for a bad cause. Factors that a court will use to imply the covenant are the length of time of employment, not giving an employee a sufficient time to adapt to new performance standards, any assurances about future employment, any promotions and commendations and, most importantly, if the discharge was motivated to deprive the employee from obtaining commissions or benefits. The violation of this covenant, in addition to providing contract remedies, may be deemed by the courts to be a tort violation, thus affording the employee tort remedies. Yet it should be mentioned that most courts in the U.S. have been very reticent in using this covenant in an employment discharge situation.

Conclusion

The goal of employment law in the United States has been to achieve a proper balance between the employer's right to hire, manage, and fire employees, and the employee's right to be treated fairly and to maintain his or her job. Considering the "lawless" nature of the employment at-will doctrine, this objective has been difficult to attain, often necessitating government intervention by means of major federal Civil Rights and labor law statutes.

Furthermore, not only the legislative branch of government, but also the judicial branch has questioned the conventional adherence to the employment at-will doctrine, a legal precept that can legally legitimize an immoral (though legal) discharge. Courts, accordingly, have increasingly recognized further common law exceptions to the employment at-will doctrine and thereby have provided more "wrongful discharge" remedies for the unfairly terminated employee.

Nevertheless, the employment at-will doctrine is still, in the U.S., *the* key legal doctrine governing the employment relationship, especially in a non-unionized setting.

United States Civil Rights Laws

The Equal Pay Act of 1963

The purpose of the Equal Pay Act is to prohibit employers from discriminating on the basis of sex in the payment of wages for equal work performed. "Equal work" means jobs of a similar nature, such as a seamstress and a tailor, both of which require equal skill, effort, and responsibility when performing under similar working conditions.

"Equal," however, means substantially equal, not identical. Yet it also does not mean "comparable," i.e., that the statute does not apply to jobs that are different but which may be fundamentally similar in responsibility, skill, and effort, such as an administrative assistant and a maintenance man.

Wage differentials also are allowed if based on seniority or merit systems, quantity and/or quality of production systems, as well as any other proper non-gender-based factor.

Title VII of the Civil Rights Act of 1964

The CRA of 1964 is the most important civil rights act in the United States. The CRA prohibits discrimination by employers, labor organizations, and employment agencies on the basis of race, color, religion, sex, or national origin. The employment activities covered by the Act are very broad in scope and encompass hiring, discharge, compensation, training, apprenticeship, referrals for employment, union membership, as well as all "terms and conditions" and "privileges" of employment. The purpose of the Act is to eliminate job discrimination in employment. However, not all discriminatory discharges are prohibited, only those based on certain "protected" categories. For example, the federal Civil Rights Act in Title VII protects against sex discrimination in employment, but the courts have not yet construed the gender category to encompass protection based on the employee's sexual orientation (as gay or lesbian) and/or "gender identity," that is, in the latter case, more extensive protection for employees who are gay, lesbian, bisexual, sexually transitioning, or transgenders. However, as noted in the first chapter, the U.S. is a federal system of government; and thus it is permissible for a state to have in its civil rights laws more protections (but certainly not less) than the federal government affords by means of national law. So, today, many states now have protections against job discrimination based on sexual orientation and/or gender identity. In addition to federal and state statutory exceptions to the employment at-will doctrine, there is a large amalgam of common law theories and causes of action that can be used by a purportedly wrongfully discharged employee. The Civil Rights Act is very broad in its scope and it forbids discrimination not only in employment (as the Act covers not only employers, but also labor unions), but also in educational opportunity (both public and private) and public accommodations. Furthermore, the Act applies to state and local governments as well as their subdivisions, agencies, and departments. As will also be seen, the Civil Rights Act of 1964 was amended by the Equal Employment Opportunity Act of 1972. But for the purpose of this book, the focus of the CRA is Title VII, which deals with employment opportunities.

An employer subject to the Act is one who has 15 or more employees for each working day in each of 20 or more calendar weeks in the current or preceding calendar year. Specific employment practices that are prohibited by the Act include the employer's: 1) failure or refusal to hire, to discharge, or to discriminate against a person because of his or her race or other protected characteristics; 2) the limitation, segregation, or classification of employees or applicants for improper reasons; 3) the maintenance of segregated work teams; 4) the granting of better bonuses and benefits based on race or other improper classifications; and 5) allowing racial, sexual, or national origin insults, abuse, hostility, or an offensive environment in the workplace.

As will be shown, discrimination can be direct and overt or indirect and inferential. For example, a superficially neutral employment policy, practice, or standard may violate the CRA if it has a disproportionate discriminatory impact on a protected class of employees. Such a practice will be deemed illegal if it has a disproportionate impact on a protected class and the employer cannot justify the practice out of business necessity. An example of such disparate impact occurred during the writing of this book when the city of North Miami Beach, Florida, dropped its requirement that new police officers be proficient swimmers. Apparently, more African-American police applicants did not know how to swim, perhaps as a vestige from days of segregation and the limited opportunities and income needed to learn how to swim as well as the barriers imposed to swimming by "whites only" beaches and pools. In response to a threatened disparate impact civil rights suit by the rejected African-American candidates, the city dropped its swimming requirement for new recruits of swimming 150 feet without stopping while wearing full uniform but no shoes. However, the city *will* require that all city police officers swim proficiently and, as such, will offer free swimming lessons.

Although it is beyond the purposes of this book to deal with the procedural aspects of U.S. discrimination law, attention must be paid to the two basic types of discrimination lawsuits, disparate treatment cases, and adverse impact cases.

In the first category, "disparate treatment cases," the employee is intentionally being discriminated against because of his or her race. In such a case, the employee will need to demonstrate evidence of the employer's specific intent to discriminate. However, intent to discriminate can be inferred, for example when the employee is a member of a protected class, is qualified for the position, or is rejected by the employer while the position remains open and the employer continues to seek applicants. However, once the employee can show this *prima facie* case of discrimination, the employee does not win automatically. Rather, the burden shifts to the employer to show some legitimate, non-discriminatory reason for having rejected the applicant. If the employer does so, the presumption of discrimination is rebutted, and the employee, in order to prevail, must then produce evidence that shows that the employer intended to discriminate and that the reason the employer offered was merely a pretext for discrimination.

In the second type of case, the "adverse impact case," the employer's policies are neutral on their face, but they nevertheless have a discriminatory effect on a protected group. That is, the selected applicants for hire or promotion significantly differ from those of the protected group members in the pool of applicants. Again, the result is to raise an inference of discrimination, which the employer must rebut. However, in an adverse impact case, the employee need not demonstrate that the employer intentionally sought to discriminate against him or her. As a general rule it is permissible for an employer to discriminate among job applications and applicants for promotion based on education, knowledge, and skills that are necessary to successfully perform the job. However, discrimination may not be readily apparent to the employer since the employer may be using facially neutral job criteria. Consequently, the employer should review hiring and promotion practices on a regular basis to make sure they are not having a disparate or adverse impact on any of the protected categories; and if so whether they are justified by business necessity. As of the writing of the second edition of this book, the Equal Employment Opportunity Commission is proceeding against Dollar General Stores and BMW. The EEOC is contending that those companies violated civil rights laws pursuant to the disparate impact theory by initially excluding job applicants based on their criminal background records. The agency is asserting that such a policy has a disproportionate adverse impact on minority job applicants. The agency, moreover, has issued guidelines to employers, recommending that they do not summarily exclude applicants based on their criminal records, but rather that employers take a more individualized approach to hiring and thus consider the time and nature of the offense, its relevance to the job in question, and the rehabilitation efforts of the applicant. An agency decision is expected in 2014, and so is an appeal to the courts.

The remedies for such discrimination encompass reinstatement, back pay, money damages, constructive seniority, attorneys' fees, and even hiring quotas in flagrant discrimination cases.

Religious discrimination generally is prohibited by the Act. Employers not only cannot discriminate in employment practices on the basis of religion, they also must make a reasonable accommodation for the religious needs of their employees, but only if such accommodation would not result in an undue hardship or burden on the employer. For example, the following religious practices usually must be accommodated: 1) prayer "breaks," 2) dietary requirements, 3) non-working mourning periods, 4) scruples concerning physical exams; and 5) special modes of dress and grooming requirements.

While ordinarily it will be deemed an undue burden for the employer to change its seniority system to guarantee that the employee will not work on certain days or that the employee has religious holidays and vacation days off, nevertheless, there are practical methods that an employer can utilize to accommodate its employees' religious beliefs. Examples include voluntary substitutes and "swaps," flexible scheduling, lateral transfers, change of job assignments, and unpaid leave for religious holidays and observances. But it must be noted that the fact that an employee refuses to cooperate with the employer in finding a reasonable accommodation certainly works to the legal benefit of the employer.

One religious discrimination case that is in the federal courts as of the writing of this book involved a woman employee, age 32, who is a Muslim and who insisted on wearing a religious head scarf, called a hijab—which is worn as a sign of modesty—at her job as a sales clerk at the Pearl Factory in the Walt Disney World Caribbean Beach Resort. While Disney policy forbids the wearing of anything but Disney-issued visors and hats, the Disney Company offered to accommodate her religious attire with a "backstage" job out of the public view. The employee refused, and ultimately, Disney fired her because of her refusal to remove the scarf. She then sued for religious discrimination under Title VII of the CRA. The case is noteworthy not only for the legal principles involved, but also because it is the first case to challenge the employee dress code at the Disney resort.

Furthermore, Disney, may have reason to worry because in May of 2006, Alamo Car Rental was found guilty of a "post-9/11 backlash discrimination" for terminating a Muslim employee who refused to remove her head scarf. The woman, a company service representative, was discharged for refusing to comply with the company's dress code. She asked to wear her head scarf during the Islamic holiday of Ramadan, but when her request was refused, she came to work wearing it anyway. She was asked to remove it, but when she refused, she was sent home and ultimately terminated.

Sexual discrimination is also prohibited by the CRA. Title VII prohibits the treatment of an employee or job applicant in a manner that would be different but for that person's gender. For example, the following practices have been deemed to be unlawful sex discrimination in the United States, though they may be legal in other countries: classifying jobs as "male" and "female"; advertising in help-wanted columns designated by gender; limiting the employment opportunities of married women but not married men; granting benefits unequally; granting benefits to employees' spouses and families unequally; paying women lower retirement benefits than men (on the assumption that women employees will live longer); not promoting women to overseas positions (on the assumption that foreign clients will not deal with a woman); requiring female employees to be single, but not male employees; and not hiring women with preschool children while hiring males with children.

Sexual stereotyping is also a form of sex discrimination. Sexual stereotyping is evidence that a woman was judged by her male supervisors and managers on the basis of stereotyped notions regarding appropriate female behavior or appearance, which can serve to establish the existence of illegal sexual discrimination. In such a case, the burden will fall on the employer to demonstrate a legitimate, job-related, non-discriminatory reason for the rejection of the female applicant or employee.

Testing and education requirements may also cause legal problems for the employer. As a general rule, it is not unlawful for the employer to hire or promote employees on the basis of results of professionally developed ability tests provided that the tests are not designed to be used in a discriminatory fashion. The plaintiff applicant's or employee's burden in such a case is to show that the tests or educational requirements select applicants for hire or promotion in patterns (across racial or otherwise protected dimensions) that are significantly different from that of the pool of applicants. However, the employer can rebut such a presumption of discrimination by showing that the tests or educational requirements are predictive of, or significantly related to, important elements of work behavior and successful job performance. Yet even if there is a showing that the tests are job-related, the courts will require that the employer use other different tests that have less of a discriminatory impact.

Similarly, minimum education requirements cannot be used as a job qualification if they eliminate a disproportionate number of minorities or other protected categories unless the employer can demonstrate a significant relationship between the education requirements and employment therein.

There are many functions that personality tests can perform. Personality tests are increasingly being used by employers, primarily as a means to increase retention of employees and to reduce turnover. There are also "screen-out" tests, which attempt to predict employee proclivity toward certain behavior, such as drug use. "Screen-in" tests seek to determine the right person for the right job. There are also tests to measure leadership, motivation, team-building skills, dependability, and even stress management. Of course, no test is a totally accurate predictor of behavior, but there are studies that show that personality tests may in fact be more reliable predictors of performance versus resumes or even personal interviews.

Nonetheless, certain points are quite clear. Personality tests are very controversial, legally, morally, and practically. The personality testing business remains largely unregulated, with no federal law or state law explicitly forbidding the use of personality tests. (However, integrity and honesty tests are prohibited in Massachusetts and Rhode Island.)

The emergent legal problem with personality tests thus is neither with precise personality test statutory law nor, for that matter, with the common law tort of invasion of privacy (presuming notice of the test is given, the test is designed for a specific and proper employment purpose, and the results are kept confidential). Rather, the legal problem with personality tests involves the CRA, specifically the "adverse" or "disparate impact" theory of liability. It is evident from a legal standpoint that if an employer does use a personality test, the test cannot have a disparate impact on any certain protected category of employees, such as certain racial or national origin groups. So, as a general rule, the Equal Employment Opportunity Commission (EEOC) maintains that a protected class must pass a test (personality or otherwise) at a rate that is at least four-fifths that of the pass rate of the unprotected classes. If this percentage is not achieved, the employer must demonstrate a legitimate need for the test, that the test is an accurate predictor of future job performance, and that there is no other comparable test that could serve the employer's purpose without negative consequences to the protected class.

Height/weight requirements also can cause legal problems for the employer. If minimum/maximum height/weight requirements have the effect of disproportionately screening out applicants on the basis of race, color, gender, or national origin, the employer may be deemed to be in violation of the CRA. The employer's obligation in such a case is to show that the requirements are validly related to the employee's ability to perform the work in question. (Actually, the courts prefer that the employer develop and use an appropriate strength and agility test whenever possible as opposed to rigid height/weight requirements, which actually may not correlate to successful job performance.)

There is no law that prohibits discrimination based on personal appearance alone, but appearance requirements may be an unlawful employment dimension if they have an effect of significantly discriminating against minorities and other protected categories. However, a "slight" adverse impact—racial, gender, or otherwise—may be permissible if a legitimate business purpose is served.

The courts, additionally, will give deference to employer appearance standards that request employees comply with the customary ways in which men and women dress and groom themselves. Again, the distinction between mutable and immutable characteristics is important. Accordingly, characteristics that can be changed, such as grooming, are not given the same protection as those that can not be changed, such as race, color, and sex.

Furthermore, it is absolutely necessary to emphasize that if the employer does in fact have appearance and grooming standards, they must be applied as equally as possible between men and women and among the protected categories. For example, if the employer wants its outside sales force to be "thin and cute," that standard must be applied to men as well as to women or else a legal appearance situation will turn into an illegal case of traditional sex discrimination. Of course, some variations may be permissible, such as in an extreme case of allowing women to wear dresses but not men, or on a lesser level to allow women to wear their hair in a pony-tail, but not men.

Furthermore, it is not a "crime," let alone a violation of the CRA, for the employer to discriminate in hiring in favor of attractive and "good-looking" applicants and employees, as long as there is no discrimination based on race or color or national origin. The clothing retailer Abercrombie & Fitch has being sued for hiring young, blond, blue-eyed, white people for sales positions while relegating minorities to stockroom positions. Abercrombie is allowed legally to have that "preppy," fraternity/sorority look, but not at the "expense" of violating the CRA and engaging in color discrimination.

Finally, if the employee's grooming or appearance is related to his or her religion, then the appearance situation has been transformed into a religious discrimination case, as was illustrated in the Disney case mentioned earlier.

The federal CRA provides a great deal of protection against discrimination in the workplace. However, not all attributes and differences are "protected categories," which means it may be quite legal, though unethical, to discriminate based on such characteristics. For example, sex discrimination does not encompass sexual preference, and thus the Act does not protect homosexual or lesbian workers who are discriminated against, discharged, or harassed in employment due to their sexual orientation. As of the writing of this book, the federal courts, even the very liberal Ninth Circuit Court of Appeals in San Francisco, have been unwilling to equate sexual preference to a protected category under the Act. However, because, as you will recall, the U.S. is a federal system, there are now several states in the U.S.—California, Connecticut, Hawaii, Massachusetts, Nevada, New Jersey, Oregon, Rhode Island, Vermont, and Wisconsin—that allow such suits under their states' anti-discrimination laws. Washington state also recently added sexual orientation to its civil rights law banning discrimination not only in employment, but also in housing and insurance.

Parental status also is not a protected category under the federal CRA. In the "classic" example, two women apply for a position but the one who has children is denied the position even if she is otherwise qualified. The rejected woman candidate is being denied the job because she is a parent and presumably, the prospective employer believes that her child-rearing responsibilities would interfere with her job performance. But take note that the woman is not being discriminated against because of her sex since the other candidate who was chosen was a woman, though a woman without children.

In addition, women with child responsibilities have attempted to use the public policy doctrine to seek legal redress for perceived unfair discharges. In one famous (perhaps infamous) case, an at-will female computer sales employee in the Boston area was fired from her job because she refused her employer's demands to work long over-time hours and to work on Saturdays. The woman refused because she had sole responsibility for raising a small child and she stated that to work such hours would mean that she would never see her child awake. She sued for violation of the public policy doctrine, contending that the public policy of the state of Massachusetts favors the welfare of children and thus supports parents' efforts to raise their children. Her case went all the way to the state supreme court of Massachusetts, which, although expressing sympathy for her (and for parents in general), ruled that there is no public policy that forbids employers from demanding that their employees work long hours.

Related to parental status is marital status. In the federal CRA, the fact that an employee is married does not place him or her into a protected category. Thus, many companies have policies in place that prevent employees from being married to other employees and both keeping their jobs. Of course, some firms try to narrow those policies to employees in the same managerial hierarchical "chain" and/or to employees in the same division or department. Some employers even prohibit relationships of a dating nature between co-workers. Such employers are worried that when marriages or romances "crash and burn," one result may be a lawsuit for sexual discrimination and harassment, for which the employer could be vicariously liable for redressing.

The problem with such marriage and dating policies lies not under the federal law, but rather under state law, especially the law of tort. An employer who too aggressively seeks to enforce its no dating/relationship/marriage policy may eventually wind up defending itself from a tort invasion of privacy lawsuit. Also, it should be noted that several states, in their state anti-discrimination laws, ban discrimination on the basis of marital status. Finally, a few companies, such as Southwest Airlines, explicitly allow office romances and consensual relationships. However, any such liberal dating policy should take into account the feelings of other employees as to perceived unfair treatment.

Finally, is a tobacco smoker in a protected category? The answer is "no" pursuant to the federal Civil Rights law, but "yes" according to approximately 30 state anti-discrimination statutes. The issue is very important in the U.S. today as many employers, in an attempt to reduce ever-spiraling health care costs, are prohibiting employees from smoking not just on the job, but anywhere and at any time. Smoking, therefore, would constitute grounds for discharge. Even in a state where this is permissible legally, the authors would counsel the employer to proceed in a very careful and cautious manner in the implementation of its no-smoking policy, particularly the investigating and random drug testing of employees, because the employer may wind up violating the common law privacy rights of its employees and thus be subject to a tort lawsuit for invasion of privacy by the discharged, at-will, still-smoking employee.

The issue is especially controversial not only due to privacy concerns, but also due to the fact that tobacco smoking is a legal activity. So is eating fast food. Being overweight, let alone obese, does lead to health care problems, and thus to greater health care costs for the employer. So could a fast-food prohibition by the employer be next?

The Bona Fide Occupational Qualification Exception to the Civil Rights Act

A *bona fide* occupational qualification (BFOQ) emerges as the greatest exception to the CRA. As interpreted by the federal courts and the EEOC, an employer is allowed to discriminate on the basis of religion, sex, or national origin if such characteristics are reasonably necessary to the normal operations of a particular business and job performance. Furthermore, in order to be a BFOQ, the characteristic must affect how the employees do the job and must relate to an essential aspect of the job or a central mission of employment. The result of a BFOQ is legal, though not necessarily ethical, discrimination.

One point must be made very clear, and that is that race and color can *never* be BFOQs. It would be illegal for the producer of a play to advertise for a "white" actor to play the role of Hamlet. (Whether it would be legal to seek only actors—that is, males—and not actresses to play the role is another matter.)

Usually the courts will require that for a BFOQ to exist, there must be a showing that all or substantially all women (or men) would be unable to perform the duties of the job efficiently or safely. For example, Broward General Medical Center in Ft. Lauderdale, Florida, dropped its policy of hiring only males to be OB-GYN nurses. The hospital, a large public facility, contended that the BFOQ doctrine would apply due to the concern that some women patients might object to being cared for by a male nurse so soon after giving birth. A male nurse, upon being reassigned from the postpartum unit, thereupon filed a complaint with the EEOC, after which the hospital changed its policy.

In another leading case, a woman desired to be an engineer on a cruise ship. She was initially denied that opportunity as the cruise line company cited the

BFOQ doctrine, in particular, accommodation and privacy issues. The key issue in the cruise line case was whether the U.S. courts even had jurisdiction over the foreign-registered cruise ships. But when a federal judge ruled that the U.S. courts indeed had jurisdiction, the cruise line dropped its "male only" policy for engineering job applicants.

Accordingly, because the BFOQ is legalized discrimination precluding employment opportunities, the courts construe the exception very narrowly. Companies have to be very careful in asserting that customer preference—for example, for a male employee to service a particular account—rises to the level of a BFOQ. Most courts today would likely rule that to remove an employee from a position because she is a female, or because a particular client objects to working with women, would be illegal discrimination. The authors of this book would thus strongly advise companies in such a situation to educate their clients and customers that a woman can do just as good of a job as a man.

Several presumably "high-end" or "classy" restaurants in Manhattan, New York City, and in Miami's South Beach have been sued by women who wanted to be waitresses but were denied such positions due to a "males only" hiring policy. These restaurants have attempted to use the BFOQ defense by claiming that the ambience they are attempting to create is an "old-world, European" dining experience which requires that all of the waiters be male. The courts have consistently rejected the BFOQ defense in such cases, in one case condemning such a males only policy as a "quaint anachronism."

However, the BFOQ doctrine has been upheld. In one leading Supreme Court case, an Alabama rule that "contact" prison guards in male, maximum security prisons had to be men was upheld by the Court because a woman could not perform that job safely or maintain prison security. Similarly, the Walt Disney Company has been successful in using the BFOQ doctrine to uphold hiring policies at its Epcot country pavilions that restrict employment to people who are from the countries represented at the pavilions.

Furthermore, Disney has been successful in resisting challenges to its hiring practices at its "themed" park areas, for example the African village of Harambe in the Animal Kingdom, where in order to obtain a job with customer contact, an applicant must be from Africa. So, not only U.S. citizens, but also African-American U.S. citizens or Afro-Caribbean citizens "need not apply." Again, Disney uses the BFOQ doctrine and the concomitant need for authenticity in the "themed" area to justify its discrimination.

But if a reader of this book is fortunate enough to go to Disney and does visit Harambe, perhaps he or she will see a white person working in the African "village." Very likely, this white person will be from South Africa, which obviously is a part of Africa, thereby comporting with the Disney requirements as this person presumably will know the African culture and language. Most significantly, one might see the white employee there because, as emphasized, color can never be a BFOQ.

Title VII and Language Discrimination

Discrimination based on language is a form of national origin discrimination and, consequently, may violate Title VII of the CRA. In one interesting case, a Japanese company doing business in the U.S. was sued in 2006 for national origin discrimination for discriminating in pay and promotions against non-Asians. One part of the lawsuit contends that weekly meetings of the company were conducted only in Japanese, thereby effectively precluding non-Japanese-speaking employees from participating.

Language discrimination lawsuits, however, usually arise when an employer adopts an "English only" rule that requires the employees to communicate in English at the workplace. Language discrimination and "English only" policies are an important topic in an area such as Southeast Florida, a tri-county region that has one of the highest percentage of foreign-born residents of any major metropolitan area in the United States. Southeast Florida, similar to many areas of the U.S., is a magnet for immigration, both legal and illegal, which results in a workforce that may be getting less and less proficient in English. Many companies have responded to this trend by adopting language policies requiring the speaking of English at work.

This controversial area of the law has been explicated by the EEOC and the courts in a series of legal interpretations. The first important rule is that if an employer requires the use of the English language at all times and at all places in the workplace, such an "English only" rule will be presumed to be both discriminatory and invalid. Adopting a "blanket" English policy, which would punish an employee for speaking another language during a "break," most certainly will land the employer in court.

The second important rule, however, holds that if the employer's "English only" policy is limited to working times (as opposed to meal and "break" times) and working areas (as opposed to the lounge, rest, snack, or cafeteria areas), then the policy may be upheld by the courts, but only if the employer can demonstrate a reasonable and legitimate business purpose for mandating the limited use of the English language.

The courts have supported a variety of employer justifications for implementing English-only policies. Some examples of business needs for such a policy are ensuring safety and security, preventing accidents, promoting effective communication, enhancing product or service quality, allowing managers and supervisors to more effectively perform their functions, responding to customer preferences (who may not speak or understand languages other than English), increasing sales, improving morale and employee relations, and promoting racial and ethnic harmony in the workplace. In one leading case, two nurses from the Philippines were warned, suspended, and then fired from their hospital jobs in Southern California for their refusal to speak English while they were at work at the nurses' station, on the "floor," and while they were working at various other work areas of the hospital. They insisted on speaking the native language of the Philippines, Tagalog, in contravention of the hospital's English-only policy to ensure patient care and safety. In 2013, Whole Foods Market initiated a review of its language policy after two Spanish-speaking workers in New Mexico stated they were suspended after complaining about the company's English-only policy, which forbids employees from speaking Spanish to each other as well as customers while on the job (unless the customer speaks another language). Whole Foods Market states that employees are allowed to speak any language they want during breaks and meal times as well as before or after work, and that the employees in question were suspended for rude behavior. Nonetheless, the state director of the New Mexico League of United Latin American Citizens is threatening a nationwide boycott unless the company changes its policy.

Presuming the employer does have such a legitimate business need for a limited English-only policy, the courts will require that the employer give the employees a reasonable time to adapt to the new policy. Overly abrupt attempts by the employer to force employees to speak and to learn English, for example by monitoring the employees, intimidating them, humiliating them, or yelling at them to speak English, may result in the creation of a "hostile environment" based on national origin, which is a violation of Title VII.

Finally, if the employer adopts an English-only policy, and the employer at that time has employees who do not speak English, the courts will require the employer to teach its non-English-speaking employees English. In one case involving the New York Yankees baseball team, the Yankees were criticized for pressuring one of their "star" Latin-American players to stop speaking Spanish and to learn "perfect" English. Of course, such a strict English-only policy may inhibit the employer from achieving higher quality of production or service and may unduly put a hardship on Spanish-speaking or other foreign-language-speaking employees.

For example, in 2006, the president of a major coal company in Kentucky, commenting on the difficulty of finding mining employees (starting at $18 per hour, plus benefits), suggested, perhaps to the chagrin of the business community and the consternation of anti-immigration advocates, that it may be time to "relax" the English-only policy in the mines in order to bring in Hispanic workers.

National origin discrimination charges also may arise when an employer discriminates against an employee or job applicant who has limited English language proficiency or who has a foreign accent. The key test, according to the courts and the EEOC, is whether the lack of English-language fluency or the presence of a foreign accent interferes with the employee's ability to perform the job at hand.

Ethnic slurs can also equate to national origin discrimination if the slurs create a hostile, offensive, abusive, or intimidating work environment or unreasonably interfere with an employee's work performance.

One final point about language is that the courts consider "language" to be a "mutable" characteristic, as opposed to race, color, and sex, which are deemed to be "immutable." The idea is that the former can be changed—such as by learning a new language or improving one's language skills—whereas the latter cannot, under reasonable circumstances, be changed. The result is that ordinarily, the courts will accord more discretion to employers to make hiring and other employment decisions based on mutable characteristics.

Title VII and Sexual Harassment

Sexual harassment in the workplace in the U.S. is considered to be a form of sexual discrimination and thus is a violation of Title VII of the CRA. Sexual harassment consists of unwelcome sexual advances, requests for sex, as well as other physical or verbal conduct of a sexual nature. Sexual harassment law divides this legal wrong into two main categories: 1) *quid pro quo*, and 2) hostile environment.

The first type of sexual harassment, *quid pro quo*, arises when an employment benefit, such as an initial job, promotion, or the continuation of employment, is conditioned by a manager or supervisor on an employee's willingness, or lack thereof, to engage in sexual conduct. That is, the *quid pro quo*, in common parlance, means the "boss" demands sex in "trade" for the job or promotion. In one case, the largest lettuce-growing company in the U.S. paid almost $2 million dollars to settle allegations of sexual harassment at its facilities in Arizona and California. The agreement with the EEOC stemmed from charges that a company production manager demanded sexual favors from a female worker as a condition of employment and job benefits.

The second type of sexual harassment, hostile environment, arises when the work environment degenerates into a hostile, abusive, or offensive setting based on sex. It is important to note that this legal violation can occur even if no employment or employment benefit is lost. Furthermore, this legal wrong can be the product of sexual actions not just by managers and supervisors, but also by coworkers and even those not actually employed by the firm, such as its vendors and other outside independent contractors. But the key issue is what exactly makes an environment sexually "hostile"? The pervasive presence of sexual comments, jokes, pictures, literature, and media will suffice, as surely will the presence of sexual aggression or battery. The U.S. Supreme Court has delineated four factors to be used in answering the "hostile" question: 1) the frequency of the conduct; 2) the severity of the conduct; 3) whether the conduct was physically threatening or sexually bellicose or ridiculing, or humiliating; and 4) whether the conduct interferes with the employee's work performance. The employer can be liable for the hostile environment harassment created by even a customer if the employer knew or should have known of the harassment and failed to take proper action to prevent or redress the harassment.

A hostile sexual environment must be objectively offensive to the "reasonable person" as well as subjectively offensive to the victimized employee. However, what makes the definition of hostile, abusive, and offensive so problematic in the law is that the "reasonable person" standard has been interpreted to mean a reasonable person standing "in the shoes" of the aggrieved employee, which perforce introduces a subjective element into the supposedly objective component to the definitional test.

The U.S. Supreme Court has stated that the sporadic use of abusive language, sex-related jokes, or occasional teasing may constitute the ordinary "trials and tribulations" of the workplace, and as such, may not create a hostile environment. Yet, ascertaining the line between "innocent" sexual behavior—for example a gender-based comment, such as telling a woman that she is "very beautiful," and even perhaps flirting with her a bit—and illegal sexual conduct, such as subjecting her to unwelcome sexual harassment, can at times be a difficult challenge.

Other gray areas arise. Is the employee who puts up, in his or her office, a reproduction of a classic Renaissance painting depicting nudity, such as Botticelli's "Birth of Venus" or "Primavera," committing an illegal act? Actually, nobody knows until someone "makes a federal case of it," literally and figuratively.

However, in many other cases, the severe nature of the hostile sexual environment is flagrantly evident. For example, Ford Motor Company agreed to a $17.5-million settlement with the EEOC to resolve sexual harassment allegations at two of its Chicago-area production facilities. The conduct complained of encompassed unwanted sexual groping and massaging, vulgar name-calling, the presence of sexual graffiti, lewd photos and pornography, and parties with strippers and prostitutes. The female victims received $7.5 million as compensation with the other $10 million to be used for educational and training purposes.

Similarly, Mitsubishi Motor Manufacturing of America agreed to pay $34 million to settle allegations of sexual harassment at its auto assembly plant in Normal, Illinois. The EEOC claimed that the workplace was pervasively "saturated" with sexuality, most of it "demeaning" to women. For example, women employees were forced by crude threats to view pornography, including pictures from sex parties organized on company time. Male employees would regularly fire air guns and shoot water at the breasts and buttocks of their female coworkers. Approximately 350 women were eligible for the $34 million settlement. Additionally, the company's supervisors and managers routinely ignored complaints about sexual abuse. As part of the settlement, Mitsubishi also agreed to revise its sexual harassment and complaint policy so as to ensure "zero tolerance" of sexual harassment. The EEOC's settlement with Mitsubishi has been, to date, the largest settlement of a sexual harassment case in the United States.

Toyota too, in 2006, announced that it had settled a $190-million lawsuit that resulted in the resignation of the company's North American CEO, who had been accused by a female employee of not only making inappropriate comments but also trying to force her to have sex with him. The employee also stated that she complained to Toyota's senior North American vice president, who then did nothing. The CEO has denied any wrongdoing and has since returned to Japan, while the senior VP no longer oversees the HR department. As a result of the settlement, Toyota instituted a new policy for combating sexual harassment, which included training all U.S. executives to recognize, prevent, and handle sexual harassment, and to immediately report and investigate allegations of sexual harassment. If the allegation is made against the chairperson, CEO, or president, the report must be made directly to the company's board of directors.

The employee who commits the sexual harassment is personally liable, of course, but what about the employer's liability? In two very important decisions in 1998, the U.S. Supreme Court very firmly established the two principal rules for the employer's liability for sexual harassment.

First, if the sexual harassment is committed by a manager or supervisor in the aggrieved employee's management hierarchy, and if the employee suffers some type of tangible job loss, harm, or injury, such as a discharge, demotion, undesirable transfer, or even missed time from work due to stress or fear, then the employer is absolutely liable for the sexual harassment. For our purposes, the term "absolute" means that presuming the employer itself is not the victim of some type of "Machiavellian" conspiracy by the employees to defraud the employer of money, then the employer has no real defense. Thus, assuming the sexual harassment finding is legitimate, the employer is liable regardless of knowledge of the wrongdoing and regardless of any highly commendable efforts to prevent sexual harassment in the workplace.

Second, if the sexual harassment is committed not by the aggrieved employee's direct managers or supervisors, but rather by the employee's coworkers, or if the aggrieved does not suffer any tangible job loss, the employer then has a defense against liability. If the employer can show that it had policies and procedures in place to combat and correct sexual harassment in the workplace, that these policies and procedures were communicated to the employees, and that there existed reasonable channels of communication for the employees to report and to complain about sexual harassment that the aggrieved employee did not use, then the employer can escape liability.

These two important Supreme Court rules have engendered some significant consequences. The second rule, which provides a potential defense, certainly has motivated employers to promulgate polices, develop procedures, and to institute training to educate employees and thereby to prevent sexual harassment in the workplace. It is thus incumbent on the employer to have clear and firm policies prohibiting sexual harassment, to disseminate such policies to the employees, and to provide channels for reporting complaints as well as provide procedures for handling and investigating such complaints.

As to the first liability rule enunciated by the Court, because the rule states that there is no defense, employers have been seeking to purchase sexual harassment insurance as protection from this type of absolute legal liability, especially since the U.S. Congress has materially expanded the amount of money that can be recovered as damages in civil rights lawsuits. In a significant and unanimous sexual harassment non-retaliation decision, the U.S. Supreme Court ruled in 2006 that the legal standard to determine if an employee who complained of harassment was retaliated against is now a "reasonable person" standard. That is, retaliation is defined as any action taken by the employer that would intimidate a reasonable employee from not complaining about sexual harassment or other forms of discrimination. It is predicted that this standard will make it easier for employees to file retaliation complaints accusing their employers of intimidating conduct. Furthermore, now the federal courts will have to determine whether an employer's actions would have caused a reasonable employee to have been intimidated on a case-by-case basis.

One such case dealt with a woman employee, a railroad forklift operator, who accused her male supervisor of sexual harassment. She was suspended for 32 days and reassigned to a more physically demanding job. Even though she prevailed in the employer's internal Human Resources appeal process, being cleared of insubordination and then reinstated and also receiving back pay for the suspension period, the Court ruled that an employee's going a month without a paycheck constitutes a serious hardship to the reasonable employee and is thus considered both intimidating and retaliatory. The wrongful supervisor in question was suspended and sent to sensitivity training.

As a matter of fact, and perhaps as an unintended consequence of the Supreme Court decisions, a whole new field in the insurance business has been created called sexual harassment insurance, which has thus far emerged as a very lucrative area.

The employer also must be very cognizant of, and sensitive to, different cultural mores and practices in the workplace regarding the interactions of women and men. For example, as a major hub for U.S.-Latin American business dealings, Southeast Florida is particularly prone to a "culture clash" of sexual mores in the workplace. For example, a simple kiss on the cheek may simply mean a friendly greeting in some Latin American cultures, but in the United States, it might readily "translate" into an unwanted sexual advance.

Wal-Mart Sex Discrimination Class Action Lawsuit

The U.S. Supreme Court, in 2011, dismissed a massive sex discrimination lawsuit against Wal-Mart Stores, Inc., ruling that the approximately 1.6 million women in the class, who allegedly were discriminated against in pay and promotions, had too little in common to form a class of plaintiffs for a lawsuit pursuant to federal procedural law. The key question was whether the lawsuit met the requirements for a class action lawsuit, specifically that there were questions of law and fact common to the class of women employee plaintiffs. In a 5-4 decision, with Justice Antonin Scalia writing for the majority, the Court concluded that the allegations against Wal-Mart were too vague and the evidence too weak to establish a common injury, which is an essential requirement for a class action lawsuit. The 1.6 million women bringing suit had worked at Wal-Mart since 1998 in the approximately 3,400 Wal-Mart stores in the United States. Justice Scalia stated that the statistical data that the plaintiff women presented allegedly showing pay and promotion differences were not sufficient proof of discrimination. Rather, the Justice said, the women must identify specific employment practices, such as a biased testing procedure, that unlawfully discriminated against the women. Wal-Mart has an express policy prohibiting discrimination but the company granted local managers substantial discretion. Yet it is important to note that the Supreme Court decision did not decide whether the women were discriminated against based on their gender at Wal-Mart. Rather, the women could not proceed as a class constituted for the lawsuit. The original lawsuit filed against Wal-Mart occurred in 2001. The women plaintiffs accused the company, which is the world's largest retailer, of systematically paying female workers less than their male counterparts and providing women employees with fewer opportunities for promotion. The suit was based on the company's personnel policies, which granted individual managers wide discretion over promotions and raises, which allowed sex biases and stereotyping that pervaded the corporate culture, and which denied fair opportunity to women. As a consequence, the women plaintiffs argued that women employee remain concentrated on the retailer's low wage "rank and file," while men were paid more and dominated the managerial ranks. Yet Justice Scalia said that "merely" demonstrating that Wal-Mart had a policy of managerial discretion overall produced sex-based disparity was insufficient. Actually, the fact that Wal-Mart did not have uniform employment policies and allowed its managers considerable discretion worked against the women plaintiffs, since the lack of uniform policies militated against any finding of commonality critical to a class action lawsuit. As a result of the decision, the women plaintiffs can still sue individually for discrimination by bringing actions to the Equal Employment Opportunity Commission, or they could try to form a smaller and more focused class action suit, with more elements of fact and law in common to the class members, perhaps by targeting smaller geographic regions or groups of stores.

Affirmative Action—Constitutional, Ethical, and Practical Concerns[79]

The term "affirmative action" itself has come to represent a wide variety of programs. At one extreme, such programs set rigid, fixed, job quotas that must be filled by women and minority group members. On the other end of the debate, there is the "mild" extreme of taking special proactive efforts to ensure that women and minority group members are included in the pool of applicants for hiring or promotion.

Almost everyone morally condemns the former and morally approves the latter.

In the middle, however, is the type of affirmative action plan that takes race, ethnic heritage, or sex into account when selecting among qualified candidates, thereby giving such individuals a preference over equally or more qualified white men. Such a preference plan raises a loud emotional outcry both from those who praise it as just redress for past discrimination and stereotyping as well as from those who condemn it as immoral, "reverse discrimination." What is required, however, to resolve this difficult issue is rational ethical analysis of legal preference-type affirmative action plans.

The United States Supreme Court, in a very significant affirmative action decision in June 2003, permitted the use of race as a preference factor in the college admissions process. At the same time, the court also issued a stern warning

---

[79] This material comes from *Business Ethics: Transcending Requirements through Moral Leadership* book by Frank J. Cavico and Bahaudin G. Mujtaba.

that colleges cannot use rigid affirmative action systems that resemble quotas and they also must adopt neutral race policies as soon as practicable.

Justice Sandra Day O'Connor, writing for a 5-4 court majority, stated that the University of Michigan Law School did not violate the "equal protection" guarantee of the 14th Amendment to the Constitution. Significantly, Justice O'Connor stated that the goal of creating a diverse student body was a sufficiently "compelling government interest" to justify the law school's consideration of race as a beneficial admissions factor. She added, however, that race-conscious admissions policies should not go on forever. Justice O'Connor stated that twenty-five years from now, the Court would expect that racial preferences will no longer be necessary.

In the majority opinion in the law school case, Justice O'Connor rejected the argument of the Bush Administration that race-neutral alternatives could be as effective in creating diversity as affirmative action. The Constitution, said Justice O'Connor, does not prevent the law school's "narrowly tailored" use of race in admission decisions so as to achieve a compelling interest in obtaining educational benefits that are produced by a diverse student body.

The Michigan law school uses race as a potential "plus" factor to promote diversity, stated Justice O'Connor, while the goal of the law school affirmative action policy was to produce a "critical mass" of minority students on campus. She supported the decision by citing studies showing that diversity promotes learning outcomes and better prepares students for an increasingly diverse workforce, for a diverse society, and for the legal professions. Diversity is necessary, she maintained, for developing leaders with "legitimacy" in the judgment of the people. Moreover, she stated that effective participation by members of all racial and ethnic groups in the civic life of the nation is critical if the U.S. truly will achieve the goal of being one "indivisible" nation. She emphasized, in addition, that businesses have made it clear that the skills and knowledge essential in today's increasingly global marketplace can only be honed through contact and experience with widely diverse peoples, cultures, ideas, and views.

Meanwhile, U.S. Solicitor General Theodore Olsen, however, condemned the Michigan policies a "thinly disguised quota." Some critics contended that the decisions mean that universities can still racially discriminate so long as they are not obvious about it. Civil rights advocates, however, hailed the decision as a major victory and claimed it not only strengthened affirmative action in a college setting, but also gave added impetus to the use of race in pursuit of diversity elsewhere, especially in employment.

Yet the University of Michigan's president, Mary Sue Coleman, said she was delighted by the decision because the principle of diversity was upheld, and she stated that the school would fix its undergraduate policy so that it is not construed as a mechanical quota-based system. Unlike the law school, the undergraduate school awards a specific, predetermined number of points to applicants whose ethnicity or race is underrepresented on campus. Specifically, a 20-point bonus is doled out to candidates of such underrepresented races on a 150-point scale, where 100 points guaranteed an admission.

The University of Michigan's undergraduate admissions policy did not survive the Court's scrutiny in another companion case. The majority of the Court found that this effectively resembled a quota system, a practice previously struck down as being unconstitutional. In this companion case, Chief Justice William Rehnquist, writing for a 6-3 majority, stated that this numerical policy made race the decisive factor in admissions decisions, and thus was unconstitutional. Justice Clarence Thomas, the court's only black member, issued a bitter condemnation of affirmative action as a well-intended but patronizing and ultimately discriminatory attempt by whites to help African Americans. Thomas's dissent began with a quote from an address by Frederick Douglas, criticizing abolitionists in 1865 for interfering with blacks' efforts to help themselves. Thomas stated that he believes that blacks can achieve success "without the meddling of university administrators." He also declared that a state's use of racial discrimination in higher education admissions is categorically prohibited by the Equal Protection Clause of the Constitution.

The undergraduate decision also could cause employers to rethink their reliance on quantitative evaluations of job applicants and employees. While the law school decision does allow colleges to consider race as a preferential factor in making decisions, the court made clear that diversity should not be defined solely in terms of race and ethnicity. Universities, therefore, will have to look more broadly at special talents and life circumstances, such as family background and income and education levels, in searching for a diverse student body. In fact, Justice O'Connor's writing effectively required that universities now must give each applicant a personal "holistic" look.

The Supreme Court's University of Michigan affirmative action cases of 2003 emerge as landmark decisions with wide-ranging implications not only for education, but also for business and for society as a whole, especially because the use of race has been upheld legally as a permissible component to an affirmative action preference plan.

In order to ethically evaluate the "preference" form of affirmative action, it is first necessary to state exactly what such a plan constitutes versus what it does not. The employment context will be used to show the components and workings of the preference type of affirmative action plan.

Typically, a preference plan is voluntarily adopted by an employer to integrate its workforce in order to redress past discrimination and social stereotyping. In the private employment sector, the plan normally is not preceded by any admission or finding of purposeful past discrimination by the employer. The plan is predicated, however, on a foundation, designed to eliminate obvious racial or sexual imbalances in the employer's workforce. That is, the number of women and minority group members in the employer's workforce is compared with the number of women and minority group members in the area labor market. If the comparison reveals a manifest imbalance, then the preference plan possesses a "foundation." (Of course, if a particular position requires special training or education, the comparison is made with those individuals in the area labor force who possess the relevant qualifications.)

The plan does not include fixed numerical quotas for hiring or promotion. Rather, all applicants and candidates are to be qualified, and the plan sets forth flexible goals or objectives for women and minority group representation in the employer's workforce. For moral, as well as very practical reasons, preferences are not to be extended to unqualified women and minority group members. But presuming that all applicants are qualified, the preference form of affirmative action allows women and minority group members to be accorded a preference or "plus" factor in employment decisions. Note that under this type of plan, no person is automatically excluded from consideration; all will have their qualifications evaluated.

Yet an applicant's race, sex, or "diversity" can and will be used as one "plus factor" in the applicant's file. So, as one clearly can perceive, the moral controversy arises when the "plus factor" dictates the hiring of a qualified woman or minority group member over an equally or more qualified white male applicant.

The preference plan, however, is not designed as an absolute preclusion to the hiring or promotion of white men. It is not an absolute principle but a contingent one because race or sex is merely one plus factor. That is, if a white male applicant is especially qualified, he certainly can be chosen over a qualified woman or minority group applicant. Yet the employer, in so doing, must be aware that it has set hiring goals and will be expected to make overall progress in achieving these affirmative action goals and attaining proportionate representation of women and minority group members.

As part of an affirmative action plan, a company can engage in various proactive diversity efforts to attract and maintain a more ethnically and gender-balanced workforce. Such efforts might encompass targeted recruiting, increasing the pool of qualified women and minority applicants and candidates, mentoring, and even training in diversity awareness. One method that will enhance the diversity of a firm's workforce and still maintain equality of opportunity and treatment is to define those positions in the firm where diversity, together with intelligence, personality, education, and experience, would be a legitimate job qualification.

Diversity, as so defined, can be viewed as a qualifying factor for an applicant, similar to intelligence. Intelligence can be assessed by the employer, but it never will be equal among all applicants. If diversity can be cited as a bona fide qualification for a job description, predicated perhaps on a firm's diverse customer base, then tangible business needs, such as marketing effectiveness and competitiveness, would drive the job-related diversity program. Therefore, a rational person would see the practical business necessity as well as the morality of such an affirmative action plan.

Diversity awareness training not only enables a firm's employees to recognize but also to appreciate differences among individuals, as well as to value the uniqueness in every person. Such uniqueness can be derived from one's race, sex, or ethnic heritage, as well as from one's religious, educational, or socioeconomic background, and even from one's physical appearance or color. Furthermore, this uniqueness should be considered as a highly valuable source of information, innovation, contribution, and value to a firm. A company should create a corporate culture that not only recognizes these differences, but also celebrates them. Additionally, the company should establish a work environment where every employee can realize his or her own complete potential. Such a firm will be more competitive due to an empowered and more effective workforce, higher morale, and a deserved reputation for being a better and moral place to work.

A company's decision to implement a diversity awareness program will also benefit all the firm's stakeholders, and society will benefit as more and more companies adopt diversity awareness programs. The rich and unique ideas and ways of thinking drawn from various people's backgrounds and cultures will make the quality of life and of work better for all.

The very difficult and contentious issue of affirmative action again reached the U.S. Supreme Court, and also once again in the context of education. In 2006, the Supreme Court heard arguments in a secondary school desegregation case in which two school boards, one in Seattle, Washington, and the other in Louisville, Kentucky, were attempting to preserve voluntarily imposed race-based integration plans. The school board plans were controversial because race was used as a factor to assign students to schools in order to achieve more racially diverse schools. The school districts contended that racial integration is an essential component to a public school education; and that such an objective is a compelling government interest so as to justify a limited use of race in implementing policies that produce integrated schools. The parents that challenged the race-based school assignment plans contended that the Equal Protection clause of the 14th Amendment to the U.S. Constitution as interpreted by the Court forbids any consideration of race in school enrollment decisions. However, proponents of the plan said that the limited use of race is necessary to redress the legacy of racism and school segregation in the United States. Moreover, proponents argued that there are positive benefits for the students and ultimately for society as a whole for students to attend racially diverse schools. Achieving a diverse student body, one recalls, was deemed to be a sufficiently "compelling" interest for the Court to uphold the University of Michigan's law school's affirmative action policy in which race was allowed to be used as one "plus" factor in an otherwise "holistic" evaluation of a candidate for admission. In the Seattle case, involving a city, it is important to note, which never imposed official segregation, students are allowed to enroll in any of ten high schools. However, if a particular high school has more applicants than seats, school official are empowered to use several tie-breaking factors, including race, in order to achieve an enrollment that approximately reflects the city-wide student population. In Seattle, whites account for 40% of the population, with blacks, Hispanics, Asians, and Native Americans accounting for the other 60%. In the Louisville case, the city once had a legally imposed dual, "separate but equal," school system, in which certain schools were reserved for whites and others for blacks. As a result of civil rights litigation, a federal court in 1975 imposed the remedy of mandatory busing in order to achieve integration of the schools. However, in 2000, a federal judge dissolved the desegregation order, finding that the schools had been successfully integrated. In order to maintain integrated schools, school officials in Louisville decided to continue the desegregation policy, which seeks to keep black enrollment in each school between 15% and 50%. A parent whose child was denied admission to neighborhood schools because the child's enrollment would have an adverse effect on desegregation sued because her child was assigned to a school impermissibly due to the child's race.

Even the initial questions and comments by the Justices of the Supreme Court reflected the conservative-liberal dichotomy to the Court. For example, the "liberal" members talked in terms of the benefits of diversity and emphasized the need and desirability of local school officials to develop policies that use race to achieve diversity in school composition. Whereas the "conservative" members asserted that despite the laudable benefits of integration and diversity, the means used to attain these "good" ends must be race neutral, non-discriminatory, and thus moral ones. Of course, the key vote in, as well as author of, the Michigan law school, 5-4, decision, Justice Sandra Day O'Connor, was no longer on the Court. The key vote, according to legal experts, was Justice Anthony Kennedy, who appears to be very reticent about using race as the classifying factor in admissions decisions. Although it is always difficult to predict the Court, many legal experts nonetheless expected that the Court would enunciate a "split decision" as in the precedent Michigan case. That is, the Court would most likely strike down the Louisville plan since race is the sole factor in assigning students; but uphold the Seattle plan where race is used as "merely" one factor, granted a potential "tipping" one, among a variety of criteria employed to determine school assignments. However, in 2007, the Supreme Court, in a surprising, momentous, landmark, and very close 5-4 decision, struck down both the Louisville and Seattle affirmative plans as unconstitutional. Chief Justice John G. Roberts, Jr., writing for the majority, declared that the two school districts had failed to meet their "heavy burden" of justifying the "extreme means" the districts had chosen to classify children by means of their race when making school assignments. Chief Justice Roberts very succinctly explained the Court's reasoning: "The way to stop discrimination on the basis of race is to stop discriminating on the basis of race." Yet the decision may not entirely eliminate the use of race as a factor in making educational decisions. Justice Kennedy, joining the majority, but also writing a concurring opinion, opined that there might be some "narrow circumstances" that would allow the use of race as a criterion in education. Justice Kennedy also declared that "This nation has a moral and ethical obligation to fulfill its historic commitment to creating an integrated society that ensures equal opportunity for all of its children." Nevertheless, the decision very likely will force educational institutions to devise race-neutral criteria, such as socio-economic factors, in designing affirmative policies and plans. As a matter of fact, in the majority opinion, Chief Justice Roberts stated that other means aside from race should be used to promote diversity in schools. Everyone seems to agree that classroom diversity is a very important educational objective, but how to achieve it fairly and constitutionally is emerging as a daunting challenge—legally, morally, and practically.

In 2013, the Supreme Court again tackled the difficult and contentious issue of affirmative action—and again in the context of education. The case, *Fisher v. University of Texas* (2013), dealt with the Texas affirmative action policy of offering admission to the "flagship" Austin campus of the University of Texas to any high school graduate in the top ten percent of his or her high school graduating class in the state. One high school student, a white female, who was not in the top ten percent in her school, was denied admission to the University of Texas at Austin. She claimed that she had higher SAT and GRE scores than black students admitted pursuant to the "ten percent" rule, and thus she contended that she had been discriminated against because of her race in violation of the 14th Amendment to the United States Constitution. The Supreme Court was expected to enunciate a "sweeping" decision, either upholding or striking down affirmative action. However, the Court enunciated a compromise decision. The Court in a 7-1 decision did not invalidate affirmative action. But the Court, with Justice Anthony Kennedy writing for the majority, made it much more difficult for a university (and other entities) to legally sustain an affirmative action program. The Court held that affirmative action programs that have a race component must undergo the rigid legal test of "strict scrutiny." Strict scrutiny, in essence, in the context of affirmative action in education, has three main components: first, the university must demonstrate that having a diverse student body is a "compelling government interest" for an affirmative action admissions program with a race factor; second, the university must show that its admissions program is tailored narrowly to obtain the educational benefits of diversity; and third, the university must show that there is no other practical race-neutral alternative that would produce the same educational benefits of diversity. The Supreme Court then sent the case back to the lower federal courts to determine if the University of Texas "passed" this "strict scrutiny" test. Supporters of affirmative action in education and other areas were naturally pleased the Supreme Court did not totally invalidate affirmative action, but were concerned that the practical result of such a demanding legal standard would jeopardize affirmative action programs. One thing is sure, though, and that is to expect more affirmative action lawsuits in education and other areas.

The Age Discrimination in Employment Act of 1967[80]

The Age Discrimination in Employment Act (ADEA) of 1967 is a U.S. federal law which prohibits an employer from failing or refusing to hire a protected individual, or from discharging an employee within the protected age category or otherwise discriminating against such individuals because of their age. Commensurately, the ADEA covers hiring, termination, compensation, as well as other terms and conditions of employment. The ADEA is enforced by the EEOC. The EEOC is permitted to bring a lawsuit on behalf of an aggrieved employee, or the aggrieved employee may bring a suit himself or herself for legal or equitable relief. In either case, the ADEA provides the right to a jury trial.

The initial purpose of the statute was to promote the employment of older persons, as long as such employment was predicated on their capabilities and not on their age. The statute also aimed to prohibit arbitrary age discrimination in employment as well as to assist employers and employees to find approaches to solve problems stemming from the impact of age on employment.

The term "employee" is defined very broadly under the statute and extends protection to public as well as private-sector employees. However, in order to be protected, the employees must be at least 40 years of age, but there is no upper-level age limit to the statute's coverage. The ADEA defines "employer" as a "person" involved in an industry affecting commerce with twenty or more

---

[80] This material comes from *Age Discrimination in Employment* book by Mujtaba and Cavico (2006).

employees for each working day in each of twenty or more calendar weeks in the current or a preceding calendar year. A "person" is defined as one or more individuals, a partnership, an association, a corporation, or a labor organization that exists among other entities and business relationships.

It is important to note that the ADEA does not bar the termination of older employees. Rather, the Act only bars discrimination against them. Accordingly, an employer can defend an ADEA lawsuit by establishing that an employment decision was based on reasonable and legitimate non-discriminatory reasons other than age, such as poor performance. For example, in a 2012 Florida case, a health reporter for a local Miami network was terminated soon after turning 50 years of age. She contended that the station discriminated against her because of her age in attempt to staff the station with younger personnel. She also contended that age discrimination, especially against women, is pervasive in the broadcast news industry. However, the court denied her claim, explaining that general theories of age discrimination are insufficient to base a claim; rather, specific evidence of the intent to discriminate was necessary. Furthermore, the station had a legitimate, job-related reason for her dismissal, to wit, television audiences were more interested in news about politics and terrorism than health matters after the 9/11 terrorist attacks.

Furthermore, despite the connection between age and high salary, the ADEA does not automatically prohibit the discharge of a highly paid employee solely based on financial considerations. While employers thus are allowed to save money by eliminating highly paid positions, however, each employment decision must be handled on an individualized, reasonable, and fair basis. Consequently, any "blanket" rules that would adversely affect older employees could trigger an ADEA lawsuit.

Finally, an employer may involuntarily retire an employee who is at least 65 years of age, has been employed during a two-year period in a legitimate executive or high-level, policymaking position, and who is immediately entitled to an enumerated employer-financed pension. Consequently, one commentator has noted that U.S. firms, pursuant to the influence of U.S. Civil Rights laws, are moving in the European direction of an expectation of lump sum buyouts for older workers when their jobs end, which are typically called "early retirement buyout."

The employer can also defend an ADEA lawsuit by interposing the BFOQ doctrine. Pursuant to the BFOQ doctrine, the employer will be obligated to show that the challenged age criteria is reasonably related to the essential operation of the employer's business and that there is a factual basis for believing that only employees of a certain age would be able to perform the particular job either safely or effectively (or both). Examples would include airline pilots, police, firefighters, and bus drivers, as well as certain others for whom definite physical requirements are a necessity for efficient job performance.

In 2005, the U.S. Supreme Court enunciated a major decision regarding age discrimination in employment in the case of *Smith v. City of Jackson, Mississippi*. The case initially was brought by older police officers in Jackson, Mississippi, who argued that a pay-for-performance plan instituted by the city granted substantially larger raises to employees with five or fewer years of tenure. Such policy, the officers contended, favored their younger colleagues. The lower courts had dismissed the lawsuit, ruling that these types of claims were barred by the statute. But the Supreme Court, in a 5-3 decision, ruled that the officers were entitled to pursue the age discrimination lawsuit against the city. Justice John Paul Stevens, writing for the majority, stated that the ADEA of 1967 was meant to allow the same type of "disparate impact" legal challenges for older workers that minorities and women can assert pursuant to the CRA. Yet Justice Stevens also noted in the decision that the same law does allow employers the legal right to at times treat older workers differently.

The decision significantly expands the protection afforded older workers, pursuant to the ADEA. The decision thus allows protected workers over the age of 40 to institute age discrimination lawsuits even if evidence is lacking that their employers never purposefully intended to discriminate against the workers on the basis of their age. The decision also substantially lessens the legal burden for employees covered by the statute by allowing aggrieved employees to contend in court that a presumably neutral employment practice nonetheless had an adverse or disparate or disproportionately harmful impact upon them.

It is important to note that pursuant to the CRA employers can successfully defend a disparate impact case only by showing the "business necessity" for a neutral but harmful employment policy, which is a much more difficult test to meet versus the "reasonable" explanation standard of the ADEA. The Court has allowed the employer to defend such an age discrimination case if the employer can interpose that the employer had a legitimate, reasonable, and job-related explanation for a "neutral" employment policy.

Nonetheless, the U.S. Supreme Court's age discrimination decision emerges as a significant victory for older workers covered by the ADEA. Such protected workers now do not have to have direct or "smoking gun" evidence of intentional age discrimination in order to file a civil rights lawsuit. Rather, all that is required is evidence of disproportionate, harmful impact stemming from a neutral age employment policy. Employers, whether U.S. employers or foreign employers doing business in the United States, must now be much more conscious of the consequences of their employment policies on older workers, particularly regarding the criteria used to determine hiring, termination, layoffs, as well as pay scales and retirement plan changes. Employers also must be prepared to provide and explain the "reasonable" factors, besides age, that would justify the employment policy that causes the disparate harmful impact on older protected workers.

It is interesting to note that the ADEA does not specifically prohibit an employer from asking a job applicant's age or date of birth. Yet because such questions may inhibit older workers from applying for employment or may be construed as evidence of an intent to discriminate based on age, any requests for age information will be examined closely by the EEOC and the courts to ensure that the age inquiry was made for a valid, lawful, and non-discriminatory purpose.

As noted in the preceding discussion of discrimination law, proving discrimination, including age discrimination, is difficult. However, the Second Circuit United States Court of Appeals rendered a very important decision regarding age discrimination, ruling that the rejection of a job candidate because he was "overqualified" raised a sufficient inference of age discrimination, thereby justifying a federal jury trial on that issue. The case in question involved a 58-year-old print production manager who was laid off by his employer and then was rejected for all 30 jobs he subsequently applied for, including one in which the hiring manager said he was "overqualified" and for which the hiring manager selected a younger "outside" candidate. The explanation of "overqualified" for the rejection was adequate in and of itself to raise an inference of discriminatory intent. Using that appeals case as a precedent, one federal district court judge emphasized that "overqualified" is actually a "code word" for "too old." The use of "code words" as a subterfuge for discrimination, as well as inferential evidence thereof, is a new and most interesting aspect of Civil Rights law.

The Pregnancy Discrimination Act of 1979

This statute protects married and unmarried women workers by mandating that employers not discriminate against them should they become pregnant and give birth. All aspects of employment are covered by the Act. Pregnancy must be treated "merely" as any other temporary disability, and employers with health and disability policies must also cover pregnancy. Additionally, an employer cannot force a pregnant employee to stop working until the child is born, provided the employee is capable of performing her duties properly. Finally, the employer cannot specify how long a leave of absence must be taken after childbirth. Paid leave, however, is not required by the statute, though such paid leave is very common in Europe, and even for fathers in some countries.

The Americans with Disabilities Act of 1990

The American with Disabilities Act (ADA) is a very significant and very comprehensive piece of civil rights legislation. The primary goal of the statute is to prevent discrimination against otherwise-qualified disabled workers in order to allow such workers to participate fully in the workforce.

The ADA not only covers employers, but also the providers of public transportation and public accommodation as well as the providers of telecommunications services. Furthermore, not only is discrimination prohibited, but also employers and others are legally required to accommodate the needs of their disabled employees to a certain degree. However, not all employers are covered by the ADA. Because an employer must have 15 or more employees to be governed by the ADA, small employers are not affected.

The ADA protects "qualified individuals" with a "disability." Accordingly, the first task is to ascertain who is a "qualified individual" and what is a "disability." A qualified individual is a person who can perform the essential aspects of the job with or without a reasonable accommodation, while a disability means a person has a physical or mental impairment that substantially limits his or her ability to engage in major life activities. The term "disability" itself also encompasses people with a record of such impairment or people who are regarded as having such an impairment. Examples range from hearing, speech, and visual problems, paraplegia, to diseases such as cancer, heart disease, and HIV and AIDS.

People who are using illegal drugs or alcoholics who use alcohol in the workplace or who are under the influence of alcohol in the workplace are not disabled. However, recovering alcoholics and former users of illegal drugs are regarded as disabled and thus are protected by the ADA. Obesity may be covered, but only if it is "morbid" obesity, that is when one's weight is two or more times the weight of a normal person. Finally, being a kleptomaniac—being consumed with an obsessive desire to steal—is not covered.

Once a job applicant or employee is deemed to be disabled, the employer is forbidden from discriminating against the disabled applicant or employee. In particular, the employer is not allowed to ask a job applicant about the presence of a disability or the type or degree of such a disability. An employer, however, is permitted to ask an applicant about his or her ability to perform the job in question. Pre-employment medical examinations are not allowed, but once a job offer is made, the employer is permitted to require a medical exam as well as condition the employment on the results of the exam. At the same time, the employer cannot discriminate among new employees in the mandating of medical exams. Once a qualified individual meets a disability standard, the employer, as noted, is under a legal obligation not to discriminate against that applicant or employee.

However, most significantly, the employer's obligation under the ADA goes even further than mere negative duty not to discriminate. The ADA imposes on the employer an affirmative duty to make a reasonable accommodation to the needs of its disabled employees. If the disabled employee can do the job with a reasonable accommodation, then the employer must make that reasonable accommodation, for example by installing wheelchair ramps, offering flexible working hours, or otherwise modifying the nature of the job.

By the same token, there is a limitation on the employer's obligation to accommodate. If the accommodation would present an undue burden or hardship for the employer, then the employer does not have to accommodate. "Undue hardship" is defined as one involving significant expense or difficulty for the employer, and this critical legal standard is determined on a case-by-case basis by the EEOC and by the courts.

The Civil Rights Act of 1991[81]

The CRA of 1866 (also known as "Section 1981") gave African American employees the right to sue employers for damages in cases of employment discrimination. This old Act also played a prominent role in the debates surrounding the later 1991 Act.

The 1991 Act actually amended the CRA of 1964 to correct unfavorable Supreme Court decisions. For example, in *Patterson v. McLean Credit Union*, the Supreme Court ruled that employees could not sue for damages due to racial harassment because, even if the employer's conduct was discriminatory, the employer had not denied employees the "same right…to make and enforce contracts…as is enjoyed by white citizens," (which language comes from the 1866 Act). This decision left employees with no effective recourse, because they rarely could show wage losses recoverable under Title VII.

The 1991 Act redefined the requirement to include "the making, performance, modification, and termination of contracts, and the enjoyment of all benefits, privileges, terms, and conditions of the contractual relationship." The 1991 Act confirmed that racial harassment on the job was included in antidiscrimination laws and clarified that Section 1981 applied to both government and private sectors.

In *Wards Cove Packing Co. v. Antonio*, the Court ruled that employees must identify the employer's particular policy or requirement that allegedly produced inequalities in the workplace and to show that it, on its own, had a disparate effect. The 1991 Act stated that an employee could prove his/her case by show-

---

[81] Contributed by Josephine Sosa-Fey, Texas A&M University-Kingsville.

ing that an individual practice or group of practices resulted in a disparate impact on the basis of race, color, religion, sex, or national origin, and that the employer had failed to demonstrate that such a practice was required by business necessity. Accordingly, the law stipulates that a statistical imbalance in an employer's workforce related to race, color, religion, sex, or national origin would not alone be sufficient to establish an impact violation.

In *Price Waterhouse v. Hopkins,* the Court held that once an employee had proved that an unlawful consideration had played a part in the employer's personnel decision, the burden of proof shifted to the employer to prove that it would have made the same decision even if it had not been motivated by the unlawful factor. Furthermore, such proof by the employer would constitute a complete defense for the employer.

The 1991 Act provided that the employer's proof that it would have made the same decision, with or without the unlawful factor, was a defense to back pay, reinstatement, and other remedies, but not to liability *per se.* This provision of the law allowed employees to recover attorneys' fees in proved discrimination cases, even if no other award was made.

Under the 1991 law, Congress limited the rights of "non-parties" to attack consent decrees by barring any challenges by parties who knew or should have known of the decree or who were adequately represented by the original parties. The non-parties could object only while the consent decree was being imposed, not afterward. Accordingly, in *Martin v. Wilke,* the Court permitted white fire-fighters, who had not been party to the litigation establishing a consent decree governing hiring and promotion of black firefighters in the Birmingham, Alabama, Fire Department, to bring suit challenging the decree.

The 1991 Act also authorizes jury trials on Title VII claims and allowed the injured parties to recover emotional distress and punitive damages while also imposing caps on such relief under both Title VII and Section 1981. The 1991 Act also made technical changes affecting the length of time allowed to challenge unlawful seniority provisions, to sue the federal government for discrimination, and to bring age discrimination claims. The law allows successful plaintiffs to recover expert witness fees as part of an award of attorneys' fees, and allows collection of interest on any judgment against the federal government.

Supreme Court Civil Rights "Disparate Impact" Decision

The U.S. Supreme Court, in 2009, ruled in an important affirmative action dealing with the "disparate impact" doctrine. In the case of *Ricci v. DeStefano,* the Court decided by a 5-4 determination that the city of New Haven, Connecticut had discriminated against white firefighters in violation of Title VII of the Civil

Rights Act. The city had discarded the promotion test results on which minorities had scored poorly. City officials contended that if the city did not discard the results the minority applicants would have sued the city. In New Haven, in 2003, 58 white firefighters, 23 blacks, and 19 Hispanics took the promotion tests to determine who would qualify as lieutenants and captains. Nineteen qualified for and were eligible for promotion. No blacks and two Hispanics qualified. There were 15 slots to fill. The city's civil service board, however, refused to certify the results, thereby denying the promotions to all who had earned them. The city explained that it feared a disparate impact lawsuit civil rights lawsuit from the minority candidates. As a result, 17 white candidates and one Hispanic sued, claiming violations of their statutory rights under Title VII of the Civil Rights Act as well as constitutional violations pursuant to the Equal Protection clause. The lead plaintiff was Frank Ricci, who is dyslexic, and who said he studied for 8 to 13 hours a day for the test, hiring an acquaintance to tape record the study materials. The firefighters lost their case at the federal district court level and in the U.S. Court of Appeals for the Second Circuit. They then appealed to the U.S. Supreme Court, which reversed the lower court decisions. Justice Anthony Kennedy, writing for the majority, stated that fear of litigation alone cannot justify an employer's reliance on race to the detriment of individuals who passed the examinations and qualified for promotions. He further stated that "the city rejected the test results because too many whites and not enough minorities would be promoted. Without some other justification, this express, race-based decision-making violates Title VII's command that employers cannot take adverse employment actions because of an individual's race. Justice Kennedy said that the purpose of Title VII was to promote hiring on the basis of job qualifications rather than on the basis of race or color. The goal of the statute, said Justice Kennedy, was to create a workplace free of discrimination where race was not a barrier to promotion. In the New Haven case, Justice Kennedy stated that "the city rejected the test results solely because the higher scoring candidates were white." Justice Samuel Alito, writing a concurring opinion, noted that the tests had been very fairly designed and that an effort had been made to eliminate all possible elements of racial bias in the promotion process. He noted that the city made no real effort to examine the legitimacy of the test and to see if the tests measured job-related knowledge and skills, but rather the city discarded the test results, which he condemned as an illegal act. Justice Kennedy also noted that the city took specific steps to ensure that black and Hispanic firefighters were consulted in designing the questions. Justice Kennedy noted in his decision a contradiction in U.S. civil rights law between the original language in Title VII, promulgated by Congress in 1964, which prohibits intentional discrimination on the basis of race and other protected characteristics, and a 1991 law, which was based on a 1971 Supreme Court decision, that prohibited employment tests that had a "disparate impact" on the hiring of racial minorities, unless the tests were demonstrated to be job-related and a business necessity. Tests must be not only relevant to the job, but there also must be a showing that no equally valid and less discriminatory tests or alternatives were available.

Disparate impact is different from disparate treatment. Disparate treatment is illegal intentional discrimination based on race; whereas disparate impact applies to presumably neutral employment practices that nonetheless have a disparate or adverse effect on minorities. Both are illegal pursuant to Civil Rights laws. The Supreme Court, however, in the New Haven decision, did not strike down the disparate impact doctrine on constitutional grounds. The disparate impact doctrine is thus still the law. Rather, the Court invalidated the New Haven employment decision of discarding the tests by saying the city had violated Title VII of the 1964 statute. Yet in the future, for an employer to throw out a test that has a disparate impact, the employer must have, says the Court, "a strong basis in evidence" that the employer will be sued before discarding test results solely based on race. Justice Stevens stated that absent "strong evidence of a disparate-impact violation," an employer will not be able to disregard tests solely on the racial disparity of the results. However, an employer will still be allowed to bring in racial considerations and potential racial impact into the testing process but now the employer must do so "during the test-design stage," said Justice Kennedy. Yet after the tests are given, only in "certain, narrow circumstances," said Justice Kennedy, employers may disregard the results only if there is a "strong basis of evidence" that using the results would cause the employer to lose a disparate impact lawsuit.

Supreme Court Third Party Retaliation Civil Rights Decision

The United States Supreme Court, in 2011, enunciated a major decision regarding the retaliation against employees who file civil rights claims in the case of *Thompson v. North American Stainless, LP.* The decision is very noteworthy because it is regarded as the Court's most recent and leading "retaliation" pronouncement. The Court ruled that in a so-called "third party" retaliation situation, employers can be sued if they retaliate against a relative or close associate of an employee who instituted a discrimination claim. The decision by the Court was a unanimous one. It was also the latest legal victory by employees on the retaliation issue, that is, the redress available to an employee who complains about discriminatory treatment at work. The Civil Rights Act of 1964 I Title VII, Section 704(a) creates a legal cause of action for retaliation by employers against claims of discrimination in an employment context. To prevail in a

Title VII retaliation lawsuit, the plaintiff employee must prove that he or she engaged in an activity protected by Title VII, the defendant employer possessed knowledge of the protected activity, the defendant took an adverse employment action against the plaintiff, and a causal connection existed between the protected activity and the protected employment action. The *Thompson* case arose because Eric Thompson and his fiancée, Miriam Regalado, worked together at North American Stainless. Thompson was a metal engineer. His fiancée filed a charge with the Equal Employment Opportunity Commission alleging gender discrimination. About three weeks later, North American Stainless terminated Thompson's employment. Thompson then filed a charge with the EEOC contending he was terminated in retaliation for his fiancée filing a charge against their employer. The company contended that he was fired because of poor performance and because he wrote an allegedly derogatory memo regarding the company's management practices. The EEOC filed a right-to-sue letter, and then Thompson filed a lawsuit against North American Stainless. The federal district court rejected Thompson's claim on the grounds that he personally did not engage in the protected activity. The district court explained that Title VII did not provide protection against retaliation for employees who have not themselves participated in the protected activity. Thompson appealed to the Sixth Circuit Court of Appeals which affirmed the district court's decision, holding that Thompson did not have a viable cause of action against his employer for retaliation because Thompson did not personally engage in his fiancée's protected activity.

An appeal was granted to the Supreme Court. Thompson's fiancée was then his wife. The Supreme Court, with Justice Antonin Scalia writing for a unanimous court, rejected the reasoning of the lower federal courts. The anti-retaliation provision in the Civil Rights Act, said Justice Scalia, covers a wide scope of employee conduct that could deter a "reasonable" employee from objecting to discrimination. Specifically, the Justice said, "obviously" a reasonable worker might be dissuaded from objecting if he knew that his fiancée would be fired. However, to prevent the retaliation provision from being abused, Justice Scalia also said that in order to institute a retaliation lawsuit the third party must fall within the "zone of interests" protected by the law. In Thompson's case, Justice Scalia said he was qualified to file a lawsuit since he was an employee of the company along with his now-wife and the purpose of the Civil Rights Act is to protect employees from their employers' unlawful actions. Justice Scalia further explained that Thompson was not an "accidental victim" of the retaliation because harming him was the unlawful act that punished his then fiancée. The Supreme Court, accordingly, reversed the decision of the court of appeals and remanded the case back to the federal district court for a trial on the merits.

The Family Medical Leave Act of 1993

The Family Medical Leave Act (FMLA) guarantees that employees may take up to 12 weeks of unpaid leave (in one 12-month period) for serious medical problems that render the employee unable to perform his or her work duties, as well as to take care of family needs, such as the birth or adoption of a child, or the care of a child, spouse, or parent with a serious medical problem. The FMLA applies to private sector employers who have 50 or more employees, as well as to federal, state, and local government employers.

To be covered, an employee must have worked for the employer for one year prior to taking the leave. The leave generally can be taken on an intermittent basis, except in the case of the birth or adoption of a child, where the consent of the employer is necessary for the employee to take intermittent leave. Finally, once an eligible employee returns from leave, he or she must be restored to the same or equivalent work position, but with no accrual of seniority for the leave period. It must be stressed that the leave is unpaid, as opposed to leave policies in many European countries.

United States Labor Laws

Currently labor law and labor relations in the U.S. are based on three major pieces of federal legislation: the National Labor Relations Act of 1935 (also called the Wagner Act); the Labor Management Relations Act of 1847 (also called the Taft-Hartley Act), and the Labor Management Reporting and Disclosure Act of 1959 (also called the Landrum Act). The Norris-LaGuardia Act of 1932 was the precursor to all of these important statutes as that Act was the first piece of legislation promulgated in the U.S. to protect the rights of employees and to allow employees and unions to engage in union activity. The goals of all of these statutes are to approximately balance the power between labor and management, to encourage peaceful negotiation and collective bargaining between labor and management, to recognize self-organization of employees as vital to collective bargaining, to restrain certain unfair labor practices by both employers and unions, thereby maintaining labor peace and sustaining economic productivity.

The Norris-LaGuardia Act of 1932

In the U.S., by 1930, the courts had become a major impediment to the realization of union goals as a variety of legal doctrines and procedures were being utilized to hinder union organizing and collective bargaining. The four main legal hindrances were injunctions, contracts called "yellow dog" contracts, the doctrine of vicarious liability, and the conspiracy rule.

"Temporary injunctions" stopping a strike were characteristically issued by a court only after hearing the employer's position. Of course, the union was entitled to a subsequent hearing to present its side, but the strike had already been halted, which usually had an inimical effect on the strike, especially if the employer dragged out the legal proceedings.

A "yellow dog" contract was a contract in which the employer required the employee to sign, in which the employee promised not to join a labor union on penalty of losing his or her job. The courts ordinarily upheld such contracts, so consequently, they were widely used to inhibit employee and union organizing activity.

The "doctrine of vicarious liability" was used to hold the union which called a strike responsible for any violence that resulted, even when the violence was not caused by union members and even when the union had exerted every effort to prevent the violence. The result was that the strike could be broken because of acts not authorized by the union and, in addition, the union and its members could be held liable for any damages caused.

Finally, the "conspiracy rule," which held that an agreement to perform an unlawful act was a crime, was utilized by the courts to enjoin union activity.

So, in the Norris-LaGuardia Act, Congress declared generally that employees must have the rights of freedom of association and self-organization with their fellow employees, and that the employees must be free from employer interference and restraint in pursuing these objectives. Specifically, in the Act, Congress prohibited "yellow dog" contracts while also forbidding the federal courts from granting injunctions against a variety of described union activities, for example stopping or refusing to work, forming and joining a union, assembling to organize, publicizing a labor dispute, and agreeing to engage in these acts as well as advising others to perform these acts. However, an injunction could be issued under certain limited circumstances, for example when there is a likelihood that substantial or irreparable injury to persons or property will occur. The Act also held that individual union members or the union would not be accountable for unlawful acts unless the acts were directed or ratified by the members of the union. Finally, the Act prohibited the courts from using the conspiracy doctrine to enjoin or punish legitimate organizing and union activities.

The result of the Norris-LaGuardia Act was that more latitude was accorded to employees to form unions and for unions to strike. However, the Act did not require the employer to recognize a union or to bargain with the union.

The National Labor Relations Act (Wagner Act) of 1935

The NLRA was a response to the economic collapse, the Great Depression of the 1930s, as well as the emergent New Deal. Congress's major objective with the

NLRA was to equalize the disparity of bargaining power between employees and employers as well as to effectuate the national policy of collective bargaining as the means to ensure labor peace and economic productivity.

The basic provisions of the Act are found in Sections 7 and 8. Section 7 guarantees certain fundamental rights for employees, specifically the rights to form, join, or assist labor organizations, the freedom to bargain collectively through a representative of their own choosing, and the right to engage in mutual concerted activity for the purposes of collective bargaining and for the employees' mutual aid and protection.

Section 8 imposes certain important duties on employers, particularly the duty to bargain collectively and in good faith with the representative of the employees. Section 8 also forbids the employer from committing certain prohibited practices (which Congress believed would discourage true collective bargaining) by declaring such practices as unfair labor practices. The result of Section 8 is very momentous for U.S. labor law and labor relations because, based on the NLRA, management is now legally obligated to bargain with a union designated as the exclusive representative for the employees in a given bargaining unit.

The bargaining unit was to be determined by a new federal agency, called the National Labor Relations Board (NLRB), which was the administrative agency created by Congress to administer the NLRA. The NLRB consists of a five-member panel, whose members are appointed by the President and confirmed by the Senate and who serve five-year terms. The two main purposes of the agency are to conduct elections and to adjudicate claims of unfair labor practices. The NLRB, however, is only authorized to act when formally requested to do so by an employee, employer, or union by the petitioning for an election or the filing of an unfair labor practice complaint.

It is important to note the limitations of the NLRA. It is not a complete labor code, as many countries have. Rather, the statute is concerned primarily with the organizing stage of labor relations, and it deals exclusively with private sector employer practices. The substantive terms of any collective bargaining agreement are left entirely up to the parties and their private negotiations. The terms of such an agreement, as well as whether or not an agreement is achieved, are to be considered in light of the economic costs to either side from failing to agree.

Another limitation of the NLRA is that public-sector workers are not covered, even though they are covered by corresponding federal and state statutes. Most states have specialized administrative agencies, equivalent to the NLRB, and which are typically called Public Employee Relations Commissions, which exist to govern labor relations in the public sector.

One major difference between labor relations in the public versus the private sector should be noted, and that is that in most state statutes, public-sector employees are not allowed to strike. Rather, mandatory binding arbitration is used to remedy impasses in negotiations between public-sector employees and their unions and their government employers.

Although it is beyond the scope of this book to provide a detailed explication of U.S. labor law, certain fundamental points must be addressed. First, not all private-sector employees are covered by the Act. Examples of those not covered are agricultural and farm workers, "domestics," independent contractors, and supervisors and managers. A "supervisor" or "manager" is defined broadly as a person with the authority to hire or fire, punish or reward, assign employees, adjust grievances, or to recommend such actions, as long as independent judgment is used. Also, the confidential employees of managers and supervisors, such as executive administrative assistants, are not covered by the NLRA.

Second, due to the managerial focus of this book, the authors believe it is necessary to spell out and to succinctly explain the types of unfair labor practices (ULP) enumerated in Section 8 that may be committed by employers and their representatives. Section 8(a)(1) makes it an unfair labor practice for the employer to interfere with, restrain, or coerce employees in the exercise of their Section 7 rights. Examples of such a violation would be threats of discharge or demotion for supporting the union, "scare" tactics, coercive interrogation, spying, forbidding any solicitation, buttons, or insignia (absent a valid reason), and granting benefits to the employees before an election. In 2014, the National Labor Relations Board accused Wal-Mart Stores of violating this section of the law by retaliating against workers who took part in strikes and protests against the company in more than two dozen states in the preceding two years. The NLRB is alleging that the company violated the law by unlawfully threatening, disciplining, and/or terminating employees for engaging in legally protected strikes and protests. The NLRB contends that the company unlawfully threatened the employees with reprisals if they engaged in protests and strikes. A great deal of the labor agitation against Wal-Mart apparently arose from the company's mandating employees to work on "Black Friday," that is, the day after Thanksgiving, as well as complaints about low wages and poor working conditions. Wal-Mart has disputed the claims and the company will contest the agency's allegations.

Section 8(a)(2) makes employer domination or financial support of a labor union a ULP. For example, contributing to a union or promoting and sponsoring a union are illegal actions. The employer using a supervisor as the main bargainer for a union is also not permitted. However, employee committees, for example those that facilitate communication, "teamwork," or productivity, may be permissible if the objective is merely to inform management and not to represent the employees or engage in labor relations, even if the employees are allowed to confer on working time without any loss of pay.

Section 8(a)(3) makes it a ULP for the employer to discriminate in the hire and tenure of an employee as well as in the terms and conditions of employment in order to encourage or discourage membership in any labor organization. For example, an employer's prohibition against using the company's e-mail system for pro-union communication, while simultaneously allowing the company to use the system for anti-union communication, was deemed to be a discriminatory ULP.

Section 8(a)(4) is the "no reprisal" provision of the Act, which thus makes it a ULP for an employer to discharge or discriminate against an employee because the employee has filed charges against the employer pursuant to the NLRA.

Finally, as noted in Section 8(a)(5), the refusal of the employer to bargain in good faith with the representative of the employees is deemed to be a ULP.

The employer's legal duty not to commit ULPs is balanced with the employer's right of free speech in Section 8(c) of the NLRA. Note that this NLRA "free speech" right is in addition to any constitutional right the employer has to free speech. Section 8(c) states that the employer's expression of views, arguments, or opinions is not a ULP as long as there is neither a threat of reprisal nor a conferral of benefits.

Accordingly, freedom of speech—under the NLRA or constitutionally, for that matter—is not absolute. At times, there is a "fine line" between legitimate anti-union rhetoric by the employer and an anti-union threat. For example, what if the employer predicts adverse consequences for the employees voting for a union? Is the employer's appeal one to the rationality of the employees or an appeal to the employees' fear? That is the key issue. If an employer has a reasonable belief in the adverse economic consequences of unionization, if such a belief is based on objective facts and available evidence, and if these consequences have a reasonable likelihood of occurring, the employer is within its protected free speech rights.

Finally, because both the employer and the union are under a duty to bargain collectively in good faith, it is important to note the definition of "collective bargaining" in Section 8(d). That section defines this critical labor law term as the mutual obligation of the employer and the union to meet at reasonable times and to confer (that is, talk about) wages, hours, and the terms and conditions of employment. Both parties are also obligated to draft a written agreement if an oral agreement already exists. However, and this point is critical, there is no obligation to agree to any proposal or to make concessions as long as there have been good faith negotiations. However, evidence of good faith usually is found from making proposals and then counterproposals, and by designating someone with authority to negotiate.

National Labor Relations Act and Social Media

One of the major tenets of the National Labor Relations Act (NLRA) states that an employer cannot terminate an employee to discourage or encourage union activity. To do so would be an illegal "unfair legal practice." Of course, an employee must make an initial case that his or her discharge was motivated by the employee's pro-union support or activity. If the employee does make such an initial showing, the employee does not automatically prevail; rather, in order to defend itself from a charge of an unfair labor practice pursuant to the NLRA the employer now has to demonstrate a legitimate job-related reason for the employee's discharge. As such, the employee is no longer in the terminable at-will category. The NLRA also protects employees who engage in "concerted protected activity" for their mutual aid and protection. Such activity would of course involve the employees advocating, supporting, or joining unions. Moreover, such activity has been deemed by the National Labor Relations Board, the federal agency which enforces the NLRA, to encompass online communication between and among employees on social media if the employees are acting together to seek to change and improve conditions at work. Accordingly, these employees even if only at-will cannot be discharged since they are engaging in conduct protected by the NLRA. Note that an employee merely acting alone on social media to complain about work is insufficient due to the "concerted" requirement. Moreover, employees communicating on social media merely to "vent" or complain about their boss or employer, especially if vile and intemperate language is used, is also insufficient for legal protection, as there must be some evidence that the employees are acting to better working conditions. Thus, in order to utilize the NLRA, the affected employees must come under the Act's coverage. Finally, it is important to point out that managers and supervisors as well as independent contractors and agents are excluded from the NLRA's coverage; rather only "employees" recovered.

The Labor Management Relations Act (Taft-Hartley Act) of 1947

The Labor Management Relations Act (LMRA) amended the NLRA. The LMRA was promulgated as a response to the rise of increasing powerful national unions in the U.S. and the more frequent use by unions of the strike and the "secondary boycott," which is a boycott used to exert pressure on employers far removed from the actual labor dispute between the union and the employer. Consequently, the basic provisions of the LMRA were the prohibitions of certain union unfair labor practices, in particular, the secondary boycott. The failure of the union to bargain in good faith with the employer was also deemed to be an unfair labor practice by the NLRA.

The goal of Congress was to achieve a balance of obligations by imposing certain constraints on the union that were comparable to those imposed on employers by virtue of the NLRA. The LMRA also upheld collective bargaining as the preferable method to keeping labor peace and settling labor disputes. However, in the Act, Congress recognized that collective bargaining will not always avoid or solve labor disputes. Accordingly, Congress established an alternative process, called the Federal Mediations and Conciliation Service, which was empowered to assist in resolving any labor dispute that affected interstate commerce. The LMRA required both management and the union to notify the Service whenever any change in the terms and conditions of employment previously set by a collective bargaining agreement was sought.

Furthermore, the Act authorized the President to intervene, appoint a Board of Inquiry to investigate and to report on the facts, and, if the President concluded that national health and safety were threatened, the President could seek a federal injunction against any strike for 80 days, a "cooling off" period, after which the strike could continue unless outlawed by special Congressional legislation in a labor dispute designated as a national emergency.

The LMRA also banned the "closed shop," which was a union demand that required union membership even before hiring by the employer. The "closed shop" must be distinguished from a "union shop," which requires employees to join and to continue as union members as long as their employment lasts. The states, however, were given the option of banning "union shops" also, which several southern and western states, such as Florida and Texas, have done. Such states are known as "right to work" states.

Finally, the LMRA provided legal remedies for the enforcement of labor agreements, and authorized lawsuits for violating the terms of a collective bargaining agreement.

The Labor Management Reporting and Disclosure Act (Landrum-Griffin act) of 1959

The purpose of the Labor Management Reporting and Disclosure Act (LMRDA) was to impose regulations on the internal affairs of unions and to promote democracy and honesty in union affairs. The LMRDA amended the LMRA in response to the rise of very powerful union leaders, an increase in union corruption, and the lack of democratic procedures by unions. Unions were now required to file reports to the Secretary of Labor regarding union assets and liabilities, internal laws and procedures (especially those regarding union elections), receipts and expenditures, and salaries of and loans to union officers.

While any detailed explication of the LMRDA is beyond the scope of this book, one other basic provision of the Act needs to be mentioned, the "Bill of Rights" for union members, which granted them equal rights in voting, meetings, opportunities to be heard, and in opposing the union. The Act also forbids unions from disciplining members for exercising rights given to them pursuant to the LMRDA.

The Social Security Act of 1935

The Social Security Act is the key federal law that creates an insurance program to provide for employees and their families upon the retirement, death, disability, or hospitalization of the employee. Limited benefits are provided by the government to the employee as well as to his or her survivors.

The Federal Insurance Contributions Act (FICA) requires both employees and employers to contribute to the Social Security Fund to help pay for the employees' benefits. The employee's FICA contribution is based on the employee's annual wage, which amount the employer withholds from the employee's salary and then matches, after which time, the money gets turned over to the Internal Revenue Service.

It must be stressed that social security is not a saving account system, like the Chilean model. Rather, it is a "pay as you go" system: The current contributions of workers fund the benefits of retired workers. Accordingly, retired workers receive monthly payments from the Social Security Administration, which administers these important statutes. The problem with the system is that fewer and fewer current workers are being asked to fund more and more retired workers, thereby putting a great strain on the system, which will be exacerbated with the coming retirement of the "Baby Boomers" generation. Either benefits will have to be cut, or the retirement age increased even more in order to keep the system functioning. The problems of the social security system, as well as the various, highly contentious reform proposals, are far beyond the purposes of this book.

The Federal Unemployment Tax Act of 1935

The Federal Unemployment Tax Act (FUTA) requires employers to pay unemployment taxes, which go into a fund administered by the state governments to pay compensation to workers who are temporarily unemployed. The states determine which workers are eligible for compensation as well as the amount and duration of such compensation. To be eligible for benefits, workers must be actively seeking employment and be available for work. Additionally, workers who have been discharged for misconduct or who have quit without just cause are not eligible for unemployment benefits.

The Fair Labor Standards Act of 1938

The Fair Labor Standards Act (FLSA) is one of the most important labor statutes in the United States. Generally speaking, the FLSA covers all employers and employees who are engaged in the production of goods for interstate commerce, protecting workers, and prohibiting oppressive child labor. However, there is one important exception to the Act. Executives, administrators, managers, professionals, outside sales personnel, and computer employees are exempt from the overtime provisions of the Act.

But other than such an exception, the FLSA mandates that a minimum wage, set by Congress (at $5.15 per hour as of this writing, there is a federal bill raising the minimum by approximately one dollar in a Congressional House/Senate Conference Committee, which the President stated he would sign into law once the House and Senate can agree on the exact bill.), be paid and that overtime pay of "time and a half" be paid to employees for each hour worked beyond 40 hours a week. Thus, even if an employee works 10 hours per day, but only four days a week, he or she is not entitled to overtime. Furthermore, each week is treated separately for overtime purposes. So if the employee works 30 hours one week and then 50 hours the next week, the employee is entitled to overtime for the second week; the employer cannot average the two weeks out.

The FLSA also empowers the Department of Labor to make regulations to govern the use of child labor. There are three main types of restrictions on child labor:

1. Children under the age of 14 cannot work except in very limited circumstances, such as delivering newspapers, working for their parents, and being employed by the entertainment or agricultural industry.
2. Children ages 14 or 15 can work for limited hours in certain non-hazardous occupations approved by the Department of Labor, such as in restaurants and gas stations.
3. Children ages 16 or 17 can work unlimited hours in non-hazardous jobs. Once a child reaches the age of 18, he or she can work in any job, hazardous or not, for unlimited hours.

In 2006, in a major lawsuit pursuant to the FLSA as well as state labor laws, International Business Machines Corp. (IBM) was sued in federal court for allegedly not paying overtime wages to tens of thousands of rank-and-file workers. The suit was brought by current and former IBM employees, and seeks class action lawsuit status in order to represent computer installers and maintenance workers for IBM throughout the United States, who are seeking millions of dollars compensation for back pay. The IBM employees contend that they were compelled to work more than 40 hours a week, and were called in to work on weekends without receiving overtime pay.

The lawsuit is expected to shine a light on the technology industry, where allegations of not paying required overtime pay have been widespread. One practice that will be scrutinized closely is the classification, by IBM as well as other companies, of workers not as "employees" but as "independent contractors," because the latter category is not covered by federal and state labor wage laws.

The Employee Retirement Income Security Act of 1974

The Employee Retirement Income Security Act (ERISA) is a very important federal statute designed to protect the pensions of private-sector employees. Yet it must be noted that this Act does not require an employer to establish a pension plan. However, once an employer does have a pension plan, ERISA empowers the Department of Labor to regulate the management of such a plan.

ERISA mandates, for example, that pension plans be in writing, that a pension plan manager be named, and that this manager be held to duties of due care and prudence as well as fiduciary duties. Furthermore, no more than 10% of the assets of the pension plan can be invested in the securities of the employer that established the plan.

ERISA also regulates the vesting of an employee's pension. "Vesting" means the time when the employee has a non-forfeitable right to receive his or her pension benefits. Vesting rules are very complicated, but there are two fundamental ERISA vesting rules:

1. The employee's own contribution to his or her pension plan vests immediately.
2. The employer's contribution to the employee's pension fund can be forfeited up to a five-year period, but once that five-year period is reached, the employer's contribution is totally vested.

The Consolidated Omnibus Budget Reconciliation Act of 1985

The Consolidated Omnibus Budget Reconciliation Act (COBRA) provides for the continuation of group health care benefits for private-sector employees who have left the employer's employment for a variety of reasons, voluntary as well as involuntary (except in the cases of workers discharged for gross misconduct).

COBRA is a very complex statute, but in essence requires that the employee, or his or her beneficiaries, be given the opportunity to continue with the employer's group health, dental, and/or optical insurance for a time period of up to 18 months (or longer if the employee is disabled). Employees, of course, are still required to pay the group health insurance premium to remain covered by the employer's policy.

State Workers' Compensation Statutes

State workers' compensation statutes are designed to protect workers injured on the job. The "trade-off" with these statutory schemes is that while an injured worker is compensated in a limited manner pursuant to a state administrative system and a state fund, the worker is precluded from suing the employer in court for negligent infliction of injuries. The employee, however, can still sue if the employer intentionally injured the employee.

It must be emphasized that these statutes only protect workers who are accidentally injured during the course and scope of employment. While fault is not an issue, the fact that an injury was intentionally self-inflicted would obviously prevent the employee's recovery.

The injured worker typically is required to notify the employer of the injury within prescribed time periods, to initially see a doctor approved by the employer, as well as to file a formal claim to a state administrative agency or board, which may conduct a hearing to ascertain eligibility as well as the extent of the worker's injury and whether or not it has resulted in a permanent or temporary disability.

Workers' compensation schemes are usually funded by the states, requiring employers to purchase insurance from a private insurance company or a state insurance fund. Some states allow the employer to self-insure.

The Occupational Safety and Health Act of 1970

The Occupational Safety Health Act (OSHA) is a very important piece of federal legislation in the United States. The objective of the Act is to impose a duty on the employer to provide a workplace free from recognized hazards causing or likely to cause death or serious bodily injury. Furthermore, the employer is obligated to comply with all OSHA health and safety standards. There are also reporting, notification, and posting requirements imposed on the employer relating to workplace incidents. The coverage of the Act is very broad, extending to any employer who employs at least one employee.

OSHA is enforced by the Department of Labor, which is authorized to conduct inspections of businesses pursuant to an administrative warrant, and which can impose civil penalties on an employer for violating the Act. There are also criminal penalties for willful violations of the Act that result in an employee's death.

Finally, OSHA contains a non-retaliation provision, which forbids the discharge or any discrimination against an employee who exercises his or her rights under the Act.

There are only two exceptions to the Act: one for employers who are covered by other safety and/or health acts, such as the Mine Safety Act; and the other for employers of domestic household employees.

The Worker Adjustment and Retraining Notification Act of 1988

The Worker Adjustment and Retraining Notification Act (WARN) is colloqui-ally known as the "plant-closing law." The purpose of WARN is to mandate that employers give notice to the employees before a plant is closed. WARN applies to employers with 100 or more employees, requiring that employers give 60 days notice before closing a plant, temporarily or permanently, which would result in the loss of employment of 50 or more employees. The notice is also required for large employee layoffs, specifically a reduction of 1/3 of the workforce, or 50 employees.

There are two exceptions to WARN when the employer does not have to give notice: 1) where the closing or layoff was caused by business circumstances which the employer reasonably could not foresee; and 2) where the employer is seeking to obtain financing to keep the plant in operation and the employer, in good faith, believes that giving the notice would be inimical to the securing of financing.

The Immigration Control and Reform Act of 1986

The main feature of the Immigration Control and Reform Act (ICRA), for the purposes of this book, is that the statute makes it unlawful for an employer to hire illegal immigrants. All U.S. employers are required to complete an immi-gration form (Immigration and Naturalization Service Form I-9) for each employee, which attests that the employer has inspected the documentation of the employee and that the employee is a citizen or permanent resident, pos-sesses an appropriate work visa, or is otherwise qualified to work in the United States. Furthermore, employers must maintain proper records of such informa-tion. There are both civil and criminal violations for violating this law.

Supreme Court E-Verify Immigration Decision

The United States Supreme Court, in 2011, in a 5-3 decision, upheld an Arizona law, called the Legal Arizona Workers Act, that requires employers to use a federal system, called E-Verify, to check the legal status of their employ-ees. The law also states that the state of Arizona can revoke charters or licenses from employers that repeatedly hire non-citizens who lack work permits. The Arizona law was signed in 2007 by then Governor Janet Napolitano, who called it the "business death penalty." Supporters of the Arizona law strongly approved the Supreme Court's decision, stating that it was an affirmation of the rights of states to curtail illegal immigration. Supporters of such laws have argued that Congress meant to give the states some discretion over business licenses and charters in the context of immigration, though states cannot impose criminal or civil penalties on businesses that hire illegal immigrants. Supporters of these laws contend that businesses are trying to get cheap labor at the expense of law-abiding American citizens and legal workers.

Opponents of the Arizona law, including the U.S. Chamber of Commerce, however, criticized the decision, stating that it would result in a growing patchwork of state and local laws seeking to regulate immigration which would be a hindrance to doing business across state lines. Critics argued that these employment-related immigration laws should be part of a broader immigration reform produced by Congress which is given in Article I in the Constitution the power to regulate immigration (by establishing a "uniform rule of Naturalization). They argue that Congress has thus preempted the field of immigration law precluding any state legislation on immigration matters. The Obama Administration also argued that the Arizona law undermined federal immigration law by creating a parallel state enforcement system that punished employer beyond what Congress has deemed to be proper. Some businesses in Arizona have criticized the law saying it gives the state a bad reputation globally. Nevertheless, writing for the majority, Chief Justice John Roberts stated that in order to deter illegal immigration, Congress has preserved the ability of the states to impose their own sanctions through the revocation of licenses and charters.

The Electronic Communications Privacy Act of 1986

The Electronic Communications Privacy Act (ECPA) was designed to protect employees' privacy in the age of electronic communication and the Internet. ECPA makes it a legal wrong—criminally as well as civilly—to intercept or access electronic communications—whether stored, in transit, at the point of transmission, or after receipt—as well as to intercept or access e-mail, whether stored or in transmission.

There are four important exceptions in the ECPA:

1. Employers can access the stored e-mail communications of employees who use the employer's electronic communication service.
2. Government and law enforcement agencies can obtain electronic communications during an investigation of suspected illegal activity, though pursuant to a valid search warrant.
3. The "business-extension" exception of the Act allows employers to monitor employees' electronic communications made in the ordinary course of business (but it does not permit the employer to monitor the employees' personal communications).
4. If the employer obtains the employees' consent to having their electronic communications intercepted by the employer, the employer can avoid liability under the ECPA.

The Employee Polygraph Protection Act of 1988

The Employee Polygraph Protection Act is a statute designed to protect employees' privacy. The Act makes it illegal for most private-sector employers to use polygraph tests. (Federal and state governments are not covered.)

There are numerous exceptions where polygraphs are permitted in the private sector, for example matters involving national security, public health and safety, drug manufacture and distribution, as well as investigations of theft, embezzlement, and espionage. In the latter three investigative cases, the employer must possess a reasonable suspicion of the employee's involvement before ordering a polygraph.

Global Legal Perspectives

The Extraterritoriality of U.S. Civil Rights Laws[82]

The U.S. CRA of 1991 mandates that U.S. Civil Rights laws have extraterritorial effect. This important employment discrimination issue concerns the rights of workers employed by a U.S. employer or by a foreign employer in a foreign country workplace. The difficult issue is whether the extensive U.S. legal protections afforded to employees in the U.S. carry overseas. This legal question typically is regarded as an issue of the "extraterritoriality" of U.S. law.

The early, leading Supreme Court case ruling on the extraterritoriality of U.S. law was not an employment discrimination case, but rather dealt with federal antitrust law. In the 1909 *American Banana Company v. United Fruit Company*, although both parties to the dispute were U.S. citizens, the alleged violation of the Sherman Antitrust Act occurred in Panama. The Court unanimously ruled at the time that the Sherman Act did not apply to acts occurring beyond the borders of the U.S. Furthermore, a majority of the court expressed reservations concerning even extending a statute extraterritorially. Another concern, raised by Justice Holmes, writing for the majority, was that extending a statute extraterritorially would contravene the fundamental sovereignty principle of international law. This decision consequently set forth the general rule governing extraterritorial jurisdiction, namely that a very strong presumption exists against the extraterritorial application of U.S. law. This presumption, furthermore, can be overcome only in exceptional instances.

The leading employment discrimination extraterritoriality case was the Supreme Court's 1991 decision in *EEOC v. Arabian American Oil Company*. In the so-termed Aramco case, the Supreme Court was called upon to decide

---

[82] This material comes from *Age Discrimination in Employment* book by Mujtaba and Cavico (2006).

whether Congress intended to apply Title VII of the CRA of 1964 to United States citizens working for U.S. companies in foreign countries. The Supreme Court, in a 6-3 decision, affirming the lower court's decision, ruled that Title VII did not reflect the requisite clear expression of U.S. Congressional intent to overcome the presumption against extraterritoriality of statutes. Consequently, the Court held that the protections of Title VII did not extend to a U.S. citizen working for a U.S. company overseas.

The Court compared Title VII of the CRA to the ADEA, which, as will be seen, was amended by Congress in 1984 so as to add provisions that specifically addressed conflicts with foreign laws, thereby revealing Congress's extraterritorial intent, which was "ambiguous" in the language of Title VII. The judicial limitation thereby expressed on the extraterritorial scope of federal law, absent a clearly stated statutory intention to the contrary, stresses the deference the courts give to sovereignty concepts and international law comity concerns that might be contravened if U.S. courts attempted to extend U.S. law too broadly and intrusively, especially labor and employment laws, to other nations. As the Court noted in *Aramco*, it is a "longstanding principle of American law that 'legislation of Congress, unless a contrary intent appears, is meant to apply only within the territorial jurisdiction of the United States'."

Very soon after the Supreme Court had ruled in the Aramco case, Congress attempted to overrule the decision by at least partially extending U.S. employment discrimination law overseas. Accordingly, the CRA of 1991 (Title VII of the CRA of 1964, as amended by the CRA of 1991), was promulgated to protect certain employees of U.S. firms overseas. Congress thereby expressly amended and enlarged the scope of Title VII (as well as the ADA) to provide a clear indication of Congress's extraterritorial intent to reach U.S. business firms that operate outside the U.S. as well as those under the "control" of a U.S. entity.

The 1991 amendments to the CRA expanded the definition of the key term "employee" to include any U.S. citizen employed by a U.S. company in a foreign country or a foreign company that is controlled by a U.S. firm. Foreign employees working within the U.S. are protected, whether working for U.S. or foreign multinational firms, as are U.S. citizen employees. However, and most significantly, outside the U.S., only U.S. citizens working for U.S. firms or firms controlled by U.S. firms are protected because foreign employees were expressly excluded from protection when employed in a foreign country, even by a U.S. firm. Accordingly, Section 109 of the CRA of 1991 amended both Title VII and the ADA to extend certain extraterritorial protections to employees.

When the U.S. Congress has legislated with an explicit intent to have extra-territorial impact for U.S. law, the courts will recognize that intent. However, if there is a "gray area," the courts can determine the legal result by judicial interpretation. Yet, even where there has been an express Congressional intention to have extraterritorial effect, the courts can interpret the law in a manner that allows defenses and qualifications. Accordingly, the courts developed three main defenses to allegations of employment discrimination overseas. These defenses are as follows:

1. Was the discriminatory employment decision made by a foreign person not "controlled" by a U.S. employer?

2. Does either Title VII of the CRA or the ADEA conflict with the host country's laws, so that the U.S. employer confronts "foreign compulsion"? That is, would compliance with U.S. law violate the host country's laws?

3. Does the performance of the job reasonably necessitate a particular characteristic, such as age, gender, or religion, thereby permitting the employer to interpose the standard BFOQ defense to employment discrimination?

Since the 1991 amendments to the CRA have made Title VII and the ADEA co-extensive in their extraterritorial protection, the courts have interpreted these seminal employment protection statutes with reference to one another. These post-amendment cases provide guidance generally on the nature of extraterritoriality, and specifically when extraterritoriality will be applied in a particular case.

An essential extraterritoriality legal issue is whether the foreign company is sufficiently controlled by a U.S. "parent" company, i.e., so as to be subject to U.S. antidiscrimination employment statutes. However, exactly determining the nationality of a business's controlling person or entity is a difficult undertaking. The ADEA initially declares that when an employer "controls" a corporation whose place of incorporation is a foreign country, any prohibited employment practices engaged in by such a corporation shall be presumed to be engaged in by the employer. The ADEA also holds that the protections of the Act shall not apply to the foreign operations of an employer that is a foreign "person" not controlled by a U.S. employer. Finally, the Act articulates four factors to determine the crucial corporation "control" test: (1) the interrelationship of operations; (2) the existence of common management; (3) the centralized control of labor relations; and (4) the common ownership or financial control of the employer and the corporation.

The application of the "control" test, therefore, is critical to determining whether these seminal employment antidiscrimination statutes will be enforceable against a foreign subsidiary of a U.S. parent corporation. If the foreign firm is not controlled by a U.S. company, then U.S. citizens employed overseas by the foreign company will not be protected by U.S. antidiscrimination laws. Instead, these employees will have to seek redress pursuant to the labor and employment laws of the nation in which the foreign firm was incorporated or does business. Therefore, a foreign firm, as well as its putative U.S. "parent," must consider whether, by applying the four "control" criteria, it is sufficiently controlled by a U.S. multinational corporation.

The ADEA also has an explicit "foreign compulsion" defense, which allows U.S. firms the legal "license" to discriminate in employment when the enforcement of U.S. discrimination laws would result in a violation of foreign law. This defense, typically called the "foreign laws" defense, means that a U.S. employer will not be liable if compliance with Title VII would cause the U.S. firm to violate the laws of the country where the workplace is located. An example of this "compulsion" defense is provided by the EEOC in its Enforcement Guidance in its Compliance Manual, which states that an employer will have a "foreign laws" defense "for requiring helicopter pilots if employed in Saudi Arabia to convert to Moslem religion where Saudi Arabian law provided for beheading of non-Moslems who entered holy area."

The degree of flexibility provided by this defense is well illustrated by the federal appeals case of *Mahoney v. RFE/RL, Inc.*, where the court ruled that when U.S. law would cause a U.S. firm to violate a foreign collective bargaining agreement—which technically is not even a law—the foreign compulsion defense nonetheless applies. It is important to emphasize that while the U.S. federal court rejected the EEOC's view of the matter, the decision is noteworthy because in many countries, the demarcation between legalistic law and social customs and practices is not as distinct as it is in the U.S.

The aforementioned BFOQ defense explicitly arises from Title VII of the CRA. The BFOQ defense has been deemed by the courts to also have extraterritorial application too. Thus, pursuant to the BFOQ doctrine, an employer may engage in discrimination if certain characteristics are reasonably necessary to the normal operations of the particular business or enterprise. For example, in *Kern v. Dynalectron Corporation*, the court held that conversion to Islam was a BFOQ for a pilot flying helicopters to Mecca because non-Moslems flying into Mecca would, if caught, be beheaded.

The ADEA was first amended by Congress in 1984 to make it applicable extraterritorially. The term "employee" was amended to include any individual who is a citizen of the U.S. employed by a U.S. employer or its subsidiary in a workplace in a foreign country. Unless a person is a U.S. citizen, he or she is not included in the definition of the term "employee" if he or she works overseas. That is, nothing in the ADEA, or the amendments thereto, or the courts' interpretations thereof, regulate age discrimination by U.S. firms against foreign nationals in foreign countries in a foreign workplace. The ADEA also has been interpreted by the courts not to cover foreign nationals when they apply in foreign countries for jobs in the United States in the case of *Reyes-Ganoan v. North Carolina Growers Association*, 2001.

The ADEA also protects U.S. citizens working overseas for a U.S.-controlled foreign employer. The ADEA provides that the prohibitions of the Act shall not apply where the employer is a foreign person not controlled by an U.S. employer. "At a minimum," declared one court, "...the ADEA does not apply to the foreign operations of foreign employers—unless there is an American employer behind the scenes." The ADEA, therefore, does not apply to a foreign corporation operating outside the U.S. even when the foreign firm employs U.S. citizens unless a U.S. company controls the foreign corporation.

Regarding the important "control" issue, the aforementioned four critical factors are specified in the Act, and thus are used by the courts in ADEA cases to determine control. They are: 1) interrelation of operations; 2) common management; 3) centralized control of labor relations; and 4) common ownership or financial control of the employer and the corporation. The purpose of the statutory "control" element, according to one court, is to protect the principle of sovereignty, meaning that "no nation has the right to impose its labor standards on another country." The Act, however, does protect employees working in the U.S. for a domestic branch of a foreign company.

An exception to extraterritoriality also exists if the application of the ADEA would violate the law of the other country where the workplace is located. This principle, termed the "foreign laws" or "foreign compulsion" defense, means that a U.S. employer will not be legally liable if compliance with the ADEA would cause the employer to violate the laws of the nation where the workplace is located. In one aforementioned ADEA case, the U.S. Court of Appeals for the District of Columbia ruled that where the U.S. law would cause a U.S. company to violate a foreign collective bargaining agreement—which technically could be argued as not equating to a "law"—the foreign compulsion defense applied.

Sexual Harassment and Cultural Conflicts[83]

Sexual harassment legal liability has been one of the momentous legal outcomes of the 1964 CRA. This notion expressly prohibits discrimination based on sex (that is, gender).

Cases of sexual discrimination first appeared in the court systems due to federal suits brought against organizations based on certain lacks of hire, lacks of promotion, lacks of training, unfair job assignment, and termination. These early cases were brought by the EEOC, the federal agency created by the passing of

---

[83] Contributed by Steven V. Cates, Nova Southeastern University.

the CRA. Very few individual suits were brought, even though the EEOC gave relief in the form of a "Right to Sue" option after investigation may have found insufficient evidence to forward a claim against a certain employer or individual of the employer.

Some ten years after the passing of the Act, the courts began to see claims of discrimination based on "retaliation" and "retaliatory effects" on the employer-employee relationship. Such claims took the form of "broken promises," "favors," or "threats" promised by male superiors to female subordinates in exchange for sexual relationships. Two areas the courts have defined as sexual harassment have been *quid pro quo* (meaning "this for that") and *hostile working environment*, meaning any action or environmental factor that would lead to the inability of the female employee to work in a non-threatening atmosphere.

Those companies found guilty of allowing their management to practice such discrimination could be fined. The courts reasoned that companies are represented by their management in dealings with employees, and therefore found such companies liable under the legal doctrine of Agency Theory. The courts quickly took up these cases due to their discriminatory implications. Consequently, the EEOC became backlogged with enormous caseloads brought forth by individuals.

Courts have a tendency to "create" law when a statute is not all-encompassing or precise, and this is precisely what happened with the CRA. The courts began to provide rulings that extended the interpretation of the law, which provided for a wealth of new and creative strategies for trial attorneys to find ways to expand the law's intent even further.

A major area of new interpretation came about as part of the discriminatory effects in the form of "pre-discrimination" of employees by male-dominated management. The courts defined such behavior as "harassment of a sexual nature," which later became known as sexual harassment. The courts defined this behavior as *unwarranted and unwelcomed overtures of a sexual nature of any kind that lead to discriminatory treatment of the victim.* By the very nature of the definition of the illegal behavior, the law allows for a broad interpretation of what sexual harassment really is. Accordingly, such behavior is subject to legal scrutiny. From a trial lawyer's perspective, this represents an excellent opportunity to find ways to hold companies accountable for their employees' behavior.

Most enterprising trial attorneys quickly realized that the courts were limited to their jurisdiction in awarding amounts greater than the limits imposed by the Act. Even in the Amendment to the 1991 CRA, the limits were held, at the time, to a maximum penalty of $250,000. The trend shifted from claimants filing claim with the EEOC and asking for relief through the federal courts to asking the EEOC to waive their rights to a hearing and asking for a "Right to Sue" waiver. This was done in order to file suit under tort law and to ask for a jury trial. This allowed the plaintiff's attorney to request judgment and relief for "pain and suffering" caused by the actions of the organization and the lack of accountability of its management's actions toward the plaintiffs.

The courts took an interest in the claims and quickly established precedents, up to and including Supreme Court decisions, which have had a major effect on how the companies must hold their managers accountable for their actions.

But what is still missing from the courts' decisions surrounding sexual harassment is the issue of how the court system, premised on the old English court system, is to deal with cultural differences that arise from those others who do not hold traditional Anglo-Saxon values. An example is if one looks at the Hispanic community and its cultural values. It is a common practice for some Hispanics to be very open about touching each other, including members of the opposite sex as they have a tendency to hug and kiss people whom they know and like. In the Hispanic community, as in many other parts of the world, "flirtation" is simply a way of socialization. The clothing that women wear may be considered provocative in other cultures, but is considered flattering to a woman's figure in the Hispanic culture. It is also standard custom for men to stare at women they consider beautiful.

If the U.S. courts were to apply to such a culture, however, this type of behavior would clearly be judged to be in violation of the CRA. In fact, if one looks at the court's rulings over time, one finds that most of the cases found for the plaintiff have been violations of their rights, yet for the exact same issues that are found to be very popular and acceptable in the Hispanic culture. And because Hispanics now are the largest minority group in the U.S.—surpassing blacks in 2005—what will the courts do if they begin to receive many complaints against Hispanics for these types of behaviors?

To demonstrate further, in the Arab world, the greatest sign of trust is to "share one's air." This is a practice wherein Arab men literally touch noses with their business associates in an intimate gesture of trust where air from one's breath is shared with the other individual. In the U.S. where one's "space" is considered a protected area, such a practice could effectively foster a noticeable hostile environment as defined by the Act. Are the courts ready to deal with such a cultural issue?

Furthermore, in many parts of the Asian and African business community, women are not considered equals. Therefore, when women managers attempt to deal with men, they are shunned. U.S. companies promote based on business results, but local custom fosters a countervailing discriminatory environment not based on the company itself, but rather on external cultural forces that are beyond the scope of the individual company.

In today's global economy, U.S. firms must be ready to reach and attempt to make business partnerships wherever business opportunities exist. Does this mean the U.S. courts will attempt to hold U.S. firms accountable for discriminatory treatment due to cultural patterns from other countries or international firms doing business in the U.S.? The answer could well be yes!

The issue of sexual harassment and the cultural differences inherent in such a discussion will be interesting because the courts still have not comprehensively addressed it at present. This topic may become the new, fertile ground that leads to the next big wave of discrimination claims and lawsuits.

Labor Laws in China, the United Kingdom, and France

In China, unions are increasingly more powerful, and are beginning to challenge large, multinational firms doing business in China. One case deals with Wal-Mart, which is confronting a government-sponsored trade union group called the All-China Federation of Trade Unions (ACFTU), an "umbrella" group for Chinese trade unions. This union is currently seeking to make inroads with large private employers in China.

Although the ACFTU is not a government entity, it is supported by the government, and has ties to the Communist Party. Its chairperson is, in fact, a member of the party's Central Committee Politburo. The ACFTU is different from a traditional U.S. union in that it does not engage in U.S.-style collective bargaining on behalf of the employees regarding wages, benefits, and work conditions. Rather, the Chinese union seeks to develop good relations between labor and management, for example by holding conferences between workers and management.

Foreign companies are not required to set up or recognize unions in China unless the employees specifically request them. However, once a company is unionized, the company must contribute 2% of its payrolls as union dues.

In the case of Wal-Mart, the company has stated that it will not agree to be unionized, but that it will obey a Chinese law that prohibits companies from obstructing or hindering employees who want to form unions. Meanwhile, the ACFTU has stated that it will bring "political pressure" on Wal-Mart to unionize. The union pressure in China apparently has succeeded, because in August of 2006, Wal-Mart, which previously dismissed the need for unions since 1996 (when it entered China), not only agreed to be unionized by the All-China Federation of Unions, but also stated that it would work with the union to establish unions at all of its stores (now numbering 60) in China.

It is important to again stress that the federation is not a type of union alliance that is common in the U.S. Rather, it is a labor entity controlled by the Communist Party, which permits no competing unions and does not allow free election of union leaders. Pursuant to Chinese law, private companies must allow unions, and companies must also set aside 2% of their total payroll to finance union activities, whereas Chinese workers contribute less than 1% of their salaries in union dues.

(One very interesting and extremely important issue to be determined is whether the union or, for that matter, Wal-Mart will seek collective bargaining.)

In 2004, the United Kingdom promulgated a new statutory dispute-resolution procedure, which dramatically changes the way in which workplace discharges, disciplinary actions, and grievances are handled. As explained by one legal commentator,[84] the major aspect of the new law, called the Employment Act 2002 (Dispute Resolution), is the mandating of a three-step statutory procedure to be used in dismissals, etc. The three parts to the process are: 1) the issue in contention must be put in writing; 2) the employer must meet to discuss the issue with the employee; and 3) the employer must conduct an appeal meeting if necessary. Additionally, for dismissals and disciplinary actions, the employer is also required to provide the employee with a written statement of the reasons for the discharge or intended action, followed by a meeting to discuss the action taken or contemplated. An appeal of the employer's decision is also required. Failure to follow these steps will make an employee's discharge automatically "unfair," subjecting the employer to a potential 10 to 50 percent increase in the award of compensation to the employee. If the issue is one of discrimination, and the employee ultimately prevails, this increase is potentially very significant because, in discrimination cases, the prevailing employee can ultimately recover unlimited damages.

In the United Kingdom, the employment-at-will doctrine, which originated under the old English common law, does not govern the employment relationship as it still does in the United States. Other common law countries, such as Canada, Australia, South Africa, and New Zealand, also have abandoned the employment-at-will doctrine, which is now, according to legal commentators, a "uniquely American" legal doctrine.[85]

The U.S. traditional rule of employment at will, furthermore, is found to be "shocking" to Latin Americans and Europeans, who are accustomed to legal protections against employee dismissals. As a matter of fact, when the French government proposed very modest changes to its system of lifetime job security by having young employees being designated as employees at-will for a short apprenticeship period, major rioting ensued throughout the country. As a result, the government dropped the proposal.

---

[85] See Dowling, Donald C., and Rose, Proskauer (2005).
[84] See Collins, Erika C. (Summer 2005).

Pursuant to French law, there is a presumption that employment is indefinite in duration. Fixed-term contracts are permissible, but they must be in writing (as opposed to indefinite-term employment). Fixed-term contracts are permitted only in limited circumstances, for example to perform a precise and temporary task, to replace an employee who is temporarily absent, to assist with a temporary increase in work, and to fill a seasonal job. Consequently, in France, most employees are employed indefinitely, and it is also common for employees to work for companies for long periods of time.

French employees, furthermore, are definitely not employees at-will in the U.S. sense when it comes to discharge. Rather, when it comes to dismissal as well as other aspects of employment, French employees enjoy numerous statutory benefits. According to one commentator,[86] for U.S. companies operating in France, the variety and level of benefits that French workers are entitled to may come as "quite of a shock." For example, French law mandates that companies with 50 or more employees must create a profit-sharing fund that is provided to all employees. Paid leave is generous, with employees being entitled to five weeks of paid leave annually after one year of service. Maternity leave is also generous, with very liberal, paid maternity leave. In the event an employee is laid off, the employer must provide notice of termination and severance payments.

Further regarding discharge, French employees are entitled to mandatory severance payments if they are terminated. The minimum dismissal payment amounts to one-tenth of the average monthly remuneration per year of service for employees with two or more years of service, and for employees with more than ten years of service, an additional payment of one-fifteenth remuneration is required. Furthermore, if the dismissal is for economic reasons, the severance is twice the aforementioned amounts. The French government also provides dismissed employees with unemployment compensation for a period of up to five years.

Anti-Discrimination Laws in Mexico and Ireland

Mexico, as part of its treaty obligation by agreeing to the North American Free Trade Agreement and the North American Agreement on Labor Cooperation, enacted a new, more protective, anti-discrimination employment law in 2003 called the Ley Federal Para Prevenir y Eliminar La Discriminacion. Compared with U.S. antidiscrimination law, the Mexican law, according to one legal commentator,[87] has a far greater scope of protection. The Mexican law prohibits discrimination in employment based on ethnic or national origin, sex, age,

---

[86] See Scott, Carole A. (2006).
[87] See Dehart, Philip, (2006).

disability, social or economic condition, health condition, pregnancy, language, religion, opinion or political persuasion, sexual preference, marital status, xenophobia, anti-Semitism, or any other distinction that has the effect of hindering or negating the recognition or exercise of rights and equal opportunities. Yet, according to this commentator, despite the extensive statutory protection, a question still remains as to whether or not the law will be enforced and whether or not Mexico will satisfy its treaty obligations in this regard.

In 2004, Ireland[88] amended its employment equality law by means of the Equality Act in order to bring Irish law more into conformity with European Community directives on equality. Specifically, the 2004 Act requires employers to take measures to adapt the workplace for employees as well as potential employees who suffer from a disability. However, as in the U.S., there is no legal duty to "adapt" if to do so would place a "disproportionate burden" on the employer. Yet the "disproportionate burden" standard emerges as a very significant change in Irish law because formerly, an employer was not under an obligation to adapt its facilities for disabled workers if more than a nominal cost was involved. The 2004 Act also expanded the definition of harassment and sexual harassment to include conduct that violates a person's dignity and creates an intimidating, hostile, degrading, humiliating, and offensive environment.

Sexual Harassment Laws in Japan, China, Peru, and India

In 1991, Japan enacted an antidiscrimination law that requires employers to prevent sexual harassment. However, sexual harassment in Japan was not treated with the same degree of seriousness and priority as in the United States. For example, few Japanese companies had training programs specifically designed to prevent sexual harassment, whereas most U.S. employers, especially large ones, do. Furthermore, there is still a clash of cultures when it comes to business practices in Japan versus the U.S., as shown by the still-common Japanese executive practice of asking lower-level female employees to serve tea to guests.

In 1997, Japan amended its Equal Employment Opportunity Law to, as noted by one commentator,[89] specifically regulate sexual harassment. Accordingly, the Japanese Civil Code now provides a basis of judicial relief in both contract and tort form for the two main types of sexual harassment: *quid pro quo* and hostile working environment. There is just one important caveat: In Japanese law, an "act" deemed contrary to "public order or good morals" shall be deemed null and void and actionable. However, certain types of *quid pro quo* harassment,

---

[88] See Collins, Erika C. (2005).
[89] See Yamakawa, Ryuichi (1999).

such as a refusal to hire or promote, may not involve an "act," and rather may be construed as a mere "omission." In this case, contract relief may not be available, which means that tort relief is available.

Regarding the hostile environment form of sexual harassment, the Civil Code provides that any person who intentionally or negligently infringes on another person's rights is subject to tort liability. The word "rights" has been defined as encompassing not only statutory rights, but also legally protected interests that are considered in need of protection. Again, if the "hostile" type of sexual harassment amounts to a recognized tort—such as assault or battery, invasion of privacy, or defamation—there will be no problem in asserting that the conduct infringes on a legally protected interest and thus constitutes a tort. However, if the alleged abusive or offensive sexual conduct does not constitute a recognized tort, the critical question will have to be judicially resolved as to whether a legally protected interest is at stake and, if so, which one.

Regarding the employer's liability for sexual harassment under Japanese law, the employer is held to a legal duty to make sure the workplace is conducive to working and that employees are treated with dignity and can do their jobs. If a manager fails to meet this legal duty, the employer will be vicariously liable for the manager's failure.

In China, the term "sexual harassment" did not exist a decade ago, not just in the law, but in the Chinese language itself. But apparently, sexual harassment has become a problem in China as more and more women are joining the workforce, so, in 2005, female Communist Party leaders introduced legislation to make sexual harassment illegal in China. There has been, in effect, a law put into place that protects "human dignity," but such a law has been rarely used in the workplace and the penalties for violating the law have been minimal, usually small monetary fines and the requirement of an apology to the victims of the disrespectful conduct. The proposed stronger law against sexual harassment, which is expected to eventually be promulgated, would compel companies to take measures to prevent sexual harassment as well as other "bad" behaviors in the workplace.

In Peru, the Law of Labor Competitiveness and Productivity was the first Peruvian legislative norm to address sexual harassment generally, as noted by two commentators.[90] Due to an ongoing desire to attract foreign investment, the law applies to all private-sector enterprises and treats foreign and Peruvian companies alike, meaning that there is no preferential treatment for "local" companies. Thus, foreign subsidiaries are treated as local employers and their employees are covered by this law.

---

[90] See Orihuela, Sandra, and Montjoy, Abigal (2000).

The prohibited sexual harassment encompasses not only physical acts against the employee but also verbal acts against the employee or the employee's family, acts of discrimination based on sex, immoral acts, and acts adversely affecting the employee's dignity. However, there is a major problem with the Peruvian law. The employee who considers herself a victim of sexual harassment at work must first terminate her labor contract in order to file suit against her employer. Thus, the victim is confronted with a stark choice: either tolerate the sexual harassment and keep her job, or quit her job, joining the ranks of the many unemployed in Peru, and hope that she prevails in her lawsuit.

In India, as noted by one legal commentator,[91] in 1997 the Supreme Court ruled that sexual harassment in the workplace violated the fundamental rights granted in the Indian Constitution to gender equality and the rights to life, liberty, and equal treatment. Article 15 of the Constitution specifically prohibits discrimination on the basis of sex as well as religion, race, caste, and place of birth. Also, Article 19 states that all Indian citizens are entitled to practice any profession.

Sexual harassment is defined by the Indian Supreme Court as unwelcome sexual behavior that a harassment victim reasonably perceives may negatively impact one's health and safety in the workplace. In order to combat sexual harassment in the workplace, employers must create a complaint procedure, resolve sexual harassment claims, institute disciplinary actions, and, where necessary, effectuate prosecution of sexual harassment offenders. It is very interesting to point out that the sexual harassment complaint committee must be headed by a woman and must be at least half-comprised of women. The employer also must notify its employees of the sexual harassment policy. Also, the sexual harassment protections in India extend to cases of third-party harassment.

Article 32 of the Constitution grants the Court the power to enact guidelines providing remedies to those who have suffered a violation of Constitutional rights, which the Court has done in the case of sexual discrimination and harassment.

Comparing Labor Relations in Mexico and the United States[92]

The impetus for the labor movement in Mexico came from the revolution of 1917, during which workers supported those who subsequently came to power. Now, the Mexican Constitution stipulates the basic, inalienable rights of workers. Similarly, the 1970 Federal Labor Law was passed as a result of labor's sup-

---

[91] See Feld, Louise (2002).
[92] Contributed by Josephine Sosa-Fey, Texas A&M University-Kingsville.

port for the government during the 1968 student action, which protested contemporary government policies.

Contrary to labor relations in the U.S., Mexican law gives rights directly to the individual employees, not to the labor organizations. Unlike the U.S., Mexico rejects the doctrine of "employee at will" and grants every employee the right to keep a job for a specified term, unless terminated for cause. The 1970 Federal Labor Law requires an individual employment contract for each employee, or implies a contract if one is not executed. Such a contract contains terms of employment, the services to be performed, salary and benefits information, and the stipulation of termination for "just cause" only. The law defines what constitutes just cause: using false documents to get the job; being dishonest or violent on the job; negligently or intentionally damaging the employer's property; immoral or impaired behavior on the job; or three unexcused absences. The law also stipulates remedies if the worker feels unjustly dismissed: reinstatement, or three months' salary, in addition to any back pay owed. Furthermore, the law provides for a year-end bonus, paid vacations and holidays, a profit-sharing plan, and protection when businesses change ownership. Collective bargaining agreements are allowed under the law, but employee protections cannot be curtailed by any such agreement. Strikes also are allowed but are extensively regulated by the Mexican Conciliation and Arbitration Board, thereby limiting their use.

Although Mexican laws give workers benefits that are not provided to U.S. workers, their total compensation is substantially lower. Despite the many benefits for Mexican workers, the total compensation (wages plus benefits) is still much lower compared with their U.S. counterparts. For an average worker in Mexico, the total cost of wages plus benefits has always been less than 25 percent (and, in recent years, less than 10 percent) of comparable costs in the U.S. Thus, many U.S. companies continue to locate jobs in Mexican "maquiladoras" (manufacturing operations) in order to take advantage of lower labor costs.

Mexican laws guarantee similar benefits as those given to U.S. workers, including minimum wages, equal pay for equal work, regardless of sex or nationality, compensation for workers who are injured, a safe workplace, and the right to join and be represented by labor organizations. The laws also ensure health care for workers and their families, provide retirement benefits, retirement savings plans administered by Mexican banks, and, in some cases, subsidized housing.

However, Mexican laws require many other benefits not required by U.S. Laws. For example, Mexico requires six weeks' paid leave for pregnant women before and after the birth of a child and daily rest breaks at work to breast-feed the baby. U.S. law only requires unpaid leave. Mexico also requires that employers pay both an annual salary and a profit-sharing bonus and an annual year-end bonus of 15 days of pay. While many U.S. companies also provide profit sharing to their workers, it is not required that they receive severance pay when they lose their jobs.

Some employers in Mexico provide other benefits not required by law in order to attract new workers, such as hiring bonuses, life and disability insurance, bus transportation to and from work, and an on-site cafeteria and banking services.

Critics of the Mexican system claim that workers often do not receive the benefits to which they are entitled unless someone pays a "mordida" (bribe) to a union government official. In fact, U.S. labor unions have filed numerous complaints under NAFTA criticizing Mexico for not enforcing its own labor laws, especially provisions in the law designed to allow the formation of labor unions. In fact, Mexican laws do make it more difficult for independent labor unions to be established.

In contrast to the U.S., where a group of workers acting together often have the protection of the National Labor Relations Act, Mexico requires that unions be registered and approved by the government before they obtain legal standing. Mexican law also permits labor agreements to have clauses that prohibit an employer from hiring nonunion applicants and require them to terminate those who will not pay their dues. In practice, this is the equivalent of a "closed shop" agreement, which is illegal in the U.S.

The Federal Labor Act of 1970 provides that conciliation and arbitration boards must review all collective bargaining agreements and that all union organizations must register with the boards. These boards are known as labor courts because their roles are similar to judicial entities, and they do not depend exclusively on the labor contracts for their enforcement authority. Rather, they are empowered by the Mexican Constitution to impose certain remedies. The Mexican Constitution requires that labor and management submit disputes to arbitration, specifying that the Conciliation and Arbitration Board consist of an equal number of labor and employer representatives in addition to one representative from the government. The Mexican Constitution specifies the board's duties, which include ruling on the legality of strikes, imposing specified remedies on employers should they fail to adopt a board decision, and reviewing labor contracts for legal improprieties.

Limited judicial review of arbitral awards is available, despite a statutory provision to the contrary. The Mexican Constitution, which overrides statutory law, requires that all acts of authority be subject to review by the federal judiciary. Appeals of arbitral decisions are made to Circuit Bar Courts or to the Supreme

Court if the constitutionality of an award is in question. Historically, arbitration decisions favor workers. On the other hand, strikes have been less common in recent years because arbitration boards usually declare them to be illegal.

Management Strategies

From the employer's perspective in the U.S., the usual objective is to create and preserve the at-will nature of the employment relationship. There may be societal and even business sanctions for even an immoral discharge of an at-will employee, but there are no legal sanctions unless, of course, another superseding legal principle is violated.

In order for a manager to minimize his or her firm's legal exposure to wrongful discharge lawsuits, the manager must carefully examine the firm's personnel policies and procedures and handbooks and manuals in reference to the specific wrongful discharge theories and principles applying nationally in the U.S. and within each specific state where the firm does business. In order to obviate the implied contract theory, the employment application should expressly define the nature of the relationship.

The applicant should be plainly advised that if hired, he or she will be an at-will employee and, as such, will be subject to discipline and dismissal without notice and cause and at the discretion of the employer. The employer should indicate that it reserves the right to unilaterally abolish or modify any personnel policy without prior notice. Furthermore, the employer should state clearly in all the employment documents that it retains the unilateral right to change and to modify the employment relationship, but that nothing it does shall modify the at-will nature of the employment relationship.

Furthermore, the employer could state that its manuals and handbooks and, for that matter, even its code of ethics, are not part of any contract with the employee. The employment manual or handbook should contain language that explicitly advises the employees that they do not have an employment contract, that they are employees at will, and that the employment relationship can be terminated by either party at any time and for any reason. Finally, the employer should state that the employee's at-will status cannot be changed except by the creation of a written document approved and signed by the president of the company or a designated high-level executive or manager.

Yet when it comes to the traditional employment at-will doctrine, a company can take the totally opposite track and abrogate it by means of its own internal "law." As an example, the Red Lobster restaurant chain, which is owned by Darden Industries, is no longer an employer at will. Rather, for a manager's discharge of an employee to be upheld in the company, the discharge must be a "just" one. An employee can appeal his or her dismissal to an employee review board, which is composed not only of managers and supervisors, but also of a cross section of Red Lobster employees—such as servers, hosts and hostesses, and bartenders—all of whom volunteer for the panel and who are told to do what they think is "fair." Red Lobster executives vigorously defend such peer review for keeping valuable employees from unfair dismissals and for substantially cutting legal expenses associated with employment-discharge disputes.

Regarding the U.S. law on sexual harassment—particularly the at-times nebulous nature of an "offensive" sexual environment as well as the legal principle of absolute liability for certain sexual harassment wrongs—the authors strongly recommend that employers in the U.S. promulgate, circulate, and enforce policies to combat sexual as well as other types of harassment. These policies should emphasize that employees who report sexual harassment will not be retaliated against in any way and also stress that complaining employees can report to an authority in the firm's management hierarchy other than the employees' own supervisor. Larger companies should institute formal training and education programs, whereas smaller firms can explain their policies at staff meetings.

Foreign companies and executives doing business in the U.S. must be prepared to deal with U.S. antidiscrimination and sexual harassment law. Although most industrialized nations now have antidiscrimination laws, these laws may not be as strict as the U.S. laws, especially the aspect of U.S. laws that makes the creation of a hostile, offensive, or abusive sexual environment at work illegal. Foreign companies and executives that do business in the U.S. can avoid legal problems by developing and instituting specialized training and education programs for new and current employees, conforming human resource practices to U.S. legal and cultural standards, putting into place confidential reporting and "whistleblowing systems," and, by involving a neutral third party, such as an ombudsman or an outside legal counsel or consultant, to receive and to investigate complaints. For example, Toyota, in response to a 2006 lawsuit in the U.S. brought against its top North American executive for allegedly sexually harassing and then retaliating against his former personnel assistant, has now instituted a special training program for all its executives, formed a special task force with outside experts, and is reviewing all the company's policies on sexual harassment as well as discrimination.

Therefore, given the number and scope of U.S. antidiscrimination laws, managers must be very proactive to ensure equal opportunity and to avoid lawsuits. First and foremost, employers must have very strong antidiscrimination policies and procedures, including a very tough policy that prohibits retaliation against employees who file complaints and one which allows for the discharge of retaliatory employees.

Second, there must be objective job-related criteria for positions, promotions, and performance. These criteria must apply equally without regard to race, gender, national origin, or any other protected characteristic. Employers should cast a "wide net" for job applicants, for example by advertising at job fairs and in journals and publications geared for minorities and other protected classes. At the same time, employers should be careful about using current employee networks or even minority employee networks—be they family, friends, neighborhood, city, or regional networks—for hiring, because using such networks to obtain employees may impermissibly shut out applicants of another protected category.

Employers also should provide managers, supervisors, and employees with training as to employment practices, especially specialized training for managers on hiring and firing employees. The training also should emphasize that retaliation against employees who complain about discrimination and harassment is strictly prohibited.

Regarding labor relations, the authors presume that most U.S. companies and foreign companies doing business in the United States would prefer to operate on a nonunion basis. That preference is surely one reason why the German and Japanese auto manufacturers have almost exclusively selected U.S. Southern "right to work" states to build their auto manufacturing plants. Today in the U.S., most people in the private-sector labor force are not unionized, and the typical employment situation in the U.S. is nonunion. Furthermore, even if an employer had employees who are unionized, there may be many others who are not.

The employer's objective presumably is to remain a "union-free" organization, and there are two general approaches that an employer can take to remain nonunion. One is a negative approach, in which the employer wages a direct, active, and hostile antiunion campaign. The other, the one strongly recommended by the authors, is a positive approach, consisting of the employer promulgating progressive, fair, and ethical personnel practices and policies, providing wages and benefits comparable with what the employees could expect if they were unionized, and instituting channels and mechanisms for the employees to participate in decision making and to voice their needs, concerns, and complaints to the employer, and to seek redress and justice. The "message" thus will be that the employer is legitimately a "good" employer to work for and, concomitantly, that the employees thereby do not need a union (or union dues).

Accommodating the Religious Practices of Employees: A Model[93]

Should a corporation in the United States be held liable for terminating an employee who refuses to work on Saturday Sabbath? How about a business that refuses to hire a female who insists on wearing a head veil to work? Or a male who, in observance of his religion, refuses to shave his beard? What about a company that fails to accommodate an employee who requests a leave of absence with pay in order to observe Yom Kippur? More and more, these are the types of challenges that many corporations and businesses face in today's work environment.

The global marketplace has generated competition to such a point that companies must increase their productivity to ensure a healthy bottom line. As a result, many businesses now require their employees to work on Saturdays and Sundays, and even on some religious holidays. Often, these work requirements come into conflict with an individual employee's desire to observe certain religious practices. In turn, these competing interests can, and often do, lead to costly legal battles.

At the forefront of these legal disputes is Title VII of the CRA of 1964, which prohibits employment-related discrimination, including discrimination predicated on one's religious beliefs. More specifically, the Act requires that an employer "reasonably accommodate" the religious practices of employees unless the accommodation would create an "undue hardship" on the part of the employer. Because Congress did not define or give substantive guidance to the terms "reasonable accommodation" or "undue hardship," the courts have been left to grapple with interpreting these terms in a variety of factual contexts. Thus far, the courts have generally held that an accommodation will be found to be unreasonable if it causes the employee to suffer a diminution in his or her employment benefits or status, or unjustly imposes a significant work-related burden on the employee. However, an accommodation that would create an "undue hardship" or more than a *de minimus* cost for the employer does not have to be implemented.

Despite this overarching principle, as delineated by the courts, there still remains a "sea of murky water" that may serve as a fertile "breeding ground" for protracted litigation between employers and employees. Accordingly, a business would be better served in taking a "proactive" approach, rather than a reactive one, in avoiding such hefty legal battles. In doing so, a corporation should take into account controlling case law and should therefore review an employee's request for religious accommodation prudently in order to ensure consistency with legal precedent.

---

[93] Contributed by Shakila Faqeeri, Florida State University.

The following model, predicated on governing case law, will serve as a comprehensive guidepost for entrepreneurs and managers in deciding which accommodations they should likely implement in order to avoid legal conflicts. In general, a company's legal obligation toward an employee should be satisfied if it carefully considers the following:

A) *What does the employee's religion require?*
   1. Ask the employee to specify in writing what his/her religion requires, i.e., time off, dress/appearance requirements.
   2. Request that the employee specify activities that violate his/her religious requirements, i.e., payment of union dues.
B) *What is the nature of the accommodation sought?*
   1. Ask the employee to specify in writing exactly what a reasonable accommodation would be, i.e., paid/unpaid time off, being allowed to wear religious garb, and/or being excused from certain job activities.
C) *How will the requested accommodation burden the company?*
   1. Calculate the financial and practical burden imposed by the request.
   2. Ask whether it will cost more to give paid time off, will the religious garb be an important public relations consideration, or will the accommodation cause an overall increase or decrease in the company's profits.
D) *Are there any acceptable alternatives in meeting the employee's demands?*
   1. Consider and offer alternative accommodations, such as requesting coworkers to swap work and/or transfer to a position with more favorable conditions.
   2. If the employee objects to the alternative accommodation, ask for a written objection stating why the alternative is unreasonable.

This model should help to avoid legal problems in this challenging area of employment discrimination law.

Appearance Discrimination in the Workplace[94]

Just as appearance affects an employer's judgment about the qualifications of a particular employee, so does it affect a customer's perception of the company and its products or services. Many employers use appearance-based hiring as a marketing technique. Legally, an employer as a general rule can discriminate based

---

[94] Republished with permission of the Clute Institute, from *Journal of Applied Business Research*, 28(5), September/October 2012; permission conveyed through Copyright Clearance Center, Inc.

on appearance in the form of attractiveness, but an employer must be very careful since an appearance standard might be connected to an Age Discrimination in Employment Act (ADEA), American with Disabilities Act (ADA) or Title VII of the Civil Rights Act of 1964 (Title VII) protected category, thereby triggering a discrimination lawsuit. Business managers must control the risks associated with this form of discrimination known in some circles as "lookism" and recognize how "lookphobia" could result in legal liabilities.

The ADEA prevents discrimination based on one's age if the worker is forty years of age or older. Additionally, the ADA prevents discrimination against employees based on their disability and requires employers to offer "reasonable accommodation" to the employee in the workplace. If an employer holds a belief that all "old" people over the age of 40 years are "ugly", and does not hire them because they are "ugly", this could be a form of illegal discrimination in violation of the ADEA. This could be proven by disparate treatment, if the employer purposefully and intentionally acted on his/her discriminatory beliefs and disparate impact if the an employer's policy or rule of classification of "attractiveness" of job applicants has a disproportionate impact on 40 plus year old job applicants. The ADA may also be violated by an employer when considering workers or job applicant's physical appearance. If the job applicant's or employee's disability is the basis for the employer's "less attractiveness" judgment of them, and they are not hired or they are treated adversely because of their outwardly appearance directly linked to their disability, this could lead to an ADA lawsuit.

Title VII protects employees and job applicants from discrimination based on the protected categories of race, color, sex, national origin, and religion. If an appearance-based case can be connected to race or color discrimination then the plaintiff employee may have a viable civil rights lawsuit. Appearance in the form of an attractiveness standard can result in illegal sex discrimination pursuant to civil rights laws when the appearance standard is applied to women but not men; that is, the female employee or job applicant must demonstrate that she was treated differently than a similarly situated male employee or applicant. Furthermore, appearance requirements that are based on sexual stereotypes are impermissible in the workplace and expose the employer to possible civil claims.

In examining the employment-appearance-gender case law more closely, the conclusion is that subjecting women but not men to appearance and attractiveness requirements is illegal sex discrimination. Regarding height and weight requirements, if an employer is going to establish them, they must be applied to both male as well as female employees; otherwise, the employer could be liable for disparate treatment based on sex pursuant to Title VII. For example, an employer will have acted illegally if the employer's maximum weight standards were applied to the exclusively female position of "flight hostess" but not to a similar though exclusively male position of "director of passenger service". However, so long as the appearance discrimination is not connected to sex discrimination and that any appearance standards are applied equally to men and women, then the appearance discrimination is legal.

If appearance discrimination can be connected to national origin discrimination then the aggrieved employee may have a viable civil rights lawsuit. The Equal Employment Opportunity Commission provides an example of how appearance discrimination would violate the law as national origin discrimination. The example supposes that an applicant, called Radika, a native of India, applies for a job as a receptionist. At the interview, the company representative tells her that she would not be right for the position because the company is looking for someone with "an all American front office appearance." Radika is dressed appropriately, but the only element of her appearance that is not in conformity with the company's standard is that she is of Indian ancestry. Accordingly, the EEOC counsels that if she can demonstrate that the company representative viewed her appearance as inappropriate because of her Indian features, Radika can establish a violation of the law (Equal Employment Opportunity Commission, Fact Sheet, 2011).

Although federal civil rights laws do not protect against appearance discrimination unless the discrimination can be linked to a protected category, there are a few states and localities that do protect against appearance discrimination. Michigan, Santa Cruz and San Francisco, California, and Washington, D.C., have all passed laws prohibiting discrimination because of weight. Michigan in particular, passed the Elliott-Larsen Civil Rights Act 453 of 1976 which banned employment discrimination specifically based upon height and weight, along with other traditional protected classes. Although the statute does not explicitly include attractiveness as a protected appearance characteristic, it specifically mentions that height and weight are appearance factors that are protected. Furthermore, the District of Columbia, Urbana, Illinois, Madison, Wisconsin, and Santa Cruz, California have passed laws prohibiting discrimination based on some aspect of personal appearance.

Employers, therefore, can and should take precautions to preclude attractiveness/appearance lawsuits. Job applicants should not be automatically excluded based upon pre-conceived notions that "old" or "disabled people" reflect an undesirable outward appearance. If an employer deems it necessary or even beneficial to have an attractiveness standard, or perhaps a concomitant height or weight standard, the employer must make sure that discriminatory elements are not built into the standard or that the standard is applied in a discriminatory manner. Men and women, blacks and whites, and people of different races and nationalities must be treated in a comparable and fair manner. Employers should be mindful that the majority of their customers or clients do not nicely fit within the "good looking" category. A diverse looking workforce has its benefits, even if some of these diverse physical characteristics may be "less attractive" to some; it will most likely be embraced by others. Appearance and attractiveness cannot legally or morally be used as a pretext for impermissible discrimination. The "take away" of this overview of the law relative to "lookism" or "lookphobia", if a person, perhaps regarded as "unattractive," cannot tie his or her appearance-based lawsuit to a protected category under federal, state, or local civil rights laws, that person will not have legal redress.

Sexual Orientation and Gender Identity Discrimination in the Workplace[95]

Generally, neither sexual orientation, nor sexual preference, nor gender identity is currently covered by federal anti-discrimination law. Title VII of the Civil Rights Act of 1964 prohibits discrimination by covered employers on the basis of race, color, religion, sex, or national origin (Title VII of the Civil Rights Act of 1964). However, Title VII's prohibition against discrimination based on "sex" does not include discrimination based on sexual orientation or preference. Each year Congress grapples with this issue and debates proposed federal legislation that would significantly expand the protections of civil rights laws in the United States. The proposed law is called the Employment Non-Discrimination Act (ENDA). The ENDA closely follows Title VII and would prohibit discrimination nationwide in employment based on sexual orientation, preference, or gender identity and passed the Senate in 2013 but failed to come up for a vote in the House of Representatives.

Over the years, there has been a progressive evolution towards protecting workers from this type of discrimination. On a federal level the movement has been slow and minimal with the 1998 federal executive orders signed by President Clinton protecting federal workers and the passage of the 2010 Don't Ask Don't Tell Repeal Act allowing gays, lesbians, and bisexuals to serve openly in the military. Additionally, there are yearly efforts to pass the proposed federal legislation that would significantly expand the protections of civil rights laws in the United States. The proposed law is called the Employment Non-Discrimination Act (ENDA). The ENDA closely follows Title VII and would prohibit discrimination nationwide in employment based on sexual orientation,

---

[95] "Sexual Orientation and Gender Identity Discrimination in the American Workplace," by Frank J. Cavico, Stephen C. Muffler, and Bahaudin G. Mujtaba. In *International Journal of Humanities and Social Science*, 2(1), pp. 1-20 (2012). Reprinted by permission.

preference, or gender identity and passed the Senate in 2013 but failed to come up for a vote in the House of Representatives.

On a state level, twenty-one states and the District of Columbia prohibit sexual orientation and sexual preference discrimination by statute. States with sexual orientation or sexual preference anti-discrimination statutes are: California, Colorado, Connecticut, Delaware, District of Columbia, Hawaii, Illinois, Iowa, Maine, Maryland, Massachusetts, Minnesota, Nevada, New Hampshire, New Jersey, New Mexico, New York, Oregon, Rhode Island, Vermont, Washington, and Wisconsin. This patchwork of state laws is only complicated by the 181 plus cities and counties, as well as the District of Columbia, which have passed local codes and ordinances which prohibit sexual orientation or sexual preference discrimination in employment within their individual geographical borders. Business managers should be cautioned that just because a state, like Florida, does not have a state law preventing workplace discrimination based on sexual orientation or preference, there still may very well be county and municipal protections afforded to employees within certain jurisdictional boundaries within that state like Miami-Dade, Broward, Monroe counties and cities like Key West, Fort Lauderdale, Miami, Miami Beach, and Wilton Manors. Similarly, the state of Idaho does not have a law banning sexual orientation discrimination, but the cities of Coeur d'Alene, Boise, Sandpoint, Ketchum, and Moscow have adopted such civil rights protections.

Businesses that hire employees in multiple states and counties throughout the United States find this area of law unsettled, confusing and ever changing. Further, in some states and local municipalities have expanded protections to bisexual, sexually transitioning, transgender and transvestite a/k/a 'cross-dressing' employees. Thus, prudent mangers should adopt policies of tolerance and non-discrimination to avoid legal and ethical quandaries.

Employers should interview, select, hire, train, and promote employees solely on the basis of their knowledge, skills, abilities, and experience. Concomitantly, employees must be rewarded only for their work-related performance; and disciplined solely for their work-related conduct. It is essential for the employer to have in its Code of Conduct or Code of Ethics a clear, firm, strong, and broad policy against discrimination and harassment. The policy must state that every employee is entitled to, and thus must have, a work environment that is free from discrimination, hostility, or harassment of any kind. Furthermore, the policy must state that all employment decisions, such as interviewing, selecting, hiring, promoting, training, rewarding, disciplining, or sanctioning, will be made exclusively on the basis of the employee's knowledge, skills, abilities, experience, performance, or conduct. The policy must state that discrimination and harassment of any kind, including based on sexual orientation or gender identity or gender expression, is explicitly forbidden and also that such discrimination or harassment will be subject to appropriate disciplinary action. Specifically, the anti-discrimination policy should state that sexual orientation discrimination or harassment is misconduct directed at persons who are gay, lesbian, bisexual, sexually transitioning, or transgender, who are perceived as such, or persons who associate with persons who are gay, lesbian, bisexual, sexually transitioning, or transgender. The policy also should state that a hostile work environment can be created by ridicule, abuse, insults, or derogatory comments that are directly or indirectly related to a person's sexual orientation, sexual preference, gender identity, or gender expression. The policy, moreover, must state that employees have a duty to come forward and to report to management any conduct that they view as discrimination, harassment, or tending to create a hostile, abusive, or offensive work environment. The employer, of course, must provide channels for such reporting, maintain confidentiality, and investigate all reports in a prompt, fair, and impartial manner. The employer also must clearly and strongly state that any attempts at reprisals for employees reporting alleged misconduct will not be tolerated and will be severely punished.

Employment non-discrimination policies, therefore, should cover both sexual orientation and gender identity; and such policies of course must cover more than application and discharge, but also should protect employees regarding promotions and transfers, as well as all the terms and conditions of employment. Furthermore, including gay, lesbian, bisexual, sexually transitioning, and transgender employees in a company's or organization's overall diversity policy, program, and strategy makes very good sense—legally, morally, and practically. The goal, therefore, should be for a company or organization to make equality of treatment, dignity and respect, inclusive diversity, toleration and mutual understanding core values of the organization.

Social Media in the Workplace[96]

Social media affords people readily and easily usable ways to stay in touch with family, friends, colleagues, and co-workers, including the ability to rap-

---

[96] "Social Media and the Workplace: Legal, Ethical, and Practical Considerations for Management," by Frank J. Cavico, Stephen C. Muffler, Bahaudin G. Mujtaba, and Marissa Samuel. In *Journal of Law, Policy, and Globalization*, 12(1), pp. 1-46 (May 2013). Reprinted by permission.

idly share information and commentary. Business today is also taking advantage of social media—for marketing, management, and human resource purposes. Furthermore, the conception of the "workplace" has been broadened with the advent of technology and especially the existence of "telecommuting." Given the popularity, prevalence, sophistication, and ever-growing use of social media, it is no surprise that social media in an employment context raises many difficult, as well as novel, legal, ethical, and practical issues including in particular, how employer's restrictions on social media use in the workplace could violate labor laws. To illustrate the problems that can emerge from social media, the Wall Street Journal (Valention-DeVries, 2013) reported on a study by Carnegie Mellon University that involved an experiment using fake resumes and social media profiles. The university study found, firstly, that 10% to one-third of U.S. firms searched social media for job applicants' information early in the hiring process; and secondly, in those cases where the job candidates' Facebook profiles indicated they were Muslim were less likely to be called for interviews than Christian applicants. Obtaining such information consequently can engender illegal intentional discrimination or even unconscious discrimination.

Social media obviously makes it easier for employees to communicate with each other, and thus perhaps to complain about and to express their views on company policies and practices, management, coworkers, and work conditions. Employee social media postings and communications related to work may be protected by federal labor law even if the employees have only at-will status. However, employers who have entered union bargaining agreements and/or have unionized workforces especially must be very mindful of the effects of the National Labor Relations Act of 1935 (NLRA) (29 U.S.C. Sections 151-169) and its limitations on employers ability to enforce "social media" policies against union members. The Wagner Act, Section 7 of the NLRA, grants employees the right to self-organization, to assist, form, or join labor unions, to bargain collectively with representatives of their own choosing, and, most importantly for the purposes herein, "to engage in other concerted activities for the purpose of collective bargaining or other mutual aid or protection" (29 U.S.C. Section 157). Section 7 of the NLRA (29 U.S.C. Section 157) thus protects a worker's right to engage in concerted activities, which are activities by and between coworkers to improve their wages and working conditions. Section 8(a)(1) of the NLRA, moreover, prohibits an employer from interfering, coercing, or restraining employees in the exercise of their Section 7 rights (29 U.S.C. Section 158).

In 1956, The Supreme Court in the case of *NLRB v. Babcock & Wilcox Company*, has ruled that no restrictions can be placed on the rights of the employees to discuss organization and unionization among themselves and to solicit members to form or join a union. Section 8(a)(1) of NLRA, therefore, prohibits an employer from interfering with employees as they engage in concerted activity. Any company policy that is too broad and consequently unreasonably tends to chill workers in the exercise of their Section 7 rights can be subject to a NLRA complaint. This traditional labor relations legal principle has been applied to employer's modern-day social media policies and social media company rules. Furthermore, general company policies that are ambiguous in the terms or application and contain no limiting language to avoid violating Section 7 rights will be considered unlawful under the NLRA

Accordingly, employees have the right under federal labor law to discuss self-organization and to collectively challenge workplace policies and practices and to seek to change them for their mutual benefit. Section 7 and Section 8, therefore, can protect employees who engage in protected "concerted activity" by communicating online by means of social media. One critical question, of course, is what exactly constitutes protected "concerted activity" by employees utilizing social media or other online communications. For example, social media conduct by employees that would not be protected: 1) comments that did not pertain to the terms and conditions of employment; 2) vulgar references; 3) disclosure of trade secrets or confidential company information; 4) physical threats or harassment against customers, clients or coworkers; and 5) disparaging remarks about the company's reputation, product or policy that rise to the level of the tort of defamation.

Managers should craft social media policies which allow for the healthy exchange of ideas and commentary which fall within the broad definition of "concerted activities" by workers during their off time so as not to violate the NLRA. However, clear lines should be demarcated by the employer to inform the workforce that the above referenced communications which do not fall within the "concerted activities" definition and could damage the company, will not be tolerated. Companies should have an "open door" policy to allows employees to complain or address a workplace issue which can then be addressed through healthy mediation, rather than promoting an atmosphere of repression, censorship and retaliation which will inevitably lead to employees venting their grievances online. Company social media policies should clearly identify which media the policy applies too; the sanctions for a violation; dispelling any reasonable "expectation of privacy" in such social interaction online; and of course set the rules and clear boundaries social media use both on and off work hours. One final word of caution to business managers should be addressed. Employers must be cognizant of the fact that there is a movement on a federal and state level, restricting the employer's use of social media, particularly with regard to requiring employees and job applicants to provide their passwords or other login information to their social media sites. Thus, employers should avoid summarily demanding the same login information from their workers or job applicants, especially without just cause, as it promotes a negative workplace atmosphere, promote ill feelings towards the company and may very soon be a basis for a violation of privacy action by the offended person.

Summary

Legal complexity naturally results from the globalization of business—in the employment field and otherwise. Consequently, foreign firms must be keenly aware of U.S. law, and U.S. firms must also be aware of not only foreign laws, but also the extraterritoriality of U.S. laws. A "simple" solution to the extraterritoriality problem examined herein might be to apply U.S. employment discrimination laws to any company incorporated in the U.S., regardless of where its employment operations take place. Yet this "answer" is not feasible due to the very strong presumption in U.S. law against the extraterritorial application of U.S. law, which typically is predicated on concerns regarding sovereignty, comity, and jurisdiction. This presumption is overcome only in exceptional instances.

The CRA, the ADA, and the ADEA have now been amended to include protection for U.S. employees working overseas for U.S. firms. Thus, Title VII, the ADA, and the ADEA currently are coextensive in their extraterritorial effect. Accordingly, these Acts have a very broad extraterritorial reach, encompassing not only U.S. firms doing business in the U.S. and overseas, but also U.S.-controlled firms. Therefore, a crucial issue for a foreign firm to ascertain is whether or not it is sufficiently controlled by a U.S. firm.

It is essential to emphasize that the courts consistently have held that only U.S. citizens are protected. Thus, only a U.S. citizen may properly institute a discrimination lawsuit under Title VII of the CRA and the ADEA, based on employment decisions made at a foreign workplace by a U.S. employer or by a foreign employer controlled by a U.S. multinational firm. Therefore, resident aliens and foreign nationals working overseas for U.S. companies are excluded from the protections of the CRA as well as from the ADEA.

Legally, and most significantly, the distinct possibility exists of different global business practices and employment standards, as well as different degrees of legal protection, for U.S. employees and non-U.S. employees working for the same international business firm and even in the same workplace. Failure to be cognizant of both U.S. employment discrimination law (including its extraterritorial aspects) and the labor law of the host country will result in increased exposure to legal liability for the multinational firm. Consequently, the manager of the multinational firm must ensure, to the extent possible, that the firm complies with both U.S. antidiscrimination employment law as well as the employment law of the host country.

TWENTY TWO

CONSUMER PROTECTION

A company's advertising and marketing activities may result in harm to consumers, for example by misstating the characteristics of a particular product or service or even by unfairly influencing consumers to purchase products or services that they otherwise would not obtain. Such conduct also may harm a firm's competitors, primarily by diverting potential customers, but also by disparaging a firm's goods or services. Consequently, not only consumers but also competing companies have attempted to seek legal redress for what they believe are legally improper advertising and marketing activities. The problem, especially in the American system, is to ascertain whether an ad is false, deceptive, coercive, subliminal, or manipulative—and thus, typically, illegal—as opposed to being "merely" selective, a "half-truth," "tough" or "hard-hitting," suggestive, in poor taste, insensitive, or even offensive—and thus ordinarily legal, though perhaps unethical. In the U.S., as well as other countries, there are a variety of legal theories that can be used to seek relief from allegedly illegal advertising or marketing activities that result in harm to the consumer or a business.

Common Law Contract

Assuming there is a valid contract between the parties, naturally any representations regarding the product or service that become embodied in the contract as legally binding promises will be enforceable. Accordingly, any failure to perform contractual promises will engender a breach of contract lawsuit. As you will recall from the prior discussion of Contract Law, a major problem regarding advertising and marketing activities and the common law of contracts is that, as a general rule, advertising and marketing actions are regarded as mere "invitations to make offers" versus legally binding offers that can be "accepted" by the consumer, thereby potentially resulting in a legally binding contract. The purpose behind the old common law general rule was not to protect consumers, but merchants, specifically to safeguard merchants from being "over accepted" and then being sued if they have limited quantities of goods.

Common Law Fraud

As you will recall from Chapter 9, the common law tort of fraud, particularly in its intentional misrepresentation formulation (that is, deceit), is a very complex cause of action containing many elements. Thus it is very difficult to establish and especially to prove fraud. For example, fraud is premised on lying about "facts," and consequently "merely" giving one's "opinion" or "predictions" about goods or services is not legally actionable as fraud, even if such opinions or predictions turn out to be erroneous. Likewise, "sales talk," exaggerations, figurative language, "puffing," and over-praising goods or services ordinarily are not considered fraud as the critical "fact" predicate is lacking for the tort.

You will also recall that fraud, in the sense of deceit, requires evidence that the wrongdoer purposefully and intentionally made a false statement of material fact with the intent to deceive and to induce the victim to reach an erroneous conclusion or enter into a contract or some type of business relationship.

Warranty Law and the Uniform Commercial Code

The Uniform Commercial Code (UCC) does provide warranty protections to consumers, as well as provides for a lawsuit in the case of breach of warranty. Yet the utility of UCC warranty law as a consumer protection tool for consumers is tenuous at best, as was pointed out in Chapter 13. For example, UCC warranties only attach to the sale or commercial lease of "goods," and not to services. Additionally, there is the problem of the "mixed" transaction, which is a combination of the sale of goods and the provision of services. In addition, as with the tort of fraud, merely giving one's opinion or prediction or "sales talk" as to the goods is viewed as legally non-actionable under warranty law.

Warranties, of course, can be, and are regularly, disclaimed. There are also notice and privity impediments in place that are hurdles against a breach of warranty cause of action.

The U.S. Federal Trade Commission and the Regulation of Advertising

The government agency in the United States that most extensively regulates advertising and marketing is the Federal Trade Commission (FTC). The FTC was one of the first independent regulatory agencies, created by the U.S. Congress in 1914 pursuant to the FTC Act. In Section 5 of the Act, Congress delegated to the agency the power to "police" the marketplace for unfair methods of competition and to prevent and punish such misconduct.

In 1938, Congress amended the Act, further empowering the FTC to regulate deceptive as well as unfair practices in commerce. The original intent of the statute was to protect businesses from the unfair methods of competition by their unethical competitors. As amended, Congressional intent now encompasses that the agency also protects consumers from deceptive as well as unfair methods of doing business.

The FTC has the following delegated and combined powers: 1) the legislative authority to make laws—that is rules and regulations—by rulemaking, the quasi-legislative power; 2) the executive power to investigate violations of its laws and to enforce them; and 3) the judicial power to hear cases in the agency before Administrative Law Judges (ALJs) and to impose "cease and desist" orders, civil fines, "corrective advertising," and other sanctions and redress for the contravention of its rules. The judicial function is called adjudication and, in addition to resolving disputes, the case decisions by the FTC's ALJs serve as laws and legal precedents.

The FTC is thus a very powerful agency with a great deal of discretionary legal authority, and accordingly, the agency emerges as the major legal "player" in the U.S. in regulating the marketplace, particularly advertising. However, it is important to point out the FTC Act did not create a private cause of action for consumers, though the FTC itself has the power to order restitution to an aggrieved consumer as part of the agency's broad remedial powers.

It also should be mentioned that another large federal agency, the U.S. Food and Drug Administration (FDA), in addition to its role in approving drugs for sale, has power comparable to the FTC to regulate the advertising and marketing of prescription drugs and to prevent and punish false and deceptive practices. For example, in one advertising action involving the FDA, the agency concluded that an ad by the pharmaceutical company Pharmacia & Upjohn for the prescription drug Caverject was misleading. The company's ad, located in Parade magazine, promoted Caverject as an alternative to Viagra pills for the treatment of male impotence. But the ad omitted one crucial fact: The drug had to be administered not in pill form, but rather must be injected by a needle inserted directly into the penis!

In a perhaps less dramatic, though nonetheless still significant FDA regulatory action, the agency determined that certain "no cholesterol" claims on Crisco and Mazola corn oils were deceptive, not because they were outright false because the products indeed contained no cholesterol, but rather because the products with the "no cholesterol" labels also contained large pictures of hearts on the product. A misimpression could be created that the products were, in fact, good for the heart, but in reality they contained high levels of fat and saturated fat. The FDA condemned the ads as being half-truths, and the manufacturers of the products "cooperated" with the agency and removed the claims from the ads.

The FTC's "deceptiveness" standard is the key legal standard when it comes to the regulation of advertising. Deceptive advertising means that the claims in an ad are outright false or that the claims therein are misleading and detrimental to the reasonable consumer. "Misleading" has been defined as a representation designed to lead the consumer astray and to induce the consumer to reach an erroneous conclusion. In order to be legally actionable, the allegedly deceptive claims in an ad must also be "material," meaning that they are likely to produce the desired effect of affecting the consumer's decision to purchase the goods and/or services.

It is very important to note that, as compared with the common law of fraud, proof of actual deception is not necessary in contemporary U.S. regulatory law. Rather, only a showing of some probability of deception is required. The old common law depends on the form of the action—that is, *scienter*, the evil intent motivating the action—whereas the regulatory law is premised on the reasonably foreseeable consequences of the action. Accordingly, intent, pursuant to the FTC legal standard, is irrelevant. Furthermore, the "reasonable consumer" is viewed by the FTC as an "ordinary" and reasonable person. However, an ad targeted to a specific group, especially a seemingly vulnerable target audience, such as the young or old or sick, is measured by the reasonableness standard of that unique group.

An interesting situation arises if an advertiser omits information that might have been considered relevant to the product or service. One recalls the old common law maxim that "silence is not fraud," at least as a general rule, and thus usually there is no duty to disclose. But under the FTC's "deceptiveness" interpretation, an omission in an ad might render the ad deceptive and illegal if what was omitted was deemed factual and material, for example health and safety information. Furthermore, omissions of such information also can be construed as being likely to affect the consumer's choice.

Another interesting situation arises if a claim is made about a product without, what the FTC believes, is proper substantiation, meaning that there is a lack of supporting data that can render the advertisement deceptive and illegal.

Finally, the FTC has the power to regulate "unfair" advertising in the marketplace, but the agency, due to Congressionally imposed constraints, as well as self-imposed political restraints, has been circumspect in regulating ads that are not false and deceptive but "merely unfair."

Two classic examples of the FTC in action in regulating deceptive and unfair advertising and marketing activities are the FTC's rules against "bait and switch" advertising and the "cooling-off" period for home solicitations. In the former, a consumer is "baited"—that is, lured into a store to purchase supposedly "sale" items which the merchant either does not have or does have but does not have the intent to sell at the "sales" price—and then the consumer is "switched" to more expensive goods. "Bait and switch" is illegal pursuant to FTC rulemaking (though not, one recollects, by virtue of the common law of contracts).

Meanwhile, the FTC's "cooling-off" regulation deals with door-to-door sales and accords the buyer a three-day period in which to rescind a purchase made by means of a home solicitation.

Other archetypal examples of FTC regulations deal with price advertising, where promotions offer "free" products with the product sold or "reduced" prices for products. These have been deemed as deceptive practices as long as the prices for the products have been artificially inflated to facilitate the "reductions" or the "free" merchandise.

In another memorable FTC case, the agency found that Kraft Foods ran a deceptive advertisement for its Kraft Singles cheese slices. The commercials for the product boasted that Kraft cheese slices were an important source of calcium, because each slice contains five ounces of milk. But the FTC stated that the ad was misleading because it wrongly implied that each cheese slice had five ounces of milk as opposed to the entire whole package of slices. Another more modern example is worthy of note because it stresses the "target audience" element to the FTC's legal standards. This was a television ad for Beck's beer that showed young adults cavorting on a sailboat (though not drinking any beer). The FTC maintained that the ad nonetheless was deceptive and misleading to the young target audience in the sense that the ad implied that young people could safely combine drinking and sailing, which the agency believed was clearly not the case. The case was settled, and the settlement included the ad's removal from the marketplace. Recently, in 2014, the FTC settled with three weight-loss companies that claimed that people could lose weight with minimal effort. The largest settlement, totaling $26.5 million, was with Sensa Products, which markets a dietary supplement called Sensa which is sprinkled on foods. The FTC stated that the chances of successfully losing weight by sprinkling something on one's food were "slim to none." The company agreed to the settlement but stated that it stands behind its product, which it called a tool to help people achieve portion control without traditional dieting, stimulants, or pills. However, the company also said that it was making changes in its advertising in conjunction with weight-loss experts.

Specifically regarding "telemarketing," it is important to note that in 1994, the U.S. Congress passed the Telemarketing and Consumer Fraud and Prevention Act, which empowered the FTC to promulgate rules governing telemarketing and to institute legal actions against telemarketers who violate agency rules. Accordingly, in 1995, the FTC promulgated a telemarketing sales rule that requires telemarketers, before making a "sales pitch," to in fact inform the consumer that the call is indeed a sales call and to clearly identify the seller's name as well as the product being sold. Misrepresenting critical info pertaining to the goods is illegal, as is omitting certain key info, such as the total cost of the goods, any restrictions on using or obtaining the goods, or whether the prospective sale is considered to be final and legally enforceable.

The U.S. Consumer Products Safety Commission

In 1972, the U.S. Congress enacted the Consumer Products Safety Act, which created a federal independent regulatory agency, the Consumer Products Safety Commission (CPSC), and empowered it to regulate the field of consumer product safety.

The CPSC has several functions, but the most important and far-reaching ones are to set legal standards for consumer products and to ban the manufacture and sale of any product that the agency deems to be potentially hazardous to consumers. Furthermore, the CPSC has the authority to issue product "recalls" and thereby to remove from the market any products that it deems to be imminently hazardous to consumers. Manufacturers are required by the CPSC to report to the agency any products that have been sold and that have also been proved to be hazardous to consumers. Distributors of consumer products are also required to notify the agency when they become aware that a consumer product possesses a defect that creates a substantial or unreasonable risk to the public or to a consumer. Finally, the CPSC conducts research on product safety and serves as a "clearinghouse" for risks associated with various products.

The Consumer Products Safety Act, however, did not create any private right of action for the consumer to sue for damages for harm caused by a product. The agency itself, however, can proceed civilly against parties who violate its rules and orders, principally by fining them.

State Consumer Protection Laws

The United States, as was pointed out in Chapter 3, is a federal system of government, with a national government (called the "federal government") as well as constituent governmental components, called "states." The states in the U.S. system are sovereign, lawmaking entities and thus can make laws pursuant to their traditional "police power," that is, the power of the state to enact laws to protect the health, safety, and welfare of the citizens of that particular state. Accordingly, in the area of advertising and marketing, the global businessperson doing business in the U.S. must be concerned not only with the FTC or other federal regulatory agencies, but also the comparable agencies at the state level.

Most states have consumer-protection statutes that protect the citizens of the state from unfair and deceptive trade practices, and most states also have state-level regulatory agencies, colloquially called "Baby FTCs," to enforce the state's consumer protection laws. Although it is beyond the purposes of this book to examine state consumer-protection laws, two pertinent points must be made. First, even if the FTC does not have jurisdiction over a dispute (perhaps due to statutory or self-imposed jurisdictional "yardsticks" that may come into play when a particular controversy might not be "big" enough for the "feds" to get involved), a state consumer-protection statute might be applicable and a state agency very well could assume jurisdiction. Second, it is quite possible that a state's consumer protection law might afford the consumer more rights and impose more duties on the manufacturer or seller versus the federal law.

You will recall that in the U.S. system, pursuant to the Supremacy Clause of the Constitution, federal law is supreme. As a result, any law that directly conflicts with a federal law must fall, yet it is permissible for a state to grant more protection to the citizens of its states than Congress or a federal regulatory agency accords to citizens of the United States.

Global Legal Perspectives

The "Made in the U.S.A." Dilemma

One difficult problem with global business ramifications arises when an ad claims expressly that a product is "Made in the U.S.A." or that the ad impliedly indicates such status by displaying U.S. flags or a map of the United States. Yet exactly how much of a product actually has to be made in the United States for a product ad to claim it is "American made"? This issue has been very contentious due to the uncertainly of such an "American" label, leading the FTC to promulgate "guidelines," which are legally enforceable, as a device to clear up this area of advertising. According to the FTC, in order to legally qualify for a "Made in the U.S.A" designation, all significant parts and processes that go into a product must be of U.S. origin. A company does not have to seek prior approval of such an ad claim, but the FTC can and will proceed against false, misleading, or unsubstantiated claims.

The FTC has also provided some examples of acceptable and unacceptable "American" claims. To illustrate, an ad for a table that states it is "Made in the U.S.A." would be illegal if the table base is imported. Similarly, an ad for a food processor would be illegal with such an ad claim if the motor was imported. Furthermore, claiming that a gold ring is "Made in the U.S.A." would be illegal if the gold was imported. However, a clock radio can be "American made" even if its plastic cover contains imported petroleum. The FTC has also warned that a "Created in the U.S.A" designation may be deceptive and illegal if the idea for the product was created in the U.S., but the actual manufacture occurred abroad.

Chinese Consumer Law[97]

China now has an established body of consumer protection law, promulgated over the last two decades and which is very comprehensive in scope as well as being pro-consumer in orientation. As a matter of fact, March 15 has been designated as Consumer Rights Day in China, and has been regularly observed since 1986.

The preeminent consumer law in the People's Republic of China is the Consumer Rights and Interests Law (CRIL), which became effective in 1994. Chapter II of CRIL establishes the fundamental rights of Chinese consumers, to wit: the right to personal and property safety; the right to obtain truthful information regarding goods and services received; the right of free choice to goods and services; the right of a fair transaction; the right to demand compensation when personal injury or property damage occurs; the right to form consumer rights organizations; the right that human dignity and national customs and habits be respected when goods are used and services are rendered; and the right to criticize and to petition government agencies and officials regarding consumer rights.

Additionally, Chapter III of CRIL contains an expansive list of business obligations to consumers, including complying with the national Product Quality Law, listening to consumers, guaranteeing that goods and services meet certain requirements for personal or property safety, providing accurate information and avoiding false or misleading information, using the products' real names and trademarks, and avoiding insulting and slandering consumers and intruding on their personal freedom.

Regarding product quality, CRIL establishes a warranty that deems that businesses shall guarantee the quality, functions, and usage of products or services under normal operation and acceptance. Furthermore, businesses that use advertisements, instructions, or samples are deemed to guarantee the actual quality of the goods or services is in conformity with that demonstrated quality.

Regarding liability, in the case of product defects that cause personal injuries, a business is held responsible for medical and other related expenses. Chapter VII specifically deals with legal responsibility and imposes general civil liability, but only in certain enumerated situations. However, if a business engages in fraudulent activities in furnishing goods or services, Article 49 of CRIL allows for increased compensation in the amount of one times the amount of the cost paid.

Chapter VI of CRIL deals with the resolution of disputes by conciliation, mediation, arbitration, and by means of consumer organizations and appeals to relevant government agencies.

---

[97] See Overby, Brooke A. (2006).

Article 24 of CRIL forbids businesses from seeking to limit their legal obligations toward consumers by contract or otherwise.

However, according to one legal commentator, there is one major weakness in CRIL for the Chinese consumer: The law, although broad in scope, and although mandating several specific instances of civil legal liability for businesses, does not have a clear pronouncement as to whether a breach of an obligation or the infringement of a right not specifically enumerated as leading to civil liability would in fact be grounds for civil liability. Consequently, according to that commentator, the effectiveness of all the broad consumer rights and consumer dignity language is considerably undercut.

Management Strategies

Advertising and marketing are not illegal. Persuading and influencing are permissible and a normal part of the process of selling and competing. Unless an ad is false, deceptive, or misleading, or does not provide the consumer with sufficient information to make an informed decision, the law affords the global businessperson a great deal of latitude in advertising and marketing products and services. For example, a "selective" ad, in which the seller focuses on an appealing characteristic of the product (such as a compact car's high mileage capability) and concomitantly downplays a negative feature of the product (such as the car's rating on a bumper crash test), is not illegal per se, as long as the seller is not misstating, hiding, or obscuring critical information.

Similarly, a "suggestive" ad, in which the seller not only promises product satisfaction, but also imparts the suggestion that the consumer will obtain various extraneous benefits from using the product (such as "sex appeal"), is not automatically illegal. Yet the seller must be careful if its suggestive ad is targeted to a vulnerable audience, such as the very young or very old, because the suggestion to such an audience may transform the legal suggestive ad into a manipulative and unfair and perhaps even illegal ad.

The FTC or equivalent federal or state agency, as the "prosecuting" party, bears the burden of demonstrating that an advertisement is sufficiently factual and is either expressly or impliedly false, deceptive, misleading, or unfair. The seller of a product or service must be aware that most things are sold by an appeal to perceived needs. Accordingly, if a seller is attempting to meet those needs, and does so in an honest and sufficiently factual manner, the seller will not have to resort to falsity and deception in order to sell its products or services. Of course, the global marketplace is very competitive, and thus the "smart" seller also will clearly differentiate its products and services from that of its competitors.

The key management strategy, legally as well as ethically, is to think of advertising and marketing as primarily a means of providing information to consumers regarding the nature, availability, and pricing of products and ser-vices. Persuasion is permissible, but providing the consumer with adequate and accurate information is paramount. Of course, there is usually nothing legally wrong with loud, intrusive, annoying, repetitive, boring, vulgar, offensive, taste-less ads that insult the consumer's intelligence and test his or her patience and sensitivities. However, we must ask the question as to whether or not such an ad campaign is legal, ethical, and especially "ethical" in the sense of being in the long-term, ethically egoistic self-interest of the seller itself.

Summary

Consumers are often misguided by marketing and advertising of products as well as services. As such, this chapter has explored the governing bodies and acts that protect the consumers and the liability that companies may face as a result of misrepresentation. This chapter focused on common law contract, common law fraud, warranty law and the UCC, the FTC and the regulation of advertis-ing, the U.S. CPSC, as well as the state consumer-protection laws.

Consumer protection should be a focal point for businesses in order to com-pete globally because without customers, they would not be able to operate. Therefore, honesty is imperative for their advertising and marketing tactics.

TWENTY THREE

ENVIRONMENTAL PROTECTION

Protection and preservation of the environment is a significant issue of global interest—socially, politically, and legally. Throughout the world, there is very strong public support for environmental protection. Safeguarding the environment, therefore, emerges as a central area of concern for the global business manager. Yet the challenge is to balance this responsibility with the manager's very practical business responsibilities to the firm and its stakeholders.

The field of environmental protection laws is immense. This chapter will examine some of the main statutes in the United States that regulate business and the environment, and also examine certain international environmental protection laws.

Environmental Regulation in the United States

In the United States, government regulation of business is extensive, as well as expensive for business to comply with. However, the law, as well as public pressure, mandates that businesses comply with a wide variety of detailed environmental regulations at the federal, state, and local levels. The United States Congress, in particular, has enacted several important statutes to protect the environment. But before these statutes are examined, common law remedies for environmental harm will be briefly addressed.

Common Law Remedies

Common law remedies to protect the environment originated early in the development of the common law of England. As mentioned in the chapter on Torts and Business, the common law torts of negligence as well as strict liability for ultra-hazardous activities—such as blasting, spraying pesticides, or transporting radioactive waste—can be used in an environmental context to provide relief for what are generally called "toxic torts." Furthermore, the old common law doctrine of nuisance can also be used to provide redress for environmental harm intentionally caused. A "nuisance" occurs when one party uses his or her property in such a manner that the use constitutes an unreasonable interference with another person's use or enjoyment of his or her property. Pollution certainly can be deemed to be a legally actionable nuisance, which means the aggrieved party can sue for money damages for the harm caused and can also sue for an injunction. However, in the latter case, before issuing an injunction, the judge will balance the utility to the community of entity doing the polluting with the degree of harm caused to a private party.

The National Environmental Policy Act

The National Environmental Policy Act (NEPA) of 1970 was a major piece of environmental protection legislation in the U.S. at the federal level. This Congressional statute created the Council of Environmental Quality, which is based in the executive branch of government, specifically in the Executive Office of the President. The Council gathers information, issues guidelines, and makes recommendations to the President.

The goal of NEPA is to make federal government agencies aware of the environment and the safeguarding of the environment and to take the objective of environmental protection into account when making decisions. NEPA also created the major federal agency regulating business and the environment, the Environmental Protection Agency (EPA).

NEPA also requires that an "environmental impact statement" (EIS) be prepared for every piece of proposed legislation and every major federal action significantly affecting the quality of the environment. The EIS must be a detailed explanation of the anticipated environmental impact of the proposed legislation or action, especially any adverse consequences thereto. In addition, the EIS must consider the commitment of resources to the proposed legislation or action as well as alternatives that would have a lesser negative environmental impact.

A federal government agency must consider the potential environmental impact before any action or project is taken, and there are opportunities for federal, state, and local government agencies as well as citizens to comment on the proposed legislation or action. Citizens can also sue to force the government to comply with the EIS requirement.

The Environmental Protection Agency

The EPA was created in 1970 to consolidate all the federal government's environmental responsibilities in the United States, especially the federal government's control over business and private action affecting the environment. The creation of the EPA represented a governmental recognition that environmental protection and pollution control are interrelated and, as such, required a coordinated approach.

The EPA conducts environmental research, advises Congress, the President, as well as state and local governments, makes grants to state and local governments, and, most importantly, as an independent regulatory agency, it possesses the power to make laws in the form of agency rules and regulations to protect the environment. The EPA can also require that government and the private sector keep records and provide samples. The EPA can also monitor and inspect to make sure its rules and the federal environmental statutes are observed. The EPA can impose civil fines, seek injunctions, and suggest that criminal prosecutions be instituted for the violation of environmental laws.

It should also be noted that states in the United States have the equivalent of a NEPA as well as an EPA specifically to deal with intrastate environmental concerns.

The Clean Air Act

The Clean Air Act of 1970 was a major Congressional enactment designed to protect the environment. The Act set forth standards and limits for automobile emissions as well as for emissions from other mobile transportation sources, prescribed gas mileage requirements for different types of vehicles, and regulated fuel additives. The Act also set forth national air quality standards for major pollutants from stationary sources. The Act also empowered the EPA to set air-quality standards as well as timetables for implementation of such standards, thereby forcing polluters to reduce pollution. The Act divided the United States into regions, established standards for each region for different types of pollutants, and required a plan for meeting these national standards and for major polluters to reduce emissions. The Act also requires that the best technology available be used to reduce pollution.

However, in perhaps the most controversial aspect of the Clean Air Act, Congress created a permit system whereby permits could be obtained to construct new pollution emission sources, even in areas where the standards were met, and also to allow pollution beyond the prescribed federal limits from a particular source. Under the permit pollution scheme, if a company does not exceed, or cuts emissions way below the prescribed pollution limits, it can sell its unused pollution rights or "credits" to another company, which perhaps does not yet have the economic resources to install expensive antipollution control devices, thereby perhaps avoiding a plant shutdown and resulting in unemployment.

The states ultimately can decide what activities should be curtailed, and what local regulations should be promulgated to meet the national standards, with the EPA's approval. At the same time, the EPA can sue to enforce the Act if the states fail to comply. Also, private citizens can sue to force the states, as well as private industry, to comply with the Act.

The Clean Water Act

The objectives of the Clean Water Act of 1972 were to eliminate water pollution, make the waterways safe for swimming and recreational use, and to make the waterways sufficiently clean for fish and wildlife. Similar to the Clean Air Act, the Clean Water Act sets forth deadlines and timetables to clean up and control water pollution from industrial sources, municipalities, and other polluters. Variances are also allowed, but the Act mandates that the most practicable and then the best available water pollution control technology be installed by polluters. The EPA is again empowered to set water control standards.

The Act also establishes guidelines for proper water uses (for example public water, recreation, fish, agriculture, or industrial water supply). The states, however, are allowed to grant permits, subject to EPA standards and guidelines, for municipal and industrial discharges. The permits must specify the types and amounts of pollutants to be discharged, and they also must spell out the steps that will be followed in order to reduce pollution.

The states have the primary responsibility to enforce the Clean Water Act, pursuant to EPA rules, standards, and guidelines, but if the states do not act, the EPA, as well as private citizens, can sue to enforce the Act.

The Marine Protection Act

The Marine Protection, Research, and Sanctuaries Act of 1972, also known as the Ocean Dumping Act, regulated the transportation and dumping of materials into the ocean. The Act completely forbids the dumping in the ocean of radiological, chemical, and biological warfare substances. The Act also established a permit system to regulate the dumping of other types of materials in the ocean. There are civil fines as well as criminal penalties for violating the Act and injunctions can also be secured.

The Safe Drinking Water Act

The Safe Drinking Water Act of 1974 required the EPA to set standards for public drinking water, in particular the types and amounts of pollutants that can be present in drinking water. The states have primary responsibility for enforcing the Act, but the federal government and private citizens can enforce the regulations as well.

The Oil Pollution Act

In 1990, as a response to the massive Alaskan oil spill from the oil supertanker Exxon Valdez, the United States Congress enacted the Oil Pollution Act. The Act, which is administered by the Coast Guard, requires the oil industry to develop plans and procedures to respond to and to clean up oil pollution spills. The Act also prescribes requirements for the hull construction of oil tankers, and requires owner-operators to obtain liability insurance before oil may be transported to the United States.

The Pesticide Control Act

The Pesticide Control Act of 1972 authorized the EPA to register and label pesticides and to prohibit pesticides, as well as to set limits on the amount of pesticide residue. The Act further empowered the EPA to register and to inspect pesticide manufacturers as well as trained pesticide applicators.

If the use of a particular pesticide poses an imminent hazard, the EPA is authorized to remove it from the market. Furthermore, if a pesticide does not present an imminent hazard, but still indicates an unreasonable adverse effect on the environment, the EPA can prevent it from being marketed. If such a substance is already registered and in the marketplace, the EPA can initiate a legal proceeding to cancel the pesticide's registration and thereby remove it from the market.

Furthermore, if a pesticide is useful and beneficial, but highly toxic to human beings, it must be labeled accordingly, such as with the words "poison" or "causes severe burns." The product label must also include the antidote instructions.

The Toxic Substances Control Act

The purpose of the Toxic Substances Control Act of 1976 was to compel an early evaluation of suspect chemicals before they become economically important. The Act requires that chemicals be tested by the manufacturer to determine any deleterious effects on human beings and the environment before being introduced into commerce. The EPA also is empowered to regulate chemical substances that pose an unreasonable risk to human beings and the environment. The agency can also ban substances that present an imminent hazard.

The Resource Conservation and Recovery Act

The Resource Conservation and Recovery Act of 1976 prohibited future open "dumps" of solid and hazardous waste. The Act attempts to convert existing dumps into more satisfactory facilities, and also requires the development of comprehensive plans for the transportation, storage, treatment, and disposal of wastes.

The "Superfund" Act

The "Superfund Act" of 1980 provided money for environmental cleanup of dangerous hazardous waste-disposal sites by means of a fund called the Hazardous Substance Response Trust Fund, which is funded through taxes on certain businesses. The technical name for the "Superfund Act" is the Comprehensive Environmental Response, Compensation, and Liability Act.

The EPA is authorized to clean up a hazardous site itself, and then seek the recovery of the costs from the parties responsible. The Act also imposed strict liability for unauthorized dumping and required that a violator either clean up the wastes, reimburse the "Superfund," or pay triple damages for the cleanup costs.

Liability under the Act is "joint and several," meaning that even if one party caused only a portion of the hazardous waste, that party may be liable for all the cleanup costs, even though that party can seek contributions from the other polluting parties.

The Noise Control Act

The Noise Control Act of 1972 empowered several federal agencies, in conjunction with the EPA, to regulate noise. For example, the Federal Aviation Administration can prescribe standards for regulating the control and abatement of aircraft noise. (The Department of Transportation does the same for cars, trucks, and motorcycles.) The EPA can also regulate machinery, appliances, and air-conditioners, among many other noise-producing goods.

The Act empowers the EPA to list the major sources of noise, set noise level and abatement standards, and set timetables to achieve such standards. It should be noted that the standards only apply to new products. At the same time, there is a requirement that the best available technology for noise control be utilized in a product.

The Act prohibits the commercial distribution by a manufacturer of a product that does not comply with the designated noise levels, as well as the importation of a product not in compliance with the designated noise levels. The Act also forbids the removal of prescribed noise-control devices as well as the sale or use of the product after such removal.

The EPA is the primary enforcer of the Act and, as such, can require reports from, tests by, and inspections of, manufacturers. The EPA can impose civil fines, sue for injunctions, and recommend criminal prosecutions.

The Atomic Energy Act

The Atomic Energy Act of 1954 was a major piece of federal legislation whereby Congress created the Atomic Energy Commission (AEC). The AEC oversees the private construction, ownership, and operation of commercial nuclear power reactors. In 1977, Congress created another agency, the Nuclear Regulatory Commission (NRC) to assume this important regulatory responsibility. The NRC now develops and implements nuclear plant licensing procedures and establishes the criteria for nuclear plant location and operation.

The Price-Anderson Act

The purpose of the Price-Anderson Act of 1957 was to encourage the development of the then-infant nuclear industry. The Act required licensees to purchase liability insurance of $60 million, capping such liability at $560 million.

The Nuclear Waste Policy Act

The Nuclear Waste Policy Act of 1982 established a national plan for the disposal of highly radioactive nuclear waste. The Act also mandated that the federal government choose and establish a permanent site for the disposal of nuclear waste.

Comprehensive Environmental Response, Compensation, and Liability Act

The Comprehensive Environmental Response, Compensation, and Liability Act (CERCLA) is a federal statute in the U.S. that deals with liability for the clean-up of hazardous waste. Pursuant to the CERCLA, the present owner or operator of real property can be held liable for the clean-up of hazardous waste on the property even if it was placed there by a previous owner. In order to avoid liability, the purchaser must be able to demonstrate that it acquired the property after the hazardous wastes were placed on the property and that the current owner lacked knowledge or any reason to know that the hazardous waste was placed there. Furthermore, the present owner of the property must show that before the sale he or she engaged in an appropriate and reasonable investigation and inquiry as to identity of the prior owners and the uses of the property.

In summary, the preceding examination of the major federal government environmental statutes, though necessarily succinct as befitting this type of book, plainly should give the discerning reader a very good idea as to the many types of environmental laws with which businesses in the U.S. must comply. As repeatedly emphasized in this book, the U.S. is a federal system, which means that the businessperson must comply not only with federal environmental protection laws, but also laws at the state and local levels.

Global Legal Perspectives

The Kyoto Protocol is an important international treaty designed to reduce greenhouse gas emissions. Globally, the treaty calls for a reduction of greenhouse gases to 5.2% below 1990 levels by the year 2012. The treaty also calls for the creation of a $400-million fund to assist developing nations in reducing greenhouse gases. In 2001, 178 nations agreed to abide by the treaty. However, the United States was not, and, as of this writing, still is not a signatory of the treaty. Rather, the U.S. intends to adopt its own rules for the reduction of greenhouse gases.

Latin America and "Fundamental Environmental Rights"[98]

The right to a clean and healthy environment is now viewed as a fundamental right, often called a "fundamental environmental right" (FER). Approximately 130 countries now have constitutional provisions that give credence to FERs.

Enforceable FERs are rare, with one exception emerging in South America. The courts in Brazil and Argentina have upheld the rights of citizens to enforce the rights to a healthy human environment. In Argentina, the courts allow citizen lawsuits without the necessity of exhausting any administrative remedies. The Brazilian Constitution, with one of its aims being to protect the Amazon Rain Forest, has one of the most detailed sets of environmental provisions of all national constitutions. The rights granted in the Brazilian Constitution to a healthy and ecologically balanced human environment have been found to be enforceable despite the countervailing pressures in Brazil for investment, increased agriculture, and development of natural resources.

To further demonstrate, Columbian courts have interpreted the right of every individual to enjoy a healthy environment to be enforceable. Actually, the courts in Columbia have equated environmental rights with other fundamental human rights, such as liberty and equality.

Costa Rican courts have interpreted the right to a healthy and ecologically balanced environment as not only fundamental, but also as self-executing and enforceable. According to the Costa Rican Supreme Court, the right of all the citizens to live in an environment free from contamination is the basis for a just and productive society.

Nigeria[99] has a very comprehensive system of regulation and protection of the environment. However, Nigeria's environmental policies are rarely enforced and are often ignored. The reason is the simple fact that Nigeria depends so heavily on transnational companies, particularly in the oil industry, for the bulk of its revenue. Furthermore, the Nigerian government typically holds a 60% interest in joint ventures with the oil companies. Consequently, the government fears that enforcement of environmental regulations would hinder, or perhaps even stop, the activities of the oil companies, thereby causing the government to lose revenue and perhaps even causing the oil companies to leave the country. It appears that profitability is paramount over the degradation of the environment

---

[98] See May, James R. (Winter 2005-2006)·
[99] See Shinsato, Alison Lindsay (2005).

in Nigeria. The situation is further exacerbated by the fact of recurring government instability in Nigeria, which impairs environmental regulations from being enforced.

Management Strategies

Pollution obviously has a legal dimension, yet because it involves harm to human beings, other sentient creatures, and the environment, it also has a moral dimension. Therefore, a company that wishes to be a legal and ethical firm must first conduct an environmental audit to ensure that the many environmental protection laws are obeyed. Yet even if the company is acting legally, nevertheless, people may still be harmed by the company's polluting. Consequently, some type of reimbursement should be paid.

Of course, many jurisdictions do not have bodies of environmental law at all, let alone those comparable to the extensive and detailed laws that exist in the United States. This lack of law or law enforcement may mean it is legal to pollute in certain international jurisdictions. However, if the "legal" pollution causes serious harm to the local people and their environment, the company, if it wishes to be a moral one, should not pollute at all, regardless of any compensation to be gained.

The authors are not advocating that a company invest so much in pollution control that it bankrupts itself. Rather, if the benefits of the firm's presence outweigh the pains, some pollution of a non-serious (and compensable nature) could morally be allowed pursuant to utilitarian ethical principles.

However, the global manager must always be aware of the consequences of the firm's actions on human beings and the environment, and must never treat either in a degrading, demeaning, abusive, or exploitative manner. As repeatedly emphasized in this book, the authors firmly believe that it is in a firm's self-interest to do the "right thing," which, in this case, would be to not harm others or the environment by polluting, even if it is legal to do so. In such a case, the authors assert that the "right" thing to do is also the "smart" thing also.

The global business manager, accordingly, must recognize this duty—legally, ethically, and, yes, egoistically—to protect and preserve the global environment in each nation around the world. Business, after all, is a part of the larger global environment itself.

Summary

Environmental issues raise a great many very important and complicated legal, ethical, moral, political, scientific, technological, and practical questions for business. All such questions exist for managers on a global scale. This chapter has attempted to succinctly review certain significant environmental laws, and to make the global business manager well aware of his or her legal and ethical duty to the environment.

TWENTY FOUR

The application and scope of laws and legal systems in the international business arena have become extremely important considerations for success, performance, and efficiency in today's global business environment. Operating in the global "marketplace" means that laws are applicable even where there are no clear boundaries, no distinct legal territories, or no effective enforcement mechanisms. The international manager and entrepreneur must be cognizant of the existence, nature, scope, and reach of a wide variety of laws.

The second edition of this book has covered a wide range of legal topics and issues dealing with legal challenges facing global managers and entrepreneurs, global organizations, and the responsibilities of professionals in these fields. This chapter concludes by providing a concise summary and, the authors trust, a positive and uplifting conclusion.

Summary

The authors selected a picture of Venice for the cover—showing the "hustle and bustle" of this beautiful and unique city, encapsulated in a World Heritage site—for a strategic reason, not merely because the city is a major world attraction and tourist destination. Yes, today the city's activity is predominantly tourist-oriented, but for many centuries, through the Middle Ages and the Renaissance, Venice was known as the premier international business, banking, shipping, and trade center in the world. Venice was the transshipment point for spices and other valuable items from the Middle East, Turkey, and India on their way to Europe. The art and architecture that contemporary tourists flock to enjoy—and, in fact, the physical city itself—were all products of the wealth the city generated from this international business, finance, and trade.

As an introduction to the book, the authors selected a quote from William Shakespeare's *The Merchant of Venice*, specifically the reference to the Rialto, which is the Rialto Bridge in Venice, the very busy market area. International business was the key to Venice's greatness, and the key business area in the city was the Rialto. The Rialto principally consisted of gold and gem sellers on the bridge and on both banks of the canal. In modern-day Venice, this area is still a very busy market: The gold sellers are still there, selling their artistic gold jewelry pieces to the tourists. So the question "What news on the Rialto?" should be familiar to many readers of this book as its essence remains, "What is happening in business today?" versus the more casual and personal greeting of "How are you doing?"

The authors of this work also selected, at the opening of this book, another quote from *The Merchant of Venice*. This second quote refers to legal decrees and precedents, signifying a certain legal import. The quote stresses the primacy and indispensable nature of the law in the conducting of business, then as well as now, and on a global basis. Venice could not have survived, let alone prospered to become the Venice now known famously as the "World Heritage" site if the city's international business foundation had not been built solidly on the "rock" of the law.

International trade, finance, and business could not, and cannot, be beneficially engaged in unless there are rules of law—rules which are clearly stated, communicated effectively, consistently implemented, and fairly enforced. In centuries past, people from all over the world conducted business in Venice, all of which occurred under the protection of Venetian law. Regardless of their city, nation, race, and religion, the laws of Venice were impartially applied to all people. An Englishman or -woman or a Turkish man or woman, a European or an Arab, a Christian, Muslim, or a Jew all would get a "fair trial" in the Venetian tribunals and a fair hearing before the Doge of Venice and the Ducal Council, the ultimate Venetian Supreme Court.

Accordingly, when the reader of this book travels as a tourist to the city of Venice, he or she must take the tour of the Ducal Palace, not only to see the impressive edifice, the beautiful and priceless artwork, and the very scary, dark, dank, and labyrinthine dungeon, but also to see the many court rooms in the Palace, which once housed the trial, appellate, specialized, and the supreme court of Venice. All of those courts were there for the reason of enforcing the law, which was a critical factor in the city's success as an international business center. The Venetians may not have "loved" the Englishman, let alone the Muslims and the Jews, but the Venetians did business with them under the governance of Venetian law. As such, they surely came to know a bit about other languages, cultures, customs, and religions, and thus perhaps came to respect others more.

People who respect one another, who understand at least a little bit about one another, who operate in a rule-based environment, as well as who do business and trade with one another in a mutually advantageous manner, usually do not go to war with each other. Thus, ultimately, and in a very modest way, the authors of the second edition of this book want to emphasize those core intrinsic, as well as instrumental, values of law, morality, fairness, and mutual dignity and respect in the conducting of contemporary business, which is now a truly global enterprise. In so doing, the authors hope to make their very modest contribution to promoting understanding and respect among peoples and nations and to working toward world peace.

PART IV
Cases for Analysis and Discussion

Case Study

CASE 1: E-Cigarettes—An Unfolding Legal Quandary
for Employers and Government

E-cigarettes are battery-powered tubes that transform nicotine-laced liquid into vapor, which is then inhaled, or, as commonly called, "vaping." Many versions of e-cigarettes are very similar to regular cigarettes in appearance, including having a glowing tip. Yet, no tobacco is burned or released, which distinguishes e-cigarettes from traditional tobacco products. Thus, smoke as well as the dangerous carcinogens—carbon monoxide and tar--are not produced as they are with traditional cigarettes. However, many e-cigarettes have vaping fluids that contain nicotine, which is the addictive agent in cigarettes. A 2009 study, as disclosed by the *Miami Herald* (Veciana-Suarez, 2013), done by the Federal Drug Administration, analyzed 19 varieties of e-cigarettes and found that one-half had the same carcinogens found in real cigarettes.

Nicotine, according to the Surgeon General, is highly addictive and has immediate adverse biochemical effects on the brain and body, especially for young people and pregnant women. Sales of conventional cigarettes have been falling due to the intense anti-tobacco advertising campaigns as well as the bans on smoking in public places as well as in the private sector. Also, federal and state tax increases have made the price of traditional cigarettes even more expensive.

But today, e-cigarettes have become a "big business." In 2013, they had grown into a $2 billion industry. To illustrate, in 2008, only 50,000 of the devices were sold, but in 2012, five million were sold (Weber and Esterl, 2014). To further illustrate, the *Miami Herald* (Veciana-Suarez 2013) reported on a Wells Fargo Securities Study that predicted that retail and online sales of e-cigarettes would grow by 240% from 2013 to 2014.

E-cigarettes can come in the form of rechargeable kits, which require a larger financial investment than a pack of regular cigarettes, but that typically are less expensive in the long run. And then there are disposable e-cigarettes, which are frequently priced similarly to regular cigarettes.

The health benefits of e-cigarettes are still being hotly debated. Some health experts say that because they provide nicotine without combustion, they are less risky to one's health, and actually may, like nicotine patches, help people quit smoking. But the use of e-cigarettes by minors has doubled in recent years. Young people may think that vaping is harmless, but there may be adverse health ramifications for young people since nicotine is present. So, though e-cigarettes may be useful in smoking cessation, they may be dangerous to young people because they are attractive products which actually come in appealing "kid" flavors such as chocolate and cherry. Other health experts condemn e-cigarettes as just another harmful pollutant. Thus, the problem for government regulators, as well as public and private sector employers, is that health experts cannot agree on whether e-cigarettes are an efficacious means to help smokers quit or merely a less harsh, but still potentially dangerous, alternative to regular cigarettes.

Health officials are also worried about vaping and minors. The *Miami Herald* (Veciana-Suarez, 2013) reported that public health officials are concerned about a growing trend of e-cigarette use by minors, which has doubled from 2012 to 2013. Miami-Dade County, for example, is considering adding e-cigarettes to the traditional cigarette ban in the Student Code of Conduct. Currently, the county school board leaves it up to the judgment of the teachers whether to confiscate e-cigarettes as they would regular ones. School officials, educators, and public health officials are particularly fearful that e-cigarettes may be the "gate-way drug" or entry point to the use of conventional tobacco products. The *Miami Herald* (Veciana-Suarez, 2013) pointed out that the Center for Disease Control indicates that about 90% of all smokers began smoking as teenagers and that in 2012 an estimated 1.78 million children and teenagers in the United States used e-cigarettes last year. Why? They are perceived as "cool," readily accessible, look like traditional cigarettes, come in a variety of designs and flavors, and are cheap. They are also perceived as being less harmful than traditional tobacco products. To illustrate the preceding point, the *Miami Herald* (Veciana-Suarez, 2013) that 53% of young adults who had heard of e-cigarettes believed they were less harmful than traditional cigarettes. Moreover, the *Wall Street Journal* (Esterl, 2013) reported that in 2013 a government survey showed that the percentage of high-school students who had tried e-cigarettes increased to 10% in 2012 from 4.7% in 2011.

On the federal level, no federal regulation exist for e-cigarettes, though current law bans the sale of traditional cigarettes to minors. Consequently, the sale of e-cigarettes, even to minors, is legal. Some history is revealing: in 1994, the Occupational Safety and Health Administration proposed a broad smoking ban that would have applied to more than a million workplaces. Yet the effort was eventually abandoned due to mounting criticism and threats, including death threats to government regulators, but also because employers had begun adopting their own smoking bans. So, by 2007, 91% of U.S. employers, according to the *Wall Street Journal* (Weber and Esterl, 2014), were subject to smoking restriction policies. There is no federal ban on e-cigarettes, though the Federal Drug Administration is investigating the matter and is contemplating a ban or some restrictions on selling the product, particularly to minors. The agency is contemplating proposed regulations, but, according to the *Miami Herald*

(Veciana-Suarez, 2013), the agency needs more research as to the health benefits and risks of e-cigarettes. Furthermore, in 2013, the *Wall Street Journal* (Esterl, 2013) reported that in 2013 the attorneys general in 40 states urged the Food and Drug Administration to regulate the manufacturing, sale, and advertising of e-cigarettes in order to keep them away from children. The attorneys general emphasized that certain advertisements for the product are geared to children, for example, by using cartoon characters like monkeys, in the ads (as opposed to traditional cigarette makers who are banned from using cartoon characters).

It is also important to note that the e-cigarette industry supports a ban on the sale of the product to minors. For example, the *Wall Street Journal* (Esterl, 2013) pointed out that one of the leading manufacturers of e-cigarettes, Lorillard, Inc., maker of "Blu" and NJOY (which, according to a 2013 study, is the leading brand with a 35.6% share of the market), has come out in support of age limits. The company, which does advertise on television, also says it requires verification of online sales. Moreover, the *Miami Herald* (Veciana-Suarez, 2013) noted that VMR, the parent company of V2, the third-largest e-cigarette seller in the country, does not sell or market to minors. They voluntarily label their products "Underage Sale Prohibited," and support bans to minors. Yet, despite the preceding V2 example, anti-tobacco advocates contend that, regardless of any position by e-cigarette companies, they are marketing their product to minors, just like the traditional manufacturers were accused of doing. Evidence cited includes e-cigarette celebrity endorsers, such as TV personality Jenny McCarthy and rock musician Courtney Love, which opponents cite as examples of "cool," "trendy," and "sexy" marketing designed to attract teenagers to the product, as well as the fact that the product is sold in such flavors as chocolate, strawberry, and pina colada.

On the state and local government level, 24 states and the District of Columbia ban smoking in the workplace, but only four states, New Jersey, Utah, Arkansas, and North Dakota, have added e-cigarettes to their smoking bans. The *Wall Street Journal* (Esterel, 2013) pointed out that more than a dozen states now ban e-cigarette sales to minors, as do the cities of Boston, Seattle, and Indianapolis. In Florida, two cities in Broward County, Sunrise and Weston, have banned the sale of e-cigarettes to minors. Weston has also banned their sale in vending machines. Chicago recently restricted e-cigarette use (Nolin and Carney, 2014). Also, in Florida, a bill has been introduced in the legislature to prohibit the sale of electronic cigarettes to minors (Veciana-Suarez, 2013). New York City too recently banned the smoking of e-cigarettes in all public places. The *Wall Street Journal* (Weber and Esterl, 2014) reported that more than 100 cities ban e-cigarettes in areas where regular cigarettes are also banned. And in Idaho, Bannock County (population 80,000) banned e-cigarettes from all county buildings, including the courthouse, county jail, and fairground facilities. The reason for the county ban was that some courthouse employees complained about indoor vapors. However, Bannock County has not extended the ban to private workplaces and restaurants because local government leaders do not have enough information yet as to the health consequences of vaping. Internationally, the *Wall Street Journal* (Esterel, 2013) noted that Mexico, Brazil, and several Asian countries restrict e-cigarette sales and that France and the European Union are considering limits to the sale of the product.

The aforementioned U.S. laws, however, mainly do not regulate e-cigarette use in the private sector. Consequently, vaping at work now is also a very difficult issue facing employers. The *Wall Street Journal* (Weber and Esterl, 2014) pointed out that some companies, like Exxon-Mobil and CVS Caremark, ban workers from using e-cigarettes and regular ones at their corporate facilities. The airlines and Amtrak also ban e-cigarettes. At Starbucks Corporation and Wal-Mart, e-cigarettes are not allowed for employees and customers. Yet at McDonalds and United Parcel Service, patrons as well as employees are allowed to engage in vaping. However, in the latter two cases, it is interesting to note that the companies charge tobacco users as well as e-cigarette smokers both a $150 extra in monthly insurance premiums. Companies today certainly have an incentive to encourage their workers to quit smoking, particularly considering the substantial rise in health care costs, but employers are unsure if allowing their employees to "smoke" e-cigarettes is the answer, especially in the office. Some employees may find the use of e-cigarettes by their co-workers annoying and disturbing as well as possibly injurious to their health. Even the mere appearance of e-cigarettes in the workplace can cause concern and produce disruption. Nonetheless, some employers may allow employees to smoke e-cigarettes so long as other employees, customers, or clients do not object. Perhaps even productivity will increase with e-cigarettes if vaping is allowed in the office, since certain employees will not have to take time off for their usual and usually frequent cigarette breaks. At a minimum, employers now must be heedful of any federal, state, and local government restrictions on e-cigarettes.

Bibliography:

Esterel, Mike. (2013, June 10). E-cigarettes fire up investors, regulators. *The Wall Street Journal*, pp. A1, A2.

Esterl, Mike. (2013, September 25). States urge e-cigarette rules. *The Wall Street Journal*, p. B2.

Nolin, Robert & Carney, Heather. (2014, January 22). City limits e-cigarette purchases. *Sun-Sentinel*, pp. 1B, 2B.

Weber, Laura & Esterl, Mike (2014, January 16). E-cigarette rise poses quandary for employers. *The Wall Street Journal*, pp. A1, A2.

Veciana-Suarez, Ana. (2013, December 9). E-cigs, a new frontier for parents' fears. *Miami-Herald*, pp. 1A, 13A.

Questions for Discussion:

1. Legally, should the FDA ban e-cigarettes to minors? Should it restrict them at all? Why or why not? How would the common law doctrine of strict liability for products impact the sale of e-cigarettes?

2. How should an ethically egoistic e-cigarette manufacturer or seller respond to the government attempts to ban or restrict the product?

3. Are e-cigarettes moral pursuant to Utilitarian ethics? Why or why not?

4. Are they moral pursuant to Kantian ethics? Why or why not?

5. What should an e-cigarette manufacturer or seller be doing to be a "socially responsible" one?

CASE 2: Jobless Discrimination

President Obama in the 2014 State of the Union address raised a growing problem for unemployed people seeking employment—discrimination against them because of the fact that they are unemployed! Companies and job agencies traditionally have preferred to hire and place people who are already employed. But today, people who have been unemployed, particularly for long periods of time, are being summarily excluded from employment. They are considered to be "risky" hires.

To illustrate the extent of the problem, the *Miami Herald* (Hananel, 2011) reported on a study by the National Employment Law Project that found that more than 150 job postings on employment websites required that applicants be currently employed. The situation is exacerbated, of course, by the many people still out of work, and for increasingly longer period of times, or being under-employed, as the economy is only very slowing recovering from the Great Recession of 2008. The *Miami Herald* (Krischer Goodman, 2012) noted that in January of 2012, around 42% of the jobless had been unemployed for six months or longer. In 2014, the *Wall Street Journal* (Leubsdorf, 2014) pointed to a Labor Department study that indicated that as of December 2013, of the 10.4 million people unemployed, 37.7% were out of work for more than six months. Sadly, many long-term unemployed simply drop out of the job market. And the AARP (Pope, 2011) points out that many job listings on Monster, Careerbuilder, and other employment websites plainly state that applicants should be presently employed and some more directly state that no one unemployed will be considered.

President Obama has been actively and strongly supporting a bill in Congress that would prohibit companies with 15 or more employees from refusing to consider an applicant or to offer a job to a person who is unemployed. The proposed law would also apply to employment agencies and would prohibit want ads that disqualify applicants just because they are unemployed. The bill gives aggrieved job applicants the right to sue for discrimination based on their jobless status and violators would face fines of $1000 per day as well being imposed with costs and attorney fees.

The legislative effort to protect the unemployed from discrimination is being supported by workers' rights advocates. They say that such laws are needed to protect the unemployed, particularly due to the perception that job knowledge and skills erode over time. Some job ads state plainly that the jobless need not apply, but other companies are more discreet and weed out the jobless during the initial evaluation period.

Business groups say that employers should have the right to determine who they should hire, and not the government. They contend that there are legitimate reasons to discriminate against the unemployed, to wit: in many fields, especially highly skilled positions, being out of work for a year or more could make someone's skills and knowledge outdated and their contacts stale. Employers also like to hire "star" employees from their competitors. Other employers and business groups assert that the results of such a law will be to produce a chilling effect on hiring as well as needless litigation by frustrated job applicants. Employers may be fearful of posting new jobs if they are confronted with lawsuits. Some critics contend that the law will only help lawyers and not the unemployed. Republicans, therefore, are strongly opposed to the proposed law and with the make-up of Congress in 2014 with Republicans controlling the House of Representatives, the bill is not expected to become enacted into law.

There are also legislative efforts on the state level. According to the *Wall Street Journal* (Banjo, 2012) and the *Miami Herald* (Krischer Goodman, 2012), New Jersey became the first state to pass such legislation and one company has been fined $1000 for violating the law. The New Jersey law makes it illegal to use language in ads that discriminate against people, but the law did not explicitly ban the practice of refusing to hire people who are jobless. Also, according to the *Wall Street Journal* (Leubsdorf, 2014), in 2012, the state of Oregon became the second state to pass a law banning discrimination, but, like New Jersey, the state only passed a narrow law prohibiting exclusionary language in job ads. Furthermore, in 2012, the *Wall Street Journal* (Banjo, 2012) and the *Miami Herald* (Krischer Goodman, 2012) reported that more than a dozen states, including Florida, Connecticut, and California, were considering legislation making it illegal to discriminate against the unemployed. The number is now up to 24 states. The proposals vary; some prohibit advertisements that require current employment; others allow aggrieved job applicants to sue under civil rights discrimination laws, as they would if they were discriminated against based on their race, religion, gender, or national origin. So far, they are just legal proposals. However, New York City and Washington, D.C. have also passed jobless anti-discrimination laws.

Jobless discrimination is difficult to prove. In a case of disparate treatment discrimination based on civil rights law, evidence that one was intentionally and purposefully discriminated against is necessary. Such evidence is very difficult to obtain for an aggrieved party, especially in a case of jobless discrimination. However, there may be another legal theory used in civil rights law that might help jobless applicants who have been denied employment—the disparate impact theory. Pursuant to the disparate impact theory, if a neutral employment policy or practice that applies to all employees and job applicants, such as not hiring the jobless, produces a disproportionate adverse effect on groups protected by the Civil Rights Act, such as minorities, women, or older workers, the burden then is shifted to the employer to come up with a legitimate job-related reason for the policy or practice. Yet disparate impact cases are difficult to sustain due to the level of statistical data required as evidence as well as the fact that the employer can defend its neutral policy or practice by asserting a legitimate reason for the policy.

Since the proposed federal law advocated by President Obama appears to be going nowhere in Congress, the President, in his January 2014 State of the Union, has taken another approach to help alleviate the problem. The President wants to draw attention to the plight of the long-term unemployed and clearly wants to help them by a new non-legislative approach, which he deems to be a "positive" one. Accordingly, the President announced that he is seeking voluntary corporate pledges from some major U.S. employers to adopt hiring policies that do not discriminate against the long-term unemployed. The President also emphasized that the fact that a company that took the pledge would not be construed as an admission that the company had in fact engaged in discrimination against people out of work for extended time periods. Over 300 companies have promised to take the pledge and so far, companies actually taking the pledge include Procter & Gamble, Bancorp, and Xerox, MetLife, Morgan Stanley, Pfizer, Walt Disney, and Xerox. The President also announced a $150 million grant program for non-profit organizations to help the long-term unemployed become more employable by assisting them in finding employment.

Bibliography:

Banjo, Shelly. (2012, June 24). Measures aim to end bias against long-term jobless. *The Wall Street Journal*, p. A3.

Hananel, Sam. (2011, October 11). Jobless seek protection from bias. *The Miami Herald*, p. 3A.

Hennessey, Kathleen. (2014, February 2). Obama pushes to help long-term jobless,. *Sun-Sentinel*, p. 3D.

Krischer Goodman, Cindy. (2012, February 22). Push to ban jobless bias gains. *The Miami Herald*, pp. 1B, 6B.

Leubsdorf, Ben. (2014, January 28). Obama tries new tack for long-term jobless. *The Wall Street Journal*, p. A5.

Pope, Elizabeth. (2011, June). What an outrage: longtime job seekers need not apply. AARP. Retrieved from *www.aarp.org/bulletin*, p. 6.

Questions for Discussion:

1. Discuss the legal issues involved in jobless discrimination? How should they be resolved?
2. Is the President's legal proposal to ban discrimination against the jobless moral pursuant to Utilitarianism? Why or why not?
3. Is it moral pursuant to Kantian ethics? Why or why not?
4. How should an Ethically Egoistic company approach this issue?
5. Is the President's voluntary approach in the State of the Union the "socially responsible" thing for a company to do? Why or why not?

CASE 3: Sick Leave, Select Days, and Small Business

The *Wall Street Journal* reported in 2014 on a growing legal, ethical, and practical controversy affecting small businesses—the granting of paid sick leave to employees. The issue is complicated by divisions among legal jurisdictions and is particularly difficult regarding mandating paid sick leave for small employers. It should be noted that, according to the *Wall Street Journal*, approximately 86% of U.S. companies of all size granted some form of paid sick leave, but about 40 million U.S. workers, or about 38% of the workforce, presently do not have paid sick leave.

Currently, on the federal level, labor laws do not require any private sector employers to grant paid sick time to their employees. Of course, there is the federal Family and Medical Leave Act (FMLA), which grants employees up to 12 weeks of *unpaid* leave in one 12-month period for medical problems, such as a serious illness or injury (as well as other circumstances) that renders the employee unable to perform his or her work duties. The FMLA prohibits the discharge of the employee and requires restatement to the same or to an "equivalent" position. The FMLA applies to private sector employers who have 50 or more employees in addition to federal, state, and local government employers.

On the state level, there is a division among jurisdictions, though most states do not have any laws mandating paid sick leave for employees. Some states, such as Florida and Wisconsin, not only do not have any law, but they also ban counties and municipalities within their states from promulgating sick-pay legislation. Presently, Connecticut is the only state that requires private sector employers to provide paid sick leave to employees. The Connecticut law went into effect in 2012. Pursuant to the law, businesses with more than 50 employees must provide one hour of paid sick leave for every 40 hours of work, up to five days a year. The law does not apply to temporary workers. A survey of Connecticut employers revealed that only 10% of affected employers said the law had increased payroll costs by more than 3%. Similar bills were introduced in the following states in 2013: Arizona, Hawaii, Maryland, Michigan, New Jersey, New York, and North Carolina.

On the municipal level many cities have adopted ordinances that require paid sick days. Cities now include New York City, San Francisco, Jersey City, NJ, and Portland, Oregon, as well as Washington, DC. These laws typically require businesses with at least five employees to provide a number of paid sick days, based on the total hours worked, up to a specified maximum, usually five to seven days a year.

Proponents of such laws state that the costs of the laws will be minimal for employers. Moreover, the costs will be outweighed by the benefits. Paid sick leave will be just another cost of doing business, and a cost that applies not merely to one business but to its competitors too. These laws, proponents argue, will be very beneficial to low wage employees who are the workers least able to afford an unpaid day off. Furthermore, compelling them to work due to economic necessity may spread more sickness in the workplace, thereby harming productivity and undermining morale.

Opponents of such laws, particularly the small business community, are concerned that being compelled to pay absent workers along with their replacements will harm the bottom-line. Legislative opponents in Florida and Wisconsin, according to the *Wall Street Journal*, expressed a fear that mandatory paid sick leave laws would harm local economies. These critics say that these laws raise the cost of doing business, especially for small employers, and thus will hinder hiring and hurt job growth. Opponents point out that a large company with hundreds or perhaps thousands of workers can easily transfer personnel to fill in for an absent employee, but a small business cannot readily do that type of transfer.

One proposal discussed in the *Wall Street Journal* involved a company that has a "Select Days" policy, which encompasses a combination of sick leave days, vacation time, and other paid leave, such as personal days. The employees, depending on seniority, are allowed to take 15-25 days a year off with pay, and they are free to use those days as they deem appropriate. Supporters of this type of policy assert that it is good for morale and inspiring trust, as a Select Day type of policy respects the employees and reflects trust in their decision-making. Supporters also say that such a policy will give an employer a competitive advantage in hiring and retaining good employees and thus a competitive advantage in the marketplace.

Bibliography:

Loten, Angus & Needleman, Sarah E. (2014, February 6). Laws on paid sick leave divide businesses. *The Wall Street Journal*, p. B5.

Questions for Discussion:

1. Should there be a federal law mandating the granting of sick leave to employees in the private sector? Why or why not? And if so, should the law apply only to businesses with 50 or more employees, like the Connecticut law, or to businesses with 10 or more employees, like the Jersey City, NJ, law? Why?
2. Are mandatory legal paid sick leave laws affecting small businesses moral pursuant to the Utilitarian ethical theory? Why or why not?
3. Are they moral pursuant to Kantian ethics? Why or why not?
4. How should an Ethically Egoistic small employer act, regardless of any mandatory laws, concerning sick leave policies for employees? Why? Is a Select Day type of policy good for the employer? What about a small employer? Why or why not?
5. How should a Socially Responsible employer act, regardless of any mandatory laws, concerning sick leave policies for employees? Why? Does the size of the employer matter? Why or why not?

CASE 4: Social Media and Lending

For some time now, employers have been conducting social media investigations as part of the examination of a job applicant's qualifications for a position. Moreover, employers have been doing the same when conducting investigations concerning wrongdoing by current employees. Nowadays, however, as *Wall Street Journal* articles have pointed out, it is not just employers engaging in this practice. Banks and lending institutions are now examining social media to determine the creditworthiness or even the identity of a loan applicant. As with its use by employers, the practice of investigating a borrower's social media postings and profile is generating concern and criticism among consumer groups, privacy advocates, and government regulators.

Lenders are especially looking for potential problems, such as whether loan applicants put the same employment information on their loan applications as they posted on social media like Facebook, Twitter, or LinkedIn, or if they posted information that they had been discharged by an employer. Furthermore, an eBay investigation by a lender could uncover, particularly for a small business, poor reviews, which could impede the business' chance of obtaining credit or more credit. Amazon and other e-commerce and accounting sites are being used to assess creditworthiness. For example, PayPal is being accessed by companies to help determine creditworthiness. Social media information is also used for the fundamental reason of verifying the identity of loan applicants. Moreover, a determination can be made as to whether a business wanting a loan gets a lot of "likes" as well as responds well to its customers.

The *Wall Street Journal* also noted that the practice of social media investigations now is mainly being used by start-up lenders, which grant smaller loans, but it is predicted that the practice will intensify and spread to larger lending institutions. These companies which have commenced the practice of social media investigations typically lend to borrowers with problematic credit histories or no bank accounts. One benefit for borrowers might be that their social media examination might help credit become more available, especially for people who might be denied credit by larger lending institutions.

Of course, the basic issue is whether information gleaned from social media is predictive of the ability and/or willingness to repay a loan. Regardless, any lending institution which utilizes social media must be careful that they do not violate federal fair credit laws, for example by discriminating against certain loan applicants based on information derived from social media. And, obviously, hacking into a loan applicant's social media accounts without permission would be a federal crime. The *Wall Street Journal* mentioned that the Federal Trade Commission is going to host seminars in 2014 on the consumer privacy issues involved in social media investigations by lenders. One key issue will be what information obtained from social media can appropriately be deemed relevant, particularly in a negative way, in relationship to securing a loan. Another issue will be whether lending institutions that do obtain and use information obtained from social media will have to verify the accuracy of that information. Currently, they do not verify since they do not provide the information to a third party, unlike consumer-reporting companies, such as Experian and Equifax, which are required to verify information pursuant to the Fair Credit Reporting Act.

Critics of social media investigations in the context of lending are concerned that such examinations will increase the chances that borrowers, including small businesses, will be unfairly denied credit or will have higher interest rates imposed due to information derived from social media. Privacy advocates are concerned that social media investigations will become overbroad and intrusive. Critics are also worried by the fact that there currently are no federal laws governing the use of social media in lending transactions. Yet borrowers are voluntarily providing social media information so that lending institutions have a more complete, and presumably a better (in a positive sense) picture of a loan applicant. The more information that applicants provide, supporters of the practice say, the better the chances of a loan approval. Some lenders make the social media examination voluntary on the part of the borrower, but others require social media access information as part of a credit background check. Some supporters of the practice say that such social media investigations can help certain borrowers get credit when other lenders deny them credit based on traditional credit sources. And other supporters say that people should be accustomed to social media investigations since employers regularly do them now. Moreover, people should be aware that anything posted online these days is really public information!

Bibliography:

Armour, Stephanie. (2014, January 9). Borrowers hit social hurdles. *The Wall Street Journal*, pp. C1, C2.

Questions for Discussion:

1. Discuss some of the legal issues involved in banks and lending institutions using social media investigations to determine a loan applicant's creditworthiness. How should these issues be resolved?
2. How should an Ethically Egoistic bank or lending institution use social media to determine creditworthiness, if at all? Should it be a voluntary practice or a required component of a background check?
3. Are such investigations moral pursuant to Utilitarian ethics? Why or why not?
4. Are they moral pursuant to Kantian ethics? Why or why not?
5. How should a "socially responsible" bank or lending institution conduct itself generally in the community and specifically with regard to social media investigations?

CASE 5: Paying College Football Players: Legal and Moral Issues

Today, a major and highly contentious and difficult issue—legally, ethically, and practically—has arisen in college athletics—paying college football (as well as basketball) players. Indisputably, college football produces a great deal of excitement on fall Saturday afternoons as well as a lot of money for the schools, the networks, and sports merchandisers. And college basketball programs generate huge amounts of money too. The coaches of certain "big-time" sports schools do very, very well financially. To illustrate, the coach at Florida State's football program gets about $3.6 million; the coach at Alabama gets about $3 million; and the coach at Alabama earns about $7 million (O'Hara, 2014). Schools also use the money to build very impressive sports stadiums and state-of-the-art facilities. Furthermore, in 2014, the traditional College Bowl championship will be replaced by the College Football Playoff series, which is predicted to generate $480 million a year, compared to "only" $170 million for the College Bowl (Maher, 2014).

Yet many of the players, who have contributed, and will contribute, billions of dollars to these big sports schools, end up with very little to show for their athletic efforts, and in many cases are lacking the knowledge and skills that a college education is supposed to supply. Moreover, one commentator emphasized that by not paying athletes, the result is a massive transfer of money from young men, many of whom are poor and minorities, to coaches, athletic directors, administrators, merchandisers, construction companies, and the media (Mahler, 2014). The argument is that it is not right to deny these young athletes entry into the free-market, so as to capitalize on their abilities and consequently to deny them this opportunity, which might represent the four best earning years of their lives, is not fair or just.

Legally, there is a union organization, called the All Players United, a movement promoted by the National College Players Association that assists players to obtain more money from the very lucrative "business" of college sports. During the 2013 season, some players actually wore wristbands with "APU" on them. Treating college student athletes as "employees" would mean they would be protected by the National Labor Relations Act, and thus could unionize and bargain collectively with the schools like any other employee. There is also an anti-trust lawsuit against the NCAA, which has a policy against paying athletes. The plaintiff is a UCLA basketball player, Ed O'Bannon, who is contending that the NCAA organization is not a single entity, but rather an association of schools that have conspired together to fix prices, and thus restrain trade, in violation of the Sherman Anti-trust Act, by not allowing athletes to be paid or participate is sports profits. In his situation, the NCAA used his image in a video and did not share any profits with him. The suit was commenced in 2009 and is now in the courts.

Some sports writers and editorial commentators suggest that in addition to room and board and, of course, a college education, players receive a salary in the form of payment of about \$20,000-\$25,000 a year to play football (O'Hara, 2014). Another commentator suggests a salary norm of about \$97,000. (This figure is based on 25% of what the college players produce from all sources, including ticket sales, product endorsements, advertising, and concessions.) (Borden, 2014). Higher or lower figures could be based on athlete participation points (for example, games started and played) as well as academic achievement points (for example, credits earned and a suitable GPA maintained). Time limits and age limits can be imposed too. One commentator suggests putting the athletes' salary into a fund that they can draw against six or maybe eight years after their college athletic career is over. Financial advice would be provided and financial payout options would include lump sum, term payments, annuities, or retirement funds.

Another suggestion is for players to sign advertising and promotional and endorsement contracts while they are playing, but with the monies received being put into a fund that all the players could benefit from to some extent. Scholarships can be offered while the students are playing and also when they are done playing. That is, in the latter case, a player could play for a school, and be strictly an employee receiving a yearly salary, and then utilize the scholarship after playing for the school, if desired (which very well may be the case when the athlete does not make the pros or whose sports career is ended due to an injury. In such a case, while playing, there would not have to be any pretense of the athletes being viewed as true students.

Sadly, many large sports schools provide little real education to their "student" athletes. They offer "special" classes with little real educational or practical value, or worse, as in the recent case of allegations against the University of North Carolina, completely fake or sham classes.

Another commentator suggests a complete free-market, where colleges would bid for the services of high school athletes (Mahler, 2014). In such a situation, contracts with the high school recruits would be negotiated individually, similar to coaches and athletic administrators. Contracts might include no-transfer clauses as well as bonuses for retention and graduation. The "market" would find the equilibrium in pricing (Mahler, 2014). Yet one argument against a free-market approach is that the biggest and/or wealthiest schools would get the best high school athletes, but as one commentator noted, these schools get the best athletes anyway (with big-name coaches, impressive facilities, and a reputation as being a conduit to a pro career) (Mahler, 2014).

Paying such stipends and/or salaries might mean that the parents of athletes would not have to subsidize their off-campus living expenses. Stipends also might mean that sports agents and fan boosters would not have to illegally provide support to athletes. Most talented football (as well as basketball) players do not choose large universities with major football programs for the schools' academic reputation and course offerings. Rather, the football players are viewing these "big-time" sports schools as their ticket to a very lucrative career in the NFL (regardless of the slim odds of a college player being a successful pro-athlete).

Bibliography:

Borden, Karl. (2014, January 24). College football players deserve a share of the spoils. *The Wall Street Journal*, p. A17.

O'Hara, Thomas. (2014, January 13). Pay them and end the hypocrisy. *Miami Herald*, p. 13A.

Mahler, Jonathan (2014, January 6-12). The case for higher earning. *Bloombergbusinessweek*, pp. 8-9.

Questions for Discussion:

1. Discuss some of the legal issues involved in the proposals to pay college football players (for example, pursuant to contract, employment, labor, and anti-trust laws).
2. How should an ethically egoistic "big-time" football school deal with the movement to pay college football players? Why?
3. Is it moral pursuant to Utilitarian ethics to pay college football players? Why or why not?
4. Is it moral pursuant to Kantian ethics? Why or why not?
5. How should a "socially responsible" big-time football school treat its players as well as the local community? Provide examples of socially responsible actions.

CASE 6: Office Depot and OfficeMax Merger Approved by Federal Trade Commission

Office Depot announced in February of 2013 that it will be buying smaller rival OfficeMax in a $1.2 billion merger deal. Prompting the deal is the fact that both retailers have too many stores and too many employees as well as the fact that competition is intense. While the companies said that their merger was a "combination of equals," analysts and investors viewed the deal as an acquisition by Office Depot of smaller OfficeMax. Office Depot shareholders would get the larger part of the combined company. The deal is a stock-for-stock deal, which calls for the exchange of 2.69 Office Depot common shares for each OfficeMax share. The result would be that Office Depot shareholders would own 51% of the combined company, with OfficeMax shareholders owning 44%, and with 5% owned by BC Partners, a preferred Office Depot shareholder.

Office supply retailers have done poorly economically as demand for their products fell after the recession. Moreover, the companies also have faced stiff competition from Amazon.com and Wal-Mart and Costco, which sell similar products to individuals, businesses, and government. Furthermore, in this age of Internet shopping, office supply stores have too many stores holding too much inventory in spaces that are too large in today's marketplace. One former Office Depot executive said that their stores have become "showrooms rather than sellers." Office Depot and OfficeMax, as well as their rival Staples, have been struggling to adapt amid changing shopper habits and slow economic recovery. Staples, the industry leader, is investing more online, where it already has about $10 billion in revenue, thereby making it the second largest online retailer by sales, behind Amazon.

At the time of the merger announcement, Staples has 39.9% of the U.S. office supply market, Office Depot 19.2%, and OfficeMax 15.7%. In the last quarter of 2012, Office Depot sales dropped 12%, and OfficeMax sales fell 7%. Office Depot's market value is about $1.3 billion, and OfficeMax's is about $933 million. Office Depot has 1,675 stores worldwide, annual sales of about $11.5 billion, and about 39,000 employees. OfficeMax has about 900 stores in the U.S. and Mexico, about $7 billion in annual sales, and approximately 29,000 employees.

Office Depot chairman and CEO, Neil Austrian, asserted that the merger would enhance the merged company's ability to serve customers globally, offer new opportunities to employees, make the merged company a more attractive partner for vendors, and increase shareholder value. The merger also would allow the merged company to compete better with warehouse clubs and online retailers, company officials stated. The merger would allow the two companies to save $400 million to $600 million a year. These savings include savings from cutting employees, streamlining distribution networks, and buying fewer ads. Also, the merger should result with better leverage against suppliers. Whether certain stores will be closed will have to be determined, but a number of stores are in the same market.

When the merger announcement was made, shares of Office Depot fell 17% while OfficeMax shares fell 7%. One key issue that has to be determined is where the merged company would be headquartered. Office Depot is based in Boca Raton, Florida and OfficeMax is based in Naperville, Illinois. At stake are thousands of jobs overall, especially those in one of the headquarter cities. Office Depot has built a $210 million headquarters in Boca Raton, after obtaining

$15 million in tax breaks from the state and county. The CEO of the combined company will have to be determined, but the companies said that their boards of directors will form a search committee to choose a CEO. Both the current CEOs will be considered. Mr. Austrian, the CEO of Office Depot, is 73 years old; the CEO of OfficeMax, Ravi Saligram, is nearly 20 years younger.

The merger was approved by shareholders of both companies. As to government approval, it is important to point out that in 1997 the Federal Trade Commission prevented the merger of Office Depot and Staples. The government contended that at that time the merger would diminish competition and lead to higher prices. Nevertheless, in November of 2013, the Federal Trade Commission approved the merger of Office Depot and Office Max. Although the FTC had blocked the proposed merger of Office Depot and Staples in 1997, the FTC felt that the market had changed, specifically due to the fact that office supply stores now confront significant competition from giant retail stores, such as Wal-Mart and Target, big discount stores, such as Costco and Sam's Club, as well as large Internet retailers, such as Amazon.

Bibliography:

Das, Anupreeta, Terlep, Sharon, & Zimmerman, Ann. (2013, February 19). Office-gear suppliers discussing a merger. *The Wall Street Journal*, pp. B1, B8.

Ostrowski, Jeff. (2013, February 21). Office Depot, OfficeMax to merge. *The Miami Herald*, p. 10B.

Pounds, Marcia Heroux. (2013, November 2). Office Depot, Office Max deal OK'd. The Miami Herald, p. C1.

Terlep, Sharon, & Solsman, Joan E. (2013, February 21). Office stores' merger news jumped gun. *The Wall Street Journal*, p. B3.

Questions for Discussion:

1. Do you agree with the government's legal conclusion? Is the Office Depot—Office Max merger legal pursuant to anti-trust law? Does it create an illegal monopoly pursuant to the Sherman Act? Does it fail the merger test in the Clayton Act? Why or why not?

2. What is the office supply "market"? Is it just the three office supply "superstores" or is it broader? Why was the determination of the relevant market critical to anti-trust legal analysis? What apparently has changed in the market since the 1997 FTC disapproval of the Office Depot and Staples merger?

3. Is the merger, although now legal, moral pursuant to Utilitarian ethics? Why or why not?

4. Is it moral pursuant to Kantian ethics? Why or why not?
5. What should a "socially responsible" merged company be doing for society and the communities where it does business? Provide examples.

CASE 7: Supreme Court 2014 Sarbanes-Oxley Whistleblowing Decision

The Sarbanes-Oxley Act (SOX), a financial reform law, was passed by Congress in 2002 in response to the Enron financial scandal and collapse. The law's main purpose was to increase corporate accountability by imposing stricter disclosure requirements for publicly traded companies as well as imposing harsher penalties for violations of securities laws. The statute also protects whistleblowing activity by employees of publicly traded firms. The pertinent whistleblowing section to SOX is called "Protection for Employees of Publicly Traded Companies Who Provide Evidence of Fraud." The law allows a civil action by an employee of a publicly traded company if the employee is retaliated against by discharge or demotion or other sanctions for reporting what the employee reasonably believes is wrongdoing in the form of fraud against shareholders or any violation of federal securities laws. The disclosure must be made to a federal regulatory or law enforcement agency or to a person with supervisory authority over the employee. The lawsuit allows the recovery of compensatory damages in the form of reinstatement, back pay with interest, restoration of seniority, and any other special damages sustained as a result of the litigation, including the costs of the lawsuit, expert witness fees, and reasonable attorney fees. Moreover, SOX also imposes fines and imprisonment (up to 10 years) on any person who knowingly and intentionally retaliates against a whistleblower who has provided truthful information to a law enforcement agency about the commission or possible commission of a federal offense.

In March of 2014, the U.S. Supreme Court significantly expanded the whistleblowing protections under the Sarbanes-Oxley Act in the case of *Lawson v. FMR*. The case dealt with two former employees of companies that administered mutual funds for Fidelity investments. The employees contended that they faced job retaliation when they reported allegations of fraud and wrongdoing affecting Fidelity funds. They claimed they were dismissed after accusing the Fidelity mutual fund and investment firm of wrongdoing. Specifically, one employee, Lawson, a senior finance director at a brokerage services company, accused Fidelity of inflating and overstating expenses by $100 million and thus "paddin" the fees that were charged to investors. The other employee, Zang, an outside research analyst, alleged that Fidelity operated "veiled index funds" where fees were charged as if the funds were actively managed, but in reality they were not. Lawson resigned after complaining of harassment and the Zang was dismissed, whereupon they sued. A federal appeals court dismissed the lawsuit, saying that SOX only protects employees who actually work for publicly traded companies. Zang and Lawson together appealed to the U.S. Supreme Court.

In a 6-3 decision, Justice Ruth Bader Ginsburg, writing for the majority of the Supreme Court, ruled that SOX also protects the employees of contractors who are hired by publicly traded companies, thereby materially expanding the number of employees governed by the statute. Justice Ginsburg stated that SOX shelters employees of private contractors that serve public companies just as it shelters the employees of public companies. She maintained that Congress in writing the statute meant to protect whistleblowers broadly. For example, outside lawyers, accountants, and investment advisors who disclose fraud and wrongdoing at publicly traded companies will now be protected by SOX as whistleblowers just like the employees of the publicly traded companies they advise. To rule otherwise, said Justice Ginsburg, would leave a "huge hole" in SOX. Justice Ginsburg further explained that it made no sense to think that Congress would want to exclude outside professional from SOX protection since these would be the very people who would be cognizant of fraud and wrongdoing and thus could stop it.

Justices, Sonia Sotomayor, Samuel Alito, and Anthony Kennedy dissented, saying the majority wrongfully interpreted the scope of the SOX act beyond its meaning. Justice Sotomayor criticized the decision for expanding the reach of the law in a "stunning" manner. She stated that SOX only covers employees of public companies. She did say the interpretation of the statute by the majority did serve a "laudatory purpose," but the wording of the statute did not support such a broad reading.

The decision was criticized by business groups who feared that it would lead to many frivolous legal actions, especially by employees of small companies who do work for publicly traded ones. The concern is that the decision will grant protection to lower-level employees who now will be able to file federal whistleblower retaliation claims upon learning of wrongdoing, perhaps trivial wrongdoing by public companies. One critic expressed fear that ìenterprisingî employment attorneys will now seek out the employees of contractors to file claims of retaliation tied to any financial matter involving a publicly traded company. Even if a case is weak, employers will settle so as to avoid the potential of even larger legal bills. Moreover, the financial wrongdoing that employees can "blow the whistle" on encompasses mail and wire fraud, which have very broad definitions under the law, and consequently could include many matters dealing with the finances of a public company and the work of its employees. Another critic stated that the decision greatly expanded the number of companies now regulated by SOX from about 5000 public companies to potentially six million private ones, including even very small businesses, who now must become aware of SOX as well as other securities laws.

However, the head of the National Whistleblower Center called the decision a "big win" for whistleblowers and he also stated that the decision would make it more difficult for companies to silence whistleblowers. As a result, companies, because they are contractors or subcontractors to publicly traded companies, and regardless of size, must be cognizant of SOX. They thus must prepare themselves for SOX whistleblower claims and be keenly aware of the consequences of retaliating against whistleblowers.

Bibliography:

Fisher, Daniel. (2014, March 4). Supreme Court extends whistleblower protection to millions of small companies. *Forbes*. Retrieved from *http://www.forbes.com/sites/danielfisher/2014/03/04*.

Jaeger, Jaclyn. (2014, March 4). Supreme Court expands whistleblower protections under Sarbanes-Oxley. *Compliance Week*. Retrieved from *http://www.complianceweek.com*.

Sarbanes-Oxley Act, Public Law 107-204, 116 Statutes 745 (2002).

Savage, David G. (2-14, March 5). Supreme Court widens whistle-blower protection. *Sun-Sentinel*, p. 3D.

Questions for Discussion:

1. Do you agree with the majority or minority rationales in Supreme Court decision? Why?
2. Is the decision moral pursuant to Utilitarian ethics? Why or why not?
3. Is it moral pursuant to Kantian ethics? Why or why not?
4. How should an Ethically Egoistic contractor of a public company deal with this decision?
5. What is the îsocially responsibleî approach of a publicly traded company when dealing with potential whistleblowing of wrongdoing at the company?
6. Do you think a criminal penalty of up to 10 years in prison is too severe and draconian when applied to a manager or supervisor who retaliates against a SOX whistleblower? Why or why not?

GLOSSARY OF TERMS

abandoned property – when the owner of property has actually discarded the property and without any intention of reclaiming it.

abatement – the process of reducing gifts to beneficiaries because the testator's estate is not sufficient to pay all the estate obligations and gifts under the will.

abstract of title – usually a component of the title insurance process; the abstract shows the complete history of the real estate, encompassing prior deeds, mortgages, taxes, judgments, liens—paid and unpaid.

accession – a means of acquiring property by an addition or increase in property already owned, for example, the produce of land or the young of animals or by substantially improving personal property.

accretion – occurs when the boundary to property is a river, stream, lake, or ocean, and the land is increased by the shifting flow of the water or the depositing of silt or sand on the bank.

acceptance – in contract law, the expression of assent by the offeree to the terms of the contract; in commercial paper law, when a drawee signs the face of a draft, thereby becoming an acceptor.

accommodation – pursuant to the Uniform Commercial Code, when a seller notifies and then ships nonconforming goods to a buyer as a courtesy; construed as a counteroffer.

accord and satisfaction – an agreement whereby the contract parties agree that one will render and the other will accept a performance different from the original contract.

accountant-client privilege – legal privilege of confidentially that to a degree protects a client's disclosures to the client's accountant.

action *in personam* – a legal action in which the plaintiff is seeking to hold the defendant liable on a personal obligation.

action *in rem* – a legal action in which the plaintiff is seeking to enforce a right against certain property owned by the defendant.

active trust – a trust in which the trustee has duties, even if the trustee's only duties are to convey title to the beneficiaries.

Act of State Doctrine – the international law principle that holds that the legal system of one country will not examine and challenge laws, acts, and judicial decisions of a foreign country made within its own territory.

actual authority – the power that the principal has expressly or impliedly granted to the agent to accomplish the purposes of the agency.

ademption – when a specific devise in a will is adeemed (that is, revoked) because it is not in the testator's estate at the time of his or her death, regardless of the testator's intent.

adjustment plan – pursuant to bankruptcy law, the plan that a debtor files with the bankruptcy court in a Chapter 13 bankruptcy proceeding.

adverse possession – a method of acquiring title to real property by occupying for a period of time fixed by statute, usually 21 years; the occupancy must be continuous, open, visible, exclusive, uninterrupted, and "hostile" (that is, asserting ownership of the property against the legal interests of the title holder).

agency by estoppel – when a person either intentionally or carelessly creates the appearance of an agency relationship.

agency coupled with an interest – when an agency relationship is created primarily for the benefit of the agent who has been given some type of legal interest in the subject matter of the agency.

agent – a person who works for another, called a principal, but who also acts for and represents the principal in order to effectuate legal relations with third parties.

aggregate view of partnership – the view that partners are merely an association of individuals.

annual meeting – pursuant to corporate law, the yearly meeting fixed in the bylaws, the chief purpose of which is to elect the board of directors.

answer – the defendant's response to a lawsuit, filed with the clerk of the court, in which the defendant either admits or denies the plaintiff's allegations.

anti-lapse statutes – laws that generally hold that if the recipient of a gift is a lineal descendant of the testator, and that person is dead at the execution of the will or fails to survive the testator, the gift to the descendant does not lapse (that is, fail), but rather the descendants of the deceased beneficiary of the testator take the gift *per stirpes*.

Anticybersquatting Consumer Protection Act – the federal statute that protects Internet domain names.

anti-piracy agreements – also called non-solicitation agreements; agreements in contracts that prevent departing employees from soliciting or serving the former employees' customers.

apparent authority – pursuant to agency law, authority created in the agent when the principal by his or her own words or conduct manifested to third parties has misled third parties to believe that the agent is authorized to act on the principal's behalf; pursuant to the Uniform Partnership Act, the rule that an act by a partner for apparently carrying on the business of the partnership in the usual way binds the partnership.

articles of incorporation – also called in some states a certificate of incorporation or corporate charter; the document required to be filed with the appropriate state authority in order to form a corporation.

articles of organization (also called a **certificate of formation**) – the principal limited liability company charter document, which is filed with the secretary of state, and contains basis information as to the name of the LLC, its address, its agent for service of process, its term, and whether the LLC will be a member managed one or one managed by a manager selected by the members of the LLC.

artisan's lien – also known as a laborer's lien; the common law lien, or charge against property, given to people who worked on or who performed services on personal property.

assault – an act by a defendant which causes a reasonable apprehension of fear in the victim of an immediate harmful or offensive contact to the person of the victim.

assignee – the third party to whom contract rights are transferred by the original contract party.

assignment – the transfer of contract rights to a third party.

assignor – the original contract party who transfers his or her contract rights.

assumption of the risk – a defense to negligence which arises when the defendant knowingly and voluntarily encounters a known risk.

assuming a mortgage – when the buyer buying property becomes primarily liable for the payment; that is, the buyer is liable on the mortgage as fully as the original mortgagor.

attorney-client privilege – legal privilege of confidentiality that protects a client's disclosures to the client's attorney.

basis of the bargain – pursuant to Uniform Commercial Code warranty law, when the buyer has relied on the warranty of the seller in making his or her decision to buy the goods.

battery – an intentional act by a defendant that causes a harmful or offensive contact to the person of the plaintiff.

battle of the forms – pursuant to the Uniform Commercial Code, the situation that arises when an acceptance of the offer contains additional and/or contradictory terms.

bilateral contract – a contract based on mutual return promises.

Bill of Rights – the first 10 amendments to the U.S. Constitution which guarantee certain individual rights from government infringement.

blanket warrant – the name given to an administrative agency search warrant that allows government regulators to inspect certain types of businesses or neighborhoods for health and safety violations without any showing of probable cause or reasonable suspicion.

board of directors – the governing body of the corporation, which collectively has the power to control, manage, and to bind the corporation.

breach of duty – occurs when a defendant's conduct fails to conform to the required standard of care.

bribe or bribery – pursuant to the Foreign Corrupt Practices Act, the payment of anything of value to a foreign government official to wrongfully direct business to oneself or one's company or organization; a civil and criminal wrong in the United States.

business judgment rule – the rule absolving a director from liability for actions that do not benefit the corporation so long as the director has acted in a good faith, reasonable, prudent, and informed manner.

business sustainability continuum – a model for a business to achieve continual success by adhering to the values of legality, morality, and social responsibility.

buy-sell agreement – another legal device used to restrict the transfer of shares of stock and thus to ensure that the ownership of the shares of stock of a company remains with a small group of shareholders; it allows or even obligates a corporation or other parties named in the agreement to purchase at fair market value another party's stock that a party is obligated to sell when certain events occur; an agreement that makes it contractually required for the corporation or shareholders to buy shares of stock; also known as a right-of-first-refusal.

bylaws – the private rules and regulations governing the internal affairs of the corporation.

CAN-SPAM Act – fully known as the Controlling the Assault of the Non-Solicited Pornography and Marketing Act; the federal statute which prohibits certain types of spamming activities.

capital stock – stock consisting of authorized capital, common stock, and preferred stock.

case law – also called the common law; law expressed by judges in court decisions.

Categorical Imperative – the key ethical principle of the German philosopher, Immanuel Kant, whereby morality is based not on the consequences of an action but rather on the application of a formal ethical test to the action to ascertain its morality; a three part principle to determine morality consisting of the universal law test, the Kingdom of Ends test, and the Agent Receiver test.

causation – the presence of a causal connection between the defendant's careless conduct and the resulting harm to the plaintiff.

Chapter 7 bankruptcy – the liquidation of a debtor's debts pursuant to federal bankruptcy law; also called straight bankruptcy.

Chapter 11 bankruptcy – reorganization and continuation of a bankrupt business pursuant to federal bankruptcy law.

Chapter 13 bankruptcy – the adjustment of the debts of an individual with regular income pursuant to federal bankruptcy law.

charge to the jury – when the judge instructs the jury as to the relevant rules of law governing the particular case.

checks and balances doctrine – the fact that the Constitution gives each branch of the federal-national government powers to limit the actions of the other branches.

choice-of-law provision – part of a contract that states which country's or state's law will govern any disputes arising from the creation of performance of the contract.

circuit courts – "inferior" or lower courts in the state court system, possessing original jurisdiction.

civil law – in the U.S. legal system, law dealing with legal wrongs committed by one private party against another private party.

civil lawsuit – a lawsuit involving disputes between individuals.

clerk of the court – the court officer whose function is to keep accurate records of cases and to enter cases on the court calendar.

click-on agreement – also called a "click-wrap" agreement; a contractual agreement that arises when a buyer indicates on a computer a willingness to accept a seller's offer by clicking in a box that says "I agree" or "I accept."

closely held corporation – a corporation with relatively few shareholders where all or most of them participate in management.

closing – the legal term to indicate the transaction where the real estate contract is effectuated and the deed to the property is transferred from the seller to the buyer.

codes of ethics (or conduct) – internal rules, certain ones of which go beyond the law, which govern the professions, such as law and medicine; and now which are typically part of the corporate organization and thus an aspect of corporate governance.

collateral promise – the secondary promise to pay or perform made by the guarantor of a contract.

comity – the international law doctrine that holds that a country must respect and thus defer to the laws and judicial determinations of another country.

commercial speech – speech which is intended to further economic and monetary interests, such as advertising, but which is still constitutionally protected to a degree.

common stock – corporate shares that have no preference over any other shares of corporate stock with regard to payment of dividends or distribution of assets upon liquidation.

comparative negligence – not a complete defense to negligence, but the reduction of a party's liability based on his or her contributing fault.

compensatory damages – damages awarded when there is a breach of contract and an actual loss, the purpose of which is to make the aggrieved party whole.

Computer Software Copyright Act – federal statute that extends copyright protection to computer programs.

Copyright Term Extension Act – federal statute that extended the time periods for protecting copyrighted works.

complaint – also called a petition; the document filed with the clerk of the court which sets forth the nature of the claim and the remedy sought.

Computer Fraud in Abuse Act – federal statute that makes accessing a computer without authority and taking confidential information a crime and civil wrong.

concurrent powers – powers that can be exercised by both the federal government and the states in the United States.

condition precedent – a clause in a contract stating that a party's duty to perform does not become operative until a stated condition occurs.

condition subsequent – a clause in a contract stating that a party's duty of continual performance comes to an end when a stated condition occurs.

condominium – property which is a multistory residential property, but can be single story and can involve commercial properties as well; a unit owner has fee simple title to the space enclosed by the interior surfaces of all exterior walls of the unit as well as its floor and ceiling; all other parts of the structure and the land on which it is located are known as common elements and are owned in common with the other unit owners.

conflict of laws rules – body of laws which indicate what state's laws apply to a multi-state case.

confidentiality agreements – also known as non-disclosure agreements; provisions in employment contracts in which the employee promises not to disclose confidential information.

confusion – the mixing of goods by different owners so that the parts belonging to each owner cannot be identified and separated.

consent defense – the defense that holds that a defendant is not liable for a wrongful act if the plaintiff has consented to that act.

consequential damages – damages above and beyond compensatory damages which resulted from the breach of contract and which were foreseeable at the time of the contract.

consideration – a requirement of a legally binding contract.

consolidation – the combination of two or more corporations, with both ceasing to exist and a new corporate entity emerging.

constructive delivery – when a token or symbol of an intangible piece or property exists, the delivery of the token or symbol is construed as delivery of the intangible property.

constructive trust – one imposed by a court in favor of the settlor or the beneficiaries when the trust was procured by fraud, duress, undue influence, or mistake, or when the trustee has abused his or her fiduciary relationship or contravened his or her duties of care.

contempt power – the inherent power of a judge to fine or imprison a party for failing to carry out the judge's order.

contract – an agreement between two or more parties that is enforceable at law.

contribution – when there are two or more sureties, and one pays the entire amount, the paying surety can seek proportionate contribution from his or her co-surety.

cooperative – property which often has the appearance of a condominium, but whereas each of the condominium unit owners holds fee simple title to their respective units, a corporation generally owns the land and improvements of a cooperative; the individual unit occupants own stock in the corporation which permits them to enter into long-term leases for their respective units.

copyright – an exclusive legal right granted by the federal government to the creators of original works of authorship.

counteroffer – a purported acceptance by the offeree which varies, qualifies, conditions, or adds to or subtracts from the offer, and which is treated as a rejection of the offer.

court – a tribunal established by government to hear and decide cases and controversies.

court of equity – a court empowered to issue equitable remedies.

corporate constituency statutes – state statutes in the United States where the board of directors of a corporation may consider the interests of other stakeholders other than the shareholders.

corporate governance – a term encompassing the mechanisms that can regulate the corporation, encompassing statutory and case law, government regulation, internal company rules, such as embodied in Codes of Ethics and Codes of Conduct, and social responsibility policies.

corporate social responsibility – a concept encompassing a company acting legally and morally and also taking an active part in civic and community activities and charitable actions.

corporation – a form of business organization; an artificial legal entity created pursuant to state law upon the filing of an articles of incorporation.

corporation by estoppel – when a third party has dealt with a business as a corporation, and thus is prevented from denying the existence of the corporation.

covenants not to compete – also called non-competition agreements; promises in contracts for the sale of a business or employment contracts in which one party promises not to compete with the other.

covenant of good faith and fair dealing - the common law covenant implied in all contracts, including franchise agreements, which means that the parties must reasonably and honestly carry out their contract obligations; the explicit Uniform Commercial Code covenant requirement for all contracts for the sale of goods for the parties to act in an honest and commercially reasonable manner.

covenant of quiet enjoyment – a warranty that landlords must provide to tenants; the tenant's right to the undisturbed use and enjoyment of real property without unreasonable disturbance by hostile claimants or neighboring tenants.

covenants in a deed – usually refer to promises made by the grantee; covenants can be affirmative, whereby the grantee promises to do something regarding the property; and covenants can be negative, whereby the grantee promises not to do something.

cover – the Uniform Commercial Code rule that allows an aggrieved buyer to purchase comparable goods elsewhere in a commercially reasonable manner and receive damages.

criminal law – law dealing with legal wrongs committed against society and punished by society.

cross-examination – the stage in a trial where the attorneys ask the opposing witnesses questions in an effort to disprove their prior answers.

cumulative voting – a voting device created under corporate law designed to ensure some minority shareholder representation on the board of directors.

cure doctrine – Uniform Commercial Code rule that allows the seller who shipped non-conforming goods to correct the shipment.

cy pres **doctrine** – the legal principle that maintains that a court can name a charitable beneficiary or substitute one charitable organization or group for prior beneficiaries if the prior beneficiaries cease to exist or cease to be charitable.

debtor's estate – in bankruptcy law, all property owned by the debtor which becomes part of the debtor's estate and subject to the bankruptcy proceeding.

de facto **corporation** – a corporation not technically a legal one but recognized as legal except as against the state.

deed - the written instrument that evidences the conveyance of title to the real property and establishes the buyer's legal right of ownership.

defamation – the intentional tort of falsely impugning the character or reputation of another.

defect – in products liability law, pursuant to the strict liability doctrine, when a product is flawed, contains an inadequate warning, or is defectively designed.

defective design – pursuant to strict liability law, when a product could have been made safer with modifications that were economically and practically feasible based on the state-of-the-art when the product was made.

***de jure* corporation** – a corporation whose existence is evidenced by an accepted articles of incorporation and a corporate charter from the state.

delegatee – the new third party to whom contract duties are transferred by one of the original contract parties.

delegation – transfer of contract duties by one of the original contract parties.

delegated powers – pursuant to the United States Constitution, the powers delegated by the states to the federal-national government.

delegator – the original contract party who transfers his or her duties to a third party.

delivery of the deed – an essential requirement to the transfer of title to real property; a deed is not effective until delivered; delivery from a technical legal standpoint means the grantor giving up possession and control of the deed.

description in a deed – refers to the description of the property to be conveyed; the property must be correctly described; and any description that identifies the property is sufficient.

detour and frolic – when an employee, while performing duties for the employer, goes out of his or her normal scope of duties to do some personal business.

Digital Millennium Copyright Act – the federal statute that extends copyright protection to the creators and owners of digital information.

director – a person designated in the articles of incorporation or chosen by the shareholders to be part of the governing body of the corporation.

disaffirmance – the right that a minor has to cancel a contract.

disassociation – the power, though not necessarily the right, that a member of a limited liability company has to disassociate himself or herself from the firm.

disclaimer – pursuant to Uniform Commercial Code law, when a seller of goods can exclude a warranty from the sales transaction.

discovery – the process in a lawsuit where the parties ask for and receive pertinent factual information regarding the case.

discharge – when contract obligations come to an end; when the contract duties of the parties are terminated.

district courts of appeal – intermediate courts in the state court system, possessing appellate jurisdiction.

dissolution – pursuant to the Uniform Partnership Act, the change in the relation of the partners caused by any partner ceasing to be associated with the carrying on of the business of the firm.

diversity of citizenship – where the parties to a lawsuit, that is, the plaintiff and defendant in the lawsuit, are citizens of different states.

dividends – the share of corporate profits to be apportioned to the shareholders as a return on their investment.

Do-Not-Call Implementation Act – law passed by Congress in 2003 enabling the Federal Trade Commission to create a Do-Not-Call List, which is a registry of names of persons not wanting to receive telemarketing calls.

due diligence – a legal defense that an accountant possesses that he or she made a reasonable investigation, acted in a reasonable manner, and had reasonable grounds to believe in the truthfulness and accuracy of financial statements and reports.

due process of law – the notice and fair hearing that are constitutionally required before government deprives a person of "life, liberty, or property."

duty of care – the existence of a legal duty to act according to a legally established standard of care.

duress – forcing a person to enter into a contract by means of threats of force.

earnings claim document – document that the Federal Trade Commission requires the franchisor to provide to a prospective franchisee with sufficient accurate information so that the franchisee can make an informed business decision.

easement – a non-possessory interest in land which gives the possessor of the easement the right to use a specific portion of another's land for the purposes designated in the easement; the most common method is by grant, meaning that an instrument, such as a deed, specifically describes the location of the easement and who is to be benefited by it.

easement by reservation – when an instrument reserves an easement in lands being conveyed to another.

easement by prescription – similar in concept to adverse possession; it can arise in situations where the owner of real property allows another to make some use of a portion of the owner's lands for a specified period of time without interruption.

easement by implication – generally arises out of a legal action in which the court determines that the parties to a conveyance intended to create an easement, but for some reason failed to do so, such as where property sold would require access across the property still owned by the seller; the court therefore creates the easement.

E-contract – a contract containing all the required elements of a traditional contract that was entered into "virtually" or in "cyberspace" utilizing computer transactions.

economic duress – also known as business compulsion; wrongful threats of economic harm or financial ruin which force a party to enter into a contract.

Economic Espionage Act – federal statute that makes the theft of a trade secret a federal criminal wrong.

elective share – when a surviving spouse is dissatisfied with his or her provisions in a will or also, if no will, his or her intestate share of the estate, the surviving spouse may elect to take an elective share of the estate, typically 30%.

Electronic Communication Privacy Act – a federal statute that makes it a crime to intercept certain electronic communications.

Electronic Fund Transfer Act – federal statute that governs consumer funds transfers.

Electronic Signature in Global and National Commerce Act – also know as the E-Sign law; federal law that made legal electronic signatures.

employee – a person who is employed to render services and who remains under the control of another in performing those services.

employer – one who hires another to render services and who controls the manner in which those services are performed.

employment at-will – where an employee is hired for an indefinite period and there is no contract or no contract provision limiting the circumstances by which the employment relationship can be terminated, then the employee can be discharged at any time, with no warning, notice, or explanation, for no reason or cause, for no good reason or cause.

engagement letter – the agreement between an accountant and his or her client; professional standards require an engagement letter for each audit and review.

entitlements – the rights to benefits specified by law, or as some property developers view them, the limitations on the use of the land or its improvement.

Ethical Egoism – the ethical theory that maintains that morality consists of advancing one's own long-term self-interest but in a rational, prudent, and self-enlightened manner.

Ethical Relativism – the ethical theory that maintains that what a society believes is right for that society is the moral standard for that society.

ethics – the branch of philosophy, consisting of ethical theories and principles, that one uses to reason to moral conclusions.

equal dignity rule – agency rule requiring an agent's authority to enter into a contract to be in writing if the contract the agent enters into is governed by the Statute of Frauds.

equal protection of the law – the Constitutional guarantee that the government must have legitimate legal reasons to classify people.

exclusionary rule – a criminal law rule that holds that any evidence obtained in violation of the 4th amendment's protection against unreasonable search and seizure is inadmissible against a defendant in a criminal trial.

exculpatory clause – a clause in a contract where one party attempts to free himself or herself from liability for negligent harms.

executed contract – a contract whose terms have been fully performed by all contract parties.

executory contract – one in which the terms of the contract have not yet been fully performed by all the contract parties.

executive power – the power conferred in the U.S. Constitution to the President to take care that the laws be faithfully executed and to serve as Commander-in-Chief.

expectation damages – damages which compensate the aggrieved contract party for the amount lost as a result of the other contract party's breach of contract; that is, the damages are the amount required to place the aggrieved party in the position he or she would have been in if the contract had been performed. This form of compensatory damages is also called the "benefit of the bargain" standard for damages.

express contract – an agreement based on words – oral or written.

express warranty by affirmation of fact or promise – pursuant to the Uniform Commercial Code, the warranty that arises when the seller makes a statement of fact or promise regarding the goods.

extension clause – a clause in an instrument that makes it payable later than its stated maturity date, and which may have an adverse effect on the negotiability of the instrument.

facilitating and expediting payments – pursuant to the Foreign Corrupt Practices Act, a legal "bribe"; a relatively small payment to a lower level foreign official with merely ministerial authority in order to induce the official to do more smoothly and quickly routine government actions that one is entitled to.

fair use doctrine – exception to copyright law that allows fair use of copyrighted works in limited circumstances.

False Claims Acts – federal and state statutes that give a whistleblowing employee who discloses wrongdoing in the form of embezzlement or fraud against the government a percentage of the award against or settlement with the employer.

federalism – a system of government composed of a national government and constituent government entities, for example, states.

federal question case – when the person bringing a law suit is basing the case on the federal constitution, federal statute or administrative regulation, or a U.S. treaty.

fee simple or fee simple estate – the largest and most complete ownership right which an individual can possess in real estate under U.S. law; gives the owner the right to the surface of the land, the subsoil beneath, and air space above, subject to certain government regulations.

fiduciary – a legally recognized relationship of trust and confidence, for example in the principal-agency relationship, the breach of which is treated as fraud.

firm offer – an offer that includes a statement that it will be held open for a certain period of time.

fitness for a particular purpose – the Uniform Commercial Code's implied warranty that arises when a buyer relies on a seller's judgment to select suitable goods.

fixtures – items that originated as personal property but became permanently affixed to the real property, and consequently cannot be removed without damage to the real property.

Foreign Corrupt Practices Act – a federal statute in the United States that makes the payment of a bribe by a business person or business to a foreign government official in order to wrongfully secure a contract or business a criminal and civil wrong; but with exceptions for "facilitating and expediting payments" and legitimate and reasonable expenses related to the demonstration and/or explanation of a firm's products or services.

forum selection provision – a provision in a contract stating that any disputes arising from the contract will be decided by the courts and law in a specifically designated jurisdiction.

franchise – a method of conducting business in which one party, the franchisor, grants to another party, the franchisee, the right to do business under a certain name, in a certain territory, and pursuant to the terms of a franchise agreement.

franchise agreement – the contract between the franchisor and franchisee which sets forth the parties' rights and duties in the franchise business relationship.

fraud – the civil wrong encompassing intentional misrepresentation, also known as deceit, negligent misrepresentation, and innocent misrepresentation; in commercial paper law, called fraud in the inducement.

free invention – when an employee makes an invention related to his or her employment and the employee is not contractually obligated to invent and the employee does not extensively or substantially use the employer's resources.

frustration of purpose – legal doctrine which holds that a party's duty to perform a contract comes to an end when the purpose or value of the contract has been destroyed, although performance is still technically possible.

GAAP – the generally accepted accounting principles, promulgated by the Financial Accounting Standards Board.

GAAS – the generally accepted auditing standards, promulgated by the Auditing Standards Committee of the American Institute of Certified Public Accountants.

garnishment – a court order requiring persons who owe a debtor money or who possess the debtor's personal property to turn the property over to the court for eventual payment to the debtor's creditors.

general warranty deed – a deed in which the grantor warrants the following: 1) the grantor has good title to the property; 2) the grantee will have quiet and peaceful possession free from all claims; 3) the grantor will defend the grantee against all claims against the property; 4) all prior grantors had good title; and 5) there are no defects in any prior grantor's title.

gift *causa mortis* – a gift motivated by the prospect of imminent death.

***inter vivos* gift** – a gift between two living persons.

good faith – honesty in fact; a Uniform Commercial Code requirement for being a holder in due course of commercial paper.

goods – moveable, tangible, personal property; the sale of which is governed by the Uniform Commercial Code.

good title – in commercial paper law, the rightful possession of a negotiable instrument.

guaranty contract – a contract where a third party, called a guarantor, makes a secondary promise to perform the agreement.

habitability warranty – an implied warranty that arises by operation of law in residential sales of home and leases and generally cannot be waived by the buyer or tenant; seller or landlord warrants that the leased premises are fit for human habitation.

homestead – a certain amount of real property protected from seizure by a debtor's creditors pursuant to a state's homestead exemption.

implied contract – an agreement that is implied from the acts and conduct of the parties.

implied warranty of good title – Uniform Commercial Code warranty that the seller of goods is deemed to guarantee good title thereto.

implied warranty of habitability – pursuant to certain state statutes and court decisions, a warranty that is implied in real estate transactions that a home sold or residential property leased is free of defects.

impossibility of performance – legal doctrine which holds that a party's duty to perform a contract comes to an end when that performance is impossible to perform.

imputed knowledge and notice – one consequence of the agency relationship whereby the principal is charged with knowledge of facts that have been disclosed to the principal's agent.

incidental beneficiary – a third party beneficiary who is only incidentally benefited by a contract, and who cannot sue to enforce the contract.

incorporators – the persons who sign and execute the articles of incorporation.

independent contractor – a person who renders services in the course of an independent occupation.

information – the very broadly construed predicate for a legally protected trade secret.

injunction – an order from a judge commanding a defendant to stop doing a wrongful act.

inside information – the confidential, secret, proprietary, private, and non-public information of a business.

insiders – a broad term under securities law referring to corporate employees, officers, directors, and shareholders, as well as certain "outsiders" who deal with the corporation.

insider trading – illegal stock trading on inside information by a corporate insider.

integration or merger clause a clause in a contract which states that the contractual agreement embodies the entire agreement of the parties and prevails over all prior as well as contemporaneous agreements, promises, and/or representations of the parties.

intellectual property law – a very broad legal term indicating the variety of methods that will legally protect intellectual property.

intentional infliction of emotional distress – the intentional tort which arises when a defendant purposefully acts in an extreme, outrageous, and atrocious manner and thereby causes the plaintiff to suffer severe emotional distress.

intentional interference with contractual or business relations – the intentional tort which arises when a defendant intentionally, knowingly, and improperly interferes with the contract, business relationship, or business expectancy of another.

intentional tort – a legal wrong committed when a person or his or her property is purposefully invaded or harmed by another.

Internet Corporation for Assigned Names and Numbers – the entity primarily responsible for regulating the issuance of domain names on the Internet.

invasion of privacy – the intentional tort of purposefully intruding on or unduly publicizing the private life of a person.

invention assignment agreement – an agreement in an employment contract whereby the employee agrees to transfer to the employer the rights to any inventions created or developed by the employee during the course of his or her employment.

integration or merger clause a clause in a contract which states that the contractual agreement embodies the entire agreement of the parties and prevails over all prior as well as contemporaneous agreements, promises, and/or representations of the parties.

invitations to make offers – not real offers, but rather invitations to the public to make offers..

joint tenancy – joint ownership of real property with right of survivorship; each of the joint tenants has an undivided interest in the property; the title to the property automatically passes to the last surviving joint tenant; a joint tenancy requires the "four unities": time, title, interest, and possession.

joint venture – a business arrangement very similar to a partnership but more narrowly focused to a single transaction or undertaking.

judge – the primary court officer, whose function is to preside over and manage trials.

judicial power – a court's power of adjudication, judicial review, and statutory interpretation; in the U.S. Constitution, the power vested in the U.S. Supreme Court and other such "inferior" courts as Congress deems to establish.

jurisdiction – the original authority of a court to hear a case.

jurisdiction over the subject matter – when a case falls within a court's general, special, limited, or monetary jurisdiction.

jury – the body of citizens sworn by the court to decide questions of fact and to render a verdict in a trial.

"last resort" – an ethical principle which sets forth the conditions under which one has a moral duty to act even though there is no legal duty to do so.

law – the entire body of principles that govern conduct and which can be enforced by the courts or other government tribunals.

lease – property interests which do not provide ownership of property per se, but which do provide the right of possession and use; the owner of the property, known as the lessor or landlord, enters into an agreement with the occupier of the land, known as the lessee or tenant, under which the lessor agrees that the lessee can occupy the land for a specific period of time in exchange for rent payments or other consideration.

legal detriment – the key test under contract law for consideration; whether the promisee has made a return promise or performed an act in return for the promisor's promise.

legal reasoning – process of critical legal thinking that judges use to analyze and resolve a case.

legislative power – the power of the U.S. Congress and the state legislatures to promulgate statutory laws.

legitimate business interest – in some states, a requirement that an employer must demonstrate in order to have a binding covenant not to compete with an employee.

libel – written defamation.

license – legal right that permits someone to enter on property owned by another for some specific purpose.

life estate – an estate in land in which the owner owns the land (and structures and attachments thereto) only for the owner's lifetime, and at the death of the present owner, the title to the land passes as directed by the original owner.

limited liability company – a new hybrid form of business entity combining aspects of a corporation and a partnership.

limited partnership – a special variant of a partnership created by the Uniform Limited Partnership Act.

limited liability partnership – a special variant of a partnership created by state statute and designed for professionals, such as lawyers and accountants.

liquidated damages – an explicit provision in a contract which fixes the amount of damages to be recovered if one party breaches the contract.

liquidation – in partnership law, also known as winding up, when all partnership affairs are settled, and which ultimately leads to the partnership's termination.

Long Arm Statute – a state statute that permits a lawsuit to be instituted against an out-of-state defendant in the plaintiff's home state.

lost property – when the owner through carelessness or accident unintentionally and involuntarily leaves the property somewhere; there is no intention of the owner to part with the title to the property.

manager-managed limited liability company – a limited liability company where only the designated manager has the actual authority to bind the company contractually.

market share liability – legal doctrine that holds that damages to an injured person caused by a defective product must be apportioned based on the market share of the manufacturers who made the product when the victim cannot ascertain the exact source of the product.

material – in securities law, if information, if stated accurately or disclosed, would have deterred or tended to deter an average ordinary and prudent investor from purchasing the securities at issue.

mechanic's lien – a lien against real estate for labor, services, and/or material used in improving realty.

member-managed limited liability company – a limited liability company where all members have the power and right to manage the entity as well as to bind the company contractually.

merchant – a person or business that regularly deals with goods of a particular kind.

merchantable quality – the standard of quality for goods pursuant to the Uniform Code's implied warranty of merchantability.

merger – in corporate law, the legal combination of two or more corporations, with only one corporation continuing to exist after the merger.

mirror image rule – contract law rule that holds that the acceptance must be identical to the offer.

mislaid property – property which is intentionally and voluntarily left in some place by the owner and then forgot by the owner.

mitigation rule – a rule which requires the aggrieved party in a breach of contract situation to make a good faith and reasonable effort to mitigate his or her own damages.

morals or morality – the ethically derived conclusion as to what is good or bad or right or wrong.

mortgage – a legal instrument used to finance the purchase of real property; the mortgage does not actually evidence the debt; rather, it merely secures it, which means it provides a source from which funds can be realized by the lender through the foreclosure of the mortgage and sale of the property encumbered by the mortgage.

Motorist Implied Consent Statute – a state statute that maintains that when a non-resident operates a motor vehicle within the borders of the state, he or she impliedly consents to appoint the state's Secretary of State as an agent for accepting service if the non-resident is involved in a motor vehicle accident in the state.

mutual agreement – the first requirement to a valid contract, consisting of an offer and an acceptance.

mutual mistake – a mistake made by both parties to the contract, and which makes the contract voidable by the party adversely affected.

mutuality of obligation – contract law rule which holds that for a promise to be legal detriment it must impose a real obligation on a party and not a fake or illusory one.

necessary and proper clause – found in Article I of the Constitution; the power that the federal-national government has to enact laws that are necessary and proper to the carrying out of its enumerated powers in the Constitution.

negligence – the name given to a civil unintentional tort lawsuit against a person for acting in unreasonable manner; also conduct which falls below the standard of care of the reasonable prudent person.

negligence *per se* – the breach of a legal duty of due care which is established by a statute.

negligent infliction of emotional distress – the legal wrong of carelessly causing mental anguish, usually requiring some impact on the person of the plaintiff.

nimble dividends – corporate dividends which are paid from current corporate earnings, and which are prohibited in most states.

nominal damages – token damages awarded when there is a breach of contract but no real loss.

non-existent principal – the situation that arises when an agent acts for a non-existent principal, for example, a promoter who acts for a corporation that is not yet formed.

non-reliance clause – a contract clause which states that the parties attest that they have not relied on any representations or promises that may have been made during the course of contract negotiations and drafting that are not explicitly set forth in the written contract.

nonfeasance – not acting; and the general rule that holds that there is no legal liability for not acting.

novation – an agreement by which one of the original contract parties agrees to accept performance by a new party and also agrees to release the other original contract party.

obligor – the original contract party who must perform contract duties for the assignee.

offer – the legally recognized beginning to a contract; a proposal to enter into a contract.

officer – a person in a position of authority and trust in regular and continuing employment in the corporation.

option – a firm offer in which the offeror has received something of value from the offeree to keep the offer open.

parol evidence rule – contract law and evidence law rule that holds that generally a contract which is the final agreement between the parties cannot be modified or contradicted by parol evidence.

partially disclosed principal – when an agent acts for a principal in a transaction with a third party, and the third party knows the agent is an agent but does not know the identity of the principal.

partnership – an association of two or more persons to do business as co-owners for a profit.

partnership by estoppel – pursuant to the Uniform Partnership Act, a partnership based on the words or conduct of a person who represents himself or herself as a partner.

patent – an exclusive legal right given by the federal government to the inventors of new and useful inventions, processes, and improvements.

perfect tender rule – Uniform Commercial Code rule that goods must conform in every detail to the terms of the contract.

periodic tenancy – a tenancy that continues from a period-to-period; often this time frame is one month; and the tenancy continues unless one of the parties gives proper notice.

permitting – the official government sanction to perform a regulated activity typically pertaining to property development and use.

personal property – generally is property which is moveable and not affixed to the land; can be tangible, meaning generally that it can be seen and touched, such as a furniture, or intangible, meaning generally that it exists as a right or idea, such as a patent.

personal defenses – in commercial paper law, those defenses to the payment of a negotiable instrument that cannot be asserted against a holder in due course.

philosophy – the study of thought and conduct, including the fields of ethics, logic, and metaphysics (the ultimate reality).

piercing the corporate veil – when the "corporateness" of the corporation is disregarded, and the corporation is treated as an association of individuals.

police power – the sovereign authority that a state legislative body has to promulgate laws to promote and protect the health, safety, and welfare of the citizens and residents of a state.

pooling agreement – in corporate law, an agreement between two or more shareholders who agree that their shares will be voted in a certain way.

power of attorney – an express written instrument that confers authority to an agent.

predominant feature test – the major aspect of a mixed contract with sale of goods and performance of service elements.

preemption – in constitutional law, the presence of detailed and pervasive regulation in a field to the extent that no state legislation will be allowed.

preemptive rights – in corporate law, the rights of shareholders to preempt, or to purchase before others, a new issue of shares in proportion to their present interests.

preferred stock – shares of stock that are not common and that have a variety of preferences regarding payment of dividends and distribution of assets.

principal – in agency law, a person who retains another, called an agent, to represent the principal, to stand in the principal's place, in order to bring about contractual relations.

privity – the existence of a contractual relationship between parties.

profits à prendre – a type of easement that generally allows someone to enter upon the land of another and remove some part of it such as timber.

promisee – the contract party to whom a promise is made.

promisor – the contract party who makes a promise.

promissory estoppel – a substitute for consideration; the reasonable reliance by a party on a promise to his or her great inconvenience or substantial change of position.

pre-incorporation transaction – a transaction done on behalf of the corporation or in the corporation's name which occurs before the articles of incorporation are filed.

premises liability – the area of negligence law dealing with the liability of landowners to people who come upon their property.

preponderance of the evidence – the standard burden of proof in a civil case.

private law – law dealing with the legal problems, relations, and interests of private individuals.

privileges and immunities – the rights of national and state citizenship provided by the Constitution.

promoter – a person who develops and organizes a corporation.

proximate cause – the legal doctrine that holds that even a carelessly acting defendant is not liable for the remote, unusual, and unforeseeable consequences of his or her wrongful act.

Public Company Accounting Oversight Board – new federal agency, created by the Sarbanes-Oxley Act of 2002, which reports to the Securities and Exchange Commission, and which oversees and regulates public accounting firms.

public law – law affecting the people as a whole; law intended to serve the societal interest as well as to achieve justice.

public policy – actions as determined by the high court of a state that promote and protect the health, safety, and welfare of the people of that state.

public policy doctrine – when an employee, even an at-will employee, cannot be discharged for engaging in an activity that public policy encourages, or conversely for not engaging in an activity that public policy discourages.

Quantum Meruit (also called **Quasi-Contract**) – a common law legal device used to recover the value of products or services that were provided in good faith in the absence of any contract in circumstances where the products and services were plainly necessary, but the party receiving them could not contractually agree to purchase them.

quasi-contract – not a real contract; a legal fiction created by the law to prevent unjust enrichment.

quitclaim deed – a deed in which the grantor gives up any claim which he or she may have to the real property; the grantor neither makes any warranties that the title is good nor even that the grantor has a title claim; the grantor conveys only the interest that the grantor has, and no more.

quorum – for shareholders' meetings, the majority of shares entitled to vote in a meeting.

quo warranto – by whose authority; a legal proceeding brought by the state to compel a corporation to correct any deficiencies or to cancel its charter.

ratification – in contract law, when a minor upon reaching the age of majority approves a contract made while a minor; in agency law, when a principal accepts the benefits of an unauthorized contract made by his or her purported authorized agent, thereby authorizing the contract.

real property – generally is considered to be land and the improvements constructed upon it.

record date – the date that ownership of stock is determined for voting and dividend purposes.

recording statutes – state statutes the purposes of which are to establish clarity and certainty to property ownership and to prevent fraud; copies of deeds as well as other instruments pertaining to real property can be recorded in government offices where they become part of the public record.

reformation – an order from a court rewriting the terms of a contract.

regulatory taking – when government so extensively regulates private property that no viable economic use can be made of the property; considered to be an eminent domain "taking" for the purposes of the 5th amendment.

rejection – a statement by the offeree to the offeror that the offeree does not accept the offer.

reliance damages – damages which compensate the aggrieved party for any expenditure made in reliance on a contract that was subsequently breached; he purpose is to return the aggrieved party to the position he or she was in before the contract was formed.

renunciation – the power, though not necessarily the right, the agent has to terminate the agency relationship.

rescission – an order from a judge canceling a contract.

res – the *corpus* or principal of a trust.

res ipsa loquitur – "the thing speaks for itself"; the legal doctrine that holds that the fact that a particular injury has occurred may in and of itself establish the breach of duty element to negligence.

respondeat superior – "let the master answer for the wrongs of the servant"; the legal principle that holds that the employer is responsible for the torts committed by the employer's employees acting within the course and scope of their employment.

revocation – in contract law, the retraction or withdrawal of the offer by the offeror; in agency law, the power, though not necessarily the right, the principal has to terminate the agency relationship.

right of first refusal – a legal agreement stating that if a shareholder wants to transfer his or her shares of the company, the company or the shareholders (or whomever is specifically is designated in the agreement) first must be given the opportunity to purchase the stock based on the terms and conditions offered by a third-party purchaser.

risk of loss rules – pursuant to the Uniform Commercial Code, the rules which determine which party, the buyer or the seller, bears the loss when the goods, without the fault of either party, are lost or harmed during shipment.

Sarbanes Oxley Act of 2002 – a major federal statute impacting corporate governance and securities laws as well as creating the Public Company Accounting Oversight Board.

satisfactory performance – a clause in a contract which states that the performance must be satisfactory to a party.

scienter – the requisite "evil mind" or wrongful intent needed for certain civil and criminal wrongs, such as common law fraud and securities fraud.

scope of employment – when an employee acts within the normal course of his or her duties.

Securities Act of 1933 – a major federal securities law which is primarily a disclosure type statute.

Securities and Exchange Act of 1934 – a major federal securities law which is primarily an anti-fraud statute.

self-defense – the use of force reasonably necessary to protect oneself from attack.

separation of powers doctrine – the fact that the Constitution divides the powers of the federal government into three separate and equal branches – legislative, executive, and judicial – with distinct powers.

service invention – an invention that occurs as an express contractual part of the employee's employment.

shareholder – a holder of record of shares in a corporation, representing an ownership interest in the corporation.

share subscription – an offer to pay for and to purchase a specified number of the un-issued shares of stock of a corporation.

slander – spoken defamation.

shop right invention – when an employee makes an invention related to his or her employment and the employee is not contractually obligated to invent, but the employee does extensively and substantially use the employer's resources.

short form merger – also known as a parent-subsidiary merger; a simplified merger procedure when a parent company wants to merge a wholly or substantially owned subsidiary into itself.

shrink-wrap agreement – an agreement, typically containing a licensing agreement, contained in a document in a box in which goods, for example, software, are packaged; by opening the package and using the good, the buyer is construed to have accepted the agreement.

social benefit corporation – a special type of corporation with a public benefit, which is for-profit and has shareholders, but where the board of directors *must* when making business decisions consider the interest of stakeholders and not just the shareholders and also must fulfill the public benefit.

social responsibility – the doctrine that holds that a person or business should contribute to charities and take an active part in community and civic affairs; in business, typically called "corporate social responsibility."

sole proprietorship – the most basic form of business organization where the owner is in essence the business.

sovereign immunity – an international law doctrine that holds that as a general rule a country is exempt from the legal jurisdiction of another country's legal system.

specialized federal courts – specialized courts created by the U.S. Congress to decide specialized matters, such as the Patent Court and Tax Court.

special meeting – in corporate law, any other meeting than an annual meeting.

special warranty deed – a deed in which the grantor warrants that the grantor has the right to sell the property; the grantor does not warrant the genuineness of any prior grantor's title.

specific performance – an order by a judge commanding the defendant to live up to the terms of a contract made with the plaintiff.

speculative damage rule – contract law rule which requires that damages be reasonably certain of computation.

stakeholders – also at times called constituent groups; those groups, such as shareholders, employees, consumers, suppliers and distributors, local communities, and society as a whole, that have a stake in the decision-making of a business, typically a corporation.

state action – government action, and not the actions of private parties and business.

state supreme court – the high court in the state court system.

Statute of Frauds – state statute which requires that certain types of contracts be evidenced by a writing.

Statutes of Limitations – state statutes which set forth the period of time in which a law suit must be instituted.

Statutes of Repose – state statutes which set forth the time period in which a products liability lawsuit must be instituted against a manufacturer or seller.

statutory interpretation – the power and role of a court to interpret the meaning of a statute.

statutory law – law enacted by legislative bodies, for example, the United States Congress and state legislatures, as well as county and municipal ordinances and codes.

stock option – the right granted to a person for a given period of time to purchase a stated amount of stock at a stated price; the price is usually equal to the fair market value of the stock when the option is issued, thereby allowing the holder of the warrant to benefit from any increase in the value of the stock; the option is granted only to a company's directors, officers, and employees in connection with their services to the company.

statutory process – the power that legislative bodies have as well as the processes they use to enact law.

stock warrant – a right granted to a person for a given period of time to purchase a stated amount of stock at a stated price; the stock warrant is different from the stock option in that the latter is granted only to a company's directors, officers, and employees in connection with their services to the company, whereas the former is sold to investors.

strict liability in tort – modern common law doctrine holding manufacturers and sellers of defective products liable without fault for harms caused.

subject to a mortgage – when the buyer buying property is not personally liable for the mortgage debt, which still exists on the property; the original mortgagor is still liable.

substantial performance – common law contract doctrine holding that a contract need only be substantially performed.

summary judgment motion – a request by a litigant to the judge for the judge to decide the case as a matter of law since there are no genuine issues of fact for a jury to resolve.

supremacy clause – the clause in Article IV of the Constitution that the Constitution and the laws made pursuant thereto are the "supreme law of the land."

suretyship contract – a primary promise made by a third party, called a surety, to perform a contract.

sustainability – the objective of a business to achieve long-term financial success; attained by the business acting in a legal, moral, and socially responsible manner.

tenancy-at-sufferance – a tenancy arising by a "hold over" of an occupant of property under a lease that has expired without the permission of the landlord; created by operation of law by the continued holding over of a tenant, whose initial possession was lawful but has since expired.

tenancy-at-will – a leasehold interest that is terminable at the option of either party for any reason whatsoever; a lease which continues until either party elects to terminate it; where a lease has expired or has been terminated and the tenant continues to retain possession of the property, a tenancy at will or at sufferance exists..

tenancy by the entirety – joint ownership of real property by husband and wife.

tenancy for years – when the lease agreement sets out a specifically determinable period of time and automatically terminates at the end thereof.

tenancy in common – joint ownership of real property in which each of the co-owners has an equal right to the entire property, but there is no right of survivorship.

tender of delivery – pursuant to the Uniform Commercial Code, when a seller places and holds conforming goods at the buyer's disposition and gives the buyer notice to take delivery.

tender offer – a public invitation to shareholders of a public corporation to sell their shares.

term tenancy – also referred to as a tenancy-for-years; an interest in land where the tenant has exclusive rights to the land for a certain time period, which is often for a year or more.

thin capitalization – when a corporation is inadequately capitalized and does not possess sufficient assets to carry on business.

third party beneficiary – when the parties to a contract agree to have the performance or benefit rendered to a third party.

time is of the essence – a clause in a contract requiring performance on a set date.

time of performance – when a contract must be performed; a "reasonable time" when no specific time is stated.

tipees – people in conspiracy with insiders who illegally trade stocks based on inside information.

title insurance – insurance purchased from an insurance company; if there is any loss to the insured grantee caused by undiscovered defects in the title to real property, the grantee will be reimbursed by the insurance company.

tort – a civil wrong; a wrongful act against a person or his or her property for which a legal cause of action may be brought.

trademark – a legally recognized mark that identifies goods or services granted by the federal or state governments.

trademark dilution – unauthorized use of a distinctive or famous trademark regardless of a showing of competition between the holder and unauthorized user, or the creation of confusion on the part of the consumer.

trademark infringement – a violation of a person's legally protected right to goods or services protected by trademark law by unauthorized use of the mark.

trade secret – information that is legally protected by federal or state trade secret law, particularly the Uniform Trade Secret Act on the state level.

transfer – any change in the possession of a negotiable instrument other than its issue or presentment.

trespass to chattels – trespass to personal property as opposed to real property.

trespass to land – the intentional tort which arises when a person purposefully and physically invades another's land or real property.

trustee – the person named in the trust, who has legal title to trust assets, and who is a fiduciary and is charged with the duty of effectively managing and administering the trust.

Truth-in-Lending Act – federal statute that requires that the terms of a residential real estate loan be set forth in a clear and understandable manner.

undisclosed principal – when an agent representing a principal deals with a third party but makes no disclosure that the agent is in fact an agent for a principal.

***Ultramares* rule** – the majority state legal view in the U.S. dealing with the accountant's liability for negligence to third parties.

undue influence – when a will or a provision in the will was obtained through force, duress, menace, or a degree of persuasion exerted on another which is sufficient to destroy the testator's free will and true intentions.

Uniform Commercial Code – state statutory law governing contracts for the sale of goods as well as regulating commercial paper and other commercial transactions.

Uniform Computer Information Transaction Act – the major statute governing computer information transactions

Uniform Electronic Transaction Act – statute that holds that an electronic signature is equal to a written signature.

unilateral contract – a contract in which an act is done in consideration of a promise.

unilateral mistake – a mistake made by one party to the contract, and which generally has no affect on the validity of the contract.

United States Constitution – the "supreme law of the land"; the document that creates the government and provides individual rights in the Bill of Rights.

United States Courts of Appeals – intermediate federal courts in the United States, possessing appellate jurisdiction only.

United States District Courts – federal courts of original jurisdiction in the United States

United States Supreme Court – the highest court in the United States, possessing both original and appellate jurisdiction.

unenforceable contact – a valid contract, but not enforceable by the courts because a party has an affirmative defense.

usury – illegal interest charged beyond the maximum allowable legal rate.

Utilitarianism – the ethical theory that maintains that morality is based on consequences and that holds that an action is moral if it produces the greatest amount of good for the greatest number of people.

value – pursuant to commercial paper law, when the consideration that has been agreed upon for the payment of an instrument has been performed.

values – things that possess worth either intrinsically (in and of themselves, such as happiness) or instrumentally (because they are the means to obtain something else of value, such as money).

venue – where geographically a lawsuit will be heard by a court.

vicarious liability – the legal principle which holds that an employer is indirectly liable for the wrongs committed by the employer's employees acting within the course and scope of their employment, regardless of the employer's fault.

voidable contract – an enforceable contract, but one or both parties to the contract has the choice to withdraw from the contract with no legal liability.

void contract – a legal nullity; an agreement that has no legal effect and thus is not enforceable by the courts.

voir dire – the process of selecting a jury to hear a case wherein the judge and the attorneys ask the prospective jurors questions to ascertain their qualifications, abilities, and biases.

voting trust – a legal relationship that arises when shareholders transfer legal title to their shares to a trustee, who becomes the record holder of the shares.

whistleblowers – people, usually employees, who disclose wrongdoing by their companies or organizations, usually to government regulators, but also to the media.

Whistleblower Protection Acts – federal and state statutes that provide protection to employees wrongfully discharged for disclosing to government agencies legal wrongdoing on the part of their employers but in conformity with the requirements of the various statutes.

wholesomeness – the Uniform Commercial Code's implied warranty that food and beverages sold must be fit for human consumption.

writ of execution – when a legal judgment is not satisfied, the creditor can obtain a court order from judge directing the sheriff to seize the debtor's non-exempt property and sell it.

zoning – typically local government laws that designate certain types of permissible uses for property within a county or municipality or zoning district.

❧ BIBLIOGRAPHY ❧

44 Liquormart, Inc. v. Rhode Island, 517 U.S. 484, 116 S.CT. 1495. (1996).

Abdalati, Hammudah (1993). Islam in Focus. LCCN: 75–4382. The Islamic Propagation and Guidance Center.

Abelson, Reed, "Surge in Bias Cases Punishes Insurers, and Premiums Rise," The New York Times, January 9, 2002, Business Day, pp. 1, 5.

Adams, S. M. (1999). Settling cross-cultural disagreements begins with "where" not "how." *Academy of management executive, Vol. 13,* retrieved September 9, 2004 from EBSCO database.

Adarand Construction, Inc. v. Pena, 515 U.S. 200, 115 S.Ct. 2097 (1995).

Adler, I. (2006). Comparing Management Differences: Mexico with Canada & the United States. Retrieved July 20, 2006, from http://www.mexconnect.com/mex_/culmngt.html

Adler, I. (2006). Racism and Business in Mexico. Retrieved July 20, 2006, from http://www.mexconnect.com/mex_/travel/bzm/bzmadler0705.html

Adler, N.J. (1984). "Women in international management: Where are they?" *California Management Review,* 26 (4): 78–89.

Adler, N.J., (1984a). "Women do not want international careers: And other myths about international management." *Organizational Dynamics,* 13 (2, Autumn): 66–79.

Adler, Nancy J. & Bartholomew, Susan (1992). Academic and professional communities of discourse: Generating knowledge on transnational human resource management. *Journal of International Business Studies,* 23(3), 551–569.

Administrative Procedure Act, 5 United States Code Annotated, Sections 551–706 (Thomson West 2006).

Adnan Güriz, (2005). Constitutional Law, in 14 INTRODUCTION TO TURKISH LAW, (Tugrul Ansay et al. eds.). Kluwer Law International.

Advertising, "Complaints bring down Spanish ads in Miami," The Miami Herald, March 18, 2006, p. C1.

Aero Kool Corp. v. Oosthuizen, 736 So.2d 25 (Florida Appeals 1999).

Age Discrimination Act of 1967, 29 United States Code Annotated, Sections 621–634 (Thomson/West 2006).

Alfonso, M.E. (2005). Deloitte Mexico Named Socially Responsible Enterprise for the Fifth Consecutive Year. Retrieved July 20, 2006, from http://www.deloitte.com/dtt/press_release/0,1014,cid%253D77003%2526pv%253DY,00.html

Allen, Michael, "U.S. Retirees Fuel Yucatan Land Grab," The Wall Street Journal, April 18, 2006, pp. D1, D2.

Allen, Moira, "Here Comes the Bribe," Entrepreneur, October 2000, p. 48.

All Pro Sports Camp, Inc. v. Walt Disney Co., 727 So.2d 363 (Florida Appeals 1999).

American Civil Liberties Union v. Michael B. Mukasey, 534 F.3d 181 (3rd Circuit 2008), *cert. denied Mukasey v. ACLU*, 2009 U.S. LEXIS 598 (2009).

Americans with Disabilities Act of 1990, 42 United States Code Sections 12102–12118).

Americans with Disabilities Act of 1990, 42 United States Code Annotated, Sections 12102–12118 (Thomson/West 2006).

A&M Records, Inc. v. Napster, Inc., 239 F.3d 1004 (9th Circuit 2001).

Angleynn Meya, "Reverse Migration: Americans in Mexico," Vol. 18 Probate and Property, pp. 57–62 (July-August 2004).

Anonymous, (1993). Price quotations and terms of sale are key to successful exporting. Business America (October,4): 12–15.

Anticybersquatting Consumer Protection Act of 1999, 15 United States Code Section 1125–1129.

Anticybersquatting Consumer Protection Act, 15 United States Code Annotated Section 1125 (Thomson West 2006).

Appleby, Julie, "Judge overturns Wal-Mart law," USA TODAY, July 30, 2006, p. 3B.

Areddy, James T., "Beijing Defines Corporate Secrets," *The Wall Street Journal*, April 27, 2010, p. A13.

Armour, Stephanie, "Borrowers Hit Social Hurdles," *The Wall Street Journal*, January 9, 2014, pp. C1, C2.

Article 35 in the Official Gazette (*Resmi Gazete*) dated July 19, 2003 and numbered 25173, and dated January 7, 2005 and numbered 26046.

Article 35 in the Official Gazette (*Resmi Gazete*) dated July 19, 2003 and numbered 25173, and dated January 7, 2005 and numbered 26046.

Associated Press, "judge OKs $143 million in CD antitrust lawsuit," Sun Sentinel, December 5, 2003, p. 9A.

Associated Press, "Martha Stewart to Fight Civil Case," The Wall Street Journal, May 27–28, 2006, p. B3.

Associated Press, "Martha Stewart to Fight Civil Case," The Wall Street Journal, May 27–28. 2006, p. B3.

August, Ray (2004). International Business Law (4th edition). Pearson-Prentice Hall.

Ayman, Roya & Chemers, Martin M. 1983. Relationship of supervisory behavior ratings to work group effectiveness and subordinate satisfactions among Iranian managers. *Journal of Applied Psychology*, 68(2): 338–341.

Bagley, Constance E. and Dauchy, Craig E. (2008). *The Entrepreneur's Guide to Business Law*. United States: Thomson/West.

Bagley, Constance E., Managers and the Legal Environment (4th edition), West-Thomson Learning (2002).

Bahamas Handbook and Businessman's Annual, (2003–2004). Dupuch Publications, Nassau, Bahamas.

Baier, Elizabeth, "Court's gay marriage ruling has impact on South Florida," Sun-Sentinel, March 31, 2006, p. 1B.

Bakhtari, Hassan 1995. Cultural effects on management style: A comparative study of American and Middle Eastern management styles. *International Studies of Management and Organization*, 25(3): 97–118.

Ball, Jeffrey, "Chrysler-Case Jury Orders Big Payment, The Wall Street Journal, February 19, 1999, p. B1.

Banjo, Shelly, "Measures Aim to End Bias Against Long-Term Jobless," *The Wall Street Journal*, March 24, 2012, p. A3.

Barber, Tom, "Beyond Noncompete Agreements: Using Florida's Trade Secrets Act to Prevent Former Employees from Disclosing Sensitive Information to Competitors," The Florida Bar Journal, March 1998, pp. 10–19.

Baris, Tan, Overview of the Turkish Textile and Apparel Industry, Harvard Center for Textile and Apparel Industry, 8–9, 2001. This is a report providing an overview of the Turkish textile sector.

Barr, robert, "Shares of gambling websites tumble," The Miami Herald, October 3, 2006, p. 2C.

Baro-Diaz, Madeline, "Terror arrests prompt outcry," Sun-Sentinel, June 30, 2006, pp. 1B, 2B.

Bartels, Natalia M, and Madden, M. Stuart, "A Comparative Analysis of United States and Colombian Tort Laws: Duty, Breach, and Damages," Vol. 13 Pace International Law Review, pp. 59–91 (Spring 2001).

Batson, Andrew, "Antitrust Measure Wins Backing Of China's Cabinet," The Wall Street Journal, June 8, 2006, p. A7.

Batson, Andrew, "Antitrust Measure Wins Backing of China's Cabinet," The Wall Street Journal, June 8, 2006, p. A8.

Batson, Andrew, "China Antitrust Law May Alter Global Acquisitions Landscape," The Wall Street Journal, November 3, 2005, p. A11.

Bauer, T. Zimmermann K (1999). Immigration Policy in Integrated National Economies. AICGS Research Report No. 10 Washington D.C, 15–30

BBC News. Mexico Fines US Hotel in Cuba Row. Retrieved July 20, 2006, from http://news.bbc.co.uk/2/hi/americas/4778268.stm

Beatty, Sally, and Simons, John, "FTC Eyes Liquor ads' Kid-Appeal," The Wall Street Journal, August 7, 1998, pp. B1, B6.

Belasco v. Gulf Auto Holding, Inc., 707 So.2d 858 (Florida Appeals 1998).

Ben-Zion, Yael, T., "The Political Dynamics of Corporate Legislation: Lessons from Israel," 11 Fordham Journal of Corporate and Financial Law, pp. 185–339 (2006).

Bennett-Alexander, Dawn D., and Harrison, Linda F. (2012). The Legal, Ethical, and Regulatory Environment of Business in a Diverse Society. New York: McGraw-Hill Irvin.

Bergen, Kathy, and Kleiman, Carol, "$34 Million Mitsubishi Settlement A Wake-Up Call To Employers," Chicago Tribune, June 11, 1998, Business News, pp. 1, 5.

Bianco, Anthony, "Ken Lay's Audacious Ignorance," Business Week, February 6, 2006, pp. 58–59.

Bierman, Noah, "Verdict against gun firm in teacher's death is rejected," The Herald. January 28, 2003, 1A, 2A.

Bhargava, V. (2005). *The Cancer of Corruption.* Retrieved April 2, 2006, from http://web.worldbank.org/WBSITE/EXTERNAL/EXTABOUTUS/0,

Black's Law Dictionary (5th edition), West Publishing Company, St. Paul, MN (1979).

Black, J. Stewart & Mendenhall, Mark (1990). Cross-cultural training effectiveness: A review and a theoretical framework for future research. *Academy of Management Review*, 15(1): 113–136.

Black, J. Stewart & Porter, Lyman W. (1991). Managerial behavior and job performance: A successful manager in Los Angeles may not succeed in Hong Kong. *Journal of International Business Studies*, 22(1): 99–113.

BMW of North America, Inc. v. Gore, 517 U.S. 559, 116 S.Ct. 1589, 1996.

Boreale, Michael, "Beachfront Property in Arizona? Loosening Restrictions on Foreign Acquisition of Mexican Real Estate and the Implications for Arizona Investors," 22 Arizona Journal of International and Comparative Law, pp. 389–412 (Summer 2005).

Boslet, Mark, "U.S. Court Likely Will Force Google To Turn Over Data," The Wall Street Journal, March 15, 2006, p. B2.

Boudreaux, Karol C., "The Human Face of Resource Conflict: Property and Power in Nigeria," 7 San Diego International Law Journal, pp. 61–102 (2005).

Bowen, Brian D., "Drafting and Negotiating Effective Confidentiality Agreements," Texas Bar Journal, June 1996, pp. 524–532.

Branch, Karen, "Suit against gun industry takes broad aim," The Herald, January 23, 1999, p. 11B.

Branch, Shelly, "Is Food the Next Tobacco"? The Wall Street Journal, June 13, 2002, pp. B1, B9.

Branom, Mike, "Family files suit over Epcot," Sun-Sentinel, November 20, 2002, p. 3D.

Branon, Mike, "Disney: Epcot ideas not stolen," The Miami Herald, November 14, 2000, p. A22.

Bravin, Jess, "California Can't Curb Children's Access to Videogames," *The Wall Street Journal*, June 28, 2011, p. A6.

Bravin, Jess, "High Court Eases Way To Liability Lawsuits," *The Wall Street Journal*, March 5, 2009, p. A1.

Bravin, Jess, "Justices Extend Protection Over Workplace Retaliation," *The Wall Street Journal*, January 25, 2011, p. B1.

Bravin, Jess, "Justices Split on Violent Games," *The Wall Street Journal*, November 3, 2010, p. B4.

Bravin, Jess, and Jordan, Miriam, "Justices Uphold Immigrant Law," *The Wall Street Journal*, May 27, 2011, pp. A1, A2.

Bravin, Jess, and Radnofsky, Louise, "Court Backs Obama on Health Law," *The Wall Street Journal*, June 29, 2012, pp. A1, A4.

Bravin, Jess and Sataline, Suzanne, "Ruling Upends Race's Role in Hiring," *The Wall Street Journal*, June 30, 2009, pp. A1, A4.

Bravin, Jess and Wingfield, Nick, "Top Court Is Next Level for Games," *The Wall Street Journal*, November 1, 2010, p. B1.

Bravin, Jess, and Zimmerman, Amy, "Justices Curb Class Actions," *The Wall Street Journal*, June 21, 2011, pp. A1, A4.

Bravin, Jess, "Court Upholds Eminent Domain," Wall Street Journal, June 24, 2005, pp. A3, A10.

Bravin, Hess, and O'Connell, Vanessa, "High Court Rejects Limits on Out-of-State Wineries," *Wall Street Journal*, May 17, 2005, pp. A1, A6.

Bray, Ilan, "A Company's Threat: Quit Smoking or Leave," The Wall Street Journal, December 20, 2005, pp. D1, D6.

Bravin, Jess, "Split Court Ends Ban on Retail-Price Floor," *The Wall Street Journal*, June 29, 2007, p. 2.

Bray, Chad, "Former Hedge-Fund Manager Is Sentenced," *The Wall Street Journal*, January 25, 2013, p. C3.

Bray, Chad, "Fund Co-Founder Sentenced in Insider Case," *The Wall Street Journal*, May 14, 2013, p. C3.

Bray, Chad, "Goldman Thief Gets 8 Years," *The Wall Street Journal*, March 19-20, 2010, p. B5.

Breed, Allen G., "Company wants to recruit Hispanics," The Miami Herald, February 18, 2006, p. 3C.

Briefs, "Europe: MasterCard Faces Price-Fixing Charge," The Miami Herald, July 1, 2006, p. 2C.

Brinton,C., Christopher, J. ,Wolff, R and Winks, R.(1984). A History of Civilization. Vol I . NJ Prentice Hall.

Broder, David, "Rulings say racial discrimination has eased,"The Miami Herald, July 3, 2009, p. 21A.

Brown v. Entertainment Merchants Association, 2011 U.S. LEXIS 4802 (2011).

Browning, Michael, "Jury: RJR tobacco not liable," The Herald, May 6, 1997, pp. 1A, 12A.

Bryant, Howard, "Yankees tell El Duque to speak English," Sun Sentinel, July 2, 2001, pp. 1C, 5C.

Buchan, David, "French put new take on bribes,"The Financial Times, February 8, 1997, p. 9.

Buckley, Cara, Consumers stake claim for CD settlement,"The Miami Herald, January 23, 2003, p. C1.

Buckman, Rebecca, "China Hurries Antitrust Law," The Wall Street Journal, June 11, 2004, p. A7.

Burkitt, Laurie and Matthews, Christopher M., "Glaxo Junkets Highlight Ills of Chinese Medical System," *The Wall Street Journal*, August 19, 2013, pp. B1, B7.

Burkins, Glen, "Grower Tanimura & Antle Agrees to Pay Nearly $1.9 Million in Harassment Case,"The Wall Street Journal, February 24, 1999, p. B2.

Burlington Industries v. Ellerth, 524 U.S. 742, 118 S.Ct. 2257 (1998).

Burstein, John, "Gym found liable in man's death," Sun-Sentinel, March 30, 2006, p. 6B.

Business Briefs, "Cruise Lines: Regulators Approve Roman Terminal," The Miami Herald, May 6, 2006, p. 3C.

Business Briefing, "Alamo loses bias lawsuit," Sun Sentinel, May 31, 2006, p. D1.

Butler, John K. Jr. & Cantrell, R. Stephen (1997). Effects of perceived leadership behaviors on job satisfaction and productivity. *Psychological Reports*, 80: 976–977.

Calamari, John D., and Perillo, Joseph M. (1987). Contracts (3rd edition). West Publishing Company Hornbook Series, St Paul, MN.

Campbell, A. M. (2006). *What Constitutes Employer's Reasonable Accommodation of Employee's Religious Preferences Under Title VII of Civil Rights Act of 1964, 134 A.L.R. Fed. 1*

Carey, Pete and Johnson, Steve, "'Expert networks' suspected before," *Sun-Sentinel*, November 30, 2010, p. 3D.

Carlton, Jim, "Cities Take Lead on Antibias Law," *The Wall Street Journal*, May 29, 2013, p. A6.

Carney, Dan, "Predatory Pricing: Cleared For Takeoff," Business Week, May 14, 2001, p. 50.

Carrell, Michael R. & Heavrin, Christina (2004). Labor Relations and Collective Bargaining: Cases, Practice, and Law, (7th Edition). Upper Saddle River: Pearson-Prentice Hall.

Cassell, Bryan-Low, "U.K. Sets Bribe Law Guidance," *The Wall Street Journal*, March 31, 2011, p. B2.

Cateora, P. (1993). International marketing. New York: Irwin

Cateora, Phillip and John Graham (2005), International Marketing, 12th Edition, McGraw Hill Irwin.

Cavico, F.J., (2003). The Tort of Intentional Infliction of Emotional Distress in the Private Employment Sector. Hofstra Labor and Employment Law Journal, Vol. 21, No. 1, pp. 109–182.

Cavico, F. J., (2002). Tortious Interference with Contract in the At-Will Employment Context. University of Detroit Mercy Law Review, Vol. 79, No. 4, pp. 503–569.

Cavico, Frank, "Business Plans and Strategies as Legally Protected Trade Secrets: Florida and National Perspectives," Vol. 9, Numbers 1 & 2, University of Miami Business Law Review 1–66 (Winter 2001).

Cavico, Frank, "Extraordinary or Specialized Training as a Legitimate Business Interest in Restrictive Covenant Employment Law: Florida and National Perspectives," Volume 14, No. 1 St. Thomas Law Review 53–107 (Fall 2001).

Cavico, F.J. (1999). "Defamation in the Private Sector: The Libelous and Slanderous Employer." Dayton Law Review, Vol. 24, No. 3, pp. 405–489.

Cavico, Frank J., "Fraudulent, Negligent, and Innocent Misrepresentation in the Employment Context: The Deceitful, Negligent, and Thoughtless Employer," Vol. 20 Campbell Law Review 1–90 (Winter 1997).

Cavico, Frank J., "Private Sector Whistleblowing and the Employment At-Will Doctrine: A Comparative Legal, Ethical, and Pragmatic Analysis," Vol. 45 South Texas Law Review 543–645 (Summer 2004).

Cavico, Frank J. "The Covenant of Good Faith and Fair Dealing in the Franchise Business Relationship," Vol. 6, Barry law Review, pp. 61–104. (2006).

Cavico, Frank C., Muffler, Stephen C., and Mujtaba, Bahaudin G. (2012). Appearance Discrimination, "Lookism," and "Lookphobia" in the Workplace. *Journal of Applied Business Research*, Vol. 28(5), pp. 791–802.

Cavico, Frank C., Muffler, Stephen C., and Mujtaba, Bahaudin G. (2012). Language Diversity and Discrimination in the American Workplace: Legal, Ethical, and Practical Considerations for Management. *Journal of International Business and Cultural Studies*, Vol. 7, No. 2, pp. 1–39.

Cavico, Frank C., Muffler, Stephen C., and Mujtaba, Bahaudin G. (2012). Sexual Orientation and Gender Identity Discrimination in the American Workplace: Legal and Ethical Considerations. *International Journal of Humanities and Social Sciences*, Vol. 2(1), pp. 1–20.

Cavico, Frank J. and Mujtaba, Bahaudin G. (2012). Age Discrimination in the American Workplace: Legal Analysis and Recommendations for Employers and Employees. *International Review of Social Sciences and Humanities*, Vol. 3(2), pp. 161–85.

Cavico, Frank J. and Mujtaba, Bahaudin G. (2011). *Baksheesh or Bribe: Cultural Conventions and Legal Pitfalls*. Davie, Florida: ILEAD Academy, LLC.

Cavico, Frank J. and Mujtaba, Bahaudin G. (Third Edition 2013). *Business Ethics: The Moral Foundation of Effective Leadership, Management, and Entrepreneurship*. Boston, Massachusetts: Pearson Custom Publishing.

Cavico, Frank J. and Mujtaba, Bahaudin G. (2013). *Business Law for the Entrepreneur and Manager* (Third Edition). Davie, Florida: ILEAD Academy, LLC.

Cavico, Frank J. and Mujtaba, Bahaudin (2012). Discrimination and the Aging American Workforce: Legal Analysis and Management Strategies. *Journal of Legal Issues and Cases in Business*, Vol. 1, May 2012, pp. 28–66.

Cavico, Frank J. and Mujtaba, Bahaudin (2012). National and Global Perspectives of Corporate Social Responsibility. *International Journal of Management Sciences and Business Research*, Vol. 1, No. 3, pp. 1–24.

Cavico, Frank J. and Mujtaba, Bahaudin G. (2012). Office Romance: Legal Challenges and Strategic Implications. *International Journal of Management, IT, and Engineering*, Vol. 2(8), pp. 10–35.

Cavico, Frank J. and Mujtaba, Bahaudin G. (2011). Reasonable Accommodation Dilemmas for Muslim-American Employees' Religious Beliefs. *Proficient: An International Journal of Management*, Vol. 3(IX), pp. 7–33.

Cavico, Frank J. and Mujtaba, Bahaudin (2012). Social Responsibility, Corporate Constituency Statutes, and the Social Benefit Corporation. *International Journal of Management and Administrative Sciences*, Vol. 1, No. 7, pp. 21–25.

Cavico, Frank J. and Mujtaba, Bahaudin G. (2010). Baksheesh or Bribe: Payments to Government Officials and the Foreign Corrupt Practices Act. *Journal of Business Studies Quarterly*, Vol. 2, No. 1, pp. 83–105.

Cavico, Frank J. and Mujtaba, Bahaudin G. (2011). Employment Discrimination and Muslims in America. *Journal for Global Business Advancement*, Vol. 4(3), pp. 279–297.

Cavico, Frank J. and Mujtaba, Bahaudin G. (2011). Managers Be Warned! Third Party Retaliation Lawsuits and the United States Supreme Court. *International Journal of Business and Social Sciences*, Vol. 10, No. 3, pp. 17–28.

Cavico, F. J., and Mujtaba, B. G. (2005). *Business Ethics: Transcending Requirements through Moral Leadership*. Pearson Custom Publishers.

Chamber of Commerce of the United States v. Whiting, 2011 U.S. LEXIS 4018 (2011).

Chazan, Guy, "Russia to Tighten Access to Oil and Gas Reserves," The Wall Street Journal, June 14, 2006, p. A7.

Cheeseman, Henry R. (2004), Business Law (5th edition), Pearson/Prentice Hall.

Cheeseman, Henry R. (2007), The Legal Environment of Business and Online Commerce (5th edition), Pearson/Prentice Hall.

Chemers, Martin M. 1969. Cross-cultural training as a means of improving situational favorableness. *Human Relations*, 22(6): 531–546.

Chemers, Martin M. & Ayman, Roya 1985. Leadership orientation as a moderator of the relationship between job performance and job satisfaction of Mexican managers. *Personality and Social Psychology Bulletin*, 11(4): 359–367.

Christopher Deliso, *Investing in Turkey: Incentives, Conditions, Getting Started*, from http://www.escapeartist.com/efam/38/CD_Turkey.html.

Cihan New Agency: Economy News, "Turkey Attracts Record Foreign Investment of $8.1 Billion in January"—May 2006, July 13, 2006, from http://www.cia.gov/cia/publications/factbook/geos/tu.html#EconCIA Government, (2006), Retrieved on July 30, 2006 From www.cia.gov *Circuit City Store, Inc. v. Adams*, 532 U.S. 105, 121 S.Ct 1302 (2001).

Citizens United v. Federal Election Commission, 130 S.Ct. 876 (2010).

Civil Rights Act of 1964, Title VII, 42 United States Code Annotated, Sections 2000e–2000e–17 (Thomson/West 2006).

Clarkson, Kenneth W., Miller, Roger LeRoy, and Cross, Frank B. (2012). *Business Law Text and Cases: Legal, Ethical, Global, and Corporate Environment* (12th edition).

Clark, Kim, "Noncompete contracts: Be loyal or see you in court, employers warn workers," U.S. News & World Report, December 18, 2006, pp. 63–64.

Clarkson, Kenneth W., Miller, Roger LeRoy, Jentz, Gaylord A., and Cross, Frank B., Business Law (9th edition). Thomson-West, 2004.

Clayton Act of 1914, 15 United States Code Annotated, Section 14, as amended by the Celler-Kefauver Act of 1950, 15 United States Code Annotated, Section18 (Thomson/West 2006).

Clean Air Act, 42 United States Code Annotated Sections 7401 et seq. (Thomson/West 2006).

Clean Water Act, 33 United States Code Annotated Sections 1251–1387, as amended by the Water Quality Act of 1987 (Thomson/West 2006).

Coca-Cola Company v. Koke Company of America, 254 U.S. 143, 41 S.Ct. 113 (1920).

Coffee, John C., Jr., "Outsider Trading, That New Crime," The Wall Street Journal, November 14, 1990, p.A16.

Cohen, Adam, "China's Draft Antitrust Law Sows Worries in West," January 30, 2004, p.A12.

Cohen, Adam, and Jacoby, Mary, "EU's Kroes Puts Consumers First in Merger Cases," The Wall Street Journal, September 26, 2005, p. A17.

Cohen, Laurie P., "Court Says Prosecutors Pressure White-Collar Defendants Unfairly," The Wall Street Journal, June 28, 2006, pp. A1, A12.

Collins, Erika C., "International Employment Law," 39 International Lawyer, pp. 449–481 (Summer 2005).

Coltri, Laurie S. (2010). *Alternative Dispute Resolution: A Conflict Diagnosis Approach* (Second Edition). Boston: Prentice Hall.

Commission for Environmental Cooperation (CEC). Retrieved July 20, 2006, from http://www.cec.org/home/index.cfm?varlan=english

Communications Decency Act of 1996, 47 United States Code Section 230.

Comprehensive Environmental Response, Compensation, and Liability Act, 42 United States Code Annotated Sections 9601–9675 (Thomson/West 2006).

Computer Fraud and Abuse Act of 1984, 18 United States Code Section 1030.

Computer Software Copyright Act of 1980, 17 United States Code Annotated Section 101 (Thomson/West 2006).

Consolidated Omnibus Budget Reconciliation Act of 1985, 29 United States Code Annotated, Sections 1161–1169 (Thomson/West 2006).

Contreras, Russell, "Whole Foods reviewing language policy," *Miami Herald*, June 8, 2013, p. 3C.

Continental T.V., Inc. v. GTE Sylvania, Inc., 433 U.S. 36, 97 S.Ct. 2549 (1977).

Copyright Act, 17 United States Code Annotated Sections 101 et. seq. (Thomson/West 2006).

Copyright Term Extension Act, 17 United States Code Annotated Section 302 (Thomson/West 2006).

Consumer Product Safety Act, 15 United States Code Annotated Sections 2051–2083 (Thomson-West 2006).

Controlling the Assault of Non-Solicited Pornography and Marketing Act of 2003, United States Code Annotated Sections 7701–7713, (Thomson West 2006).

Cooper, Phillip J. (2000), Public Law and Public Administration (3ʳᵈ edition), F.E. Peacock Publishers, Inc., Itasca, Ill..

Copeland, Libby, "The fat suit," Sun-Sentinel, November 17, 2002, pp. 1E, 8E.

Corkery, Michael, "New Twist in Vacation Homes," The Wall Street Journal, February 25–26, 2006, pp. B1, B4.

CNN Law Center, "Two ex-Coke workers sentenced in Pepsi plot deal," *CNN. com*. Retrieved May 23, 2007 from: www.cnn.com/2007/LAW/05/23/coca.cola.sentencing/index.html.

Crock, Stan, and Moore Jonathan, "Corporate Spies Feel a Sting," Business Week, July 14, 1997, pp. 76–77.

Cross, Frank B., and Miller, Roger LeRoy (2007). Legal Environment of Business (6ᵗʰ edition), Thomson-West.

Curtis, Henry Pearson, "Ex-Disney employee sues over dress code," The Orlando Sentinel, May 23, 2004, p. A7.

Danaher, M. G. (2006). *Employers Fail to Accommodate if Only One of Two Religious Concerns Are Addressed, 8 No. 11 Law. J. 2.*

Dash, Eric, "Pay Rules Adopted by S.E.C.," The New York Times, July 27, 2006, pp. C1, C10.

Davidson, Daniel V. and Forsythe, Lynn M. (2011). *The Entrepreneur's Legal Companion.* Boston, MA: Prentice Hall.

Davies, Frank, "Senate Ok's Homeland Security Bill, "The Herald," November 20, 2002, pp. 1A, 20A.

Davis, Ann, "English-Only Rules Spur Workers to Speak Legalese," The Wall Street Journal, January 23, 1997, pp. B1, B6.

Davis-Bacon Act of 1931, 40 United States Code Annotated, Sections 276a-276a-5 (Thomson/West 2006).

DeCarlo, Thomas E. & Leigh, Thomas W. (1996). Impact of salesperson attraction on sales managers' attributions and feedback. *Journal of Marketing, 60*, 47–66.

DeGeorge, Richard T. (2006), Business Ethics (6ᵗʰ edition), Pearson/Prentice Hall.

Dehart, Philip, "The NAALC and Mexico's Ley Federal Para Prevenir Y Eliminar La Discriminacion," 34 Georgia Journal of International and Comparative Law, pp. 657–688 (2006).

Delaney, Kevin, "Ruling Lets Lee Go to Work at Google," The Wall Street Journal, September 14, 2005, p. B2.

Desai, M.A., Hines, J.R. (2002). Expectations and expatriations: Tracing the causes and consequences of corporate inversions. National Tax Journal, 55(3). Retrieved August 10, 2005 from ProQuest Database.

Diamond v. Diehr, 450 U.S. 175, 101 S.Ct. 1048 (1981).

Diamond, Randy, "McGreevey signs law requiring 'smart' guns," Bergen Record, December 24, 2002, pp. A1, A7.

Digital Millennium Copyright Act of 1998, 17 United States Code Sections 1201–1205.

Digital Millennium Copyright Act, 17 United States Code Annotated Section 1201 (Thomson/West 2006).

DiMatteo, Larry A. (2003). The Law of International Business Transactions. Thomson-Southwestern-West.

District of Columbia v. Heller, 208 U.S. LEXIS 5628 (2008).

Dobbs, Dan B. (2001). The Law of Torts, West Group (and Supplement 2006).

Dobbs, Dan B., Keeton, Robert E., and Owen, David G. (1984), Prosser and Keeton on the Law of Torts (5th edition), West Publishing Company.

Domrin, Alexander N., "From Fragmentation To Balance: The Shifting Model of Federalism in Post-Soviet Russia," 15 Transnational Law and Contemporary Problems, pp. 515– 549 (2006).

Do-Not-Call Implementation Act (2003). Public Law No. 108–10. 15 *United States Code* Section 6101.

Dooren, Jennifer Corbett, "FTC Acts on Diet Products," *The Wall Street Journal*, January 8, 2014, p. B6.

Dorsey, Patrick, "Woman files suit against Marlins," Sun-Sentinel, May 6, 2006, p. 6B.

Doyle, Michael, "Justices stand by healthcare law," *The Miami Herald*, June 29, 2012, pp. 1A, 2A.

Doyle, Michael, "Ruling backs white firefighters," *The Miami Herald*, June 30, 2009, p. 3A.

Dowling, Donald C., and Rose, Proskauer, "The Practice of International Labor and Employment Law for Multinational Employer Clients," 730 Practicing Law Institute Litigation and Practice Course Handbook Series, pp. 773–815 (2005).

Dunham, Kemba J., "Banking on Boomers in Baja," The Wall Street Journal, reprinted in The Miami Herald, February 15, 2006, Business Monday, pp. 6–7.

Dussauge, P., Hart, S., and Ramanantsoa, B. (1987). Strategic Technology Management. New York: John Wiley and Sons

Dzvimbo, K. (2003). The International Migration of Skilled Human Capital From Developing Countries September, 2003. Retrieved from www. worldbank.org on 28 September, 2006

Earley, P. Christopher 1987. Intercultural training for managers: A comparison of documentary and interpersonal methods. *Academy of Management Journal*, 30(4): 685–698.

Economic Espionage Act, 18 United States Code Annotated Sections 1831–1839 (Thomson/West 2006).

Editorial. (2006, July 13). What Mr. Kellier did not say. Daily Observer

EEOC v. Waffle House, Inc., 534 U.S. 279, 122 S.Ct. 754 (2002).

Efrati, Amer, "U.S. Loses Bear Fraud Case," *The Wall Street Journal*, November 11, 2009, pp. A1, A6.

Ehrenreich, Barbara, "Zipped Lips," Time, February 5, 1996, p. 80.

EIU Business: Industry Overview, *Turkey: Manufacturing*, June 30, 2006; From http://www.toyotatr.com/tr/company.asp; Business Digest, Turkish News in Brief, Toyota Turkey, July 13, 2006.

Electronic Communication, "Employer's e-mail policy is unfair to union organizing effort, judge rules," Florida Employment Law Letter, Vol. 15, No. 2, April 2003, p. 5.

Electronic Communications Privacy Act, 18 United States Code Annotated Sections 2510–21 (Thomson West 2006).

Electronic Communications Privacy Act of 1986, 18 United States Code Annotated 2510–2521 (Thomson/West 2006).

Electronic Signature in Global and National Commerce Act, 15 United States Code Annotated, Section 7002 (Thomson West 2006).

Emerick v. Kuhn, 737 A.2d 456 (Connecticut Appeals 1999).

Emshwiller, John R. and Scannell, Kara, "Mozilo Agrees to Pay $67.5 Million," *The Wall Street Journal*, October 16–17, 2010, pp. B1, B2.

Employee Polygraph Protection Act of 1988, 29 United States Code Annotated, Sections 2001 et seq. (Thomson/West 2006).

Employee Retirement Income Security Act of 1974, 29 United States Code Annotated, Sections 1001 et seq. (Thomson/West 2006).

Emshriller, John R, Smith, Rebecca, and Murray, Alan, "Lay's Legacy: Corporate Change – But Not the Kind He Expected," The Wall Street Journal, July 6, 2006, pp. A1, A10.

Englund, M. (2005). "Welcome Home, Big Money; Companies may repatriate some $350 billion held abroad at a low tax rate in 2005—a huge inflow that could boost the U.S. economy." Business Week Online. Retrieved August 9, 2005 from LexisNexis Database.

Ergun Özbudun, *Constitutional Law*, in 19–22 INTRODUCTION TO TURKISH LAW, (Tugrul Ansay et al. eds.., 2005). Kluwer Law International.

Ervin, C. (n.d.). *OECD Actions to Fight Bribery in International Business Transactions*. Retrieved April 2, 2006, from http://magnet.undp.org/Docs/efa/corruption/Chapter10.pdf

Executive Agencies in Jamaica: The Story Thus Far and the Central Management Mechanism. (2001). Retrieved July 19, 2006 from http://www.cabinet.gov.jm/docs/pdf/ExecAgenciesThusFar.pdf

Faccio, M., Larry, H.P., Young, L. (2001). Dividends and expropriation. The American Economic Review, (1). Retrieved August, 7, 2005 from ProQuest Database.

Fair Labor Standards Act of 1938, 29 United States Code Annotated, Sections 201–260 (Thomson/west 2006).

False Claims Act of 1863, as amended by the False Claims Reform Act of 1986, 31 United States Code Annotated, Sections 3729–3733 (Thomson/west 2006).

Family Medical Leave Act of 1993, 29 United States Code Annotated, Sections 2601 et seq. (Thomson/West 2006).

Farah, C. E. (1994). *Islam*. ISBN: 0–8120–1853–2. Barron's Educational Series, Inc.

Faragher v. City of Boca Raton, 534 U.S. 775, 118, S.Ct. 2275 (1998).

Federal Arbitration Act, United States Code Annotated, Sections 1–16 (Thomson/West 2006).

Federal Courts Improvement Act of 1982, 28 United States Code Annotated, Sections 1292–95 (Thomson West 2006).

Federal Trademark Dilution Act of 1995, 15 United States Code Annotated, Sections 1114–25 (Thomson West, 2006).

Federal Patent Act of 1952, 15 United States Code Annotated Section 1125(a) (Thomson/West 2006).

Federal Trade Commission Franchise Rule, 16 Code of Federal Regulations Section 436.1.

Federal Trademark Dilution Act of 1995, 15 United States Code Annotated Sections 1114–25.

Federal Trade Commission Act, 15 United States Code Annotated Sections 41–58 (Thomson-West 2006).

Federal Unemployment Tax Act of 1935, 26 United States Code Annotated, Sections 3301–3310 (Thomson/West 2006).

Feeley, Jeff, "Shoe-seller Nine West to pay $34 million to settle antitrust suit, The Miami Herald, March 7, 2000, p. 10C.

Feld, Louise, "Along the Spectrum of Women's Rights Advocacy: A Cross-Cultural Comparison of Sexual Harassment Law in the United States and India," 25 Fordham International Law Journal, pp. 1205–1281 (2002).

Felsenthal, Edward, "Big Weapon Against Insider Trading is Upheld," The Wall Street Journal, June 26, 1997, p. C1.

Feltes, Patricia, Robinson, Robert K. and Fink, Ross L. (1993). "American female expatriates and the civil rights act of 1991: Balancing legal and business interests." *Business Horizons, Vol. 36, 2, pp. 82–86.*

Fiedler, Fred E. (1967). *A theory of leadership effectiveness.* New York: McGraw-Hill.

First National Bank of Boston v. Bellotti, 435 U.S. 765, 98 S.Ct. 1407 (1978).

Flint, Joe, "Breaking Longtime Taboo, NBC Network Plans to Accept Liquor Ads," The Wall Street Journal, December 14, 2001, pp. B1, B6.

Folsom, Ralph H., Gordon, Michael Wallace, and Spanogle, John A. (2000). International Business Transactions in a Nutshell (6th edition). West Group.

Fong, Mei, "China May Force Foreign Firms to Allow Unions," The Wall Street Journal, July 7–8, 2006, p. A2.

Fong, Mei, and Zimmerman, Ann, "China's Union Push Leaves Wal-Mart With a Hard Choice," The Wall Street Journal, May 13–14, 2006, pp. A1, A6.

Foreign Corrupt Practices Act of 1977, 15 United States Code Annotated Section 78m (Thomson/West 2006), as amended by the Ominbus Trade and Competitiveness Act of 1988, 19 United States Code Annotated Section 2903 (Thomson/West 2006).

Foreign National and Commonwealth Citizens (Employment) Act (1973). Laws of Jamaica.

Foreign Sovereign Immunities Act of 1976, 28 United States Code, Sections 1602–1611.

Forster, Julie, "Gotta Get That Gator," Business Week, November 27, 2000, pp. 91, 94.

Fowler, Geoffrey A., and Qin, Juying, "China Threatens Rolling Stone's Ability to Publish Local Edition," The Wall Street Journal, March 31, 2006, p. A13.

Fowler-Hermes, J., "Appearance-based Discrimination Claims Under EEO Laws," The Florida Bar Journal, April 2001, pp. 32f.

Foy, Paul, "Olympic defendants off the hook," The Herald, December 6, 2003, p. 7A.

France, Mike, "Europe: A Different Take On Antitrust," Business Week, June 25, 2001, p. 40.

Fracchia, Fabrizio, "Administrative Procedures and Democracy: The Italian Experience," 12 Indiana Journal of Global Legal Studies, pp. 589–598 (2005).

Franklin, E. (2005). Repatriation risk: Why Global Firms Need To Be Concerned and What Can be Done to Alleviate the Problem. Term Paper prepared for International Legal Environment of Business. Nova Southeastern University.

Fredrix, Emily, "Costco says no to Coke products," *Sun-Sentinel*, November 18, 2009, p. 3D.

Frick, Helen L. 1995. The relationship of national culture, gender, and occupation to the work values of the employees of an international organization. Unpublished D.E. Dissertation, School of Education and Human Development, The George Washington University, Washington D.C.

Furchgott, Roy, "Workers Sign Away a Day in Court," The New York Times, July 28, 1996, p. 9.

Futterman, Matthew, "Talent Agencies Cry Foul, Lawsuits Fly, *The Wall Street Journal*, May 7, 2010, p. B1.

Gardner v. Loomis Armored, Inc., 913 P.2d 377 (Washington 1996).

Garvin, Glenn, "Reporter's age-bias win reversed," *Miami Herald*, January 19, 2012, p. 8B.

Gebert, Diether & Steinkamp, Thomas (1991). Leadership style and economic success in Nigeria and Taiwan. *Management International Review*, 31(2): 161–171.

Gerlin, Andrea, "Seminars Teach Managers Finer Points of Firing," The Wall Street Journal, April 26, 1195, pp. B1, B8.

Gender Watch, "Now No Means No in China," Business Week, March 28, 2005, p. 12.

Gilbert, Daniel, "Ego, Alcohol To Blame, Says KBR's Ex-Chief," *The Wall Street Journal*, February 24, 2012, pp. B1, B2.

Gibson, Richard, and Brat, Ilan, "Whirlpool-Maytag Deal Gets Antitrust Approval," The Wall Street Journal, March 30, 2006, p. A2.

Gierczyk, Yvonne, "The Evolution of the European Legal System: The European Court of Justice's Role in the Harmonization of Laws," 12 International Law Students Association Journal of International and Comparative Law, pp. 153–180 (2005).

Gilmer v. Interstate Johnson Lane Corporation, 500 U.S. 20, 111 S.Ct 1647 (1991).

Gingrich, Newt, and Kies, Ken, "Our Taxed Expats," The Wall Street Journal, June 28, 2006, p. A14.

Glick, Norman D. (2001). Situational Leadership in cross-cultural environments: The relationship between cross-cultural experience, culture training, leadership style, and leader effectiveness in the U.S. Foreign Service. Doctoral Dissertation, School of Business and Entrepreneurship, Nova Southeastern University; Ft. Lauderdale, Florida.

Glick, Norman D. (2001). The impact of culture on sales force management. *Journal of Applied Management and Entrepreneurship*, 6(2): 116–129.

Global Economics (2013). *Bloomberg Businessweek*, November 21-November 27, pp. 17–19.

Global News Wire. (2005). Human factor vital to ASIMCO'S China management retrieved July, 13 2006 from http://0-web.lexis-nexis.com. novacat.nova.edu/universe/document?

Gonzales v. Raich, 545 U.S. 1, 125 S.Ct. 2195 (2005).

Goodman, Cindy K., "Today, it's OK to sign on the electronic line," The Herald, October 1, 2000, pp. 1E, 7E.

Gordon, Marcy, "SEC moves to require more exec pay disclosure," The Miami Herald, January 18, 2006, p. 3C.

Goss v. Lopez, 419 U.S. 565, 95 S.Ct. 729 (1975).

Government and Politics (2005). Retrieved July 12, 2006 http://countrystudies. us/caribbean-islands/34.htm

Grant, John A., Jr., and Steele, Thomas T., "Restrictive Covenants: Florida Returns to the Original 'Unfair Competition' Approach for the 21st Century," *The Florida Bar Journal*, November 1996, pp. 53–56.

Grantz v. Bollinger, 539 U.S. 244 (2003).

Greater New Orleans Broadcasting Association, Inc. v. United States, 527 U.S. 173, 119 S.Ct.1923 (1999).

Greenberger, Robert S., "Justices Back Arbitration Use In Work Arena," The Wall Street Journal, March 22, 2001, pp. A3, A10.

Greenberger, Robert S., "Supreme Court Gives Workers Legal Options," The Wall Street Journal, January 16, 2002, p. B14.

Greenhouse, Seven, "For Employers, Ruling Offers Little Guidance on How to Make Their Hiring Fair," *The New York Times*, June 30, 2009, p. A13.

Greenhouse, Steven, "Looks aren't everything—unless you want a job," The Miami Herald, July 15, 2003, p. 21A.

Greenberger, Robert S., "More Courts Are Granting Advertisers First Amendment Protection," The Wall Street Journal, July 3, 2001, pp. B1, B3.

Greenhouse, Linda, "Justices curb Postal Service immunity," Sun-Sentinel, February 23, 2006, p. 2A.

Greenman v. Yuba Power Products, Inc., 27 Cal. Rptr. 697, 377 P.2d. 897 (California Supreme Court 1963).

Griffin, R.W., Pustay, M.W. (2003) International Business: A Managerial Perspective (4th Ed.). Upper Saddle River, New Jersey: Pearson Prentice Hall.

Groppi, Tania, and Scattone, Nicoletta, "Italy: The Subsidiarity Principle," 4 International Journal of Constitutional Law, pp. 131–137 (2006).

Grovis, Jaclyn, "Publix: Market leader shows shopping savvy," Sun-Sentinel, April 2, 2006, p. E1.

Grow, Brian, "A Body Blow To Illegal Labor," Business Week, March 27, 2006, pp. 86–88.

Grutter v. Bollinger, 539 U.S. 306 (2003).

Grutter v. Bollinger, 539 U.S. 206, 123 S.Ct. 2325 (2003).

Grossman, Mark, "Confidentiality agreements have no standard form," The Herald, March 3, 2003, Business Monday, pp. 27–28.

Güriz, Adnan *Constitutional Law*, in 2 introduction to turkish law, (Tugrul Ansay et al. eds.., 2005). Kluwer Law International.

Guth, Robert A., "Microsoft Sues To Keep Aide from Google," The Wall Street Journal, July 20, 2005, p. B1.

Haddad, Charles, and Pascual, Aixa M., "When You Want to Sue-But Can't," Business Week, June 10, 2002, p. 46.

Hall, Edward T., and Mildred Reed (1990). Understanding Cultural Differences, Intercultural Press, Inc.

Hall, Daniel (2002). Administrative Law: Bureaucracy in a Democracy (2nd edition), Pearson Education.

Hamzah, Zain. (2005). *Legal issues on online Transactions*. Retrieved on August 3 2006 from: http://0-proquest.umi.com.novacat.nova.edu/pqdweb

Hananel, Sam, "Lay to submit papers to inquiry," Sun-Sentinel, November 8, 2003, pp. 8B, 9B.

Hanks, Douglas III, "When is a condo not a condo"? The Miami Herald, April 9, 2006, pp. 1E, 4E.

Harish, N. (May 2012). Corporate Social Responsibility Practices in Indian Companies: A Study. *International Journal of Management, IT and Engineering*, Vol. 2, Issue 5, pp. 519–36.

Harris v. Forklift Systems, 510 U.S. 17, 114 S.Ct. 367 (1993).

Harrison, J. Kline 1992. Individual and combined effects of behavior modeling and the cultural assimilator in cross-cultural management training. *Journal of Applied Psychology*, 77, (6), 952–962.

Hasegawa, T. (n.d.). *Investigation of Corruption in Japan*. Retrieved April 8, 2006, from http://www.unafei.or.jp/english/pdf/PDF_rms/no56/56–36.pdf

Hasnas, John, "Department of Coercion," The Wall Street Journal, March 11–12, 2006, p. A9.

Hatton, T. & Williamson J. (2002). What Fundamentals Drive Migration, NBER Working Paper no. W9159. National Bureau of Economic Research Discussion Paper No. 2003/23

Hawley, S. (2000). *Exporting Corruption: Privatisation, Multinationals and Bribery*. Retrieved April 5, 2006, from http://www.globalpolicy.org/nations/corrupt/corner.htm

Hays, Kristen, "Enron pair pay price for fraud," The Miami Herald, May 26, 2006, pp. 1A, 2A.

Hays, Kristen, "Convictions likely to be erased," Sun-Sentinel, July 27, 2006, p. 2D.

Heart of Atlanta Motel v. United States, 379 U.S. 241, 85 S.Ct. 348 (1964).

Hegerich, Robyn M., "Employment Law – Title VII Does Not Extend to Third-Party Retaliation Claim by Finance of Discrimination Claimant," 43 *Suffolk University Law Review* 1059 (2010).

Heim, Kristi, "U.S. gives up effort to split Microsoft," The Miami Herald, September 7, 2001, pp. 1A, 2A.

Hemlock, Doreen, "Teaching linguistic nuances," Sun Sentinel, December 13, 2004, Your Business, p. 5.

Henn, Harry G., and Alexander, John R. (1983). Laws of Corporations, West Publishing Company Hornbook Series.

Henry, E. and Preston, M. (2005). Congressman resigns after bribery plea. Retrieved April 12, 2006, from http://www.cnn.com/2005/POLITICS/11/28/cunningham/

Henry-Wilson, M. (2006, August 2). Informed Debate needed on Foreign Workers. Daily Observer.

Herlihy, Edward D., "Eminent Domain Debate Hits the Links," The Wall Street Journal, March 28, 2006, p. D8.

Herman, A. (1989). Growth in international trade law. Financial Times (March, 30): 10, International Chamber of Commerce terms (Incoterms).

Herman, Tom, and Silverman, Rachel Emma, "Telecommuters May Face New Taxes," Wall Street Journal, November 1, 2005, pp. D1, D2.

Hermida, Julian, "Convergence of Civil Law and Common Law in the Criminal Theory Realm," 13 University of Miami International and Comparative Law Review, pp. 163–232 (2006).

Hersey, Paul & Blanchard, Kenneth H. (1993). Management of organizational behavior: Utilizing human resources (6th ed.). Englewood Cliffs, NJ: Prentice-Hall.

Hesler, T., Hiremath, J. (2005). Cash Repatriation and Tax Incentive. AFT Exchange. Retrieved August 24, 2005 from ProQuest Database.

Hiaasen, Scott, and Viglucci, Andres, "U.S. Supreme Court: ruling on land is vital locally," Herald, June 24, 2005, pp. 1B, 10B.

Hiam, A., and Schewe,C.(1992). The Portable MBA in Marketing . New York : John Wiley and Sons.

Hill, John S. & Still, Richard R. & Boya, Unal O. (1991). Managing the multinational sales force. International Marketing Review, 8(1): 19–31.

Hodgetts, R.M., Luthans, F., & Doh, J.P. (2006). International Management: Culture, Strategy and Behavior, 6th edition. McGraw-Hill Irwin: Boston.

Hofstede, Geert (1980). Culture's consequences: International differences in work-related values. London, U.K.: Sage Publication Ltd.

Hofstede, Geert (1993). Cultural constraints in management theories. Academy of Management Executives, 7(1): 81–94.

Holmes, Stanley, "Free Speech or False Advertising," Business Week, April 28, 2003, pp. 69–70.

Holzeer, Jessica and Johnson, Fawn, "Larger Bounties Spur in Fraud Tips," *The Wall Street Journal*, September 7, 2010, p. C3.

Honeycutt Jr., Earl D. and Ford, John B. (1995). Guidelines for managing an international sales force. Industrial Marketing Management, 24: 135–44.

Hu, F. (2005). Capital Flows, Overtaking and the Nominal Exchange Rage Regime in China. Cato Journal, 25(2). Retreived August 18, 2005 from ProQuest Database.

Hymowitz, Carol, "Technology facilitates intellectual theft," The Herald, September 12, 2005, Business Monday, p. 2.

Hymowitz, Carol, and Lublin, Joann S., "Many Companies Look the Other Way at Employee Affairs," The Wall Street Journal, March 8, 2005, pp. B1, B6.

Hynick, Jeff, "May I Borrow Your Mouse? A Note on Electronic Signatures in the United States, Argentina and Brazil," 12 Southwestern Journal of Law and Trade in the Americas, pp. 159–176 (2005).

IBM, (2006). "IBM pushes online contract mgmt." Retrieved on August 3 2006 from: http://0-web.lexis-nexis.com.novacat.nova.edu/universe/document

Immigration, "France's Plan: Pay 'Em To Go Home," Business Week, April 24, 2006, p. 16.

Immigration Reform and Control Act of 1986, 29 United States Code Annotated, Section 1802 (Thomson/West 2006).

Import Administration: Import monitoring, licensing and compliance programs. Retrieved July 20, 2006, from http://ia.ita.doc.gov/import-monitoring.html

Inagaki, Kana, "More Japanese turning to courts," The Miami Herald, August 21, 2006, p. 14A.

Ingersoll, Bruce, "FDA Takes On 'No Cholesterol' Claims," The Wall Street Journal, May 15, 1991, p. B1.

Interpreters and Translators. Retrieved on June 22, 2006 from: http://stats.bls.gov/oco/ocos175.htm

Intel Corp. v. Hamidi, 30 Cal.4th 1342, 1 Cal.Rptr.3d 32 (California Supreme Court 2003).

International Shoe Company v. Washington, 326 U.S. 310, 66 S.Ct. 154 (1945).

International Trade Administration. Retrieved July 20, 2006, from http://trade.gov/index.asp

International Trade Commission. Retrieved July 20, 2006, from http://www.usitc.gov/

Investments at a price. (2005). Emerging Europe Monitor: Central Europe. Retrieved August 6, 2005 from Business Source Premier.

Investment Climate: Part I China. (2000). U.S. & FCS Market Research Reports: International Market Insight. Retrieved August 12, 2005 from National Trade Databank Database.

Islamic Network Group, 2002. *Islamic Speakers Bureau Publication.* Presenting Islam & Muslim Culture in the Content of Social Studies and Work History: School Grades 7th – 12th. Speakers Kit. Islamic Networks Group; website: www.ing.org.

Jacobs, Margaret A., "Brutal Firings Can Backfire, Ending in Court," The Wall Street Journal, October 24, 1995, pp. B1, B4.

Jacobs, Margaret A., "Red Lobster Tale: Peers Decide Fired Waitresses Fate," January 20, 1998, pp. B1, B4.

Jamaican Telecommunications Acts, 2006. *Highlights of the Jamaican Telecommunications Acts 2000.* Retrieved on August 3 2006 from: http://unpan1.un.org/intradoc/groups/public/documents/CARICAD/ UNPAN009919.pdf

Jargon, Julie and Thurm Scott, "Heinz CEO's Golden Exit Deal," *The Wall Street Journal*, March 5, 2013, p. B1.

Jenkins, Jr., Holmes W., "The Land (and Antitrust Case) That Time Forget," The Wall Street Journal, April 26, 2006, p. A17.

Johnson, Avery, Mundy, Alicia, and Bravin, Jess, "Drug Industry Gets Hit by Ruling," *The Wall Street Journal*, March 5, 2009, p. A2.

Johnson, Elizabeth Prior, and Burt, Frank, "English-Only Work Rules: Per Se Discriminatory or an Employer's Prerogative"? The Florida Bar Journal, November 1994, pp. 58–62.

Johnson, Tim, "Censored Search," The Miami Herald, April 13, 2006, pp. 1C, 6C.

Johnson, Tim, "Wal-Mart succumbs to state-run union," The Miami Herald, August 17, 2006, p. 2C.

Johnson, Linda, "Pfizer to sell consumer unit to J&J," Sun-Sentinel, June 27, 2006, pp. 1D, 2D.

Jones, Ashby, "Court Might Consider Concealed Weapons," *The Wall Street Journal*, April 12, 2013, p. A5.

Jones, Ashby, and Kendall, Brent, "Roberts Straddles Ideological Divide," *The Wall Street Journal*, June 29, 2012, pp. A1, A4.

Jones, Ashby and Lubin, Joann S., "Critics Blow Whistle on Law," *The Wall Street Journal*, November 1, 2010, p. B1, B11.

Jones, Ashby, "New 'Personalized' Gun May Trigger Old Law," *The Wall Street Journal*, November 21, 2013, p. A4.

Jordan, Miriam, "Good taste lost in ad translation," The Wall Street Journal, reprinted in the Sun-Sentinel, March 19, 2006, p. 1E.

Jordan, Miriam, "Blacks vs. Latinos at Work," The Wall Street Journal, January 24, 2006, pp. B1, B2.

Jordan, Miriam, "Testing 'English Only' Rules," The Wall Street Journal, November 8, 2005, pp. B1, B13.

Kaufman, Leslie, and Underwood, Anne, "Sign or Hit the Street," Newsweek, June 30, 1997, pp. 48–49.

Kazor, Bill, "Debate heats up on eminent domain," The Miami Herald, March 16, 2006, p. 9B.

Kealey, Daniel J. & Protheroe, David R. (1996). The effectiveness of cross-cultural training for expatriates: An assessment of the literature on the issue. *International Journal of Intercultural Relations* 20(2): 141–165.

Kellier, D. (2006, July 12). Ministry has ensured fair Mix of Foreign and Local Workers. Daily Observer.

Kelo v. City of New London, Connecticut, 545 U.S 469, 125 S. Ct 2655 (2005).

Kendall, Brent, "Chinese Vitamin-C Suppliers Found Liable for Price-Fixing," *The Wall Street Journal,* March 15, 2013, p. B1.

Kendall, Brent, "Regulators Focus on AB InBev's Documents," *The Wall Street Journal,* February 4, 2013, pp. B1, B4.

Kenis, Izzettin (1977). A cross-cultural study of personality and leadership. *Group and Organization Studies,* 2(1): 49–60.

Kenworthy, Tom, "Minimum wage laws multiply in states," USA Today, September 13, 2006, 1A.

Kenya: Institutional Situation. (n.d.). Retrieved June 13, 2006, from http://www.etat.sciencespobordeaux.fr/_anglais/institutionnel/kenya.html

Kidwell, David, and Merzer, "A loss for Big Tobacco," The Herald, July 8, 1999, pp. 1A, 6A.

Kiley, David, "A Green Flag for Booze," Business Week, March 7, 2005, p. 95.

Klass, Mary Ellen, "Tort reform bill passes house," The Miami Herald, March 17, 2006, pp. 1C, 6C.

Knight, Victoria, "Personality Tests as Hiring Tools," The Wall Street Journal, March 15, 2006, p. B3A.

Kocian, Lisa, "Dunkin' Donuts checks workers," The Miami Herald, May 31, 2006, p. 3C.

Koeppel, David, "Limit the damage ex-employees can do," The Herald, May 9, 2005, Business Monday, p. 22.

Koppel, Nathan, "Legal Pot Use in Colorado Could Still Get You Fired," *The Wall Street Journal,* April 26, 2013, p. A8.

Kramer, Michael, "Corruption and Fraud Stunt Third-world Growth," The White Paper, Vol. 16, No. 3, May/June 2002, p. 22f.

Kranhold, Kathryn, "Sotheby's Chief is Convicted of Price-Fixing," The Wall Street Journal, December 6, 2001, p. B1.

Kravets, David, "Court sides with doctors who advise pot use," Sun Sentinel, October 30, 2002, p. 7A.

Kravets, David, "IBM hit with class-action suit," Sun-Sentinel, January 25, 2006, p. 3D.

Kristof, Kathy, "This Investment Vehicle is Rife with Fraud," Sun-Sentinel, March 12, 2002, p. 7D.

Labaton, Stephen, "Supreme Court Lifts Ban on Minimum Retail Pricing," The New York Times, June 29, 2007.

Labaton, Stephen, "Supreme Court to Review Antitrust Case Against Phone Companies," The New York Times, June 27, 2006, p. C3.

Labor-Management Relations Act of 1947, 29 United States Code Annotated, Sections 141 et seq. (Thomson/West 2006).

Labor-Management Reporting and Disclosure Act of 1959, 29 United States Code Annotated, Sections 401 et seq. (Thomson/West 2006).

Lanham Trademark Act of 1946, 15 United States Code Sections 1051–1128.

Lanham Trademark Act, 15 United States Code Annotated, Sections 1051 et. seq. and 1114 et. seq. (Thomson/West 2006).

Larson, John W., Comiter, Richard B., and Cane, Marilyn B., "Florida's New Partnership Law," The Florida Bar Journal, November 1995, pp. 20–33.

Lascu, Dana-Nicoleta (2006). International Marketing, 2nd Edition, Atomic Dog Publishing, 2006.

Lavelle, Louis, "Happy Endings Not Guaranteed: Arbitration doesn't always live up to its billing," Business Week, November 20, 2000, pp. 69, 73.

LaVelle, Michael J., "A Russian Experience," 42 Arizona Attorney, pp. 30–35 (2006).

Law on Foreign Land Ownership Passes Despite Opposition, TURKISH DAILY NEWS, Dec. 30, 2005, from http://www.turkishdailynews.com.tr/article.php?enewsid=32092.

Law No. 4916 Published in Article 35 the Official Gazette (Resmi Gazete) dated July 19, 2003 and numbered 25173.

Leary, Alex, "Corporate-fund limits for elections reversed," The Miami Herald, January 22, 2010, p. 3A.

Leicester, John, "Protesters seek status quo," The Miami Herald, March 18, 2006, p. 12A.

Leif, Carter H., and Harrington, Christine B., Administrative Law and Politics (3rd edition), Longman Publishers, 2000.

Lewis, Seth, "Protect Yourself," *Miami Herald*, Business Monday, February 20, 2006, p. 4.

Leonhardt, David, and Dawley, Heidi, "A Little Booze for the Kiddies," Business Week, September 23, 1996, p. 158.

Lippman, Joanne, "FTC Is Cracking Down on Misleading Ads," The Wall Street Journal, February 1, 1991, p. B5.

Liptak, Adam, "Court Voids Ban on Sale to Youth of Violent Games," *New York Times*, June 28, 2011, pp. A1, A15.

Liptak, Adam, "Supreme Court tightens Rules in Class Actions," *The New York Times*, June 21, 2011, pp. A1, B4.

Liptak, Adam, "Supreme Court Finds Bias Against White Firefighters," *The New York Times*, June 30, 2009, pp. A1, A13.

Lobosco v. New York Telephone Company/NYNex, 727 N.Y.S.2d 383 (New York Court of Appeals 2001).

Loci, Toni, "Employment discrimination suits get boost," The Miami Herald, June 23, 2006, p. 5A.

Lohtia, Ritu, Daniel C. Bello, Teruhisa Yamada and David Gilliland (2005), The Role of Commitment in Foreign-Japanese Relationships: Mediating Performance for Foreign Sellers in Japan, Journal of Business Research. Vol. 58: 1009–1018.

Lohr, Steve, "New Microsoft Browser Raises Google's Eyebrow," The Wall Street Journal, May 1, 2006, pp. A1, A16.

Lo, C. (1996). The Renmbi and China's Reluctance to Let Go. Asian Wall Street Journal. Retrieved August 10, 2005 from ProQuest Database.

Lopez-Bassols (2000). The International, ITC Skills and Employment – OECD Directorate for Science, Technology and Industry, DSTI/DOC (2002) 10, 7 July, 2002

Lowell, C. (2002). Skilled Labour Migration from Developing Countries. Retrieved from www.ilo.org/public/english/protection/migrant/download

Lublin, Joann S., "Harassment Law in U.S. Is Strict, Foreigners Find, "The Wall Street Journal, May 15, 2006, pp. B1, B3.

Lublin, Joanne S., "Retaliation Over Harassment Claims Takes Focus," The Wall Street Journal, April 17, 2006, p. B4.

Liu, Josephine, "Two Roads Diverged in a Yellow Wood: The European Community Stays on the Path to Strict Liability," 27 Fordham International Law Journal, pp. 1940–2006 (2004).

M.C. Mirrow, "The Code Napoleon: Buried But Ruling in Latin America," 33 Denver Journal of International Law and Policy, pp. 179–194 (Spring 2005).

MacLucas, Neil, "Swiss Vote 'Yes' on Executive Pay Controls," *The Wall Street Journal*, March 6, 2013, p. B3.

Maganrini, Gary, Jurisdiction Over Foreign-Nation Manufacturers, The Florida Bar Journal, March 1994, pp. 38–45.

Maher, Kris, "Workers Are Filing More Lawsuits Against Employers Over Wages," The Wall Street Journal, June 5, 2006, p. A2.

Maher, Kris, "Lawsuits Say Hospitals Colluded To Maintain Low Pay for Nurses," The Wall Street Journal, June 21, 2006, p. B2.

Mail Fraud Act of 1990, 18 United States Code Annotated, Sections 1341–42 (Thomson/West 2006).

Man, Anthony, "Court opens door to spending," *Sun-Sentinel*, January 22, 2010, p. 3A.

Marine Protection, Research, and Sanctuaries Act, 16 United States Code Annotated Sections 1401–1445, 33 United States Code Annotated Sections 1407 et seq. (Thomson/West 2006).

Martens, J., Scaprpetta, S., and Pilat, D. (1996). Mark-up ratios in manufacturing industries. OECD Woking paper No. 162 : 10–12

Martin, P. & Straubhaar, T. (2002) Managing Migration for Economic Growth

Martinez, Amy, "Lawsuit claims sunscreen kept us in the dark," The Miami Herald, March 31, 2006, p.p. 1C, 6C.

Martinez, Amy, "Lawsuit claims sunscreen kept us in the dark," The Miami Herald, March 31, 2006, p. 1C.

Martinez, Amy. (2006). Building up the Bahamas. The Miami Herald, Miami Florida.

Mason, W. (2004). *Products Liability Law in Japan.* Retrieved July 20, 2006, from http://library.findlaw.com/2004/Feb/18/133288.html

Masters, Brook A., "Corporate Crime: Society's Thirst For Justice Grows," The Miami Herald, July 15, 2005, p. 3C.

Mathews, Anna Wilde, "FDA Plan Would Aid Drug Makers In Liability Suits," The Wall Street Journal, January 14, 2006, pp. A1, A4.

May, James R., "Constituting Fundamental Environmental Rights Worldwide," 23 Pace Environmental Law Review, pp. 113–82 (Winter 2005–2006).

McAdams, Tony, Neslund, Nancy, and Zucker, Kiren Dosarijh (2012). *Law, Business, and Society* (10th edition). New York: McGraw-Hill Irvin.

McAdams, Terry, Neslund, Nancy, and Neslund, Kristopher (2007). Law, Business, and Society (8th edition), Irwin-McGraw Hill.

McCall, William, "Nike settles speech lawsuit," The Herald, September 13, 2003, pp. 1C, 2C.

McCann, J. (2003). Risk *v. Reward: Contemplating the Trade-Offs of Conducting Business in the Middle East.* Retrieved July 17, 2006, from http://www.thunderbird.edu/about_us/publications/tbird_mag/vol56_no_1/index.htm

McCartney, Timothy. (1976). Ten, Ten the Bible Ten- Obeah in the Bahamas, TimPaul Publishers, Nassau Bahamas.

McCartney, Timothy (1976). Bahamian Sexuality TimPaul Publishers, Nassau Bahamas.

McClam, Erin, "Stewart Guilty On All Counts," The Miami Herald, March 6, 2004, pp. 1A, 11A.

McClam, Erin, "Waksal gets 87 months, $4.3M fine, The Miami Herald, June 11, 2003, pp. 1C, 4C.

McDonald v. Chicago, 130 S.Ct. 3020 (2010).

McGeehan, Patrick, "Co-creator of musical Grease files lawsuit against cruise lines," The Miami Herald, February 16, 2006, p. C2.

McMorris, Frances A., and Schmitt, Richard B., "Court Takes Broad View of Insider Trading," October 9, 1996, p. A7.

Mehren, Elizabeth, "Same-sex couples suffer setback," The Miami Herald, March 31, 2006, p. 6A.

Mehta, Rajiv, Trina Larsen, Bert Rosenbloom, and Joseph Ganitsky (2006), The Impact of Cultural Differences in U.S. Business-to-Business Export Marketing Channel Strategic Alliances, Industrial Marketing Management. Vol. 35: 156–165.

Meritor Savings Bank v. Vinson, 477 U.S. 57, 106 S.Ct. 2399 (1986).

Metro-Goldwyn-Mayer Studios v. Grokster, 125 S.Ct. 2764 (2005).

Meyers, Mariyetta, "Russia and the Internet: Russia's Need to Confront and Conquer Trademark Infringement in Domain Names and Elsewhere on the Web," 9 Gonzaga Journal of International Law, pp. 200–35 (2005–2006).

Michaels, Daniel, and Wilke, John R., "U.S., EU Probe Airlines for Price-Fixing on Cargo," The Wall Street Journal, February 15, 2006, p. A3.

Michaels, Dave, "SEC to ban misleading reports on CEO pay," *Bergen Record,* December 22, 2013, p. B7.

Miller v. California, 413 U.S. 15, 93 S.Ct. 2607 (1973).

Miller, Roger LeRoy, and Jentz, Gaylord A. (2007). Business Law Today (7th edition), Thomson West.

Mills, Pamela J., and Morris, Duane, "Franchising Around the Globe: Relationship, Definition and Regulation." SL037 American Law Institute-American Bar Association, pp. 493–520 (2005).

Miranda v. Arizona, 384 U.S. 436, 86 S.Ct 1602 (1966).

Misawa, Mitsuru, "Shareholders' Action and Director's Responsibility in Japan," 24 Penn State International Law Review, pp. 1–57 (2005).

Mitchell, Terence R. & Foa, Uriel G. 1969. Diffusion of the effect of cultural training of the leader in the structure of heterocultural task groups. *Australian Journal of Psychology,* 21(1): 31–43.

Mitchener, Brandon, "Germany Says Business Bribes on the Rise," The Wall Street Journal, April 14, 1997, p. A17.

Mizrahi, Rhonda 1995. The relationships between perceived leadership style and leader effectiveness when considering employee cultural diversity. Unpublished D.B.A. Dissertation, School of Business and Entrepreneurship, Nova Southeastern University, Ft. Lauderdale, Florida.

Mohtadi, H. (1990). Expropriation of Multinational Firms: The Role of Domestic Market Conditions and Domestic Rivalries. Economic Inquiry, 28(4). Retrieved August 12, 2005 from ProQuest Database.

Mollers, Thomas M., "European Directives on Civil Law—Shaping a New German Civil Code," 18 Tulane European and Civil Law Forum, pp. 1–37 (2003).

Moore, S. Craig, "English-Only Rules in the Workplace," Volume 15, Labor Lawyer, pp. 295–308 (American Bar Association 1999).

Morris, Tom & Pavett, Cynthia M. (1992). Management style and productivity in two cultures. Journal of International Business Studies, 23(1): 169–179.

Mossberg, Walter A., "Using a Fingerprint to Log On to Your PC," The Wall Street Journal, March 15, 2006, pp. D1, D14.

Mossberg, Walter S., and Boehret, Katherine, "Using a Fingerprint to Log On to Your PC," The Wall Street Journal, March 15, 2006, pp. D1, D14.

Muffler, Stephen C., Cavico, Frank C., and Mujtaba, Bahaudin G. (2010). Diversity, Disparate Impact, and Ethics in Business: Implications of the New Haven Firefighters Case and the Supreme Court's Ricci v. DeStefano Decision. SAM: Advanced Management Journal, Vol. 75(3), pp. 11–20.

Mujtaba, Bahaudin G. and Cavico, Frank J. (2012). Discriminatory Practices against Muslims in the American Workplace. Journal of Leadership, Accountability, and Ethics, Vol. 9(1), pp. 98–117.

Mujtaba, Bahaudin G. and Cavico, Frank J. (2010). The Aging Workforce: Challenges and Opportunities for Human Resource Professionals. Davie Florida, ILEAD Academy, LLC.

Mujtaba, Bahaudin G., Cavico, Frank C., and McFarlane, D. (2011). International Age Discrimination: Management Challenges and Opportunities. The International Journal of Management and Business, Vol. 2, No. 1, pp. 36–53.

Mujtaba, Bahaudin G., Cavico, Frank J., and Muffler, Stephen C. (2012). Language Diversity in America: Challenges and Opportunities for Management. SAM: Advanced Management Journal, Vol. 77(2), pp. 38–47.

Mujtaba, Bahaudin G. (2005). The Ethics of Management and Situational Leadership in Afghanistan. Aglob Publishing Inc. ISBN: 1-59427-047-3. Hollandale, Florida USA. Website: www.aglobpublishing.com Phone: (954) 456-3653.

Mujtaba, Bahaudin G., and Cavico, Frank J., (2006). *Age Discrimination in Employment: Cross Cultural Comparison and Management Strategies.* BookSurge Publishing.

Muller, Joann, "Ford: The High Cost of Harassment," Business Week, November 15, 1999, pp. 94–96.

Murray, Alan, "High-Tech Titans Unite on Lifting Visa Caps," The Wall Street Journal, June 14, 2006, p. A2.

Murray, Sara, "Credit Checks on Job Applications Get Scrutiny During Bad Times," *The Wall Street Journal*, October 21, 2010, p. A5.

National Environmental Protection Act, 42 United States Code Annotated Sections 4321–4370 (Thomson/West 2006).

National Labor Relations Act of 1935, 20 United States Code Annotated, Section 151 (Thomson/West 2006).

National Society of Professional Engineers v. United States, 435 U.S. 679, 98 S.Ct. 1355 (1978).

Nation Briefs, "Washington State: Legislature Passes Gay Rights Bill," The Miami Herald, January 26, 2006, p. 3A.

Nevins, Buddy, "Judge says U.S. has jurisdiction over cruise lines," Sun Sentinel, July 24, 1990, p. 3A.

Newman, Karen L. & Nollen, Stanley D. (1996). Culture and congruence: The fit between management practices and national culture. *Journal of International Business Studies*, 27(4), 753–779.

New York Times Company v. Sullivan, 376 U.S. 254, 84 S.Ct. 710 (1964).

Noise Control Act, 42 United States Code Annotated Section 4901 (Thomson/West 2006).

Norris-LaGuardia Act of 1932, 29 United States Code Annotated, Sections 101-115 (Thomson/West 2006).

Norton, Helen, "Stepping Through Grutter's Open Doors: What the University of Michigan's Affirmative Action Cases Mean for Race-Conscious Government Decision-making," 78 *Temple Law Review* 543 (Fall, 2005).

Notable & Quotable, "From Justice Anthony Kennedy's majority opinion in the case of Ricci v. DeStefano," *The Wall Street Journal*, June 30, 2009, p. A15.

Nuclear Waste Policy Act, 42 United States Code Annotated Sections 10101 et seq. (Thomson/West 2006).

O'Brien, Gordon E., Fiedler, Fred E., & Hewett, Tom 1970. The effects of programmed culture training upon the performance of volunteer medical teams in Central America. *Human Relations*, 24(3): 209–231.

O'Boyle, Shannon, Perez, Luis, and Wallman, Britany, "Court extends property seizures," *Sun Sentinel*, June 24, 2005, pp. 1A, 15 A.

O'Connell, Vanessa, "Massachusetts Tries to Halt Sale of 'Sweet' Cigarettes," The Wall Street Journal, May 20, 2004, pp. B1, B2.

O'Connell, Vanessa, and Lloyd, Mary Ellen, "Philip Morris Loses Appeal of Oregon Damage Award," The Wall Street Journal, February 3, 2006, p. B3.

O'Connell, Vanessa, "From the Ashes of Defeat," The Wall Street Journal, August 21, 2006, pp. B1, B4.

O'Connor, Lona, "Drawing the line on sexual harassment can be difficult," Sun-Sentinel, Your Business, April 2, 2004, p. 13.

O'Donnell, Jayne, and Woodyard, Chris, "Toyota's sex-harassment lawsuit could set standard," USA TODAY, August 8, 2006, p. 7B.

Occupational Safety and Health Act of 1970, 29 United States Code Annotated, Sections 553, 651-678 (Thomson/west 2006).

Offerman, Lynn R. & Hellman, Peta. S. (1997). Culture's consequences for leadership behavior: National values in action. Journal of Cross-Cultural Psychology, 28(3): 342–351.

Oil Pollution Control Act, 33 United States Code Annotated Sections 2701–2761 (Thomson/west 2006).

Oliveira, Maria Angela Jardim de Santa Cruz, "Recognition and Enforcement of United States Money Judgments in Brazil," 19 New York International Law Review, pp. 1–35 (Winter 2006).

Olkon, Sara, "Widow loses appeal in gun case," The Miami Herald, June 2, 2005, p. 9B.

Oncale v. Sundowner Offshore Services, Inc., 523 U.S. 75, 118 S.Ct. 998 (1998).

Oppenheimer, Andres, "IBM executives deny home office knew of bribes," The Herald, October 1, 2000, pp. 1E, 12E.

Orwell, G. (1984, at 4 (1949)).

Organized Crime Control Act, 18 United States Code Annotated, Sections 1961–1968 (Thomson/West 2006).

Organizations of ITA. Retrieved July 20, 2006, from CHART: http://www.ita.doc.gov/ooms/ITAALL.pdf

Orihuela, Sandra, and Montjoy, Abigal, "The Evolution of Latin America's Sexual Harassment Law: A Look at Mini-skirts and Multinationals in Peru," 30 California Western International Law Journal, pp. 323–344 (2000).

Orol, R. (2006). Public interest groups, government agencies spar over environmental solutions.   Retrieved July 20, 2006, from http://www.cec.org/trio/stories/index.cfm?ed=18&ID=198&varlan=english

Oster, S. (1990). Modern Competitive Analysis. London, UK: Oxford University Press.

Overby, Brooke A., "Consumer Protection in China After Accession to the WTO," 33. Syracuse Journal of International Law and Commerce (2006), pp. 347–392.

Palazzolo, Joe, "Business Slams Bribery Act," *The Wall Street Journal*, November 28, 2011, pp. B1, B8.

Palazzolo, Joe, "The Business of Bribery," *The Wall Street Journal*, October 2, 2012, pp. B1, B4.

Palazzolo, Joe, "Bribery Law Dos and Don'ts, *The Wall Street Journal*, November 15, 2012, pp. B1, B2.

Palazzolo, Joe, Matthews, Christopher M., and Ng, Serena, "Nepotism: When Is It a Crime"? *The Wall Street Journal*, August 20, 2013, pp. B1, B2.

Palsgraf v. Long Island Railroad Company, 248 N.Y. 339, 162 N.E. 99 (Court of Appeals of New York 1928).

Panken, P. M. (2003). *An Employer's Checklist for Reasonable Accommodation of Religion in the Workplace 49 No. 4 PRAC. LAW. 25*

Panztor, Andy, "Boeing, Lockheed To Gain Approval On Rocket Merger," The Wall Street Journal, March 30, 2006, p. A2.

Parents Involved in Community Schools v. Seattle School District No. 1, 127 S.Ct. 2738 (2007).

Parliament Passes Law on Foreign Ownership of Property, Turkish Daily News, Dec. 30, 2005, from http://www.turkishdailynews.com.tr/article. php?enewsid=32015.

Pasztor, Andy, "Boeing, Lockheed To Gain Approval On Rocket Merger," *The Wall Street Journal*, March 30, 2006, p. A2.

Patent and Trademark Act, 35 United States Code Section 101.

Pear, Robert, "FDA's hands are full monitoring drug ads," Sun-Sentinel, March 28, 1999, p. 14A.

Pedowitz, Arnold H., "So Long. Now Don't Compete." The New York Times, February 16, 2003, p. 10.

Pentair, Inc. (2006). *Code of Business Conduct and Ethics.* Retrieved July 17, 2006, from http://www.pentair.com/code.html

Peters, Eric, "Getting Sued for Saving Lives," The Wall Street Journal, February 25, 1999, p. A20.

Piercy, N. (1982). Export Strategy : Markets and Competition Reseda, CA: George Allen and Irwin.

Pohlman R., and Mujtaba, B. G. (2007). The Impact of Sarbanes Oxley's Act on Human Resources Management. Chapter in *The 2007 Pfeiffer Annual: Human Resource Management.* Edited by Robert C. Preziosi.

Pohlman R., and Gardiner, G. (2000). *Value Driven Management.* AMACOM.

Popper, Nathaniel and Hamilton, Walter, "Insider trading nets record prison term," *Sun-Sentinel*, October 14, 2011, p. 2D.

Posthuma, R. A., Dworkin, J. D., Torres, V. & Bustillos, D. L. (2000). Labor laws in Mexico an in the U.S.: An international comparison. *Labor Law Journal*, 51, pp. 95–112.

Pounds, Marcia Heroux, "Office Depot, OfficeMax deal OK'd," *Miami Herald*, November 2, 2013, p. C1.

Powell, Eileen Alt, "Groups plan to oppose AT&T deal," The Miami Herald, March 17, 2006, p. C1.

Power, Stephen, "Daimler Fires Workers Following Its Bribery Probe," The Wall Street Journal, March 7, 2006, p. A3.

Prasad, S. B. (1981). Managers' attitudes in Brazil: Nationals vs. expatriates. *Management International Review*, 21(2), 78–85.

Pregnancy Discrimination Act of 1978, 42 United States Code Annotated, Section 2000e (Thomson/West 2006).

Prengamam, Peter, "Lawsuits target illegal hirings," The Miami Herald, August 23, 2006, p. 3C.

Price Waterhouse. (1996). Doing Business in India. Price Waterhouse: USA.

Price Waterhouse. (1984). Doing Business in Kenya. Price Waterhouse: Kenya.

Private Securities Litigation Reform Act of 1995, 15 United States Code Annotated Sections 77z-2, 78u-5 (Thomson/West 2006).

Prosser and Keeton on the Law of Torts. West Publishing Company Hornbook Series, 5th ed. (1984).

Pucci, Adriana Noemi, "Arbitration in Brazil: Foreign Investment and the New Brazilian Approach to Arbitration," 60 Dispute Resolution Journal, pp. 82–87 (February-April 2005).

Pulliam, Susan, Rothfeld, Michael, and Strausburg, Jenny, "Big Consultant Payouts Hint Insider Probe Will Broaden," *The Wall Street Journal*, January 10, 2011.

Putti, Joseph M. & Tong, Ang Chin 1992. Effects of leader behavior on subordinate satisfaction in a civil service-Asian context. *Public Personnel Management*, 21(1): 53–63.

Reich, R. (1991). The Work of Nations . New York : Knopf

Reilly, David, and Nassauer, Sarah, "Tip-Line Bind: Follow the Law In the U.S. or EU"? The Wall Street Journal, September 6, 2005, pp. C1, C3.

Reilly, David, and Nassauer, "Tip-Line Bind: Follow the Law In the U.S. or EV"? The Wall Street Journal, September 6, 2005, pp. C1, C3.

Restatement of Contracts, American Law Institute (1932).

Restatement of the Law (Second) of Torts, Section 402A, Torts, American Law Institute Publishers, St. Paul, MN (1977).

Restatement of the Law (Third) of Torts, American Law Institutes Publishers, St. Paul, MN (1997).

Restatement (Second) of Contracts, American Law Institute (1981).

Restatement (Second) of Torts, American Law Institute Publishers, (1977).

Resource Conservation and Recovery Act, 42 United States Code Annotated Sections 6901 et seq. (Thomson/West 2006).

Reuschlein, Harold Gill, and Gregory, William A., Agency and Partnership, West Publishing Company Hornbook Series (1979).

Review and Outlook, "Antitrust Spin Cycle," The Wall Street Journal, March 13, 2006, p. A18.

Review and Outlook, Wall Street Journal, June 24, 2005, p. A12.

Review and Outlook, "Calling All Plaintiffs," The Wall Street Journal, May 2, 2006, p. A16.

Revised Model Business Corporation Act, National Conference of Commissioners on Uniform State Laws (1984).

Revised Uniform Limited Partnership Act, National Conference of Commissioners on Uniform State Laws (1976).

Richey, Warren, "Nurse sues Broward Hospital," Sun Sentinel, September 17, 1994, p. 3B.

Riegel v. Medtronic, 552 U.S. 312, 128 S.Ct. 999 (2008).

Risk Management Institute. Retrieved June 22, 2006 from http://www.irmi.com/Expert/Articles/2004/Wagner05.aspx

Robinson-Patman Act of 1936, United States Code Annotated, Section 13 (Thomson/West 2006).

Rosen, Gary C., and Reimer, David H., "Covenants Not to Compete: Current Conflicts and Emerging Issues Affecting Enforcement," The Florida Bar Journal, November 1994, pp. 71–74.

Rosenn, K. S. (2005). Federalism in Brazil. Duquesne Law Review. Duquesne University: PA.

Ross, A. (2004). Bringing the Profits Home. The China Business Review, 31(5). Retrieved August 12, 2005 from ProQuest Database.

Roza, Edni, "Brazilian Banking Institution and Anti-Money Laundering Framework: Compliance with International Standards," 11 Law and Business Review of the Americas, pp. 299–318 (2005).

Rubins, Noah, "The Enforcement and Annulment of International Arbitration Awards in Indonesia," 20 American University International Law Review, pp. 359–401 (2005).

Rudansky, Alex Kane, and Pugh, Tony, "What the ruling will mean for U.S. consumers," The Miami Herald, June 29, 2012, pp. IA, 2A.

Ruhnke, Jill Sanner (1995). The impact of NAFTA on labor arbitration in Mexico. *Law and Policy in International Business,* 26 (Spring), pp. 917–944.

Rustad, Michael L., and Paulson, Sandra R., "Monitoring Employee E-mail and Internet Usage: Avoiding the Omniscient Electronic Sweatshop: Insights from Europe," 7 University of Pennsylvania Journal of Labor and Employment Law, pp. 829–904 (2005).

Safe Water Drinking Act, 21 United States Code Annotated Section 349, 42 United States Code Annotated Sections 200, 300f-300j (Thomson/West 2006).

Sampson, Hannah, "Cleared for takeoff," *Miami Herald,* November 13, 2013, pp. 1A, 2A.

Sanger, David E., "29 Nations Agree to a Bribery Ban," New York Times, May 24, 1997, pp. 1, 34.

Sanmaninatelli, Maria, "Vote is a test for new premier," The Miami Herald, June 26, 2006, p. 16A.

Santiago, Roberto, "Florida workers have scant job protection," The Miami Herald, September 5, 2005, p. 5B.

Sarbanes-Oxley Act of 2002, 28 United States Code Annotated Sections 1658 et seq. (Thomson/West 2006).

Sarbanes-Oxley Act of 2002, 15 United States Code Annotated Section 7201 et. seq. (Thomson/West 2006).

Sarwar, Ghulam (1995). *Islam: Beliefs and Teachings.* Dawat Offset Printers, Delhi-6.

Sasseen, Jane, "White-Collar Crime: Who Does Time"? Business Week, February 6, 2006, pp. 60–61.

Savage, David G., "Court rules no ban on drug suits," *The Sun Sentinel,* March 5, 2008, p. 3A.

Savage, David G., "Violent video games divide high court," *Sun-Sentinel,* November 3, 2010, p. 6A.

Savery, Lawson K. & Swain, Pamela. A. (1985). Leadership style: Differences between expatriates and locals. *Leadership & Organization Development Journal,* 6(4): 8–11.

Scandall, Kara, "Lawsuit Charges U.S. Unite of Japanese Company With Bias," The Wall Street Journal, January 20, 2005, pp. B1, B2.

Scannell, Kara, "Shell, Six Other Firms Settle Bribery Probe," *The Wall Street Journal,* November 5, 2010, p. B3.

Scannell, Kara and Catan, Thomas, "U.S. Nears Deals in Bribery Case," *The Wall Street Journal,* October 15, pp. B1, B2.

Schaffer, R., Earle, B. Agusti, F. (2005). International Business Law and Its Environment: A Managerial Perspective (6th Ed.) Ohio: Thomson South-Western West

Schaffer, R., Earle, B., Agusti, F. (2005). *International Law and Its Business Environment* (6th ed.). Ohio: Thomson Corporation.

Schaffer, Richard, Earle, Beverly, and Agusti, Filberto (2002). International Business Law and its Environment (5th edition). West-Thomson Learning.

Schacter, V. (2005). *Practising Law Institute, Privacy in the Workplace*

Schatz, Amy, "FCC Approves Verizon-MCI Pact and SBC's Purchase of AT&T," The Wall Street Journal, November 1, 2005, p. A2.

Scheck, Justin, "China Secrets Case Gets Guilty Plea," *The Wall Street Journal*, March 2, 2012, p. B1.

Schwaneberg, Robert, "Suit over loft bed falls short," The Star-Ledger, August 16, 2006, pp. 13, 16.

Schmidt, Robert, and Howley, Kathleen M., "U.S. sues Realtor trade group," The Miami Herald, September 9, 2005, pp. 1C, 4C.

Schroeder, Michael, and Fuhrmans, Vanessa, "Foreign Firms Trading in U.S. Get a Warning On Deception," The Wall Street Journal, September 3, 2000, pp. A14, A17.

Sciolino, Elaine, "Chirac to withdraw labor law," Sun-Sentinel, April 11, 2006, p. 12A.

Scott, Carole A., "Money Talks: The Influence of Economic Power on the Employment Laws and Policies of the United States and France," 7 San Diego International Law Journal, pp. 341–403 (2006).

Searcey, Dionne, "U.K. bribes law has firms in a sweat," *The Wall Street Journal, Europe News*, December 29, 2010, p. 6.

Securities Act of 1933, 15 United States Code Annotated Sections 77a-77aa (Thomson/West 2006).

Securities Act of 1934, 15 United States Code Annotated Sections 78a-77mm (Thomson/West 2006).

Securities and Exchange Commission Rule 10b-5, 17 Code of Federal Regulations Section 240.10b-5 (Thomson/West 2006).

SEC v. W.J. Howey Co., 328 U.S. 293, 66 S.Ct.1100 (1946).

Segal, Martin E., "The truth behind McDonald's hot coffee suit," *Miami Herald*, Business Monday, November 13, 2006, p. 8.

Selim Levi, Yabancilarin Tasinmaz Mal Edinmeleri, 72 (Legal Publishing, 2006) (discussing the right of foreigners to purchase irremovable property in Turkey).

Selmer, Jan (1987). Swedish managers' perceptions of Singaporean work-related values. *Asia Pacific Journal of Management*, 5(1), 80–88.

Selmer, Jan (1996). What expatriate managers know about the work values of their subordinates: Swedish executives in Thailand. *Management International Review*, 36 (3): 231–242.

Shah, A. (2006). *Causes of Poverty: Corruption*. Retrieved April 8, 2006, from http://www.globalissues.org/TradeRelated/Poverty/Corruption.asp

Shellenbarger, Sue, "Employers Often Ignore Office Affairs, Leaving Co-Workers in a Difficult Spot," The Wall Street Journal, March 10, 2005, p. D1.

Shellenbarger, Sue, "Supreme Court Takes on How Employers Handle Worker Harassment Complaints," The Wall Street Journal, April 13, 2006, p. D1.

Shellhardt, Timothy D., "Jury to Consider If 'Overqualified' Signals Age Bias," The Wall Street Journal, July 27, 1998, pp. B1, B2.

Shenkar, O. and Luo, Y. (2003). *International Business*. USA: John Wiley & Sons, Inc.

Sherman Act of 1890, 15 United States Code Annotated, Section 1 and Section 2 (Thomson/West 2006).

Sherman, Mark, "Race-based school programs reined in," *The Miami Herald*, June 29, 2007, pp. 1A, 2A.

Shinsato, Alison Lindsay, "Increasing the Accountability of Transnational Corporations for Environmental Harms: The Petroleum Industry in Nigeria," 4 Northwestern Journal of International Human Rights, pp. 186 et seq. (2005).

Sidel, Robin, "Retailer Named Uncle Sam Claims Piece of Debit Pact," February 2, 2006, pp. C1, C6.

Sidoti, Liz, "More, nastier ads likely in elections," *Sun-Sentinel*, January 22, 2010, p. 3A.

Silberston, A.(1970). Price behaviour of firms. Economic Journal 80 No. 319: 511–570.

Silver-Greenberg, Jessica, Protess, Ben, and Barboza, David, "Hiring in China by JP Morgan under scrutiny," *Miami Herald*, August 18, 2013, p. 4A.

Smith, Bradley A., "Newsflash: First Amendment Upheld," *The Wall Street Journal*, January 23–24, 2010, p. A15.

Smith, Elliot Blair and Kuntz, Phil, "Some CEOs Are More Equal Than Others," *Bloomberg Businessweek*, May 6 – May 12, 2013, pp. 70–74.

Smith, Ethan, "Concert Deal Wins Antitrust Approval," *The Wall Street Journal*, January 26, 2010, pp. B1, B2.

Smith, Annie Kates, "Trading in false tips exacts a price," U.S. News & World Report, February 5, 2001, p. 40.

Smith, Craig S., "Chinese Discover Product Liability Suits," The Wall Street Journal, November 13, 1997, pp. B1, B13.

Smith, Peter B. (1992). Organizational behavior and national cultures. *British Journal of Management*, 3: 39–51.

Smith, Sasha, "Spying: How Far is Too Far," Fortune Small Business, June 2001, p. 85.

Social Security Act of 1935, 42 United States Code, Sections 301–1397, as amended by the Federal Insurance Contributions Act, 26 United States Code Annotated, Sections 3101–3125 (Thomson/West 2006).

Soloman, Deborah, and Squeo, Anne Marie, "Crackdown Puts Corporations, Executives in New Legal Peril," The Wall Street Journal, June 20, 2005, pp. A1, A10.

Springen, Karen, "Smoking: Light Up and You May Be Let Go," Newsweek, February 7, 2005, p. 9.

Spencer, Jane, "Signing Away Your Right to Sue," The Wall Street Journal, October 1, 2003, pp. D1, D2.

Squeo, Anne Marie, "In Patent Disputes, A Scramble to Prove Ideas Are Old Hat," The Wall Street Journal, January 25, 2006, pp. A1, A8.

State Farm v. Campbell, 538 U.S. 408 (2003).

State Farm Mutual Automobile Insurance Company v. Campbell, 538 U.S. 408, 123 Sup.Ct.1513 (2003).

Standard Oil Company of California v. United States, 337 U.S. 293, 69 S.Ct. 1051 (1949).

Standard Oil Company of New Jersey v. United States, 221 U.S. 1, 31 S.Ct. 502 (1911).

State Oil Company v Khan, 522 U.S. 3, 118 S.Ct. 275 (1997).

Steighorst, Tom, "Magic Embarks on New Voyage," Sun-Sentinel, May 16, 2006, pp.1D, 2D.

Steinback, Robert L., "AT&T agrees to buy BellSouth," The Miami Herald, March 6, 2006, pp.1A, 2A.

Stikeman Elliott LLP, Canada. (2005). Reducing Risk in International Investments. Retrieved August 6, 2005 from LexisNexis Database.

Stop Counterfeiting in Manufactured Goods Act, 18 United States Code Sections 2318–2320, as amended by Public Law No 109–181.

Strumpf, Dan, "Liability Issues Create Potholes On the Road to Driverless Cars," *The Wall Street Journal*, January 28, 2013, pp. B1, B7.

Suda, Y. (2005). *Monitoring E-Mail of Employees in the Private Sector: A Comparison between Western Europe and the United States, 4 WASH. U. GLOBAL STUD. L. REV. 209*

Sullivan, Allanna, "Shell Oil, Texaco Agree To Join Units," The Wall Street Journal, March 19, 1997, pp. A3, A6.

Synder v. Phelps, 131 S.Ct. 1207 (2011).

Tadena, Nathalie, "Engineer Gets 4 Years In Motorola Secrets Case," *The Wall Street Journal*, August 30, 2012, p. B3.

Tamen, Joan Fleischer, "Ruling lets employers avoid court," Sun-Sentinel, March 22, 2001, pp. 1D, 8D.

Taylor, Jeffrey, "New Rules Harness Power of Free Markets to Curb Air Pollution," *The Wall Street Journal*, April 14, 1992, pp. A1, A12.

Taylor, Jeffrey, and Kansas, Dave, "Environmentalists Vie for Right to Pollute," *The Wall Street Journal*, March 26, 1993, pp. C1, C19.

Telemarketing and Consumer Fraud and Abuse Prevention Act, 15 United States Code Annotated Sections 6101-6108 (Thomson-West 2006)

Telemarketing Sales Rule, 16 Code of Federal Regulations Sections 310.1-310.8 (Thomson-West 2006).

The Bahamas, (2006). Retrieved on September 17, 2006 from: www.factmonster.com.

The Communications Decency Act of 1996, 47 United States Code Annotated Section 230 (Thomson West 2006).

The International Court of Justice. (2006). Retrieved June 29, 2006, from http://www.icj-cij.org/icjwww/igeneralinformation/inotice. pdf

The World Trade Organization. (2006). *The Panel Process*. Retrieved June 29, 2006, from http://www.wto.org/english/thewto_e/whatis_e/tif_e/disp2_e.htm

Thernstron, Abigall, "The Supreme Court Says No To Quotas," *The Wall Street Journal*, July 1, 2009, p. A13.

Thompson v. North American Stainless, LP, 2011 U.S. Lexis 913 (2011).

Thurm Scott, "Criminal-Records Checks in Cross Hairs," *The Wall Street Journal*, June 12, 2013, pp. A1, A3.

Torruco-Gamas, J. (2005). *The Presence of the Federal System in Mexico*. Duquesne Law Review. Duquesne University: PA.

Toxic Substances Control Act, 15 United States Code Annotated Sections 2601–2692 (Thomson/West 2006).

Trademark Dilution Act, 15 United States Code Annotated Section 1125 (Thomson/West 2006).

Trademark Law Revision Act of 1988 15 United States Code Annotated, 15 United States Code Annotated, Section 1121–27 (Thomason West, 2006).

Triandis, Harry C. (1982). Dimensions of cultural variation as parameters of organizational theories. *International Studies of Management and Organization*, 12(4): 139–169.

Triandis, Harry. C. (1993). The Contingency Model in cross-cultural perspective. In M. M. Chemers & R. Ayman, editors, *Leadership theory and research: Perspectives and direction*, San Diego, CA: Academic Press.

Trottman, Melanie and Banjo, Shelly, "Wal-Mart Hit Over Worker Protests," *The Wall Street Journal*, January 16, 2014, pp. B1, B2.

Truth-in-Lending Act of 1968, 15 United States Code Sections 1601-1693.

Tuna, Carl, Koppel, Nathan, and Sanserino, Michael, "Job-Test Ruling Cheers Employers," *The Wall Street Journal*, July 1, 2009, p. B1.

Tung, Rosalie L. (1982). Selection and training procedures of U.S., European, and Japanese Multinationals. *California Management Review*, 25: 51-71.

Turkish Constitution, art. 70, (1924).

U.S. Library of Congress, (2006), Turkey. Retrieved on July 30, 2006, from http://countrystudies.us/turkey/56.htm

Unfair Competition, Florida Statutes Annotated, Section 542.335 (Thomson West, 2006).

Uniform Commercial Code, National Conference of Commissioners on Uniform State Laws (1952).

Uniform Computer Information Transaction Act, National Conference of Commissioners on Uniform State Laws (1999).

Uniform Electronic Transaction Act, National Conference of Commissioners on Uniform State Laws (1999).

Uniform Limited Liability Company Act, National Conference of Commissioners on Uniform State Laws (1995).

Uniform Limited Partnership Act, National Conference of Commissioners on Uniform State Laws (1916).

Uniform Partnership Act, National Conference of Commissioners on Uniform State Laws (1914).

Uniform Trade Secrets Act, Florida Statutes Annotated, Section 688.001–688.009 (Thomson West, 2006).

United Nations Conference on Trade and Development (2004) World Investment Report 2004. New York Geneva

United States International Trade Commission: About us. Retrieved July 20, 2006, from http://www.usitc.gov/ext_relations/about_itc/index.htm

United States v. Aluminum Company of America, 148 F.2d 416 (2nd Circuit1945).

United States v. American Library Association, 539 U.S. 194, 123 SCt. 2297 (2003).

United States v. Chestman, 447 F.2d 551 (2nd Circuit Court of Appears 1991), certiorari denied, 503 U.S. 1004 (1992).

United States v. Colgate & Company, 250 U.S. 300, 39 S.Ct. 465 (1919).

United States v. Lopez, 514 U.S. 549, 115 S.Ct. 1624 (1995).

United States v. Microsoft, 2001 WL 721343 (D.C. Circuit 2001).

United States v. O'Hagen, 521U.S. 642, 117 S.Ct 2199 (1997).

United States v. Sacony-Vacumn Oil Co., 310 U.S. 150, 60 S.Ct. 811 (1940).

United States v. Stevens, 130 S.Ct. 1577 (2010).

UpFront, "Immigration: France's Plan" Pay 'Em To Go Home," Business Week, April 24, 2006, p. 16.

Urbina, Ian, "Ohio Supreme Court Rejects Taking of Homes for Project," The New York Times, July 27, 2006, p. A18.

Valentino-DeVries, "Social Media and Bias in Hiring," *The Wall Street Journal*, November 21, 2013, p. B4.

Vardi, Nathan, "Founder of Dooney & Bourke Gets Jail in Bribery Case," *Forbes.com*. Retrieved November 10, 2009 from: http://www.forbes.com/2009/11/10/bourke-corrupt-foreign-business-bribery.html.

Wagner, D. (2004). The implications of Recurring Terrorism for Business. International.

Walker, Elaine, "Joe's lament: You can't fight the government," The Miami Herald, June 25, 2003, pp. 1C, 4C.

Walker, Elaine, "Joe's Stone Crab faces another legal setback," The Miami Herald, March 29, 2001, pp. 1C, 3C.

Weaver, Jay, and Brecher, Elinor J., "Smokers' damages, class suit snuffed," The Miami Herald, July 7, 2006, pp. 1A, 17A.

Wei, S-J. (2001). *Corruption and Globalization*. Retrieved April 2, 2006, from http://www.brookings.edu/comm/policybriefs/pb79. htm

Weimer, De'Ann, and Forest, Stephanie Anderson, "Forced Into Arbitration? Not Any More," Business Week, March 16, 1998, pp. 66–68.

Weitz, Barton A., Stephen Castleberry, and Mildred Reed (2004). Selling: Building Partnerships, 5th Edition, McGraw Hill Irwin.

Whistleblower Protection Act of 1989, 5 United States Code Annotated, Section1201 (Thomson/West 2006).

White, James J., and Summers, Robert S. (1980). Uniform Commercial Code (2nd edition), West Publishing Company Hornbook Series, St Paul, MN.

White, Michael, "GM hit with record judgment," The Herald, July 10, 1999, pp. 1A, 14A.

Wikipedia Encyclopedia, (2006), Turkey. Retrieved on July 30, 2006, from http://en.wikipedia.org/wiki/Turkey

Wikipedia Encyclopedia, (2006), Economy of Turkey. Retrieved on July 30, 2006, from http://en.wikipedia.org/wiki/Economy_of_Turkey

Wickard v. Fillburn, 317 U.S. 111, 63 S.Ct. 82 (1942).

Wilke, John R., and Chen, Kathy, "As China's Trade Clout Grows, So Do Price-Fixing Accusations," February 10, 2006, pp. A1, A14.

Wilke, John R., and Clark, Don, "Samsung to Pay Fine for Price-Fixing," The Wall Street Journal, October 14, 2005, pp. A3, A6.

Wilke, John R., "Five Paint Firms Are Scrutinized For Price-Fixing," The Wall Street Journal, June 4, 2001, p. A4.

Wilke, John R., "Funeral Industry Is Hit With Casket-Pricing Suit," The Wall Street Journal, May 4, 2005, p.p. D1, D4.

Wilke, John R., "U.S. Court Rules Antitrust Laws Apply to Foreigners," The Wall Street Journal, March 19, 1997, p. A7.

Wilkinson, J. Harvie III, "The Seattle and Louisville Cases: There Is No Other Way," 121 Harvard Law Review 158 (November, 2007).

Will, George F., "Legal Theft in Norwood," Newsweek, April 24, 2006, p. 94

Will, George, "Profit can rule the day," *Sun Sentinel*, June 26, 2005, p. 5H.

Williams, M. (2006, August 6). Bouygues Transfers Skills to Local Workers

Wilson, David L., "Microsoft ruled a monopoly by a federal judge," The Miami Herald, November 6, 1999, pp. 1A, 14A.

Winkelmann, R. (2002). Why do firms recruit internationally? Retrieved from www.unizh.ch/sts/research/publications/pdf/schmollers

Winter, Christopher, "Price-gougers face penalties," Sun-Sentinel, September 14, 1999, pp. 1D, 9D.

Wollenberg, Skip, "Liquor makers drop old ban, will advertise over TV, radio," The Herald, November 8, 1996, p. 3A.

World Bank, Turkey Country Economic Memorandum: Promoting Sustanined Growth and convergence with the European Union, Volume II: Expanded Report, Report No. 33549-TR, 4, February 23, 2006.

Worchel, Stephen & Mitchell, Terence R. (1972). An evaluation of the effectiveness of the culture assimilator in Thailand and Greece. *Journal of Applied Psychology*, 56, (6): 472–479.

World Briefing: Europe, "Italy: Voters Reject Constitutional Challenge," The New York Times, June 27, 2006. p. A6.

WTO (1988, September) Jamaica's Trade Policy Review Report. WTO Press

WTO (2005, January) Jamaica's Trade Policy Review Report. WTO Press

Wurcel, G (2004). Management of Workers in WTO Negotiations: A development perspective. Retrieved from www.gcim.org/attachments/GMP%20No%2015. pdf

Wyss, Jim, "Bill limits eminent domain," The Miami Herald, May 3, 2006, p. 3C.

Yamakawa, Ryuichi, "We've Only Just Begun: The Law of Sexual Harassment in Japan," 22 Hastings International and Comparative Law Review, pp. 523–558 (1999).

Yanowitz v. L'Oreal, Inc., 131 Cal. Rptr.2d 575 (California Appeals 2003).

Yeh, Rhy-Song (1988). Values of American, Japanese and Taiwanese managers in Taiwan: A test of Hofstede's framework. *Proceedings, Academy of Management*, Anaheim, CAL.

Yeh, Quey-Jen (1995). Leadership, personal traits and job characteristics in R&D organizations: A Taiwanese case. *Leadership and Organizational Development Journal*, 16(6): 16–28.

Yost, Pete, "Justice Depart. Settle e-book case with Macmillan," *Miami Herald*, February 9, 2013, p. 3C.

Yuen, Rachel A., "Beyond the School Yard: Workplace Bullying and Moral Harassment Law in France and Quebec," 38 Cornell International Law Journal, pp. 625-649 (2005).

Zakah Guide. *IslamiQ Zakah Payment Gateway: Unlocking the Potential of your Charitable Donations.* London. IslamiQ.com

Zamora, Stephen, and Cossio, Jose Ramon, "Mexican Constitutionalism After Presidencialismo," 4 International Journal of Constitutional Law, pp. 411–437 (2006).

Zeira, Yoram, Harari, Ehud & Nundi, Dafna I. (1975). Some structural and cultural factors in ethnocentric multinational corporations and employee moral. *The Journal of Management Studies,* 66–82.

Biographies

Author Biographies

Professor Frank J. Cavico is a Professor of Business Law and Ethics at the H. Wayne Huizenga School of Business and Entrepreneurship of Nova Southeastern University (NSU). He was the principal creator of the required MBA law and ethics course "The Values of Legality, Morality, and Social Responsibility in Business," and he presently serves as Lead Professor for that course. In 2000, he was awarded the Excellence in Teaching Award by the Huizenga School. In 2007, he was awarded the Faculty Member of the Year Award by Huizenga School. His fine record is also complemented by numerous research endeavors, principally law-review articles across the broad sectors of business law and ethics as well as a business ethics textbook, *Business Ethics: Transcending Requirements Through Moral Leadership*, co-authored with Dr. Bahaudin G. Mujtaba, which has been adopted for use by many national and international business schools. Professor Cavico holds a J.D. degree from St. Mary's University School of Law and a B.A. from Gettysburg College. He also possesses a master of laws degree from the University of San Diego School of Law, and a master's degree in political science from Drew University. Professor Cavico is licensed to practice law in the states of Florida and Texas. He has worked as a federal government regulatory attorney and as counsel for a labor union. He has practiced general civil law and immigration law in South Florida.

Professor Bahaudin G. Mujtaba is Professor of Management and Management with the H. Wayne Huizenga School of Business and Entrepreneurship of Nova Southeastern University. He has worked as an internal consultant, trainer, and teacher in the corporate arena and also worked in retail management for 16 years. He was awarded the prestigious Faculty of the Year Award for the 2005 Academic Year at the School of Business and Entrepreneurship of NSU. Professor Mujtaba attended Habibia High School in Afghanistan, Fort Myers High School, Edison Community College, the University of Central Florida, Nova University, and Nova Southeastern University in the United States. His doctorate degree is in management, and he has two post-doctorate specialties: human resource management and international management. Dr. Mujtaba is author or co-author of twenty books and nearly three hundred articles and presentations. During the past 25 years, he has had the pleasure of working in the United States, Brazil, the Bahamas, Pakistan, Afghanistan, St. Lucia, and Jamaica. He was born in Khoshie of Logar province, and raised in Kabul, Afghanistan.

Author Contact Information:

Nova Southeastern University
H. Wayne Huizenga School of Business and Entrepreneurship
Office Phone: (954) 262-5000, or (800) 338-4723.

Contributors' Biographies

1. *Hajar Amrani* is a graduate of Nova Southeastern University. Born and raised in Morocco, she completed a master's degree in international business administration at NSU. In 2001, she obtained her bachelor's at Mohamed V. University in Rabat, Morocco, majoring in English literature and linguistics. Her family's encouragement and her husband's support have been her source of strength to come to the U.S. in 2004 to pursue a graduate degree in business.

2. *Dr. Donald L. Ariail,* a certified public accountant, is an Assistant Professor of Accounting at Texas A&M University—Kingsville, System Center, San Antonio. He was the recipient of the 2006 KPMG Outstanding Dissertation Award, presented by the Gender Issues and Worklife Balance Section of the American Accounting Association. Dr. Ariail had worked in the public accounting profession since 1972 and he was the owner of a successful local CPA practice in Atlanta, Georgia prior to entering academia in 2005. He holds a doctorate degree in accounting from the H. Wayne Huizenga School of Business and Entrepreneurship of Nova Southeastern University.

3. *Dr. James M. Barry* is a professor of marketing at Nova Southeastern University. Dr. Barry is a 25-year veteran of the corporate world, with experience in industrial, government, and commercial marketing. During that time, he has served in a variety of executive marketing roles with several *Fortune 500* companies and start-up ventures. While at GE, BFGoodrich, Rockwell Collins, and AT&T, Dr. Barry spearheaded a number of business planning efforts and acquisition studies aimed at transforming corporate market focus. Dr. Barry's teaching experience covers marketing communications, salesmanship, internet marketing, and international marketing courses.

4. *Dr. Steven V. Cates* did his undergraduate work at the University of North Carolina, majoring in business and economics. He received his MBA at Northern Illinois University and his J.D. at John Marshall School of Law in Chicago. He holds a post-graduate certification in employment law from the University of Wisconsin School of Law and a certification in labor law from the University of Michigan—School of Law. He received his

DBA from Nova Southeastern University in 1999, with a concentration in human resource management, and a second concentration in marketing in 2003. Dr. Cates has held managerial and executive positions in human resources with Kroehler Manufacturing Co., Miller Brewing Company, Wilsonart International, Equity Inc., and Forsyth Technical Community College. He then joined Averett University, where he held the rank of Assistant Professor and Department Chair before his retirement in 2005. Dr. Cates presently teaches human resources management classes at Nova Southeastern University.

5. *Dr. Ramdas Chandra* joined Nova Southeastern University in July 2006. He received a Ph.D. in International Business and Marketing from the Stern School of Business at New York University. His research focuses on international market entry and expansion, international retailing, international franchising, e-commerce, various strategic aspects of international marketing, exporting, foreign direct investment, trade and its impact on economic development, and sustainable business. Born in India, Dr. Chandra has worked in three different countries, allowing him to bring a very diverse, international perspective to his research and teaching.

6. *Dr. Elizabeth Danon-Leva* received her Doctorate in International Business Administration at Nova Southeastern University. She has published papers in several conference proceedings, books, and journals, and works as a business consultant and Adjunct Professor in International Business and Management. Her research interests include business ethics, leadership, cross-cultural studies, and change management.

7. *Dr. John Wayne Falbey* is a faculty member and Program Chair for Real Estate Development at the H. Wayne Huizenga School of Business and Entrepreneurship, Nova Southeastern University. In addition to being a member of the Florida and Colorado Bar Associations, Dr. Falbey is Managing Member and President of The Falbey Group, LLC, a real estate development firm in Florida. He has been actively engaged in real estate development for more than 30 years.

8. *Dr. Shakila Faqeeri* was born in Kabul, Afghanistan. Dr. Faqeeri pursued her Bachelor of Arts degree from the University of Central Florida, where she was recognized as the Top Honor Graduate of her class. In 2005, she received her Juris Doctorate from Florida State University. During her law school tenure, she served in many leadership positions and was also a member of the executive boards of two prestigious law journals. She now practices criminal defense law in Clearwater, Florida.

9. *Stephanie C. Ferrari* is a Web developer at the H. Wayne Huizenga School of Business and Entrepreneurship of Nova Southeastern University. She received her Bachelor of Science degree in computer science and completed her MBA degree at Nova Southeastern University. Mrs. Ferrari currently teaches Online Communications and Internet Competency for the Huizenga School's doctoral programs. She and her husband, Silvano Ferrari, also own and manage a Precision Tune Auto Care franchise in Lauderhill, Florida.

10. *Erica Franklin* is a graduate of Nova Southeastern University's Masters of International Business Administration Program. She is originally from Memphis, Tennessee, and received her Bachelor of Business Administration Degree from Christian Brothers University, also in Memphis. Ms. Franklin is seeking to follow a career in international marketing as either a marketing analyst or to work in marketing management and consulting.

11. *William Freeman* has worked in the nonprofit and cause-related arena for over two decades. Currently, he is an adjunct professor in the Master's of Nonprofit Management program at George Mason University in Arlington, Virginia. He is an examiner with the Malcolm Baldrige National Quality Program (2005-2006), certified in the Balance Scorecard methodology and organizational change implementation. Mr. Freeman is a doctoral candidate at Nova Southeastern University's H. Wayne Huizenga School of Business and Entrepreneurship. He earned his MBA from Southeastern University in Washington, D.C.

12. *Dr. Norman D. Glick* studied international management at Nova Southeastern University. He has an M.A. in Economics and Japanese Area studies from Columbia University. He is retired from the U.S. Foreign Commercial Service, where he served as Senior Commercial Officer at the U.S. Embassies in Tokyo, Seoul, Lagos, and Cairo. He is currently an Adjunct Professor at Montgomery College in Rockville, Maryland.

13. *M. Ashraf Haidari* is political counselor at the Embassy of Afghanistan in Washington. He has held various positions at the Embassy, including Director and First Secretary. He is also a "peace scholar" at George Washington University. He speaks several languages and has traveled throughout the world to speak on issues related to Afghanistan and the creation of peace and prosperity for Afghans.

14. *Regina Harris* is currently the Director of Claims for a professional liability insurance group. She graduated from Nova Southeastern University's Masters of Management program with a focus on leadership programs at the School of Business and Entrepreneurship. Ms. Harris was inducted into

Huizenga School's International Honors Society. She also has a Bachelors of Business in Marketing from the University of Miami. She is interested in the topics of workforce diversity management, power bases, leadership, teamwork, and coaching.

15. *George Knowles* is an assistant in the legal department of the United European Bank and Trust Limited, Nassau, The Bahamas. Mr. Knowles regularly attends sessions regarding legal and ethical manners as a way of supporting the cause of promoting ethical and legal conduct in business and to advance knowledge.

16. *Simone Maxwell* is a graduate student at Nova Southeastern University. She pursued her undergraduate degree in Hospitality Administration at the Southern New Hampshire University. She is currently enrolled at NSU, where she is pursuing the Master's of Business Administration with a specialization in leadership. She also serves as a research assistant to the faculty. Ms. Maxwell was born and raised in St. Mary, Jamaica.

17. *Dr. Timothy McCartney* is a clinical psychologist and an organizational development consultant. He was educated in The Bahamas, the U.S., Switzerland, Jamaica, England, and France, where he received his doctorate in clinical psychology from the University of Strasbourg. Dr. McCartney returned to the Bahamas in 1967 and was appointed to serve in Ministry of Health of The Bahamas. He was the first Bahamian to obtain a doctorate in psychology, and was thereafter directed to develop the profession of psychology and allied health. Dr. McCartney was honored by the National Association of The Bahamas (Miami, Florida) for his "commitment to the betterment of society" on November 13, 1999, and he received the "key" to the City of Miami, Miami-Dade County from the office of the Mayor. Dr. McCartney's most recent award was presented to him by the Governor General of The Bahamas at an impressive ceremony at Government House in The Bahamas on September 9, 2002, which was attended by dignitaries from around the world. He was honored as a "Health Hero" by the Pan American Health Organization of the United Nations (at their 100th anniversary celebration) for his outstanding contribution to the field of psychology.

18. *Dr. Donovan A. McFarlane* is currently an Adjunct Professor in Business Studies at City College and a Doctoral Scholar in Educational Leadership Studies and International Business at St. Thomas University. He holds an MBA as well as a B.S. degree in Business Administration from Nova Southeastern University, a Doctor of Philosophy (Ph.D.) from The

American Institute of Holistic Theology, and a Doctor of Metaphysical Science (Msc.D.) from The University of Metaphysics. He was born in Manchester, Jamaica, where he grew up and attended DeCarteret College and Church Teachers' College.

19. **Dr. Ronald Needleman** is an Associate Professor of Economics in the H. Wayne Huizenga School of Business and Entrepreneurship at Nova Southeastern University. He also serves as Chair of the Public Administration Programs. Dr. Needleman earned his Ph.D. in Economics at the City University of New York, Graduate Center, and B.A. in Economics at Queens College. Dr. Needleman has conducted extensive research in the areas of state and local finance, energy, and urban problems, e.g., poverty, welfare, health services, and employment.

20. **Dr. Stephen C. Muffler** is a full-time attorney in private practice handling corporate civil litigation and business transactions in the tri-county area of South Florida, having been a member of the Florida Bar for over 13 years. He graduated with a Juris Doctorate and was conferred a second law degree in international law (LL.M.–Master of International Laws). Dr. Muffler is also a member of the Florida Bar's International Law Section and is the chairman of the Fort Lauderdale Citizens Police Review Board, which investigates complaints against Fort Lauderdale Police officers and reviews the Fort Lauderdale Police's Internal Affairs Department Findings and Reports. Dr. Muffler is an adjunct professor teaching MBA students their required basic corporate law and ethics classes at Nova Southeastern University. His publications include articles published in legal journals concerning the Foreign Corrupt Practices Act and the influences of the Russian Mafia on international business.

21. **Dr. Miguel A. Orta,** a native of Cuba, teaches import/export management, comparative management and international negotiations, international legal environment, and law, ethics, and society classes at Nova Southeastern University. Dr. Orta has a B.A. in political science and mass communications from Florida State University, a Juris Doctor from Duke University, and a masters in international business from Nova Southeastern University. As founder of American Strategic Consultants, he has conducted market research, feasibility studies, and business planning for the development of international enterprises in Venezuela, Colombia, Argentina, Brazil, Ecuador, Mexico, and Panama. Dr. Orta is presently involved in strategic planning for Chinese, Indian, Malaysian, and Thai companies entering both the United States and Latin American markets. During the 1990s, he served as a special business and trade consultant to Fernando Color de

Mello, the first democratically elected president in Brazil after the fall of its military dictatorship.

22. ***Cuneyt Oskal*** was born in Izmir, the third-largest city of Turkey. After he graduated from the Department of Engineering Sciences at Aegean University in Izmir, he enrolled in the one-year intensive MBA program of Istanbul University in the Department of Business Administration. Then he had an opportunity to work for the Turkish Army Force as a Chemical Engineer for about two years. After his military service, he completed a master's degree in management information systems at Nova Southeastern University. Cuneyt is currently working for NSU as a Web master and is also teaching college computer technology classes as an adjunct professor.

23. ***Bina Patel*** was born in Nairobi, Kenya. She moved to the United States at a very early age and was raised in Gainesville, Florida, where she attended the University of Florida for her undergraduate studies. She is pursuing a masters degree in International Business at NSU, and her research areas include international business, international management, ethics, corruption, and cultural awareness. She also serves as a research assistant to the faculty at NSU. Currently, Ms. Patel resides in Pembroke Pines, Florida.

24. ***John W. Palma, Jr.*** graduated from the Charles E. Schmidt School of Science at Florida Atlantic University with a Bachelor of Arts in psychology. His interests include history, behavioral finance, and the psychological consequences of wealth, status, and power.

25. ***Dr. Pedro F. Pellet*** is a professor at H. Wayne Huizenga School of Business and Entrepreneurship. He has attended higher education centers in Cuba, Great Britain, Puerto Rico, Spain, and in the U.S. Dr. Pellet received a Baccalaureate Superior from the University Complutense de Madrid, Spain; a B.Sc. in Biology from the University of the Sacred Heart, Santurce, Puerto Rico; two B.A.'s in economics and political sciences; and an M.A. in economics from the University of Puerto Rico, Rio Piedras Campus. He also received a Ph.D. in international affairs, with specialties in economic development and the developmental process, from the University of Miami, Coral Gables, Florida. Dr. Pellet currently teaches undergraduate, masters, and doctoral courses. He also supervises dissertations and conducts scholarly research in the area of applied economics. He has been a full-time teacher at Nova Southeastern University since April 1982.

26. ***Dr. Carrol Pickersgill*** is an attorney-at-law and Senior Vice President of Legal, Regulatory, and Corporate Affairs of the Port Authority of Jamaica. She holds a degree of Doctor of Business Administration (DBA) from

Nova Southeastern University, a Master of Science Degree (M.Sc.) in Maritime Administration from the World Maritime University (Sweden), a Bachelor of Laws Degree (L.L.B.) from the University of West Indies (Barbados), and a Certificate of Legal Education from the Norman Manley Law School (Jamaica).

27. **Dr. Andrés Raúl Pérez Díaz** graduated as a Medical Doctor (the equivalent of the U.S. degree of Doctor of Medicine) in 1968 from the University of Havana. He received the 2nd Degree Specialist in Clinical Biochemistry, awarded by the Department of Higher Medical Education, Ministry of Public Healthy, Cuba. He has taught as a full professor in the Departments of Biochemistry in the University of Havana Medicine Faculties as well as in several Universities of Costa Rica. With tens of papers published, he has conducted research in different lines of basic medical sciences and in the field of higher medical education.

28. **Dr. Randolph Pohlman** has written two books, entitled *Understanding the Bottom Line: Finance for Non-financial Managers and Supervisors and Value Driven Management: How to Create and Maximize Value Over Time for Organizational Success.* Dr. Pohlman was a senior executive at Koch Industries, the second-largest privately held company in the U.S. He was recruited to Koch via Kansas State University where, for more than ten years, he served the college in a variety of administrative and faculty positions, including holding the L. L. McAninch Chair of Entrepreneurship and serving as Dean of the College of Business. Dr. Pohlman is an active presence in the South Florida community, serving as a trustee and member of the Board of Governors for the Greater Miami Chamber of Commerce. He served as a member of the 2004 GMCC Cutting Edge Award Committee, and was Chief Judge for the 2002, 2003, and 2005 GMCC Cutting Edge Awards. He also serves on the Board of Governors and is a trustee for the Greater Fort Lauderdale Chamber of Commerce. He is on the Board of Directors of the International Assembly for Collegiate Business Education. In addition, Dr. Pohlman serves on the board of directors for two companies: Clark Consulting and Viragen, Inc. He currently serves as Dean of the H. Wayne Huizenga School of Business and Entrepreneurship at N.S.U.

29. **Dr. G. Rauf Roashan** graduated from Habibia High School. He then enrolled in the medical school of Kabul University, where he obtained his M.D. degree. He also has a master's degree from Yale University School of Medicine. Dr. Roashan held government positions in Afghanistan before the communist coup in 1978, having been in charge of health planning and international health departments for the Ministry of Public Health

of Afghanistan. He also served as the president of the Institute of Child Health in Kabul. He has served on the World Health Organization's Executive Board and as member of an international committee established by the world body to study the status of smallpox eradication in India, Nepal, and Bhutan.

30. **Dr. Belay Seyoum** is Associate Professor of International Business Studies at the H. Wayne Huizenga School of Business and Entrepreneurship of Nova Southeastern University. Prior to coming to Nova Southeastern University, Dr. Seyoum taught international business at Concordia and at McGill University in Montreal, Canada. Dr. Seyoum has published four books and numerous articles in the area of international business in several prestigious academic journals such as the *Journal of World Trade, International Business Review, International Trade Journal,* and the *Thunderbird International Business Review.*

31. **Dr. Josephine Sosa-Fey** teaches management and collective bargaining at Texas A&M University–Kingsville, San Antonio System Center. She has co-authored numerous referenced articles on human resource management, leadership, and cultural values and has published numerous papers in conference proceedings. She has also presented at regional and national conferences. She possesses a doctoral degree from the H. Wayne Huizenga School of Business and Entrepreneurship of N.S.U.

32. **Dr. Nicolaos Spiliopoulos** is a practicing attorney on the island of Tinos, Greece. He previously served on the legal staff of the European Commission. Dr. Spiliopoulos received his L.L.B. degree from the University of Athens and his L.L.M. from the University of Heidelberg.

33. **Dr. Andrew E. Trumbach** is a highly technical accounting and information systems professional with a diversified background that includes over 20 years in public accounting and private industry in the Unites States and the Caribbean. Dr. Trumbach has earned a Bachelor of Science degree in Accounting, a Master of Business Administration from California State University, and a Doctorate in Business Administration degree from Nova Southeastern University. He is also the president and co-founder of Onebin.com, president and founder of American Document Management, Inc., and VP and CFO of American Marketing & Management, Inc.

34. **Dr. Thomas M. Tworoger** is Chairman of the Entrepreneurship Department at the H. Wayne Huizenga School of Business and Entrepreneurship at Nova Southeastern University (the Huizenga School). He directs the undergraduate and graduate entrepreneurship programs and curricula

for the Huizenga School. Dr. Tworoger also teaches undergraduate and graduate-level courses in entrepreneurship, finance, and strategy. In 2005, he received the Excellence in Teaching Award at the Huizenga School. Prior to entering the teaching profession in 1997, Dr. Tworoger was a Kenworth truck dealer for 22 years. He took a small, single-location dealership with just $2 million in revenue and grew it into a multi-location organization with $130 million in revenue. In 1984, he became the first truck dealer in the U.S. to sell Japanese medium- and heavy-duty trucks. The company was repeatedly the number one dealer in sales for both Kenworth and Hino. In addition, the company had Isuzu and Mitsubishi Truck franchises as well as dealer agreements with Caterpillar, Cummins, and Detroit Diesel engines. In 1996, he sold his company to a division of DaimlerChrysler, Freightliner, LLC. Presently, Dr. Tworoger is in partnership with his son, David, in a lakefront development in central Florida called Lake Byrd Shores (lakebyrdshores.com). He is also engaged in business consulting and public speaking.

35. **Dr. Don Valeri**, B.A. (Hons), LL.B., M.B.A., Ph.D., is a lawyer in Vancouver, British Columbia, Canada, where he currently teaches business law and business ethics. His doctoral research was in leadership studies, with an emphasis on servant leadership and other forms of ethical leadership.

36. **Dr. Pan G. Yatrakis** is professor of economics and finance and Chair of the Finance and Economics Faculty at the H. Wayne Huizenga School of Business and Entrepreneurship at Nova Southeastern University. He received his B.A. and MBA degrees from Columbia University and his Ph.D. from the Stern School of Business at New York University.

❧ INDEX ❧

F

M